HOLINESS AND ECCLESIOLOGY
IN THE NEW TESTAMENT

Holiness and Ecclesiology in the New Testament

Edited by

Kent E. Brower *&* Andy Johnson

WILLIAM B. EERDMANS PUBLISHING COMPANY
GRAND RAPIDS, MICHIGAN / CAMBRIDGE, U.K.

Published 2007 by
Wm. B. Eerdmans Publishing Co.
2140 Oak Industrial Drive N.E., Grand Rapids, Michigan 49505 /
P.O. Box 163, Cambridge CB3 9PU U.K.

Library of Congress Cataloging-in-Publication Data

Holiness and ecclesiology in the New Testament /
    edited by Kent E. Brower & Andy Johnson.
        p.   cm.
    Includes bibliographical references and index.
    ISBN 978-0-8028-4560-3 (pbk.: alk. paper)
    1. Church — Biblical teaching.   2. Holiness — Biblical teaching.
    3. Bible. N.T. — Criticism, interpretation, etc.
    I. Brower, K. E. (Kent E.)   II. Johnson, Andy.

    BS2545.C5H65   2007
    234′.8 — dc22

                                                2007019921

www.eerdmans.com

Contents

Contributors

J. Ayodeji Adewuya   Associate Professor of Greek and New Testament, Church of God Theological Seminary

Paul M. Bassett   Emeritus Professor of the History of Christianity, Nazarene Theological Seminary, Kansas City, Missouri

Richard Bauckham   Formerly Professor of New Testament Studies and Bishop Wardlaw Professor, University of St. Andrews

George J. Brooke   Rylands Professor of Biblical Criticism and Exegesis, University of Manchester

Kent E. Brower   Vice-Principal and Senior Lecturer in Biblical Studies, Nazarene Theological College, Manchester

Dean Flemming   Lecturer in New Testament, European Nazarene College, Büsingen

Michael J. Gorman   Dean of the Ecumenical Institute of Theology and Professor of Sacred Scripture at St. Mary's Seminary and University

Joel B. Green   Professor of New Testament Interpretation, Fuller Theological Seminary

Donald A. Hagner   George Eldon Ladd Professor of New Testament, Fuller Theological Seminary

ANDY JOHNSON   Professor of New Testament, Nazarene Theological Seminary

GEORGE LYONS   Professor of New Testament, Northwest Nazarene College

I. HOWARD MARSHALL   Professor Emeritus, University of Aberdeen

TROY W. MARTIN   Professor of New Testament, Saint Xavier University

PETER OAKES   Greenwood Lecturer in the New Testament, University of Manchester

RUTH ANNE REESE   Associate Professor of New Testament, Asbury Theological Seminary

DWIGHT SWANSON   Senior Lecturer in Biblical Studies, Nazarene Theological College, Manchester

†GORDON J. THOMAS   Lecturer in Biblical Studies, Nazarene Theological College, Manchester

RICHARD P. THOMPSON   Professor of New Testament, School of Theology and Christian Ministries, Northwest Nazarene University

J. ROSS WAGNER   Associate Professor of New Testament, Princeton Theological Seminary

ROBERT W. WALL   The Paul T. Walls Professor of Scripture and Wesleyan Studies, Seattle Pacific University

BRUCE W. WINTER   Principal and Lecturer in Systematic Theology, Queensland Theological College, Brisbane

† deceased

Abbreviations

AB	Anchor Bible
AGJU	Arbeiten zur Geschichte des antiken Judentums und des Urchristentums Roms im Spiegel der neueren Forschung. Edited by H. Temporini and W. Haase. Berlin, 1972–
ACNT	Augsburg Commentaries on the New Testament
ANRW	*Aufstieg und Niedergang der römischen Welt: Geschichte und Kultur*
ANTC	Abingdon New Testament Commentaries
BBB	*Bulletin de bibliographie biblique*
BDAG	Bauer, W., F. W. Danker, W. F. Arndt, and F. W. Gingrich. *Greek English Lexicon of the New Testament and Other Early Christian Literature.* 3rd ed. Chicago, 1999.
BDF	Blass, F., A. Debrunner, and R. W. Funk, *A Greek Grammar of the New Testament and other early Christian Literature.* Chicago, 1961.
BECNT	Baker Exegetical Commentary on the New Testament
BETL	Bibliotheca ephemeridum theologicarum lovaniensium
BICSSup	British Institute of Classical Studies: Supplement Series
BIS	Biblical Interpretation Series
BNTC	Black's New Testament Commentaries
BRS	Biblical Resources Series
BU	Biblische Untersuchungen
BZNW	Beihefte zur Zeitschrift für die neutestamentliche Wissenschaft
CC	Continental Commentaries
CCWJCW	Cambridge Commentaries on the Writings of the Jewish and Christian World 200 BC to AD 200
CNT	Commentarie du Nouveau Testament
DJD	Discoveries in the Judaean Desert
EDNT	*Exegetical Dictionary of the New Testament.* Edited by H. Balz and G. Schneider. ET. Grand Rapids, 1990-93.
EKKNT	Evangelisch-Katholischer Kommentar zum Neuen Testament

GNC	Good News Commentary
GNS	*Good News Studies*
HNTC	Harper's New Testament Commentaries
HTKNT	Herders theologischer Kommentar zum Neuen Testament
ICC	International Critical Commentary
IVPNTC	InterVarsity Press New Testament Commentary
JB	Jerusalem Bible
JPTSup	Journal of Pentecostal Theology Supplement Series
JSJSup	Journal for the Study of Judaism in the Persian, Hellenistic, and Roman Periods: Supplement Series
JSNTSup	Journal for the Study of the New Testament: Supplement Series
JSOTSup	Journal for the Study of the Old Testament: Supplement Series
KEK	Kritisch-exegetischer Kommentar über das Neue Testament (Meyer-Kommentar)
KJV	King James Version
LSJ	Liddell, H. G., R. Scott, H. S. Jones, *A Greek-English Lexicon*. 9th ed. with revised supplement. Oxford, 1996.
LXX	Septuagint
MG	Moulton, W. F., A. S. Geden, H. K. Moulton, *Concordance to the Greek New Testament*. 5th ed. Edinburgh, 1978.
NA^{27}	*Novum Testamentum Graece,* Nestle-Aland, 27th ed.
NAB	New American Bible
NASB	New American Standard Bible
NCB	New Century Bible
NCBC	New Cambridge Bible Commentary
NClaB	New Clarendon Bible
NEB	New English Bible
NIB	*The New Interpreter's Bible*
NICNT	New International Commentary on the New Testament
NICOT	New International Commentary on the Old Testament
NIGTC	New International Greek Testament Commentary
NIV	New International Version
NIVAC	NIV Application Commentary
NovTSup	Supplements to Novum Testamentum
NRSV	New Revised Standard Version
NSBT	New Studies in Biblical Theology
NTC	The New Testament in Context
NTL	New Testament Library
NTTS	New Testament Tools and Studies
OBT	Overtures to Biblical Theology
OTL	Old Testament Library
PBTM	Paternoster Biblical and Theological Monographs
PillarNTC	The Pillar New Testament Commentary

RSV	Revised Standard Version
SBLDS	Society of Biblical Literature Dissertation Series
SBLEJL	Society of Biblical Literature Early Judaism and its Literature
SBLMS	Society of Biblical Literature Monograph Series
SBLSymS	Society of Biblical Literature Symposium Series
SBT	Studies in Biblical Theology
SDSS	Studies in the Dead Sea Scrolls and Related Literature
SJLA	Studies in Judaism in Late Antiquity
SNTSMS	Society for New Testament Studies Monograph Series
SP	Sacra pagina
SSEJC	*Studies in Early Judaism and Christianity*
SSU	Studia Semitica Uppsaliensia
StBL	Studies in Biblical Literature
STDJ	*Studies on the Texts of the Desert of Judah*
STJHC	Studies and Texts in Jewish History and Culture
TANZ	Texte und Arbeiten zum neutestamentlichen Zeitalter
THKNT	Theologischer Handkommentar zum Neuen Testament
TNTC	Tyndale New Testament Commentaries
UBS⁴	*The Greek New Testament,* United Bible Societies, 4th ed.
WPC	Westminster Pelican Commentaries
WUNT	Wissenschaftliche Untersuchungen zum Neuen Testament
ZBK	Zürcher Bibelkommentare
ZC	Zondervan Commentary

Dedication to Alex R. G. Deasley

Paul M. Bassett

In the early 1970s, we had a student at Nazarene Theological Seminary (NTS) in Kansas City who seemed to have an academic standard, a teacher and mentor under whom he had studied in Britain who, for him, was the standard of excellence in all things intellectual (and spiritual as well). He had sat under this mentor in Manchester, England, at what was then British Isles Nazarene College (now Nazarene Theological College). But we wondered sometimes if he did not think it to have been the Alexandria of Clement and Origen, or the Hippo of Augustine, or the Paris of Thomas Aquinas. He loved to intone the name of that mentor with his Scottish tongue on every suitable, or even nearly suitable, occasion. "Alex R. G. Deasley," he would say, and in Scottish fashion, he pronounced it "Alec," even though it was spelled "Alex." He would sometimes invoke the name in class, shooting it off with an attached opinion so that it vibrated and ricocheted around the room in rebuke of some poor fellow student's belief in the theological equivalent of a flat earth or ignorance of any of the world outside of Pecos County, Texas. And of course, for him "Alex R. G. Deasley" trumped the authority of any *"Guru du Jour"* in those years, such as Von Rad or Bultmann or Tillich. Because the student was quite bright and open, and because several of the faculty already knew "Alex R. G. Deasley," it did not fall on our ears as some tiresome mantra, but was taken in good part. "Alex R. G. Deasley": I can still hear it and you can too if you walk into any classroom at Nazarene Theological Seminary and listen quietly.

My own firsthand acquaintance with Alex really begins in 1976, when we worked together at an ecumenical youth and young adult retreat sponsored by the Church of the Nazarene in the United Kingdom. The experience confirmed my inclinations that working with him would be a treat to be treasured. By the time he arrived at NTS in 1977, some around our Seminary were expressing their concern that the "hype" that had preceded Prof. Deasley's arrival might impede his immediate effectiveness at NTS. He had distinguished himself as a scholar, beginning even before his high school days at the prestigious King Edward School in Birmingham. He had earned an Honours M.A. from Cambridge, and a Ph.D. under the direction of F. F. Bruce, at Manchester. He had not simply muddled through, but had excelled in one of the toughest intellectual climates in the world. Along with other duties, he had served as pastor of congregations in Scotland, Canada, and England. And he had already, still in his twenties, clearly made a mark as a teacher and preacher on both sides of the Atlantic. Any visit to North America had seen his calendar filled with preaching engagements — everywhere — and many places more than once, as schedule allowed. Distinction still surrounds his name and service at Nazarene Theological College, Manchester. In Canada, he served as Professor of New Testament at what was then Canadian Nazarene College; and there, he was a principal figure as the college entered formal relationships with the University of Manitoba, where he also taught in the Department of Religion.

He has always insisted that he is a preacher on loan to theological education; and he made that clear in coming to NTS in 1977. To our unsurprised but exceeding great joy, he served us splendidly in both ways. We experienced the sheer spiritual delight of hearing the Holy Spirit speak through the artful exposition of the Word by Prof. Deasley across these years in a variety of settings. And, that devotion to digging into the Word itself, in a spirit of prayer and humble service, has rubbed off on students, too. If you ask most students who went to NTS between 1977 and 2002 from whom they yearned most to hear the Gospel among those they heard here, you will hear "Alex R. G. Deasley" in every short list. What one hears in his preaching is not simply an encounter with the text, but an encounter with the Lord himself; what one sees in the pulpit is an instrument finely tuned so that we will not mistake the instrument for the music; nor the instrumentalist for the composer.

There clearly has been no strut in him, of course. Students went to his classes knowing the demand would be great, but so would be the reward of their labor. (And who else around NTS has chosen words with tweezers [as several have said], thinks in paragraphs, and speaks carefully enough that even Oliver Hardy could "write it down for you"?) The faculty knew they could count on him to do whatever he does with seamless integrity, skill, and insight.

His friends and fellow academics know well something of the vastness of his learning and the depth of his wisdom, and we moan, "How we wish he'd had more time to write." And then we call on him to be the editor of the *Wesleyan Theological Journal* for most of a decade, or some entity calls on him to write a report in confidence on some prickly subject. And he responds to such calls to service with grace. He puts the *Wesleyan Theological Journal* on the professional academic map; and the report on Prickly Subject becomes the basic study document for guiding the thinking of the Church on that issue. His recent books — on marriage and divorce,[1] and on the Dead Sea Scrolls[2] — are superb contributions to the education of Christ's Church, and merit far larger readership than they are receiving.

As we have already noted, Prof. Deasley has often said that he is a preacher on loan to theological education. I do not doubt for a moment that such is his deep feeling. But as one yoked to him in theological education at NTS for twenty-five years, I respectfully suggest that the metaphor simply doesn't work. He has given too generously and freely (to us) out of his trust fund of gifts and graces, and invested (in us) far too deeply the resources of an exceedingly well-furnished mind and loving heart for us even to begin to think in terms of "loan." The words "gifts" and "commitment" spring too readily to mind.

So now, in honor of the long, superbly executed, fruitful, and faithful scholarly work of Alex Deasley, we offer a salute peculiar to scholars marking a high moment in the career of one of their own — we dedicate to him a celebratory collection of scholarly essays written by friends, former students, and colleagues in his academic field. The Table of Contents presents a truly distinguished list of contributors. We thank them deeply; and we thank Andy Johnson and Kent Brower, respectively, Alex Deasley's successor at NTS and his successor at Nazarene Theological College, Manchester, for their editorial work, as well as their own essays in the volume.

Oh yes. The occasion for this celebration? Our friend and mentor's seventieth birthday, May 10, 2005. And may God grant us the gift of his company for many years to come.

Musicologists have long noted that at the end of his religious pieces, Johann Sebastian Bach almost always wrote the Latin words *Sōli Deō Gloria* — "to God alone be the glory." I am sure that those who have done the honors in writing for this collection, and the one to whom the collection is dedicated, are no less firm in their yearning that while they have celebrated great gifts by exercising their own gifts, it will be the God from whom those great gifts come who will indeed "alone receive the glory."

1. Alex R. G. Deasley, *Marriage and Divorce in the Bible and the Church* (Kansas City: Beacon Hill, 2000).

2. Alex R. G. Deasley, *The Shape of Qumran Theology* (Carlisle: Paternoster, 2000).

Introduction: Holiness and the *Ekklēsia* of God

KENT E. BROWER AND ANDY JOHNSON

Locating the Project

In the ecclesial contexts of the United Kingdom and North America, thinking about the people of God is often reduced to how an individual is related to God and the category of holiness is either ignored, reduced to inward piety, or thought to be the preserve of legalists. Throughout the biblical story, however, the people of God are expected to embody God's holy character publicly in particular social settings.[1] Hence, holiness is a theological and ecclesial issue prior to being a matter of individual piety. Therefore, this volume intentionally approaches the issue of holiness from an ecclesial standpoint and participates in a larger discussion indicating a renewed interest in the theme of the holiness of God and of the people of God.[2] Given this ecclesial context, there is a need for

---

1. The current interest in the specific area of ecclesiology as it relates to the character of God is exemplified in such works as Miroslav Volf, *After Our Likeness: The Church as the Image of the Trinity* (Grand Rapids: Eerdmans, 1998) and Samuel M. Powell and Michael E. Lodahl, eds., *Embodied Holiness: Toward a Corporate Theology of Spiritual Growth* (Downers Grove, Ill.: InterVarsity, 1999). On the current interest in ecclesiological matters in the NT and in general see Richard N. Longenecker, ed., *Community Formation in the Early Church and the Church Today* (Peabody, Mass.: Hendrickson, 2002); John G. Stackhouse, ed., *Evangelical Ecclesiology: Reality or Illusion?* (Grand Rapids: Baker Academic, 2003); Mark Husbands and Daniel J. Treier, eds., *The Community of the Word: Towards an Evangelical Ecclesiology* (Downers Grove, Ill.: InterVarsity, 2005).

2. E.g., recent works include: David Willis, *Notes on the Holiness of God* (Grand Rapids: Eerdmans, 2002); Stephen C. Barton, ed., *Holiness Past and Present* (London: T&T Clark, 2003); John Webster, *Holiness* (Grand Rapids/Cambridge: Eerdmans, 2003); Thomas Jay Oord and Michael Lodahl, *Relational Holiness: Responding to the Call of Love* (Kansas City: Beacon Hill Press of Kansas City, 2005); Kent E. Brower, *Holiness in the Gospels* (Kansas City: Beacon Hill Press of Kansas City, 2005).

serious engagement with NT texts whose ultimate aim is to stimulate churches to imagine anew what it might mean to be a publicly identifiable people who embody God's very character in their particular social setting. This volume provides a context in which this kind of engagement can take place. It explores how the concepts of holiness and the people of God are related as they come to expression in a variety of biblical documents. A significant part of most of the essays focus on how such an exploration provides direction for shaping a local church (in the UK and North American contexts) into an ecclesial community.

There are some clear limitations immediately apparent in this volume. Most obvious is the absence of essays on the Old Testament. The essays are restricted to Qumran and the NT[3] simply on account of the limitations of what is possible to include in one volume and because of the primary academic interests of the dedicatee. But each of the essayists is acutely conscious of the fact that the whole discussion has its roots firmly fixed in the soil of the Old Testament and the historical context of the Second Temple period.

The essays are written from diverse viewpoints. They deal with NT and Qumran documents which are themselves diverse in terms of their views of holiness and the people of God. Among the contributors, there is a diversity of specialization, methodological approach, and theological assumptions. Thus, the contributors often take different approaches to a range of issues. We have made no attempt to flatten the differences. There is general agreement in this volume that God not only calls a people as a whole to reflect God's holy character but that the Spirit enables the fulfillment of that call *to some extent* prior to the eschaton. All contributors agree that the people of God are called to live lives that reflect their new status as the saints. However, there continues to be disagreement over just how much grace-enabled transformation a community as a whole and the persons within it might expect to experience prior to the eschaton.

In this introductory essay, we do not attempt to summarize each of the other essays in the volume. Nor do we explicitly try to represent the views of each essay. Rather, we offer an interpretive overview of what we take to be some of the main themes that have emerged from the essays and attempt to tie them together in a coherent fashion.

3. We are also conscious of the lack of total coverage of the NT. Most serious, perhaps, is our lack of essays on Colossians and the Johannine epistles, both of which would have much to say on the subject of this volume. Due to a variety of factors, we were simply not able to offer separate essays on each NT document.

Themes Emerging in the Volume

Holiness as an Orienting Concern for Second Temple Judaism and for Early Christianity

In the introductions to a good number of the essays, the contributors note the lack of "holiness" vocabulary in their assigned document and use language like: "At first glance, then, this document may not seem to have much to contribute to the issue of holiness and ecclesiology" (e.g., Bauckham, Thompson, cf. Brower). Of course, they then continue right on with their essays! This reflects the growing awareness that the holiness of God and of God's people is an orienting concern of every part of the NT, a backdrop presumed by its writers whether or not they use such language.

The two essays on Qumran and those on the Gospels traverse familiar ground in showing that the concern for what it means to be a *holy* people of God is a widespread and fundamental issue in the milieu of Second Temple Judaism in which Jesus lives and from which Christianity emerges. The quest for holiness is the key to the self-understanding of the Qumran community as well as that of the Pharisees. In fact, the Jesus movement may be understood as a competing holiness/renewal movement within Second Temple piety. In such a context, holiness and purity practices, although distinguishable (Bauckham), are directly related and a key source of controversy between Jesus and the Pharisees.

In general, the holiness of the people of God in the Second Temple period is understood in terms of boundary maintenance, i.e., as separation from impurity. This leads to a purity-based social system whose purpose is to safeguard the conditions under which God's people could experience God's (dangerous) holy presence. God's holy presence could not be contaminated by impurity. At Qumran, perfect obedience to God's will as revealed in Torah is the key ingredient of holiness and the language of perfection is noteworthy. This is not simply legalism, however. Outward obedience is to be matched by inward purity of heart, expressed both in the purity of lives lived and in the context of worship. The community may have had a sense of participation with the Angels of the Presence in offering worship to the holy God, a service that required perfection. They are to be a kingdom of priests. Likewise, the Pharisees are concerned with the purity of the whole land, extending the priestly standards of purity beyond the temple.

Jesus' concern with holiness takes a different tack. Whereas the Pharisees require repentance and ritual purity *before* inclusion within the holy community, Jesus eats with sinners so that they might repent (Thompson). He thereby redefines holiness by crossing purity boundaries bringing the compassion/purifying love of God to bear on the lives of those who have been excluded from God's people. Hence, Jesus, "the Holy One of God," is not contaminated by impurity but rather, as the bearer of the Holy Spirit of God, is characterized by a holiness that is contagious and transforming as it confronts the impure and the sinful.[4] Jesus embodies active holiness and brings outcasts, the impure and the unholy, into the sphere of his holiness and thereby transforms those whom he touches. The disciples are called to be on his mission but it is only as they are following this Holy One along the way that leads to the cross that they themselves can be called holy (Brower). Their holiness, therefore, is always a derived holiness that comes from their continuing relationship with the Holy One.

Holiness as Derived Holiness

One thing that the OT, Second Temple Judaism, and the NT all agree on is that holiness is never an independent possession of an individual or a community. A community and people are holy only insofar as they are in relation to the Holy One. In varying degrees, most of the essays in this volume argue that "being in relation" to the Holy One connotes some degree of reflection of the character of that One. Hence, defining the character of the Holy One of God is crucial for discussions involving the holiness of God's people.

While the Gospels make clear that Jesus' life and teachings begin to redefine holiness in terms of saving compassion towards those on the margins of God's people, several essays in this volume on the Pauline epistles argue that holiness is further (and scandalously) reconfigured in terms of "cruciformity."[5] Given that the NT as a whole maintains that it is Jesus who reveals the character of the God of Israel (the nature of God's holiness), it is the whole Christ event which thereby reveals just how far God will go in the exercise of outward-looking, saving compassion. The cross becomes the preeminent place where God's holiness is publicly displayed, where the crucified Son *reveals the very character of the Triune God*. In Stephen Barton's terms, holiness has been dislocated and relocated in the *crucified Lord*,[6] a conception that makes little sense

---

4. As we note below, however, not all purity practices are abandoned by the followers of the "Holy One of God." In Acts and in some of Paul's letters, certain purity practices continue to have a role in marking out the holy people of God.

5. Joel Green uses similar language in his essay on 1 Peter when he argues that the holiness tradition of the OT upon which Peter draws heavily is "now fundamentally branded by the crucifixion of Jesus" (p. 320).

6. Stephen C. Barton, "Dislocating and Relocating Holiness: A New Testament Study," in *Holiness Past and Present*, pp. 193-213 (p. 205).

apart from a Trinitarian understanding of God. Hence, as Michael Gorman argues, Paul undertakes a "Trinitarian reconstruction of holiness" and the character of the sanctity/holiness which derives from this God may best be described as "cruciformity," aggressively self-giving, saving love (Gorman, pp. 148-66). Affirming this as the direction that the NT moves gives support to David Willis's contention that it is a theological mistake to make transcendence and immanence opposites and to subsume holiness almost exclusively under the category of transcendence.[7] Rather the NT suggests that the transcendent One is freely immanent to fulfill God's covenanting, saving purposes. Hence, the witness of the NT suggests, as Willis contends, that the Triune God is not best described as "the wholly other" but as "the Holy Other" who confronts us as purifying love.[8]

Holiness as Purity

While the extent of personal transformation prior to the eschaton is still an issue of debate in this volume, in the NT God demands both internal and external purity from God's people. The Triune God confronts us as *purifying* love. God's call to holiness and the gift of sanctifying grace both demands and, by means of the Spirit, effects transformation/purification of one's inner dispositions and attitudes in ways that enable God's people to embody cruciform love in the public practices of the *ekklēsia*. In contrast to much of Enlightenment-influenced Protestant Christianity, the NT does not bracket "inner" intentions and dispositions off from their embodiment in public practices. The NT understands persons as embodied wholes. To co-opt Douglas Harink's words: "God's gracious work through Christ and the Spirit is . . . depicted as spread over the whole range of human life, active and passive, attitudinal and bodily, inner and outer, personal, social, and political."[9]

While cruciform practices are the *distinctive* dimension of a holiness that has been redefined through the crucified messiah, the NT continues to affirm certain basic Jewish understandings of holiness as purity or difference from Gentiles, e.g., avoiding sexual immorality and idolatry (Wall). Behind these purity practices may be seen the enhancement and protection of the new covenant community from the contagious infection of sin. Such practices that uphold the community's set-apartness are not unrelated to the distinctive dimension of holiness as the practice of costly love. For example, as Gorman points out,

---

7. *Notes on the Holiness of God*, p. 1, passim.
8. *Notes on the Holiness of God*, pp. 2-3.
9. Douglas Harink, *Paul Among the Postliberals* (Grand Rapids: Brazos, 2003), p. 35.

"[f]or Paul, sexual immorality (Greek *porneia*) . . . and cruciform love cannot co-exist, for *porneia* is a form of self-love, of self-indulgence that harms others and diminishes the holiness of both the individual and the community" (Gorman, p. 165). And, given the religious and political climate of the NT, purity practices that guard against compromising one's loyalty to the crucified Lord are necessary.[10] In an honor/shame society in which crucifixion is the most shameful way to die and where aggressively seeking social status is simply "common sense," unless people are being transformed from the inside out it is difficult to imagine that they will either become or remain totally devoted to a *crucified* Lord. It is difficult to imagine that they will remain a part of a community whose communal life calls for and displays the very opposite of blatant status enhancement, i.e., love for the sake of the other.

But separation from the practices of the world is never an end in itself but a means by which the character of God is manifest in his holy people. Many of the essays in this volume offer a corrective to the view that holiness is best demonstrated by isolation from society. As Swanson notes, "For the Church, the Holiest Place is not found in separation from the world, but within the world" (Swanson, p. 38).

At the same time, holy living is often counter-cultural, whether it be set against the uncannily post-modern-like pagan context of Corinth (see Winter) or the legalistic tendencies of some religious separationist practice. This counter-cultural shape of the embodiment of holiness comes through in a number of essays. Winter is particularly acute in his analysis of the residual pagan influence within the lives of Paul's Corinthian converts who have yet to understand and embody the implications of their new life in Christ as his holy ones. Their understanding of their new freedom in Christ has not been matched by an equally robust understanding of the implications of their new status and existence in Christ. Paul's call to his Corinthian converts to lead lives worthy of their calling, and his expectation that they (and we) should do so, is even more striking than Winter's reading suggests.

Holiness for Communal Persons

If indeed "cruciformity" is a crucial dimension of God's holiness that emerges in the NT, responding to God's call to be holy requires the exhibition of costly,

---

10. E.g., taking care not to eat meat in the temple of a god/goddess (1 Corinthians 10) or exercising caution (1 Corinthians 8–11) or avoiding altogether (Acts 15; Revelation 2) the eating of *eidolothyta*.

self-giving, status-lowering practices toward others. Hence, God's sanctifying grace calls for and enables an ethical response within an inherently communal framework (Wagner). That is, God's call to holiness comes to a people/community, not to *isolated individuals*. Holiness is profoundly ethical in character and lived in the public sphere. But this is far more than simply individual ethical living in a societal context. Such a recognition is crucial, especially when the typically Protestant way of thinking about holiness/sanctification in the North American and UK contexts has been to focus on isolated individuals and then argue about what God's grace is or is not able to accomplish in their lives. By gathering the *twelve* around him as a microcosm of restored Israel, Jesus displayed God's intention to *form a people* who would embody God's character and draw the nations to God.

This call to embody the character of the Triune God cannot, however, be reduced to a kind of communal abstraction, i.e., a call that somehow comes to "the whole community" but seemingly affects no one person in particular. While God's call to holiness and God's sanctifying grace does not come to *isolated individuals,* it does indeed come to *communal persons.* Indeed, it characteristically comes *from* the Holy Spirit *through* the grace-enabled concrete practices of people who accompany us on our way to the eschatological new creation when our communion with the Triune God and with each other will be completely perfected. Therefore, rightly ordered relationships within the new covenant community requiring such costly practices as forgiveness, reconciliation, and restoration of the wayward sister or brother are not optional. God's call to holiness and sanctifying grace does not come to communal persons apart from the community that is being sanctified together.

Public Nature of Holiness

In continuity with Israel's vocation in the OT, the people of God in the NT continue to be set apart from the surrounding culture as a "kingdom" and "priests" for the purpose of publicly witnessing to/embodying God's rule and healing presence to the nations. As we have noted, the purpose of being distinctively different is not to escape from the world. Nor is it limited to some "spiritual" realm as opposed to the work-a-day world of politics and economics. Indeed, the NT recognizes that "powers and principalities" opposed to the present and coming rule of God are manifest in social, political, economic, and religious structures as well as in the actions of individuals. Hence, when the NT is situated in its first-century socio-political setting, holiness is not limited to the typically modern realm of "the religious." Rather, it involves publicly engaging various unholy powers that would impede the *shalom* that God's coming rule will bring for the whole creation. It is what Joel Green refers to as a "holiness of engagement," that results in cruciform communities whose life together is a public exhibit that challenges dominant ways of organizing life (e.g., the patron/client system, the imperial cult).

In this context, separation is far more than just avoiding evil. God's people are indeed to live pure lives, but this runs far deeper than the micro-ethical concerns that have led to the legalism that has marred holiness movements for two millennia. It is also about the church exposing and resisting the corrupt powers and ideologies that challenge God's rule in the world. In simple terms, God's people shun and oppose idolatry, that is, any loyalty that usurps the allegiance to God and his purposes. If the sexual mores and status-seeking problems in Corinth have a distinctly post-modern ring to them, the political, economic, and military hegemony of Rome that is the backdrop to Revelation provides an eerie backlight to contemporary imperialistic hegemonies. The people of God are called to continue to bear prophetic holy witness against all arrogations of divine prerogatives and authority by modern nation states, however they clothe themselves. The public sphere cannot be abandoned, no matter how costly the witness might be.

The complacency of individualised piety is shattered by Flemming's theologically astute reading of the book of Revelation. By demonstrating undiluted loyalty to the Triune God in the war against the beastly powers, the people of God in Revelation "have his [the lamb's] name and the name of his Father written upon their foreheads" (Rev. 14:1). In Revelation's symbolic world, such a "mark" is publicly visible; it is not hidden or private. By its very nature the "true church" which is pure and blameless (Rev. 14:4-5) is *not* "invisible." Hence, as they "follow the lamb wherever he goes" (Rev. 14:4), as a people they become a visible and "living exegesis"[11] of the narrative of the crucified Christ. And therefore, they become a public embodiment of the very character of the Triune God.

Hence, as the Spirit enables the church to recapitulate the story of the crucified one through self-giving actions exhibiting costly love towards each other and those outside it, it cannot help but stand out in a visible and public way. It is indeed the visible body of the crucified Lord, the Holy One of God. As such, it is not only the primary locale of the sanctifying Spirit of God, a sphere of holiness where communal persons are being sanctified together, but also a powerful and public instrument of mission (Revelation 11). Its members are in-

---

11. The language is from Michael J. Gorman, *Cruciformity: Paul's Narrative Spirituality of the Cross* (Grand Rapids: Eerdmans, 2001), p. 92.

deed "firstfruits for God and the lamb" (Rev. 14:4) whose Spirit-empowered public witness is the catalyst for the fuller harvest to come when God's covenanting purpose testified to throughout the Bible is fulfilled, i.e., when the holy God dwells with God's holy people in a holy place.[12]

12. This last phrase is from Gordon J. Thomas, "A Holy God Among a Holy People in a Holy Place: The Enduring Eschatological Hope," in *Eschatology in Bible & Theology: Evangelical Essays at the Dawn of a New Millennium,* ed. Kent E. Brower and Mark W. Elliott (Downers Grove, Ill.: InterVarsity, 1997), pp. 53-69.

The Dead Sea Scrolls and
New Testament Ecclesiology

GEORGE J. BROOKE

I. Introduction

Most of the contributions to this collection of essays are discussions of the concept of holiness from one angle or another. The dominant assumptions, and good Wesleyan ones at that, seem to be that the concept somehow embodies some of the principal features of what it is to be a church, and that the concept does not concern individual piety alone, or even at all, but is integral to how groups of Jews and Gentiles understood themselves as constituting the people of God in their local contexts. The study of the self-understanding of such groups and how they considered themselves to be a church, the people of God locally, is the backbone of ecclesiology. This contribution makes some general observations about the character of the religious group(s) who lived at Qumran. These observations do not intend to be comprehensive but are offered so as to indicate at least some of what needs to be kept in mind in the modern construction of any particular New Testament ecclesiology, especially if any such construction is used to propose models for Christian organisation and behaviour in the present day.

Given that few scholars nowadays would identify Jesus or his immediate followers with those who inhabited Qumran[1] and that the consensus about John the Baptist is that he may have been familiar with the beliefs and practices of the Qumran community but probably had never been a member,[2] why

---

1. See, e.g., the general remarks on this by O. Betz and R. Riesner, *Jesus, Qumran and the Vatican: Clarifications* (London: SCM, 1994); H. W. Kuhn, "Jesus," in *Encyclopedia of the Dead Sea Scrolls*, ed. L. H. Schiffman and J. C. VanderKam (New York: Oxford University Press, 2000), pp. 404-8; G. J. Brooke, "Dead Sea Scrolls," in *Jesus in History, Thought, and Culture: An Encyclopedia*, ed. J. L. Houlden (Santa Barbara/Oxford: ABC-Clio, 2003), pp. 201-6.

2. See the excellent summary article and bibliography by R. L. Webb, "John the Baptist," in *Encyclopedia of the Dead Sea Scrolls*, pp. 418-21.

should a consideration of the Qumran community find its way into a book which is essentially about the individuals and churches reflected in the various New Testament writings?[3] For pragmatic reasons, a general chapter on some features of the Qumran community can indeed inform the discussion about New Testament ecclesiologies in many significant ways. The focus on Qumran arises because of the character of the library that has been found in the eleven caves at and near Qumran: it seems to contain the remains of about nine hundred scrolls, many of which share a similar ideological framework which, together, are clearly datable and provide insight into the workings of a particular community and the wider movement of which it was a part in ways which virtually no other set of writings from antiquity offer the modern reader. The fact that they are close in time and place, as well as religious tradition, to the early Christian communities makes their use for the study of the New Testament entirely justifiable.

The community of the scrolls also shares several key features with some of the New Testament communities. The similarities in belief, organisation, and practice have been commented on since the scrolls first came to light.[4] It is also important to recall in particular that the community of the scrolls and some of the early Christian communities seem to have operated with similar attitudes to authoritative traditions. Similar scriptural materials are used as touchstones for community self-understanding, the very range of which allows for different self-expressions to come to the fore in different kinds of texts or at different periods. Furthermore, this range of diverse self-expressions suggests a flexibility towards tradition that needs to be rediscovered in some modem appropriations of tradition.

---

3. See G. J. Brooke, "The Scrolls and the Study of the New Testament," in *The Dead Sea Scrolls at Fifty*, SBLEJL 15, ed. R. A. Kugler and E. M. Schuller (Atlanta: Scholars Press, 1999), pp. 61-76, esp. p. 76, where mere lip-service to the Jewish context of Jesus is noted.

4. Several volumes of essays and monographs have become classics: K. Stendahl, ed., *The Scrolls and the New Testament* (New York: Harper, 1957; London: SCM, 1958; republished New York: Crossroad, 1992); J. Murphy-O'Connor, ed., *Paul and Qumran* (London: Geoffrey Chapman, 1968), republished as J. Murphy-O'Connor and J. H. Charlesworth, eds., *Paul and the Dead Sea Scrolls* (New York: Crossroad, 1990); M. Black, ed., *The Scrolls and Christianity* (London: SPCK, 1969); J. A. Fitzmyer, *Essays on the Semitic Background of the New Testament* (London: Geoffrey Chapman, 1971; Missoula: Scholars Press, 1974), republished as part of *The Semitic Background of the New Testament* (Grand Rapids/Livonia: Eerdmans/Dove Booksellers, 1997); J. H. Charlesworth, ed., *John and Qumran* (London: Geoffrey Chapman, 1972), republished as J. H. Charlesworth, ed., *John and the Dead Sea Scrolls* (New York: Crossroad, 1990); N. S. Fujita, *A Crack in the Jar: What Ancient Jewish Documents Tell Us about the New Testament* (New York: Paulist, 1986).

II. Implications from the Qumran Scrolls

A. *Change and Development*

The first implication from the Qumran scrolls for the better appreciation of New Testament ecclesiologies concerns change and development. With the complete publication of the manuscript discoveries in the Qumran caves it is possible to attempt to plot change and development in the Qumran community and the movement of which it was a part in ways not envisaged even twenty years ago. The reconsideration of the archaeology of the site has also given rise to a more subtle appreciation of the history of the community that lived there. The consideration of two examples will highlight the need for New Testament scholars to continue to take into account in ever more subtle ways the place of change and development in the ecclesiologies they observe in and behind the various documents they study, before it is assumed in a naive way that the views, for example, of Paul or of the Johannine tradition are there to be taken over straightforwardly as models of holiness in easily defined fixed terms.

The Teacher of Righteousness

The first example concerns the Teacher of Righteousness. The identity of the so-called Teacher of Righteousness remains a mystery, but a general consensus has emerged that he was active in the life of the Essene movement in the second century BCE.[5] A variety of factors have resulted in this consensus. These can be briefly listed. (1) The *Damascus Document* (CD) implies that the Teacher began his leadership role 410 years after the start of the exile in 586 BCE. Even if the numbers in CD 1:5-10 are symbolically schematic rather than factually accurate, for the symbolism to work the implication is still that the Teacher was active in the mid-second century BCE. (2) Study of the various manuscripts of the *Thanksgiving Hymns (Hodayot)* strongly suggests that the complete compilation was brought together in the first half of the first century BCE. Given the long-standing recognition that the poems in the compilation can be categorised as either "Community Hymns" or "Teacher Hymns,"[6] it is likely that the

---

5. See, e.g., M. A. Knibb, "Teacher of Righteousness," in *Encyclopedia of the Dead Sea Scrolls,* pp. 918-21.

6. The authorship of these hymns is most cautiously expressed by M. A. Knibb, *The Qumran Community,* CCWJCW (Cambridge: Cambridge University Press, 1987), p. 158: "There are some psalms behind which a distinct personality does seem to stand, and it is possible — but no more than this — that these should be regarded as psalms composed by the teacher of righteousness."

composition of many of the individual hymns belongs in the second century BCE. (3) An argument from silence supports a second-century date for the Teacher: none of the copies of the principal rule book associated in its final form with Qumran itself, the *Rule of the Community,* mentions the Teacher. Since these were describing the organisation and practices of the community from the end of the second century BCE onwards, it seems likely that they were composed after his demise.

What is the point of mentioning the Teacher in the present context? The recent re-evaluation of Qumran archaeology has resulted in the strong argument that the site was probably not occupied before the beginning of the first century BCE; indeed it is quite likely that it was only taken over by a small group of Essenes sometime in the first quarter of the first century BCE.[7] With the Teacher active in the movement in the second century and the site at Qumran occupied only at the start of the first century, the logical conclusion is that the Teacher never went to Qumran with the community that occupied the site; he had probably been dead for some years before the move was made by a small group from amongst the Essenes. The role of changing leadership within the Essene movement needs fresh consideration and such consideration may have implications for understandings of changing leadership patterns in early Christian communities.

Why did a small number of Essenes come to take up residence at Qumran in the first century BCE? Numerous possibilities have been considered over the years and it is not necessary to rehearse them all here. In sum, either the move could have been the result of any one or more of a range of pressures external to the group, such as arguments with those in political control in Jerusalem, or there could have been circumstances internal to the Essene movement which caused some to move to the north-west shore of the Dead Sea; those circumstances could have been benign, such as a concern that at least some of the membership should live a life of utmost priestly purity, or they could have been malign, such as a theological argument, or a disagreement about the date of the eschaton, or a leadership crisis in the wake of the death of the Teacher.[8] Whatever the case, the movement went through a change of leadership and the pass-

---

7. See the important reassessment of the site by J. Magness, *The Archaeology of Qumran and the Dead Sea Scrolls,* SDSS (Grand Rapids: Eerdmans, 2002), esp. pp. 63-69.

8. By way of example, the so-called Groningen hypothesis argues that there was a split in the Essene movement in which the Man of Lies led some astray while the Teacher of Righteousness on the basis of particular scriptural interpretations and halakhic understandings concerning the calendar and the cult took his followers to Qumran: F. García Martínez and J. Trebolle Barrera, *The People of the Dead Sea Scrolls: Their Writings, Beliefs and Practices* (Leiden: Brill, 1995), pp. 91-96.

ing of the founding figure might have resulted in some of the differences amongst the followers becoming apparently schismatic. The question arises: which community should students of the scrolls seek to describe, the community at Qumran at some stage of its existence, the community which was probably responsible for putting the manuscript collection together, or one of the communities described in one or more of those very manuscripts, one of which was the community established by the founding figure? The same can apply to the New Testament. For constructing an ecclesiology, do scholars start with those who variously put the collection together or with one of the communities described in the compositions that make up the collection, perhaps the one (or more) that describes the community around the founding figure? And what part should be assigned to changing leadership patterns in how communities organise and express their self-understanding?

Changes at Qumran Itself

If there were changes within the Essene movement, possibly a leadership crisis, which resulted in the move of a small number of Essenes to Qumran, it is also likely that while at Qumran for about a century and a half (c. 85 BCE–68 CE) there were also changes within the community of one kind or another. It is thus too simple ever to say that "The Qumran community believed that. . . ." Indeed, the publication of the best-preserved copy of the *Rule of the Community* from Cave 1 (1QS) already suggested that life at Qumran was not static. In 1QS 7:8, the ruling reads "whoever bears a grudge against his fellow unjustly, shall be punished (for) one year,"[9] but the length of the punishment is written in a supralinear correction. It seems as if the original punishment was "six months." If this is not simply a scribal error which is being corrected immediately, it implies that "the penalty was increased."[10] There was some change and development in the punishments meted out for improper behaviour.

The publication of all the copies of the *Rule of the Community* from Qumran Cave 4 has enabled us to see that the changes and developments were probably far more radical than this single adjustment. The most significant difference occurs between what is extant in 1QS column 5 and its counterpart in

---

9. J. H. Charlesworth, trans., in E. Qimron and J. H. Charlesworth, "Rule of the Community," in *Rule of the Community and Related Documents*, The Dead Sea Scrolls: Hebrew, Aramaic, and Greek Texts with English Translations 1, ed. J. C. Charlesworth (Tübingen: J. C. B. Mohr [Paul Siebeck]; Louisville: Westminster John Knox, 1994), pp. 1-51, (p. 31).

10. Charlesworth, "Rule of the Community," p. 31, n. 180. Cf. the comment by M. A. Knibb, *The Qumran Community*, p. 126: "'one year' has been inserted as a correction, thus indicating a change of practice."

4QS^d. In the former the text is addressed to the "men of the community" and authority in many matters appears to reside with the "Sons of Zadok, the priests who keep the covenant." The counterpart in 4QS^d is addressed to the Maskil ("wise teacher" or "master") and authority resides with the Many. How are these differences to be assessed? It seems that there are three options. First, it is possible to argue largely on the basis of the relative dates of the manuscripts that what was formerly under the authority of the Zadokite priests at the early stages of the Qumran community was supplanted by a more democratic exercise of power through the Many.[11] Second, conversely, on the basis of supposing that shorter texts normally precede their longer counterparts and that groups develop from the more egalitarian to the more institutionalised, it can be proposed that the authority of the Many was supplanted by the Zadokite priests, perhaps as a feature of the move to Qumran.[12] Third, the previous two options might be combined so that what began as a more egalitarian movement and became institutionalized through its use of the Zadokite priesthood was yet further rejuvenated with the republication of an earlier form of the *Rule of the Community*.[13]

What emerges from brief consideration of these two examples is that the Qumran community and the wider movement from which it came and of which it continued to be a part was far from a static group. Changes in leadership, in hierarchies, in organisational structure, and in the bases of authority can be noticed and need to be accounted for. For Qumran, the scholarly endeavour in understanding these developments has barely begun, but the implications for the study of the New Testament are sure: even within a relatively small and well-defined movement like the Essenes there is change and development over time, and the models for community organisation change too. Ecclesiology needs to be understood as the description of a dynamic not a static phenomenon. For those who would promote the pursuit of holiness, models of community organisation need to be flexible and dynamic, not rigid and static.

---

11. As has P. S. Alexander, "The Redaction-History of *Serek ha-Yahad*. A Proposal," *Revue de Qumrân* 19/75 (2000): 333-48.

12. As argued by S. Metso, *The Textual Development of the Qumran Community Rule*, STDJ 21 (Leiden: Brill, 1997). Other supporting factors include the increasing explicit use of scriptural passages in the supposedly later versions of the composition.

13. See G. J. Brooke, "From 'Assembly of Supreme Holiness for Aaron' to 'Sanctuary of Adam': The laicization of temple ideology in the Qumran scrolls and its wider implications," *Journal for Semitics* 8 (1996): 119-45.

B. Hierarchies

Within the changing structures of the Qumran community a slight tension is evident between stricter and more informal hierarchical organisation. The way in which a religious group or community organizes itself reflects its self-understanding and what it is trying to represent of the divine economy. At Qumran many compositions directly or indirectly reflect the way the community variously understood itself. The *Rule of the Community* (1QS) is often taken as normative of community structure,[14] but let us consider briefly a couple of other examples of this, the *Temple Scroll* and the *Eschatological Midrash*, and a little of what the implications may be of such texts for New Testament views of the church.

The most complete version of the *Temple Scroll* is an Herodian manuscript (11QT^a), but there is widespread agreement that the composition was probably compiled towards the end of the second century BCE, possibly before part of the Essene movement moved itself to Qumran and took the composition with it. The first major section of the composition is a description of the temple interwoven with descriptions of the various cultic practices which belong to the specific sections of the temple which are being described. This is sometimes described as the joining of two sources together, an architectural plan and a set of cultic rules based on a 364-day calendar. After a largely non-extant preface the composition starts its temple journey in the Holy of Holies and works outwards towards the temple courts and beyond. The view of the world in such a presentation is clearly a priestly one, since only the high priest would have access to the inner sanctum, and that but once a year, and other priests would have been the sole Israelites to work in other focal parts of the sanctuary. In this way the description of the structure of the temple and its services endorses a community hierarchy that puts the high priest at the top, followed by other priests, then the Levites, then male Israelites, then women. The relative grades of the community are clearly delineated and hierarchy (in its literal sense) portrays a particular view of the world.

If the *Temple Scroll* is an implicit attack on practices in Jerusalem contemporary with its compilation, then its promulgation is all the more interesting. Whereas in Jerusalem and its temple the role and status of the priestly hierarchy is obvious because it is encountered daily, for a community that withdrew from the temple such hierarchical roles needed enforcing through other means, such as the promulgation of a similar view of the world through texts. A text like the

---

14. E.g., 1QS 6:4 describes how at a community council everybody sits in the order of his rank; 1QS 6:8 describes that at a session of the Many the priests sit first, then the elders, then the rest of the people.

Temple Scroll justifies a particular view of the world and how the community that copies and reads it should be organised. The justification is underpinned through the method of the presentation of the scroll too, namely, in the way that it is put over in terms of the voice of God himself. There is divine authority for the structure and practice contained in the *Temple Scroll* and thus divine authority for the hierarchy it promulgates and the systems of purity it puts in place to endorse such hierarchy. It is intriguing to note that in the description of the servants in the temple, the *Temple Scroll* seems to upgrade the status of the Levites, suggesting that it may be a piece of Levitical polemic as much as anything. Thus the compilation of the *Temple Scroll* is both an implicit attack on priestly organisation and cultic practice in Jerusalem as well as a firm statement about priestly hierarchy in the community responsible for compiling and preserving it.

In a very summary fashion it may be said that the Gospels offer two overall narrative perspectives which are then variously reflected in the kinds of community structures hinted at in their texts. On the one hand the Gospels of Mark and Matthew tell a story which begins away from Jerusalem and works its way towards a climax there. At one level these Gospels can be read as stories presenting alternative authorities to those represented by the hierarchies emanating from Jerusalem: Mark's Jesus has cosmic authority over unclean spirits (Mark 1:23) and to forgive sins (2:10) over against the authority of the scribes, whereas, summarily put, Matthew's Jesus presents an alternative kingship. It is not surprising that it is these two Gospels that provide the tradition about James and John and the best seats in heaven (Mark 10:35-45; Matt 20:20-28), a narrative which undermines conventional views of hierarchical authority. In the Gospels of Luke and John the narratives are more temple-oriented from the outset like the *Temple Scroll*, but Luke seems to counteract any suggestion of priestly hierarchy by stressing the role of the cultically marginalised (women, the sick, the impure, Samaritans, Gentiles). The Fourth Gospel, though implying that Jesus is dressed in the robes of the high priest (John 19:23), counteracts any priestliness by showing how temple structures and the festivals are replaced by Jesus throughout his ministry and through Jesus' prayer by offering a picture in which all who believe are equally part of the unity which is discernible in the relationship between Jesus and the Father (John 17:20-26). Texts reveal issues of community organisation.

In a way different from the *Temple Scroll* the *Eschatological Midrash* (4Q 174) speaks of several different temples in its interpretation of the oracle of Nathan from 2 Samuel 7.[15] For the Qumran commentator both the first and sec-

---

15. The most detailed analysis of 4Q174 and its significance in relation to the New Testament is provided in G. J. Brooke, *Exegesis at Qumran: 4QFlorilegium in its Jewish Context*, JSOTSup 29 (Sheffield: JSOT Press, 1985).

ond temples are rejected and the present guarantee of the divine presence, represented by the holy angels, rests with the community itself understood as a sanctuary; it is a *miqdash 'adam,* a "sanctuary of men," or "Adamic sanctuary."[16] This language suggests a picture slightly other than the very strict hierarchical one of the *Temple Scroll,* even though ultimately God will himself establish a suitable sanctuary which will no doubt require a priesthood.[17] Part of an explanation for the different emphasis between these two compositions may lie in their date of composition: the community has changed in its outlook and organisation during the two generations or more that probably separates the two works. Whatever the case, the "sanctuary of men" in 4Q174 is an image which endorses the way in which every member of the community is cultically significant through their sacrificial actions. Because the view of the community as temple in the *Eschatological Midrash* is only envisaged as a temporary eschatological arrangement until God himself restores the temple (and its priesthood) in a suitable way, it seems to be different from the apparently more permanent style of the community as temple built upon the "living stone" according to 1 Peter (2:4-6).[18] For this essay the full interpretation of the details does not matter as much as the clarification of the overall point that texts betray community structures in many intriguing and varied ways.

C. Size Matters

In addition to recognising that all communities are better understood in a dynamic way and that their texts betray their structures, whether or not they are hierarchical, the size of a group or community makes a difference to how it is organised and how its members may understand themselves.

Discussions of the Qumran community have often mistakenly talked as if it were all that there was to Essenism. That was evidently not the case if the number of four thousand members in the movement as put about by Philo and repeated by Josephus is anything to go by.[19] Estimates for how many people might have lived at Qumran at any one time during its heyday vary between seventy-

---

16. On the wider significance of these terms see G. J. Brooke, "Miqdash Adam, Eden and the Qumran Community," in *Gemeinde ohne Tempel — Community without Temple: Zur Substituierung und Transformation des Jerusalemer Tempels und seines Kultes im Alten Testament, antiken Judentum und frühen Christentum,* WUNT 118, ed. B. Ego, A. Lange, and P. Pilhofer (Tübingen: J. C. B. Mohr, 1999), pp. 285-301.

17. The Qumran exegete reads Exod 15:17 eschatologically.

18. Cf. the well-known use of Isa 28:16 in 1QS 8:5-6.

19. Philo, *Good Person* [= *Prob.*], 75; Josephus, *Ant.* 18:20.

five and two hundred, with the dining-room being able to sit between 120 and 150 people.[20] Although it can be generally assumed that at a meal the community sat in rank order, as the *Rule of the Community* suggests for the first half of the first century BCE at least, other patterns of organisation are also apparent.

If the sectarian compositions found in the library caves reflect something of the organisation of those members of the movement who lived at Qumran,[21] then it is intriguing to note that group dynamics seem to have resulted in the formation of an inner circle. The *Rule of the Community* (1QS 8:1-2) describes the council as being composed of twelve men and three priests.[22] The most common view is that the twelve men represent the tribes of Israel and the three priests the Levitical tribes of Gershon, Kohath and Merari.[23] Parallels with the use of twelve in the New Testament have often been noted, especially in Matt 19:28 and Luke 22:30 which make explicit connection of the disciples with the tribes, as well as in Revelation 21. But other compositions in the Qumran library use multiples of twelve. The *Temple Scroll* (11QT^a 57:11-14) states that the ideal judicial body for the king has twelve priests, twelve Levites, and twelve chiefs of the people. 4QpIsa^d seems to refer to the council of the community as made up of twelve priests and twelve heads of the tribes, an arrangement which may be echoed in the judicial role of the twenty-four elders in Rev 4:4 and 11:16-18.[24]

Alongside the organisation as having an authoritative group at its centre, the scriptural system of arranging Israel into tens, fifties, hundreds, and thousands was also adopted, at least in the community's more idealistic texts, such as the *Temple Scroll* (11QT^a 57:4-5), the *War Scroll* (1QM 4:1-5), and the *Rule of the Congregation* (1QSa 1:29-2:1). That such a system may have also been applied in the structure of the Essene movement as a whole is implied in the *Damascus Document* (CD 12:23-13:2). This division of the movement may have been done in part to recall that the community was the inheritor of the covenant made at Sinai (Exod 18:21).[25]

20. The estimate of M. Broshi, "Qumran: Archaeology," in *Encyclopedia of the Dead Sea Scrolls*, p. 735.

21. Or possibly in some other Essene settlements.

22. 4Q265 fragment 7, line 7, states that "there will be in the council of the Communit[y] fif[teen men];" see J. M. Baumgarten, "265. 4QMiscellaneous Rules," in *Qumran Cave 4.XXV: Halakhic Texts*, DJD 35, ed. J. M. Baumgarten et al. (Oxford: Clarendon, 1999), pp. 69-70.

23. See, e.g., A. R. C. Leaney, *The Rule of Qumran and its Meaning: Introduction, Translation and Commentary*, NTL (London/Philadelphia: SCM/Westminster, 1966), p. 212.

24. See J. M. Baumgarten, "The Duodecimal Courts of Qumran, the Apocalypse, and the Sanhedrin," *Journal of Biblical Literature* 95 (1976): 59-78; reprinted in J. M. Baumgarten, *Studies in Qumran Law*, SJLA 24 (Leiden: Brill, 1977), pp. 145-71.

25. The place of the covenant in sectarian theology has recently been emphasised by A. R. G. Deasley, *The Shape of Qumran Theology* (Carlisle: Paternoster, 2000), pp. 138-72.

All this strongly suggests that it was obvious to the Qumran community and to the wider movement of which it was a part that within any group there would have to be subgroups. Those did not need to be arranged hierarchically, though commonly they seem to have been perceived that way. Any general comments on size in relation to group structure and organisation would be incomplete without at least the raising of the question of what place size might have played in the fragmentation of the movement. The issues arising from these observations for the study of New Testament communities and the groups and factions within them are obvious: size matters in many ways.

D. Gender and Role Assumptions

Alongside matters of flexibility, hierarchies, and size, some mention should be made of the place of roles within community self-understanding, particularly concerning the status and roles of women. The scholarly assumption about the Qumran community has been that it was composed of celibate males. This assumption has been based on three factors. First, the probable identification of the community with some part of the Essene movement has resulted in the reading of the Qumran site in light of the classical sources as a place where the community was all male. The description of Pliny has been of key significance,[26] but this has been understood as supporting the application of parts of the testimonies of Philo and Josephus to the Qumran site too.[27] Second, the almost complete absence of female skeletons from the principal cemetery at Qumran has resulted in the juxtaposition of the archaeology of the site with the evidence of the classical sources. Third, the combination of classical source evidence and archaeology has resulted in the reading of the sectarian texts most commonly connected with the site as being addressed to men only.

Although it seems likely that the Qumran community was composed principally or exclusively of men, it is not so obvious that they were all celibate. Some of the members of the community that lived there may have been celibate, but it is also possible that some had merely taken vows of abstinence.[28] Such vows might have been for the duration of their stay at Qumran or for life. Whatever the case, it is likely that the male orientation of the Qumran community was the direct result of the application of purity laws within the commu-

26. "Without women and renouncing love entirely": Pliny, *Natural History* 5:73.

27. Philo, *Hypothetica*, 14; Josephus, *War* 2:120; cf. *War* 2:160-61.

28. See the summary article by J. M. Baumgarten which takes this view: "Celibacy," in *Encyclopedia of the Dead Sea Scrolls*, pp. 122-25.

nity, purity laws whose main aim was to reflect the self-understanding of the community as a spiritual sanctuary living in the last days. The separation from Jerusalem resulted in the need for a priestly community which could function firstly as a substitute for the Jerusalem temple and secondly be ever ready to provide the priesthood in the temple to be established by God himself when the time came. The priestly perspective in many of the Qumran sectarian documents, even if it is ameliorated to some degree at some points in the life of the community, provides a view of the world grounded in the holiness of God and the requirements of purity which enable the community of priests to serve in God's presence. That outlook influences what roles members play and limits the roles of women.

But women were not entirely excluded from the scene. The *Damascus Document* shows that the norm was for Essenes to be married and for their wives to have certain rights and restrictions. In the more idealistic *Rule of the Congregation* women (and children) have an explicit place. They are to be taught the law so as to take up some of the responsibility of it for themselves. One surprising feature of the *Rule of the Congregation* that has been much debated concerns whether a woman has the right to testify against her husband.[29] Though this would indeed be unusual in contemporary Judaism as usually reconstructed, it does seem likely that a married woman could speak in a court setting against her husband. What might such testimony include? It may have been of very limited scope and only covered incidents in which the husband had committed some sexual offence with his wife, such as having sexual relations during menstruation or pregnancy.[30] Purity limits women's roles, but it does not exclude them altogether.

Paul's insistence on the necessary and equal role of all the parts of the body in his teaching to the community at Corinth reveals the major part that debate about roles played from the outset in early Christian community organisation and self-understanding. The irony of Paul's teaching is not lost on modern readers, since it is clear that he considered apostles as having some preeminence, even if only as first among equals. The ambiguous nature of Paul's teaching on the status and roles of women is also self-evident.

---

29. See P. R. Davies and J. E. Taylor, "On the Testimony of Women in 1QSa," *Dead Sea Discoveries* 3 (1996): 223-35.

30. 4QD^e 7 i 12-13 reads: "One who comes near to fornicate with his wife contrary to the law shall depart and return no more": J. M. Baumgarten, *Qumran Cave 4.XIII: The Damascus Document (4Q266-273)*, DJD 18 (Oxford: Clarendon, 1996), pp. 163-64.

E. Models of Organisation

The choice of language used for community self-description has implications well beyond the aesthetic. Members of groups tend to live up to the way in which they are described and so descriptors necessarily influence behaviour and practice. Several models of organisation for the Qumran community and its wider movement have been hinted at so far. It is appropriate to bring some of them together and to classify them, even if briefly and crudely, simply so as to be able to pose of the New Testament texts similar questions about the kinds of models for Christian organisation and practice that are used there. The majority of the models of community organisation and self-understanding which occur in the sectarian scrolls depend upon authoritative traditions of scripture which are reworked and appropriated by the community in its implicit and explicit statements about its self-identity.

Cultic Model

The most obvious model is based on cultic traditions, with the community understanding itself as a temple with a priesthood.[31] This model seems to have changed and developed during the life of the Essene movement and even during the life of the Qumran community which was part of it. To begin with, this model of organisation arises from real dissatisfaction with what was taking place in Jerusalem. Although it has long been espoused that the dissatisfaction surrounded the misappropriation of the office of high priest, it is as likely, if not more so, that it was concerned with alternative views concerning cultic practices involving matters of purity, sacrifice, and the calendar. This seems to be attested by the *Temple Scroll,* which was probably compiled from earlier sources in light of the cultic reforms of John Hyrcanus. It says little about any supposed problems with the high priesthood and its lineage. The same can be said for *MMT,* which has much to say about issues of purity, but says nothing in what survives about priestly genealogy.

With its attention on the priestly Sons of Zadok and Sons of Aaron, the Cave 1 copy of the *Rule of the Community* describes a community controlled by priestly authority. Even in the council the grouping of three priests and twelve men may be understood as giving a disproportionate voice to the priest compared with more standard models of organisation based on the tribes of Israel. By the time the forms of the *Rule of the Community* which do not mention the

---

31. See the excellent summary by R. A. Kugler, "Priests," in *Encyclopedia of the Dead Sea Scrolls,* pp. 688-93.

Sons of Zadok are being copied out once again, the notions of priesthood seem to have been re-appropriated by the whole community more explicitly, so that there is an intensification in the requirements of purity within the movement. The same can be seen in 4Q174, a composition from the Herodian period in which the community is a "sanctuary of men." Thus there are some indications that the less explicit the priestly leadership in a community, the more the requirements of ritual purity are applied to all members with greater stringency: the less hierarchy, the more responsibility.

Cosmological Model

The priestly model with its strictures about purity is essentially hierarchical and strongly implies that the community is stratified with the high priest at the top. But what does such a hierarchy represent? The cosmological significance of the temple has long been recognised, but its implications for how a temple-oriented community might understand itself are seldom mentioned. For the Qumran community, membership, both potential and actual, has cosmological requirements. These are evident in the physiognomical compositions (4Q186; 4Q534; 4Q561) in which comment is made on physical features, the discernment of which might well have influenced whether an applicant was admitted.[32] These features are set against a cosmological background informed by the stars and the zodiac.

The key component in viewing the organisation from a cosmological perspective is the way that community members become involved in heavenly space. The *Songs of the Sabbath Sacrifice* is a composition which leaves it unclear whether the community in its worship is bringing heaven to earth so that the worship of angels is in the midst of the community,[33] or whether the com-

---

32. As argued by P. S. Alexander, "Physiognomy, Initiation and Rank in the Qumran Community," in *Geschichte — Tradition — Reflexion: Festschrift für Martin Hengel zum 70. Geburtstag*, vol. 1, *Judentum*, ed. H. Cancik, H. Lichtenberger, and P. Schäfer (Tübingen: J. C. B. Mohr, 1996), pp. 385-94.

33. As argued by D. Dimant, "Men as Angels: The Self-Image of the Qumran Community," in *Religion and Politics in the Ancient Near East*, STJHC, ed. A. Berlin (Bethesda, Md.: University Press of Maryland, 1996), pp. 93-103, (p. 101): the Qumran "community aimed at creating on earth a replica of the heavenly world." Cf. F. García Martínez, "Apocalypticism in the Dead Sea Scrolls," in *The Origins of Apocalypticism in Judaism and Christianity*, Encyclopedia of Apocalypticism, vol. 1, ed. J. J. Collins (New York: Continuum, 1999), pp. 162-92, at p. 184: "The complexity and structured organization of the heavenly world that we find in the apocalypses are represented also in the Scrolls, which add a most notable element: the idea that the angels are already living among the members of the community. The fellowship with the angels is not restricted to the future but is a reality also of the present and allows participation in the liturgy of the heavenly temple."

munity is transported to heaven in a quasi-mystical fashion.[34] It could even be that the experience is something in between: "joining together heaven and earth through the very performance of 'a concrete liturgical act.'"[35] In the end it does not matter for our immediate purposes. The overall point is that the closer the community's life and worship reflect the way of the cosmos, the greater the demands for purity within the community.

Military Model

The *War Scroll* and some other sectarian compositions develop the idea that the community is to be organised as the army of Israel. According to Jethro's initiative (Exod 18:21) Israel is to be organised administratively in thousands, hundreds, fifties, and tens; this system is reflected in Num 1:1-54, where the tribes are mustered for military purposes. Similar conditions that apply to the community as army apply to the community as priesthood. There are similar restrictions on entry, though the reasons for the restrictions may vary slightly. In the military organisation of the community, the formation of the Israelites as at the foot of Sinai is reused in the *Temple Scroll* (11QT^a 57:4-5), the *War Scroll* (1QM 4:1-5),[36] and the *Rule of the Congregation* (1QSa 1:29-2:1).[37] Such a system may have also been applied in the structure of the Essene movement as a whole according to the *Damascus Document* (CD 12:23–13:2), which also uses the language of "camps" of local groups of members. The military model may have encouraged a dualistic outlook: non-members of the community are stereotyped and dehumanised as enemies. All models of organisation have an ethical dimension; however, with military terminology the ethical perspective is all the more stark. Also it should be noted that the military, cosmological, and cultic models reinforce each other in relation to purity requirements.

---

34. C. H. T. Fletcher-Louis, *All the Glory of Adam: Liturgical Anthropology in the Dead Sea Scrolls, STDJ* 42 (Leiden: Brill, 2002), p. 392, concludes that the *Songs of the Sabbath Sacrifice* are "the fullest, most sustained expression of an anthropology which takes the righteous up into the divine life and that of the angels" and he reads the thirteenth song as indicating that "the community's own chief priesthood is identified with the Glory of God of Ezekiel's throne vision."

35. B. Frennesson, *"In a Common Rejoicing": Liturgical Communion with Angels in Qumran, SSU* 14 (Uppsala: Uppsala University, 1999), p. 116.

36. For a mass of comparative information from within the *War Scroll* and elsewhere see the detailed comments on military organisation in Y. Yadin, *The Scroll of the War of the Sons of Light against the Sons of Darkness* (Oxford: Oxford University Press, 1962), pp. 38-64.

37. Detailed comments on how the ideal community was reflected in the present are provided by L. H. Schiffman, *The Eschatological Community of the Dead Sea Scrolls, SBLMS* 38 (Atlanta: Scholars Press, 1989), pp. 32-36.

Tribal Model

The organisation of Israel on the basis of its twelve tribes is also used in several of the sectarian or quasi-sectarian compositions.[38] The pattern of twelve is linked with the cultic realm through the twelve gates of the ideally constructed temple as this is described in the *Temple Scroll* (11QT^a 44), based on the city gates described in Ezek 48:30-35. Perhaps not surprisingly in a text from the end of the Second Temple period, a time when Israel's system of tribes was no longer in full operation, the restoration of Israel according to the model of the twelve tribes is often associated with the eschatological era. In this way it is not surprising that at Qumran the *War Rule* refers to twelve chiefs (1QM 2:1-4) and in the army the twelve tribes and their leaders play a significant role (e.g., 1QM 3:14; 5:1-2).

A particular use of the number 12 is to be found in the organisation of the council of the community according to 1QS 8:1: in the council there are to be twelve men and three priests. The tribal model in all its extended applications uses imagery that has both political and familial backgrounds, each reinforcing the other. The tribal model implies a relational view of communities and encourages stress on kinship, whether actual or fictive, and the system of honour and shame that accompanies it.

III. Application

The five points which have been described briefly in this study can have two applications within the context of a book like this on aspects of holiness within the first Christian communities and how the organisation of those early communities may have helped or hindered the practice of qualities which might best reflect the divine purposes for humanity.

The first and perhaps more significant application will be the way in which some of what is described here might act as a control in the reading of the New Testament authors. It is clear from this cursory glance at aspects of community organisation and practice at Qumran, and in the wider Essene movement, that there was much in Palestinian Judaism of the two centuries before the fall of the temple in 70 CE which could have been known (probably at second hand for the most part) by those responsible for developing early Christian community identity, organisation, and religious practice.

---

38. See A. Jaubert, "La symbolique des douze," in *Hommages à André Dupont-Sommer,* ed. A. Caquot and M. Philonenko (Paris: Adrien-Maisonneuve, 1971), pp. 453-60.

Several of these matters have been described and discussed over the years; they were a particular feature of the first generation of comparative studies between the communities of the Dead Sea Scrolls and the New Testament where a wide range of similarities were noted.[39] For example, there was considerable interest in the parallels between the *mebaqqer* of the scrolls and the *episkopos* of the later Pauline traditions. Several similarities between Qumran and the Lukan community or its idealistic antecedents in Jerusalem were noted, such as the ongoing constitution of the earliest group as twelve with Matthias replacing Judas through a use of lots.[40] The fact that within Judaism of the first centuries BCE and CE the Essene movement alone seems to have required an elaborate framework of initiation, rather than being something which could be claimed by birthright also speaks volumes to how the second birth of the first Christians through baptism should be viewed.

This paper has looked at a few other matters with a view to supplementing and updating some elements of this comparative discussion, but also in the hope that by paying attention to a wider range of topics, the comparisons may be all the more instructive in highlighting what may be taking place in various early Christian groups. The underlying significance of purity in the Qumran system of organisation and practice is not surprisingly echoed in New Testament sources, not directly, but simply because the first followers of Jesus were Jewish and such matters were at the heart of Jewish practice and belief.

Second, this description and discussion of some Qumran matters arguably has a knock-on effect for the modern Christian context too. In reflecting on the data from the Qumran caves, modern readers can see all the more readily that there is no single blueprint with divine authorisation for how communities should organise themselves before God. By looking at a Jewish movement nearly contemporary with the New Testament communities modern readers can appreciate more how the New Testament documents might be read and how their significance might be brought into the present.[41] By reading the

---

39. See note 4 above. In addition, despite overplaying the differences between the scrolls and the New Testament, there are many helpful comments in C. M. Pate, *Communities of the Last Days: The Dead Sea Scrolls, the New Testament and the Story of Israel* (Leicester: Apollos, 2000).

40. See, e.g., S. E. Johnson, "The Dead Sea Manual of Discipline and the Jerusalem Church of Acts," in *The Scrolls and the New Testament*, ed. K. Stendahl, pp. 129-42; B. Reicke, "The Constitution of the Primitive Church in the Light of Jewish Documents," in *The Scrolls and the New Testament*, pp. 143-56.

41. Those who use the social sciences to study the New Testament have for some while stressed the need for a wide range of methods in reading the texts, beyond the merely historical, theological, or literary. A fine example of how this can be done is presented by K. C. Hanson and D. E. Oakman, *Palestine in the Time of Jesus: Social Structures and Social Conflicts* (Minneapolis: Fortress, 1998).

Qumran scrolls, modern readers can recognise how the scrolls can make a contribution towards the reconstruction of a suitable social and historical framework, so that the New Testament material is not appropriated in a naive way, either theologically or historically.

Over the decades all religious communities change and develop in response to a wide range of factors; this is no less true of the Qumran community (or communities) and the wider Essene movement, even though its concern to be scriptural, to be the true remnant of Israel, may have remained constant throughout its existence. Leadership crises will forever arise and types of leadership evolve that may be suitable to new circumstances. The scrolls highlight how it is important to look behind such features as hierarchical organisation, community size, roles, and gender differentiation, to discover what principles are motivating matters of organisation and practice. Cultic, cosmological, military, and tribal models of organisation all indicate something both ideal and practical.

The evidence from the scrolls shows that communities may oscillate between the poles of hierarchy and egalitarianism. When a religious community is very hierarchical it is easy for members to abrogate their responsibilities; those communities with more egalitarian structures will often require more from every member. Furthermore, communities may oscillate between this world and another. In general and put crudely, Judaism has been affirming of this worldly order, while Platonism has influenced many Christian communities to believe that aspirations should lie with the real, which is supposedly elsewhere. The Qumran group provides an example of a Jewish group that seems to have had, at least at some time during its existence and for some of its members, a striking balance between the two. Significantly this is illuminated by the *Songs of the Sabbath Sacrifice,* a text that has more to say about the sovereignty of God than almost any other. Finally, because of the insight that there is the need both to realise participation in the worship of the angels of heaven and also to make real the sovereignty of God on earth, there are also varieties of insight within the sectarian texts as to the appropriate response to personal interaction with the world around. For some asceticism is the suitable way forward to rediscover purity, for others it is greater engagement with others as natural or fictive kin.

The scrolls and the community that collected and preserved them have much to offer the better understanding of Christian ecclesiologies, both ancient and modern. Beyond the much-discussed detailed parallels between the scrolls and the New Testament, study of the scrolls and their communities poses questions about change and development, about leadership and hierarchy, about the influence of size on organisation, about the roles to be played, especially variously by men and women, and about the scriptural language systems that are used for modelling the communities so as to reflect both ideals and actualities.

Holiness in the Dead Sea Scrolls:
The Priorities of Faith

DWIGHT SWANSON

In a context in which impiety is celebrated, and those who take faith seriously are relegated to the categories of fundamentalist or curiosity — or, potential terrorist — any attempt to explain or understand a world in which holiness, that is, the relation of the human to the divine, is definitive of society is most difficult. But, such was the nature of Judaism in the Second Temple period. And, it is at Qumran,[1] where concern for holiness was a central theme, that we have material for understanding holiness for early Christianity.

Holiness at Qumran is a subject that has seldom been studied.[2] Whereas attention has been given to purity,[3] "holiness" does not even manage an entry

---

1. This article uses "Qumran" or the "Dead Sea Scrolls" or "community" in keeping with the general agreement amongst scholarship that all three are related in some respect to the movement known from other sources as the "Essenes."

2. Jacobus A. Naudé, "Holiness in the Dead Sea Scrolls," in *The Dead Sea Scrolls After Fifty Years: A Comprehensive Assessment,* vol. 2, ed. Peter W. Flint and James C. VanderKam (Leiden, Boston, Köln: Brill, 1999), pp. 171-99, and Hannah K. Harrington, "Holiness and Law in the Dead Sea Scrolls," *Dead Sea Discoveries* 8 (2001): 124-35 are the only specific treatments of the subject in the past ten years.

3. See especially J. Neusner, *The Idea of Purity in Ancient Judaism* (Leiden: Brill, 1973). Also, M. Newton, *The Concept of Purity at Qumran and in the Letters of Paul* (Cambridge: Cambridge University Press, 1985). See also Jacob Milgrom, *Leviticus,* AB 3 (Garden City, N.J.: Doubleday, 1991-2001).

I wish to acknowledge my appreciation to the Orion Centre for the Study of the Dead Sea Scrolls and Associated Literature, The Hebrew University, Jerusalem, which, by making me a Visiting Scholar in the spring of 2004, made possible the time and place in which to do the research out of which this article arises. I also wish to note that Alex Deasley first introduced me to the Dead Sea Scrolls, which unexpectedly altered the course of my academic life. That alteration was not his fault, and the altered course has been a happy one, so I give him thanks for encouraging me on that initial path of discovery.

in the *Encyclopedia of the Dead Sea Scrolls.*[4] This apparent discrepancy actually highlights its centrality — holiness is not addressed directly because it is the assumed background of the rise of the sectarian movements of the second century BCE. Everything flows from a concern for the holy: the holiness of the Temple, the Holy City, the priesthood, and the people.

Alex R. G. Deasley comes closest to a specific treatment of holiness, via his study of the cognate term, perfection. His interest goes back to his 1972 Ph.D. thesis, "The Idea of Perfection in the Qumran Texts,"[5] written under the supervision of F. F. Bruce at the University of Manchester, and reaches fuller development in the publication of his Didsbury Lectures in *The Shape of Qumran Theology.*[6] Deasley has stepped back from the minutiae to reflect on the over-all shape of the material, and particularly that which is commonly accepted to represent the beliefs of the community of Qumran. These are discussed under four headings: covenant,[7] the human predicament, perfection, and eschatology. Only the third category, perfection, can receive treatment in this essay.

Deasley argues that the covenant requires a holy people, therefore purity is the Community's chief concern. The means of attainment of purity is "to walk perfectly."[8] This is both a future ideal and a present expectation. Perfection is "the only means to the high end of saving Israel by accepting and fulfilling her covenant responsiblities" and, "the rendering to God by perfect worshippers of the perfect worship he rightly demanded."[9] Perfection is a way of life, lived according to the revealed interpretation of the Torah, and a quality of character leading to inward humility (see 1QS 3:7), and also the present condition for worship with the holy ones.[10] Alongside this, however, the Community also insisted that perfection would only be achieved in the age to come. This final perfection demands the destruction of all the powers of sin and evil and the prince of darkness, and, positively, restoration to Eden and renewal in the likeness of Adam in the beginning.[11]

---

4. *Encyclopedia of the Dead Sea Scrolls*, ed. Lawrence Schiffman and James C. VanderKam (Oxford: University Press, 2000).

5. See the earlier work of R. Newton Flew, *The Idea of Perfection in Christian Thought* (London: Oxford University Press, 1934).

6. A. R. G. Deasley, *The Shape of Qumran Theology* (Carlisle: Paternoster, 2000).

7. Cf. G. Vermes, *The Dead Sea Scrolls: Qumran in Perspective* (London: SCM, 1977).

8. Deasley, *Shape*, p. 210.

9. Deasley, *Shape*, p. 234.

10. Deasley, *Shape*, pp. 235-40.

11. Deasley, *Shape*, pp. 240-46. Cf. F. F. Bruce, *Second Thoughts on the Dead Sea Scrolls* (London: Paternoster, 1956), pp. 101-2; F. M. Cross, Jr., *The Ancient Library of Qumran and Modern Biblical Studies* (Garden City, N.Y.: Doubleday, 1958), pp. 71-73; J. T. Milik, *Ten Years of Discovery in the Wilderness of Judaea* (London: SCM, 1959), pp. 116-21.

Deasley's particular contribution is the recognition of a present realisation and a personal and inward character to perfection as an essential aspect of holiness at Qumran. This has clear implications for understanding perfection language in the New Testament. Deasley does not spell these implications out, for such was not the purpose of his study. This anacoutholon needs to be filled, and it seems useful to make the attempt here.

First, we need to define "perfection." This translation of the Hebrew *tammim*[12] reflects the tendency to follow the AV and RSV English translations of the Bible. It also reflects the LXX and NT use of the Greek *teleios* in translating *tammim* in non-cultic settings.[13] The Greek philosophical idea of *teleios* as an absolute perfection that cannot be improved has been read by many into the New Testament usage of the term. This has had the unfortunate result of the appearance through history of fringe sects claiming absolute, angelic perfection for themselves. It has also led to such a complete rejection of the possibility of perfection in the present by much of Western Christianity that the presence of the term in the New Testament has been ignored or explained away.

Neither reaction is acceptable. We must look to the Second Temple use of *tammim* to understand New Testament perfection rather than Greek philosophical traditions. The Qumran texts provide a good starting point.

Perfection in the Sectarian Scrolls

The core texts that provide the "control" for understanding sectarian beliefs are the *Community Rule* (1QS), with the *Damascus Document* (CD, and the "D" texts from Cave 4), the *Thanksgiving Hymns* (1QH), and the *War Scroll* (1QM).

1. The Community Rule[14]

1QS describes itself as "*the* rule" of the Community, and so foundation beliefs are most evident. The text begins:

> [The Master shall teach the sai]nts to live according to the book of the
> Community [Ru]le, that they may seek God with a whole heart and soul,

12. See Vermes, *The Dead Sea Scrolls in English,* published in four editions between 1962 and 1995.

13. More recently, other formulations have been offered, such as "sound" (NJB), but these reflect the dilution of the modern understanding of "perfection."

14. 1QS is the largest intact document of its type.

and do what is good and right before him as he commanded by the hand of Moses and all his servants the prophets; that they may love all that he has chosen and hate all that he has rejected; that they may abstain from all evil and hold fast to all good; that they may practise truth, righteousness, and justice upon earth and no longer stubbornly follow a sinful heart and lustful eyes, committing all manner of evil [1QS 1:1-7].[15]

These first words of the *Community Rule* introduce "saints," or "holy ones,"[16] whom a *Maskil* (Instructor) guides in "seeking God with a whole heart and soul." Thus, by allusion to Deut 6:4 combined with 4:29, this work is identified with covenant recital and renewal.[17] The *Maskil* admits these "volunteers"[18] into a "covenant of grace" by which each "may be joined to the counsel of God and may live perfectly before him in accordance with all that has been revealed . . ." [1:8-9]. They bring all their devotion and wealth into the Community of God, "that they may purify their knowledge in the truth of God's precepts and order their powers according to His ways of perfection . . ." [1:12-13].

The contrast between love of good and light and hatred of evil and darkness shows a keen determination to avoid sin. The means to do this, within the covenant, is through perfection and purity, and doing everything commanded in the fully revealed Torah.

The Covenant Ritual: 1:15–3:12

In the instructions for the ceremony upon entering the covenant, the priests bless "all the men of the lot of God who walk perfectly in all his ways" [2:2], while those who refuse to enter the covenant will not be "reckoned among the perfect, nor be purified by atonement, nor cleansed by purifying waters, nor sanctified by seas and rivers . . ." [3:3-5]. The phrase "walking in his ways" confirms the Deuteronomic[19] covenant concerns of the Rule, but the addition of a "perfect" walk helps explain the meaning of *tammim* in Qumran life. The

15. G. Vermes, *The Complete Dead Sea Scrolls in English* (London: Penguin Books, 1997). Citations will follow Vermes unless otherwise indicated. Line references, not specified in his edition, follow Florentino García-Martínez and Eibert Tigchelaar, *The Dead Sea Scrolls Study Edition* (Leiden: Brill, 1997), abbreviated as G-M/T.

16. A certain reconstruction of *qedoshim* from the fragmentary evidence:]*shim*.

17. On the base text of Deut 6:4, the phrase "seek with your whole heart and soul" is inserted from 4:29 in place of "love," and "all your might" is omitted. The effect is to emphasise the role of Torah study within the covenant.

18. A term which identifies the Community with the expectations of Ps 110, like "saints" a theme shared by early Christianity.

19. See Deut 10:12.

phrase echoes the covenant command to Abraham in Gen 17:1, "Walk before me and be perfect."[20] This key-word insertion takes the word beyond the cultic sphere into moral territory.[21]

The holy life is lived by perfection, purification, cleansing, and sanctification, defined in personal terms: the one whose sins are expiated is cleansed by the spirit of holiness, made clean by submission to the precepts of God, and then "walks perfectly in all the ways commanded by God" [3:6-10].

The Two Spirits: 3:13–4:26

This section conceives of the work of God in the Children of Light in this way:

> He will refine for Himself the human frame by rooting out all spirit of injustice from the bounds of his flesh. He will cleanse him of all wicked deeds with the spirit of holiness; like purifying waters He will shed upon him the spirit of truth (to cleanse him) of all abomination and injustice. And he shall be plunged into the spirit of purification, that he may instruct the upright in the knowledge of the Most High and teach the wisdom of the sons of heaven to the perfect of way [4:20-22].

Commentary regarding the dualism between the Prince of Light and the Angel of Darkness, and their respective children, is usually on the ongoing struggle between the two. Yet, the scrolls assert that the purification by the spirit of holiness cleanses from sin (in this instance, wicked deeds).[22] Perfection comes through knowledge here, but is still grounded in purification.

The Men of the Community: 5:1–6:8

The Rule for the Men of the Community contrasts the "volunteers" from "men of injustice." On one hand, they separate from evil,[23] and on the other they

20. Enoch, "walked with God," but is not designated as perfect in Genesis 5. In 1 Enoch he is repeatedly described as "righteous." Noah is "righteous and perfect" in 6:9, but is not described as "walking with God." Abraham is commanded to be like both men.

21. See D. D. Swanson, *The Temple Scroll and the Bible: The Methodology of 11QT, STDJ* 14 (Leiden: Brill, 1995), pp. 227-35, for a description of the exegetical device of "key-word insertion."

22. See Jonathan Klawans, *Impurity and Sin in Ancient Judaism* (Oxford: Oxford University Press, 2000), chap. 3; cf. Eyal Regev, "Abominated Temple and a Holy Community: The Formation of the Notions of Purity and Impurity in Qumran," *Dead Sea Discoveries* 10 (2003): 243-78.

23. Separation is a key component of sanctification for perfectionist groups. The term used here is *habdiyl*.

unite *(yahad)* to the covenant under the authority of the priests, particularly under Torah [5:2-3]. In this unity they "atone for all those in Aaron who have freely pledged themselves to holiness . . ." [5:6], and are examined annually regarding their perfection, whether they have moved up or down in standing [5:24-25]. Evidence of perfection is based on their "deeds." However, it is also based on *spiritual* criteria, as can be seen when we turn to the "Penitential Code" of Columns 6 and 7.[24]

The Rules for Judgement: 6:24–7:25

There is no holiness vocabulary in this section, but these may be seen as application of the Purification Offering (the *hattat*) from Temple practice to Community practice.[25] These are not simply a harsh legalism, then, but a way to make atonement and to find forgiveness when access to the Temple was lost. The inclusion of internal sins such as impatience, deception, lack of care for a companion, or malice, alongside visible acts like spitting and guffawing, confirms the argument.

The Council of the Community: 8:1–9:11

The "Council of the Community" is described as

> . . . an Everlasting Plantation, a House of Holiness for Israel, and Assembly of Supreme Holiness for Aaron. They shall be witnesses to the truth at the Judgement, and shall be the elect of Goodwill who shall atone for the Land and pay to the wicked their reward [8:5-7].

Vermes' translation of the phrase "Assembly of Supreme Holiness" obscures the more familiar rendering of a "foundation of a Holy of Holies."[26] Such a translation reflects the view that this is not Temple imagery here, but a reference to the status of the members themselves. Whether this is the case, the phrase could scarcely fail to call to the hearer's mind some association with the Holiest Place in the Temple.

This group of men are described as the "men of perfect holiness" in 8:19–9:11, suggesting that they have attained a higher level of holiness distinct from the rest of the Community. The "Council of Holiness" consists of those who "walk in the way of perfection," not breaking even one word of Torah [8:20-

---

24. See Deasley, *Shape,* pp. 236, 237.
25. E.g., Klawans, *Impurity and Sin,* as in n. 22 above.
26. *Sod qodesh qodeshim.*

22]. A single sin of inadvertence results in two years of penance, until one's perfection is once again established [8:23–9:2]. This Council "establishes the spirit of holiness according to everlasting truth" and "atones for guilty rebellion and for sins of unfaithfulness" [9:3-4]. When this is done, they "set apart a House of Holiness in order that it may be united to the most holy things and a House of Community for Israel, for those who walk in perfection" [9:6]. This piling up of the terms of holiness, purity, and perfection when describing the inner council of the Community is revealing. It presents a view of life with Temple imagery at its centre in which the function of the Community is to do atonement/expiation; this can be done only in "the holiest Place," which requires a perfect walk before God.

The Blessing: 10:5–11:22

The closing hymn of the Rule moves the imagery up a notch. The gift of righteousness joins the writer to the Holy Ones, the very angels:

> From the source of his righteousness is my justification, and from his marvellous mysteries is the light in my heart. My eyes have gazed on that which is eternal, on wisdom concealed from men, on knowledge and wise design (hidden) from the sons of men; on a fountain of righteousness and on a storehouse of power, on a spring of glory (hidden) from the assembly of flesh. God has given them to his chosen ones as an everlasting possession, and has caused them to inherit the lot of the Holy Ones [11:5-8].

Thus, holiness is the goal and expectation of the Community. Though there is a cosmic struggle between good and evil which encompasses the individual, those who keep Torah, as revealed within the Community, and learn knowledge through wisdom, may receive the lot of the men of holiness. The life of the Community is a life of a perfect walk, living as the very Holiest Place where atonement for sins is effected. And, there is the hint of communion with the angels of the presence.

2. The Damascus Document

The overlap of content and vocabulary between this tenth-century CE document found in the Cairo Geniza with the *Community Rule* makes certain that they come from the same circle of Judaism of the Second Temple Period. Here we have the "men of holiness" [4:6], those who "walk in perfect holiness" [7:5, 20:5],[27] the "Council of Holiness" [20:25], and the concern for purity throughout.

In the opening "Exhortation" the language usage offers a sort of "historical" context for understanding the Rule of the Community. For the community behind this text, the Exile has not ended. God continues to hide his face from the Sanctuary, but has raised up a Teacher of Righteousness to guide a remnant who keep the covenant. The Teacher is opposed by "traitors," and "seekers after smooth things" who not only force the Teacher and his followers to "wander in a pathless wilderness," but seek to take their lives. In short, they "loath all who walked in perfection" [1:20].

The writer goes on to open the eyes of the readers to the works of God, "that you may choose that which pleases him and reject that which he hates, that you may walk perfectly in all his ways and not follow after thoughts of the guilty inclination and after eyes of lust" [2:14-15]. The language is familiar from the *Community Rule*. This is followed, however, by a list of those who failed to walk perfectly through said guilty inclination. At the head are the Heavenly Watchers, followed by Noah's sons, and the children of Jacob in Egypt and at Kadesh Barnea [2:18–3:12]. Singled out for obedience, however, is Abraham. "Abraham did not walk in it [i.e., the guilty inclination], and he was accounted a friend of God because he kept the commandments of God . . ." [3:2]. Here the expectation of a "perfect walk" is explicitly linked to Abraham, and is also placed in direct contrast to the "guilty inclination" — a variation of the "evil *yetser*" of Rabbinic Judaism.

The "remnant" place themselves in Abraham's line, "holding fast to the commandments of God" [3:12], receiving the revelation of times and festivals, and desires of God for how men should live. Because of their repentance, God forgave their sin, and "built them a sure house in Israel whose like has never existed from former times till now. Those who hold fast to it are destined to live forever, and all the glory of *Adam* shall be theirs" [3:19]. This enigmatic and ambiguous phrase ("all the glory of Adam," or "all the glory of man/kind?") offers a glimpse of a belief that the perfect walk offers a return to Eden.

One Cave 4 manuscript of D ties together with the hymn of 1QS, as well as the Thanksgiving Hymns. 4Q266 Fr 8 Col i excludes people with physical or mental blemishes (madman, lunatic, simpleton, fool, blind, maimed, lame, or deaf) from entering the Community for the simple reason that, "the holy angels [are in their midst]." Vermes' reconstruction (in the brackets) is verified by comparison to the *War Scroll* (1QM):

---

27. Columns 19 and 20 are CD-B, which Vermes inserts into CD-A at Column 8.

No boy or woman shall enter their camps . . . no one who is lame, or blind, or crippled, or afflicted with a lasting bodily blemish, or smitten with a bodily impurity, none of these shall march out to war with them. They shall all be freely enlisted for war, perfect in spirit and body and prepared for the Day of Vengeance. And no one shall go down with them on the day of battle who is impure because of his "fount," for the holy angels shall be with their hosts [7:3-6].

Crispin Fletcher-Louis has argued that the worship of the community was an experience of transfer from earth to heaven, and even from mortality to immortality.[28] Whether this conclusion is valid or not, that the Community believed its worship took place with the Angels of the Presence has to be seen as the driving force for its purity concerns. In their presence, nothing less than a "perfect walk" would suffice.

3. The Thanksgiving Hymns

Commentators on the *Thanksgiving Hymns* tend to emphasise the stark and pessimistic terms of the author's portrayal of the human condition:[29]

But what is the spirit of flesh that it should understand all this, and that it should comprehend the great design of your wisdom? What is he that is born of woman in the midst of all your terrible works? He is but an edifice of dust, and a thing kneaded with water, whose beginning is sinful iniquity, and shameful nakedness, and a fount of uncleanness, and over whom a spirit of straying rules (1QH 5:19-21).[30]

Seldom noted, however, is the rather optimistic view of purity and holiness for those who seek God. The description just cited is followed with:

By your goodness alone is man righteous, and with your many mercies [you strengthen him]. You will adorn him with your splendour and will [cause him to reign amid] many delights with everlasting peace and length of days [5:23-24].

---

28. Crispin H. T. Fletcher-Louis, *All the Glory of Adam: Liturgical Anthropology in the Dead Sea Scrolls*, STDJ 42 (Leiden: Brill, 2002), p. 476.

29. E.g., Helmer Ringgren, *The Faith of Qumran: Theology of the Dead Sea Scrolls*, expanded ed. (New York: Crossroad, 1995), pp. 94-95.

30. Vermes' use of the archaic "Thy" and "Thou" is emended in these citations.

García-Martínez and Tigchelaar fill the first gap with "purified" instead of Vermes' "strengthen." This alternative has the merit of fitting in with the theme of this hymn, God's holiness and the role of his holy ones in creation (line 7). Regardless of the reconstruction, the phrase "many delights *(rôv 'edeniym)* with everlasting peace and length of days" contains another hint of return to "Eden."

Hymn 6 is another example of stark contrast. First, the weakness of the human is described:

> And yet I, a shape of clay kneaded in water, a ground of shame and a source of pollution, a melting-pot of wickedness and an edifice of sin, a straying and perverted spirit of no understanding, fearful of righteous judgements, what can I say that is not foreknown . . . ? [9:21-23].

Then comes purification by the grace of God:

> By your mercies and by your great goodness you have strengthened the spirit of man in the face of the scourge, and have purified [the erring spirit] of a multitude of sins [9:31-32].

Hymn 5, on the other hand, focuses almost wholly on the graciousness of God by which the poet is able to choose (Vermes) or love (G-M/T) truth [6:25-26]. He exults, "I have loved you freely and with all my heart!" [6:26 and 7:13]. The wicked, to be sure, are created for wrath and slaughter [7:20], but there is no description of the polluted human. The emphasis of this Hymn is on the work of the Holy Spirit upon his own servants.

> And I know that man is not righteous except through you, and therefore I implore you by the spirit which you have given [me] to perfect your [favours] to your servant [forever], purifying me by your holy Spirit, and drawing me near to you by your grace [8:19-20].

This hymn, then, combines the themes of holiness, purity, perfection, and love within the grace of God through his Holy Spirit, which allows the singer to "stand in your presence [for]ever" [8:22]. This phrase, in a fragmentary section of the text, alludes to the theme already mentioned in 1QS, which is more explicit later in this scroll:

> For the sake of your glory you have purified man of sin that he may be made holy for you, with no abominable uncleanness and no guilty wickedness; that he may be one with the children of your truth and partake of the lot of your Holy Ones . . . [19:10-12].

Purification from sin is joined with the idea of the members of the community worshipping together with the Angels of the Presence — only possible when each is purified to the angels' level of holiness.

Conclusions

The reading of these texts reveals that perfection provides a linking thread that runs right through the sectarian passions. The holiness of the members of the Community is key to its self-understanding. Holiness is not simply one of a number of "beliefs" held, but the one concept which governed every aspect of life: the members of the *Yahad* maintained the highest level of purity required of any Jewish group, indeed, a perfection of purity, because they worshipped before God in the company of the angels of his presence.

The concern for purity is not an external legalism, however. The allusion to the command to Abraham for perfection is a covenantal concern: it is a perfect obedience. This perfect obedience is anticipated for the future, as in Judaism as a whole, but it is also expected for the present as the Community serves as the Holiest Place. The phrase "perfect walk" denotes this expectation, possible only by the grace of God.

Holiness beyond Qumran

Having made the case for the centrality of holiness to the Qumran Community, we could be left with the question, "So what?" To address this question, we come to our second implication from the Qumran evidence: *concern for perfection in the Second Temple period is not limited to the Dead Sea Sect.*

A recently published text from outside the Community, 4QInstruction,[31] shows that the Community's concern for holiness is part of a wider phenomenon within the Judaism of its time. It combines both wisdom and apocalyptic genres. It is typically wisdom in its concerns for instruction and understanding

---

31. The official edition is J. Strugnell and D. J. Harrington, *Qumran Cave 4.XXIV: Sapiential Texts, Part 2. 4QInstruction (Musar Le Mevin): 4Q415ff. With a re-edition of 1Q26*, DJD 34 (Oxford: Clarendon, 1999). There were at least six copies of this text: 1Q26, 4Q415-418, and 423. See Eibert Tigchelaar, *To Increase Learning for the Understanding Ones: Reading and Reconstructing the Fragmentary Early Jewish Sapiential Text 4QInstruction*, STDJ 44 (Leiden: Brill, 2001), pp. 15-17, who argues for at least eight copies; Torleif Elgvin, "Priestly Sages? The Milieus of Origin of 4QMysteries and 4QInstruction," in *Sapiental Perspectives: Wisdom Literature in Light of the Dead Sea Scrolls*, ed. J. J. Collins, G. F. Sterling, and R. A. Clements (Leiden: Brill, 2004).

(thus its Hebrew title, *Musar le-Mevin*, "Instruction for a *Maven*/Student"), and extended treatment of themes such as poverty, borrowing and lending, wives and daughters. It is typically apocalyptic in that the wisdom offered is the revelation of a mystery, the *raz nehiyeh* or "mystery that is to be," with judgement for those who ignore this wisdom. What is missing is the vocabulary common to the texts termed "sectarian," interest in purity, or evidence of priestly concerns. These factors, amongst others, serve to place the work apart from the Community which copied and used the text.

While there is no purity language, there is other related terminology. Two passages are relevant. The first is the opening section of 4Q417 (Instruction[c]), thought to be the first column of the work.[32]

> 1And *you, understanding one (Maven)* . . . 2. . gaze on, [And] in the wonderful mysteries of the God of the Awesome Ones you will ponder, the *beginnings of* . . . 3. . . . And gaze on[*the mystery that is to come,* and the deeds of old, *on what* is to be, and what is to be] . . . 5. . . [And to what is to be, *in what*] . . . in every . . . 6[And by day and by night meditate upon the mystery that is to] come. And study it continually, and then you will know truth and iniquity, wisdom 7[and foolish]ness. *You will [recognize] every a[ct]in all* their ways, together with all *their* punishment(s) in all ages everlasting. And the punishment 8of eternity. Then you will discern between the [goo]d and [evil according to their] deeds. . . . For the God of knowledge is the *foundation* of truth, and *by/on* the mystery that is to come. 9He has *laid out* its (= truth's) *foundation,* and its deeds [He has *prepared with all wis*]dom. And *with* all [c]unning *has he fashioned it,* and the *domain* of the *deeds (creatures)* 10*with* a[*ll*] *its secrets.* . . . He [*ex*]*pounded* for their un[der]standing every d[ee]d/cr[eatu]re . . . so that *man* could walk 11in the [fashion (inclination)][33] of *their/his* understanding. And he will/did *expound for ma[n . . .]* And in *abundance/property/purity*[34] of understanding *were made kn[own the se]crets* of 12his (?man's) plans, together with how he should walk [p]erfec[t[35] in all] his [ac]tions. These things investigate/*seek early and* continually.

32. 4Q417 Frag 1 i [formerly 2 i], combined with 4Q418 43, 44, 45 (in italics), following DJD 34 (with archaic language ignored).

33. *Yetser* appears only by reconstruction, but the reading is accepted by Tigchelaar, *To Increase Learning,* p. 52, and Goff, *Worldly and Heavenly Wisdom,* p. 54.

34. The choices reflect the uncertainty in translating *kosher* here.

35. The reading is questioned by Tigchelaar, *To Increase Learning,* p. 53, arguing that two more letters could fit the lacuna, and that none of the letters that are visible are certain. My own observation of the photograph tends to agree with the DJD reading.

Although the terminology is different, the focus on knowledge which is the re-sult of meditation on "the mystery which is to come" is familiar.[36] Discernment between good and evil, and the role of the *yetser* has resonance with the *Community Rule* [1QS 1]. In this case, however, the inclination is not apparently evil or "guilty." Rather, it appears in parallel with perfection, linked by the verb "walk." So, a man is to walk in the inclination of his understanding, and to walk perfect in all his deeds. This juxtaposition is unexpected, and is one of the clues which suggest this is not a "sectarian" work. The use of *yetser*, inclination, in line 11 suggests Genesis 6, where the evil inclination is in sharp contrast to Noah's righteous perfection, rather than Genesis 17. That contrast may have led the author to deduce that an evil *yetser* calls for a perfect *yetser*. This idea is strengthened by the use of "secrets of his plans" (*mhshbt*, as in Gen 6:5), with the perfect walk.

Equally intriguing is the language of Genesis 2 and 3 here. The knowledge which brings discernment between good and evil (line 8) comes from God, the foundation of truth. God laid this foundation with wisdom and formed (*ytsrh*) it with cunning (*'armh*, as in the play on words in Gen 2:25, 3:1, 7, 10, 11 between "naked" and "prudent/cunning").[37] In contrast to the Genesis narrative, all these terms are positive because this knowledge comes from God. This agrees with the wisdom view of Proverbs, where *'arum* is prudence given from God. This is the knowledge the first man and woman would have received had they sought "the mystery which is to come" from God rather than the serpent. As a result, the couple were not "*'arum*/prudent," but "*'arummim*/naked."[38] In light of these associations, to "walk perfect" envisions what might have been differ-ent in Gen 3:8 when God's voice was heard as he walked in the garden in the evening breeze.

This allusion to the garden leads us to the second passage, 4QInstruction[d] (418 Fr 81 + 81a with 4Q423 8, 1-4).

> 1[for the utterance of] your lips *He has* opened up a spring *so that* you may bless the Holy Ones, and *(so that) as (with)* an everlasting fountain *you* may praise *His* n[ame. The] n has He separated you from every 2fleshly spirit, *so that you may be* separated from every thing that He hates, *and (might)* hold

---

36. The full phrase, "mystery which is to come," does not appear there, but "wonderful mysteries" do, e.g., 1QS 11:4-5, 9:18-19, CD 3:18, 1QH 5:8, 9:21, 10:13, 15:26. Cf. Goff, *Worldly and Heavenly Wisdom*, esp. chap. II.

37. Goff, *Worldly and Heavenly Wisdom*, pp. 116-23, discussed the use of Genesis 1–3 in terms of "spiritual people" and "fleshly spirit," noting the use of *'enosh* for "man" in this passage.

38. See further D. Swanson, "'Original Sin' in the Primeval Narrative," *European Explorations in Christian Holiness* 2 (2001): 192-94.

yourself aloof from all that *His* soul abominates. [Fo]r He has made every-one, 3and has made them to inherit each his own inheritance; but He is your portion and your inheritance among the children of *mankind,* [And over] his *(Adam's?/God's)* [in]heritance has He set *them* in authority. But you 4by (doing) this honour Him, by consecrating yourself to Him, just as He has appointed you as a *Holy of Holies* [*over all the*] *earth,* and (just as) among all the [Go]dly [Ones] 5has He cast your lot, and has magnified your glory greatly. He has appointed you for Himself as a first-born among [   ] sa[*ying,* "*I will bless you*] 6and My bounty to you I will give. As for you, *do not* My good things belong to you? Yea, in faithfulness to Me walk continu-ally [   ]."

Whether the identity of the recipient of this blessing is the *Maven*/student, a priest, a poor farmer, or anyman need not detain us.[39]

First, the familiar concept of separation from that which God hates is present. Second, we come once again to the idea of the *Holy of Holies* in human form. This seems to refer to an individual rather than a community. "You" in every case here is singular, not plural. The *Maven,* whoever he might be, is ap-pointed as a Holy of Holies, indeed, over all the earth and among all Godly Ones! In response, he is to consecrate, or sanctify, himself to God. And so, he will walk in faithfulness to God continually.

Creation language is not far away here, either, as the *Maven* receives his inheritance among the children of *'adam.* As such he receives a blessing, that of all humankind as in Genesis 1, and that of a first-born.

Such terms directed to any specific person are remarkable. Perhaps they apply to some extraordinary figure, such as a high priest,[40] or a messianic figure with New Testament undertones. But, the ambiguity of the language prevents a firm conclusion. If the setting for this work is outside Temple circles,[41] then we have an early example of creating a holy place wherever there is faithfulness to divinely revealed teaching. Whichever setting is envisioned, the import is simi-lar — great glory is given to a human being to be the holiest Place.

---

39. Proponents, in order, are C. H. T. Fletcher-Louis, *All the Glory,* p. 178; Elgvin, "Priestly Sages," pp. 85-86; Eibert Tigchelaar, "The Addressees of 4QInstruction," in *Sapiential, Liturgical and Poetical Texts from Qumran, STDJ* 35 (Leiden: Brill, 2000), p. 75.

40. Fletcher-Louis's conclusion, as above.

41. See Elgvin, "Priestly Sages," pp. 85-86.

Conclusions

These passages use perfection language, as does Qumran, but the source of this is Primeval, grounded in creation as in Genesis 1–6, rather than Patriarchal and covenantal from Genesis 17. The holiness it discusses is personal, and not descriptive of a whole community, though it is not clear if this is expected of every *Maven* or only one person. Most important, these texts give a glimpse of a spirituality which precedes or exists alongside the Qumran community. Perfection is not a sectarian concern only, but a wider phenomenon. Perfection of walk and holiness on the level of the Holiest Place are part of a wider common heritage of imagery and practice.

Whether the idea of perfection, *tammim,* is based in the Primeval or the Patriarchal setting, there is a lifestyle of holy living that is spelled out in the texts we have surveyed. This lifestyle is based on the relationship of the individual and the community to their holy God. In covenant terms, perfect obedience to Torah is the demand. It is not absolute perfection, but "walking"; failure is admitted, but there is a means of expiation. Even so, perfect obedience is a present expectation.

Perfection in the New Testament Reconsidered

The Scrolls show the centrality of concern for purity/impurity in the Second Temple Period. By the turn of the era, this was the value by which each group identified itself in relation to others.[42] The teaching of Jesus and the apostles cannot adequately be understood unless it is seen in this same context. The Christian focus on salvation — the means of entering the kingdom of God — and on sin — the human situation from which we are saved — has obscured its purpose, deliverance from sin and life in the kingdom. More of the NT is focussed on the life of the kingdom than on the means of entrance. The means of living the kingdom life is through sanctification — the chief concern of Torah, and of the parties of Judaism of Jesus' time.

We now consider the New Testament language of perfection in light of these texts, in order to clarify the denotation of the word for NT interpretation.

---

42. J. Neusner, "Method and Structure in the History of Judaic Ideas: An Exercise," in *Jews, Greeks and Christians,* ed. R. Hamerton-Kelly and Robins Scroggs (Leiden: Brill, 1974), p. 75.

Walking Perfect

"Walking" is a common New Testament expression for the way of living the Christian life. It is a persistent call from Paul in Ephesians, urging believers to "walk worthy of your calling" (4:1), to "walk in love" (5:2), to "walk as children of light" (5:8). John the Elder exhorts his disciples to "walk in the light" (1 John 1:7), to "walk just as he [Jesus] walked" (2:6), to "walk in truth" (2 John 4; 3 John 3, 4), and to "walk according to his [the Father's] commandments" (2 John 6), which is to love one another.

What is not found in the New Testament, however, is "walking" in close relation to "perfection." On the other hand, in the Hebrews 11 role-call of faith that is not unlike CD 3, Enoch is a pattern of faith because "he had pleased God" (11:5, 6). This reflects the LXX translation of walk in Gen 5:22 and 24 with *euaresteo* (εὐαρεστέω), which is also used of Noah in Gen 6:9 and Abraham in 17:1. Noah and Abraham follow Enoch in Hebrew's list, but their perfection is not an issue. The writer of the Hebrews seems to follow the Enoch line here.

Blameless or Perfect?

One question centres on the proper translation of *tammim*. Two different Greek terms are used in the LXX passages of most interest to us — Gen 6:5 and 17:1. New Testament writers use them both.

a. Amemptos (ἀμέμπτος), as LXX at Gen 17:1

In the *Community Rule*, *tammim* was inserted from Gen 17:1 into the Dtr context. The LXX text translates this with *amemptos*, which would suggest an English translation of "blameless" (as in the NRSV). This may be the usage lying behind the following NT passages.

- 1 Thess 3:12-13. "May the Lord make you increase and abound in love for one another and for all, just as we abound in love for you. And may he so strengthen your hearts in holiness that you may be blameless before our God and Father at the coming of the Lord Jesus with all his saints."

We should not be surprised to find *blameless* in relation to *holiness* and *love*, and in an eschatological framework, having seen the same grouping in 1QS. In the *Community Rule*, however, "love" of God in Deut 6:4 was replaced by "keeping the Torah" from 4:29. Here, "love for one another" is Paul's version of Lev

19:19, the second commandment of Jesus. The function of blamelessness here is the same as that of walking *tammim* in 1QS — it allows one to stand in the presence of God.

- 1 Thess 5:23. "May the God of peace himself sanctify you entirely; and may your spirit and soul and body be kept complete and blameless at the coming of our Lord Jesus Christ."

The eschatological framework continues to predominate. The common interpretation of "at the coming of the Lord" refers to a future, end-time sanctification. Qumran compels us to see this also as a present expectation — the entire sanctification does not merely happen "*at* the coming," but the believer is kept blameless now, *to be found so at* the coming of the Lord.

- Luke 1:6, of Zechariah and Elizabeth

Luke's depiction of the parents of John as righteous and blameless echoes that of Noah in Gen 6:9 and, perhaps, Job 1:1, "perfect and upright" *(tam wyashar),* though the LXX translates with *teleios.* What is striking is that they "live blamelessly according to all the commandments and regulations of the Lord." Although direct relationship with Qumran or Essenes is not demanded by such a depiction, it does highlight contemporary expectation of what it means to be a faithful and pious Jew. Such are the forebears to Jesus and his followers.

b. Teleios (τέλειος), *as LXX at Gen 6:9*

The second term used by the LXX for translating *tammim* is *teleios,* and its verbal root. In light of the Qumran literature, this is what lies behind the NT use of this word. There are two differing presentations of perfection which need to be illustrated.

- Hebrews: The perfection of Jesus

Jesus is the perfect one. In 2:10 Jesus, the pioneer of salvation, is made perfect through suffering, having been made for a little while lower than the angels (2:9; LXX of Ps 8). This, once again, is the Primeval pattern from creation — Jesus as perfect *'Adam.*

In 5:9 we are told Jesus is made perfect through his obedience, and made high priest according to the order of *Melchizedek.* This motif is returned to in chap. 7: the Son has been made perfect forever, a high priest "holy, blameless, undefiled (ὅσιος, ἄκακος, ἀμίαντος), separated from sinners, exalted above the heavens" (7:26). As the perfect high priest Jesus is able to enter the Holy Place to perform expiation (9:11), purifying (v. 14, // "sanctifies" of v. 13) our conscience (or, consciousness). Thus far Hebrews sounds much like 4QInstruction[d].

- Hebrews: The perfection of those saved by Jesus' perfection

In Hebrews, perfection is a fruit of salvation. This occurs in 5:11–6:8, alongside the treatment of Christ's perfection as a priest like Melchizedek. These matters, it is said, can be understood by the *perfect* (5:14), who have been disciplined to distinguish between good and evil.[43]

This Genesis 3 terminology also echoes 4QInstruction[d]. The writer then urges the readers to go beyond the basics to *perfection*. Those once enlightened, who fall away, cannot renew their repentance. Enlightenment consists of tasting the heavenly gift, sharing the Holy Spirit, tasting the goodness of the word (ῥῆμα) of God, and the powers of the age to come — eschatological language in present expectation.

In chaps. 9 and 10, the better offering of Christ is contrasted with what the old covenant could not do. In 9:9 the offering of gifts and sacrifices is contrasted unfavourably with Christ's offering of his own blood — they cannot "perfect the conscience/consciousness of the worshipper." In 9:14, worshippers are purified from dead works. At Qumran, worshippers must be perfect to worship; in Hebrews, worshippers are made perfect.

In 10:1, since the Torah is but a shadow of the true, it cannot make perfect those who draw near. In contrast, Christ has by his one offering "perfected for all time those who are sanctified." This is by the Holy Spirit (10:14, 15).

Chapter 11 ends the survey of those who are commended for their faith but did not receive the promise with an explanation: "God had provided something better so that they would not, apart from us, be made perfect." In the opening verses of chap. 12, Jesus as perfector of our faith is now the goal of our race. Discipline by trial is for the purpose of sharing Christ's holiness (12:10), without which no one will see the Lord (12:14). The last reference to the perfection of people is in a contrast between Mt. Sinai and the new Mt. Zion, and heavenly Jerusalem. Arrival in this city is to join with angels and the firstborn of heaven and God, with "the spirits of the righteous made perfect" and with Jesus. This sounds like a vision of the future, but it is said to already be reality, "You have come to Mount Zion" (12:22).

Throughout these chapters there is a focus on the worshipper as coming

---

43. διάκρισιν καλοῦ τε καὶ κακοῦ; cf. Gen 3:6 LXX: γινώσκοντες κὰλον καὶ πονηρόν.

into the Holy/Holiest Place, as we found at Qumran. Whether or not there is direct relationship, they inhabit the same thought-world.

What, then, is the nature of Hebrews' perfection? Like 1QS, it is perfect obedience, although amidst suffering; and it is perfection of faith. Ultimately, the perfection of the believer is made possible only by Jesus' perfect obedience and sacrifice. But that sacrifice brings the believer into the heavenly Jerusalem.

• Matthew: Perfect love in the Sermon on the Mount

The NT coupling of perfection language with love is most illuminated by comparison to Qumran. The use of "perfection" in the respective corpae brings us to the nub of what distinguishes the holiness of the NT from that of Second Temple Judaism. At Qumran, as in the OT, the essence of holiness is that it requires "separation" from the unholy. Perfect holiness, then, will be perfect separation lest the pure becomes impure by exposure to uncleanness.

Matthew 5:48, "Be perfect as your heavenly father is perfect," is a crux for grasping the implications of Qumran perfection. Because it is absurd to expect that one can be as perfect as God, a fact fully borne out by Christian experience, this is written off as hyperbole or pure idealism. Since it is unachievable, it is therefore ignored. This study may shed some light on this text.

Matthew 5:48 is generally recognised as being based on Lev 19:2, "Be holy because I, the Lord your God, am holy."[44] This last section of Jesus' antitheses begins with his citation of Lev 19:18, "You shall love your neighbour as yourself," so the allusion is not fanciful. The appearance of *teleios* where Leviticus has *hagios,* holy, is a key-word insertion whose purpose is to draw attention to another biblical text. The question is, what text? Davies and Allison, for example, argue that Deut 18:13, "Be *tammim/teleios* before the Lord your God," is the key text, on the basis of other use of Deuteronomy in Matthew 5.[45] This is possible, for Jesus' antitheses, other than this one, are aimed at Deuteronomy.[46] But, a basic factor in key-word insertion is that the context of the key-word must aid the interpretation of the base text. In this setting, Deuteronomy 18 is not help-

44. See marginal notes in English translations. The Greek makes this clearer:

Lev 19:2:   ἅγιοι ἔσεσθε ὅτι ἐγὼ ἅγιος κύριος ὁ θεὸς ὑμῶν
Matt 5:48:   ἔσεσθε οὖν ὑμεῖς τέλειοι ὡς ἐγὼ ὁ πατὴρ ὑμῶν ὁ οὐράνιος τέλειός ἐστιν

45. W. D. Davies and Dale C. Allison, Jr., *The Gospel According to Saint Matthew,* ICC (Edinburgh: T&T Clark, 1988), pp. 561-63. See also the NA[27] margin.

46. Whereas Jesus' citations of commandments might be seen as deriving from Exodus or Deuteronomy, the reference to Deut 24:1, and the citations of Deuteronomy in the testing narrative of chap. 4 tend to confirm this contention.

ful, being prohibitions against magic. Ruling this out, we must turn to Noah and Abraham as likely sources for the insertion. In light of the range of literature we have surveyed, either is a possibility, and we must make an exegetical decision as to which line of contemporary thinking the SOM is following. Given the strong covenant setting of the Sermon, the comparison with the *Community Rule* focus on Abraham leads us to see Gen 17:1 here.

The implications of this can be quickly drawn. The SOM is indisputably a covenant setting: Jesus is giving Torah on the Mount. Jesus gives a command, which centres on the great command of Deut 6:4, "Love the Lord your God with all your heart, soul, and mind," and Lev 19:19, "Love your neighbour as yourself" (Matt 22:37-39). Perfection is perfect obedience to this command.

The use of Lev 19:2 in a word about love of neighbour indicates that the holiness of God is to be understood as perfect love. Just as the Torah demands holiness because the Lord is holy, so Jesus demands love because God is perfect love. If we consider the possibility that the misquote of Lev 19:19 in 5:43, "love your neighbour and hate your enemy," may be an indirect reference to Qumran teaching, then this kind of perfection is outlined in even bolder contrast. In Matthew 5 we discover that perfection, or holiness, is the expression of love which encompasses the other, including the enemy. Rather than demanding "separation," this kind of holiness is not contaminated by the impure. Instead, as seen in the ministry of Jesus (e.g., Matt 4:23-24; 8:1-3; and Mark 7), holiness overcomes impurity. As is said elsewhere, "perfect love casts out fear" (1 John 4:18).

Conclusions

The Christian life is a life of holiness. Just as much as for the Judaism of the first century, this was the case for Jesus and the early Church. Although there are noticeable differences, at the heart of the differences is a commonality.

First, early Christianity shared with the rest of Judaism a central concern for holiness, often depicted as perfect obedience. Christian interpretation of *teleios* through the centuries has focussed on "perfect" with a Greek philosophical connotation. The reading of this Greek term without grasping its Hebrew basis has had unfortunate consequences for the history of the Church. It is time to reclaim the call to holiness central to New Testament teaching.

Second, the New Testament shares the goal of walking in the presence of the holy God. But, for the Church, the Holiest Place is not found in separation from the world, but within the world. "Where two or three are gathered in my name, I am in their midst" (Matt 18:20). Indeed, in Christian holiness, an inversion takes place. Holiness does not withdraw, it reaches out. In reaching out and touching the unclean, it does not become unclean, but it is contagious and makes holy. And the nature of holiness is perfect love like God's, which must extend to love of neighbour and love of the enemy.

Perfection, then, is not for the margins of faith. Perfect holy love is the heart of the new covenant, and the central commandment of that covenant.

Holiness and Ecclesiology:
The Church in Matthew

Donald A. Hagner

For a challenging call to a high standard of holiness it would be hard to top the Gospel of Matthew. The Sermon on the Mount (chaps. 5–7) presents an idealism so daunting that it has often been regarded as a kind of foil for the gospel — the exceptionally high standard of the law, as interpreted by Jesus, being intended to drive us to the necessity of grace. Indeed, so insistent is Matthew's call to this new level of righteousness that it is easy to misread him as arguing for salvation by works. But this would be to ignore the main affirmation that Matthew makes, namely the announcement of "the gospel of the kingdom" *(to euangelion tēs basileias),* a phrase unique to Matthew (4:23; 9:35; 24:14; cf. 26:13). The dawning of the kingdom in the historical figure of Jesus is purely a matter of grace. It comes to the unworthy, as something to be received rather than earned.

With the coming of the eschatological reality of the kingdom, however, it is equally clear that a new standard of righteousness comes into effect: the righteousness expected of those who belong to the dawning kingdom. The connection between righteousness and the kingdom is vital. This essay explores the interconnection between the gospel of the kingdom of God, the new eschatological community, and the call to a new form of righteousness. In the process we hope to gain some insight into the dynamic of righteousness among the earliest disciples of Jesus and draw lessons for the contemporary church.

I count it a personal privilege and joy to offer this essay in honor of my good friend and NT colleague, Alex Deasley, who has long been interested in the pursuit of holiness and who for many years has faithfully labored to that end in his teaching, preaching, writing, and living.

The Gospel of the Kingdom

One of the unique and most conspicuous features of the Gospel of Matthew is found in the five discourses (chapters 5–7; 10; 13; 18; and 24–25). These provide an incomparable compendium of the teaching of Jesus. While this emphasis on the teaching of Jesus is one of the distinctives of the Gospel, the teaching presupposes and relies upon the more important fact of the announcement of the kingdom. Although the phrase "the gospel of the kingdom" is found only once in the five discourses (24:14), the word "kingdom" *(basileia)* occurs frequently there and throughout the Gospel (55x total; Mark: 20x; Luke 46x). The kingdom serves as the prior, determining fact in the narrative, including the teaching sections. Matthew, like the other Synoptics and John too, describes the dawning of an eschatological reality. This is the fundamental, governing fact that controls the narratives. All that Jesus says and does is in one way or another related to the dawning of the kingdom of God.

The point is, as Matthew likes so much to stress, that with the coming of Jesus we have arrived at the fulfillment of the promises of scripture. One sees this throughout Matthew's narrative, as for example at the very beginning in the genealogies, with their stress on Abraham and David. Both the Abrahamic and Davidic covenants find their realization in Jesus. At the beginning of the Sermon on the Mount, the Beatitudes affirm the reality of the kingdom in the present (see 5:3, 10), and not merely something to be expected in the future. John the Baptist's doubt about whether Jesus was the Messiah, the One who would bring the kingdom, is answered by Jesus with words pointing to apocalyptic fulfillment (11:4-5). Jesus identifies John as fulfilling the role of Elijah (11:14; 17:12), the one preparing the way for the promised One, adding "For all the prophets and the law prophesied until John" (11:13). John is therefore at the pivot point of the turning from the age of prophecy to the age of fulfillment. Just as the healings are signs of the presence of the kingdom of God, according to 11:4-5, so too the exorcism of demons points to that same reality: "But if it is by the Spirit of God that I cast out demons, then the kingdom of God has come upon you" (12:28). In the parables discourse, Jesus stresses the fulfillment he brings: "But blessed are your eyes, for they see, and your ears, for they hear. Truly I say to you, many prophets and righteous people longed to see what you see, and did not see it, and to hear what you hear, and did not hear it" (13:16-17). As the narrative approaches its climax, Jesus accepts Peter's confession of him as Messiah (16:16), and as he enters Jerusalem as messianic king (note Matthew's quotation of Zech 9:9) he does not turn away the shouts of "Hosanna to the Son of David!" (21:9; cf. 21:15-16).

At the same time, it is clear that even with all of the realized eschatology in Matthew, the kingdom also awaits a future manifestation. The kingdom comes *into* the present age without bringing it to an end. Currently the kingdom is present in a paradoxical form. Jesus admits as much when he says to the disciples: "To you it has been given to know the secrets [*ta mystēria*] of the kingdom" (13:11). One of the mysteries of the kingdom revealed in the parables discourse of chapter 13 is the surprise that the kingdom arrives without bringing judgment upon the wicked. Judgment is delayed. Indeed, as the parables of the mustard seed, the leaven, the hidden treasure, and the pearl reveal (13:31-33, 44-46), the kingdom first comes in a small, inconspicuous way, without overwhelming the world (as it eventually will). The greatest of surprises, of course, is the fate of the Messiah, who comes not triumphantly, but humbly, not to ascend the throne of David, but to die (16:21). And then too comes further surprising teaching: the disciples of Jesus must also be prepared to suffer, take up their cross, and follow after him (16:24-27). The reality of the kingdom is to be lived out here and now, in this still very imperfect world, in advance of the time of the parousia of the Son of Man.

What needs to be stressed here is that a new eschatological reality has arrived with, in and through Jesus, and that together with that reality comes a new standard of righteousness and a new pattern of obedience.[1] One cannot talk of righteousness and obedience without giving attention to the new reality of the kingdom. "The king of whom Matthew's gospel speaks is Jesus. The kingdom into which he invites his readers is the kingdom of heaven. Matthean spirituality springs out of encounter with that king and involves entry into that kingdom."[2]

The New Eschatological People of God

Among the Synoptic Gospels it is in Matthew that the emergence of a new community is most explicit. As is well known, the word *ekklēsia* ("church") occurs in the four Gospels only in Matthew (16:18; 18:17). Of course, speaking in Aramaic, Jesus would not have used the Greek word *ekklēsia*, but an Aramaic word for "community."[3] Nevertheless, by the time of the writing of the Gospel, the evangelist would have been prepared to understand the Greek word in the explicit meaning of "church," the meaning it has elsewhere throughout the NT. The new community founded by Jesus is nothing other than the "church."

1. Stephen C. Barton, "Dislocating and Relocating Holiness: A New Testament Study," in *Holiness: Past and Present,* ed. Stephen C. Barton (London: T&T Clark, 2003), pp. 198-200.

2. Stephen C. Barton, *The Spirituality of the Gospels* (London: SPCK, 1992), p. 10.

3. Probably *qahal,* but also possible are *'edah* (= Greek *synagōgē*) or *kenishta.*

As the community of the kingdom, this is a new eschatological people. While on the one hand there is an obvious and inevitable discontinuity with Israel, on the other hand, this community regards itself as the initial fulfillment of God's promises to Israel. Although the language is lacking, it is a kind of new Israel, or better, the true Israel. Jesus says "I tell you, you are Peter [*Petros*], and on this rock [*petra*]⁴ I will build my church" (16:18). Very significant here is Jesus' reference to "my church," where the pronoun, preceding the noun in the Greek, is emphatic: *mou tēn ekklēsian* ("*my* church"). The church is the community *of Jesus,* a designation that stands in remarkable contrast to the phrase, *qahal YHWH,* "community of the Lord" (LXX: *ekklēsia kyriou,* e.g., Deut 23:1-2; 1 Chr 28:8; Mic 2:5; cf. Neh 13:1; Lam 1:10). The community of Jesus as the community of the Messiah is the eschatological counterpart to Israel — or better, the eschatological manifestation of Israel.

A few scholars have argued in recent years that Matthew's community is to be understood as a sect within Judaism rather than an actual manifestation of Christianity.⁵ Although they have rightly emphasized the Jewishness of Matthew's Gospel, in my opinion they seriously underestimate the degree of newness and the discontinuity with Israel that is found repeatedly in Matthew.⁶ This eschatological community — the community of the kingdom — represents the fulfilled expression of Israel. It is in continuity with Israel but it is also a new people. Very important is the fact that it centers no longer on Torah, but on Jesus (cf. 10:32-33, 37-39). It is this community that will enjoy his presence wherever two or three are gathered in his name (18:20);⁷ it is this community

---

4. The word play on "Peter" and "rock" is effective in the Greek, but would have been even clearer in the Aramaic where both words would have been exactly the same: *Kepha.*

5. Andrew Overman, *Matthew's Gospel and Formative Judaism: The Social World of the Matthean Community* (Minneapolis: Fortress, 1990); *Church and Community in Crisis: The Gospel According to Matthew, The New Testament in Context* (Valley Forge, Pa.: Trinity Press International, 1996); Anthony J. Saldarini, *Matthew's Christian-Jewish Community* (Chicago and London: University of Chicago Press, 1994); "The Gospel of Matthew and Jewish-Christian Conflict," in *Social History of the Matthean Community: Cross-Disciplinary Approaches,* ed. David L. Balch (Minneapolis: Fortress, 1991), pp. 38-61; David Sim, *The Gospel of Matthew and Christian Judaism: The History and Social Setting of the Matthean Community* (Edinburgh: T&T Clark, 1998); "Christianity and Ethnicity in the Gospel of Matthew," in *Ethnicity and the Bible,* BIS 19, ed. Mark G. Brett (Leiden: Brill, 1996), pp. 171-95; "The Gospel of Matthew and the Gentiles," *Journal for the Study of the New Testament* 57 (1995): 19-48.

6. See my "Matthew: Apostate, Reformer, Revolutionary?" *New Testament Studies* 49 (2003): 193-209; and "New Things from The Scribe's Treasure Box (Mt 13:52)," *Expository Times* 109 (1998): 329-34.

7. Cf. the parallel rabbinic saying that the Shekinah glory is present where two or three gather to study Torah (*m. Aboth* 3:2; *b. Sanh.* 39a; *b. Ber.* 5b).

that Jesus promises he will be with "always, to the close of the age" *(tēs synteleias tou aiōnos)* (28:20).

This community of the kingdom is called to faithfulness to the Torah (cf. 5:17-19) but, as we will see, in a unique way. Jesus does not call the community to follow the Torah directly, but to follow *his* teaching (cf. 7:24-27). For it is the Messiah's teaching that represents the true interpretation of the Torah (cf. 23:8, 10). To follow the teaching of Jesus is in effect to be faithful to the Torah. The great commission thus includes the words "teaching them to observe all that I have commanded you" (28:20).

Righteousness in Matthew

The *hagios* ("holy") word group is not prominent in Matthew. The verb *hagiazō* ("sanctify") occurs only in 6:9, "hallowed be thy name," and in 23:17, 19 where it refers to the gold of the temple which the temple "makes sacred," and a gift that the altar "makes sacred." The noun *hagiasmos* ("holiness") does not occur. The word *hagios* ("holy") occurs mainly as an adjective modifying "Spirit" and "city," and once the holy "place," i.e. the inner sanctuary of the temple (24:15). It occurs twice as a noun, "what is holy" (7:6), and, in plural form, "the saints who had fallen asleep" (27:52).

Matthew's word for the conduct of believers is not "holiness," but *dikaiosynē,* "righteousness." Among the Synoptic Gospels, the word occurs only in Matthew, except for its single occurrence in Zechariah's prophecy in Luke 1:75. Matthean scholarship has tended to follow the conclusion of Benno Przybylski that all seven occurrences of the word in Matthew refer to ethical conduct.[8] This seems true in most of the instances, but not, in my opinion, for all of them. I find exceptions in the two references outside the Sermon on the Mount. In 3:15 and 21:32 the righteousness in view can be understood as the righteousness of God, i.e., God's saving activity (as, e.g., in Paul [!], in Rom 1:17), rather than human righteousness. In view in both references is John the Baptist as the forerunner of the messianic salvation brought by Jesus. Furthermore, it also seems unlikely that *dikaiosynē* in 5:6 refers to ethical righteousness. Instead, in keeping with the context of the other beatitudes, the hunger in view is for eschatological *justice,* for the real-

---

8. Benno Przybylski, *Righteousness in Matthew and His World of Thought,* SNTSMS 41 (Cambridge: Cambridge University Press, 1982). Oddly enough, Przybylski denies that "righteousness" is of any great importance to Matthew, regarding it as "essentially a Jewish concept" (pp. 115, 123).

ization of God's rule on earth (in accord with the point of the future tenses of vv. 4, 5, 7, 8, and 9).[9]

The four remaining occurrences of the word do have ethical righteousness in view, and to these we now turn our attention. The beatitude of 5:10, "Blessed are those who are persecuted for righteousness' sake," has in view the ethical righteousness of those who follow Jesus. The allusion to this logion in 1 Pet 3:14 also points to this understanding. The parallelism between 5:10 and 5:11 is striking, where *heneken dikaiosynēs* ("on account of righteousness") parallels *heneken emou* ("on account of me"). Righteousness is associated with relationship to Jesus. Clearly ethical righteousness is also in view in 5:20, "For I tell you, unless your righteousness exceeds that of the scribes and Pharisees, you will never enter the kingdom of heaven." The difference in righteousness here is not quantitative, but qualitative. Although the language here sounds quantitative (lit. "abound more than"), the contrast is really qualitative, as the great difference between the ethical teaching of Jesus in the Gospels and the oral tradition of the Pharisees indicates (note too the reference to the "heavy burdens" imposed by the Pharisees in 23:4, and the contrast to the "easy yoke" and "light burden" of Jesus in 11:30). It is thus not a matter of increasing the legal stipulations, building a higher fence around Torah than the Pharisees did, but rather of exhibiting the new righteousness associated with the kingdom as its resultant fulfillment.

"Righteousness" in 6:1 (RSV: "piety") refers merely to the concrete practices of almsgiving, prayer, and fasting (6:1-18). The avoidance of hypocrisy (see vv. 2, 5, 16) is clearly important in the pattern of righteousness taught by Jesus.

The reference in 6:33, however, is one of the most illuminating: "But seek first his kingdom and his righteousness, and all these things shall be yours as well." In this exhortation we are confronted directly with the connection between the kingdom and righteousness. Jesus here calls his disciples to make the kingdom their priority: they are to put it "first." To make a priority of living under the sovereign rule of God, his kingdom, is at the same time to seek God's righteousness. The second phrase, "his righteousness" is epexegetical of the first, "his kingdom." That is, to prioritize the first is in effect also to prioritize the second.

The call to righteousness is therefore inseparable from the gift of the

---

9. I am well aware of the danger of "Paulinizing" Matthew. For a defense of these conclusions, see my "Righteousness in Matthew's Theology," in *Worship, Theology and Ministry in the Early Church: Essays in Honor of Ralph P. Martin,* ed. M. J. Wilkins and T. Paige (Sheffield: JSOT, 1992), pp. 101-20; and "Balancing the Old and the New: The Law of Moses in Matthew and Paul," *Interpretation* 51 (1997): 20-30. An excellent treatment of the subject can be found in J. Reumann, *"Righteousness" in the New Testament: "Justification" in the United States Lutheran-Roman Catholic Dialogue* (Philadelphia/New York: Fortress/Paulist, 1982), pp. 125-35.

kingdom. It is this fact that conditions all references to righteousness in the Gospel, enabling us to speak of righteousness not only as demand, but as gift at the same time. And this is why the righteousness of the disciples is qualitatively different from the righteousness, for example, of the Pharisees. The imperative is preceded by an indicative; the demand is preceded by gift. That was true, of course, for the OT era too, where the giving of the law is preceded by a statement of the already existing covenant relationship between YHWH and Israel. But now a new era of fulfillment has arrived. The reality of the dawning kingdom makes possible not merely a correct exegesis and new definition of the law, in the teaching of Jesus, but also brings to the recipients of the kingdom a new ability to live according to the will of God.

The ethical teaching of Matthew is thus directed to those who have received the kingdom. These are particularly kingdom ethics, applicable to those who belong to the kingdom. They cannot successfully be separated from this context, in which alone they make sense. The Sermon on the Mount is understood correctly only when it is seen in the context of the whole Gospel.[10]

The Righteousness of the New Community

Eschatology has begun with the arrival of the kingdom brought by Jesus. This turning point in the ages entails the creation of a new community of God's people, the church. Matthew calls that new community to righteousness. We have seen that this demand of righteousness presupposes the gift of the kingdom. But now we must explore further the nature of this righteousness. More exactly, what does discipleship look like in concrete, lived-out terms?

To begin with, the obedience of discipleship is now centered not upon the commandments, but upon Jesus and his teaching. "The law is no longer the center of gravity; Jesus is."[11] Although the righteousness of the Torah is still in view, the call is not to obey the commandments *per se*, but to obey the teaching of Jesus. It is *his* interpretation of the law that is definitive: "You have heard it said . . . but *I* [emphatic in the Greek] say to you" (5:22, 28, 32, 34, 39, 44). It is *his* words that will not pass away (24:35). In the commission that ends the Gospel,

10. *Pace* Hans Dieter Betz, who attempts to isolate the Sermon on the Mount from the Gospel and to deal with it independently as an entity with self-standing, universal relevance. See his *The Sermon on the Mount,* Hermeneia (Minneapolis: Fortress, 1995) and G. N. Stanton's critique of Betz in *A Gospel for a New People: Studies in Matthew* (Edinburgh: T&T Clark, 1992), pp. 307-25.

11. K. Snodgrass, "Matthew and the Law," in *Treasures New and Old. Contributions to Matthean Studies,* ed. D. R. Bauer and M. A. Powell (Atlanta: Scholars Press, 1996), p. 126.

those who are discipled are "to observe all that *I* have commanded you" (28:20). As the "one teacher" (23:8) of the community, it is *his* teaching that is to provide the rule of the community.

This does not, however, involve a new nomism, i.e., a centering on the commandments of Jesus parallel to the way contemporary Judaism centered on the Mosaic commandments. If there is an intended parallel between Jesus and Moses going up a mountain to deliver the law of God,[12] it would be a mistake to suppose that it is simply a matter of replacing the law of Moses with the new law of Jesus, all else remaining essentially the same. Because, as we have seen, the teaching of Jesus occurs in the context of eschatological fulfillment, an entirely different dynamic is at work. For the same reason, while Moses was significant only as a mediator of the law, Jesus is the focal figure of the new covenant. Discipleship revolves around him (10:37-38) rather than around the law. The key issue is following Jesus rather than obeying the law. Of course, for Matthew, to follow the teaching of Jesus is at the same time in effect to be faithful to the entirety of the law properly understood (even hyperbolically down to the smallest letter and the smallest mark; 5:18). In no way does Matthew regard Jesus as being disloyal to or undermining the righteousness of Torah. Rather Matthew's Jesus upholds it and defines it (5:17).

The words "disciple" and "follow" are regularly used in connection with following Jesus. The first, "disciple" *(mathētēs),* occurs far more frequently in Matthew (73x) than in Mark (46x) or Luke (37x).[13] The second, "to follow" *(akolouthein),* is also more frequent in Matthew (25x) than in the other Synoptic Gospels (Mark, 18x; Luke, 17x). A disciple is one who is in special relationship with Jesus, as a learner in relation to a teacher (10:24-25), and as one who will eventually become a teacher.[14] Jesus, the Messiah, is the "one teacher" of the community (23:8-10). When Jesus sits down to teach — the typical position of one who teaches — "his disciples" come to him (5:1). The word is commonly used specifically to refer to the twelve, though it can refer to, and often implies,

---

12. See D. C. Allison, Jr., *The New Moses: A Matthean Typology* (Minneapolis: Fortress, 1993), pp. 172-80.

13. The word occurs twenty-eight times in Acts, but nowhere else in the NT. The cognate verb *mathēteuein,* "to make disciples," occurs three times in Matthew, and in the remainder of the NT only once, in Acts 14:21. The verb *manthanein,* "to learn," occurs three times in Matthew, and only once in Mark. For a full study, see Michael J. Wilkins, *Discipleship in the Ancient World and Matthew's Gospel,* 2nd ed. (Grand Rapids: Baker, 1995); cf. too, by the same author, *Following the Master: Discipleship in the Steps of Jesus* (Grand Rapids: Zondervan, 1992).

14. A. T. Lincoln, "Matthew — A Story for Teachers?" in *The Bible in Three Dimensions,* ed. D. J. A. Clines et al. (Sheffield: JSOT, 1990), pp. 103-26. P. S. Minear, *Matthew: The Teacher's Gospel* (New York: Pilgrim, 1982).

a wider circle. The "disciple" is preeminently one who "learns" — the root meaning of the word. What is learned are the mysteries of the kingdom (13:51-52) — its dawning and its present, unobtrusive form — as well as the righteousness appropriate to the kingdom (chaps. 5–7; cf. 11:1). But the disciples must also learn the strange necessity of Jesus' death (16:21; 20:17), together with the disturbing fact that they must follow in his footsteps, taking up their own cross (16:24). What is finally most important, however, is that disciples are those who do the will of the Father as explicated by Jesus (7:21; 12:50; 21:31).[15]

The verb *poiein*, "to do," is very important in Matthew.[16] It is not just a matter of hearing the words of Jesus, but of doing them. Matthew would be in full accord with James (cf. Jas 1:25) — well, and for that matter, Paul too! (Rom 2:13). "Everyone who hears these words of mine and does them will be like the wise person. . . ." "Everyone who hears these words of mine and does not do them will be like a foolish person . . ." (7:24-27). "The Son of man is to come with his angels in the glory of the Father, and then he will repay every person for what he or she has done" (16:27). The stress upon doing is found throughout the Gospel (cf. also 19:16-22; 24:26; 25:40, 45).

The disciples are those who "follow" Jesus. Indeed, the essence of discipleship is following Jesus (4:19-22; 8:22; 9:9; 19:21, 27-30). In view is learning from Jesus, doing what Jesus teaches and in this way manifesting the righteousness of the Torah. Equally important is following Jesus in self-giving obedience to the will of the Father, even to the point of dying to self (16:24-28; cf. 10:38).

Jesus, as we have noted, fulfills the law in the sense of bringing it to its intended meaning (5:17). In the Sermon on the Mount, Jesus radicalizes the law, focusing not merely on actions, but even on the thoughts that underlie the actions.[17] What should especially be noted, however, is that Jesus does not get bogged down in what might be called nomistic detail. He does not multiply the commandments or engage in any casuistry. (This in itself suggests that it is a mistake to approach every specific command of the Sermon in a flat-footed, simplistic, and absolute literalism.)[18] Instead, in his sovereign authority Jesus is

15. Matthew would have agreed fully with the statement made by Jesus in John 8:31: "If you continue in my word, you are truly my disciples."

16. It is worth noting that while Matthew uses *peripatein*, "to walk," in its literal sense, he avoids using it as the equivalent to the Hebrew verb *halach*, though we might have expected him to do so. Does he deliberately want to avoid any suggestion of a parallel between Jesus' teaching and the Pharisees' *halacha*? Cf. R. T. France, *Matthew: Evangelist and Teacher* (Grand Rapids: Zondervan, 1989), pp. 257-60.

17. See K. E. Brower, "Jesus and the Lustful Eye: Matthew 5:28," *Evangelical Quarterly* 76 (2004): 291-309.

18. See my "Ethics and the Sermon on the Mount," *Studia Theologica* 51 (1997): 55.

able to cut through to the very essence of the law. He defines the weightier matters of the law as "justice, mercy, and faithfulness" (23:23), sounding very much like an Old Testament prophet. The essence of the law, however, is found in the striking twofold love commandment. It is here that the ethical teaching of the law finds its root. "You shall love the Lord your God with all your heart, and with all your soul, and with all your mind" and "You shall love your neighbor as yourself." "On these two commandments," Jesus concludes, "hang all the law and the prophets" (22:40). This is the heart of the law for Jesus and these two commandments accordingly provide a hermeneutic for the understanding of all the other commandments.[19] In a similar way, the Golden Rule points to what is to be regarded as the essence of the law: "In everything do to others as you would have them do to you; for this is the law and the prophets" (7:12). Here is the center of Matthew's call to righteousness; nothing is more basic than this. "The greatest holiness to which the disciples are called is a life of faith in Jesus, manifested by love for others. All laws are secondary to and must be interpreted in light of this commandment of love."[20] Brower too finds the double love commandment central to holiness: "Single-minded devotion to God and love of neighbor, flowing from the people of God in loving relationship with the holy God through Jesus Messiah by the Spirit, is the motivational center of Christian holiness."[21] Stephen Barton's conclusion seems justified: "It seems fair to say, then, that the double command to love God and neighbor expresses in a nutshell what practical spirituality is about according to Matthew."[22]

The righteousness of the new community is of a radical character. The Sermon on the Mount is its blueprint. Those who will manifest it are described as "the salt of the earth" and "the light of the world" (5:13). They are learning to deal not merely with their actions, as basically important as that is, but also with their thoughts, with their heart, with their innermost being. They are faithful; their word is as good as gold. Far from being vengeful, they are loving and good, even towards their enemies. They are not hypocrites, playacting, pretending to be something they are not. Their piety is more private than public. They are forgiving of others, just as they have experienced God's forgiveness.

---

19. See B. Gerhardsson, "The Hermeneutic Program in Matthew 22:37-40," in *Jews, Greeks and Christians: Religious Cultures in Late Antiquity, Essays in Honor of William David Davies,* ed. R. Hamerton-Kelly and R. Scroggs (Leiden: Brill, 1976), pp. 129-50, and T. L. Donaldson, "The Law that Hangs (Matthew 22:40): Rabbinic Formulation and Matthean Social World," *Catholic Biblical Quarterly* 57 (1995): 689-709.

20. Leonard Doohan, *Matthew: Spirituality for the 80's and 90's* (Santa Fe: Bear, 1985), p. 22.

21. K. Brower, *Holiness in the Gospels* (Kansas City: Beacon Hill, 2005), p. 126.

22. Barton, *Spirituality,* p. 22.

They are not materialistic. They are not anxious, but place their trust in God's provision for them. They make the kingdom of God and the righteousness associated with that kingdom their priority. They are not judgmental. They act towards others as they would like others to act towards them. They are serious about the call to righteousness.

This comprehensive picture of righteousness in the Sermon on the Mount contains virtually all of the ethical teaching that can be found in the remainder of the Gospel, implicitly if not explicitly. It is this pattern of righteousness that is in view when Jesus commissions his disciples to make other disciples, "teaching them to observe all that I have commanded you" (28:20). Ritual purity, so important to contemporary Judaism, plays no role in the teaching of Jesus. "Holiness, in the view of Jesus, was not maintained by ritual purity — clean hands — but by the integrity of being that identified wholly and unreservedly with the purposes of God in compassion and redemption for His lost and dying world."[23]

The Dynamic of the New Righteousness

If we have a grasp of the "what," the content of the righteousness of the kingdom, what can be said of the "how," that is, the implementation of that righteousness? Matthew does not speak directly concerning this, but there are some things that can be said from what Matthew does provide. Here the interrelationship of ideas mentioned earlier becomes all-important.

(1) First and foremost is the fact of a new eschatological reality in the presence of the kingdom now, in and through Jesus, in advance of its fullest coming, in the Eschaton. This is the fundamental basis, the underlying predication, upon which the call to righteousness rests. We have entered an unprecedented era of fulfillment, and with it comes *a new potentiality.*

> The Sermon as it lies before us now in Matthew represents the design for Christian living which the apostolic Church gave its catechumens — that is, it was preceded by the preaching of the Gospel and conversion. But what is true of the Sermon as a whole is true also of the separate sayings which make it up. Originally they were all preceded by something else — the proclamation of the glad news of God's inbreaking Reign and the new relationship with God which it made possible.[24]

23. K. Brower, *Holiness in the Gospels,* p. 115.
24. A. M. Hunter, *A Pattern for Life: An Exposition of the Sermon on the Mount, Its Making, Its Exegesis and Its Meaning,* rev. ed. (Philadelphia: Westminster, 1965), p. 104.

The gift of the kingdom speaks of grace with clarity. The ability to live in the manner laid out by the Sermon on the Mount depends upon the new empowering of God's grace now available to us. With the dawning of a new era, new things are possible (cf. 13:52). The Beatitudes that stand at the beginning of the Sermon on the Mount affirm the blessed status of those who are the recipients of the kingdom. The kingdom is theirs *now* (5:3, 10) and the fullness of eschatological blessing will be theirs at the consummation of the age, as the future tense verbs indicate.[25] But the emphasis is on the first part of each beatitude, the present blessedness that is ascribed to the disciples. The possibility of a radical transformation of the disciples must start here. The ethical teachings that follow depend on this present reality brought by Jesus. The disciples do not start empty-handed in their quest for righteousness. Far from it. Jesus refers to the treasury from which they may draw: "The good person out of his or her good treasure [Luke (6:45) adds "of the heart"] brings forth good" (12:35). It is fully in keeping with the thrust of the Gospel to conclude that the "good treasure" is rightly understood as the fruit of the grace of the newly dawning kingdom and reception of it.

(2) A further new reality that is essential to living as disciples is the relationship with Jesus. We have already noted that following Jesus is practically a definition of discipleship. The acceptance of Jesus as Messianic Teacher and Lord is obviously a *sine qua non* so far as righteousness is concerned. The disciples were "learners" by virtue of their being with Jesus. During the course of his ministry they were in the process of being formed by him. Personal commitment to him meant everything (10:32-33, 37-39). But can Jesus be a resource to later disciples who do not have the privilege of his bodily presence? Matthew supplies the later church with a superb compendium of the teaching of Jesus. But more than that, he implies that Jesus himself remains a resource for later disciples. "Where two or three are gathered in my name, there am I in the midst of them" (18:20). But the most impressive promise here is found in the final words of the Gospel: "and lo, I am with you always, to the close of the age" (28:20). And, it must be noted, these words follow immediately after the commission "teaching them to observe all that I have commanded you." The continuing presence of Jesus with his disciples through the centuries is part of the realized eschatology of the present kingdom and remains an important factor in personal transformation and the practice of righteousness. The invitation of 11:28-30 is applicable to all who would be disciples of Jesus — not just the twelve, not just the disciples in Matthew's church, but all the disciples of Jesus

---

25. As we have noted above, the beatitude of 5:6 refers probably to those who hunger and thirst for justice, not personal righteousness, and thus is not relevant to our discussion here.

throughout the history of the church: "Come to me, all who labor and are heavy laden, and I will give you rest. Take my yoke upon you, and learn from me; for I am gentle and lowly in heart, and you will find rest for your souls. For my yoke is easy and my burden is light." Jesus is the ultimate resource for discipleship.

(3) The church, the new community of faith created by Jesus, constitutes a family for disciples and an environment in which righteousness can be encouraged. This new community, analogous to Israel, is called to obedience. It is "part of a holy fellowship — a fellowship marked by submission and obedience to Jesus' words about the divine reign, cost what it may."[26] Fictive kinship becomes an important factor.[27] Matthew alone among the Synoptics specifies the "disciples" in the following statement: "And stretching out his hand toward his disciples, he said 'Here are my mother and brothers! For whoever does the will of my Father in heaven is my brother, and sister, and mother'" (12:49-50). The members of the new community, the *ekklēsia,* constitute a new family that does the will of the Father, i.e., that lives righteously. This family has an enabling role; its members provide a significant resource for the achievement of righteousness. An example of this can be seen in the discourse of chapter 18. Here, among other things, we find warnings concerning the gravity of causing "one of these little ones [= disciples]" to stumble (18:6-7). But the helping role of the community of brothers and sisters is most strikingly apparent in the example of dealing with one member of the community who sins against another (18:15-17). Here it is the larger church that finally holds the individual accountable. Matthew only begins to speak of the potentiality of the community for the life of the disciple. It is left more to Paul and others to draw out more of the rich resources of the church, now described as "the body of Christ," for discipleship.

(4) It is the Holy Spirit who applies the reality of the present kingdom to the Christian in everyday life. Anything that anyone ever experiences of the reality of God is due to the agency of the Holy Spirit. The outpouring of the Spirit at Pentecost not only constitutes the formal birthday of the church; it also provides the church with the supernatural power to live out its identity. What does Matthew have to say about the Holy Spirit?

With the other evangelists, Matthew sees the exceptional activity of the Spirit in the story of Jesus as a mark of its eschatological character. Jesus is conceived by the Holy Spirit (1:18, 20), and anointed by the Holy Spirit at his bap-

26. B. Gerhardsson, *The Ethos of the Bible,* trans. Stephen Westerholm (Philadelphia: Fortress, 1981), p. 62.

27. See David deSilva, *Honor, Patronage, Kinship, and Purity: Unlocking New Testament Culture* (Downers Grove, Ill.: InterVarsity, 2000), pp. 157-239.

tism (3:16; cf. 12:18). More important for our purposes, however, is the promise that Jesus would baptize others with the Holy Spirit (3:11). It is also important to note that when the disciples make disciples of others, they are to baptize them "in the name of the Father and of the Son and of the Holy Spirit" (28:19). The Holy Spirit is self-evidently important to discipleship. Matthew knows that disciples will be empowered with the Spirit. The Spirit will have an important role to play in very practical matters. Speaking of the time in the future when persecution comes upon the disciples, Jesus exhorts them not to be anxious, because what they are to say "will be given in that hour; for it is not you who speak, but the Spirit of your Father speaking through you" (10:19-20). Although Matthew does not talk about the Holy Spirit specifically in connection with righteousness, it seems a safe inference to conclude that the Spirit, as the identifying mark of the reality of present eschatology, is at the same time a central factor in the disciple's pursuit of living in accord with the will of the Father.

Righteousness for Today?

Several questions remain about the contemporary relevance of the teaching in Matthew concerning discipleship. Is that material applicable today? To all Christians? Is it practicable?

To begin with, there has been considerable debate about whether Matthew's description of the disciples is to be regarded as "historicizing" or as involving "transparency."[28] The issue is whether the disciples are thought of as strictly historical, in an unrepeatable past, and therefore that what is said of the disciples refers only to them ("historicizing"), or whether what is said of them applies equally to disciples in the church of Matthew's time and later ("transparency"). Are the commands of Jesus valid only for the twelve, or do they apply to later Christians equally?

It is clear that there is a sense in which the original circle of twelve disciples was and remains unique. There are, furthermore, points in the narrative where we have the unrepeatable. A case in point would be the sending out of the twelve and the accompanying discourse (10:1-15). Some of this material is necessarily limited to the time of the historical twelve — the only time, for example, when the restriction of the gospel of the kingdom to "the lost sheep of the house of Israel" (10:5-6) would have been permissible. Already in Matthew's day the gospel was proclaimed to the Gentiles (24:14; 28:19). The same thing is

---

28. See U. Luz, "The Disciples in the Gospel according to Matthew," in *The Interpretation of Matthew*, ed. Graham Stanton (Philadelphia/London: Fortress/SPCK, 1983), pp. 98-128.

true, for example, concerning portions of the discourse on the Mount of Olives (chapters 24–25), e.g., 24:15-28, where the exhortation to those in Judea to "flee to the mountains" (24:16) is necessarily limited to the original situation of the first century. Thus we sometimes encounter material of a mixed nature, some applying to the historical twelve exclusively, some to the disciples of later times.

Luz concludes that there is not "a thorough-going historicizing in the understanding of the disciples in Matthew's Gospel. At only one point is Matthew consistent: discipleship is always related to the teaching of the historical Jesus. . . . It is as pupils of the historical Jesus that the disciples become transparent and are models of what it means to be a Christian."[29] Matthew's church and the church throughout history has always rightly understood itself as addressed by the call to discipleship in this Gospel. Much or most of what Jesus spoke to the disciples is applied more broadly than to the twelve.

If we assume the extensive transparency of the disciples, we are still left with further complicating questions of applicability. Besides the kind of historical limitedness we have noted in connection with the twelve, it is clear that not all instructions about discipleship apply to all Christians. Thus, for example, not all are called to celibacy (19:10-12) or to sell all that they have as a part of their discipleship (19:21). Practical instructions provided in the missionary discourse (e.g., 10:8-14) would perhaps be generally applicable, but even then only to those who are called to leave secular professions for full-time evangelism. Thus some of Matthew's instructions concerning discipleship may need to be taken to apply only to a special group within the church, the so-to-speak religious professionals, rather than also to its "ordinary" members. At the same time, however, the ethical stipulations of the Sermon apply across the board to all believers. Every Christian without exception is called to exhibit the higher righteousness of the kingdom.

Even commandments that are pertinent to all in the church can raise the question of whether they are to be applied to the personal or societal level. To cite a famous example, are we to turn our other cheek to one who strikes us only in personal relationships, or can the commandment be taken as a justification for pacifism? What about forgiveness, not resisting evil, and so forth? This is a well known problem in the ethical appropriation of the Sermon on the Mount. Although this is not the place to go into the problem fully, I may simply indicate that my impression is that the primary level of application is to the individual, but that there are also often implications for the societal level that should be heard.[30]

29. Luz, "The Disciples in the Gospel," p. 105.
30. See my "Ethics in the Sermon on the Mount," *Studia Theologica* 51 (1997): 44-59.

The final problem to be dealt with here is the absolute nature of this call to righteousness and the issue of practicality. What are we to say concerning the idealism of the discipleship that Matthew puts before us? Discipleship calls for total commitment (13:44-46). It calls for death to the self, the losing of one's own life for the sake of Christ (16:24-26). In terms of holiness or righteousness, it calls us to perfection. "You, therefore, must be perfect, as your heavenly Father is perfect" (5:48). The Sermon on the Mount is precisely a call to perfection because it is meant to reflect the present reality of the kingdom. The idea that *teleios* here refers to "maturity" rather than perfection is, in my opinion, not correct. "Perfection" here points to a quality of life marked by the kind of righteousness described in the antitheses — behavior that manifests an inner orientation dominated by the priority of the kingdom (cf. 6:33). The challenge here is indeed startling. It is analogous to the call in 1 Peter to be *holy,* as the Lord is holy (1 Pet 1:15-16, quoting Lev 11:44-5). What is within our reach at present, however, is a pattern of life (not to be undervalued) rather than any absolute achievement of righteousness. This is evident from the fact that the Sermon implicitly acknowledges that perfection understood as sinlessness is an impossibility under present circumstances, i.e., in the present age. Thus in the middle of the Sermon, the disciples are taught to pray "forgive us our debts [*opheilēmata*]," i.e., "shortcomings" (6:12; cf. the Lukan parallel, 11:4, "sins"). The fact that we are to pray regularly for such forgiveness indicates that, at least for the present, sin unfortunately will remain a reality in the life of the disciples.[31] A similar concessive note is sounded in 26:41, "Watch and pray that you may not enter into temptation; the spirit indeed is willing, but the flesh is weak." We encounter here an instance of the familiar tension between realized and future eschatology: we are called to a perfection already in the present, which will be fully ours only in the future.

The idealism of the discipleship to which Matthew calls us is therefore a perpetual reminder of the necessity of grace. To strive after a high goal beyond our reach should make us humble, but it should not defeat us. With the resources available to us, we can do more and better than we have. For what we do, we are fully dependent upon God's enabling; for what we cannot do we are dependent upon God's forgiveness.

---

31. "The fuller righteousness which Jesus asks of the disciple is not his as a possession permanently at his disposal, as a something which he can *have;* it is his only as God's perpetually renewed gift." Martin H. Franzmann, *Follow Me: Discipleship According to Saint Matthew* (St. Louis: Concordia, 1961), p. 55.

Matthew's Challenge to the Contemporary Church

The Gospel of Matthew calls disciples of Jesus — disciples of the present — to be "the salt of the earth" and "the light of the world" (5:13-16). The more one contemplates Matthew's call to righteousness, the more one realizes the impact that the church could make upon the world if it were to make a more significant attempt to exhibit that righteousness. It is for this reason that Jesus exhorts his followers with these words: "Let your light so shine before others, that they may see your good works and give glory to your Father who is in heaven" (5:16).

The radical pattern of righteousness that emerges in Matthew is striking, as we have seen. It repeatedly does nothing less than turn the standards and values of the world on their head. To pick just one stunning example, the world thinks that greatness consists in being served, whereas Jesus teaches the opposite: "It shall not be so among you; but whoever would be great among you must be your servant, and whoever would be first among you must be your slave; even as the Son of man came not to be served but to serve, and to give his life as a ransom for many" (20:26-28). Not pride, but humility is to be the way of the disciple who would follow Jesus (18:3-4).

Matthew's pattern of righteousness may be called "prophetic" in the classical sense: as going directly against the prevailing conduct of the secular world. Jesus calls his disciples to a discipleship that counts, that makes a difference. This is to be a discipleship of more than words — a serious discipleship of action and deeds. "Not everyone who says to me 'Lord, Lord,' shall enter the kingdom of heaven, but the one who does the will of my Father who is in heaven" (7:21). The potential impact of this kind of discipleship is incalculable.

But this challenge — to realize this kind of discipleship, to live out the righteousness of the Sermon on the Mount — seems hopelessly impossible, does it not? If we look at this challenge solely in terms of human potentiality, the answer must be that no one is adequate. Here, however, the words of Jesus concerning the difficulty of a rich man being saved may be relevant: "With human beings this is impossible, but with God all things are possible" (19:26). It remains for the church to act in faith and for the disciples of Jesus to press on toward the goal.

The Holy One and His Disciples:
Holiness and Ecclesiology in Mark

KENT E. BROWER

Does Mark have anything to say about holiness or ecclesiology? The answer to that question depends upon whether one restricts the discussion to the term "holiness" or "church." Such a restricted study would be a travesty. Issues of purity and community are prominent in Mark. Purity is only one aspect of the larger question of the definition of the people of God in late second temple Judaism and emergent Christianity. Mark has plenty to say about this. In simplest terms, Mark paints a picture of the restoration and re-creation of the holy people of God centred on Jesus. He makes this case through the narrative re-application of key biblical themes leading to a renewed understanding of holiness.

The Holy One of God

In a recent discussion, Edwin K. Broadhead writes, "The Holy One of God presents a singular description of Jesus that acquires some degree of significance through the structures and strategies of the Gospel of Mark." But, he continues, "Ultimately this image is significant for what is *not* done with it: the title is not omitted, but it is also not developed. Consequently, the Holy One of God remains an isolated and largely inconsequential description."[1]

1. Edwin K. Broadhead, *Naming Jesus: Titular Christology in the Gospel of Mark,* JSNTSup 175 (Sheffield: Sheffield Academic Press, 1999), p. 100.

Thanks to colleagues in the Ehrhardt Seminar and the NTC Postgraduate Seminar who offered helpful comments after an oral presentation of this essay. This essay depends upon and develops some themes in the earlier discussion in Kent Brower, *Holiness in the Gospels* (Kansas City: Beacon Hill Press of Kansas City, 2005), chap. 4, particularly in the first section. I am delighted to offer this essay as a tribute to my friend and fellow Manchester graduate, Alex Deasley, a model of careful scholarship and robust churchmanship.

On the basis of sheer lack of references or explicit exploitation, Broadhead's point could hardly be contested. This phrase, ὁ ἅγιος τοῦ θεοῦ, occurs only on the lips of an unclean spirit who is commanded to be silent (1:24-25).[2] Despite this infrequent usage, however, the phrase may have greater significance than Broadhead supposes. Although it is not Mark's single most important description of Jesus nor even the central one, when considered in its narrative context and juxtaposed to other images in Mark, it is an important ingredient in Mark's motif of the renewed holy people of God centred on Jesus and his disciples.

Several literary observations signal its importance. First, the fact that the phrase is placed on the lips of an unclean spirit points to its accuracy. Mark takes for granted that the unclean spirits have knowledge that remains hidden from the mundane world. The unclean spirit, thus, gives an identity to Jesus of which those around are unaware, an impression confirmed by Jesus' command to be silent (1:25). According to a general comment in 3:11, Mark notes that "whenever the unclean spirits saw him, they fell down before him and shouted, 'You are the Son of God!'" The phrase the "Holy One of God" is a subset of "Son of God." Mark considers this to be routine identity: unclean spirits "recognize Jesus' transcendent status."[3]

A different nuance occurs in the exorcism story in chapter 5. A range of interesting issues is raised by this story[4] but the context of impurity suggests that the exorcisms in general signify "the perfection of Israel restored."[5] For our purposes, however, Legion's question is the point: "What have you to do with us?" (᾽Ιησοῦ υἱὲ τοῦ θεοῦ τοῦ ὑψίστου;) (5:7). Here the emphasis is again upon Jesus' identity. Although the "Holy One of God" and the "Son of the Most High God" are not identical, Mark sees them as complementary and accurate descriptors. Taken together, these exorcisms "vividly demonstrate the binding of 'the strong man,' Satan, and the 'plundering' of his 'household' (3:23-27). Consequently Jesus warns those who dismiss his miracles as sorcery that they are in danger of blasphemy against the Holy Spirit, the divine power at work in him (3:28-30)."[6]

---

2. The only other gospel usage is John 6:68-69. Explicit OT usage is also rare. The phrase is used of Aaron in Ps 106:16 (MT: לְאַהֲרֹן קְדוֹשׁ וְהוָה = LXX: 105:16 τὸν ἅγιον κυρίου). Isaiah 40:25 uses ὁ ἅγιος for God (MT: קָדוֹשׁ); see also Isa 57:15a (NRSV: "For thus says the high and lofty one who inhabits eternity, whose name is Holy"; MT: אָמַר רָם וְנִשָּׂא שֹׁכֵן עַד וְקָדוֹשׁ). Except where they are my own, all translations are taken from the NRSV.

3. L. W. Hurtado, *Lord Jesus Christ: Devotion to Jesus in Earliest Christianity* (Grand Rapids/Cambridge: Eerdmans, 2003), p. 287.

4. See Stephen Barton, "Dislocating and Relocating Holiness: A New Testament Study," in *Holiness Past and Present*, ed. Stephen C. Barton (London: T&T Clark, 2003), p. 200.

5. Ben F. Meyer, *The Aims of Jesus* (London: SCM, 1979), p. 157.

6. Hurtado, *Lord Jesus Christ*, p. 287.

Two other "Son of God" ascriptions occur in Mark. At the trial scene in 14:61 the high priest asks "Are you the messiah, the Son of the Blessed One?" At one level, this two-fold identification stays within conventional second temple images for messiah and Son of the Blessed One. But the response of the Markan Jesus moves beyond both descriptions through the evocative phrase ἐγώ εἰμι ("I am") as well as the suffering Son of Man figure already established in Mark 8:27-32.

The second linked identity occurs at the crucifixion. In 15:39, the centurion at the cross says, "Truly this man was υἱὸς θεοῦ." "Debates about whether the phrase should be translated as 'a son of god' or 'the Son of God' are interesting but ultimately fruitless. The very ambiguity of the Greek sentence tells against any view that the centurion had much more in mind than the experience of watching 'a good death.' But for Mark the term connotes far more than could be gleaned from an analysis of its background in the second temple period."[7]

These identifications all come from reluctant witnesses. The high priest, the representative of the gathered religious establishment (see 14:53-55), and the centurion, the representative of Roman power, both oppose Jesus and therefore the purposes of God. So do the unclean spirits. They know Jesus and therefore fear him. Their opposition to Jesus is the reminder that, in Mark's view, human opposition is but the mundane manifestation of cosmic opposition to the purposes of God (see 8:33).

No such reluctance attaches to the final two cognate identifications in Mark. According to Mark 1:10-11, Jesus sees "the heavens torn apart (σχιζομένους τοὺς οὐρανοὺς) and the Spirit descending like a dove on him. And a voice came from heaven, 'You are my Son, the Beloved.'" This identification is for Jesus himself. According to Mark, Jesus alone sees the rending of the heavens and hears the voice identifying and affirming his mission. An identical ascription occurs in Mark 9:7 (cf. 12:6) but in the transfiguration story, the voice is for the three disciples — and because of his identity, they are to listen to him.[8]

Son of God is thus a key term right from the opening lines of the Gospel.

---

7. Brower, *Holiness in the Gospels*, p. 145, note 221. See also R. T. France, *The Gospel of Mark*, NIGTC (Grand Rapids/Carlisle: Eerdmans/Paternoster, 2002), pp. 659-60.

8. This placement of the story is hardly accidental. Jesus has just been identified as "Messiah" by Peter in 8:27-30 and has immediately reinterpreted that confession in terms of a suffering Son of Man (8:31). Peter finds this objectionable leading, in turn, to a rebuke from Jesus. Jesus then calls the crowd along with the disciples to follow him in cross-bearing. The voice from the cloud is a pointed reminder to the three that Jesus' message is God's message. If they wish to set their minds on divine rather than human things, they will need to listen to Jesus, the Son of Man.

Mark begins by telling his readers that the whole narrative is about Jesus Christ, the Son of God.[9] The phrase forms an inclusio with the words of the centurion in 15:39 which serve as literary markers enclosing the bulk of Mark's narrative, indicating that Mark intends to develop through the story precisely what he means by "Son of God." If this is so, then the Holy One of God as a specific subset of Son of God is far from isolated.

The Herald of the Holy One of God

Immediately following the identity of Jesus in 1:1, Mark introduces the Baptist. According to 1:4 he is *the voice in the wilderness.* Both aspects of that identity are important. On the one hand, he is in the *wilderness.* Although the wilderness is almost certainly a geographical location, it has significance beyond that. Ulrich Mauser argues that the reference to the wilderness in Mark 1:3 "carries with it the full weight of a great religious tradition embracing high hopes and promises as well as the deep shadows of judgement and despair. . . ."[10] The theme itself runs throughout Isaiah. Most scholars draw attention to its presence in Deutero-Isaiah,[11] but it is also present in Isaiah 11, tied to the notion of the returning remnant (see 11:11), itself "a powerful symbol of restoration."[12] Isaiah 35 is especially interesting. The entire chapter is devoted to the return from exile of the redeemed people of God through the wilderness on the way of the Lord.[13] In that wilderness, a dangerous and dry place, the Lord makes a way of holiness on which the unclean cannot travel nor wild beasts cause harm (35:8). Instead, the redeemed shall walk there and the ransomed of the Lord will return to Zion with rejoicing.

Mark's citation of this text and John's wilderness location evokes the entire holy remnant notion, immediately creating a context of heightened expectation. The wilderness is the place of testing in which only the faithful survive.

---

9. Ἀρχὴ τοῦ εὐαγγελίου Ἰησοῦ Χριστοῦ (υἱοῦ θεοῦ). Although υἱοῦ θεοῦ may be disputed on textual grounds alone, on literary grounds it should be read.

10. Ulrich Mauser, *Christ in the Wilderness: The Wilderness Theme in the Second Gospel and its Basis in the Biblical Tradition,* SBT 39 (London: SCM, 1963), p. 82. See now Joel Marcus, *The Way of the Lord: Christological Exegesis of the Old Testament in the Gospel of Mark* (Edinburgh: T&T Clark, 1993), pp. 23-26 who, however, thinks the prophetic context is primary.

11. See especially Rikki E. Watts, *Isaiah's New Exodus and Mark* (Tübingen: J. C. B. Mohr [Paul Siebeck], 1997). See also Thomas R. Hatina, *In Search of a Context: The Function of Scripture in Mark's Narrative,* JSNTSup 232/SSEJC 8 (Sheffield: Sheffield Academic Press, 2002).

12. Meyer, *Aims of Jesus,* p. 118.

13. See Marcus, *Way of the Lord,* p. 37.

Thus, the call by John in the wilderness recalls the narrowing process that always attends the wilderness — the remnant survives in the wilderness.[14] John's call, then, is a new beginning for the people of God. The wilderness tradition signals that the good news announced by the Baptist centres on God's renewal of his people.[15] John is in the wilderness because that is where he must be if he is to play his role in the unfolding drama.

On the other hand, John is the *voice* in the wilderness. He is the prophet expected by Isaiah to announce the good news of God's action. Hence, the conflated OT citations (1:2-3)[16] serve as the framework within which John's work is to be considered. Surprisingly, Mark tells us this citation is from Isaiah[17] even though the first words echo Exod 23:20 and Mal 3:1; Isa 40:3 follows. John appears as the voice in the wilderness announcing the good news. And the good news is that the time of the eschatological restoration of the people of God has arrived.

The interweaving of Mal 3:1 strengthens this view.[18] This allows Malachi to be read within the Isaianic new exodus/return from exile framework.[19] John's goal is "to gather together the remnant of Israel destined for salvation."[20] This is the beginning of the re-creation of the people of God. The arrival of the kingdom of God is NOW and John's work is the opening scene (see 1:1).[21] In short, the kingdom of God has arrived in the coming of Jesus (see 1:14).

John's second role is that of *Elijah*.[22] But why is this important? Perhaps Malachi 3 and 4 offer a clue. Immediately following the phrase cited in Mark 1:2, Malachi continues, "the Lord whom you seek will suddenly come to his temple." The notions of purification and judgement continue. According to 3:3, the Lord "will purify the descendants of Levi until they present offerings to the LORD in righteousness."[23] Impurity is then condemned: judgement will be meted out against "the sorcerers, against the adulterers, against those who swear falsely, against those who oppress the hired workers in their wages, the

14. Thanks to Professor Bernard Jackson for some of the ideas in this section.

15. The Qumran community cites this text as its motivation for establishing a community in the wilderness. See 1QS 8:13-14.

16. Most scholars identify Mal 3:1, Exod 23:20, and Isa 40:3 as the OT texts conflated here.

17. See France, *Gospel of Mark*, p. 60, for a summary of MSS variations.

18. Malachi itself seems to develop ideas from Deutero-Isaiah. See Meyer, *Aims of Jesus*, p. 126.

19. See Watts, *Isaiah's New Exodus*, p. 89.

20. Meyer, *Aims of Jesus*, p. 119.

21. M. D. Hooker, *St Mark*, BNTC (London: A. & C. Black, 1991), p. 37.

22. See K. E. Brower, "Elijah in the Markan Passion Narrative," *Journal for the Study of the New Testament* 18 (1983): 85-101. Mark makes this connection in a variety of indirect ways.

23. The "Lord" in 3:1 (MT) is not Yahweh as in 3:3, 4 (MT).

widow and the orphan, against those who thrust aside the alien, and do not fear me, says the LORD of hosts" (3:5). The surest sign of the people's distance from God, according to Mal 3:8-9, is the failure to pay the required tithe. Judgement and destruction are all that is left (3:8, 10). But God, true to his character (3:6), delays his judgement by promising to send "the prophet Elijah before the great and terrible day of the LORD comes. He will turn the hearts of parents to their children and the hearts of children to their parents, so that I will not come and strike the land with a curse" (Mal 4:5-6).

Mark does not cite Mal 4:6 or any other additional text from Malachi. Nevertheless, might these chapters of Malachi offer overtones that echo in Mark? Jerusalem and the Temple are important in Malachi and Mark.[24] In Mark, the Temple is both the symbolic centre of opposition to Jesus and, from chapter 11, the locale of the action. Jesus' parabolic action and prophetic word in the Temple (11:15-18) foreshadows judgement; his teaching in the Temple from 11:23–12:44 involves a series of confrontations, predominately focused on his identity and authority. Jesus concludes his teaching by noting the greed of the scribes; he then stands in the Temple treasury noting the generosity of the poor when compared to the rich.

Despite some common themes, these are at best distant echoes of Malachi. At first, the Temple episode might seem to be broadly akin to the purification of the Sons of Levi, but that is not Mark's primary concern.[25] The superficial connection of faulty tithing practice and the mistreatment of widows in Malachi with Mark's stern critique of the scribes should not be pressed (12:38-44). According to Mark 13 Temple reform is doomed to fail and the fate of the Temple has already been sealed because of the [anticipated] rejection and crucifixion of Jesus by the spiritual leaders in collusion with the occupation powers.

A better connection might be made to the Baptist's proclamation. Malachi calls the people to turn from their covenant unfaithfulness. John calls the people to repent and be baptised, thus creating a holy people fit for a holy God. Repentance presupposes avoiding the kind of judgement expected in Malachi. John's call to repentance is akin to the plea of the Lord of hosts in Mal 3:7: "Return to me, and I will return to you." But these echoes of Malachi may provide little more than intertextual colour.

24. See K. E. Brower, " 'Let the reader understand': Temple and Eschatology in Mark," in *'The Reader Must Understand': Eschatology in Bible and Theology,* ed. K. E. Brower and M. W. Elliott (Leicester: Apollos, 1997).

25. This episode cannot be reduced to "the Cleansing of the Temple" even in a symbolic way. Mark pictures this as a prophetic representative action symbolising the ultimate end of the whole Temple system, and those around him know it (see 11:18-19).

More promising is a developing Elijah tradition based on the scriptures, not least Malachi. If such a tradition exists,[26] then the citation of Mal 3:1 has heightened importance in Mark 1:2-3. John, who is fulfilling the role of Elijah, appears in the wilderness, proclaims a baptism of repentance for the forgiveness of sins, and announces the coming of the mightier one who will baptise with Holy Spirit. The response to John's preaching is set out in historically exaggerated terms, no doubt — πᾶσα ἡ Ἰουδαία χώρα καὶ οἱ Ἱεροσολυμῖται πάντες — but this misses Mark's point. For him this is a renewal of the people of God who are coming *from Jerusalem and Judaea* and are coming *into the wilderness* to be baptised by John. This may indeed be a symbolic new exile before a new return.[27] In Mark's view God is doing a new thing (see Isa 43:3, 19): "in and through the remnant of Israel God reconstitute[s] his holy people."[28] They are the new purified people of God, a kingdom of priests and a holy nation, whose sins are forgiven (see Mic. 7:18) — the renewal movement is underway. After he baptises Jesus, John's function in Mark is almost finished.

Mark gives an important clue to how this whole John-Elijah relationship is to be understood. In chapter 6, John's death is narrated in great detail — it is the death of a righteous and holy person (6:20).[29] Shortly after, Elijah appears with Moses on the Mount of Transfiguration (9:4). While descending from the mountain, Jesus discusses with Peter, James, and John the meaning of resurrection, then says cryptically, "Elijah is indeed coming first to restore all things. . . . But I tell you that Elijah has come, and they did to him whatever they pleased, as it is written about him."

The significance of this passage has long been recognised, even if its interpretation has been in dispute. Steven Bryan argues that "through John the 'restoration of all things' was both complete and successful."[30] This, of course, begs the question about the kind of success John has.[31] The answer depends on who John is. Many scholars focus upon his mission as forerunner to the Messiah. But is that how Mark sees him? Probably not. As France notes, "neither the OT passages produced in vv. 2-3 as models for John's role as forerunner nor the spe-

---

26. See Steven M. Bryan, *Jesus and Israel's Traditions of Judgement and Restoration*, SNTSMS 117 (Cambridge: Cambridge University Press, 2002). See especially Markus Öhler, *Elia im Neuen Testament: Untersuchungen für Bedeutung des alttestamentlichen Propheten im frühen Christentum*, BZNW (Berlin: Walter de Gruyter, 1997).

27. I owe this idea to my late colleague, Gordon Thomas.

28. Meyer, *Aims of Jesus*, p. 118. An interesting intertextual possibility may be suggested between Isa 43:19-20 and Mark 1:13.

29. For a full discussion, see Brower, "Elijah."

30. Bryan, *Jesus and Israel's Traditions*, p. 90. See also Hooker, *Mark*, p. 220.

31. See Hooker, *Mark*, p. 37.

cific role which he assigns to the ἰσχυρότερος in v. 8 could be expected in themselves to suggest a *human* figure. It is Yahweh who will follow the forerunner in both Mal 3:1 and Isa 40:3, and in OT thought it is Yahweh himself who will pour out his Spirit in the last days."[32]

The theocentric character of this section supports this view. According to Joel Marcus, Yahweh is the warrior who leads his people in a new exodus, redeeming his people. This is predicated of Jesus, a point made explicit throughout by the subtle modifications Mark makes to the cited texts.[33] Mark's use of this motif has Christological implications foreshadowing what the rest of the Gospel shows: "Where Jesus acts, there God is acting."[34] In short, John is the forerunner of Jesus who, in turn, is acting as God acts, rather than the forerunner of God's messianic agent who awaits the arrival of God. John is already restoring the people of God in preparation for God's returning to his people. John's baptism "came from heaven" (11:30).

Elijah's role as the restorer of the people to covenant faithfulness has been accomplished. But this is still a preparatory role. John has completed his task of setting the stage for the coming one, Jesus Messiah, Son of God, the Holy One of God. The restored holy people of God are ready for the mightier one to baptise them with Holy Spirit and lead them on his mission. That, Mark tells us, is inaugurated when Jesus arrives in Galilee after John is arrested (1:14).

The Followers of the Holy One of God

Like so much else in the first chapter of Mark, the announcement by Jesus of "God's good news"[35] is programmatic for the rest of the story. Mark gives a summary: "The time is fulfilled, and the kingdom of God has come near; repent, and believe in the good news" (1:15).[36] That which the Baptist has announced has come and the decisive time has arrived. ". . . a new era of fulfillment has begun, and it calls for a response from God's people."[37]

The response is immediate: Jesus calls four fishermen and they follow. The sequence itself confirms the significance of "the Holy One of God" for Mark. Al-

32. France, *Gospel of Mark*, p. 70.

33. The text of Isa 40:3 is modified by changing τοῦ θεοῦ ἡμῶν to αὐτοῦ. Mal 3:1 is changed in a variety of ways under the influence of Exod 23:20. See France, *Gospel of Mark*, p. 64, for a plausible explanation.

34. Marcus, *Way of the Lord*, pp. 26-40. The citation is from p. 40.

35. See France, *Gospel of Mark*, p. 91.

36. The message is the same as the Baptist's. See Meyer, *Aims of Jesus*, p. 128.

37. France, *Gospel of Mark*, p. 93.

though readers already know that the whole narrative is about Jesus, Son of God (1:1), and that he is ὁ υἱός μου ὁ ἀγαπητός (1:11), the disciples do not. "The first disciples respond only to Jesus' personal authority without knowing his identity or his important role in the divine drama of the end of the age."[38] Jesus' explanation is minimal — if they follow him, they will become fishers of people.[39]

Taken in isolation and in historical terms, the story strains credulity. But seen in the narrative flow, a variety of ideas emerge. The call is a continuation and extension of the ministry of John. But while those who respond to John's message come from all Judaea and Jerusalem, Jesus' first disciples are "socially insignificant people from an insignificant corner of provincial Galilee."[40] Historically, Galilee is Jesus' home territory but its character is different from Judaea. Hooker calls it "semi-pagan."[41] Jesus' call, then, is to those outside the inner core of ethnic Israel represented by Judaea and Jerusalem. Set in the context of the eschatological restoration of the people of God, Jesus' call of specific individuals to join him is part of that bigger picture. John's task is complete but the good news is only beginning. John calls out a remnant but it is an "open remnant."[42]

The most significant point, however, is that these disciples are now "with Jesus."[43] In the next episode, they are astonished at his teaching because he teaches with ἐξουσία (1:22). That is followed immediately by the first exorcism (1:26), a clear sign of the arrival of the kingdom in strength.[44] This demonstration of Jesus' authority in word and deed is important in itself but the key point for the disciples is that Jesus is identified by the unclean spirit as the Holy One of God. John has already announced that Jesus would baptise them with the Holy Spirit. That baptism does not occur directly in Mark's narrative.[45] What

38. Whitney T. Shiner, *Follow me!: Disciples in Markan Rhetoric,* SBLDS 145 (Atlanta: Scholars, 1995), p. 193.

39. This is an apt metaphor given the occupation of the four. But in light of the whole restoration motif, one should not dismiss out of hand a possible echo of Jer 16:16 where fishers are given the task of gathering Israel from afar. See Meyer, *Aims of Jesus,* p. 118. *Contra* France, *Gospel of Mark,* pp. 96-97.

40. France, *Gospel of Mark,* p. 94. See the disparaging remark in Mark 14:70.

41. Hooker, *Mark,* p. 54.

42. See Bryan, *Jesus and Israel's Traditions,* p. 121, n. 97, commenting on Meyer.

43. Shiner, *Follow me,* p. 191, observes, "It is striking that the creation of community has primacy over both teaching and christological confession in the Gospel of Mark."

44. See Bruce D. Chilton, *God in Strength: Jesus' Announcement of the Kingdom* (Sheffield: JSOT, 1987). Meyer, *Aims of Jesus,* p. 156, writes, "The combat evoked is not the endless seesaw of history's long haul but the apocalyptic turning-point."

45. See R. A. Guelich, *Mark 1:1–8:26,* WBC 34A (Waco: Word, 1989), p. 25, "Through Jesus' life (ministry) and death, one receives the 'baptism with the Holy Spirit,' i.e., the salvation promised for the new age (1:14-15; 1:16-18)." See also France, *Gospel of Mark,* pp. 72-73.

does occur is that the disciples are in the company of Jesus, the one with ἐξουσία who is the Holy One of God. They are part of God's holy people because they are with the Holy One.

Next Jesus calls Levi (2:14). He, too, follows without explanation. The narrative sequence is interesting. Just before the call of Levi, in the story of the paralytic, opposition begins (2:1-12). At that point in the story some of the scribes are sitting around Jesus — a symbol of their closeness to him (cf. 3:34). But they are scandalised by Jesus' presumption in declaring the paralytic's sins to be forgiven because that is God's prerogative. Now in this episode, controversy escalates. Levi is a tax collector. Not only does Jesus call him to follow, he goes to dinner at Levi's house and is joined by "many tax collectors and sinners" (2:15). These are now the ones sitting with Jesus and his disciples.[46] The scribes of the Pharisees, who enter the story here for the first time, are pointedly *not* eating with Jesus and his disciples. But they note Jesus' dinner companions and question his actions: "Why does he eat with tax collectors and sinners?" (2:15-16). Jesus' response is that he is calling sinners, not the righteous (2:17).

Only two points can be noted from this episode. First, behind this concern for table fellowship lies the issue of purity and holiness.[47] Sitting at table is an expression of intimacy and fellowship. By eating with tax collectors and sinners, Jesus is thought to endanger his character as a holy person through contact with the contagion of sin. Not only are his dinner companions by definition impure but the Pharisaic food rules are probably also ignored. Second, "for the Pharisees the meal had become a microcosm of Israel's intended historic structure as well as a model of Israel's destiny."[48] According to Borg, "Jesus' association with sinners and tax collectors appeared to threaten both the internal reform of Judaism and its solidarity over against the Gentiles. Moreover his table fellowship with outcasts challenged the understanding of God upon which the reform and solidarity were based."[49]

The message of Jesus is to those who are excluded from the holy people of God. His message is good news because God is re-creating an inclusive new people. Jesus offers forgiveness by calling the sinners and in doing so reshapes the holy people of God as those who are intimately bound to himself. The ob-

---

46. Mark has already hinted that the number of followers Jesus has is far greater than the four already called (cf. 1:28, 33, 37, 45). Now he notes "for there were many who followed him" (2:15).

47. See Marcus J. Borg, *Conflict, Holiness and Politics in the Teachings of Jesus*, rev. ed. (Harrisburg: Trinity, 1998), pp. 74-77; pp. 94-96 for a summary of the issues.

48. Borg, *Conflict*, p. 95.

49. Borg, *Conflict*, p. 100.

jections are centred on what Wright calls "the scandalous implied re-definition of the Kingdom itself."[50]

The third call story is arguably the most important. Mark has already told us about the expanding ministry of Jesus in Galilee but great numbers from Judaea, Jerusalem, Idumea, beyond the Jordan, and the region around Tyre and Sidon also come to him (3:7). Mark does not say so explicitly, but the implication is plain — people from Gentile territory are also amongst those healed. The ministry has become so intense that Jesus needs to escape.

This time Jesus goes to the mountain, calls those whom he wants, and they come to him. From these followers he creates (ἐποίησεν)[51] the Twelve whom he names. They are "to be with him, and be sent out to proclaim the good news and to have authority to exorcise demons." These twelve apostles, then, function as representatives of the entire people of God. The locale is deliberate[52] and the number 12 could hardly be mistaken for anything other than the re-creation of the old and full people of God made up of "radically disparate elements."[53]

Second, they are called to be with him. The disciples already know something of Jesus' identity although the implications have yet to dawn. But this is the Son of God, on God's mission and re-creating the people of God to fulfil God's mission. A community has always been essential for the mission of God to his created order. In Meyer's fascinating words, "Israel, in short, understood salvation in ecclesial terms."[54]

From this point on, then, Jesus has the renewed people of God gathered around him *en nuce*. They are with the Holy One of God, on his mission, with his message, and acting in his authority. But the path of discipleship is fraught with problems. The disciples have ample opportunity to understand who Jesus is and to grasp its significance. Finally, Mark brings the initial section to a close with an exasperated Jesus leaving the question, "do you still not understand" hanging in the air (8:21).

The whole central section, from 8:22 to 10:52, has Jesus and his disciples on a journey from Caesarea Philippi to Jericho during which Jesus teaches them about messiahship and discipleship. Initially, they come to the revelatory moment that Jesus is Messiah (8:27-31), but like the partially restored sight of the

---

50. N. T. Wright, *Jesus and the Victory of God* (London: SPCK, 1993), p. 274.

51. Guelich, *Mark*, p. 159, notes both "appoint" and "made" as translations but opts for the former.

52. So Hooker, *Mark*, p. 111, *contra* Guelich, *Mark*, p. 156.

53. Meyer, *Aims of Jesus*, p. 154. See also Bryan, *Jesus and Israel's Traditions*, p. 98, who draws attention to Sir 48:10.

54. Meyer, *Aims of Jesus*, p. 134.

blind man in the immediately preceding story, the insight is genuine but distorted. They now know who Jesus is but only gradually discover what this means for Jesus and any would-be followers. Jesus forbids them to say anything about this to anyone. Instead, the teaching takes a new and rather sinister direction: the Son of Man must suffer. This is by no means an easy conclusion and Peter tries to dissuade Jesus (8:32).

Worse is yet to come. Not only must Jesus suffer — those who are his followers must as well. And this is not just for the Twelve or an inner circle. In Mark 8:34 Jesus calls the crowd with his disciples but warns anyone who would follow to be prepared to die for his sake and the good news (8:35) with vindication promised at the end to those who are faithful (8:38; cf. 10:28-31).

The contours of their journey are illuminating. They respond to Jesus' call, follow him without fully understanding where they are going and only perceiving dimly who it is that they are following. They listen to his teaching, occasionally understanding but frequently getting it wrong. The lessons they have to learn are significant, for Jesus has to help them understand the way the restored people of God will look and act. Although they are frequently befuddled, they do not oppose Jesus, and indeed, avow undying fealty — just before they all betray him (14:50). Jesus predicts this but promises to go before them to Galilee (14:27-28). After the empty tomb, the young man at the tomb commands the women, "But go, tell his disciples and Peter that he is going ahead of you to Galilee; there you will see him, just as he told you" (16:7). The new community will be reconstituted in Galilee *outside* Jerusalem and its soon to be destroyed Temple (13:2).

Re-Defining the People of God

The Twelve and those around Jesus are the renewed remnant of Israel, the re-defined people of God with the Holy One of God at the centre. Mark develops this theme in several ways. Three of them deserve mention.

First, membership is fluid and quite different from what might have been expected. All are welcome; clearly, not all respond (despite 1:5). The story line in chapters 2 and 3 is illuminating. Initially those sitting around Jesus include the scribes. By the next pericope the scribes of the Pharisees are near Jesus but not sitting with him and his disciples (2:15-17). Soon the Pharisees are offering their critique of his Sabbath observance, first in the grain fields (2:23-28), then in the synagogue (3:1-6). But this time they are watching him to catch him out; distance is implied. When he fails to meet their criteria for appropriate Sabbath observance, the Pharisees *go out* to conspire with the Herodians (3:6). Opposition grows. Meanwhile his family tries to restrain Jesus for his own good (3:19). Scribes from Jerusalem — the implication is that they are the "heavies" — come to level accusations. Jesus' response is very robust: by failing to recognise the source of his power they align themselves with the forces against God. Such opposition to God has no remedy (3:22-30). The sequence closes with the return of the family. In 3:31-35 Mark tells us that his mother and his brothers are *standing outside* asking for him while at the same time a crowd is *sitting around* him. Jesus asks a rhetorical question, "Who are my mother and my brothers?" The response is blunt: "And looking at those who sat around him, he said, 'Whoever does the will of God is my brother and sister and mother'" (3:35). The sequence starts with those expecting to be first in the kingdom of God sitting with Jesus and ends with them on the outside in opposition to him. Many who are first shall be last and the last first (10:31). The new people of God are those gathered around Jesus and who do the will of God.

Second, the last supper is the act of institution for this new covenant people. The context is Passover; the language is heavily laden with scriptural images (new exodus; new covenant; blood of the covenant; blood poured out for the many — see Exod 24:8; Jer 31:31-34; Zech 9:11; Isa 53:12). Jesus evokes these very images and establishes the new covenant community through his prophetic representative action with bread and wine. These disciples, already called out and participating in the new life of the kingdom of God centred on Jesus, are now constituted as the new covenant community. "Here is the basis of a thoroughgoing Christian ecclesiology in relation to the people of God in the OT."[55] In Mark this is finally accomplished through Jesus' death (see 10:45). "The final irony," according to Neyrey, "is that death, the ultimate pollution, serves as the very source of purity for Jesus' followers."[56]

Third, the locus of God's dwelling is now in the temple not made with hands.[57] This challenge goes to the heart of the whole Temple system. Although everything in Mark from 11:1 onwards is set in the context of this challenge, only one aspect can be drawn out here. In the death scene in the passion narrative, Mark's attention shifts from τὸ ἱερόν to the temple ναός, the Holy of Holies.[58]

---

55. France, *Gospel of Mark*, p. 570.

56. Jerome H. Neyrey, "The Idea of Purity in Mark's Gospel," in *Semeia* 35, ed. John H. Elliott (Decatur, Ga.: Scholars 1986), p. 115.

57. For a full development of this argument, see Brower, "Reader."

58. See G. I. Davies, "The Presence of God in the Second Temple and Rabbinic Doctrine," in *Templum Amicitiae: Essays on the Second Temple Presented to Ernst Bammel*, JSNTSup 48, ed. W. Horbury (Sheffield: JSOT, 1991), p. 33, who suggests that "belief in the divine presence in the Second Temple was much more widespread than is commonly allowed" including, crucially, Matt 23:21.

As Jesus dies, judgement is being exercised by God on the very heart of the Temple by opening the ναός.[59] For Mark, the Holy of Holies is no longer the locus of God's dwelling. A new ναὸς ἀχειροποίητος is emerging. It is the new covenant community (see 14:24), a new people of those who respond to Jesus' call. With judgement on the ναός, it could only be a matter of time before there would not be "one stone upon another" in τὸ ἱερόν.

Re-Defining Holiness

What happens to the *practice* of holiness itself? In the first edition of *Conflict, Holiness and Politics,* Marcus Borg writes, "A 'quest for holiness' or a 'quest for purity'[60] was the dominant cultural dynamic in the Jewish homeland in the first century. It created a social world order as a purity system, one with sharp social boundaries."[61] Although Borg now argues that holiness is primarily an elitist issue[62] rather than the concern of what Dunn calls "common Judaism,"[63] holiness remains a defining issue of identity for the people of God.

To a greater or lesser degree, all of Second Temple Judaism is concerned with purity. God is holy and therefore dangerous and only dwells safely with his people under conditions of holiness. The Gospels picture purity as a key issue of controversy between Jesus and the Pharisees. At its most basic, the debate is over whether holiness is dependent upon separation from impurity through boundary maintenance or whether the system itself has come to misconstrue God's demands for his people. In Borg's view, the conflict is about whether compassion or purity is central.[64]

The debate over the precise relationship between Jesus and the Second Temple purity system continues. But our question is slightly different: how does this play out in Mark? Jerome Neyrey argues that "Mark presents Jesus challenging the Jewish purity system . . . [and] reforming it in favor of other core

59. See Brower, "Elijah," *passim* and R. E. Brown, *The Death of the Messiah* (New York/London: Doubleday/Geoffrey Chapman, 1994), p. 1100. The same word, ἐσχίσθη, is used in 1:10 to describe the rending of the heavens at the spirit's descent on Jesus.

60. The terms "holiness" and "purity" are directly related even if distinctions can be drawn. See Richard Bauckham, "The Holiness of Jesus and his Disciples in the Gospel of John" in this volume who draws attention to the distinctions. For this essay, the pursuit of holiness and purity are treated as synonymous.

61. Borg, *Conflict*, p. 8.

62. See Borg, *Conflict*, p. 14.

63. See J. D. G. Dunn, "Jesus and Holiness: The Challenge of Purity," in Barton, *Holiness*, p. 173.

64. Borg, *Conflict*, p. 15.

values."[65] A brief summary of selected key points demonstrates the overall shape of Mark's re-definition.

First, the locale of holiness. Biblical holiness is always connected to God, whose character defines holiness. Therefore, the holiness of people, places, and things is always derived from God, the Holy One.[66] Because the Temple is God's dwelling place, "holiness is measured in terms of proximity to the Temple."[67] But this changes. As Barton puts it, "God is to be found somewhere new, though not in an unanticipated place. God is present in the person of the Son of God, himself the One in whom dwells the Holy Spirit of God. This claim represents a dislocation and relocation of holiness. It represents also an extension and intensification of holiness."[68] Jesus is the Holy One of God. The Holy Spirit is upon him and his actions are the work of the Spirit within him (3:29). The location of holiness is now in the new temple not made with hands, Jesus in the midst of the people of God. Those around Jesus are made holy by being made into the restored and renewed people of God. Holiness is determined by obedience and proximity to Jesus. Those near Jesus do the will of God (3:35).

But therein lies a problem. For Jesus' opponents, obedience to God's will in Torah is crucial and, as they see it, Jesus is actually quite disobedient at critical points — disregard for Sabbath observance and food rules are the most obvious violations. But Mark argues that obedience to Jesus, whose understanding of Torah penetrates to its very heart, is the determining factor in participation in the kingdom (10:19-22). Obedience is better than cultic purity (see 12:33-34): the "cultic community has to be also the moral community which celebrates God's holiness in lives devoted to doing God's holy will."[69]

Second, the boundaries of holiness. If purity can only be maintained through separation from impurity, then boundaries are important. But Jesus crosses boundaries. Examples abound. Jesus eats with sinners. They become insiders while the righteous, initially around Jesus, put themselves outside of the will of God. The Temple itself, which should have fulfilled the role of "house of prayer for all the nations" has become a prisoner of its own purity rules complete with political overtones. Factionalism on traditional purity grounds is out.[70]

---

65. Neyrey, "Idea of Purity," p. 91.

66. See Dunn, "Jesus and Holiness," p. 169.

67. Neyrey, "Idea of Purity," p. 95. See also Philip Jenson, *Graded Holiness: A Key to the Priestly Conception of the World*, JSOTSup 106 (Sheffield: JSOT, 1992), who gives a convincing demonstration of this point from the OT.

68. Barton, "Dislocating," p. 197.

69. Barton, "Dislocating," p. 196.

70. See Dunn, "Jesus and Holiness," p. 185. He writes, "Jesus protested against such boundary drawing within Judaism and in effect called for a reordering of priorities."

Third, the contagion of holiness. If boundary markers between insiders and outsiders have been moved, the very permeability of the boundary suggests that holiness does not need a defence from the contagion of evil. Instead holiness itself is contagious. Jesus does not acquire impurity. He touches the unclean; he deals with Gentiles; he shares meals with sinners. And by doing so, he imparts cleanness and wholeness.[71]

But the contagion of holiness is not passed to his disciples as if it were an independent possession. It is always derived from and always in relationship to the Holy One. An interesting example of this comes in two contrasting exorcism stories. According to 6:7, Jesus sends the Twelve out and gives them authority over the unclean spirits. They are successful on this mission, returning in 6:28 to tell Jesus all that they have taught and done. Contrast this with the story of the botched exorcism in 9:14-29. Jesus leaves his disciples while he goes up to a high mountain with the three in the inner group. Meanwhile, the remaining disciples undertake to exorcise an unclean spirit but fail. In fact, Jesus' cryptic explanation of their failure, "This kind can come out only through prayer" (9:29), is best seen as acknowledgement that exorcism is a derived authority, not one vested in the apostles as independently empowered exorcists. The point is confirmed by Mark just a few lines later. John tells Jesus that they saw an exorcist casting out demons in Jesus' name, but they forbade him "because he was not following us." Jesus' response to the disciples is a sharp reminder that he is the source of power (9:38-39).

Fourth, the inwardness of holiness. The clearest evidence for this occurs in Mark 7. Food rules are no longer relevant: Jesus, according to Mark, declares all foods clean (7:19b).[72] Food rules exclude the very people intended to be part of God's new people. For Jesus, the only true indication of holiness is inward. "Purity of heart is reckoned as so much more important than the ritual washing of hands as to render the latter inconsequential."[73] Of course, it must be more than inward. Holiness must be expressed in external actions that reflect and model the character of the holy God. These actions define and embody holiness for the new covenant people of God in the new life of God's kingdom. But external purity that is not matched by internal purity is the mark of hypocrisy rather than holiness in Jesus' view.

71. See Neyrey, "Idea of Purity," p. 112.

72. Holiness language is not at all prominent in pagan sources. In *Arrian's Discourses of Epictetus* I.xxii, Epictetus argues that the conflict between Jews and Syrians is "not over the question whether holiness [ὅσιον] should be put before everything else and should be pursued in all circumstances, but whether the particular act of eating swine's flesh is holy or unholy [ἀνόσιον]." Thanks to Gerald Downing for drawing my attention to this reference.

73. Dunn, "Jesus and Holiness," p. 188.

Finally, the transforming character of holiness. Perhaps this is the key message of Mark. The holiness of Jesus affects both persons and society. The contagion of Jesus' holiness brings healing to the impure. Lepers are cleansed — note the link between illness and impurity (1:41-44); forgiveness is offered to sinners — note the link between the healing of the paralytic and the forgiveness of sins (2:1-12). Particularly poignant is the release of those possessed by unclean spirits. The exorcism in Mark 5 expresses, as Barton puts it, ". . . something of the sanctifying presence of God in Jesus bringing a new sense of self. . . ."[74]

But the re-ordering of the holy community is even more radical. By Jesus' action, people are brought into the community of faith. They are often those excluded under traditional rules. Holiness as separation from impurity is changed to holiness as community with Jesus. This is mission-driven holiness. The Sabbath is for doing good; the table is a banquet for all who would come. God's eschatological people are on his mission. And they reflect and model the character of God: merciful and just, forgiving and accepting, open and inclusive. They are the holy people of the holy God. This calls for a re-ordering of society.[75]

Holiness and the Twenty-First Century People of God

This reading suggests that Mark has a great deal to say about holiness and ecclesiology. Three areas in particular emerge from this reading of Mark.

First, the identity of the holy people of God is wholly bound up with the relationship to the Holy One of God. Those who are his people are those gathered around him who do the will of his father. They share the redemptive mission of Jesus. They do it together. God's will is neither individualistic nor egocentric as if "discovering God's will for my life" were downloading a personal blueprint. Mark's Gospel reminds us that the holy people are gathered together to be on Jesus' mission with his authority. Those who have responded to his personal call enter into the people of God. They are those who are called to fulfil the purposes of the people of God, set out first for Israel and then for us who follow those first disciples. This is an inclusive people without pre-determined purity and ethnic boundaries. All who wish to follow Jesus may become part of his people, the new people of God. Membership in the people of God requires an ongoing relationship rather than a static ontology. Their holiness is determined by their closeness to the holy one. Holiness, then, is neither a thing nor a performance target. Those who do the will of God are those who follow Jesus

---

74. Barton, "Dislocating," p. 200.
75. See Dunn, "Jesus and Holiness," p. 190.

and his way. He radiates holiness and thereby transforms the community through his ongoing presence and continued leadership. Although Mark says little about the Spirit, there can be little doubt that the holy presence of Christ is mediated in and through the presence of the Spirit in the community of faith.

Second, holiness can no longer be defined primarily in terms of separation or performance codes. The only boundary marker that matters is whether the people are willing to be cross-bearers and to follow after Jesus.[76] Holiness displayed primarily in observance of moral codes that are used as boundary markers is excluded. Mark challenges any understanding of the holy people of God that concentrates upon separation and purity as ends in themselves. On the other hand, God's people *are* identified by the kind of lives they live. But this is bound up with God's rescue mission. Do his people reflect the mercy and compassion of the Holy One who reaches to the dispossessed, strengthens the powerless, touches the unclean, and shares fellowship with notorious sinners? Or do they make separation from evil an end in itself?

Jesus demonstrates that holiness is contagious. It overcomes evil, is not contaminated by contact with sinners. Instead of being overwhelmed by the contagion of sin and impurity, the holiness of Jesus' person transforms the unclean, the sick, the sinner, and thwarts the power of evil in every confrontation. We, therefore, like Jesus are to be agents of wholeness and cleanness. There is a warning attached to this, of course. Mark is at pains to remind us that, apart from Jesus, we are no match for the power of evil and have no defences against the contagion of sin. Our holiness is ever and utterly dependent upon our relationship with the Holy One himself. Without the presence of Christ through his Spirit, the power and infection of evil overwhelm us.

Third, the holy people of God participate in God's sanctifying mission. God's holiness transforms persons — sinners, sick, and suffering. This transformation occurs in the day-to-day experience of the community in following Jesus in cross-bearing servanthood. It also transforms communities because God's people are on his mission. The marginalised feature prominently because God is unwilling to see any of his created order lost. They are especially important — the mission of God is not to those who are already the righteous; it is to those who aren't. Any brand of holiness that forgets its identity with the poor and dispossessed and becomes obsessed with maintaining its own purity, refusing to touch the suppurating wounds of humanity, has turned into a supercilious morality divorced from the heart of God.

In 12:28-34, Mark sums it all up in a key story. Jesus is asked, "Which com-

76. See Barton, "Dislocating," p. 206, "Holiness as separation . . . is displaced by *holiness as solidarity:* the solidarity of Jesus. . . ."

mandment is the first of all?" The response of Jesus is to recite the Shema and Lev 19:18. The scribe agrees and restates the commands, adding, "this is much more important than all whole burnt offerings and sacrifices." The significance of his response cannot be overestimated. To say, *in the Temple and following Jesus' prophetic representative action in the Temple,* that these two commandments are more than all whole burnt offerings and sacrifices is a highly symbolic challenge. These two commandments are at the heart of Second Temple piety but because the kingdom has arrived, Jesus' teaching has a much more daring conclusion: these demands can be met. This is no longer a future hope. The time has arrived. Mark writes, "When Jesus saw that he answered wisely, he said to him, 'You are not far from the kingdom of God.'" No wonder that Mark tells us, "And after that no one dared ask him any question" (12:34b).

Gathered at the Table: Holiness and Ecclesiology in the Gospel of Luke

RICHARD P. THOMPSON

It is unlikely that one would find either holiness or ecclesiology included in anyone's "top ten list" of characteristics of the Gospel of Luke. This is not surprising, since a quick perusal of this Gospel reveals few instances of the vocabulary of holiness apart from references to the Holy Spirit.[1] And when one considers what the Lukan understanding of the church might be, the Acts of the Apostles rather than the Gospel of Luke tends to capture the attention.[2] One might conclude, then, that Luke's Gospel has little to offer discussions about holiness and ecclesiology.

There are two reasons why one should reassess this conclusion. First, one should not merely assume that the *second* half of Luke-Acts contributes more distinctly to conversations about holiness and ecclesiology than Luke's Gospel. To be sure, the prominent role of the church in Acts might suggest that the Gospel of Luke only provides the reader with preliminary material regarding the church, from which the reader would draw in reading the subsequent narrative. However, when one considers the lack of evidence suggesting that Luke and Acts *should* be read together and the growing body of questions about the

---

1. Other than the adjective ἅγιος describing God (1:49), the one reference to holiness (1:72-75) refers to God's "holy covenant" (διαθήκης ἁγίας) and to serving God "in holiness" (ἐν ὁσιότητι).

2. E.g., Richard Paul Thompson, "Christian Community and Characterization in the Book of Acts: A Literary Study of the Lukan Concept of the Church" (Ph.D. diss., Southern Methodist University, 1996); Hans Conzelmann, *The Theology of St. Luke,* trans. Geoffrey Buswell (Philadelphia: Fortress, 1961), pp. 207-34.

This essay is dedicated with gratitude to Dr. Alex Deasley, an admirable example to his students as a careful exegete of Scripture, a cogent proclaimer of the gospel, and a faithful servant of God and the church.

often-assumed unity of Luke-Acts, it seems best to reassess such assumptions by turning to consider what the Lukan Gospel might contribute *on its own terms apart from Acts.*[3] Second, the nature of the Gospels as *narrative* texts demands that one must read these texts differently from other New Testament genres. Whereas ancient letters addressed their original recipients directly in their *specific* historical situation, narratives invited the recipients out of their "everyday world" to witness and experience persons and events in *another* world, the narrative world. Thus, narratives function in implicit ways that may be more descriptive than logically developed so that scenes and images rather than specific terminology and logic may dominate the textual landscape. In other words, the issue might not be that Luke's Gospel offers little to discussions about holiness and ecclesiology; the issue might be *how* this Gospel conveys such matters and *where* one might find them.

The proposal here is that there are implicit but distinctly Lukan contributions to discussions about holiness and ecclesiology within a characteristic motif of the Gospel of Luke: the meal scene and, more specifically, those instances where the narrative depicts Jesus and others gathered together at a meal table.[4] In what follows, I will contend that, at the heart of the Lukan Gospel and, more specifically, the meal scenes that include Jesus at the table during the ministry portion of that narrative is the issue of what constitutes the people of God and who may truly gather with him at the table, which symbolically represents God's salvific purposes.[5] Thus, the conflict that erupts in these scenes is over contrasting understandings of what it means to be the people of God — understandings that carry with them radically different concepts of purity and holiness.

1. Meals, Food, and Purity in the Ancient World

In the ancient world, meals and food went beyond mere physical nourishment. Like most societies or human groups, a variety of rules and boundaries related to eating: what persons ate, how persons ate, and with whom persons ate.[6] Such

---

3. E.g., Mikeal C. Parsons and Richard I. Pervo, *Rethinking the Unity of Luke and Acts* (Minneapolis: Fortress, 1993).

4. See John Paul Heil, *The Meal Scenes in Luke-Acts: An Audience-Oriented Approach,* SBLMS (Atlanta: Scholars, 1999).

5. See Marcus J. Borg, *Conflict, Holiness and Politics in the Teachings of Jesus,* rev. ed. (Harrisburg: Trinity, 1998), esp. pp. 88-134.

6. Mary Douglas, "Deciphering a Meal," in *Implicit Meanings: Essays in Anthropology* (Boston: Routledge & Kegan Paul, 1975), pp. 249-75, esp. p. 249.

matters reflected the social groups and social status associated with those involved. Beliefs, values, practices, and traditions of those groups defined these rules and boundaries.[7] The designation of what was and was not "pure" or "holy" typically came out of these broader social contexts. In many ways, purity ultimately dealt with what was deemed appropriate within a larger social system or worldview. These understandings of purity functioned to order life and make sure everything — including people, foods, conditions, and places — was "in its proper place."[8] Such concerns provided the boundaries that delineated "clean" from "unclean," holy from unholy, and "insider" from "outsider." In the ancient world, the meal was the microcosm of all these interplaying social and religious markers and boundaries.[9] Thus, many of the purity issues regarding meals were ultimately considerations about the unifying boundaries of particular groups.[10] Invariably, controversy at a meal indicated some kind of boundary transgression, which group members perceived as a threat to their identity and solidarity. A meal, then, was more than the mere consumption of food; it was to eat in a particular social context.

For Israel, purity and holiness were intrinsically related to Jewish identity and solidarity. Purity laws and regulations regarding meals were crucial because of the communal aspects just mentioned. One finds evidence of such regulations in writings of the Qumran community, Josephus, and Philo.[11] However, central to the Jewish meal and its regulations was a theological perspective, which understood table fellowship as fellowship before God.[12] This theological perspective was inseparable from the worship of God, including everything associated with the temple system. The temple purity system established and maintained the social boundaries, classifications, and identity of the Jewish people as the people of God. These social boundaries and classifications designated which persons or categories of persons were holy and which were not.[13]

7. John H. Elliott, "Household and Meals vs. Temple Purity: Replication Patterns in Luke-Acts," *Biblical Theology Bulletin* 21 (1991): 102-8.

8. Jerome H. Neyrey, "The Symbolic Universe of Luke-Acts: 'They Turn the World Upside Down,'" in *The Social World of Luke-Acts: Models for Interpretation,* ed. Jerome H. Neyrey (Peabody, Mass.: Hendrickson, 1991), pp. 274-85.

9. See Borg, *Conflict,* pp. 94-96.

10. Dennis E. Smith, "Table Fellowship as a Literary Motif in the Gospel of Luke," *Journal of Biblical Literature* 106 (1987): 633-34, n. 52.

11. See references in James D. G. Dunn, "Jesus, Table-Fellowship, and Qumran," in *Jesus and the Dead Sea Scrolls* (New York: Doubleday, 1992), pp. 261-64; and Smith, "Table Fellowship," p. 617, n. 15.

12. Dunn, "Jesus, Table-Fellowship, and Qumran," pp. 254-55.

13. Cf. John H. Elliott, "Temple versus Household in Luke-Acts: A Contrast in Social Institutions," in *The Social World of Luke-Acts,* pp. 218-24.

The Pharisees as a group were particularly concerned with maintaining the boundaries of table fellowship by following the same purity regulations required for priests and temple worship.[14] Thus, Jewish meal scenes like those presented in Luke include a broad range of interrelated social concepts, codes, and values which the narrative may not explicitly emphasize but for which the reader or interpreter must account, especially as they relate to any conflict that may arise.

2. Meal Scenes with Jesus at the Table

Hardly a chapter goes by in Luke without some kind of reference to food, meals, eating, or hunger.[15] Some references are merely passing ones; others are meal scenes. The mention of food or a meal often comes from the Lukan Jesus himself (15:11-32; 16:19-31). At other times, the narrator depicts Jesus at the meal table. These meal scenes are particularly noteworthy because of their variety and their narrative placement. They depict Jesus at the table with one of three groups of people: "outsiders" or "sinners," Pharisees, and his disciples. One finds Jesus eating with the first two groups of people within the Lukan depiction of Jesus' ministry. The last type of scene, depicting Jesus eating with disciples, includes the Lord's Supper and Emmaus episodes which draw from the images and emphases of the preceding meal scenes.

a. Jesus at the Table with "Outsiders" or "Sinners" (Luke 5:27-39; 19:1-10)

The similarities of two episodes — Jesus' encounter with Levi in chapter 5 and Jesus' encounter with Zacchaeus in chapter 19 — suggest that these scenes frame and epitomize the Lukan presentation of Jesus' ministry to the outcasts of Jewish society. These similarities include the following: both were tax collectors and apparently wealthy;[16] both hosted Jesus for a meal;[17] and both meals

14. Jacob Neusner, "Two Pictures of the Pharisees: Philosophical Circle or Eating Club," *Anglican Theological Review* 64 (1982): 525-37.

15. For a list of such references, see Robert J. Karris, *Luke, Artist and Theologian: Luke's Passion Account as Literature* (New York: Paulist, 1985), pp. 49-51.

16. Although the narrator explicitly describes only Zacchaeus as wealthy (19:2), Levi's "great banquet" (5:29) implicitly suggests something about his financial means.

17. While no meal is specifically mentioned in the Zacchaeus episode, it was customary to offer a meal to one's guest (see 19:7).

provoked controversy. Considering the theological and social nature of Jewish meals, the tensions and underlying emotions bring issues to the surface that demand closer inspection.

(1) Jesus at the Table at Levi's House (Luke 5:27-39)

The first meal scene in Luke's Gospel follows several initial scenes in Jesus' Galilean ministry, when Jesus called some as followers and healed others. Like the scene of Jesus' call of Simon Peter (5:1-11), Jesus initiated the encounter with Levi, whom the narrator describes simply as a "tax collector" (τελώνης). To be sure, tax collectors of that day had a contemptible reputation because of their vocation. However, the Lukan narrator does not present them so much as Jewish traitors but as corrupt persons who dishonestly garnered such fees and more from the people (cf. 3:13).[18] Nonetheless, as a sequential reading of this gospel would have already discovered, tax collectors were among those whom the narrator had mentioned earlier as seeking John's baptism (3:12) — a "baptism of repentance for the forgiveness of sins" (3:3).[19] The correspondence of Levi's radical and obedient response to that of Jesus' first followers (5:11), especially in the shadow of the previous scene where Jesus forgave the sins of the paralytic (5:17-26), implies that Levi was repentant and that Jesus had forgiven him. Such matters suggest possible reasons why Levi hosted the banquet in Jesus' honor.[20]

In addition to Levi and Jesus, the narrator also mentions that "a large crowd of tax collectors and others" (5:29) attended the banquet.[21] Such developments would not have surprised the Lukan audience, since they would have expected the dinner host to invite persons of similar social status.[22] However, this guest list apparently was the point of contention for the Pharisees and their scribes, whose presence is left unexplained but who "were grumbling" (ἐγόγγυζον) not to Jesus but to his disciples about them eating with "tax collectors and sinners" (5:30; cf. 15:1-2). The contrast between the *narrator's* and *Phari-*

18. Halvor Moxnes, *The Economy of the Kingdom: Social Conflict and Economic Relations in Luke's Gospel*, OBT (Philadelphia: Fortress, 1988), pp. 52-53.

19. Cf. Heil, *Meal Scenes*, p. 22.

20. In contrast to the other synoptic gospels, only Luke unambiguously presents Levi as the host (5:29). See E. Springs Steele, "Luke 11:37-54 — A Modified Hellenistic Symposium?" *Journal of Biblical Literature* 103 (1984): 390-91.

21. David A. Neale notes that Luke did not repeat "tax collectors and sinners" (Mark 2:15, 16; Matt 9:10) because it would have affirmed the Pharisees' perspective (*None but the Sinners: Religious Categories in the Gospel of Luke*, JSNTSup 58 [Sheffield: JSOT, 1991], p. 130).

22. Cf. Richard L. Rohrbaugh, "The Pre-industrial City in Luke-Acts: Urban Social Relations," in *The Social World of Luke-Acts*, p. 140.

sees' perception of the dinner guests underscores the issue for the Pharisees: eating or dining with "sinners." In other words, the controversy was not over the *food* that was served but over the *people at the table*.[23] Interestingly, the narrative offers nothing explicitly about these other guests or the reasons behind the Pharisees' negative assessment.[24] Rather, the Pharisaic use of the term "sinner" suggests that they merely identified such persons as on the periphery of the community or even outside its boundaries.[25] The Pharisees considered them as outsiders because they were in conflict with the community's values, norms, and conduct.[26] Since the meal reflected these community boundary markers, eating with sinners was nothing less than a serious threat to the whole community and a breach of those boundaries that defined and maintained it.[27] Thus, the Pharisees sought to protect the community from whatever endangered it by upholding those purity regulations that distinguished "insider" from "outsider."[28]

The controversy over eating with sinners precipitated a response from Jesus, although the Pharisees had not questioned him directly. His response turned the Pharisees' purity system upside-down as it pertained to table fellowship. Whereas the Pharisees used the term "sinner" to distinguish and isolate the outsider, Jesus used the same term to designate those whom he had come to call to repentance (5:32). The Pharisees' distinctions of holiness and community left such persons on the periphery and outside the workings of God; Jesus' table fellowship with the outsider or sinner redefined such understandings of holiness, community, and the workings of God by including rather than excluding the outcast for the sake of repentance.[29] This idea of seeking to restore sinners through repentance was certainly not controversial to the Jewish people (cf. Ezekiel 34). Nonetheless, the differences between the Pharisees and Jesus were not about the ministry of repentance but about the nature of holiness and community. The Pharisees required repentance *before* inclusion within the community; Jesus ate with sinners so that they might repent.

23. Neale notes that rabbinic prohibitions typically focused on food, not people (*None but the Sinners*, pp. 62-63).

24. For an assessment of different explanations for the criticism, see Neale, *None but the Sinners*, pp. 118-24.

25. Dunn asserts that the term "sinner" had a "well-established factional use" within the Judaism of Jesus' day ("Jesus, Table-Fellowship, and Qumran," p. 259).

26. Cf. Joel B. Green, *The Theology of the Gospel of Luke* (Cambridge: Cambridge University Press, 1995), p. 85; Dunn, "Jesus, Table-Fellowship, and Qumran," p. 259.

27. Cf. *m. Dem.* 2.3: "He that undertakes to be an Associate . . . may not be the guest of an ʿam ha-aretz nor may he receive him as a guest in his own raiment."

28. Moxnes, *Economy*, pp. 52-55.

29. Cf. Joachim Jeremias, *The Eucharistic Words of Jesus* (New York: Charles Scribner's Sons, 1966), p. 205.

(2) Jesus at the Table at Zacchaeus's House (Luke 19:1-10)

The story of Jesus' encounter with Zacchaeus is unique to Luke and is obviously Lukan in both style and vocabulary.[30] In many ways, this pericope builds upon the accumulation of narrated scenes, images, and emphases throughout the Gospel's central portion which focuses on Jesus' ministry and journey to Jerusalem.[31] Thus, Jesus' interaction with another tax collector should not surprise the reader of this Gospel, since the narrator has interspersed throughout the account of Jesus' ministry a variety of encounters with marginalized persons, including tax collectors (5:27-32; 15:1-2). In addition, the parable of the Pharisee and the tax collector (18:9-14) in the previous chapter affirms the latter one's humility before God. Thus, the responses of both Zacchaeus and Jesus confirm what the reader has seen and concluded about Jesus' ministry throughout the Lukan Gospel.[32]

Several features of this story, however, intensify its dramatic effect that culminates in Jesus' visit to Zacchaeus's house and Jesus' pronouncement. First, there is the irony of the name Zacchaeus, meaning "pure" or "innocent" in its Hebrew form but contrasting with the crowd's perception of him as a sinner (19:7). Second, the narrator identifies Zacchaeus as a "chief tax collector" (19:2). Although the term ἀρχιτελώνης appears in no other extant Greek text, one may surmise that this designation either refers to someone in charge of the collectors of tariffs and customs or simply suggests that the reader should multiply all assumptions about tax collectors in this instance. Third, the narrator mentions that Zacchaeus was "rich" (πλούσιος; 19:2). Given some of Jesus' teachings about the rich and the sorrowful response of one who was "very rich" (πλούσιος σφόδρα; 18:23), this piece of information complicates the initial picture. Fourth, Zacchaeus's initial efforts to see Jesus were unsuccessful because of the crowd and his short stature (19:3). This physical description of Zacchaeus is probably more than a passing reference about his height. As Mikeal Parsons has noted, rhetorical practice of the ancient world often used an opponent's physical abnormalities, including shortness, as an occasion for ridicule.[33] In

30. John O'Hanlon, "The Story of Zacchaeus and the Lukan Ethic," *Journal for the Study of the New Testament* 12 (1981): 2-9; William P. Loewe, "Towards an Interpretation of Lk 19:1-10," *Catholic Biblical Quarterly* 36 (1974): 321-31.

31. Cf. I. Howard Marshall, *The Gospel of Luke: A Commentary on the Greek Text*, NIGTC (Grand Rapids: Eerdmans, 1978), pp. 694-95.

32. Cf. Robert C. Tannehill, "The Story of Zacchaeus as Rhetoric," *Semeia* 64 (1994): 204-5.

33. Mikeal C. Parsons, "'Short in Stature': Luke's Physical Description of Zacchaeus," *New Testament Studies* 47 (2001): 50-57.

particular, shortness in physical stature was often associated with moral deficiencies, including low self-appraisal and greediness. By mentioning Zacchaeus's shortness, the narrator has initially presented him as "a laughable, perhaps despicable, character."[34] Such characterization is corroborated and intensified by the crowd's reaction to Jesus' visit to the home of Zacchaeus, whom they identified as a "sinful man" (19:7; cf. 5:8). An ancient audience would have possibly heard two things in that complaint: (1) Zacchaeus had been born a sinner, as his stature indicated; and (2) he was still living as a sinner by swindling money from others (cf. 3:13; 19:8).[35] Such a negative assessment about Zacchaeus may have contributed to the crowd hampering his attempts to see Jesus. Thus, once the reader gathers all these pieces to the characterization of Zacchaeus together, she has before her an unmistakable picture of the quintessential outsider, the chief among sinners, the most unlikely of persons to respond favorably to Jesus.

The last half of the pericope is dependent on the favorable response of this least likely person to the call of Jesus. This response included Zacchaeus welcoming Jesus (ὑπεδέξατο αὐτόν), the same response of the disciple Martha when Jesus visited her home (10:38). However, the central feature of this passage is the two contrasting evaluations of Jesus' actions. On the one hand, the complaint against Jesus was registered not only by the Pharisees (cf. 5:30) but by "all" (πάντες; 19:7). The grumbling is reminiscent of earlier instances where the Pharisees complained about Jesus' association with "tax collectors and sinners" (cf. 15:2; γογγύζω in 5:30). However, the more inclusive "all" suggests that the *whole* community — not only the Pharisees — rejected Zacchaeus as a sinner and outcast, meaning that they rejected his rights as a Jew, as part of the people of God.[36] As a result, the criticism against Jesus is similar to the earlier one directed against his disciples: he was associating and presumably eating with persons whom the community judged to be outside of the boundary markers that defined that community. They saw Jesus' actions as a threat to the character and identity of the Jewish people by opening them up to outsiders.[37] On the other hand, Jesus' response to Zacchaeus (19:9-10) — which also indirectly addressed the complainants[38] — reversed the community's assessment of Zacchaeus's plight. Jesus' declaration of salvation (and the two supporting rationale) ulti-

34. Parsons, "Short," p. 54.
35. Parsons, "Short," p. 55.
36. Cf. Tannehill, "The Story of Zacchaeus," p. 206.
37. Cf. Halvor Moxnes, "Meals and the New Community in Luke," *Svensk exegetisk årsbok* 51 (1986): 160; Borg, *Conflict*, pp. 107-9.
38. Tannehill suggests that the use of indirect address in a hostile situation was appropriate ("The Story of Zacchaeus," pp. 208-10).

mately contradicted the community's objection to his association with a reputed sinner like Zacchaeus. The community identified Zacchaeus as the ultimate outsider and treated him in ways to ensure that he remained isolated from them. However, by going to Zacchaeus's house and presumably eating at his table, Jesus embodied and then declared a different perspective that redefined the boundaries of community and purity by being inclusive of the "lost," the sinner, and the outsider. Hence, Jesus reversed the purity regulations and boundary markers of the community that kept the "lost" lost, the sinner sinful, and the outsider outside.

b. Jesus at the Table with Pharisees
(Luke 7:36-50; 11:37-54; 14:1-24)

Because of the complaints about Jesus' eating companions, one might not expect to find Jesus eating with persons such as the Pharisees, who sought to preserve the identity and solidarity of the Jewish people by maintaining the community's boundaries and purity regulations. However, a surprising aspect of the meal scenes in Luke's Gospel is that three scenes, unique to this Gospel, each depict Jesus having dinner at a Pharisee's home (7:36-50; 11:37-54; 14:1-24).[39] Interestingly, one finds these three meal scenes placed within the larger narrative context of Jesus' ministry, which is bracketed by the two scenes describing Jesus at the table with outsiders and the ensuing controversy that accompanied those meals. The repeated occurrence of meal scenes in the Lukan account of Jesus' ministry suggests that the reader should draw conclusions from the cumulative effect that comes with repetition. At the same time, this narrative arrangement encourages the reader to keep these distinct settings in creative tension, particularly as one considers the narrative implications of reading and evaluating these scenes together. In each of these three meal scenes, the *fait divers* and the sayings of Jesus that follow in tandem deal with significant issues regarding the community known as the people of God and the nature of holiness that shaped them.[40]

---

39. Cf. John Nolland, *Luke 1–9:20*, WBC 35A (Dallas: Word, 1989), p. 353.

40. Some suggest that Luke shaped these meal scenes according to the symposium genus; e.g., X. de Meeûs, "Composition de Lc. XIV et genre symposiaque," *Ephemerides theologicae lovanienses* 37 (1961): 847-70; J. Delobel, "L'onction par la pécheresse: La composition littéraire de Lc. VII., 36-50," *Ephemerides theologicae lovanienses* 42 (1966): 415-75; Steele, "Luke 11:37-54"; Smith, "Table Fellowship."

(1) Jesus, Simon the Pharisee, and the
Sinful Woman (Luke 7:36-50)

The narrator begins the first pericope by simply stating that a Pharisee invited Jesus to dinner. While the reader may interpret the invitation as an indication of the Pharisees' openness or friendliness toward Jesus, she should recall the last series of appearances by Pharisees in the Lukan Gospel, which presents them as his opponents in one way or another (5:17–6:11; cf. 7:30). Ironically, this scene comes on the heels of the criticism that Jesus was "a glutton and drunkard, a friend of tax collectors and sinners" (7:34). Here Jesus was not eating with sinners but with this Pharisee and presumably others like him who as a group had an established reputation for holiness and purity.[41] However, with the appearance of a "woman in the city" whom the narrator explicitly states "was a sinner" (7:37), the reader would readily recognize that her appearance and subsequent actions shattered the inscribed holiness and purity regulations of that meal, at least according to the Pharisees. The widespread interpretation that the woman was a prostitute misses the significance of the "sinner" label, which groups her with the "tax collectors and sinners" (7:34), those whom Jesus had been criticized for befriending.[42] Here, it initially appears as though an outsider had threatened the boundaries of the community by ignoring them.

The central part of this episode, however, is not the interaction between Jesus and this woman but the interaction between Jesus and Simon the Pharisee.[43] The *fait divers* that initiated the sayings of Jesus as the chief guest was not the woman's appearance or actions but Simon's unspoken suspicions about the identity of *both* the woman *and* Jesus.[44] What Jesus said to Simon contrasted both two different responses of hospitality toward Jesus (Simon's and the woman's) and two different perspectives about the woman (Simon's and Jesus'). On the one hand, Simon's neglect as the host to show the customary hospitality and honor to the chief guest dishonored Jesus.[45] The host's unstated thoughts subtly provide to the reader the reasons for his neglect: his

41. Green states that the Pharisee invited Jesus because he assumed Jesus was similarly concerned with religious purity (*Theology*, p. 90).

42. Cf. Kathleen E. Corley, *Private Women, Public Meals: Social Conflict in the Synoptic Tradition* (Peabody, Mass.: Hendrickson, 1993), p. 127.

43. Cf. Barbara E. Reid, "'Do You See This Woman?' Luke 7:36-50 as a Paradigm for Feminist Hermeneutics," *Biblical Research* 40 (1995): 37-39; contra Evelyn R. Thibeaux, "'Known to Be a Sinner': The Narrative Rhetoric of Luke 7:36-50," *Biblical Theology Bulletin* 23 (1993): 152.

44. Cf. Steele, "Luke 11:37-54," p. 386; contra David B. Gowler, *Host, Guest, Enemy and Friend: Portraits of the Pharisees in Luke and Acts* (New York: Peter Lang, 1991), pp. 219-20.

45. Cf. Mark Allan Powell, "The Religious Leaders in the Gospels of Luke: A Literary-Critical Study," *Journal of Biblical Literature* 109 (1990): 96.

doubts about Jesus' true identity (7:39). Conversely, the woman's actions, which Simon saw as disgraceful and shameful, fulfilled the honor and hospitality that the host should have provided. The result of these contrasting actions was the reversal of status, both for Simon and for the woman.[46] On the other hand, Simon's perspective of the woman was that "she *is* a sinner" (emphasis added; 7:39), which probably contributed to his negative appraisal of her actions. Conversely, the parable reveals Jesus' perspective, which in turn validates the connotation of the narrator's initial characterization of the woman: this woman who "used to be" a sinner was no longer the sinner she once was.[47] The woman's actions expressed her gratitude for forgiveness that she had already received. In other words, the narrator shifted the scene's focus from the initial conflict over interpreting the woman's actions to Jesus' retelling of what happened to reveal that the woman was not a sinner but someone enjoying the salvific benefits of forgiveness. While Simon and Pharisees like him had already determined who were sinners from a human point of view, Jesus articulated and embodied a divine point of view that saw the woman differently, thereby affirming her for what she had already become.[48] Thus, this meal scene turns the table on those who had erroneously complained about those whom Jesus befriended, revealing instead the Pharisees' impiety and mistaken understandings of holiness and community.[49] Such a reversal did not place Simon and the Pharisees outside the realm of God's salvation. Rather, this scene raises the question for Simon and the reader whether they might acknowledge what Jesus has revealed and challenged regarding the nature of holiness and community.[50]

(2) Jesus, an Unnamed Pharisee, and Washing before Dinner (Luke 11:37-54)

The second instance of Jesus eating at a Pharisee's house begins much like the first one, with an invitation extended to Jesus (11:37). Like the previous instance, the *fait divers* that initiated some sayings from Jesus (11:39-52) was not something that happened during the meal but involved the host's unspoken thoughts about Je-

46. Gowler, *Host,* pp. 221-24.
47. Reid notes the imperfect verb ἦν may have the connotation "used to be" ("Paradigm," p. 41).
48. Cf. Powell, "Religious Leaders," p. 99.
49. Cf. Neale, *None but the Sinners,* pp. 141-42.
50. Robert C. Tannehill, "Should We Love Simon the Pharisee? Hermeneutical Reflections on the Pharisees in Luke," *Currents in Theology and Mission* 21 (1994): 432-33; Reid, "Paradigm," p. 48.

sus.[51] In this instance, the narrator explains that Jesus "first had not been washed (ἐβαπτίσθη) before dinner" (11:38), a violation of Jewish purity regulations.[52] Jewish thought and practice believed that ceremonial cleansing removed a person's impurities in preparation for the meal. The reader of this Gospel should catch the irony of what surprised this Pharisee: although *Jesus'* neglect of "baptism" in preparation for the meal startled him, the *Pharisees* along with the lawyers had refused "the will of God . . . for themselves" because they had not been baptized by John (μὴ βαπτισθέντες ὑπ' αὐτοῦ; 7:30), which was a baptism of repentance (3:3).[53] This surprise, with all its irony, precipitated a series of seven harsh statements from Jesus, which is the focus of attention in this scene.

A brief glance at the major points of contention in Jesus' words indicates the Lukan perspective that the Pharisees held to a narrow understanding of holiness and purity that focused on ritual purity and practice while ignoring the social and economic relations of their day. Jesus' initial statement, which is not introduced by οὐαί ("woe") as the others, functions as a general indictment against the Pharisees that receives explication in the succeeding "woe" statements. He noted the irony of their concern for clean cups and dishes while full of morally and socially destructive drives and attitudes: ἁρπαγή, which connotes the violent seizure of whatever one wants because of insatiable greed; πονηρία which, in association with ἁρπαγή, seems to suggest something like moral worthlessness. Although the Pharisees had maintained *external* ritual purity, Jesus accused them of *internal* impurity because they upheld a social system that ostracized and oppressed others.[54] The remaining three statements against the Pharisees followed the harsh reality of this initial statement: they meticulously practiced tithing on the minutiae of life but failed to practice essential matters like justice (11:42); they loved to receive honor from others but did not love God (11:42-43; cf. 7:36-50);[55] they contaminated unsuspecting people with their hidden uncleanness (11:44). Thus, the Lukan arrangement and collection of these sayings in this particular context link these concerns for purity regulations to the exploitation of others. The holiness and ritual purity essential to the Pharisees' understanding of com-

---

51. Contra Heil, *Meal Scenes*, p. 83. See Joel B. Green, *The Gospel of Luke*, NICNT (Grand Rapids: Eerdmans, 1997), p. 470.

52. The verb βαρτίζω refers to the Pharisaic practice of ritual washing before a meal. A. I. Baumgarten identifies this as immersion (*The Flourishing of Jewish Sects in the Maccabean Era: An Interpretation*, JSJSup 55 [Leiden: Brill, 1997], pp. 98-99).

53. Heil, *Meal Scenes*, pp. 83-84. Cf. John A. Darr, *On Character Building: The Reader and the Rhetoric of Characterization in Luke-Acts* (Louisville: Westminster John Knox, 1992), p. 104.

54. Cf. Moxnes, *Economy*, p. 112.

55. Cf. Powell, "Religious Leaders," pp. 96-97, who sees the religious leaders as unloving, a derivative of their self-righteousness.

munity promoted practices and a system that ultimately violated the essential nature of the community itself. By presenting this meal scene and the ensuing conflict between Jesus and his host, the Lukan narrator encourages the reader to consider an alternative understanding of holiness and community that focuses on the needs of others rather than an understanding that merely focuses on inner holiness that ultimately had to do with self-interest and the oppression of others.

(3) Jesus, a Leader of the Pharisees, Honored Seating, and Dinner Invitations (Luke 14:1-24)

The Lukan narrator introduces the last of the three meal scenes at a Pharisee's home in ways that remind the reader of earlier episodes. Reminiscent of one such episode in chapter 6, a person with a physical malady confronted Jesus on the Sabbath with Pharisees constantly "looking over his shoulder," as the periphrastic construction ἦσαν παρατηρούμενοι implies (14:1). The narrator offers no explicit reason for the man's presence. However, the juxtaposition of two men — one known only by his impurity, the other known only by his purity and prominence — could not be more striking.[56] Thus, Jesus' act of healing included the "outsider" within the realm of God's salvific work and precipitated what Jesus had to say.

All three sections of Jesus' comments focus on invitations to dinners and the seating arrangements for such occasions. The prominence of the host implies a similar social standing for the dinner guests, who were probably Pharisees as well.[57] In such a context, seating position at the table indicated social rank relative to other guests.[58] Thus, Jesus witnessed nothing out of the ordinary; even his disciples exhibited similar concerns (cf. 9:46-48; 22:24-27). However, Jesus advocated behavior that contested the social norms of that day and challenged the typical social concern for seeking honor at the meal table by instructing them to take the seat of least honor (14:7-11).[59] In verses 12-14 the at-

---

56. The host was "one of the *rulers* of the Pharisees" (emphasis added; 14:1), which implies high social standing.

57. John T. Carroll notes that the pronoun αὐτοί (14:1, 7, 16) probably refers to the Pharisees ("Luke's Portrayal of the Pharisees," *Catholic Biblical Quarterly* 50 [1988]: 612, n. 36).

58. Smith cites references to the ranking at meals in the writings of Plato, Plutarch, Philo, and the Qumran community ("Table Fellowship," pp. 617-20).

59. Robert C. Tannehill, "The Lukan Discourse on Invitations (Luke 14:7-24)," in *The Four Gospels 1992: Festschrift Frans Neirynck,* ed. F. Van Segbroeck et al., BETL (Leuven: Leuven University Press, 1992), p. 1607; and de Meeûs, "Composition de Lc., XIV," p. 868 identify a common pattern here that underscores a reversal of behavior from that which supports those of high status to that which conflicts with them.

tention turns to invitations and the dinner guest list. Dinner invitations were signs of social status; received and offered invitations declared and sustained one's high standing through a system of social obligation. Those of high social standing did not socialize with groups other than their own because doing so would risk a significant loss of status.[60] Again, Jesus' instructions subverted the system by advocating the invitation of society's outcasts and needy, not those expected and able to reciprocate.[61] This kind of invitation would cross those community boundary markers of purity and holiness by including those who had previously been excluded — the needy, the oppressed, and the unclean — at a table that had been reserved only for people who lived by the same purity codes.[62]

The parable in verses 15-24 functions to tie together many of the issues that have arisen throughout this meal scene. Unlike the previous section, the question was not about the nature of the guest list but what might happen if those on the original guest list did not attend the dinner, a collective act of social disapproval of the dinner arrangements.[63] Neither the parable itself nor the narrator offers any explicit reason for such an act of disgrace toward the host. Nonetheless, the collective act against the host precipitated his invitation of unacceptable guests as Jesus had instructed (which includes the subversion of the established system of obligation, reciprocity, and purity), as the repetition of the guest list in both verses 13 and 21 implies. Thus, the host would experience the loss of social standing and be identified with those who socially degraded him and others (14:23) because of his actions against these established social norms. The parable clearly functions as implicit commentary, through which the narrator offers insights through a reliable character. Thus, the parable illustrates, as John Carroll puts it, "a crisis of division and reversal within Israel" that had come as a response to Jesus' ministry of inclusion to outcasts and sinners.[64] On the one hand, the division has to do with differences over the nature of community and who were truly invited to table fellowship. On the other hand, the reversal has to do with what the reader encounters in the ministry portion of Luke's Gospel: the ones expected to respond favorably to Jesus' invitation did not, but the ones not expected to respond favorably did. As a result, the Pharisees and others in the Lukan Gospel were vulnerable to a reversal of

60. Rohrbaugh, "Pre-industrial City," p. 136.

61. Cf. Luke T. Johnson, *The Gospel of Luke,* SP (Collegeville, Minn.: Liturgical, 1991), p. 224.

62. The list of invitees in Luke 14:13 is similar to the list of forbidden persons in Lev 21:17-23 and 1QSa II 5-22. Moxnes notes that the issues here are socioeconomic but acknowledges that poverty may have contributed to persons' ritual impurity (*Economy,* pp. 102, 129).

63. Rohrbaugh, "Pre-industrial City," pp. 141-42.

status of a different sort: the religious "insiders" of the story may find themselves outside.

c. Jesus at the Table with Disciples (Luke 22:14-38; 24:13-35)

Throughout the Lukan account of Jesus' ministry, the meal scenes involving Jesus include him as someone's guest. The two general kinds of persons who hosted these dinners could not be more different: Pharisees and tax collectors, the latter whom the Pharisees considered "sinners" (15:1-2). All five scenes depict some kind of controversy over dinner guests and companions. In the end, the questions about who did and did not gather at the table with Jesus were about holiness and purity as they related to the Jewish community as the people of God.

While the remaining two meal scenes — the Last Supper (22:14-38) and Jesus at the home of two disciples in Emmaus (24:13-35) — stand in contrast to the earlier scenes since Jesus functions as host rather than guest, the questions and issues about the nature of holiness and the community remain. The cumulative effect of the previous episodes and the emphases of these two scenes direct the reader's attention to those whom Jesus served as host. In the scene of the Last Supper, the intimacy and communal nature of the Passover meal are unmistakable, both historically[65] and in the Lukan rendition of the occasion; only the Lukan narrator mentions that Jesus told those with him that he "eagerly desired to eat this Passover" with them (22:15).[66] The reader finds little other information about those whom Jesus gathered at this table, other than that among them was one who would betray Jesus (22:21-23), another who would deny knowing him (22:31-34), and still others who were concerned with position and status (22:24-27).[67] In many ways, here one finds Jesus gathering unlikely persons to his table, much like the parable of the great banquet (14:15-24) and the meal scenes involving Levi and Zacchaeus illustrated earlier. And these disciples even received the promise of the eschatological meal at Jesus' table in his kingdom (22:30). What is readily apparent is that this episode becomes within the Lukan Gospel the archetypal example of the motif of table

64. Carroll, "Portrayal," p. 615.

65. The meal was celebrated with family or neighbors (Exod 12:3-4), but disciples often shared the meal with their teacher (Johnson, *Luke*, p. 333).

66. Although the antecedent of the pronoun "them" (22:15) is "apostles" (22:14), the reference to "my disciples" suggests that the meal included others besides the apostles (cf. 24:9, 13, 33). See Quentin Quesnell, "The Women at Luke's Supper," in *Political Issues in Luke-Acts*, ed. Richard J. Cassidy and Philip J. Sharper (Maryknoll, N.Y.: Orbis, 1983), pp. 59-61.

fellowship that has been developing as the narrative unfolds — a motif that offers an alternative understanding of holiness and community in contrast to what the Pharisees and others believed.[68] That is to say, the persons whom the reader finds gathered at Jesus' table at the Last Supper exemplify those with whom Jesus had been criticized for associating and befriending through his ministry in the Lukan Gospel and the ones whom the religious and wealthy of society would have never invited to their table.

Similar kinds of issues emerge in the pericope involving the two disciples who invited the unrecognized risen Jesus to stay with them in Emmaus (24:13-35). Although their dejection and misunderstanding about what happened to Jesus would initially convince the reader to see them in a less-than-favorable light, they did something that offers a glimmer of hope: they offered hospitality to a stranger in need (24:28-29), something not dissimilar to Jesus' own actions during his ministry. And it is at the table with Jesus, as he inexplicably acted as host rather than guest by breaking the bread and offering it to these two in ways reminiscent of the Last Supper, that these two confused and despondent followers recognized the presence of the risen Jesus among them (24:30-31). Here the reader again finds unlikely persons gathered at the table with Jesus, and here they recognized the risen Jesus.

What seems apparent in these final two meal scenes is that the Lukan narrator has connected the alternative understanding of holiness and community as seen in Jesus' ministry and teaching with the death and resurrection of Jesus. In the episode of the Last Supper, the giving of Jesus' body (22:19; cf. 22:27) exemplifies the reversal of social expectations and norms that is to characterize the community as Jesus has advocated.[69] The repeated "this" (τοῦτο) in verse 19 associates the body of Jesus that was being given in death on behalf of those gathered at the table (ὑπὲρ ὑμῶν) with the practices of table fellowship among them.[70] Thus, this self-giving of Jesus on behalf of those at Jesus' table is to characterize those who gather in table fellowship: "do this" does not refer specifically to the institution of the Eucharist as a sacrament but to the embrace of the gospel embodied by Jesus and the identification with Jesus' mission as seen in table fellowship.[71] In the episode in Emmaus, the narrator directs the reader's attention to two related matters. On the one hand, the breaking of

---

67. Cf. Karris, *Luke*, p. 69, who notes that Jesus is among transgressors at the Last Supper.

68. Cf. Smith, "Table Fellowship," p. 628.

69. While there are significant text-critical issues regarding Luke 22:19b-20, I accept the majority position which affirms the longer form.

70. The present tense of the participle (διδόμενον) indicates that the giving of Jesus' body was in process. Although the verb does not *directly* connote Jesus' death, the subsequent arrest and crucifixion confirm that implied connotation.

bread reminds the reader of what happened at the Last Supper, including Jesus' declaration that he would eat and drink with his community of followers once the "the kingdom of God might be fulfilled/come" (22:16, 18, 28-30). On the other hand, the eyes of the reader fall upon the disciples' recognition of Jesus as he broke and gave the bread to them (24:30). The narrator offers no explanation why the recognition occurred at this moment, but the Lukan emphasis on "looking" or "beholding" and the imperfect tense of the indicative ἐπεδίδου ("he began to give") suggest that the act of giving may have resulted in the disciples' first glimpse of the wounds from Jesus' crucifixion (cf. 24:39-40). Thus, the recognition of the crucified and now risen Jesus at the table with these two disciples suggests nothing less than the fulfillment of Jesus' promise during the Last Supper and the validation of this community that gathers at his table. That is to say, the death and resurrection of Jesus are the means by which the Lukan understanding of holiness and community as embodied in the person of Jesus may be actualized in table fellowship with him.

d. Gathered at the Table: Holiness, and Ecclesiology

In retrospection, the reader of Luke's Gospel would recognize that the meal scenes that include Jesus at the table during his ministry are more than episodes of conflict over holiness or purity codes regarding the Jewish meal. The questions and even Jesus' sayings that deal with issues regarding those who were and were not invited or those who gathered at the table all seem to direct one's attention to understandings of holiness and purity that are ultimately about the nature of the community of God's people. Nothing in the narrative suggests that the Lukan Jesus was unaware that he was behaving and speaking in such conflicting ways. Rather, one may conclude that Luke presents Jesus as one who embodied, advocated, and then modeled in the final two meal scenes an alternative understanding or redefinition of holiness and community.

In particular, the Lukan Jesus redefined the Jewish concept of holiness that functioned to distinguish the community of faith and those who made up that community from others. The common Jewish understandings of holiness distinguished the holy from the unholy, the faithful from the faithless, and the insider from the outsider. One would observe such distinctions in all aspects of life, from Sabbath observance to the obedience of religious customs and even to meal companions and dinner guest lists. Thus, even pious practices commonly associated with holiness reinforced these distinctions that maintained a larger social and religious system but that in the end disrupted the community itself because it offered those deemed as outsiders little or no justice (cf. 11:39-44).

Conversely, Luke's Gospel presents an alternative understanding of holiness defined by the inclusive nature of God's salvific work rather than by the exclusive nature of God's people. This understanding of God and God's salvific work for all humanity now defines the concept of holiness, rather than an exclusive understanding of holiness that limits the scope and realm of God's activity. Rather than defining holiness in ways that maintain one's place within the holy elect of God by distinguishing the clean and holy from the unclean and unholy, now one finds holiness depicted in ways that embrace the holy purposes of a holy God, whose salvation extends to all and makes the unclean clean.[77]

3. Holiness and Ecclesiology: Reading the Gospel of Luke as the Church's Scriptures

The fact that some of the controversial issues in the meal scenes during Jesus' ministry arose among the disciples during the Last Supper (22:24-27; cf. 14:7-11) implies that readers of Luke's Gospel should see and understand the depicted redefinition of holiness and community with the church in mind. There are a number of implications that arise — both for Luke's original recipients and for those contemporary readers who seek to engage and embody this Gospel as part of the church's Scriptures.

First, the defining marks of holiness and the church are both theological and ethical in nature. One finds in the Lukan Jesus an explicitly theological reorientation of holiness, not because he eliminated the ethical dimension but because his embodiment of God's purposes and activities redefined the ethical in theological ways. Jesus' practices and teachings did not merely challenge prevalent views of holiness as practice but in the end the corresponding views of God and God's purposes. Interestingly, conflict both in the Lukan narrative world and in contemporary settings is often over the ethical or what one considers to be part of the holy: what practices are or are not acceptable, what persons are and are not considered as part of the redeemed, and the like. However, the Lukan perspective reframes such debates by turning the attention *first* to the theological: God, God's nature, God's purposes, etc. Holiness, then, does not simply function to maintain one's understanding of God but arises out of faithfulness to the perceived nature and purposes of God. Thus, if as the Gospel of Luke suggests, the purposes of God extend to all humankind, holiness and those markers that define it in terms that are more exclusive must be revised. The significance of this redirection cannot be overstated, because the challenge

71. Cf. Karris, *Luke,* pp. 67-69.

here is for an adequate theological orientation that defines and shapes the ethical response(s) of the church.

Second, one must find ways to define holiness and the church that do not isolate the church and her practices from the rest of society. To be sure, the church is to embody the transforming grace of God, the evidence of which will be apparent in certain kinds of ways. However, the tendency of differentiation typically accompanies definition, thereby declaring what is and is not associated with the defined. Thus, concepts of holiness often state or imply both what is and is not considered as holy, usually distinguishing practices and persons accordingly. Moreover, one might seek to preserve a particular concept of holiness in distinction from society or maybe from other groups. Concepts of the church consistently focus on her nature as the faith community, which implicitly distinguishes those of the church from those not deemed persons of faith. To be sure, definitions may usefully affirm aspects of God's activity and purposes, but they may also exclude persons and situations from the realm of God's salvific purposes, especially when the church is defined as "separate" from the world. The Gospel of Luke reminds us that God's purposes extend beyond those definitions that typically distinguish the community of faith or the church from the rest of society and that often hamper the movement of the gospel beyond the church's extremities.

Third, an adequate understanding of the church (including holiness) must delineate not only the church's *distinctive* aspects but also her role within society and the world in terms of mission. In both ancient and contemporary practice, some persons confined the concept of holiness to pious or religious practices that distinguish them as people of God. However, as Jesus' stern words in chapter 11 make clear, one's understanding of holiness or the church cannot be limited to the pious practices of individual Christians or to other practices that keep the church holy apart from an unholy world. Rather than viewing holiness as something like the church's property to be protected from encroachments of sinful society, one might view holiness as the church's endowment from God for faithful mission within society and the world. Such an understanding of holiness calls the church to engage society and social issues, not as a means of protection from the world's uncleanness but as faithful response to God's purposes of salvation for all. In addition, it may steer some of the church's attention away from individualized notions and practices of personal piety or even debates over "culture wars" toward proactive involvement in various social and world arenas, where oppression and injustice characterize the human condition and where God's holy purposes of liberation and salvation extend. After all, in the Gospel of Luke those who gathered at the table with Jesus included persons in such circumstances as these.

The Holiness of Jesus and His Disciples in the Gospel of John

Richard Bauckham

At first sight the Gospel of John may not seem to have much to contribute to the theme of "holy church." The word ἅγιος ("holy") occurs just four times, with reference to God (17:11: "Holy Father"), Jesus (6:69: "the Holy One of God"), and the Holy Spirit (14:26; 20:22[1]).[2] The word "church" (ἐκκλησία) does not occur at all.[3] However, there are four occurrences of the verb ἁγιάζειν ("to make holy, to consecrate, to sanctify") (10:36; 17:17, 19 [bis]), two of which refer to the consecration of Jesus' disciples (17:17, 19). A close examination of these occurrences of ἁγιάζειν in their contexts will show that the Gospel does in fact treat the holiness of Jesus' disciples as a significant theme which is closely related to the holiness of Jesus, the Father, and the Spirit. The occurrences of ἅγιος ("holy") will fall into place as we consider the significance of the uses of ἁγιάζειν ("to make holy").

Purity and Holiness

Before proceeding to examine our theme in the Gospel of John, there is a preliminary point to be made about the biblical notion of holiness. New Testament scholars are not always careful about distinguishing between holiness and purity in Old Testament and Jewish thought. Both terms are closely connected with the sanctuary and the cultic practice of the Temple, but in different ways. Holiness belongs properly to God, and all persons and things given to God become holy. It is a paradoxical concept, in that holiness expresses what God in-

---

1. There is also a variant reading that adds ἅγιον to πνεῦμα at 7:39, but this is readily explicable from the tendency of scribes to add ἅγιον in references to the Holy Spirit.

2. In the Johannine letters, ἅγιος is used only at 1 John 2:20, where "the Holy One" is probably Jesus, as in John 6:69.

3. It is found within the Johannine literature only at 3 John 6, 9, 10.

trinsically is, distinct from all creation, and yet it is also shared — in varying degrees — by all that belongs to God. For the people of God holiness is an obligation because God is holy: "You shall be holy, for I YHWH your God am holy" (Lev 19:2; cf. 11:44-45; 20:26). The holiness of the people of God entails both cultic and moral obligations that set them apart from the world in dedication to the service of God. It can be said both that God makes people holy (consecrates or sanctifies them) and that people make themselves holy (consecrate or sanctify themselves) (e.g., Lev 21:8).

Purity, on the other hand, is what creaturely persons and things have if they are not defiled by such things as death, sexual emissions, childbirth, scale disease, or animals forbidden as food. Impurity of this kind — ritual impurity — is more like dirt than sin. For most people most of the time, it is unavoidable and not blameworthy, but it must be removed by ritual washing and, in some cases, sacrifice. However, there is also a type of defilement — moral impurity — that results from immoral behaviour.[4]

Each of these major terms — holy and pure — has its own opposite, making two distinct pairs of antonyms (cf. Lev 10:10; 11:47; Ezek 22:26; 42:20; 44:23): "holy" (קָדוֹשׁ, ἅγιος) and "profane" or "common" (חל, κοινός or βέβηλος); "pure" or "clean" (טהור, καθαρός) and "impure" or "unclean" (טמא, ἀκάθαρτος). For the sake of clarity, I shall restrict my English usage in this essay to "holy" and "profane," "pure" and "impure." Corresponding to each of these pairs of antonyms are two verbs, describing the movement from one state to the other. To make the profane holy is to "consecrate" or to "sanctify" (קדשׁ, ἁγιάζειν or ἁγίζειν),[5] while to make the holy profane is to "desecrate" or to "profane" (חלל, βεβηλοῦν). To make the pure impure is to "defile" or to "pollute" (טמא, μιαίνειν), while to make the impure pure is to "purify" (טהר, καθαρίζειν). We can represent these relationships by two diagrams:[6]

	< consecrate <			< purify <	
holy		profane	pure		impure
	> profane >			> defile >	

These show the way in which the two distinct systems of holiness/profanity and purity/impurity operate. But the systems are also related. All holy things are

---

4. On this generally neglected category, see especially J. Klawans, *Impurity and Sin in Ancient Judaism* (Oxford: Oxford University Press, 2000).

5. Jewish and early Christian Greek generally use ἁγιάζειν, which is otherwise rare, in place of the otherwise more common ἁγίζειν.

6. The diagrams are adapted from G. J. Wenham, *Leviticus*, NICOT (Grand Rapids: Eerdmans, 1979), p. 19.

also pure, and all profane things are either pure or impure. The relationship can be expressed in a combination of the two diagrams,[7] thus:

```
      < consecrate <                        < purify <
  holy                    profane & pure                 impure
        > profane >                         > defile >
```

From this diagram it appears that the state of being profane and pure is midway between holiness and impurity. It is the normal state of most persons and things. From this state it is possible to be elevated to holiness or degraded to impurity. The impure cannot become holy without first becoming pure, but the two processes involved — purification from impurity and consecration as holy — are distinct.[8] The impure should not come into contact with the holy and cannot do so without fearful results. If something holy is defiled, it is necessarily also profaned.

We are now in a position to distinguish John's use of these two sets of terms — those relating to holiness and those relating to purity. Three times he refers to Jewish practices of preserving purity (18:28)[9] and removing impurity (2:6; 3:25).[10] These references are simply matters of historical explanation.[11] But on two other occasions John refers to the purification of Jesus' disciples from the moral impurity caused by sin. Both are instances of John's frequent use of double meaning: using a term that has both an obvious, literal sense, but also an overtone of spiritual meaning. The first instance is when Jesus washes his disciples' feet. The word "clean" or "pure" (καθαρός) in 13:10-11 refers, on the

7. This diagram is adapted from Wenham, *Leviticus*, p. 19.

8. Some New Testament scholars speak of sanctification or consecration as including purification (e.g., H. Stettler, "Sanctification in the Jesus Tradition," *Biblica* 85 [2004]: 159). But for the sake of clarity and conformity with Old Testament usage it is better to see purification as (in the case of impure persons or things) a necessary precondition or presupposition for consecration.

9. On the reasons why the chief priests may have feared defilement if they entered the praetorium, see R. Bauckham, "James, Peter, and the Gentiles," in *The Missions of James, Peter, and Paul*, ed. B. Chilton and C. Evans, NovTSup 115 (Leiden: Brill, 2005), pp. 91-116. It is probably not the case that Gentiles or their houses were regarded as *ipso facto* ritually impure, but the chief priests may have feared contamination from the idolatry practised in the praetorium or simply have been exercising extreme caution, as priests who must officiate at the Passover, to avoid any possible source of impurity, such as human corpses or those of unclean animals.

10. In this case, it may be that the dispute is over whether John's baptism purifies from moral impurity (for this as John the Baptist's interpretation of his practice of baptizing, see Klawans, *Impurity*, pp. 138-43), but the Gospel writer does not explain the point.

11. I disagree with the common view that the reference to purification in 2:6 has something to do with the meaning of the miracle at Cana.

literal level, to the cleanness of the body after it has been washed, but also, on a symbolic level, to the state of disciples who have been purified of sin by the forgiveness that Jesus' death is to procure for them.[12] Washing — especially the total immersion of which Jesus speaks in verse 10 — is an appropriate symbol for this purification because washing was in many cases the form of ritual prescribed in the Torah for the removal of ritual impurity. But it was not a means of purification from moral impurity, and so it here functions symbolically.[13] The second instance is in 15:2-3, where the language of purification (καθαρίζειν and καθαρός) presumably refers, on a literal level, to pruning the vine,[14] but on a symbolic level it parallels 13:10. In 15:3 Jesus interprets the parabolic image to mean that the disciples have been purified (from sin) by his word.

These passages raise many questions we cannot answer here. What is important for our purpose is that, in line with biblical and Jewish ideas of purity and holiness, John understands the disciples to be purified from sin prior to their consecration to be holy (17:17-19). Purity is a presupposition for holiness but it is not the same thing. We might speak of a retrospective and a prospective aspect of salvation: purification deals with the entail of past sin, consecration with dedication to the service of God in the future.

The Festival of Hanukkah (John 10:22)

It is in the context of the Temple at the festival of Hanukkah that Jesus in John's Gospel first uses the language of holiness, claiming that he is "the one the Father has consecrated (ἡγίασεν) and sent into the world" (10:36). Just as on other occasions in this Gospel Jesus' words relate to the themes associated with the festival he is attending in the Temple,[15] so many scholars have postulated a connection between Jesus' reference to his consecration by the Father and the theme of the festival of Hanukkah.[16]

---

12. For this understanding of the footwashing, see R. Bauckham, "Did Jesus Wash His Disciples' Feet?" in *Authenticating the Activities of Jesus,* ed. B. Chilton and C. A. Evans, NTTS 28, 2 (Leiden: Brill, 1999), pp. 414-18.

13. This is also the case in Ezek 36:25, which may be in the background to this passage.

14. The choice of the word καθαρίζειν (v. 2), not the most natural for viticulture, is probably determined by the symbolic meaning given to the image in v. 3. See C. S. Keener, *The Gospel of John,* vol. 2 (Peabody, Mass.: Hendrickson, 2003), p. 996.

15. Besides the commentaries, see G. A. Yee, *Jewish Feasts and the Gospel of John* (Wilmington, Del.: Michael Glazier, 1989); M. L. Coloe, *God Dwells With Us: Temple Symbolism in the Fourth Gospel* (Collegeville, Minn.: Liturgical Press, 2001), chaps. 6–7.

16. According to F. J. Moloney, *The Gospel of John,* SP (Collegeville, Minn.: Liturgical Press, 1998), p. 321, "Very few scholars make the link between the description of Jesus as 'conse-

Hanukkah, the most recently established of the Temple festivals and the only one not authorized in the Hebrew Bible, was also unique in being a festival that celebrated the Temple itself. It commemorated the restoration of the Temple to the worship of YHWH in the year 165 or 164 BCE,[17] following its profanation, two or three years earlier, by order of Antiochus IV Epiphanes. As part of his general proscription of specifically Jewish religious practices, Antiochus had made the Jerusalem Temple a centre of a pagan cult, for which an altar had been erected over the altar of burnt offering. This pagan altar was known as the "desolating sacrilege" (1 Macc 1:54: βδέλυγμα ἐρημώσεως; cf. Dan 11:31; 12:11). The restoration of the Temple to the worship of YHWH was accomplished by Judas Maccabaeus, when he had defeated the Syrian army sufficiently for him to gain control over the Temple. It included the purification of the Temple from the defilements of pagan worship, the removal of the defiled and desecrated altar of burnt offering and the installation of a new altar, the reconsecration of the Temple to YHWH's service, and the inauguration of sacrifices on the new altar of burnt offering. This recommencing of sacrifice to YHWH occurred on the same date (25 Chislev) as that on which pagan sacrifices had begun to be offered on the "desolating sacrilege" (1 Macc 1:59; 4:52-54). The festival celebrating this restoration of sacrifice lasted eight days from 25 Chislev (1 Macc 4:52-58). The Maccabees decreed that a festival on these dates should henceforth take place annually (1 Macc 4:59).

From the point of view of the cultic acts involved, what Judas Maccabaeus had done to the Temple entailed three processes: (1) the purification of the Temple from defilement; (2) the (re-)consecration of the Temple to YHWH, after its

---

crated' and the celebration of the Dedication." But at least since 1990 it has become common to recognize the link. Scholars who do so include E. C. Hoskyns, *The Fourth Gospel,* rev. ed. (London: Faber & Faber, 1947), p. 385; R. E. Brown, *The Gospel according to John (I–XII),* AB 29 (New York: Doubleday, 1966), pp. 400, 411; G. R. Beasley-Murray, *John,* WBC 36 (Waco: Word Books, 1987), p. 177; Yee, *Jewish Feasts,* p. 91; D. A. Carson, *The Gospel according to John* (Leicester/Grand Rapids: InterVarsity/Eerdmans, 1991), p. 399; C. H. Talbert, *Reading John* (London: SPCK, 1992), p. 165; M. W. G. Stibbe, *John,* Readings (Sheffield: Sheffield Academic Press, 1993), pp. 118-19; B. Witherington, *John's Wisdom* (Louisville: Westminster John Knox, 1995), p. 191; F. J. Moloney, *Signs and Shadows: Reading John 5–12* (Minneapolis: Fortress, 1996), pp 149-50; Coloe, *God Dwells With Us,* chap. 7; C. S. Keener, *The Gospel of John,* vol. 1 (Peabody, Mass.: Hendrickson, 2003), pp. 822, 830; C. G. Kruse, *The Gospel according to John,* TNTC (Leicester: InterVarsity, 2003), p. 244; A. J. Köstenberger, *John,* BECNT (Grand Rapids: Baker, 2004), p. 316. It is remarkable that A. Guilding, *The Fourth Gospel and Jewish Worship* (Oxford: Clarendon, 1960) chap. 9, in a chapter devoted to the relationship between the "Feast of the Dedication" and the Gospel of John, made no reference to 10:36.

17. For discussion of the date and an argument for December 165, see J. VanderKam, "Hanukkah: Its Timing and Significance to 1 and 2 Maccabees," *Journal for the Study of the Pseudepigrapha* 1 (1987): 23-40.

profanation; (3) the restoration of sacrificial worship in the Temple. The account in 1 Maccabees 4:36-59 (the fullest account we have) includes all three of these elements, and uses the standard vocabulary for each. In the case of (1) and (2) our discussion of purity and holiness now enables us to distinguish the two and to recognize the characteristic vocabulary appropriate to each. The Gentiles had both profaned (βεβηλοῦν: 4:38, 44, 54) and defiled (μιαίνειν: 4:45) the altar. The Jews purified (καθαρίζειν: 4:36, 41, 43) the sanctuary and (re-)consecrated (ἁγιάζειν: 4:48) the courts of the Temple. It is notable that the emphasis is on the profaned and defiled altar. This is not, however, specifically said to be purified, because what happened was that the pagan altar was removed, the old altar of burnt offering was also removed and put into store, and a new altar was built (4:44-47). Apparently they did not know how to purify and to reconsecrate the old altar, but stored it with a view to a day when a prophet who could say what should be done with it would arise. As to the second of the necessary cultic acts, consecration, the account refers specifically only to the consecration of the Temple courts. We should probably assume that the consecration of the new cultic objects, including the altar of burnt offering as well as the altar of incense, the lampstand, the table for the bread of the presence, and the holy vessels (4:49), is taken for granted as part of their installation. The sanctuary building was also reconstructed (4:48). The consecration of the courts is probably singled out for mention precisely because they were not, like most of the temple and its furniture, new.

Following purification and consecration, which included the installation of a new altar of burnt offering, the third stage was the inauguration of sacrificial worship at the new altar. For this the account in 1 Maccabees uses the verb ἐγκαινίζειν (4:36, 54; 5:1) and the noun ἐγκαινισμός (4:56, 59), which in English versions of this passage are usually translated "to dedicate" and "dedication" (so, e.g., NRSV, JB; NEB has "to rededicate" and "rededication"),[18] but these translations are at best misleading, at worst incorrect. These English words suggest dedication to the service of God, which is the action we have called consecration. What is really meant by ἐγκαινίζειν and ἐγκαινισμός is "to inaugurate" and "inauguration." These are the plain meanings of the Greek words (from καινός, "new"), and they are also required by the context in 1 Maccabees, where what happens, when the new altar is "inaugurated," is that sacrifices are offered on it (4:53, 56). The altar is not dedicated but inaugurated

18. J. A. Goldstein, *I Maccabees,* AB 41 (New York: Doubleday, 1976), pp. 272-73, 287, uses "restore" in 4:36 and 5:1, but "dedicate" in 4:54 and "dedication" in 4:56, 59. He supposes that ἐγκαινίζειν can have both meanings and that it is used here to translate more than one Hebrew root (284). This is mistaken both in thinking that the Hebrew חנך means "to dedicate" (see below) and that the Greek verb has both meanings.

by means of its first use. This is what took place on 25 Chislev, the very day on which the old altar had been profaned through the offering of the first pagan sacrifices on the "desolating sacrilege" (1:59; 4:53-54). The parallel between the two is that in each case sacrifices were first offered on a new altar. Both the altar and the sanctuary could be said to be "inaugurated" (altar: 4:54, 56, 59; sanctuary: 4:36; 5:1) because worship in the sanctuary focused on the sacrifices on the altar of burnt offering. In both cases the reference is to the inauguration of sacrifices on the new altar. (Note also that the meaning "to inaugurate" suits very well the two New Testament occurrences of ἐγκαινίζειν: Heb 9:19; 10:20, both with cultic reference.)

The reason that ἐγκαινίζειν has usually been translated "to dedicate" is not because of any evidence of Greek usage but because it has correctly been seen as a translation of the Hebrew root חנך.[19] This is the root from which the word Hanukkah (חנכה or חנוכה), the most common name for the festival, is derived. חנך has usually been understood to mean "to dedicate" and major reference works[20] still give this meaning, even though as long ago as 1972 S. C. Reif demonstrated it to be incorrect.[21] If "to dedicate" is understood in English to mean "to set apart for God," "to consecrate to sacred use," then it is a misleading translation of חנך. This Hebrew verb means "to use for the first time," "to initiate the use of." (As a compact translation I prefer "inaugurate" to Reif's "initiate," which has inappropriate connotations in English.) An instructive parallel to the events of the first Hanukkah is the use of חנך in 1 Kgs 8:63, in the account of Solomon's inauguration of the Temple. We are told that Solomon offered a vast number of sacrifices, and in this way he "and all the people of Israel inaugurated (ויחנכו) the house of YHWH." We then learn that, because the great bronze altar of burnt offering was not able to cope with all the sacrifices, Solomon "consecrated (קדש) the middle of the court that was in front of the house of YHWH" (8:64). Thus, as Jacob Milgrom explains,

19. Cf. Brown, *The Gospel according to John (I–XII)*, p. 402. In LXX (where there is an extant Hebrew *Vorlage*) ἐγκαινίζειν translates חנכ four times, while four different nouns formed from ἐγκαινίζειν are used to translate חנכה fifteen times. ἐγκαινίζειν is used three times to translate the Piel of חדש ("to renew, to restore").

20. E.g., D. J. A. Clines, ed., *The Dictionary of Classical Hebrew*, vol. 3 (Sheffield: Sheffield Academic Press, 1996), p. 271. W. Dommershausen, writing on חנך in *Theological Dictionary of the Old Testament*, vol. 5, ed. Johannes Botterweck and Helmer Ringgren (Grand Rapids: Eerdmans, 1986) correctly recognizes that the basic meaning is "to use for the first time," "to initiate" (19-20), but goes on to discuss it as though this were no different from "to dedicate" (20-21).

21. S. C. Reif, "Dedicated to חנך," *Vetus Testamentum* 22 (1972): 495-501. Reif's case is strongly endorsed by J. Milgrom, *Leviticus 1–16*, AB 3 (New York: Doubleday, 1991), pp. 592-95.

before Solomon could make the area around the altar an extension of the altar he had to consecrate it. By the same token one can assume that before Solomon could initiate the use *(ḥnk)* of the Temple, he first had to consecrate it *(qdš)*.[22]

The parallel account in 2 Chronicles goes on to add that "they sacrificed the initiation offering (חנכת המזבח) for the altar seven days" (7:9; see also 2 Macc 2:9: Solomon "offered sacrifice for the inauguration [ἐγκαινισμοῦ] and completion [τελειώσεως] of the temple.")

Milgrom finds the same sequence of consecration (קדש) followed by initiation of use or inauguration (חנך) in the case of the Tabernacle in the wilderness. First Moses anointed (the usual means of consecration) and consecrated the Tabernacle and the altar with all their accoutrements (Num 7:1). Then the heads of the tribes brought their offerings, which are called "initiation offerings for the altar" (חנכת המזבח: Num 7:10, 11, 84, 88). These were gifts not for the consecration (dedication) of the altar but for the next ceremonial stage, the inauguration, when these offerings would be offered on the altar of burnt offering, thus initiating its use.[23] In the account of the consecration of the priests, the Tabernacle, and the altar in Leviticus 8–9 the word חנך is not used, but there is the same sequence of consecration by anointing (8:1, 10-12, 30) and then inauguration by first use (9:1-24). The latter takes the form of Aaron offering one of each type of sacrifice on the consecrated altar.[24] Another instance where חנכה refers to the inauguration of the Temple's sacrificial services is in the case of the Second Temple in Ezra 6:16-17.

It is likely that the precedents of the inauguration of the Tabernacle and especially its altar as well as the inauguration of Solomon's Temple lie behind the account of Judas Maccabaeus's restoration of the Temple in 1 Macc 4:41-59. The fact that the latter speaks only once of consecration (ἡγίασαν) and with the Temple courts (τὰς αὐλάς) as its object (4:48) may reflect 1 Kgs 8:64, where Solomon consecrates (קדש, LXX ἡγίασαν) the middle of the Temple court (LXX τῆς αὐλῆς) and this is the only act of consecration explicitly mentioned.

Our conclusions about the distinction between consecration and inauguration can be confirmed by study of Josephus's account of the restoration of the Temple by Judas Maccabaeus (*Ant.* 12.316-326). This is based on the account in 1 Maccabees, but Josephus varies the key vocabulary. For the two stages on which 1 Maccabees focuses, purification and inauguration, Josephus uses the

22. Milgrom, *Leviticus 1–16*, p. 593. For God's consecration (ἁγιάζειν) of Solomon's Temple, see also 3 Macc 2:9, 16.
23. Milgrom, *Leviticus 1–16*, p. 593.
24. Cf. Milgrom, *Leviticus 1–16*, pp. 542-44, 571, 592-93.

verb ἁγνίζειν (not to be confused with ἁγίζειν or ἁγιάζειν!)[25] as well as καθαρίζειν where 1 Maccabees has καθαρίζειν, and, where 1 Maccabees uses ἐγκαινίζειν (translating חנכ), Josephus has the two verbs ἀνανεοῦν ("to renew") and ἀνακτίζειν ("to re-establish"). What Josephus says were renewed or re-established are variously the Temple itself, the sacrifices, the customs (τῶν ἐθῶν, evidently meaning the sacrificial practices) and the Temple service (τῶν περὶ τὸν ναόν). Clearly, Josephus has understood ἐγκαινίζειν and ἐγκαινισμός in 1 Maccabees in the way we have argued it should be understood: as referring to the re-commencement of sacrificial worship in the Temple, centred on the sacrifices offered on the new altar of burnt offering. This, Josephus claims, is what happened on 25 Chislev, continued for eight days, and is commemorated annually in the Temple on these dates thereafter. Why has he not used the terms ἐγκαινίζειν and ἐγκαινισμός, preferring the verbs ἀνανεοῦν ("to renew") and ἀνακτίζειν ("to re-establish")? The answer is probably that ἐγκαινίζειν and ἐγκαινισμός, strictly understood, suggest innovation rather than renovation or restoration. Since Josephus's whole account stresses that what happened was the restoration of the sacrificial worship as it had been before the desecration by Antiochus Epiphanes, he probably thought verbs with the prefix ἀνα ("re-") more appropriate.

Josephus does make one significant change to the account of events in this passage of 1 Maccabees. According to the latter, the priests offered incense on the new altar of incense, lit the lamps on the new lampstand, and set out the bread of the presence on the table before 25 Chislev (4:50-51), whereas the sacrifices on the altar of burnt offering commenced only on 25 Chislev. This makes the former actions not properly part of the inauguration, which is therefore restricted to the commencement of use of the altar of burnt offering and does not include the resumption of more minor aspects of the Temple worship. Josephus, however, says that on the 25 Chislev all these activities recommenced: they lit the lights of the lampstand, burned incense, set out the bread on the table, and offered burnt-offerings on the altar (*Ant.* 12.319). Not only does Josephus re-date the first three of these acts to 25 Chislev, he also brings the kindling of lights on the lampstand forward into first place in the list. This must be connected with the fact that Josephus calls the annual commemorative festival not Hanukkah but "lights" (φῶτα). He himself explains this name "from the fact that the right to worship appeared (φανῆναι) to us at a time when we hardly dared hope for it" (*Ant.* 12.325). But his placement of the lighting of the lampstand as the first act on 25 Chislev shows that Josephus is certainly not ignorant of the more obvious

25. LXX occasionally uses ἁγνίζειν to translate טהר, which is more commonly translated καθαρίζειν.

connection of the name "Lights" with the lights that were doubtless in his day lit on the first day of the festival in the Temple. (Whether the practice of lighting lamps in homes had already begun we cannot be so sure. This, the later usual way of observing Hanukkah [*b. Shabb.* 21b], may have begun only some time after the loss of the Temple in 70 CE.)[26] Not content with this obvious explanation, Josephus has added an explanation that relates to the historic significance of the original restoration of the Temple worship. But "Lights" was doubtless a popular name for the festival, alluding to a ceremony of lamp-lighting with which the festival began, whereas Hanukkah, "Inauguration," was the more original and official name, describing the meaning of the festival.

Several names for the festival are attested in the literature. The Hebrew name (the days of) Hanukkah (חנכה) is first attested directly in the first century CE, in *Megillat Ta'anit* (which forbids fasting on the eight days of Hanukkah). But there can be no doubt that it is this Hebrew word that is translated into Greek as ἐγκαινισμός in 1 Maccabees (4:56, 59) and as ἐγκαινία in John 10:22 (the plural form is common for festivals in Greek). In 1 Maccabees the name of the festival is (the days of) the Inauguration of the Altar (ὁ ἐγκαινισμὸς τοῦ θυσιαστηριοῦ), for which the Inauguration (Hanukkah) was doubtless an abbreviation. But the second of the two letters prefixed to 2 Maccabees (1:10–2:18) calls the festival the Purification of the Temple (1:18: ὁ καθαρισμὸς τοῦ ἱεροῦ) or, more briefly, the Purification (2:16).[27] This concurs with the way the rather summarized account of the events in 2 Maccabees (10:1-8) calls what happened on 25 Chislev not the inauguration or restoration, but the purification (καθαρισμός: 10:5, cf. 7). This account seems to use "purification" as an overall description of all that was done to the Temple (cf. also 14:36), and presumably means that the climax of the work was the completion of the purification on 25 Chislev. Perhaps the Purification was the name of the festival used in Egypt, where 2 Maccabees, an abridgement of the work of Jason of Cyrene, probably originated.[28] Since it was the sanctuary that was puri-

26. The supposition of S. Zeitlin, "Hanukkah: Its Origin and Significance," *Jewish Quarterly Review* 29 (1938-39): 8-9, that before 70 CE the people celebrated Hanukkah by marching through the streets with torches — a form of nationalistic celebration of the Maccabean liberation of Israel from the Syrians — and that later, for political reasons, this was transmuted into the custom of lighting lamps at home, seems to be pure speculation, while the distinction he makes between a religious festival and a political one is a misapprehension of the relationship between politics and religion in this period.

27. J. A. Goldstein, *II Maccabees,* AB 41A (New York: Doubleday, 1984), p. 171, is probably right to claim that, following ἄγειν, these terms should be understood as the proper name of a festival.

28. T. Fischer, "First and Second Maccabees," in *Anchor Bible Dictionary,* vol. 4, ed. D. N. Freedman et al. (New York: Doubleday, 1992), p. 443.

fied, while the altar was not purified but replaced, this name rather shifts the focus of the festival from the altar (as in 1 Maccabees) to the Temple. We should note, however, that 2 Maccabees also preserves the name found in 1 Maccabees alongside its distinctive name when it announces the contents of the work: "the purification (καθαρισμόν) of the great temple and the inauguration of the altar (τὸν τοῦ βωμοῦ ἐγκαινισμόν)" (2:19). The author probably knows that the Inauguration of the Altar was the original and standard name for the festival.

More remarkable is the way the first of the two letters prefixed to 2 Maccabees (1:1-9) apparently calls Hanukkah "the days of Tabernacles in the month of Chislev" (1:9; cf. 1:18). Evidently the eight days of Hanukkah could be thought to resemble the eight days of Tabernacles, with some of the ceremonies of the latter used for the former (2 Macc 10:6-7), though the most characteristic feature of Tabernacles, the booths themselves, did not recur at Hanukkah.[29] It may be because of this association of the two festivals that the theme of light, with appropriate ceremonial in the Temple, came to be part of the celebration of Tabernacles too (and is echoed in that context in John 8:12). In rabbinic times at least the Hallel psalms (Pss 113–118) were part of the liturgy of both festivals.[30]

In conclusion to this section, we can be fairly confident that by the first century CE the official name of the festival was the Days of the Inauguration of the Altar, or Inauguration (Hanukkah) for short. The latter would be the most appropriate translation of ἐγκαινία in John 10:22.

Jesus the New Altar (John 10:36)

Scholars who have made a connexion between Jesus' use of the word "consecrate" (ἁγιάζειν) in John 10:36 and the fact that he is speaking at the festival of Hanukkah (10:22: ἐγκαινία) have relied on the misleading translation of the latter as "Dedication" in all English versions, and taken the two Greek words to refer to the same action of consecration or dedication. Now that we have established that "Inauguration" (short for "Inauguration of the Altar") would be a better translation of the name of the festival, we must understand the connexion differently. Jesus' consecration by the Father is to be seen as parallel not to the inauguration of the Temple or altar but to the consecration of the Temple or altar that would have preceded the inauguration. Of the three ritual stages of Judas Maccabaeus's restoration of the Temple — (1) purification,

---

29. VanderKam, "Hanukkah," pp. 32-34.
30. See J. VanderKam, "Dedication, Feast of," in *Anchor Bible Dictionary,* vol. 2, p. 124.

(2) consecration, (3) inauguration by first use — the name of the festival refers to the third, but Jesus' consecration is equivalent to the second.

Scholars who have taken ἁγιάζειν as equivalent to the action indicated by the title of the festival have pointed out that John could not have used the verb ἐγκαινίζειν in 10:36 because it would be very unnatural to use this verb with a person as the object, whereas ἁγιάζειν can properly used of the consecration of a person (for example, of Aaron: Lev 8:12 LXX).[31] This is correct, but once we recognize the distinction between consecration and inauguration, there is a further reason why it is the former that is applied to Jesus, not the latter. The inauguration to which the festival's title refers was accomplished by the offering of sacrifices for the first time on the new altar of burnt offering. We have seen that the title "Inauguration" properly referred to the inauguration of the new altar by its first use, but even if it were applied more loosely to the Temple as a whole and the inauguration of worship in it, the focus of this worship would still be sacrifice on the altar of burnt-offering. If Jesus is treated symbolically as the new Temple or the new Altar, sacrifice "in" or "on" him could not be a fact of the past, but an event still in the future at this point in John's narrative. God has already consecrated Jesus to be the place of sacrifice, but the sacrifice has not yet been offered.

The reference to Jesus' consecration in the context of the feast of Hanukkah must certainly be connected with the theme of Jesus as the new Temple, fulfilling the meaning of the Jerusalem Temple with eschatological newness, that runs prominently through the Gospel of John and has been highlighted in, among others, the passages which portray Jesus in the Jerusalem Temple at other major festivals: Passover (2:13-22) and Tabernacles (7:37-39; 8:12).[32] For understanding this theme it is important to remember the two key and interrelated features of the meaning of the Jerusalem Temple: it was the place in which God was graciously present for his people in their midst, and it was the place of the sacrifices that, also in God's grace, enabled access by God's people to his presence in the Temple. Jesus is the eschatological fulfilment of these features in being both the new "place" of God's dwelling with his people and also the sacrifice, the final once-for-all sacrifice, that enables this presence of God among his people. While the two features are closely related, John's use of the symbolism of Hanukkah does not, as some scholars have argued, relate to Jesus as the new presence of God with his people but to the sacrifice he is going to offer when he is next in Jerusalem. In typically Johannine fashion there are references forward

31. E.g., Hoskyns, *The Fourth Gospel*, p. 392.
32. See especially Coloe, *God Dwells With Us*, chaps. 4 and 6 and the discussion of these passages in Keener, *The Gospel of John*, pp. 517-31, 721-30, 738-42.

to the death and resurrection of Jesus on the two previous occasions when the new Temple theme is evoked in the context of Temple festivals (2:19-22; 7:37-39) but in neither case is the imagery explicitly sacrificial. John reserves this for the last occasion when Jesus is in the Temple prior to his death as the new Passover lamb on his last visit to Jerusalem. The occurrence of Hanukkah between Tabernacles and Passover makes it very appropriate for this purpose.

Hanukkah was unique as a Temple festival whose theme was the Temple itself. But the festival did not focus on God's presence as such but on the sacrificial worship. Whereas in the accounts of Solomon's inauguration of the first Temple the visible presence of God's glory is the main focus (1 Kgs 8:10-13; 2 Chron 5:13-14; cf. 2 Macc 2:8; 3 Macc 2:9; and similarly for the Tabernacle: Exod 40:34-38), there is no reference to the presence of God in the Temple in the accounts of Judas Maccabaeus's restoration of the second Temple. There is no suggestion that the presence of God departed from the Temple when it was desecrated and returned when sacrificial worship was resumed.[33] We must therefore reject the interpretation of John 10:36 offered by Mary Coloe, that, just as "in the Tabernacle and the Temple, God's glory dwells in [Jesus], consecrating him as a new House of God."[34] The thought here is not of Jesus as God's presence but of Jesus as the one God has consecrated for the offering of sacrifice. Probably we should think not of his consecration to be the Temple as the place of sacrifice, but more specifically of his consecration as the new altar of burnt-offering. Just as the altar installed by Judas Maccabaeus was a new one, so is Jesus the eschatologically new altar on which the final sacrifice is to be offered, not yet but soon, within the narrative time of the Gospel.[35]

Jesus' consecration to God's service is the reason for the title "the Holy One of God" that Peter ascribes to him in 6:69. The most characteristic way of making something or someone holy was anointing with oil (e.g., Exod 29:36; 40:10; Num 7:1 [these refer to the altar of burnt offering]; Exod 30:23-30; Lev 8:12; 16:32). Conversely, the significance of anointing is that it consecrates some-

---

33. For the (rather sparse) evidence that God was thought to inhabit the second Temple as well as the first, see G. I. Davies, "The Presence of God in the Second Temple and Rabbinic Doctrine," in *Templum Amicitiae: Essays on the Second Temple Presented to Ernst Bammel*, JSNTSup 48, ed. W. Horbury (Sheffield: Sheffield Academic Press, 1991), pp. 32-36.

34. Coloe, *God Dwells With Us*, p. 153.

35. Various other suggestions of ways in which John 10:22-39 (and perhaps also chap. 11) echoes Hanukkah themes have been made: see Keener, *The Gospel of John*, vol. 1, pp. 821-23; E. Nodet, "La Dédicace, les Maccabées et le Messie," *Revue biblique* 93 (1986): 321-75; S. Motyer, *Your Father the Devil? A New Approach to John and the 'Jews,'* PBTM (Carlisle: Paternoster, 1997), pp. 124-25. These are less certain and not so directly related to our present theme of holiness, and so will not be discussed here.

one, sets them apart for God's service, makes them belong to the God whom the Hebrew Bible often calls "the Holy One." Aaron was called "the holy one of God" (Ps 106:16) and Elisha "the holy man of God" (2 Kgs 4:9) because they had been anointed with oil. The Messiah, i.e. "the Anointed One" (and note that John makes sure his readers know what Messiah means: 1:41), or, more properly, "the Lord's Anointed One," is therefore by definition also "the Holy One of God." Though this is not attested as a messianic title in early Jewish literature, it is such a natural usage that we may probably assume it was used in that way. John 6:69 is the Johannine equivalent of the confession of Peter in the Synoptics, where Peter confesses Jesus to be the Messiah (Matt 16:16; Mark 8:29; Luke 9:20). John's variation, "the Holy One of God," belongs to his tactic of running through a whole series of messianic titles at various points in his Gospel in order to apply all of them to Jesus (cf. 1:29, 34, 41, 45, 49; 4:42; 11:27; 20:28).[36] But it also creates a link with 10:36. It becomes clear that John places Jesus' anointing as Messiah prior to his coming into the world[37] and that he connects it especially with Jesus' mission to glorify God by sacrificial death.

From Christology to Ecclesiology

There are a series of close parallels between what Jesus says to "the Jews" at Hanukkah (10:23-38) and Jesus' prayer to the Father in chapter 17. The most important of these (listed in the table below) occur in the statements Jesus makes about himself and his relation to the Father in chapter 10 and in statements about the disciples and their relation to Jesus and the Father in chapter 17. The parallels are appropriate, since 10:23-38 is the last of the occasions on which Jesus debates his own identity with the Jewish authorities in the Temple, while chapter 17, following on chapters 14–16, concludes the part of the Gospel devoted to Jesus' teaching to and about his own disciples. The christological claims of chapters 2–10 come to a climax with those at Hanukkah: "I and the Father are one" (10:30) and "The Father is in me and I am in the Father" (10:38). Both become the basis for key requests that Jesus makes for his disciples in prayer to the Father, asking in each case that something true of Jesus and the

---

36. In the Synoptics, Jesus is called "the Holy One of God" only by the unclean spirit (Mark 1:24; Luke 4:34). In context, the title is very appropriate, not because "holy" "is roughly synonymous with 'clean' . . . and the antonym of 'unclean'" (J. Marcus, *Mark 1–8*, AB 27 [New York: Doubleday, 2000], p. 188), but because the impure (unclean) should never come into contact with the holy or must suffer fearful consequences if it does. The demon fears Jesus most of all because he is "the Holy One of God."

37. For a limited parallel, see Jer 1:5.

Father should also be true for the disciples. It is characteristic of this Gospel that Jesus takes the relation he has to the Father as a model for the way the disciples relate to himself (and the Father) (cf. 13:20; 20:21).[38]

John 10	John 17
(30) The Father and I are one.	(11) so that they may be one as we are one
	(21) that they may all be one
	(22) so that they may be one as we are one
	(23) so that they may be completely one
(36) the one whom the Father has consecrated	(17) Consecrate them in truth
	(19) And for their sakes I consecrate myself, so that they also may be consecrated in truth
and sent into the world	(18) As you have sent me into the world, I have sent them into the world
	(21) so that the world may believe that you have sent me (cf. 3, 8)
	(23) so that the world may know that you have sent me and have loved them even as you have loved me
(38) the Father is in me and I am in the Father	(21) As you, Father, are in me and I am in you, may they also be in us
	(23) I in them and you in me
	(26) so that the love with which you have loved me may be in them, and I in them

The most significant christological statement in Jesus' words at Hanukkah, other than the two claims to unity with the Father, is the one we have been considering: Jesus as "the one whom the Father has consecrated and sent into the world" (10:36). That the Father has sent Jesus into the world is, of course, stated repeatedly throughout the Gospel, but here it is conjoined with the much more unusual claim that Jesus has been consecrated by the Father. It is very notable that the only other uses of the verb "to consecrate" (ἁγιάζειν) are the cluster of three occurrences in 17:17-19, and that there too there is a close connection between being consecrated and being sent.

Before turning to the consecration of the disciples, we must note that here

---

38. Cf. A. J. Köstenberger, *The Missions of Jesus and the Disciples according to the Fourth Gospel* (Grand Rapids: Eerdmans, 1998), pp. 186-97; J. Ferreira, *Johannine Ecclesiology,* JSNTSup 160 (Sheffield: Sheffield Academic Press, 1998), chap. 6.

it is not said that the Father has consecrated Jesus, but that Jesus consecrates himself (17:19).[39] These are complementary perspectives: in the Hebrew Bible it can be said both that God consecrates people (e.g., Exod 31:12) and that people consecrate themselves (e.g., Lev 11:44; Num 11:18), and the two can be closely related (Lev 20:7-8). In this case, there is the distinction between the Father's consecration of Jesus, setting him apart for the mission on which he sent him into the world (10:36), and Jesus' appropriation of that mission for himself at the crucial moment when he is going willingly to his death. It is because Jesus' self-consecration leads him to self-sacrifice on the cross that he does it "for the sake of" his disciples, "so that they also may be consecrated in truth" (17:19). By fulfilling the mission for which the Father consecrated him, Jesus makes it possible for his disciples also to be set apart for God's service. At the same time the holiness of the disciples derives from God (17:17), who has been addressed, uniquely, as "Holy Father" at the point where Jesus began to pray for his disciples (17:11).

As "Holy Father" occurs at the beginning of this part of the prayer (17:11b-19),[40] so the prayer for the disciples to be consecrated (17:17-19) forms the climax of the sub-section, making an inclusio between "holy" (ἅγιε) in verse 11 and "consecrated" (ἡγιασμένοι) in verse 19b. Francis Moloney suggests that Jesus here takes up in turn the two words in his address to God as "Holy Father," asking God first, as Father, to exercise his fatherly care in protecting the disciples (17:11b-16), and then, secondly, as *Holy* Father, to make the disciples holy also (17-19).[41] But these two petitions are also closely connected by the theme of the disciples' relationship to "the world," a theme that runs through the whole section from verse 9 to verse 19. Jesus himself is leaving the world, but his disciples remain in it, and it is for his disciples in this situation that Jesus prays (17:11). Like Jesus, they are in the world but not of it, and therefore the world hates them, just as it hated Jesus (17:14). While Jesus was with them he protected them (17:12), but now that he is leaving the world, the Father must protect them

39. It is difficult to decide whether Jesus consecrates himself as the high priest who is to offer sacrifice or as the sacrifice itself. But the latter is more probable, since the theme of Jesus as high priest is not explicitly found elsewhere in the Gospel (but see J. P. Heil, "Jesus as the Unique High Priest in the Gospel of John," *Catholic Biblical Quarterly* 57 [1995]: 729-45), whereas the theme of Jesus as the sacrifice is (1:29, 36). R. E. Brown, *The Gospel according to John (XIII–XXI)*, AB 29A (New York: Doubleday, 1966), pp. 766-67, attempts to combine the two possibilities.

40. For the tripartite structure of the prayer, see Moloney, *The Gospel of John*, pp. 458-59; Ferreira, *Johannine Ecclesiology*, chap. 3. Both scholars follow Jürgen Becker in dividing the prayer thus: (1) Jesus prays for himself (vv. 1-8); (2) Jesus prays for his disciples (vv. 9-19); (3) Jesus prays for future disciples (vv. 20-26). According to this analysis, "Holy Father" (v. 11b) does not open the second section of the prayer, but it does mark the beginning of the sub-section in which what Jesus prays for the disciples is specified.

41. Moloney, *The Gospel of John*, pp. 465-66.

(17:11b, 15). Furthermore, in order to fulfil the mission that is the purpose of their remaining in the world, they need not only protection, but also consecration. Consecration sets them apart from the world, as the holy distinguished from the profane. It puts them, as people devoted to the holy God, on God's side of the distinction between himself and the profane world that does not know him. But this does not take them out of the world (17:15). On the contrary, just as the Father has consecrated Jesus for his mission in the world, so the Father will consecrate the disciples for their mission in the world.

In what does this consecration consist? We have already made clear that it does not include the disciples' purification from sin, which is only a precondition for consecration. The disciples have already been purified from sin (13:10; 15:3), though they continue to need ongoing forgiveness (13:10). Their consecration is still to come, from the point of view of Jesus when he prays 17:17-19. But, even more decisively, their consecration parallels the consecration of Jesus himself, whereas Jesus needs no purification and so the disciples' purification cannot be modelled on his.

The common translation of ἁγιάζειν in this passage as "sanctify" has probably misled many English readers into supposing that the reference is to a process of being made ethically holy (since this is the meaning of "sanctification" in traditional Protestant theology). In fact the reference is to an act of God that consecrates the disciples for his service, though it is an act that results in a state of holiness, i.e. of having-been-set-apart for God (hence the perfect passive participle ἡγιασμένοι in v. 19). But what is the act of consecration? Jesus' request to the Father, "Consecrate them by (or: in) the truth (ἐν τῇ ἀληθείᾳ) (your word is truth)" (17:17), is as difficult to interpret as many other uses of "truth" and "true" in John's Gospel, and there is also a question of whether the phrase "in truth" (ἐν ἀληθείᾳ) in verse 19 should be understood in the same way or simply as "truly" (equivalent to ἀληθῶς). The latter issue makes little difference to the overall sense. In the case of v. 17, an attractive option taken by some commentators[42] is that God consecrates the disciples by giving them his commandment(s) so that they may live lives obedient to him and so be holy. The thought that God has consecrated Israel by giving the commandments is common in rabbinic literature (e.g., *t. Ber.* 5:22; 6:9-14; *b. Shabb.* 137b), but it also makes good sense of the treatment of Israel's holiness in the Torah itself, where what sets Israel apart from the nations is the commandments. God consecrates Israel by giving the commandments, and Israel maintains holiness by keeping them (cf. e.g., Exod 31:13; Lev 11:44-45). Jesus, in his prayer, has already said that he has given his disciples God's word (17:14) and that they have kept it (17:6).

---

42. E.g., Keener, *The Gospel of John,* vol. 2, p. 1060.

Another interpretation of v. 17 is that God consecrates the disciples by means of the word of revelation of himself that Jesus has given them.[43] In this case, the reference backwards would be especially to verse 8.

Yet Jesus *asks* God to consecrate them (17:17). The act is still future, as the fact that the consecration of the disciples follows from Jesus' self-consecration to sacrificial death (17:19) also requires. So a better interpretation may be to understand God's word in v. 17 as simply a word of appointment and commissioning.[44] Then the way is open for us to think that the consecration of the disciples actually takes place in 20:21-23, when the risen Jesus turns his words in 17:18 into an address to the disciples: "As the Father has sent me, so I send you," and endows them with the Holy Spirit.[45] The Spirit is associated with sending here, as consecration is in 17:17-19. Perhaps we can conclude that, while the word of God sets the disciples apart for mission (17:17), the Holy Spirit enables the fulfilment of that holiness in the carrying out of the mission.[46] (Word and Spirit are closely connected in John, and both are connected with truth.) If so, all of this Gospel's holiness language coalesces around the consecration of Jesus and the disciples: The Holy Father consecrates Jesus the Holy One, who consecrates himself so that the disciples also may be consecrated, participating in the holiness of Jesus and the Father through the Holy Spirit.

Conclusion

Holiness is what distinguishes God as "other" than the world, and those who belong to God are thereby also distinguished from the world that does not

43. E.g., C. K. Barrett, *The Gospel according to St John,* 2nd ed. (London: SPCK, 1978), p. 510; B. Lindars, *The Gospel of John,* NCB (London: Oliphants, 1972), p. 528; Carson, *The Gospel according to John,* p. 566. A related view is that this revelation is the sphere in which the disciples are consecrated: H. N. Ridderbos, *The Gospel of John: A Theological Commentary,* trans. J. Vriend (Grand Rapids: Eerdmans, 1997), p. 555; Köstenberger, *John,* pp. 495-96. Brown, *The Gospel according to John (XIII–XXI),* pp. 761-62, implausibly takes the ἐv to mean both "in" and "by." He even allows the meaning "for," which would make excellent sense ("consecrate them for the truth") but is surely not possible.

44. Note that the idea of God's consecrating someone can come close to the idea of God's choosing them: 2 Macc 1:25; Sir 45:4.

45. It is very tempting to link consecration with the Holy Spirit by means of the image of anointing with the Spirit (cf. Acts 10:38), since anointing is a common means of consecrating, but the image in 20:22 is of the Spirit as breath in an act of new creation, not as oil.

46. Some such connexion is made by J. H. Bernard, *A Critical and Exegetical Commentary on the Gospel according to St. John,* vol. 2, ICC (Edinburgh: T&T Clark, 1928), p. 574; Brown, *The Gospel according to John (XIII–XXI),* pp. 766-67; G. M. Burge, *The Anointed Community: The Holy Spirit in the Johannine Tradition* (Grand Rapids: Eerdmans, 1987), p. 202.

know God. Yet God makes them holy, dedicated to him, not in order to remove them from the world, but in order to send them into the world to make God known. Jesus is the Holy One whom God has consecrated for his mission, and, obedient to his Father, Jesus consecrates himself, especially with a view to his self-sacrifice on the cross. The holiness of the disciples relates to that of Jesus in two ways. First, it is because Jesus has accomplished his self-offering that the disciples can also be consecrated. Secondly, they are consecrated in order to continue Jesus' own mission in the world. There is a difference in that the disciples' mission is not to atone for the sin of the world, but it is similar in its demand for costly dedication to the service of God. As holy, the disciples are set apart from the world, but, as in Jesus' case, this consecration is in the service of God's self-giving love for the world. They are distinguished from the world both for God's sake and for the world's own sake.

Holiness in the Book of Acts

I. Howard Marshall

The topic of holiness in the book of Acts is one of those where a study based purely on the occurrences of the specific word-group in the Greek language is likely to lead to disappointed expectations. In popular Christian religious usage "holiness" is one of a number of terms that refer primarily to the spiritual and moral quality of the life of the people of God. But holiness in the Bible (particularly in the Old Testament) is often concerned with aspects of life that are more ritual and formal in character, and we must examine this usage also. However, in order to take proper account of the spiritual and moral aspects of holiness that should characterise God's people it will be necessary to look more widely than in the specific word-field. Accordingly, to study the motif of "holiness" we must look first at the *hagios* word-group, then at the concept of purity, and finally at the way of life of God's holy people.[1]

The *Hagios* Word-Group and Related Material

J. B. Wells notes that "in the book of Acts there are more occurrences of ἅγιος than in all four gospels put together, and the vast majority of these describe the Holy Spirit."[2]

1. For scholarly discussion of the topic see O. E. Evans, *Saints in Christ Jesus: A Study of the Christian Life in the New Testament* (Swansea: John Penry Press, 1975); S. C. Barton, ed., *Holiness Past and Present* (London: T&T Clark, 2003); J. B. Wells, *God's Holy People: A Theme in Biblical Theology,* JSOTSup 305 (Sheffield: Sheffield Academic Press, 2000).

2. Wells, *People,* p. 236. According to MG the adjective *hagios* occurs 55 times in Acts. Three of these references have textual variants: the word should be retained in 4:25 (so UBS text)

It is a joy to present this essay to Alex, whose friendship and fellowship I have treasured since we both sat in Divinity classrooms in Cambridge in 1957-59.

Jesus

Peter describes Jesus himself as "the holy *(hagios)* and righteous One" in Acts 3:14. His point appears to be to make a contrast with Barabbas, the murderer, who was favoured over Jesus as the object of clemency, but the term "righteous" might have been thought sufficient to achieve this effect as is the case in 22:14. The collocation, however, does indicate that "holy" and "righteous" are words with closely related meanings. The same word is also used in 4:27 where the prayer of the church refers to the opposition of Pilate and Herod to God's holy Servant *(pais)* whom he had anointed and then in 4:30 to the position of Jesus as the agent through whom God was working signs and wonders. The usage here brings out more clearly not just the righteous, moral character of Jesus, but his close relationship to God which made him a sacrosanct person. In both cases Jesus is the Servant of God, standing in a special relationship to him as his agent. Thus to reject Jesus was to reject God's representative and thus God himself. In the latter case, (4:30) the reference is specifically to the "name" of God's Servant, a form of expression which establishes the rank of Jesus.[3]

Already at his birth Jesus is described as "holy" in virtue of his conception by the Holy Spirit (Luke 1:35). In a weaker sense every male child is said to be holy to the Lord (Luke 2:23 alluding to Exod 13:12), and in obedience to this command under the old covenant the parents of Jesus carry out the prescribed rite.[4]

Jesus is also described as the Holy One *(hosios)* in two citations of Ps 16:10 (LXX 15:10), the one in Peter's speech in 2:27 and the other in Paul's speech in 13:34.[5] The choice of term is due to the use of the LXX. The word *hosios* is more

---

but omitted in 8:18 and 15:29 (so UBS text). This gives a total of 53 references, 41 of which are to the Holy Spirit. Of the remainder, there are references to Jesus in 3:14; 4:27, 30; the prophets in 3:21; the temple in 6:13; 21:28; the site of the burning bush in 7:33; Christian believers in 9:13, 32, 41; 26:10; and an angel in 10:22. The verb *hagiazō* is used twice in the perfect participle to refer to God's people (20:32; 26:18). The synonym *hosios* is used of Jesus in 2:27 and 13:35 (citing Ps 16:10) and of the "sure mercies" of David in 13:34.

3. The use of "name" in this way is found only of God and Jesus; it indicates powerfully how God and Jesus are seen as functionally equal (H. D. Buckwalter, *The Character and Purpose of Luke's Christology* [Cambridge: Cambridge University Press, 1996], pp. 182-84).

4. Here it may be useful to recognise the existence of different levels of holiness: see P. P. Jenson, *Graded Holiness: A Key to the Priestly Conception of the World* (Sheffield: JSOT Press, 1992).

5. The citation here is immediately preceded by words taken from Isa 55:3, "I will give you the holy and sure blessings promised to David [lit. the holy, sure things of David]." The word translated here as "holy" is the same Greek word, *hosios,* and the word "blessings" has been supplied by the translators. In Ps 16:10 *hosios* translates the Heb. *hasid* ("godly one") and in Isa 55:3 it translates the plural form of Heb. *hesed* (steadfast love). The wordplay in the Greek reflects the fact that the underlying Hebrew words are from the same root.

expressive of an attitude of piety, the trust in God that is expressed in the offering of prayer to him, so that "devout" might be a better English rendering; it does not have the same sense of being called by God and belonging to him that we find in *hagios*. The citation picks up the confident affirmation of the Psalmist that God will not abandon him to Sheol (Gk. Hades) or allow him to experience corruption, and the point is that, if a person puts their confidence in God, then God will preserve them even from death.[6]

People, Places, and Things Associated with God

Other representatives of God are described similarly. The prophets who spoke of the coming Saviour and salvation are "his holy prophets of long ago" (Luke 1:70), a phrase repeated in Acts 3:21 (cf. Wis 11:1). The adjective here seems to be on its way to be simply an indication that the persons so signified are worthy of respect. Luke similarly refers to the temple as "this holy place" (Acts 6:13; 21:28),[7] where the thought is simply that the temple belongs to God and is therefore to be kept from what the Jews regarded as defilement, specifically the entry of non-covenanted people into the area reserved for the covenanted people. The ground around the burning bush is likewise holy (Acts 6:33, citing Exod 3:5), and the covenant made by God is holy (Luke 1:72; cf. Dan 11:28, 30; 1 Macc 1:15, 63). God's angels are holy (Acts 10:22;[8] Luke 9:26) and so is his name (Luke 1:49). All of this material reinforces the non-controversial and familiar fact that "holy" is a term which expresses the nature and status of God as God, and is applied by extension to the people, places, and things that are closely associated with him and are therefore sacrosanct, just as he is. We also note that the element of moral quality is often present in these uses.

All of this may be regarded as traditional language, rooted in OT usage, and important as showing that Luke was familiar with it, and it cannot be left out of reckoning. To a considerable extent this language is found in those parts

---

6. This is not the place to discuss the understanding of death and resurrection here and the way in which the Psalm is understood to refer to the Messiah. For a new proposal see D. P. Moessner, "*Two* Lords 'at the Right Hand'"? The Psalms and an Intertextual Reading of Peter's Pentecost Speech (Acts 2:14-36)," in *Literary Studies in Luke-Acts: Essays in Honor of Joseph B. Tyson*, ed. R. P. Thompson and T. E. Phillips (Macon: Mercer, 1998), pp. 215-32.

7. Compare the way in which Jerusalem is "the holy city" in Matt 4:5 (diff. Luke 4:9); 27:53; cf. Rev 21:2; but the usage is already found in Isa 48:2; 52:1; 66:20; Neh 11:1; Pr Azar 4 (Dan 3:28 LXX); 1 Macc 2:7 et al.

8. One wonders if the point here is that, if a *holy* angel can visit Cornelius, a Gentile, Peter should have no compunctions about visiting him also.

of his narrative where the new covenant is not yet established or, at least is only in process of establishment. There is nothing surprising in the retention of this traditional understanding of God and of the persons and things that are closely associated with him.

God's People

Alongside this material we now have the various occasions where disciples and those who become believers are referred to as "the holy ones" or "the saints." This usage is found in 9:13 (cf. 26:10), where Ananias refers to the way in which Saul had afflicted "your saints in Jerusalem." It is significant in that it refers to the disciples as God's people. This term was already in use for the Jews as the people of God; the OT usage is collective ("the holy people," Isa 62:12), except in Dan 7:27 where it is disputed whether it refers to the Jewish people or to heavenly beings. But Ananias uses it to refer not to the Jewish people as a whole but to the limited group of believers in Jesus. In fact, the reference of "your" is clearly to the Lord Jesus (Acts 9:17) and not to God the Father. So the phrase "your saints," which in Judaism would presumably have been automatically taken to mean "the people of God" here refers to "the people of the Lord Jesus," with the implications that the decisive factor is the relationship to the Lord Jesus and that all those who believe in him are now the people of the Lord,[9] entitled to the designation previously used for Jews in general.[10]

The phrase recurs in 9:32 to refer to believers at Lydda, and 9:41 where "the saints *and* widows" are distinguished; this surely does not mean that the widows were not saints (especially since Tabitha is said to be a disciple), but

---

9. At this stage, however, the reference is simply to the believers in Jerusalem, who were presumably all Jews and proselytes (cf. Acts 6:5).

10. The phrase "saints of God/the Lord" was in usage at the time for Jews. In the Old Testament Israel is a people holy to the Lord (Exod 19:6; Deut 7:6). The people are described as godly (Heb. *hasidim*) and holy (Heb. *qedosim*); for the latter see Pss 16:3; 34:9; Dan 7:18, 22, 25, 27. In 1 Macc 1:46 the NRSV interprets "the holy ones" as "the priests" in the light of the context. Tobit 12:15 B refers to the seven holy angels who offer up the prayers of the holy ones. See further Wis 18:9; *1 Enoch* 38:4-5; 48:1, 4; 51:2; 62:8; 1QH 4:24; 1QM 3:5; 6:6; 10:10; 12:7-8; 14:12; 1QS 5:13; 8:20-21; 11:7-8; CD 20:7-87; *Pss Sol* 17:36. The usage at Qumran would appear to reflect an understanding that the term should properly be reserved for those who were obedient to the Lord and not applied to the disobedient and apostate people. See H. Seebass, *"Hagios,"* in *The New International Dictionary of New Testament Theology,* vol. 2, ed. Colin Brown (Grand Rapids: Zondervan, 1976, 1986), pp. 227-28; Evans, *Saints,* pp. 15-28. More generally, on holiness and perfection at Qumran see A. R. G. Deasley, *The Shape of Qumran Theology* (Carlisle: Paternoster, 2000).

rather the phrase "and widows" is explicative — to the saints including, in particular the widows who constituted the closer circle of friends to which Tabitha belonged.[11] The term is not used again until we get to 20:32 where Paul speaks of "all those who are sanctified" *(hēgiasmenoi)* and the reference is clearly to the whole company of believers; it identifies them as the people of God, and the use of the perfect participle implies that an action has taken place with lasting results. Such people have been chosen by God to be his people. The wording here deserves careful note. Paul is here committing his hearers to God and to his word of grace. Although they may be thought to be in the safekeeping of God simply because they are his people, nevertheless there is a relationship to be sustained by prayer and the people themselves need to be reassured that God is caring for them by knowing that prayer is being offered to a God who answers prayer. The reference to God's word of grace is there to remind them that God has spoken gracious promises to his people through which they know his character as the faithful God. It is this God who speaks his word who has the power to build them up, i.e., to make them strong and secure in their faith and to grant them an inheritance among all those who are sanctified. This may simply mean that along with all the other sanctified people they will ultimately receive that gift of God which is promised to his children like a legacy given by a parent to his children.[12] Nothing is said at this point as to how people come to be included in the company of the sanctified, although the use of the perfect participle implies a process of becoming.

This last point is elucidated when the phrase reappears in 26:16-18 in the important description of the nature of salvation: here a distinction is made between "the people" (i.e., the Jews) and "the Gentiles" who are brought out of darkness into light, out of the power of Satan into the kingdom of God, and receive forgiveness and "a place among those who are sanctified by faith in me (Jesus)." This description is particularly important because it unambiguously links the experience of becoming members of the people of God with the act of believing in Christ. What is possibly debatable is whether the actions described in v. 18 refer only to the immediately preceding antecedent, the Gentiles, or also to the (Jewish) people. Do the Jews need to turn to God and receive forgiveness? In fact, the point is clear enough. Elsewhere the offer of forgiveness is held out to the Jews along with the need to believe in Jesus (2:38; 3:19, 26; 5:31). It follows that what Paul is emphasising here is the way in which God has made it

11. Evans, *Saints,* pp. 40-41, argues that the use of the term here is based on traditions used by Luke rather than being a result of Lucan redaction.

12. The "inheritance" metaphor breaks down at this point, since this legacy is not dependent upon the death of the legator. The term signifies more a gift which is as certain as something promised in a will or testament.

possible for the Gentiles to become part of the sanctified people in exactly the same manner as it is possible for Jews, namely by faith in Jesus, although in their case they need to turn to God (cf. 1 Thess 1:9-10). It is this association of being sanctified with the act of believing (and going on believing) in Jesus that is important. The negative implication is that the Jewish people are not counted among the sanctified unless they now believe in the Messiah who has come.

The usage here is similar to that elsewhere in the New Testament, especially in Paul's letters where "the saints" has become a way of referring to Christian believers as those "called to be saints."[13] Paul can interestingly place side by side the phrases "sanctified in Christ Jesus" and "called [to be] saints" (1 Cor 1:2) as if the one phrase added a nuance to the other. (Paul, however, is not stereotyped in his introductory descriptions and one should not read too much into the variations.)

The usage in Acts is thus in no way singular. The concept of believers as the holy or sanctified ones is reflected in the designation "the holy ones" found throughout most of the Pauline corpus, in Hebrews, Jude, and Revelation; elsewhere the adjective is applied descriptively to believers (1 Pet 1:15-16; 2:5, 9; 2 Pet 3:11; cf. the use of the verb in John 17:17, 19; Heb 10:10, 14, 29; 13:12).

There are two aspects to the idea of the "holy ones" that cannot be rigidly distinguished. The one is concerned with what we might broadly call status, i.e. the fact that the holy ones are so described in that they are members of God's people, having a special relationship with him that is dependent upon his bringing a people into being and making these specific individuals members of it. The other aspect is concerned with character, in that such people are expected to live lives that are worthy of God and are changed so that they become more and more like what God wants them to be. Simple analogies such as that of girls joining a uniformed organisation such as the Girl Guides are helpful: the girls wear a uniform which marks them out as belonging to the organisation which they have joined, but it takes time for them to learn to live according to the standards expected for Guides and laid down in the Promise and Law of the Guides. We might compare the similar tensions that exist in the concept of justification where believers are given the status of acceptance with God, so that they can say that they have been justified by faith, and yet they are under obligation to live righteous lives through the power of the risen Christ and the Holy Spirit.

13. The term "saints" is used for Christian believers in Rom 1:7; 8:27; 12:13; 15:25, 26, 31; 16:2, 15; 1 Cor 1:2; 6:1, 2; 14:33; 16:1, 15; 2 Cor 1:1; 8:4; 9:1, 12; Eph 1:1, 15, 18; 2:19; 3:8, 18; 4:12; 5:3; 6:18; Phil 1:1; 4:22; Col 1:2, 4, 12, 26; 1 Thess 3:13 (?); 2 Thess 1:10; 1 Tim 5:10; Phlm 5, 7; Heb 6:10; 13:24; Jude 3; Rev 5:8; 8:3, 4; 11:18; 13:7; 14:12; 16:6; 17:6; 18:20, 24 19:8; 20:9; 22:21 (variant reading). In Matt 27:52 the reference must be to figures of the past. Consequently, Evans, *Saints,* pp. 38-40, argues that Luke here reflects Pauline language.

The Holy Spirit

It would be easy to pass over the references to the Holy Spirit as being simply a use of conventional language. The matter is somewhat complex. As Wells observes, in the Old Testament "Spirit of your/his holiness" occurs a mere three times (Ps 51:11; Isa 63:10, 11), but in the New Testament "Holy Spirit" is found about 90 times (some passages are textually uncertain).[14] What is significant for our immediate purpose is that the Spirit is mentioned over 250 times in the New Testament.[15] Thus the Spirit is referred to specifically as the *Holy* Spirit in only about one-third of the total occurrences. In the Gospel of Luke, however, 13 of 17 references to the Spirit use the adjective "holy," and in Acts the proportion rises to 41 of some 58 references. Thus Luke overwhelmingly prefers to use the full phrase "Holy Spirit," and the most frequent use of *hagios* in Acts is as a descriptor of the Spirit. Despite the tendency for this stereotyped usage to become a mere label into whose original significance people did not bother to enquire, nevertheless it is hard to believe that recipients of the Holy Spirit were not aware that this power coming into their lives would have a sanctifying influence upon them.[16] Although there is a good deal of stress in Acts on the function of the Spirit as prophetic, equipping believers for witness and giving them courage and wisdom when they speak,[17] it is unlikely that this stress would lead to the suppression of this other important aspect of the work of the Spirit. The gift of the Spirit is clearly understood as an integral part of the experience of salvation (Acts 2:38; 8:15-17; 9:17; 10:44-48; 15:8; 19:1-7), coming upon all believers to give them boldness and joy (Acts 4:31; 13:52). Nevertheless, Luke does not explicitly link the coming of the Holy Spirit with making believers *holy* (in the way that Paul does in Rom 15:16; 1 Thess 4:7-8; 2 Thess 2:13; cf. Titus 3:5).

Purity and Impurity

The question of purity, closely associated with holiness in some parts of the Old Testament, arises more than once in Acts, and this must be investigated to see whether it is related in any way to the concept that we are studying.

The Jews at this time regarded certain foods as common or unclean *(koinos, akathartos)*. These two adjectives have much the same sense (Acts 10:14,

14. Wells, *People*, p. 236.
15. A precise figure cannot be given because of the difficulty of determining whether some references are to the Spirit of God or to some other entity such as the human spirit.
16. The Spirit is expressly linked to sanctification in Rom 1:4; 2 Thess 2:13; 1 Pet 1:2.
17. E.g., Acts 1:8; 4:8; 13:9.

28; 11:8).[18] In accordance with the law, some foods were regarded as defiling those who eat them, whereas others were "clean."[19] Peter as a law-abiding Jew did not eat what was common or unclean (10:14; 11:8).[20] Food prepared by Gentiles was unclean and therefore forbidden to Jews, although there is some dispute regarding how strictly this principle was held. This was because Gentiles were regarded as unclean and therefore whatever they touched was unclean; to bring them into the temple was to defile it (21:28). But the principle could work both ways: Gentiles could be regarded as unclean because they ate foods prohibited to Jews.[21]

The vision that Peter received from God stated that what God has cleansed is no longer to be regarded as "common" (10:15; 11:9).[22] Therefore Peter draws the conclusion that God has shown him that he should not call any person common or unclean (10:28).[23] There are three tricky points here.

18. The adjective *koinos* retains its sense of "common," i.e., available to and shared by a group, in Acts 2:44; 4:32; Titus 1:4; Jude 3. In this sense it is akin to the verb *koinōnein*, "to share" (not used in Acts), and the noun *koinōnia* (Acts 2:42). However, it developed the sense of that which is common to human society and therefore not proper to God, hence that which is not sacred and therefore defiling (1 Macc 1:47, 62; 4 Macc 7:6; see C. K. Barrett, *A Critical and Exegetical Commentary on the Acts of the Apostles*, vol. I, ICC (Edinburgh: T&T Clark, 1994, 1998), p. 508. The adjective *akathartos* is frequently used in the NT of unclean, i.e., evil spirits (Acts 5:16; 8:7), and is an explanatory synonym of *koinos* in Acts. The fact that *akathartos* was so often associated with unclean spirits may well have added a pejorative nuance to it in its usage here.

19. Childbirth, various bodily discharges, and skin diseases also led to uncleanness, and there were sacrificial rites for removing the defilement (Mark 1:44; Luke 2:22). By NT times it was also held that eating with unwashed hands could make the person unclean. In such cases ordinary washing with water was an adequate remedy (Mark 7:1-4; John 2:6).

20. There is a further contrast between foods that are clean and those that are consecrated; the shewbread is consecrated (and therefore not available for ordinary consumption, Luke 6:4), but normal bread is clean and available for general use.

21. Barrett, *Acts*, I, p. 516.

22. The verb *koinoō* has the sense to make unclean (Acts 21:28) or to regard as unclean (Acts 10:15; 11:9). For God to cleanse something or somebody overrides human estimates. The verb *katharizō* is used of spiritual cleansing of the heart in Acts 15:9, but here (Acts 10:15; 11:9) God cleanses people by denying human estimates that they are unclean.

23. The picture in Acts is confirmed by the material in the Gospel of Luke. For people living as Jews in the liminal period of the birth and mission of Jesus the laws about cleansing have still to be observed. There has to be purification of the mother after the birth of Jesus (Luke 2:22), and it is clearly an indication of proper Jewish piety that this rite is carried out. The healed leper has to go through the cleansing ceremony (Luke 5:14). However, Jesus criticises the Pharisaic cleansing of vessels as unnecessary; it is spiritual cleansing of sinful hearts by giving alms which is important and effective (Luke 11:41). Luke does not have an equivalent to the important discussion of the matter in Mark 7:1-23. The omission is part of his omission of the whole of Mark 6:45–8:26 and is not necessarily due to any bias against this specific pericope. It may be

First, the vision was of animals that were forbidden to Jews by the law rather than of food prepared by Gentiles. Nevertheless, Peter draws the conclusion that if God has cleansed the foods, then this implies that the Gentiles are clean; one can go to their houses and eat with them. It is not immediately clear how a divine command releasing Jews from the terms of the law regarding types of animals regarded as unclean would be understood as cleansing foods prepared by unclean Gentiles.

Second, it is disputed whether the effect of the divine command is to cleanse both foods and Gentiles for Jewish believers.[24] Some interpreters argue that the Mosaic law remained in force for Jewish believers; the vision was not to be accepted on the literal level as removing the prohibitions on certain kinds of foods but solely on the metaphorical level as denying that Gentiles are unclean.[25]

Third, at first sight it would appear that the effect of the vision is to declare that all Gentiles are ritually pure and clean, so that Peter can freely visit them. However, later Peter states that God has cleansed the Gentiles by faith (15:9).[26] This could imply that it is only believing Gentiles that are clean and that unbelieving Gentiles remain unclean in the eyes of Jews. If this is the case, was Cornelius understood to be clean already by virtue of his devotion to God? Is the narrative not wholly consistent at this point?[27]

Can these problems in the narrative be satisfactorily solved?

1. F. F. Bruce notes that the sheet in the vision contained *all* (kinds of) animals, reptiles, and birds, and draws the conclusion that it contained animals that were of both kinds, fit and unfit for food, and that the clean animals might have been thought to be contaminated by the presence of the unclean. Some

---

that the Peter and Cornelius story in Acts 10–11 was seen as a partial equivalent for it. There is considerable difference of scholarly opinion over whether Luke thought that the Jewish law remained binding on Jewish believers. See C. L. Blomberg, "The Law in Luke-Acts," *Journal for the Study of the New Testament* 22 (1984): 53-80; J. Jervell, *The Theology of the Acts of the Apostles* (Cambridge: Cambridge University Press, 1996), esp. pp. 61-75; M. Turner, "The Sabbath, Sunday, and the Law in Luke/Acts," in *From Sabbath to Lord's Day: A Biblical, Historical and Theological Investigation,* ed. D. A. Carson (Grand Rapids: Zondervan, 1982), pp. 99-157; S. G. Wilson, *Luke and the Law,* SNTSMS 50 (Cambridge: Cambridge University Press, 1983).

24. So, for example, R. Pesch, *Die Apostelgeschichte,* vol. 1, EKKNT (Zürich/Neukirchen-Vluyn: Benziger/Neukirchener, 1986), p. 339.

25. So, for example, J. Jervell, *Die Apostelgeschichte,* KEK 3 (Göttingen: Vandenhoeck und Ruprecht, 1998), p. 306; C. A. Miller, "Did Peter's Vision in Acts 10 Pertain to Men or the Menu?" *Bibliotheca Sacra* 159 (2002): 302-17.

26. The adjective *katharos,* "clean," is used in Acts only of being guiltless (Acts 18:6; 20:26).

27. The point is noted by Barrett, *Acts,* II, p. 717, but he doubts whether the distinction between the two types of cleansing would have occurred to Luke.

were prohibited but even the permitted ones would need to be slaughtered and prepared in the appropriate Jewish manner.[28] Once the law had been extended, as it was by this time, to prohibit allowable animals (e.g., cattle) prepared by Gentiles, it is understandable that the range of the divine permission could be seen as extending to the Gentile foods.[29]

2. There is no doubt that the story highlights the fact that Peter ate with Gentiles as the main cause of criticism by the opponents (11:3), and therefore it is most probable that he was eating their food rather than just being in their company. The suggestion that he ate food taken by his party or prepared by it sounds distinctly casuistic.

3. It may be significant that in 15:9 the point is not that God has cleansed the Gentiles ceremonially or ritually as regards their bodies but that he has cleansed their *hearts* by faith. The issue in this chapter is initially at any rate not the matter of eating with Gentiles but the requirement for them to be circumcised and to keep the law as the condition of salvation, because apart from that they are unclean. Peter's response is that their salvation is by faith and not by outward observance of the law, including especially circumcision. Therefore it would seem that a distinction can be drawn between the outward defilement of the Gentiles, which God has taken away as the heavenly voice to Peter indicated, and the inward defilement of sin which is taken away when they believe and receive the Holy Spirit. Similarly, in 1 Cor 7:14 there is no barrier to the continuation in marriage of a believer with an unbeliever,[30] since the ritual uncleanness is ineffective.[31] Whereas Paul uses *hagios* and *hagiazō* in this context, Luke does not do so; the concept of purity and impurity is not tied up with holiness.

God's Holy People

In the first part of this essay we established the important point that the term "holy" has been taken over to refer to believers in Christ and this group apparently is now the holy people of God. Here we have a phenomenon which indi-

---

28. F. F. Bruce, *The Book of the Acts,* 2nd ed. (Grand Rapids: Eerdmans, 1988), pp. 204-6; cf. Barrett, *Acts,* I, p. 506. In *Acts* (Leicester: Inter-Varsity, 1980), p. 185, I suggested that there were probably no clean animals in the sheet. Either way, the total contents could have been regarded as unfit for consumption.

29. Food sacrificed to idols and eaten in a pagan temple was, of course, in a different category. See Acts 15:20, 29; 1 Cor 8–10; Rev 2:14, 20.

30. The assumption is probably that one of the partners is converted after the marriage.

31. Here, however, the principle is that the believing partner "sanctifies" the unbelieving partner and the children of the marriage who would otherwise be unclean *(akathartos).*

cates what is sometimes called "supersession," as if the church has replaced the Jews (Israel) as God's people. To understand the situation in this way, however, would be a misleading simplification.

Throughout the history of Israel it is clear that the people were in danger of ceasing to be God's people if they turned to idolatry and disobedience to the commandments, i.e. if they broke the covenant. Sometimes their sin was so great that they had to undergo a period of punishment during which God refused to hear their cries for mercy and people died as a result. But always there was the possibility that for the sake of their fathers or his own mercy God would eventually decide that they had suffered enough and cease to chastise them. In other words, we can make a distinction between physical Israel (all the people of Israel and Judaea) and the spiritual Israel of people who kept the covenant and enjoyed its benefits. This pattern continued after the OT period, when different groups saw that Israel as a whole had turned to apostasy and called them back to God, by following the teaching of the group.[32]

The Christians believed that God had sent the Messiah, Jesus, and that this new event inaugurated the new covenant, clearly foretold in prophecy, which was to be the way of acceptance by him. This new covenant remained the way in which God established his relationship with Jews, and there was no exclusion of Jews from his people, provided that they accepted the Messiah. Scripture was interpreted to mean that God also included believing Gentiles as spiritual descendants of Abraham and therefore as members of the covenant people. This does not seem necessarily to have been the case under the old covenant, but is certainly seen as part of the new, and it does not take away the position of Jews as God's people but simply affirms that God's people includes more than the Jews and is open to all who believe. This is not supersessionism but rather spiritualisation of the concept of the people of God.

This position is clear and consistent, and may fairly be understood as that of Luke-Acts, even if the details of Luke's position continue to be debated.

We have seen that "holy" is a term used for God and people, places, and things that particularly belong to him. The use of the term for believers is primarily concerned with their status as the people of God and their consequent privileges. We do not come across the explicit linking of holiness with blamelessness that is set out as the purpose of God for believers in Col 1:22 or the prayer that God will make his people complete in holiness (1 Thess 5:23).[33] Nev-

---

32. See especially M. A. Elliott, *The Survivors of Israel: A Reconsideration of the Theology of Pre-Christian Judaism* (Grand Rapids: Eerdmans, 2000).

33. For this understanding of holiness see further, for example, Rom 6:19, 22; 2 Cor 1:12 (variant reading); 7:1; Eph 5:26-27; 1 Thess 4:3-8; 1 Tim 2:15; 2 Tim 2:21; Heb 12:14; 1 Pet 1:15-16;

ertheless, it is evident that the people of God will live lives of ethical and spiritual quality according to the presentation in Acts.[34] Acts provides us with a number of descriptions of Christian character, individual and congregational, actual and ideal, in description and in exhortation.

1. The holy people are *committed to their Lord.* Barnabas encouraged the believers in Antioch to remain faithful to the Lord with steadfastness of heart (11:23) and Paul persuaded new believers to continue in the grace of God (13:43); Lydia expressed the hope that she would be seen to be a believer in the Lord, which must mean a continuing relationship rather than an initial action of conversion (16:15). Those who are faithful to the Lord are prepared to accept his will for them, even though it may involve the prospect of suffering (21:14). They are prepared to risk their lives for Jesus (15:26; 21:13).

2. The holy people are *united to one another.* They are of one mind (1:14; 4:32), an attitude which expresses itself in generosity to one another and the creation of a community in which there is mutual care and the sharing of resources for the benefit of the poor. Within the conditions of ancient society it is unlikely that equality in income or in expenditure could be achieved or was even envisaged, but there is a strong stress in the opening chapters on the care of the poor through sharing by the better-off (2:45; 4:32).

3. The unity of the holy people was *demonstrated in their communal life* which, initially at any rate, brought them together for the activities listed and briefly described in 2:42-47.

These included, first, *learning:* Luke actually calls it teaching, a term which appears to be used for evangelistic material (5:28; 13:12; 17:19) as well as for instruction within the community. In 15:35 teaching and evangelism are linked together, and it is hard to distinguish between evangelism and Christian instruction, since clearly the one flows into the other.

Second, there was *fellowship.* This word is notoriously difficult to define with precision and various meanings are possible. It could refer to sharing together in a common meal, but against this is the immediately following mention of the breaking of bread. Or it might refer simply to the association of the believers with one another with the consequent activities. Barrett cites Calvin with approval: "mutual association, alms, and other duties of brotherly fellow-

---

2 Pet 3:11. The range of references shows that the ethical dimension of holiness was widely recognised within early Christianity.

34. J. B. Green notes that "we find in Acts no sustained teaching on 'biblical spirituality,'" but nevertheless is able to develop a profound exposition of the nature of the transformation that goes on in Acts and is intended to be reproduced in the lives of those who read Acts ("Doing Repentance: The Formation of Disciples in the Acts of the Apostles," *Ex Auditu* 17 (2002): 1-23.

ship." Whatever the precise meaning of the word, the fellowship expressed itself in mutual support.

Third, one specific expression of this association was the *breaking of bread,* a common meal which in the light of what is recorded in the Gospel must have been thought of as a meal at which the Lord was spiritually present and his death was remembered (Luke 22:19; 24:30-31).

Fourth, there is *prayer.* This communal activity is attested before Pentecost in 1:14 and then afterwards in 2:42; 4:23-31; 12:5, 12, and was also an activity of the apostles (6:4). On two occasions prayer is associated with fasting (13:2-3; 14:23).

4. Closely linked with prayer is the activity of *praising God,* both collectively (2:47) and individually (3:9). Such praise is expressive of rejoicing in response to God's goodness, particularly in experiencing salvation (8:39; 13:52; 16:34), but also at being called to suffer for the gospel (5:41).

5. The activities of the holy people are *ascribed to the influence of the Holy Spirit* upon them; they "receive" the Spirit or are filled with the Spirit. The Spirit is coupled with wisdom (6:3), faith (6:5; 11:24), grace (6:8),[35] and goodness (11:24) and the capacity to speak out boldly (4:31). The indications are that these qualities are the result of the infusion of the Spirit. There are particular infusions of the Spirit to prepare people for public speaking and the exercise of divine authority (4:8; 13:9).[36]

6. The quality of *goodness* (11:24) in the holy people is seen in such traits as the readiness to forgive wrongs (7:60), being full of good works and charity (9:36), and honesty (the implication of 5:1-11). These traits lead to a good reputation both among the people at large (2:47) and among other believers (16:2). Yet it should be noted that such qualities are not peculiar to believers: a Roman centurion treats Paul kindly (27:3), as do also the Maltese people to the victims of shipwreck (28:2).

7. Perhaps the fullest description of ideal Christian character emerges in Paul's speech at Miletus (20:18-35) with its emphasis on *total commitment* to the

---

35. The force of this term is not clear. Elsewhere in Acts grace appears to refer especially to God's powerful saving care by which people are enabled to come to faith and are saved and by which they are then preserved and protected in their Christian life and missionary activity (Acts 11:23; 13:42; 14:3, 26; 15:11, 40; 18:27; 20:24, 32). Here, then, the reference may be to the way in which God acted savingly and powerfully through the mighty works and preaching of Stephen rather than to a gracious quality of character.

36. It is debated whether Apollos "spoke with great fervour" (NIV text; cf. NRSV) or "spoke with fervour in the Spirit" (NIV margin). In favour of the latter view see Barrett, *Acts,* II, p. 888; M. Turner, *Power from on High: The Spirit in Israel's Restoration and Witness in Luke-Acts,* JPTSup 9 (Sheffield: Sheffield Academic Press, 1996), p. 389. G. D. Fee, *God's Empowering Presence: The Holy Spirit in the Letters of Paul* (Peabody: Hendrickson, 1994), pp. 612-13, says that it "can only mean 'ardent in spirit'" but (at least here) offers no justification for this categorical statement.

task of evangelism and care for other believers. Surprisingly there is only one specific mention of love as a quality of God's people; the one use of *agapētos* is found in 15:25, and *agapē* and *agapaō* are not used at all, whether of God or of his people.[37]

These fragmentary glimpses into the Lucan depiction of the life of the early church show that the holy people were characterised, whether ideally or actually, by devotion and commitment to the Lord that was joyful and glad, and by various qualities that can be summed up in terms of goodness; there was a powerful bond between the members of the holy people so that their devotion to the Lord was expressed in communal activities, among which being instructed by teachers, praying and praising the Lord, sharing in common meals, and caring for one another were central.

Conclusion

Our study has shown the range of ways in which the concept of holiness is expressed in Acts. Essentially God has a holy people, holy in that they belong to him, composed of both Jews and Gentiles who believe in Jesus Christ and stand in continuity with the faithful people of Israel in Old Testament times. The concept of purity and impurity which distinguished between pure and impure foods and pure and impure people in outward ways is abolished in line with the spiritual understanding of holiness that characterises the New Testament. Believers receive the gift of the Holy Spirit and there are some indications that thereby they are empowered and guided for their life and witness; they are to be good people. From Acts there emerges incidentally a picture of people who are to be wholly devoted to the Lord, expressing that devotion in prayer and praise, and living together in communities characterised by unity and mutual generosity. Although Luke does not specifically understand this way of life in terms of holiness, the close juxtaposition of the term "sanctified" with the descriptions of Christian conversion in 26:15-18 and of Christian character in 20:32-35 is an adequate indication that he would have regarded holiness as expressing itself in this kind of changed character.

Wells's summary of the situation is apt:

> More widely, the book of Acts tells of the Holy Spirit at work expressing God's holiness, through his people, to the world. This is quite evidently a dynamic power of holiness, as seen in the work of Jesus in the gospels. So

---

37. So far as God's attitude to humanity is concerned, the lack is compensated for by references to his grace (*charis;* see n. 35 above).

we find it explicitly associated with boldness (4.31), generosity (5.3), obedience (5.32), good repute (6.3), hope of glory (7.55), power (8.18-19; 10.38), healing (9.17), comfort (9.31), discernment and guidance (10.19-20; 13.2, 9; 15.28; 16.6; 20.23; 21.11), doing good (10.38), faith (11.24), joy (13.52), tongues and prophecy (19.6). Though the link is not explicit, it is in association with this dynamic power, received at Pentecost, that the disciples are termed ἅγιοι, 'saints', and that they bring many to faith. And as this community of faith grows, so in due time the gift of the Holy Spirit is found to be "poured out even on the Gentiles" (10.45; cf. 11.17-18; 15.8-9). Thus the book of Acts depicts in highly graphic terms the dynamic power of holiness crossing Israel's boundaries, just as the gospels imply.[38]

In his book Evans draws several conclusions regarding the use of "saints" in the New Testament as a whole and gives an admirable summary of the total picture.

1. The saints are a community which stands in continuity with the Old Testament people of God. The term is always applied collectively and never to individuals.
2. They are saints by virtue of their relationship to Jesus Christ (26:18).
3. They have been chosen and called by God.
4. They form the eschatological community to whom belongs the inheritance of the Kingdom of God (20:32; 26:18).
5. They are endowed with the gift of the Spirit.
6. They are a separated community (cf. 5:12-16).
7. They form one universal community (10:34).
8. They are a witnessing community.
9. They are a militant community.
10. They are a worshipping community.
11. They show moral purity and goodness.[39]

It scarcely needs demonstration that this understanding of the saints is reflected in and confirmed by the evidence of Acts. Some of these features are explicitly associated with the use of the actual term "holy," whereas others are part of the total picture that we find in Acts. The picture in Acts is thus in line with that found more broadly in the rest of the New Testament.

38. Wells, *People*, pp. 236-37.
39. Evans, *Saints*, pp. 124-46.

Reading Paul with Acts:
The Canonical Shaping of a Holy Church

Robert W. Wall

In a series of studies, culminating with my commentary on the Book of Acts, I have attempted to clarify the strategic role Acts performs within the New Testament.[1] Against the critical consensus since Cadbury that Luke and Acts should be read as a continuous narrative, I have suggested that Acts performs a discrete role as Scripture independent of its relationship to Luke's Gospel. The opening sentence of Acts, along with the kerygmatic portions of its speeches, may well remind its reader that Acts continues the Gospel story of the risen Jesus. However, the history of interpreting Acts typically commends a more prospective role in orienting the reader of Acts to the implied authors and audiences as well as the subject matter of the NT letters that follow.[2] Especially the second half of Acts (16–28) and its portrait of Paul and his mission point readers forward to the Pauline letters.[3]

Although the intracanonical relationship between Acts and the Pauline letters is laden with numerous important historical questions, my interpretive interest in this relationship is both rhetorical and theological.[4] Rhetorically

---

1. Robert W. Wall, "The Acts of the Apostles," *NIB* 10 (Nashville: Abingdon, 2002), esp. pp. 26-32, 213-15.

2. On which see Robert W. Wall, "Introduction to Epistolary Literature," in *NIB* 10, pp. 369-91, esp. 389-90. Along similar lines, see D. E. Smith, *The Canonical Function of Acts* (Collegeville, Minn.: Liturgical Press, 2002) and cf. the especially fluent account of the (pre-canon) reception history of Acts by C. Mount, *Pauline Christianity: Luke-Acts and the Legacy of Paul,* NovTSup 104 (Leiden: Brill, 2002), pp. 11-58.

3. On the intertextual echoes of Pauline letters in Acts, see D. Wenham, "Acts and the Pauline Corpus," in *The Book of Acts in its First Century Setting: Ancient Literary Setting,* ed. B. Winter and A. Clarke (Grand Rapids: Eerdmans, 1993), pp. 215-58.

4. Ideally, the text of Acts and the texts of relevant Pauline letters form an intertext that engages its interpreter in a reflexive reading. Thus, even as Acts informs a reading of a Pauline letter, so also a Pauline letter informs a reading of Acts.

Acts evokes powerful impressions that influence how the reader apprehends the Pauline letters. Acts tells us something of the canonical Paul's persona, circumstances, vocation, and religious motives enabling the interpreter of his letters to fill in their gaps imaginatively and in agreement with Pauline tradition. Yet Acts is also a theological narrative giving its own witness to God's gospel and illuminating the theological contribution each letter makes to a full understanding of Paul's *biblical* testimony. Allowing Acts to exercise this hermeneutical function guards against the subversion of Paul's testimony and authority in the life of the church and enables us to highlight an often neglected aspect of the New Testament's depiction of the shaping of a "holy church."

Paying attention to the argument of the Jewish scholar Daniel Boyarin brings this neglected aspect into clearer focus. Boyarin criticizes Paul's efforts to redefine Israel by spiritual, individual, and internal properties, which he claims subverts the identity of a biblical Israel that is characterized by public practices and purity routines peculiar to a people belonging to God.[5] Whether directed toward Paul or his later interpreters, the Letter of James criticizes those believers who profess a "faith apart from works" (Jas 2:14-17; cf. Rom 9:30– 10:13), which produces a disembodied and useless "religion" unapproved by God (Jas 1:26). Not only does this criticism follow the speech of the James of Acts in concluding the so-called "Jerusalem Council" (on which see below), it supports Boyarin's criticism of Paul as well.[6]

In this article, I will contend that if understood within their canonical setting — introduced by Acts and balanced by the second collection of letters from the "Jerusalem Pillars"[7] — Paul's letters may be interpreted in a way that assuages Boyarin's worry. Indeed, by reading Acts 15 and then the Pauline letters

---

5. D. Boyarin, *A Radical Jew: Paul and the Politics of Identity* (Berkeley: University of California Press, 1994).

6. David J. Rudolph has defended the importance of messianic (Jesus-believing) Jews who affirm their commitment to Jewish religious traditions and communal life as a matter primarily of covenant faithfulness in "Messianic Jews and Christian Theology: Restoring an Historical Voice to the Contemporary Discussion," *Pro Ecclesia* 14 (2005): 58-84. Not only is Rudolph's affirmation similar to the theological subtext of James's speech in Acts 15 (and recalled in Acts 21:21-25), but his discussion of Christian ecclesiology, informed by the presence and practices of the messianic Jewish synagogue, provides the best contemporary articulation of what the James of Acts considers most important in cultivating "New Covenant spirituality" and unity between Jesus-believing Jews and Gentiles.

7. Particularly James, placed first among the Catholic Epistles, served to orient its readers to the ongoing importance of a Jewish ethos in an emergent church that was increasingly Gentile. Not only does its definition of purity (Jas 1:27) conform to the instruction of "the perfect law of liberty" (i.e., Torah) but the community is measured by its public practices of purity by which it demonstrates its love and loyalty to God.

and 1 Corinthians in particular[8] as canonical co-texts, the one glossing the other, the broader NT witness defines a "holy church" *not only in terms of an inward purity of heart by faith (Acts 15:9), but also in terms of public practices that demonstrate purity thereby bearing witness to the church's faithfulness to Israel's God.*

The Jerusalem Council (Acts 15) in Canonical Context

The plotline of Paul's mission in Acts 16–28 is shaped in response to the concern expressed by James in rendering a verdict to the question raised by a Pharisaic contingent within his Jerusalem congregation: namely, whether repentant Gentiles should practice Torah purity according to Jewish tradition (Acts 15:5). The historical reconstruction of this "Jerusalem Council," especially in relationship to Galatians 2, and the role this episode performs within Acts remain contested matters of Acts criticism without a settlement in sight. I leave that prospect to others. My particular interest is the function of this narrative within the NT canon in preparing readers for the NT Letters that follow.

The Strategic Importance of the Pharisees'
Implied Question (Acts 15:5)

Interpreters of Acts commonly depict those from "the party of the Pharisees" as troublemakers and then presume the impropriety of their claim upon repentant Gentiles.[9] But there is nothing in the text itself that should incline readers in this direction. In fact, Luke's use of the "*dei* of divine necessity" — that a repentant Gentile's circumcision and Torah observance *are made necessary* by *God's* ordination (15:5) — underwrites the seriousness of the Pharisees' interest in seeking after *God's* qualifications for church membership.[10]

In any case, the implied question raised here by the Pharisees is different from the earlier question that provoked the original dispute in Antioch (15:1-2). While both questions deal with the purity of uncircumcised Gentiles, the prior issue raised in Antioch concerns a pattern of Gentile salvation: "Unless you are

8. My reasons for choosing 1 Corinthians will become clear below.

9. Typical is Mount's assessment of the Jerusalem council as "a separation of the Way from the Pharisees — that is, one more step on the road from Jerusalem to Rome" (*Pauline Christianity*, p. 151).

10. In Acts Torah's definition of purity has purchase in a way that the Temple's definition of purity does not (cf. 6:11-15; 7:47-50; 24:14-20; 21:17-26).

circumcised according to the custom of Moses, *you cannot be saved*" (15:1). Apparently the Judean teachers in Antioch require something more like Judaism's traditional protocol of Gentile proselytism, whilst Paul and Barnabas' experience of Gentile conversion (Acts 13–14) argues against this purity tradition and confirms the pattern of Gentile conversion already in place since Cornelius (15:12; cf. 11:18). We should note that James "officially" dismisses these Judean provocateurs as having no official portfolio from the Jerusalem church (15:24); moreover, the intramural conflict they provoke in Antioch is further evidence that they are not in partnership with the Spirit (cf. 15:28, 30-31).[11]

Readers of Acts understand why this is so: God's Spirit has already spoken through Israel's Scriptures — confirmed and interpreted by the events of Pentecost — that salvation in the last days of Israel's history is realized by "everyone who calls upon the name of the Lord" (2:21), i.e., the risen Jesus (2:26). In fact, that this prophecy includes even non-proselyte (i.e., uncircumcised, unclean) Gentiles has already been disclosed, witnessed, and approved by these same Jerusalem apostles and elders (now led by James) following the conversion and Spirit baptism of the uncircumcised Cornelius (so 11:1-18). Within the narrative world of Acts, then, there is good reason why "this question" provoked by the Judean teachers in Antioch no longer interests Jerusalem's leadership (so 15:24).

This conclusion brings us back to the implied question raised by the "party of the Pharisees." Their concern is no longer the salvation of unclean pagans who have turned to Jesus, but rather the regulation of Christian fellowship within the Diaspora synagogue whose mixed membership brings together repentant Jews and pagans. Sharply put, *what public practices must repentant pagans observe in forging an identity apropos of a people belonging to Israel's God?* These faithful Pharisees, then, are not concerned with an alternative means of salvation but with public practices that identify a peculiar people as God's people — especially in the Diaspora where Moses is still "taught . . . read" and observed in Christian assemblies (15:21).

The careful reader of Acts recognizes the propriety of the Pharisees' question since it expresses the thematic of "practices in keeping with repentance" from Pentecost forward: apostolic teaching, fellowship, sharing goods in common, and worship (2:42) are practices that constitute the *halakhah* of a membership whose "one heart and soul" in this regard provides material witness to "great grace upon them all" (4:32-33; cf. 2:47). To these resurrection practices,

---

11. The Western expansion of 15:1-2, 7 and 21:25 reflects the longstanding failure to separate the two questions raised by Acts 15:1 and 5 in favor of the Antiochene version, probably under the influence of Galatians 2.

begun in Jerusalem, are added the community's evangelistic ministries, its performance of the Spirit's "signs and wonders," the exorcism of demonic opposition in continuity with Jesus, hospitality, and other social virtues that are never rescinded in Acts. Yet the stunning results of Paul's mission in the Diaspora, which adds repentant pagans (with other "God-fearers") to the membership of the covenant community, requires that additional practices are added to this catalogue.

Hence, the subtext of the question raised by these believing Pharisees fits into this overarching scheme of the community's common life according to Acts: By what purity practices shall we continue to evince our "one heart and soul" as a people belonging to Israel's God? This question is asked again at this particular moment by those believers most sensitive to the threat against this very oneness, which has now been challenged by the stunning action of God who has included unclean but repentant Gentiles within the community.

The Inadequacy of Peter's Initial Response (Acts 15:6-11)

Peter's initial response to the question of a repentant Gentile's purity with respect to "table fellowship" is to reform traditional *halakhah*. In the programmatic telling of Cornelius' story in Acts 10, the central conflict between Peter and Cornelius is initially defined by the heavenly audition, "What God has cleansed *(katharizō)*, you must not call common" (10:15). Peter interprets this subsequently in traditional Jewish terms of table fellowship: "it is unlawful for a Jew to associate with or to visit any one of another nation" (10:28). Thus, when Peter rehearses that story for this "council," his decisive commentary is that God no longer requires repentant Gentiles to put on "a yoke" of the law (15:10) because God has "cleansed *(katharizō)* their hearts by faith" (15:9b). If Peter's commentary is glossed by the earlier text, which seems apropos to the question raised by the Pharisees, then the concept of purity is not here a synecdoche of inward sanctification but of social propriety. The baptism of the Spirit indicates that "God made no distinction between us and them" (15:9a) and not that God had forgiven their sins — even though this is surely implied (cf. 2:38). For this reason, in the first telling of Cornelius' conversion, Peter's response to the stunning "Gentile Pentecost" was to baptize Cornelius and his household *by water* initiating them into membership of the faith community (cf. 10:47-48).[12] If

---

12. It is a "category" mistake to link Spirit baptism with personal transformation or regeneration in Acts resulting from the insinuation of a Pauline idea of Spirit filling upon Acts (e.g., Alex Deasley who falls prey to this in the otherwise well argued article, "Entire Sanctifica-

read "intratextually," then, the fuller meaning of Peter's comment at the Jerusalem Council is made clearer: because God has purified the hearts of unclean (i.e., non-proselyte) Gentiles, they need not undergo traditional Jewish rites of purification before table fellowship/friendship with repentant Jews.

James's Call for Purity Practices as Interpretive Key (Acts 15:12-29)

In Acts 15 it is critical to recognize the importance of the obvious: Peter does not have the last word! Rather James provides the council's "official" response to the Pharisees: while God has purified the hearts of repentant Gentiles who call upon the risen Jesus for their salvation, the more urgent issue is ecclesiological and not soteriological, more sociological than spiritual: Jesus-believing pagans are to embrace the rudiments of Jewish communal life as a responsible act in maintaining the public presence of the covenant community.[13] Especially given the testimony of Barnabas and Paul regarding what "God had done through them among the Gentiles" (15:12), the *halakhic* reading of Amos concerns the purity of uncircumcised but repentant Gentiles in Diaspora congregations where Moses is read every Sabbath (15:20-21, 29; cf. 21:25).

Following others, I take it that the catalogue of purity practices introduced by James in 15:20 (cf. 15:29; 21:25) is based upon the so-called "holiness code" found in Leviticus 17–18 which issues instructions to regulate the social discourse between Israel and non-Jews that include religious and relational (including sexual) guidelines.[14] James's midrash contemporizes this Levitical legislation for the current situation in which the "Israel of the last days" is constituted by mixed congregations of Jews and "unclean" (i.e., non-proselytized) Gentiles who worship and fellowship together as members of "the Way."

This expanded definition of purity is the interpretive key of the second half of Acts. When Paul returns to Jerusalem following his farewell tour

---

tion and the Baptism with the Holy Spirit: Perspectives on the Biblical View of the Relationship," *Wesleyan Theological Journal* 14 [1979]: 27-44). "Spirit-filling" carries with it soteriological and moral inferences for Paul while in Acts it infers a more practical, prophetic meaning. From a canonical perspective, I would posit meaning in the interplay between the two.

13. The particular *halakhic* matter that James may have in mind when commenting upon the Amos prophecy is the Levitical concern for the effect of "the practices of the nations" upon Jewish purity or when "resident aliens" mingle with faithful Jews (Lev 17–18); cf. R. Bauckham, "James and the Gentiles (Acts 15:13-21)," in *History, Literature, and Society in the Book of Acts,* ed. B. Witherington (Cambridge: Cambridge University Press, 1996), pp. 154-84.

14. The Western text's addition of the "golden rule" in 15:20 is probably the effort of scribes to spiritualize the code into a general moral precept. This subverts the *halakhic* intent of the James of Acts: his is a code of pagan *practices* from which repentant pagans must abstain.

through Roman Asia (Acts 21:17-26), he finds that he is still the "straw that stirs the drink" of controversy among other Jewish believers. The elders of the Jerusalem church led by James are no longer interested in the religious practices of uncircumcised Gentile converts as before; they are now distressed over reports that Paul's mission has subverted important religious traditions among his Jewish converts who live and worship among Gentiles in the Diaspora (21:21). The relevant issue is whether Paul is guilty of "gentilizing" repentant Jews. In defending himself Paul does what any observant Jew would do: he purifies himself for temple worship (21:24-26) and then appeals to his ritual purity (24:18) in order to claim that his opponents have found no "impurity" *(adikēma)* in him (24:20; cf. 18:14). The implied claim is that Paul's mission among "impure" Gentiles in no way imperils the "purity" of repentant Jews.

The prophecy from Amos frames the second half of Acts in a manner similar to the prophecy from Joel in the first half: the narrator's repetition of the prophecy's language and ideas reminds the reader that "these things that have happened among us" bring to realization God's plan of salvation. At its surface level, the Amos prophecy continues the theme of Israel's restoration and its mission to the nations: as Joel predicts that "everyone who *calls* upon the *name* of the Lord will be saved" (2:21), so Amos prophesies in similar fashion that following the rebuilding of Israel God would find a place for "all the Gentiles who are *called* by my *name*" (15:17). The repetition of these central symbols of "call" (= salvation) and "name" (= Savior) confirms at the midpoint of Acts that Joel's prophecy is fulfilled: the "rebuilding" of repentant Israel and the inclusion of the nations in its salvation has taken place through the Spirit-filled mission of the church. The rest of Acts unfolds from Amos' prophecy against the backdrop of this eschatological horizon, as Paul's mission gathers more and more believers while moving toward Rome at "the end of the earth."

Because the citation of Amos cannot be separated from the midrash of James (15:13-21, 22-29), any echo of the prophecy heard in the second half of Acts extends James's initial reading of it. In particular, the prophecy's use of "rebuild" *(anoikodomeō;* lit. "housing") as a restoration metaphor will be recalled again and again by the various "households" *(oikia)* and "houses" *(oikos)* that provide a strategic locus during Paul's missionary activity and God's salvation. The reference to the Davidic "tent" *(skēnē)* not only resonates with Luke's identification of Paul as a Corinthian "tent-maker" *(skēnopoios;* 18:3), it also posits James's concern with the community's purity in a symbolic world of the eschatological "temple" (see 15:16, 20-21). Paul is the brightest "light" to the nations as he extends the influence of God's word to new places farther from the center of the sacred universe. Yet with each new place — and the "houses" in which new believers are called by God — another level of "the profane" is exposed that may threaten "the sacred." In each new place, James's anxiety is felt all the more, whether the effect of these conversions will contaminate the holy people of God.

The Second Half of Acts in Light of the Jerusalem Council

One rightly wonders what historical circumstances in Luke's world might prompt the concern for the "gentilizing" of Jewish believers. Two obvious clues are found within Acts from which we may infer the narrator's motive: the rousing success of Paul's urban mission in the Diaspora among God-fearing Gentiles and a relative lack of his success among God-fearing Jews, who remain a divided house in their response to the risen Jesus (28:16-28). These data when coupled with the destruction of the Jerusalem temple (fulfilling the Lord's prediction), the return of Palestine to Roman rule (rather than the reverse as predicted by Scripture), and the virtual cessation of the Jerusalem church by end of the first century may have led some believers to argue that the relevant symbols of covenant renewal between God and a "true" Israel no longer include more traditional expressions of Jewish holiness. Sharply put, Christianity has superseded Judaism and need not retain anything Jewish in order to have the identity or vocation as God's people.

The response of Acts to this crisis is worked out during a time of relative calm within the church. Even its "catholic spirit," however, cannot thoroughly disguise the tension within the early church or the anxiety felt by Jewish believers at the sudden influx of Gentiles into their fellowship. However, the narrator's interest in protecting the Jewish heritage of Christian faith is not wholly expected and must be viewed as somewhat radical. Even as God does not require uncircumcised Gentile converts to follow conventional Jewish practices for fellowship with Jewish believers, neither does God require repentant Jews to forsake their ancestral traditions out of loyalty to the Messiah. *The spiritual crisis as Acts portrays it is the possible loss of a distinctively Jewish memory without which the church cannot be the church.*

In shaping the second half of Acts as a response to this theological challenge, Luke composes accounts of three additional Pauline missions (15:22–18:17, 18:18–21:26, 21:27–28:16). For our purposes, it is important to note that Luke brackets the second of these narrative blocks with acts of ritual purification that characterize Paul as an exemplar of holiness within traditional Judaism (18:18-21; 21:26). Paul's adventure concludes in Rome where he awaits his court appearance by engaging in prophetic ministry that, as we might anticipate, divides the house of Israel according to Scripture's script (28:17-28). As a result of this division, some Roman Jews believed (28:24). Hence, Paul's mission to the Jews in Rome is not a complete failure.[15] For this reason, the reader of Acts is led to suppose that any future Christian community that might develop as a result of Paul's announcement of salvation to the Gentiles in Rome (28:28) *would not be without a significant Jewish influence.*

Paul's Jewishness in Acts 16–28, in both religious practices and missionary protocol, is a keen indicator of Luke's response to the theological crisis of his day: the church must continue its firm connection with its Jewish roots in order to be thoroughly Christian. Paul's witness to the risen Messiah does not replace these traditions but reshapes them in unconventional ways; and it is precisely in this manner that the Pharisee Paul exemplifies Torah purity in Israel's last days of salvation's history.

The concerns that occasioned the reception of Acts as Scripture during the late second century were substantively different than those that occasioned its composition. These concerns are envisaged in the so-called "Western text" of Acts which probably has added to Luke's Acts to support the project of the early catholic church to distinguish itself from Judaism as a discrete religious and theological option.[16] For this reason, the Western additions to Acts are "anti-Judaic" and helped to foster a supersessionist theology and anti-Semitic prejudice within the ancient church that remains to this day. Reading the story of Paul in Acts in light of Luke's theological agenda at the end of the first century may provide a necessary corrective to this dark side of the canonical project at the beginning of the twenty-first century.

Reading the Epistolary Paul by the Light of Acts

From a canonical perspective, the account of the founding of the Corinthian church in Acts 18 prepares the interpreter for 1-2 Corinthians by providing an important interpretation that glosses Paul's own more allusive account of the church's origins (1 Corinthians 3–4). Paul founded this church through his preaching of the word of God that Jesus is Messiah and grounded it over a period of eighteen months by his teaching (Acts 18:4-5, 11; cf. 1 Cor 3:5-15). The evident

---

15. For this issue, as well as a more extensive discussion of the issues surrounding 28:17-28, see my "Acts," pp. 360-64. As I emphasized there, the narrative does *not* depict Paul's language at the end of Acts as indicating a permanent, conclusive "Jewish rejection of the Gospel."

16. Cf. E. Epp, *The Theological Tendency of Codex Bezae Cantabrigiensis in Acts,* SNTSMS 3 (Cambridge: Cambridge University Press, 1966); P. M. Head, "Acts and the Problem of its Texts," in *The Book of Acts in its Ancient Literary Setting,* ed. Winter and Clarke, pp. 413-44.

centrality of Paul's testimony "that Jesus is Messiah" (Acts 18:5) is also true of Paul's letters where he responds to every practical problem in light of "the testimony of Messiah" (cf. 1 Cor 1:6). The impression that Paul's mission took place in a milieu of conflict (18:9-10) is also true of the letters (cf. 1 Cor 1:10-17). Although the epistolary Paul speaks of this conflict largely in terms of the influences of the surrounding pagan culture, much of it obtains to the difficulty of negotiating between Jewish and Gentile congregations in Corinth in which the "gentilizing" of the church's Jewish legacy might be underway (cf. 1 Cor 8). One may well wonder whether a congregation founded by Jews (= Acts) has evolved in four or five years into a congregation whose religious orientation is largely pagan (= 1-2 Corinthians) without a keen awareness of the gospel's debt to its Jewish heritage.

This lack of a Jewish touchstone opens the church's witness to contamination by its engaging in those very unclean practices that James sets out to avoid in forming a Christian congregation deemed pure both of heart and in public life — in particular, "pollutions of idols and sexual immorality" (15:20; cf. 15:29; 21:25).[17] Acts therefore supplies a motive that underwrites Paul's response to the presence of "sexual immorality" (*porneia;* 1 Cor 5:1-13; 6:13-20; 7:1-7) and "meat offered to idols" (*eidōlothyta;* 15:29; 1 Cor 8:1-13; 10:19-30) in Corinth. The Jewish character of the narrative of Paul's mission in Acts, when compared to the Gentile character of Paul's Corinthian correspondence, envisages an "ecclesial calculus" that stipulates the importance of a Diaspora congregation's Jewish origins as foundational for its public identity and worship practices. In canonical context, the close relationship between Acts and the Pauline letters underwrites this ecclesiology.

"Pollutions of Idols" and 1 Corinthians 8–10

Within the narrative world of Acts, Paul is especially sensitive to the threat of idol worship as subversive of the Diaspora congregation's belief in the God of Israel (Acts 14:14; 16:18; 17:16; 19:18-20). His response is attentive to the worry of James that repentant pagans will bring "pollutions of idols" with them into the community, thus contaminating their public identity as a people belonging to God. Indeed, a critical feature of the narrative's argument against the church's

---

17. The final two unclean practices mentioned by James are also dietary, having to do with foods improperly butchered *(to pnikton)* and made from animal blood *(to haima).* Both are probably related to religious practices of pagan shrines and are themselves "pollutions of idols" (cf. C. K. Barrett, *A Critical and Exegetical Commentary on the Acts of the Apostles,* vol. 2, ICC [Edinburgh: T&T Clark, 1994, 1998], pp. 730-36). *Porneia* probably refers to sexual promiscuity of all kinds rather than of a particular kind (e.g., incest, irregular marriages, et al.).

supersession from its Jewish heritage is the refusal to tolerate any practice that links believers to their pagan past while maintaining the synagogue's worship practices even when believers move into separate quarters.

This perspective, shaped by a prior reading of Acts, informs the interpreter of 1 Corinthians 8–10 where this same issue is considered, even though now problematized by additional threats.[18] Especially when glossed by Paul's story in Acts, Paul's discussion of *eidōlothyta* is controlled by the question: How is a congregation's holiness preserved and protected when set apart for God in the midst of the normal social exchanges that one encounters in the world?[19] The relationship between Paul's arguments on sexual morality and idol meat in 1 Corinthians underwrites a definition of Christian freedom that marks out a people belonging to God.[20]

It is important to note Paul's repetition of the decidedly Jewish word, *eidōlothyta* (1 Cor 8:1 and 10:19),[21] to enclose his entire response to the problem case of idol meat. Rejecting a more narrow understanding of this word as limited to pagan religious routines, Willis followed by others argues that it functions more like a metaphor that infers a whole matrix of socioeconomic and religious interactions.[22] Paul's use of this Jewish word suggests that he is rendering these interactions from the perspective of a Diaspora Jew whose pharisaic past has sensitized him to the symbolic importance of mealtimes. Here then, the per se practice of eating idol meat puts several important elements of a congregation's religious life into play, including the phenomenology of conversion from paganism to Christian faith, its theological beliefs and the performance of its moral, social, and spiritual values.

The initial reference to idol meat is linked by Paul to the congregation's reception of the knowledge *(gnōsis)* which it has received from hearing Paul's gospel (1:4-5). His repeated unhappiness with unproductive *gnōsis* (8:1a, 10, 11) is hardly anti-intellectual but is rooted in an observation, shared by the broader Greco-Roman philosophical tradition (e.g., Aristotle, Epictetus), that what the believer knows must be inextricably linked to how she or he lives: truth claims, if really true, will be embodied in a virtuous life. In dealing with the practices of idol meat, Paul wants to guard against a separation between the theological

---

18. E.g., strained relationships between different social classes and the proper balancing of knowledge and love in ecclesial life (cf. Richard B. Hays, *First Corinthians*, Interpretation [Louisville: John Knox, 1997], p. 135).

19. So P. Sampley, "The First Letter to the Corinthians," in *NIB* 10, p. 893.

20. Sampley, "First Letter," pp. 893-925.

21. The more natural choice for a non-Jewish audience would have been *hierothytos*.

22. W. L. Willis, *Idol Meat in Corinth: The Pauline Argument in 1 Corinthians 8 and 10*, SBLDS 68 (Chico, Calif.: Scholars Press, 1985).

gnōsis that "there is no God but one" (8:4) and a practice that embodies this belief, i.e., loving responses that "build up" (8:1b-3) those "weaker" believers who have become confused by it. This knowledge of God presumes that the creator God's desire to save all people through the one Lord, Jesus Christ,[23] is prompted by love. Hence, salvation itself is a loving response to the "weaker" other which therefore obligates a reciprocal response to "weaker" others.

Paul's repetition of *eidōlothyta* (8:1, 4, 7, 10) makes it clear that "eating of meat offered to idols" has occasioned a serious threat to this moral principle, and one that cuts two ways. On the one hand, there are "strong" believers in the congregation who are unwavering in their orthodox knowledge of one God and Lord but whose triumphal admission of this fact is "puffed up" *(physios)* and thereby antagonistic to its corresponding virtue, a love that encourages the congregation's religious resiliency (8:4, 7). The repetition of *physios* makes clear that violating this principle threatens to make these "strong" believers no better than the "arrogant" *(physioō)* subversives he condemns in 4:18-19.

On the other hand, the real danger of *"gnōsis* apart from love" is that "weak" believers — those who have recently come into the congregation out of paganism — may be influenced to revert back to former religious routines (i.e., "pollutions of idols") offensive both to the God of Israel and to the apostle (8:10). When glossed by James's speech in Acts 15, the "weak" in 1 Corinthians 8 are those newly repentant pagans James is concerned about. Their "hearts have been purified by faith" but their practices with respect to "pollutions of idols" must yet be changed in order to forge a public identity in keeping with the congregation's Jewish legacy and Christian fellowship with those "strong" believers whose religious orthodoxy has been shaped by this same Jewish legacy (cf. 8:6).

Most interpreters focus attention on the responsibilities of the "strong" whose knowledge has effectively liberated them from concerns over participating in public gatherings associated with idol meats, with debilitating results for the "weak." In this regard, *gnōsis* has shaped a "conscience" (or "self-awareness")[24] that is steadfastly unbothered by the threat idols pose either for their witness (8:10a) or spiritual vitality. Perhaps this has even become the mark of Christian maturity that has now been insinuated upon newer believers whose weaker self-awareness makes them more susceptible to religious disaffection. In this regard, the loving response requires those with "strong" self-awareness — whose monotheistic beliefs are secure — to abstain from those re-

23. Paul's clear allusion to Israel's Shema' in 8:6 (cf. Deut 6:4-5) that begins with "for us," indicates his assumption that the "strong" are in continuity with his robust christological monotheism, a monotheism radically reformed by his belief in Jesus' resurrection by which his messiahship, Lordship, and Sonship are disclosed (cf. 1 Cor 15; Acts 2:26).

24. So R. Horsley, *1 Corinthians,* ANTC (Nashville: Abingdon, 1998), pp. 120-22.

ligious practices that might "wound" the "weak self-awareness" of newly converted pagans and lead them to observe "pollutions of idols" for religious (rather than for social) reasons in tacit denial of their monotheistic faith. Paul's appeal to love, then, is to do those actions that serve to safeguard the core beliefs of Christianity's *gnōsis,* especially in those new converts for whom these beliefs are not yet made "strong." If the "strong" fail in their ministry of love, the "weak" will fail to retain faith in the God of Israel and thus forfeit participation in Israel's salvation.

The admonition of the James of Acts is focused differently, not upon the congregation's "strong" (i.e., repentant Jews) but upon its "weak" (i.e., repentant pagans). The history of interpreting 1 Corinthians 8 has presumed the singular responsibility of the "strong" in abstaining from practices that might precipitate the spiritual disaffection of the "weak." The result has been to shape a kind of paternalism that absolves the weak — the newly converted — from making responsible choices that would participate in God's grace. Such paternalism is corrected by the James of Acts who makes clear that repentant pagans, whose hearts (= "conscience")[25] have been purified by faith, are themselves responsible for engaging in practices that preserve the congregation's Jewish legacy and thereby forge a public identity apropos for a people belonging to God.

Paul's final use of *eidōlothyta* in the rhetorical question of 10:19 recalls his earlier discussion in chapter 8 and enables him to make an important practical point in 10:20-22: participation in meals tied to pagan religion, if only for social reasons, has a "demonic" result even though the "divine" referent of an idol is fictive. This conclusion is not so different from the one voiced by the James of Acts. Central to the church's Jewish legacy is the intolerance of Israel's God to idols. Indeed, in a passage loudly echoing the OT narrative of God's fearful response to Israel's accommodation of other deities (10:1-13), the response to Paul's various rhetorical questions in 10:14-22 on idol meat is formed from Israel's Scriptures. The issue, then, is not merely public relations or the spiritual subversion of immature Christians; the issue is that any tinkering with pagan deities, no matter how trivial, contaminates the congregation's covenant with God.

The result of reading Acts *and* 1 Corinthians 8–10 together is a more balanced conception of a congregation's responsibility for cultivating the faith of new converts. While more mature believers are responsible to abstain from practices that might incline the immature to choose the gods of pagan culture over faith, the immature must be held accountable to avoid the destructive

---

25. For the connection between the psychology of "heart" and conscience/self-awareness, see A. Thiselton, *The First Epistle to the Corinthians,* NIGTC (Grand Rapids: Eerdmans, 2000), p. 643.

power of any other idolatrous allegiance. Working out one's salvation within the faith community is a collaborative work that enjoins "weak" and "strong" to form friendships that are by turns responsive to God's love and the spiritual requirements of other believers.

"Sexual Immorality" and 1 Corinthians 5–7

Besides worship practices inappropriate for a congregation of the Christian Diaspora, the "holiness code" of Acts also prohibits *porneia* (cf. 15:20, 29; 21:25). As a metaphor for unlawful sexual practices within marriage (perhaps based on Lev 18:6-18), *porneia* threatens crucial relationships that weave the social fabric of a Christian congregation. Without question sexual relations is an important purity practice, since God's sanctifying grace is an embodied experience and especially instantiated in the relationships of a Christian household. Yet, unlike the "pollutions of idols" thematic, the connection between Acts and the NT letters in this regard is unclear. Nowhere in the narrative world of Acts is sexual impropriety a threat to the congregation's wellbeing and witness or to any specific Christian marriage. Hence, when considered within its canonical setting the mention of *porneia* in Acts anticipates its fuller commentary in the NT letters that follow.

No biblical discussion of sexual (im)propriety is more important and familiar than that of 1 Corinthians 5–7.[26] The repetition of *porneia* (5:1; 6:13, 18; 7:2; cf. *porneuō*: 6:18; *pornē*: 6:15, 16) tracks Paul's sexual ethics from his definition of sexual deviance as subversive of congregational nurture and witness (5:1-13) to his essay on Christian marriage as the appropriate antidote for *porneia* (7:1-16). As is the case with idol meat, central to both aspects of his discussion of sexual immorality is Paul's broader concern for correcting a lawless variety of Christian freedom that subverts the congregation's witness (6:13-20). By this text, then, the NT reader comes to understand the implications of James's concerns first "voiced" in Acts 15:20.

This would seem especially true if the inclusion of *porneia* in the purity code of Acts alludes to Torah's legal brief on mixed marriages in Lev 18:6-18 as many commentators contend. In fact, 1 Cor 5:1-2 loudly echoes Lev 18:8, thereby cuing up the entire Levitical prohibition against forbidden "marriages" or sex-

---

26. On the rhetorical unity and theological coherence of 5–6 as a response to a single occasion of sexual impropriety, see W. Deming, "The Unity of 1 Corinthians 5–6," *Journal of Biblical Literature* 15 (1996): 289-312. Besides the repetition of *porneia* in 7:1 to introduce Paul's discussion on marriage, my reason for extending Paul's essay on sexual ethics to include that chapter is the "canonical" sensibility that the use of *porneia* in Acts 15:20, which cues Paul's subsequent discussion, alludes to Torah's code on mixed marriages found in Leviticus 18.

ual unions. With this intertext in view, then, the repetition of *porneia* to characterize a repulsive sexual union between a man and his stepmother and then to introduce Paul's nuanced discussion of mixed marriages[27] (7:1-16) within a Diaspora congregation, may be read in canonical setting as his *halakhah* on practices of marital purity in a manner that avoids the pollution of *porneia*. 1 Corinthians 5–7, then, functions as a biblical case study that clarifies the theological motive and ecclesial practice for preventing the corrupting influence of sexual immorality to persist within a Christian congregation.[28]

What is clear from Paul, and inferred by the James of Acts, is that sexually irregular practices, such as the incestuous relationship envisaged in 1 Cor 5:1-2, threatens to contaminate the entire congregation. For this reason, Paul commands the congregation to "cleanse" itself (5:7) by "driving out the wicked person *(poneron)* from among you" (5:13b). When one's reading of 1 Corinthians is oriented by Acts, Paul's focus on the entire congregation rather than on the individual believer is not unexpected. In fact, it is entirely in line with the concerns of the James of Acts for whom holiness is not merely an individual matter of the heart but extends to Christian fellowship and concerns what public practices the congregation maintains as the identifying marks of its covenant with God. What Paul's case study clarifies is that the congregation's relationship with God, let alone its public witness, can be imperiled by the conduct of a single moral renegade. Paul focuses here on the congregation, then, which is the legal residence of his apostolic "spirit," which collaborates with the Holy Spirit as the medium of the "power of our Lord Jesus" (cf. 3:16-17). It is within this assembly, congregated in the presence of apostolic and divine spirits, where the one who practices *porneia* must be expelled.

For the purpose of this essay, let me extend this observation by summarizing in broad brushstrokes the two principal points of Paul's *halakhic* midrash on the biblical demand to "drive out the wicked person among you" (Deut 17:7). Paul's initial point is that maintaining purity requires the congregation's leadership to expulse the offending member (5:3-8), not as a matter for the civil law courts to decide (so 6:1-8) but of church discipline. Indeed, he claims to have already "delivered this man to Satan for the destruction of his flesh" (5:5) — a curious phrase probably best taken symbolically as an operation of Paul's apostolic spirit that continues to reside in the congregation even though he is physically absent.

The immediate context makes it clear that this practice of deliverance is

---

27. I.e., marriages between celibate and non-celibate, between believer and non-believer.

28. On the characterization of 1 Corinthians 5 as "halakhic midrash," see B. Rosner, *Paul, Scripture and Ethics*, AGJU 22 (Leiden: Brill, 1994), pp. 61-93.

related to the "deliverance" thematic of the Passover typology (5:6-8). In this case, to "celebrate the festival" (of Passover) means to "cleanse out the old leaven" (5:7a), since such a "cleansing" — the expulsing of the "wicked person among you" — delivers the congregation from the threat of sin and death. Paul's language frames the expulsion as a Passover activity logically subsequent (and therefore responsive) to the sacrifice of "Christ, our Passover lamb." According to the Passover *typos,* the blood of the Passover lamb identifies those who belong to the redeemed people (cf. Exod 12:1-13), who then must prepare for their exodus from "malice and evil" (par. Egypt's Pharaoh) by preparing unleavened bread (cf. Exod 12:14-20). Accordingly, Paul's exhortation to become "new" leaven by cleansing itself of the "old" (= offending brother) presumes the sacrifice of the messianic lamb has "marked" believers with Christ for their exodus from sin (cf. 6:9-11). In this sense, to tolerate the brother's *porneia* is to repudiate Passover and to remain in "Egypt."

Whatever the eventual destiny of the offending brother,[29] the prior reference to the "day of the Lord" (5:5) as a time of salvation adds an eschatological motive to this use of the Passover typology: the death of Christ as Passover lamb and then the "cleansing of old leaven" are related activities that aim the congregation toward God's grand future for them in a "new" creation — the promised land — in which the practices of *porneia* are absent (cf. 6:9-10; Rev 21:6-8). In fact, according to Pauline thought, this future cosmic purity is already being instantiated by God's grace in the congregation's life. Thus, if the "day of the Lord" will bring *porneia* and every other anti-God activity to an end, a congregation's toleration of such behavior is at cross purposes with God's redemptive design.

Paul's differentiation between the *pornos* who is a non-believer and the *pornos* who is "a so-named brother" clarifies the practice of expulsion, evidently hinted at in a prior letter in which he prohibited the Corinthians "to associate *(sunanameignumi)* with immoral people" (5:9). The repetition of *sunanameignumi* (lit. "mixed up with") in v. 11 indicates its importance for Paul, whose intent is to delineate and distinguish the moral boundary markers of a faith community from the "immoral of this world" (5:10). If *porneia* is found in both "the world" and the congregation, one might indeed ask what real gains result from becoming Christian.

Paul's conversionist pattern of salvation presumes the transforming power of divine grace; for this reason, one should probably find some "hedging" in his use of the awkward phrase, *adelphos onomazomenos* ("a so-named

---

29. On which, see J. Gundry-Volf, *Paul and Perseverance,* WUNT 2/37 (Tübingen: Mohr, 1990), pp. 116-20.

brother"). Simply because an offending believer is "named" on the congregation's membership roster does not indicate his status with God — even though the very practice of cleansing intends to update the membership roster to make it as accurate as possible. In any case, the deep logic of Paul's argument is that any who have been "purified, sanctified, and justified in Jesus' name and by the Spirit of God" (6:11) will no longer engage in unrighteous activities including *porneia* (6:9-10). Lifestyle does not get the sinner saved; trusting Jesus does. But a transformed lifestyle, washed of sin, is the certain outcome — and thus an accurate barometer in identifying whoever God's grace finds and forgives.

Paul's response to the problem of persistent sin within a congregation is different from what we find in the second collection of NT letters. As a unifying thematic of the Catholic Epistles, congregations are exhorted not to expulse wayward believers but to rescue them from their sin in order to save them for the age to come (cf. Jas 5:19-20; Jude 22-23). What is inferred by this intracanonical conversation is a balancing act of sorts: whilst sin cannot be tolerated and the congregation's holiness must be protected by internal discipline, its love and loyalty for its members must extend especially to those who have lost their spiritual way.

Finally, then, is it possible to be a Christian without living a Christian lifestyle? Is God's purification of the sinner's heart by profession of faith all that is necessary in maintaining a congregation's Christian identity? Is Boyarin's criticism of a supersessionist Paul therefore correct? Do his letters allegorize Israel's Scriptures to make it unnecessary for Christians to perform purity practices (e.g., circumcision, Torah observance, Sabbath-keeping, table fellowship) as the public and corporate mark of an "Israel of God"? Even though many Protestant interpreters of Paul would think so, this text from 1 Corinthians would suggest not. The thesis of this essay contends that by reading Acts prior to Paul according to the "canon-logic" of the NT, readers of Paul are made more alert to his own instructions that require Christian congregations to maintain Jewish practices to safeguard its covenant with Israel's God. Hays puts it this way: "Paul in effect addresses the Gentile Corinthians *as* Israel."[30] Toleration of immoral conduct, such as catalogued in 5:11, subverts the internal integrity and external witness of the church as God's holy people.

Paul's Constraints on Christian Freedom

In introducing both his essays on *porneia* and *eidōlothyta,* Paul rebukes his readers for behaving arrogantly toward others (*physioō;* 5:2; 8:1); and then in

---

30. Hays, *1 Corinthians,* p. 88.

concluding each he personalizes their slogan of Christian liberty, "all things are lawful" (*panta exestin;* 6:12; 10:23; cf. 9:1-2) in order to correct it. This rhetorical framework clarifies an organizing principle of Pauline ethics: a congregation's public practices are motivated by a commitment to grow the faith of others. Whilst God's grace has liberated believers from the self-destructive powers of sinning to live holy lives, such a freedom is neither self-centered nor privatized but is constrained by the community's vocation "to live a life worthy of the gospel of Christ" (Phil 1:27; cf. 1 Cor 11:1). Believers are never absolutely free to live any way they wish but are prompted to seek the spiritual benefit of others for God's glory (10:23-33).

Like all biblical intertexts, this one forged by the canonical process between Acts 15:20 and Paul's essays on *porneia* and *eidōlothyta* in 1 Corinthians is mutually glossing, the one text reading the other. In this sense, one might infer yet another motive behind James's cautionary note insisting on complementing an inward purity of heart by faith (15:9) with those purity practices that identify the church's faithfulness to Israel's God: such practices enable repentant Gentiles and Jews to form congregations in which table fellowship supplies an ethos of Christian formation.

However, Paul's concerns in this regard are not solely pragmatic. Especially in concluding his essay on *porneia* (6:12-20), he asserts an important Christological claim as another principle of his vision of Christian existence: our redemption is bodily not only in its source (Christ's bodily death and resurrection; 6:19b-20a) but also in its conclusion (the church's resurrection from the dead; 6:14; cf. 15:42-57). For this reason, Christian beliefs must be embodied in public practices, whether sexual or religious. To imitate Christ (11:1) is to submit to his lordship over every activity (6:13).

A Theological Footnote for Today's Church

The canonical reading offered above suggests that God's cleansing of our lives by faith through the Spirit's baptism is embodied in a holy life and sanctified relations with all others. Moreover, it highlights the fact that the connection of the Spirit to the recreation of a holy people to serve God's redemptive interests, now and into the future, is a thoroughly Jewish idea.[31] The practical question that emerges for today's church is this: what does it mean that the church must be more Jewish in order to become more Christian? At the very least, one's con-

---

31. Cf. Alex Deasley, "The Holy Spirit in the Dead Sea Scrolls," *Wesleyan Theological Journal* 21 (1986): 45-73.

version to Christ by faith must not diminish the keen sense that covenanting with God not only demands faith in a particular Savior but also a particular way of life apropos of repentance. That is, the theological beliefs we confess must be embodied in the moral behaviors that evince the presence of God's Holy Spirit within us. Such a holy life, into which new believers are baptized and cultivated by God's Spirit, is marked out by a set of resurrection practices, individual and corporate, by which we are known in the public square.

Following the lead of Acts and Paul, this essay has concentrated on two practices, idolatry and sexual immorality, which are subversive of a holy life that shares in the resurrection of the living Lord Jesus. Both continue as real threats today. Perhaps this is due to the absence in our congregations of those resurrection practices catalogued by Acts — teaching God's word, inspiring worship, sharing goods in common, prayer, fellowship, evangelism — by which according to Paul's letters the Spirit enables believers to participate more fully in the results of the Lord's death and resurrection. But perhaps the growing tolerance of sexual impropriety and split loyalties within our congregations, which winks at divorce, turns an eye to seductive dress, and easily mixes the pagan gods of security (e.g., consumerism, militarism, patriotism) with the gospel, is due to the willingness of our "strong" to tolerate the weaknesses of our "weak." One prophetic expression of "being more Jewish in order to become more Christian" is to insist on obedience of those moral conditions that must be met before Christian fellowship is possible. Perhaps today's Christian leaders should press for a soteriology predicated on works and not on faith alone. The verdict of the James of Acts is given full expression by the Letter of James, which denies utterly the present and future efficacy of a faith without works.[32]

---

32. R. W. Wall, *The Community of the Wise: The Letter of James*, NTC (London: Continuum, 1997), pp. 142-57; "A Theology of Staying Saved (James 2:22)," unpublished paper read to the annual meeting of the *Society of Biblical Literature*, November, 2003, Atlanta; "Toward a Unifying Theology of the Catholic Epistles: A Canonical Perspective," in *The Catholic Epistles and the Tradition*, BETL, ed. J. Schlosser (Leuven: Peeters, 2004), pp. 43-71.

"You Shall Be Cruciform for I Am Cruciform": Paul's Trinitarian Reconstruction of Holiness

MICHAEL J. GORMAN

The biblical text "You shall be holy, for I am holy" (Lev 11:44-45; 19:2) issues both a fundamental theological claim about Israel's God and a corollary, equally fundamental claim on Israel as God's people.[1] Although Paul does not explicitly cite that Levitical injunction, there is ample evidence that he, like any good Jew, knew and contemplated it.[2] To be holy is to be set apart, to be like God *(imitatio dei)* and thus different from other people — but precisely how?

Paul's understanding of holiness was not completely new, for his gospel was a narrative in continuity with Israel's story. Thus Paul affirms certain basic Jewish understandings of holiness as difference from Gentiles (e.g., avoidance of sexual immorality and idolatry). Yet Paul also offers a radically new interpretation of holiness molded by the gospel of the Messiah who was crucified by Rome but raised and exalted by God.[3]

This essay proposes that Paul's understanding of holiness is grounded in his gospel, particularly (1) in his unique conviction that the crucified Messiah Jesus, the Son of God, is the revelation of the *holiness* of God the Father, and (2) in the corollary conviction that believers are called to be holy through "co-crucifixion" with Christ by the power of the *Holy* Spirit, who is the Spirit of both the Father and the Son. In other words, Paul's distinctive understanding of

---

1. See also Lev 20:7-8, 26; 21:6-8.

2. For example, in 1 Thessalonians, Paul's frequent admonitions to holiness are "more than a distant echo of the Levitical command to 'be holy as I am holy'" (Calvin Roetzel, *Paul: The Man and the Myth* [Minneapolis: Fortress, 1999], p. 36). 2 Cor 6:16 does cite a related Levitical text (26:11-12), but some scholars think it is part of a non-Pauline interpolation.

3. Cf. Stephen C. Barton, "Dislocating and Relocating Holiness: A New Testament Study," in *Holiness Past and Present,* ed. Stephen C. Barton (London: T&T Clark, 2003), pp. 193-213: "[T]he reinterpretation of holiness and its corollaries represented by the claim that 'God was *in Christ*' (2 Cor. 5.19) signifies a development of momentous proportions" (p. 197).

human holiness is grounded in the cross, which reveals three interconnected realities: the narrative identity of Christ the Son, the essential character of God the Father, and the primary activity of the Spirit. Paul's experience of Son, Father, and Spirit resulted in his radical reconstruction of holiness as both a counter-intuitive divine attribute/activity (or attribute-in-relation)[4] and a counter-cultural human imperative that is inherently communal. This unique, cruciform, and trinitarian vision of holiness may be summarized in a paraphrase of Leviticus: "You shall be cruciform for I am cruciform."[5]

Paul's Preoccupation with Holiness

"The river of holiness ran wide and deep through the traditions of Israel," Calvin Roetzel eloquently writes.[6] However, Roetzel rightly remarks, holiness is a "neglected feature of Paul's theological grammar."[7] This neglect is rather ironic, since Paul himself is preoccupied with holiness, as several aspects of his lexicon and letters indicate.[8]

The Holy Ones

The first piece of evidence is the term *hagioi* (singular *hagios*), or "holy ones," which is normally — unfortunately — translated "saints."[9] Paul takes over a term applied to Israel, as God's people, in the Scriptures and other Jewish writings.[10]

---

4. On divine holiness as a relational, covenantal reality, see John Webster, *Holiness* (Grand Rapids: Eerdmans, 2003), pp. 43-52.

5. This essay will limit its analysis to the seven letters universally considered to be authentic: Romans, 1 and 2 Corinthians, Galatians, Philippians, 1 Thessalonians, and Philemon. Footnotes will contain occasional references to the disputed letters.

6. Roetzel, *Paul*, p. 36.

7. Roetzel, *Paul*, p. 36.

8. Jeffrey A. D. Weima suggests that we should not be surprised that Paul, as a member of the Pharisees — whose name meant "separated ones" — was passionate about holiness as the "boundary marker" of God's covenant people ("'How You Must Walk to Please God': Holiness and Discipleship in 1 Thessalonians," in *Patterns of Discipleship in the New Testament,* ed. Richard N. Longenecker [Grand Rapids: Eerdmans, 1996], pp. 98-119 [p. 102]).

9. Usually or always so in the NRSV, NIV, NASB, and KJV. The NAB, a Roman Catholic translation, uses "holy ones."

10. See James D. G. Dunn, *The Theology of Paul the Apostle* (Grand Rapids: Eerdmans, 1998), p. 44, n. 90 for instances of this usage. Dunn stresses the inclusion of the Gentiles in Paul's use of this epithet (pp. 44-45).

Hagioi is one of Paul's two favorite terms for believers (the other being *adelphoi*, "brothers [and sisters]"). Paul addresses believers as *hagioi* at the beginning of four letters (Rom 1:1, 7; 1 Cor 1:2; 2 Cor 1:1; Phil 1:1)[11] and also refers to them as such on twenty other occasions.[12] By placing the designation *hagioi* in the opening of his letters, Paul shows his ability to direct special attention to the church's holiness,[13] and by using *hagioi* elsewhere — in what appear to be less deliberate ways — Paul also reveals that this way of speaking of the church is second nature to him. Holiness is, therefore, essential to the identity of the church as a whole and to each individual in it.[14]

A second piece of evidence is related to the first. In two letter openings, Paul uses *hagioi* in connection with God's calling. In Rom 1:7, he says either that the Roman believers are "called holy ones" or, perhaps, "called to be holy ones" (so NRSV, NIV, NAB; Greek *klētois hagiois*). Does Paul mean that the church already *is* holy or that it is called to *become* holy? Similar language in 1 Cor 1:2 suggests that the answer is "both": Paul defines "the church of God that is in Corinth" as those who have already been "made holy [*hēgiasmenois*, from the verb related to *hagios*] in Christ"[15] and who are also "called to be holy" *(klētois hagiois)*. The purpose of God, in Paul's view, is to call out a people into Christ, which in itself sets this new community apart as God's holy people, and also to form them into a people that sees holiness as its mandate and its goal, or *telos*. Holiness *(hagiasmos)*, for Paul, is both gift and task.[16] The meaning of this holiness, according to 1 Cor 1:2, derives its shape and substance only "in Christ."

---

11. See also Col 1:2, 4; Eph 1:1, 4.

12. Rom 8:27; 12:13; 15:25, 26, 31; 16:2, 15; 1 Cor 6:1, 2; 14:33; 16:1, 15; 2 Cor 8:4; 9:1, 12; 13:12; Phil 4:22; 1 Thess 3:13; Phlm 5, 7; plus "every saint" (sing.), Phil 4:21. Thus the term occurs 25 times in the undisputed letters and another fifteen in the disputed (mostly in Col and Eph).

13. Holiness language especially pervades the opening of Rom (1:1-7) and 1 Cor (1:1-9).

14. This is further confirmed elsewhere; for example, Paul identifies both the community (1 Cor 3:16-17; 2 Cor 6:16) and the individual (1 Cor 6:19-20) as God's (holy) temple.

15. NRSV, NIV, and NAB all have "sanctified."

16. The word *hagiasmos*, "holiness/sanctification," appears in Rom 6:19, 22; 1 Cor 1:30; 1 Thess 4:3, 4, 7. The similar term *hagiōsynē* appears in Rom 1:4; 2 Cor 7:1; 1 Thess 3:13. Dunn (*Theology*, p. 330) notes that Paul can use *hagiasmos* to mean both the *beginning* of salvation, when "individuals were set apart to discipleship," and the *process* of salvation. Cf. Webster: "Holiness is indicative; but it is also imperative; indeed, it is imperative *because* it is the indicative holiness of the triune God whose work of sanctification is directed towards the renewal of the creature's active life of fellowship with him" (*Holiness*, p. 87).

The Call to Holiness

A third piece of evidence for the centrality of holiness in Paul is its appearance in programmatic statements in his letters. Perhaps the clearest example of this is 1 Thessalonians, in which "holiness is the most important theme."[17] At two key junctures (the middle and the end), Paul summarizes his basic message to the Thessalonians as a call to holiness: "[May the Lord] strengthen your hearts to be blameless in holiness [*hagiōsynē*] before our God and Father at the coming of our Lord Jesus with all his holy ones [*hagiōn*]" (3:13), and "May the God of peace himself make you entirely holy [*hagiasai hymas holoteleis*] . . . and may your spirit, soul, and body be kept blameless at the coming of our Lord Jesus Christ" (5:23). In addition, at the beginning of his ethical instruction in 1 Thessalonians, Paul identifies the essential will of God as the Thessalonians' "holiness" (*hagiasmos*, 4:3a). While sexual holiness is particularly in view (4:3b-8, where "holiness" appears twice and "Holy Spirit" once), this counter-cultural sexual holiness — believers are not to be "like the Gentiles who do not know God" (4:5) — is clearly seen as part of a larger call to holiness. Paul relates that holiness to Father, Son, and Spirit: God (the Father) calls in holiness (4:7), the Spirit effects holiness (4:8), and the Son ("the Lord") judges the unholy (4:6b).[18]

Holiness is also the focus of 1 Corinthians. Not only does the letter's opening (1:2; see above) name holiness as the Corinthians' status and goal, but the thanksgiving — which sets the letter's agenda — echoes the concern of 1 Thessalonians that believers be blameless at Christ's coming (1 Cor 1:8). Paul then returns to the theme of God's call to holiness by reassuring the Corinthians (and maybe himself) that God is faithful and will indeed complete the call (i.e., effect the Corinthians' blamelessness at the coming of the Lord). This call is specified as "fellowship [*koinōnian*] with his son Jesus Christ our Lord" (1:9). We see then that for Paul holiness means participation or sharing (the root meaning of *koinōnia*) in Christ.[19] We may justly see 1 Corinthians, therefore, as Paul's attempt to explain to the Corinthians what this programmatic call of God to holiness in Christ means for them in the midst of all the complex issues the community is facing.

More specifically, it is clear from the letter that the Corinthians see themselves as a "spiritual" community, heavily endowed with gifts of the Spirit. Paul

17. Weima, "'How You Must Walk,'" p. 98.
18. Weima, "'How You Must Walk,'" p. 110.
19. This reinforces the interpretive principle we noted earlier: for Paul, holiness is inseparable from Christ. Paul makes this claim explicitly also in 1 Cor 1:30: Christ has become for us holiness *(hagiasmos)* from God.

recognizes the community's charismatic character (1:5-7; chaps. 12–14) as well as its holy character (1:1-9, 6:11). However, the community's sanctification does not match its abundance of spiritual gifts; the people's growth in holiness — their conversion — seems incomplete.[20] The people's values are still shaped more by the spirit of their Greco-Roman age than by the Holy Spirit. Throughout 1 Corinthians, Paul calls them to three dimensions of holiness: avoiding sexual immorality but embodying an appropriate sexuality (5:1-13; 6:12-20; 7:1-40); avoiding idolatry but embracing exclusive allegiance to Jesus (10:1-22); and, above all, avoiding self-serving behavior but practicing Christ-like, cruciform love that seeks the good of the other and the community (chap. 13, esp. 13:5; 16:14; cf. 8:1-13; 9:1-26; 10:23–11:1; 14:1-40).[21] This counter-cultural (holy) love pays special attention to the weaker members of the community (11:17-34; 12:14-26) and special honor to apostles who exhibit Christ-like power-in-weakness (4:1-13), and it has a counter-intuitive commitment to absorbing injustice rather than inflicting it (6:1-11). This cruciform holiness stands in marked contrast to the dominant Roman cultural values of promoting the self by seeking honor, and of honoring the powerful. Paul's primary goal is to turn a *charismatic* community into a *cruciform* and therefore truly *holy* community, one in which all believers are in proper relationship to one another and to God the Father, Christ the Lord, and the Holy Spirit — the triune God at work among them.[22]

Space does not permit much discussion of holiness in other letters.[23] It must suffice simply to mention Romans briefly.[24] Paul claims that God's loving act of justification/reconciliation in Christ, known by the presence of the Spirit (5:1-11), liberates people from the idolatry and immorality of this age (1:18-32; 12:1-2) in order to die and rise with Christ, presenting themselves to God as his slaves who obey him in a life of holiness (6:1-23, with "holiness" or "sanctification," *hagiasmon*, in 6:19 and 6:22). That this holiness is in fact Christ-likeness is clear from the assertion that the *telos* of salvation is conformity to "the image of his [God's] son" (8:29)[25] rather than to this age (12:1-2); from allusions to Jesus'

---

20. See Stephen J. Chester, *Conversion in Corinth: Perspectives on Conversion in Paul's Theology and the Corinthian Church* (London: T&T Clark, 2003).

21. Even Paul's vision of sexual holiness is related to a larger vision of holiness linked explicitly to the cross in chaps. 5 and 6 (5:6-8; 6:19-20), and implicitly in chap. 7. There Paul advocates mutual, kenotic marital love (7:1-7) and honors bearing with an unbelieving spouse (7:12-16).

22. For the trinitarian activity of God in 1 Corinthians, see especially 6:15-17 and 12:4-6.

23. The reader should consult the other essays on Paul in this volume.

24. Galatians and Philippians will be treated, under a different heading, below.

25. Dunn (*Theology*, p. 502) notes the "cluster" of terms related to election/sanctification in 8:27-33.

teaching on love and non-retaliation (12:9-21); and from an explicit call to Christ-like love for the weak (15:1-3).

Three Fundamental Features of Holiness in Paul

We may now make three general observations about holiness in Paul that are suggested by the foregoing survey: (1) holiness is difference from the life of Gentile non-believers; (2) holiness is both the character and the activity of the triune God; and (3) holiness is essentially Christ-likeness.

First of all, human holiness in the Jewish (and therefore also early Christian) tradition is, first and foremost, difference from those who do not participate in God's call or character. This differentness, for Paul, is radical, and he can use very stark apocalyptic language to express the contrast (e.g., 1 Thess 5:4-11; Rom 13:13-14). The non-conformity to this age, however, does not mean an escape from the world, which Paul flatly rejects as preposterous (1 Cor 5:9-10).[26] Unlike, say, the community at Qumran, holiness for Paul means being different from but still located within the host environment. In fact, the community's difference enables it to bear witness to its surrounding culture (Phil 2:14-16). This dynamic tension of "in but not of the world" appears, for example, in Romans 12–13, which begins with Paul's famous call for nonconformity to this "world" or "age," and which deals nonetheless with life in this real, dangerous world where people have enemies (Rom 12:9-21) and must deal with imperial authorities (Rom 13:1-7) — who may, in fact, be the enemies.

Secondly, for Paul holiness is trinitarian in structure.[27] It is the unified, collaborative activity of Father, Son, and Spirit. Holiness is the call and will of God the Father; it occurs in Christ, who defines holiness for the church; and it is effected by the Spirit, who is the *Holy* Spirit. One word Paul uses to describe the result of this divine activity is *koinōnia*. Human holiness is participation in divine holiness. Holiness is, therefore, both the property and the activity of the Father, the Son, and the Spirit. God not only sets people apart, but also conveys to humans the very character of God. Human holiness is therefore not merely a human imperative; it is a divine product, or "fruit" (Gal 5:22).

26. Paul does want believers to disassociate from unholy believers (1 Cor 5:9-13). If 2 Cor 6:14–7:1 is authentic, then the "holiness" (7:1) Paul advocates probably means disassociation from such pseudo-saints, including so-called apostles who (unlike Paul — 6:3-10) fail to practice cruciform holiness.

27. For further discussion of Paul's trinitarian spirituality and theology, see my *Cruciformity: Paul's Narrative Spirituality of the Cross* (Grand Rapids: Eerdmans, 2001), pp. 63-74, and the literature cited there.

Thirdly, holiness is Christ-likeness. In both apocalyptic passages noted above, the alternative to being in the darkness of unholiness is "putting on" Christ (Rom 13:14) or "living with Christ" by practicing faith, love, and hope (1 Thess 1:8-10). That is, Christ-likeness, or *koinōnia* with Christ (1 Cor 1:9), is the opposite of unholiness and thereby constitutes holiness itself. The eschatological goal of conformity to Christ (Rom 8:29) begins now through an ongoing experience of sharing in Christ's status as a slave or servant of God and others, one characterized by non-retaliatory, other-centered, cruciform love.

We will have more to say about the shape of this Christ-likeness below. For now, however, the very notion raises a crucial issue. As a Jew, Paul knows that to be holy is to be *God-like;* as a Jew in Christ, he knows that to be holy is to be *Christ-like.* The question is then raised, What is the connection between these two necessary understandings of holiness? The answer, for Paul, is that *Christ is God-like, and God is Christ-like.* That is why Paul can speak of the (Holy) Spirit as the Spirit of both the Son and the Father.

The Holy Spirit[28]

The Activity of the Holy Spirit (1 Thessalonians)

In Paul's earliest letter, 1 Thessalonians, the Holy Spirit is mentioned early and associated with both power and joy (1:5-6). But the Holy Spirit is also associated with holiness per se in Paul's exhortation to (especially sexual) holiness. Holiness is both the property (4:8) and the activity (4:3, 4, 7) of the Spirit. As Gordon Fee says in commenting on the phrase "Holy Spirit" in this text: "[T]he Spirit is none other than the Spirit of God, himself 'holy.' . . . [W]e are here dealing with the character of God, and with Paul's understanding of the Christian ethic as the Spirit's reproducing that character in his people."[29]

It would be a mistake, therefore, to conclude that for Paul in 1 Thessalonians the Holy Spirit is merely the spirit of holy sexuality. The activity of the Holy Spirit is equally visible in the faith, love, and hope that Paul offers as proof of the Thessalonians' reception of the gospel and the Spirit (1 Thess 1:2-10). This experience included becoming imitators of Paul and Jesus

---

28. In Paul's undisputed letters, there are more than one hundred references to the Spirit, of which twelve or thirteen specify the Spirit as the *Holy* Spirit: Rom 5:5; 9:1; 14:17; 15:13, 16; 1 Cor 6:19; 12:3; 2 Cor 6:6; 13:13[14]; 1 Thess 1:5, 6; 4:8; and possibly also Rom 15:19 (some mss.). See also Rom 1:4, "Spirit of holiness."

29. Gordon D. Fee, *God's Empowering Presence: The Holy Spirit in the Letters of Paul* (Peabody, Mass.: Hendrickson, 1994), p. 51.

by being persecuted (1:6; 2:14-16), and Paul associates this suffering particularly with the Thessalonians' faith, or faithfulness (*pistis,* 1:7; 3:2-7) as well as their love (3:6) and their hope/steadfastness (3:13).

Thus we may conclude that Paul believes that the work of the Holy Spirit, and thus human holiness, consists in large measure of faith(fulness), hope/steadfastness, and love. Furthermore, this holiness includes becoming like Jesus (and other holy examples) through steadfast faithfulness in the face of adversity. The traditional meaning of holiness, therefore, is being expanded to mean something like sharing in the story of Jesus the crucified.[30] Holiness is taking on a cruciform shape, without thereby losing other, more traditional meanings such as sexual virtue. The identity and activity of the Spirit, therefore, is also being reshaped by being associated with the Son. This identification of the Spirit as the Spirit of the Son becomes explicit in Galatians.

The Activity of the Spirit of the Son (Galatians)

The word *hagios* and its cognates do not appear in Galatians. This absence is rather ironic, since the core issue in this letter is the meaning of holiness: What are the essential "marks" of the Israel of God (Gal 6:16)? The thrust of the letter is to reject separate table fellowship, circumcision, or even Sabbath-keeping as the true meaning of holiness. Instead, Paul proposes, participation in God the Father's gift of the Son and Spirit is the root meaning of holiness. The Israel of God is marked by the cross and the Spirit. And that Spirit is, in fact, the Spirit of the Son (Gal 4:4-6).[31] This identification of the Spirit as the Spirit of the Son is crucial to understanding Galatians in general and the meaning of holiness in Galatians in particular.

In Gal 1:4 Paul summarizes the entire letter in three phrases. It will focus on the promises of God (chaps. 3–4) fulfilled in the crucified Messiah, who "gave himself up for our sins" (chaps. 1–2) "to deliver us from the present evil age" (chaps. 5–6) — that is, to create a holy, Spirit-filled people. Galatians 1:4 shows that the meaning of holiness will be related to the inextricable bond between the cross and the Spirit as the outworking of God's eschatological salvation. The entire letter says that the salvation process — holiness — is crucifixion: *to* the flesh and the world (5:25; 6:14), and *with* Christ (2:19-20).

---

30. For a full exposition of the cruciform character of holiness in 1 Thessalonians, see Andy Johnson, "The Sanctification of the Imagination in 1 Thessalonians," in this volume.

31. The Spirit is also referred to as the Spirit of Christ, as well as God [the Father], in Rom 8:9.

Galatians 2:19-20 reveals the focal point of Paul's gospel in the death of Christ and in believers' participation in it. Paul speaks representatively, using "I" and "me." Echoing and expanding 1:4, in 2:20 he describes Christ's death on the cross as his act of self-giving love: "who loved [*agapēsantos*, the verb related to the noun *agapē*] me by giving himself for me" (2:20b).[32] Furthermore, according to a growing number of scholars, Paul here also refers to Christ's death as his act of faith, or faithfulness *(pistis)*, toward God: "I live by the faith *of* the Son of God [rather than "faith *in* the Son of God"] who loved me...."[33] This means that Paul sees the identity of Christ the crucified Son of God revealed in a story of faith (toward God) and love (toward others). Christ's faithful, loving death on the cross is therefore the quintessential act of covenant fulfillment, the quintessential *holy* deed; it is the *definitive revelation of holiness.*

Believers are those who identify so fully with Christ's cross that Paul can say, "I have been crucified with Christ" and that this same crucified (but now obviously resurrected) Christ lives "in me." That is, believers experience a kind of resurrection by means (paradoxically) of co-crucifixion. Paul thus implies that the life of believers will also be characterized by Christ-like faith and love (see 5:6).

Galatians 4:4-6 narrates the Father's dual gift of the Son and the Spirit as the fulfillment of the promise to liberate the people of God and incorporate the Gentiles into God's family (4:5). It is both surprising and extraordinarily significant that Paul in this context describes the Spirit sent into our hearts as "the Spirit of his [God's] Son" (4:6). Not only does this demonstrate an intimate link among Father, Son, and Spirit, but it also connects believers simultaneously to both the Father and the Son through the Spirit. Because the Spirit is the Spirit of the Son of God who displayed faith and love on the cross, the mark of God's children, indwelt by that Spirit, is not circumcision but "faith expressing itself through love" (5:5-6, clearly echoing 2:20). This constitutes the essential holiness of the Spirit-led community. Believers live by faith and love in conjunction with a Spirit-inspired hope for righteousness (5:5), that is (as similar texts in 1 Thessalonians suggest), the hope for God-likeness (holiness) — and thus vindication — at the eschatological judgment.

Finally, two points about Gal 5:22-25, on the "fruit of the Spirit," are worth noting. First, the language of "fruit" implies the kind of natural consequence

---

32. Author's translation, taking the Greek word *kai,* usually translated "and," as explanatory, "by giving."

33. See further discussion and relevant literature in my *Cruciformity,* pp. 110-21. However, this interpretation does not neglect the importance of the believer's faith; see, for example, 2:16: "even we have believed in [literally, *into*] Christ."

discussed above that is implied by the presence of the Spirit of God's Son. At the same time, however, human cooperation with the Spirit is required (5:25; cf. 5:16). Second, although the fruit of the Spirit includes both love and faith(fulness) *(agapē* and *pistis),* the list in 5:22-23 is obviously broader than that. The "crucifixion" of the flesh and its desires (5:25) means the birth of new desires and practices that "flesh out" the root meaning of cruciform holiness as self-giving, other-serving love of neighbor (5:13-14).

In Galatians, then, the implicit association of the Spirit with the cross of Christ in 1 Thessalonians has become explicit. The work of the Spirit — holiness — is, in essence, cruciformity. We will now look briefly at three other letters that continue this association of cross and Spirit and also connect both more directly to God the Father.

Christ Crucified as the Holiness of the Cruciform God

Christ Crucified, the Holiness of God (1 Corinthians)

Sometimes called the "kerygmatic paradox," 1 Cor 1:18–2:5 declares boldly that "Christ [is] the power and wisdom of God" (1:24). In context, the reference to Christ is clearly to Christ *crucified* (1:23; cf. 1:18; 2:2). Traditional divine attributes — wisdom and power — are turned topsy-turvy by being associated with the foolishness and weakness of crucifixion. Paul infers that *Christ crucified both reveals and redefines God.* Unlike the broader Jewish tradition, in which God's power and beneficence (the "paradox of holiness")[34] were held in *tension,* Paul holds them in *concert.* In Christ he does not know a God of power *and* weakness but the God of power *in* weakness. God is cruciform.

In 1 Cor 1:30 Paul repeats the divine attribute of wisdom and adds three others: "[Christ] became for us wisdom from God, and righteousness and holiness [NIV; "sanctification" in NRSV, NAB] and redemption."[35] At first glance, these three may seem more like divine *activities* than divine *attributes:* God's right-wising, sanctifying, and redeeming. But this differentiation between divine activity and divine attribute is a false one. God's actions are self-revelatory,

34. Hannah K. Harrington, *Holiness: Rabbinic Judaism and the Greco-Roman World* (London/New York: Routledge, 2001), p. 43.

35. The phrase "for us" in 1:30 does not mean that Paul is a relativist who believes that the revelatory character of Christ crucified is a function of our belief, and that non-belief voids its revelatory reality. Rather, Paul simply acknowledges the counter-intuitive character of this revelation, which explains why so many reject it despite its salvific value for those who perceive it correctly (cf. 1:18-25).

the expression of God's essence or character.[36] The context once again demands that we understand Paul to be referring to Christ in 1:30 as Christ *crucified*. This means that in Christ crucified, and only in Christ crucified, God acts to make humans holy (activity). It also means that *the cross reveals the holiness of God* (attribute, essence), just as it reveals the wisdom and power of God. But this is not normal deity: "For execution by crucifixion to become the criterion of holiness, and of God's holiness at that, became the supreme scandal."[37]

A scandal, yes, but also true holiness. In 1 Cor 11:1 Paul refers to the actualization of this Christ-like holiness as becoming like him (Paul) inasmuch as he is like Christ — by which Paul again means Christ crucified, Christ who did not exercise his rights but gave them up as an act of love for others. And if Christ is God's holiness for us, then becoming like the crucified Christ is sharing in God's holiness and thus becoming like God.

This strange notion of divine holiness, revealed in Christ crucified and thereby cruciform in character, is confirmed by passages from two additional letters.

Christ Crucified, the Image and Glory of God (2 Corinthians)

In 2 Cor 3:17-18 Paul comments on his interpretation of Exod 34:34 as a reference to turning to the Lord that gives "unveiled" access to God:

> "The Lord" is the Spirit, and where the Spirit of the Lord is, there is freedom. And all of us, with unveiled faces, seeing the glory of the Lord as though reflected in a mirror, are being transformed into the same image from one degree of glory to another; for this comes from the Lord, the Spirit. (NRSV, slightly altered)

These verses seem in part to distinguish and in part to conflate "the Lord" and "the Spirit," while they raise the question, "Who or what is 'the glory of the Lord'?"

A few verses later, Paul makes it clear that his gospel is "the gospel of the glory of Christ, who is the image of God" (4:4), that he and his colleagues proclaim "Jesus Christ as Lord" (4:5), and that God the creator of light has now

---

36. For example, the Bible stresses that God is faithful to the covenant and thereby acts to save in ways that express that unchangeable faithfulness. Cf. Webster, *Holiness*, pp. 39-40, and Colin Gunton, *Act and Being: Towards a Theology of the Divine Attributes* (Grand Rapids: Eerdmans, 2002).

37. Paul S. Minear, "The Holy and the Sacred," *Theology Today* 47 (1990-91): 5-12 (8).

"shone in our hearts to give the light of the knowledge of the glory of God in the face of Jesus Christ" (4:6). Thus Christ is the glory and image of God, but he is also "Lord," a title associated with the Spirit in the text from 2 Corinthians 3 cited above. What are we to make of all this?

First, Paul has become so convinced that Christ is the self-revelation of God that he attributes to Christ the scriptural divine epithet "Lord." He also identifies Christ with two scriptural word-pictures that speak of the likeness of God in the heavenly realm: the "glory" and the "image" of God.

Second, Paul attributes his certainty that Christ is God's self-revelation to his experience of God's Spirit. Thus, Paul concludes, it must be none other than God's Spirit who is calling him and others to experience the very glory of God in the Son. This is the essence of believing existence, to "see" the glory of the Lord (i.e., Christ) and be gradually transformed by the Spirit into the image of Christ, the image of God (2 Cor 3:18). Though Paul does not use the word "holiness" here, he is describing the process of becoming holy, of becoming like Christ and thus like God.

Third (and this is absolutely crucial), we must not forget that throughout this discussion of "the gospel of the glory of Christ" (2 Cor 4:4), Paul assumes that his Corinthian readers remember that the only gospel he proclaims (1 Cor 1:18-25) and the only Christ he knows (1 Cor 2:2) is Christ *crucified*. Christ *crucified* is the image and glory of God. To be sure, it is Christ crucified and resurrected/exalted, but the two are inseparable in Paul's mind.[38] Paul reminds his readers that the glory and image of God about which he writes, and into which all believers are being transformed, is the paradoxical glory of power in weakness, of life in death (2 Cor 4:10; cf. 2 Cor 12:1-10).

Fourth, and finally, the bottom line: if the crucified Christ is the glory and image of God, what does that say about God, and what does it say about the process of becoming God-like? The answers are implicit but nonetheless clear: God is like Christ crucified. To become like God is to become like that kind of God.

In his letter to the Philippians, Paul continues this motif.

Christ Crucified, the Story of God (Philippians)

The well-known text Phil 2:6-11 is both the centerpiece of Philippians and Paul's "master story." The entire passage is the subject of much debate, but the

---

38. Commenting on this passage, Victor Paul Furnish says, "For Paul, it is precisely *as* the crucified one that Christ is 'the Lord of glory' (1 Cor. 2:8 . . .)" (*II Corinthians*, AB 32A [Garden City, N.Y.: Doubleday, 1984], p. 248).

following remarks represent what may be an emerging consensus on certain key issues.[39]

Paul's master story begins, "Although Christ Jesus was in the form of God, he did not regard this equality with God as something to exploit for his own advantage" (Phil 2:6, author's translation).[40] The phrases "the form of God" and "equality with God" are synonymous, indicating something Christ already possessed but did not use for his own advantage. The background of this language is probably both the scriptural language of the divine image and glory and the competing Roman language of claims to imperial divinity.[41] Thus Christ is like the God of Israel and is truly divine, unlike the emperor, who is a pseudo-god.

This opening verse sets up a contrast between normal expectations of deity and Christ's actual actions, which are narrated in the following two verses (2:7-8) as a two-stage self-emptying, or *kenōsis*, in "incarnation" and obedient death by crucifixion:

> Although Christ Jesus [x] was in the form of God, he did not [y] regard this equality with God as something to exploit for his own advantage, but instead [z] emptied himself by taking on the form of a slave . . . [and] humbled himself by becoming obedient to the point of death — even death on a cross. (Phil 2:6-8 abridged, author's translation)

The text says that although normal human expectations would be for a god to exercise power and privilege, to seek status and honor, and to perpetually "climb upward" as proofs of divinity, *this* "form of God" did just the contrary.

The bracketed letters [x], [y], and [z] are used to indicate that this part of

39. For lengthier discussions of the views presented here, see my *Cruciformity*, pp. 88-92, 164-69, 278-80, 316-19, and 357-58; the chapter on Philippians in my *Apostle of the Crucified Lord* (Grand Rapids: Eerdmans, 2005), pp. 412-53; and "'Although/Because He Was in the Form of God': The Theological Significance of Paul's Master Story (Phil 2:6-11)," *The Journal of Theological Interpretation* 1/2 (Fall 2007). For similar interpretations of this text, see N. T. Wright, *The Climax of the Covenant* (Minneapolis: Fortress, 1991), pp. 56-98, and Stephen Fowl, "Christology and Ethics in Paul," in *Where Christology Began: Essays on Philippians 2*, ed. Ralph P. Martin and Brian J. Dodd (Louisville: Westminster John Knox, 1998), pp. 140-53; and *The Story of Christ in the Ethics of Paul*, JSNTSup 36 (Sheffield: JSOT Press, 1990), pp. 49-101. Of course there are differing interpretations of certain details and various points of emphasis among these similar approaches.

40. For the justification of this translation, see, e.g., Wright, *Climax*, pp. 56-98; and Gerald F. Hawthorne, "In the Form of God and Equal with God," in *Where Christology Began*, ed. Martin and Dodd, pp. 96-110.

41. See, e.g., John Dominic Crossan and Jonathan L. Reed, *In Search of Paul: How Jesus's Apostle Opposed Rome's Empire with God's Kingdom — A New Vision of Paul's Words and World* (San Francisco: HarperSanFrancisco, 2004), esp. pp. 235-57, 270-91; Gorman, *Cruciformity*, pp. 278-81.

Paul's master story is the basis of a pattern that appears throughout his letters, a pattern of "although [x], not [y] but [z]," meaning: "although status [x], not selfish exploitation [y] but self-emptying/self-giving [z]." This pattern provides a narrative structure in Philippians and elsewhere to a cruciform life in contrast to "normalcy."[42]

Paul's use of the story of Christ in its immediate context suggests that he is describing the very meaning of life in and with the triune God. He urges the Philippians to pattern their lives after Christ (2:1-5), which is life "in Christ" (2:1, 5), "fellowship with/participation in [*koinōnia*] the Spirit" (2:2), and the activity of God (the Father) that enables intentions and acts that please God (2:13).[43] To be like Christ is to participate in the Spirit and to embody the activity of God. It is, in other words, to be like God, to be holy. And that only makes sense if the story of Christ is the story of God, if the counter-intuitive kenosis of the Son reveals the way God really acts and really is.

Philippians 2:6-11, then, reveals not only the narrative identity and holiness of Christ the obedient Son, but also the narrative identity and holiness of God the Father. This is a *counter-intuitive, counter-cultural, and counter-imperial* form of deity. Yet, for Paul, this is what Christ as the "form of God" is all about. And that means *Paul wants us to re-think God.*[44] Here Pauline scholarship has only recently begun to raise the right theological issues emerging from this exegesis. For example, in their book *In Search of Paul,* John Dominic Crossan and Jonathan L. Reed contend that Phil 2:6-11 speaks of "kenotic divinity" and ask, "[F]or Christians, is not Christ *the* revelation of God and, then, is that kenotic Christ not the supreme revelation of a kenotic God?"[45]

Paul does clearly imply that what Christ did, though counter-intuitive and extravagantly unorthodox, was ultimately not a *violation* of divinity but an *expression* of it. Otherwise, how could Christ be "equal with God" if Christ betrayed the character of God?[46] This means that "Although he was in the form of God, . . ." in the larger thought-world of the apostle also means "*Because* he was

---

42. See, e.g., 1 Thess 2:7; 1 Cor 9:12-23 (esp. 9:19); 2 Cor 8:9; and my *Cruciformity,* pp. 88-91, 164-75, 181-99, 209-12, 230-61. "Normalcy" is from Crossan and Reed, *In Search of Paul,* pp. 242, 284, *et passim.*

43. Cf. Wright (*Climax,* p. 87), who says that Phil 2 is "not merely [about] the imitation of Christ: it is the outworking of the life of the Spirit of God."

44. For a fuller discussion of Paul's notion of a kenotic or cruciform God, see my *Cruciformity,* pp. 9-18.

45. Crossan and Reed, *In Search of Paul,* 289-91 (citation, p. 291).

46. See further Wright, *Climax,* pp. 86-87, on the exaltation as God's endorsement of Christ's kenosis as "the proper expression of divine character" (p. 87), and Fowl, "Christology and Ethics," p. 142.

in the form of God." (The Greek allows either translation.)[47] Because of the [x]-[y]-[z] pattern noted above, it is important to keep in mind the *surface* structure of the text: "Although he was. . . ." At the same time, however, the *deep* structure of Paul's theological grammar compels us to interpret the text as "Because he was. . . ."[48] The "although" of the text does not mean that the story of Christ is an anomaly, an aberration of true divinity, but rather that *our* normal perception of deity is in fact the aberration. As N. T. Wright puts it:

> The real theological emphasis of the hymn . . . is not simply a new view of Jesus. It is a new understanding of God. . . . [I]ncarnation and even crucifixion are to be seen as *appropriate* vehicles for the dynamic self-revelation of God.[49]

and

> The one who was eternally "equal with God" expressed that equality precisely in the sequence of events referred to in vv. 6-8.[50]

Some will raise the question, "Does not the reward Christ receives in Phil 2:9-11 suggest that his humanity is in view?" Christ's humanity (obedience) is indeed rewarded by God. But the probable allusions in the text to Adam and to the image ("form") of God suggest that true humanity is to be God-like.[51] The obedient Christ is exalted because in manifesting true *divinity* as the form of God taking the form of a slave (by becoming human and offering himself in death), he also manifested true *humanity* (unlike Adam) — as the obedient Son of the Father.

Thus we see what is for Paul a crucial and inextricable link between divine and human holiness: kenosis is the *sine qua non* of both divinity and humanity, as revealed in the incarnation and cross of Christ, the one who was truly God and truly human.[52]

---

47. Actually, there are three main options: the neutral "being" (NIV); the concessive "although/though" (NRSV, NAB); and the causative "because."

48. Wright (*Climax*, p. 83, n. 110) says that if his interpretation is correct, "the causative sense is clearly the one required." Hawthorne leans strongly in the same direction ("In the Form of God," p. 104).

49. Wright, *Climax*, p. 84.

50. Wright, *Climax*, p. 90.

51. Cf. "image" in 2 Cor 4:4 (Christ); Gen 1:27 (humanity).

52. As Chalcedonian and therefore anachronistic as this claim will sound to some, it seems to me to be the inevitable conclusion of the line of thought we have been pursuing. N. T. Wright's treatment of the passage (*Climax*, pp. 56-98) demonstrates how one can see in Phil 2:6-11 both the story of representative Israel/humanity and the story of incarnate divinity. James

Summary: The Shape of Holiness in Christ

Drawing on his Jewish heritage, Paul assumes that the people of God are called to be a counter-cultural, holy people, restored to right covenantal relations with God.[53] Traditional Jewish holiness is both affirmed (avoidance of sexual immorality and idolatry) and challenged (circumcision, separate table fellowship), but above all it is recomposed in a new key. Paul's experience of Christ as the faithful, obedient, loving, crucified Son of God leads him to reconstruct his understanding of both God's holiness and human holiness as embodied in the story of Christ's kenosis in incarnation and death. Living out this story is a communal, counter-cultural affair. Cruciform holiness stands in marked contrast to key Roman values (which can infiltrate the body of Christ), especially those values associated with the libertine and status-seeking lifestyle of the elite, and those related to the power and domination predicated of imperial divinity. This cruciform holiness means, in sum, becoming like Christ by the power of the Holy Spirit of the Father and the Son, and thus also becoming like God — for God is Christ-like. "You shall be cruciform for I am cruciform," says the Lord.

Holiness Today

Stanley Hauerwas rightly says that "Wesley was right to hold that the peculiar contribution of Methodists [and thus the entire Wesleyan tradition] to the church universal lies in our struggle to recover the centrality of holiness as integral to the Christian life."[54] In our context, Paul may help us understand both human and divine holiness in many ways, of which I have chosen three to explore briefly.

Dunn emphasizes Christ's humanity (without denying the possibility of pre-existence in the text): "[I]n Christ, his death and resurrection, God's original design for humanity finally achieved concrete shape and fulfillment" ("Christ, Adam, and Preexistence," in *Where Christology Began,* ed., Martin and Dodd, pp. 74-83 [p. 79]).

53. This fundamental *covenantal* understanding of holiness also applies to justification (i.e., the restoration of right covenantal relations by means of God's initiative in Christ), demonstrating the inextricable connection between justification and holiness. Cf. Webster: "Holiness is restored covenant fellowship" (*Holiness,* p. 92).

54. Stanley Hauerwas, *Sanctify Them in the Truth: Holiness Exemplified* (Nashville: Abingdon, 1998), p. 124. I should think that Alex Deasley, whom this volume honors, would agree as well.

The Holiness of the Individual and the Church

Paul's notion of holiness challenges privatistic, self-centered, therapeutic, and sectarian notions of holiness. Cruciform holiness is inherently other-centered and communal. It is differentness of character but continued existence in the world. It is public participation in the story of God in Christ by the Spirit.

Both modern and post-modern persons have tended to look for meaning by pursuing "the reflexive project of the self,"[55] with post-moderns, of course, eschewing any meta-narrative, or master story. Even Christians are tempted to look at holiness as just another version of self-help and self-realization. But as Christians, John Webster writes, we discover our identity by entering a process of becoming holy; to be sure, this process varies from person to person by his or her "fulfilling a vocation through time."[56] However, Webster insists, "[t]he becoming is, precisely, discovery, not invention; it is not our generation of a self-narrative . . . but the enactment of an office: 'You shall be holy, for I, the Lord your God, am holy.'"[57] To continue Webster's use of narrative language, but with a Pauline emphasis: we enter into a story of Another, the divine master story of cruciform holiness. This can happen only in a community that performs the story.[58]

The performance of this holy story is, by definition, a counter-cultural act that shapes (among other things) our sex lives and our political lives.

Holy Sex

The experience of the Spirit, for Paul, is always also the experience of the crucified Christ; any other experience, no matter how (allegedly) "spiritual" it may be, is not an experience of the Spirit of the God revealed in the cross.

We must be quick to add here, however, that an apparent actualization of cruciformity is not necessarily the work of the Holy Spirit. For Paul, cruciformity is the distinctive dimension of holiness, its *sine qua non*, but not its totality. In particular, as we have seen, for Paul cruciformity without sexual holiness is not holiness at all; it is pseudo-holiness. Paul shows us that sexual

---

55. The phrase "the reflexive project of the self" is from Anthony Giddens, *Modernity and Self-Identity: Self and Society in the Late Modern Age* (Stanford: Stanford University Press, 1991), p. 231, quoted in Webster, *Holiness*, p. 104.

56. Webster, *Holiness*, p. 104.

57. Webster, *Holiness*, p. 104.

58. On this, see the essays in Samuel M. Powell and Michael E. Lodahl, eds., *Embodied Holiness: Toward a Corporate Theology of Spiritual Growth* (Downers Grove, Ill.: InterVarsity, 1999).

libertinism/immorality is the denial of cruciform existence, for it fails to (1) appropriate the work of the triune God in redeeming the human body through the cross and (2) express the kind of obedience to God that marks off God's people from the "gentiles." For Paul, sexual immorality (Greek *porneia* — "'unlawful sexual intercourse' . . . including homosexual practice and sexual immorality in general")[59] and cruciform love cannot co-exist, for *porneia* is a form of self-love, of self-indulgence that harms others and diminishes the holiness of both the individual and the community.[60]

Thus an alleged instance of self-giving, covenantal love outside the bounds of licit sexual relations is not, Paul would argue, an example of holiness; it is *not* the work of the Holy Spirit. Furthermore, neither eroticism nor erotic love is synonymous with the divine Spirit, as some have suggested. Rather, the gift of sex is properly used only when it is linked to the other-regarding, community-regarding kind of love that can be expressed within the bounds of marriage.

Holy Politics

As we have seen, Paul challenges our notion of God and God's attributes. Some may object to the notion of a cruciform God and argue that in the discussion of God's holiness, we cannot forget God's majesty and power. Here John Webster is again helpful, because he rightly defines God's holiness, not as pure majesty, but as "majesty in relation."[61] Because God's majesty and God's relationality cannot be separated, we must understand God's majesty in light of God's revealed relationality. We do not simply hold the majesty and relationality of God in *tension;* with Paul, we must see them in *concert,* a unison revealed in the power of the cross. God is not a god of power *and* weakness but the God of power *in* weakness.

The embedded theology of most Christians still revolves around a non-cruciform model of God's power, and a crucial corrective is needed. If we know God in the cross, then we should also know that God's majesty is a majesty of power-in-weakness.

This brings us inevitably to God and politics, to the "normal" god of civil religion that combines patriotism and power — the god of George W. Bush and of many Americans. As the Spanish historian-theologian Jaume

---

59. Dunn, *Theology,* p. 690.
60. See Dunn's concise but insightful discussion in *Theology,* pp. 119-23.
61. Webster, *Holiness,* p. 41.

Botey Vallès has said, the god of Bush (and, we might add, of many other presidents, prime ministers, kings, etc.) is a god of military might.[62] That simply is not the God revealed by Jesus, Vallès rightly says. Neither is it the cruciform God of Paul. In other words, military power is not the power of the cross, and such misconstrued notions of divine power have nothing to do with the majesty or holiness of the triune God known in the weakness of the cross. The "civil" god, though perfectly "normal," is not only unholy; it is an idol. To embrace such a god is to endanger, if not terminate, *koinōnia* with Jesus, and thus the possibility of holiness.

In our time, any "holiness" that fails to see the radical, counter-imperial claims of the gospel is inadequate at best. Adherence to a God of holiness certainly requires the kind of personal holiness that many associate with sexual purity. But adherence to a *cruciform* God of holiness also requires a corollary vision of life in the world that rejects domination in personal, public, or political life — a mode of being that is often considered realistic or "normal." Kenotic divinity and a corollary kenotic community constitute "both the best possible commentary" on Paul and a "frontal assault" on "normalcy."[63]

In our context, this frontal assault will require from Christians a rejection of the normal sequence of piety, war, victory, and peace that pervaded ancient Rome and pervades early twenty-first-century politics and religion — a sequence that plays out, not only in the strategies of powerful nations, but in the minds and hearts of Christians who have found in the god of military power a seductive alternative to the cruciform God of Paul.[64]

Conclusion

Paul's vision of trinitarian cruciform holiness is still relevant today. It challenges our contemporary spiritualities, immoralities, and idolatries.

62. Jaume Botey Vallès, *El Dios de Bush* [*Bush's God*], Cuadernos Cristianisme i Justícia 126 (Barcelona: Centre d'Estudia Cristianisme i Justícia, 2004), esp. pp. 19-25.

63. Crossan and Reed, *In Search of Paul,* p. 296.

64. The sequence of piety, war, victory, and peace is taken from Crossan and Reed, *In Search of Paul,* pp. xi-xii; cf. pp. 412-13.

Made Holy by the Holy Spirit:
Holiness and Ecclesiology in Romans

PETER OAKES

The relationship between holiness and ecclesiology in Romans is an important topic. Paul ties together the concept of holiness and the concept of the nature of the people of God. He expends considerable energy in explaining and emphasising the specialness, the sanctity, that belongs to the people of God. In doing this, Paul gives a particular role to the Spirit of God which in Romans is a Spirit that brings holiness. As we shall see, this holiness is conceptualised in several ways. Each of these would have been very striking to the members of the Christian groups in first-century Rome. Each of them also poses quite a sharp challenge to many present-day churches.

There is a common cultural pattern in which societies divide their world into spheres of the "sacred" or "holy" and the ordinary. "Holiness" is a cultural concept that denotes the nature of something or someone as belonging to this special category or sphere. The concept of "holiness" has two aspects. On the one hand, holiness can refer to the status of something or someone as being in the special category. There are three ways of talking about this status. People can talk about specialness, separateness, distinction from ordinary things. They can also talk about closeness to, links with, identity with other holy objects or beings. This especially includes talk about links to God or the gods. Thirdly, they can talk using terms by which that society denotes the holy. On the other hand, holiness can also refer to the characteristics that the society expects of something or someone in the special category. These characteristics vary from society to society and also vary between types of objects or beings. Quite a number of the typical characteristics of the holy are defined by a society's system of purity. As well as the bipolar issue of whether entities are "holy" or "not holy," many societies also have a concept of a scale of degrees of holiness. Some entities are more holy than others.[1] Our primary interest in this article is in holiness as a status, rather than in the characteristics of holiness. To what extent and in which ways does Paul use the concept of holiness to express the nature of the Christian people of God?

The three ways of talking about holiness as status give us an outline agenda of holiness issues, each of which has a strongly ecclesiological nature. In Romans, the separation of Christians from the sphere of the ordinary is particularly expressed by Paul's use of the language of calling, election, and predestination. Links between Christians and other holy entities are, in Romans, mainly expressed in terms of being children of God. In Romans, Paul generally uses the ἅγιος word group when he wants to use holiness terminology. We need to consider the use of the term, οἱ ἅγιοι, "the holy ones," for Christians. Before our main three items, we shall do an initial survey of that usage of ἅγιος, etc., and see if it makes any particularly key contributions to the argument of the letter.

The ἅγιος (Holy) Word Group in Romans

The words in question are the adjective ἅγιος, a verb ἁγιάζω (to make holy — in senses to be explored below), and two nouns, ἁγιωσύνη (holiness) and ἁγιασμός (the process or result of making holy). There are twenty-four occurrences of the word group. Five describe the Spirit as "holy" (5:5; 9:1; 14:17; 15:13, 16) and one refers to the Spirit "of holiness" (ἁγιωσύνης, 1:4). Four describe things as holy. Three of these clearly relate to, or originate from, God: "writings" (1:2), "the Law" (7:2), and "the commandment" (7:2). The fourth describes the type of kiss to be exchanged among the Christians (16:16). Its holiness is presumably derived from the description of the Christians as "holy ones" (ἅγιοι, 1:7; 8:27; 12:13; 15:25, 26, 31; 16:2, 15). Alongside these eight texts, a further five use the word group in relation to people. Speaking in some sense about Israel, Paul says that the "initial offering" and "mixture as a whole" (ἀπαρχή and φύραμα, 11:16, Dunn's translation[2]), and the "root" and "branches" are holy. Slavery to righteousness (6:19) and to God (6:22) result in ἁγιασμός, the process or result of becoming holy. Finally, Paul's aim is that the "offering of the nations/gentiles" should be something that has been made holy, ἡγιασμένη, by πνεῦμα ἅγιον, the holy Spirit (15:16).

---

1. For a model of this, see Jerome H. Neyrey, *Render to God: New Testament Understandings of the Divine* (Minneapolis: Fortress, 2004), Appendix B.
2. James D. G. Dunn, *Romans 9–16*, WBC (Dallas: Word, 1988), p. 658.

The word group is fairly evenly spread through the letter. There is a small concentration at the beginning (1:2, 4, 7) but without obvious coordination between the terms. The only other concentrations are near the end: three times around the end of the main argument (15:13, 16), three times in describing the Jerusalem Christians (15:25, 26, 31), and three times in connection with the life of the Christians at Rome (16:2, 15, 16). The group of terms in 15:13, 16 is interesting because both texts relate to the instrumental role of the Spirit and this is further expounded in v. 19, which repeats the phrase, "by the power of the Spirit," from v. 13. We shall focus on this passage more than once. The group of terms relating to the Jerusalem Christians is interesting testimony to the place of that community in early Christian life. The group of terms in chapter 16 points to the diversity and commonness of usage of "holy ones" as a term for Christians. The phrase in 16:2, "in a way worthy of the holy ones," is particularly interesting in that way.

A number of uses draw attention by being unusual or emphatic. The "Spirit of holiness," πνεῦμα ἁγιωσύνης (1:4), occurring in a piece of Christology, suggests how far-reaching a study of Romans with a focus on holiness could be. The description of the Roman Christians ends rather emphatically with κλητοῖς ἁγίοις, "called as holy" (1:7). In 15:16, "made holy by the holy Spirit" is similarly emphasised by its position at the end of a complex statement. Attention is also drawn to it by the double occurrence of words in the ἅγιος group. More straightforward repetition also occurs in the ἁγιασμός of 6:19, 22.

> ὥσπερ γὰρ παρεστήσατε τὰ μέλη ὑμῶν δοῦλα τῇ ἀκαθαρσίᾳ καὶ τῇ ἀνομίᾳ εἰς τὴν ἀνομίαν, οὕτως νῦν παραστήσατε τὰ μέλη ὑμῶν δοῦλα τῇ δικαιοσύνῃ εἰς ἁγιασμόν.

> For, just as you presented the parts of your body in slavery to uncleanness and lawlessness, which results in lawlessness, so now present the parts of your body in slavery to righteousness, which results in holiness (Rom 6:19, my translation).

> νυνὶ δὲ ἐλευθερωθέντες ἀπὸ τῆς ἁμαρτίας δουλωθέντες δὲ τῷ θεῷ ἔχετε τὸν καρπὸν ὑμῶν εἰς ἁγιασμόν, τὸ δὲ τέλος ζωὴν αἰώνιον.

> But now, having been set free from sin, and having become slaves to God, you have your fruit resulting in holiness, the end of which is eternal life (Rom 6:22).

In this passage, Paul contrasts slavery to sin with both slavery to righteousness, which is εἰς ἁγιασμόν (6:19), and slavery to God, the fruit of which is εἰς ἁγιασμόν (6:22). The two positive slaveries are synonymous and have an identical outcome, ἁγιασμός. The term probably means the result of being made holy, rather than the process.[3] It seems more likely that εἰς would be used to introduce a state than a process, especially after "fruit" in v. 22. The timing of events in vv. 19 and 22 is, however, confusing. The slavery to righteousness and the consequent holiness in v. 19 seem to be conditional on presenting the parts of one's body, to which Paul is now calling them. In v. 22, enslavement to God and the fruit that results in holiness seem already to have come about. However, Paul's indicatives often match his imperatives. The Roman Christians are already enslaved to God. They need to act in such a way as to become enslaved to God (see also 8:4-13). In 6:19, 22, ἁγιασμός does not have a clear relationship to status. It seems more likely to denote the characteristics of holiness, "a holy lifestyle" (see also 1 Thess 4:3-7).

The only one of the passages that has clear structural significance for the letter as a whole is 15:15-16. This is very programmatic: Paul describes his mission in order to justify what he has written to the Romans (15:14-16). Also, in 15:16, Paul's description of the Spirit as ἅγιον is presumably because of the Spirit's activity in making people holy.

> τολμηρότερον δὲ ἔγραψα ὑμῖν ἀπὸ μέρους ὡς ἐπαναμιμνῄσκων ὑμᾶς διὰ τὴν χάριν τὴν δοθεῖσάν μοι ἀπὸ τοῦ θεοῦ εἰς τὸ εἶναί με λειτουργὸν Χριστοῦ Ἰησοῦ εἰς τὰ ἔθνη, ἱερουργοῦντα τὸ εὐαγγέλιον τοῦ θεοῦ, ἵνα γένηται ἡ προσφορὰ τῶν ἐθνῶν εὐπρόσδεκτος, ἡγιασμένη ἐν πνεύματι ἁγίῳ.

> But I have written to you rather boldly in part, as a reminder to you, on account of the grace given to me by God, to be a minister of Christ Jesus for the gentiles, serving in a priestly way the gospel of God, in order that the offering of the gentiles would be acceptable, having been made holy by means of the holy Spirit (15:15-16).

Paul says that he writes to the Roman Christians because God has given him the gift of being a λειτουργός for the nations or gentiles (ἔθνη).[4] The term λειτουργός probably carries cultic connotations here. The verb ἱερουργέω is certainly cultic, expressing work as a priest. With the accusative, τὸ εὐαγγέλιον, it suggests that Paul serves as a priest in relation to the gospel. The actual or in-

---

3. Agreeing with James D. G. Dunn, *Romans 1–8*, WBC (Dallas: Word, 1988), p. 347, against C. E. B. Cranfield, *The Epistle to the Romans*, vol. 1, ICC (Edinburgh: T&T Clark, 1975), p. 327.

4. In 9:24 and 11:13, Paul uses the term to refer to non-Jews; in 16:26, it may imply universality.

tended result of this priestly service in respect of the gospel is that the "offering of the gentiles" should, like a good Temple sacrifice, be of a kind that is acceptable, which means that it needs to be ἅγιος. As Dunn points out, this implies that the gentiles in question need to be ἅγιος, irrespective of whether ἡ προσφορὰ τῶν ἐθνῶν means "the offering that the gentiles bring" (in their own priestly service) or "the offering that is the gentiles."[5] Both an offering and those who offer it should be holy.

The word ἡγιασμένη, "having been made holy," is the perfect participle of the verb ἁγιάζω. In the NT, this verb has a wide range of uses. However, the most common of these (eight out of twenty-eight instances) is to denote the change of status that comes about at conversion: the move from the ordinary to the holy. The closest parallel to the form in 15:16 is 1 Cor 1:2, in which the "assembly of God which is in Corinth" is described as ἡγιασμένοις ἐν Χριστῷ Ἰησοῦ, κλητοῖς ἁγίοις, "made holy in [or by means of] Christ Jesus, called as holy." The last phrase also matches Rom 1:7. Also connected with conversion is the inclusion of ἡγιάσθητε, "you were made holy," in the list in 1 Cor 6:11. Further examples occur in Eph 5:26 and in Hebrews (2:11; 10:14, 29; 13:12). The other types of use of the verb in the NT vary considerably. In the case of the non-Christian spouse in 1 Cor 7:14, some sort of transfer to the category of the holy occurs without conversion. There is a type of being made holy in 1 Thess 5:23, where Paul expresses the wish for God ἁγιάσαι ὑμᾶς ὁλοτελεῖς, "to make you holy completely." There is also Christ's expression in John's Gospel, ὑπὲρ αὐτῶν ἐγὼ ἁγιάζω ἐμαυτόν, "for their sakes I make myself holy" (John 17:19), where Christ is devoting himself, consecrating himself, in his willingness to die. He is taking himself completely out of the realm of the ordinary by undergoing destruction for the sake of God.

This enunciation of possibilities for the meaning of the verb, drawn from beyond Romans, serves as a caution. "Holiness" terminology gets used by various writers — or even a single writer — in various ways. The terms do not consistently denote a single system in which there is a single boundary between the holy and the ordinary, with ἁγιάζω always denoting the process of moving across that boundary. However, in Rom 15:16, the immediate context does imply that the "making holy" of the "offering of the gentiles" means the conversion of the gentiles to Christian belief, a move from the sphere of the ordinary to the sphere of the holy: Rom 15:15-16 is a description of Paul's mission, and this is then expounded as evangelism in vv. 17-21.

If "having been made holy" in 15:16 is an expression of conversion, then

---

5. Dunn, *Romans 9–16*, pp. 860-61. The singular, "offering," suggests that Paul is thinking of the offering consisting of the gentiles.

the role of the πνεῦμα ἅγιον, the holy Spirit, is interesting. The Spirit is presumably described as "holy" here[6] because of its action in producing holiness. Here, the holy Spirit is specifically the means by which the convert is moved from the sphere of the ordinary to the sphere of the holy.[7] This text in 15:16 is Paul's excuse for everything he has written (or possibly for part of it)[8] up to Rom 15:13. He dared to write what he wrote because God had given him a mission intended to result in the making holy of the gentiles, meaning the conversion of the gentiles. One implication of this is that we ought to expect that the letter will conceptualise Christian existence in terms of holiness. In that confidence, let us turn to our main agenda: calling; being "holy ones"; and connection to God as children.

Called by God

There is a range of ways in which Paul expresses the status of Christians as holy. The first one is the idea that they are called by a divine being. Rom 1:6 describes them as κλητοὶ Ἰησοῦ Χριστοῦ, "called by Jesus Christ,"[9] who has just been described as being appointed as son of God. If a divine being calls someone, especially if that calling becomes in some sense constitutive of who they are, then they are marked out from the ordinary people on the streets of Rome. Those who are divinely called belong, to some extent, to the sphere of the holy. Kings,

6. Only six of the twenty-three references in Romans have this epithet.

7. An alternative reading of ἐν πνεύματι would be that the gentiles are made holy within (in some sense) the holy Spirit. An instrumental interpretation of ἐν here ("by means of") is supported by 15:13 ἐν δυνάμει πνεύματος ἁγίου, "by the power of the holy Spirit" and 15:19, Paul's mission ἐν δυνάμει πνεύματος.

8. Brendan Byrne sees it as relating to the plea for tolerance in 14:1–15:13 (*Romans*, SP [Collegeville, Minn.: Liturgical, 1996], p. 435).

9. Agreeing with Peter Stuhlmacher (*Paul's Letter to the Romans: A Commentary*, trans. Scott J. Hafemann [Louisville: Westminster/John Knox, 1994], p. 18), against Dunn (*Romans 1–8*, p. 19). He prefers "called to be Jesus Christ's," arguing that elsewhere in Paul, it is God who calls. However, Dunn may overestimate the degree of distinction that Paul makes between the actions of Christ and the actions of God. The Spirit is a central figure in the process of bringing about holiness and Paul can, even within the same verse, switch between "Spirit of God" and "Spirit of Christ" (8:9). The three occurrences of κλητός with the genitive in the Septuagint (1 Kgs 1:41, 49; Zeph 1:7) all indicate the person who did the calling. (These texts tempt us to translate κλητοί in Rom 1:6 as "guests," especially as one could imagine κλητοῖς ἁγίοις [1:7] as an allusion to Zephaniah, in which God has consecrated [ἡγίακεν] his guests for the great sacrifice on the Day of the Lord. However, the parallel to κλητὸς ἀπόστολος, "called as apostle" [1:1], makes it difficult to read κλητός in 1:7 as anything other than "called." This does not, of itself, rule out the potentially interesting allusion to Zeph 1:7.)

prophets, emperors,[10] and others who are seen as being called by God or the gods are taken out of the realm of the ordinary by virtue of the calling itself. Whatever these people do or do not do, they are, to some extent, holy, set apart. Paul sees the Christians at Rome as a people who are called by God and hence set apart from the ordinary. In ecclesiological terms: the Church is a called people and this sets them apart, in some sense, from the sphere of the ordinary.

The three occurrences of κλητός in Rom 1:1-7 (and only seven other times in the NT) make "calling" a definite motif here. The calling of Christians by God also occurs at 8:28, 30 and 9:24. The last of these explicitly includes both Jews and Gentiles (ἐξ Ἰουδαίων . . . καὶ ἐξ ἐθνῶν). This is then explained by using a double quote from Hosea, in each part of which καλέω is used in a declarative sense. The "not-my-people" and the "unloved" are called "my people" and "loved" (9:25, loosely quoting Hos 2:25 LXX = 2:23 MT). The ones said not to be God's people are called "sons of the living God" (9:26, quoting Hos 2:1 LXX = 1:10 MT). Rom 9:25-26 also resonates with an earlier reference to God as the one, καλοῦντος τὰ μὴ ὄντα ὡς ὄντα, "calling the things that are not, as though they are" (4:17).

The theme of "calling" in Romans is further reinforced by two related ideas. First, calling is rooted in the past and made particularly deliberate by Paul's emphasis on God's foreknowledge and prior decision. Christians are κατὰ πρόθεσιν κλητοῖς, "called according to God's foreknowledge" (8:28). God "foreknew" them (προέγνω, 8:29) and "marked them out in advance" to be in conformity to Christ's likeness (προώρισεν, 8:29, 30). God "prepared them in advance" (προητοίμασεν, 9:23). The second idea is that of choice, election. The Christians corporately are the ἐκλεκτοὶ θεοῦ, the ones chosen by God (8:33). Individual Christians can also be called ἐκλεκτός (16:13). In an unusual expression in 11:7, Jewish Christians are called ἡ ἐκλογή, "the election," a term that is also used in 11:5 of the process by which this group comes about.

All told, there are about sixteen times in the letter when Paul reminds the Roman Christians that they are called or chosen by God. This reminds them forcefully that their communities are not ordinary but holy. The language of foreknowledge deepens this by taking their calling back into the mists of time: a place in God's people was prepared for them before they were born. The language of choosing brings out the concept of the specialness of the holy people: the other people were not chosen.

The concept of the divine calling, and hence holiness of the Church — or

---

10. For various types of evidence implying the divine calling of the Roman Emperor, see Peter Oakes, *Philippians: From People to Letter*, SNTSMS 110 (Cambridge: Cambridge University Press, 2001), pp. 139, 141, 143-44, 155-58.

indeed of individual assemblies of followers of Christ, which would be a description more closely related to Paul's hearers at Rome — is one that often, understandably, causes a certain degree of embarrassment among churches today. Reflection on the first-century Roman situation is helpful here. The Christian assemblies were a number of gatherings that would probably have been seen, by both insiders and outsiders, as some sort of immigrant cult associations.[11] (Increasingly, local-born Romans joined them, but at the time of the letter, these Romans would have been perceived as joining what were essentially immigrant groups.) A few foreign cult associations might have reasonable prestige due to their antiquity, their devotion to a deity that was held in high public regard, or their having some high-status members. However, the Christian assemblies would not come into these categories. They were low-status assemblies of generally low-status people devoted to a newly arisen divine figure. Paul brings a message to them that reveals their high status in the sight of God. They are called by him, special, holy. By doing this, Paul strengthens the identity of these groups[12] and hence supports them in their existence.

I can only comment on present-day churches as a lay observer. However, it does seem that many congregations generally lack a sense of their identity as special, holy people of God. To put this at a very practical level: many Christians go to church primarily to meet their friends. There is nothing wrong with this being one reason, especially since friendship with other Christians is one of the central mechanisms of the proper functioning of a Christian life. However, the community that a Christian congregation should be is a holy group of people. These are people called by God to a dedicated life, worship, and service. A church is a holy assembly. Without going down the road of all the negative forms of separateness that anyone can list, churches do need to have a sense of their identity as the special, holy people of God, called by God and separated from being merely part of the sphere of the ordinary. For many churches, the recovery of their sense of being called, holy people is surely an essential step towards their more effective engagement as Christians in the world.

---

11. For introduction to the nature of associations in the Graeco-Roman world and comparison of churches with them see Philip A. Harland, *Associations, Synagogues, and Congregations: Claiming a Place in Ancient Mediterranean Society* (Minneapolis: Fortress, 2003) and Richard S. Ascough, *Paul's Macedonian Associations: The Social Context of Philippians and 1 Thessalonians*, WUNT 2:161 (Tübingen: J. C. B. Mohr, 2003). The word "cult" in this context means simply that the association's existence centred around religious activity.

12. For a study of Paul's role in seeking to shape the identity of the Roman congregations see Philip F. Esler, *Conflict and Identity in Romans* (Minneapolis: Fortress, 2003).

Holy Ones

The phrase κλητοῖς ἁγίοις in 1:7 is best translated as something like "called as holy people." Translations of κλητοῖς ἁγίοις as "called to be holy people" (or "holy ones" or "saints") can be problematic. The "called to be" can easily be read as an aspiration of holiness rather than a current reality. As Romans 6 shows, Paul does have aspirations for development in holiness among the Roman Christians. However, this is not conveyed by his usage of the plural adjective ἅγιοι as a noun. The link between 1:7 and 1:1 makes it particularly clear in this case. In 1:1 Paul's calling makes him an apostle: apostleship is not some future aspiration. In 1:7 the Roman Christians' calling makes them now holy people. The idea in the verse is not that holiness or sainthood is to be an ambition to be fulfilled. They already have this status and, given the emphatic location of ἅγιος at the end of the description of the Romans, Paul must see it as a decisive element of their identity.

In Romans, Paul consistently uses the term ἅγιοι to refer to Christians: in general (8:27, 16:2 and probably 12:13); at Rome, as a whole group (1:7) and as an individual house church (16:5); at Jerusalem (15:25, 26, 31). The repeated use, in these last verses, of οἱ ἅγιοι for the Christians at Jerusalem suggests that the term was especially commonly used to describe either this first Christian community[13] or, possibly, Jewish Christians in Israel as a whole. However, "Jerusalem" is actually only three words away from ἅγιοι in each verse so it is possible to take the term ἅγιοι even here as a general term for Christians, with "in Jerusalem" qualifying it as referring to this particular church.

The very word, ἅγιοι, reminds the Roman Christians that they were having ascribed to them a holiness that was conceptualised and/or delineated in Jewish terms. The word ἅγιος was, as far as we can tell, rarely used in non-Jewish texts. Graeco-Roman texts usually expressed the concept of holiness by use of other terms such as ὅσιος or ἱερός. The Roman Christians would have felt that they were being incorporated into a version of a Jewish system of the marking out of sacred and profane.

This does not mean that οἱ ἅγιοι in Romans is necessarily a synonym for "Israel." Some scholars on Romans may move too readily to that kind of equivalence. In the Septuagint, οἱ ἅγιοι can be used of angelic beings (e.g., Zech 14:5) and, in the Pentateuch, the only use of the masculine plural[14] of ἅγιος as a noun comes in Moses' challenge to the followers of Korah:

---

13. Dunn, *Romans 9–16*, p. 873.
14. In the Hebrew of Num 16:5, *qadosh* is singular.

ἐπέσκεπται καὶ ἔγνω ὁ θεὸς τοὺς ὄντας αὐτοῦ καὶ τοὺς ἁγίους καὶ προσηγάγετο πρὸς ἑαυτόν καὶ οὓς ἐξελέξατο ἑαυτῷ προσηγάγετο πρὸς ἑαυτόν.

God [will] visit and recognise those who are his and those who are holy and [will] bring them to himself — indeed, he [will] bring to himself those whom he chooses for himself (Num 16:5).

Here, ἅγιος is used for the distinction between those who have access to the holy parts of the Tabernacle and those who do not. (A particularly interesting point in this verse is that the ἅγιοι effectively have προσαγωγή, "access," which is a key Christian privilege in Rom 5:2, although, there, there is no close coordination with holiness terminology.) Israel is, of course, described as holy in the Pentateuch: they are βασίλειον ἱεράτευμα καὶ ἔθνος ἅγιον, "a royal priesthood and a holy nation" (Exod 19:6). Beyond the Pentateuch, οἱ ἅγιοι is used several times of Israelites in general. Wis 18:9 is a particularly clear example (although it is not the only term used in that text: the preferred term in Wisdom 18 is actually οἱ ὅσιοι, 18:1, 5, cf. 9).

The pattern of Paul's usage of holiness terminology for Christians and Israelites suggests that he is not simply using the terminology to tell the Christians that they are in some sense inheriting Israel's identity and blessings. Rather, he is making specific points about holiness, both in what he writes about Christians and in what he writes about Jews. This complexity means that when Paul calls the Roman Christians οἱ ἅγιοι, we ought not immediately to assume that they would only hear this as a quasi-national description of them as God's new people. There are other possibilities too, especially in more priestly terms or as marking a close link to the divine. The priestly or divinisation ideas would certainly be conceptions of the holy that would be more familiar to the average Greek or Roman than would the idea of "the holy ones" being "the people of God." The Israel idea cannot be excluded from Paul's use of οἱ ἅγιοι, especially since Paul uses much of his holiness language in reference to Israel as well as to Christians: ἅγιος (11:16); called by God (11:29); having "adoption," υἱοθεσία (9:4); and "election," ἐκλογή (11:28) — the list could be extended. However, for ἅγιος, aspects of holiness other than simply being part of God's people may be heard in the term.

A further issue is that OT texts can operate with what one could see either as a relative view of holiness (Israel is holy, relative to the nations; the priests are holy, relative to ordinary Israelites) or as a progressive or hierarchical view of holiness. This hierarchy is expressed spatially (the Ark of the Covenant, the Most Holy Place, the Holy Place, the Tabernacle or Temple, the

Land)[15] and in terms of corresponding beings (God, the High Priest, the Priests, maybe the Levites, the Israelites).

In contrast, Paul's use of the term οἱ ἅγιοι represents a bipolar model of holiness rather than a progressive one: people are "holy" or "not holy" rather than holiness being a quality people have in varying amounts. This is curious because one would expect the reality of life among the Christian groups in Rome to be that, like the synagogues, they would have people with varying levels of commitment, perhaps ranging from the interested occasional visitor to the zealous devotee, with every degree of commitment between. The sharp community boundary implied by Paul's use of οἱ ἅγιοι is also represented in other ways. In 6:1-11, for example, baptism provides a clear marker at some sort of point of entry and is conceptualised in the stark language of death and life. Although Paul can, as in 1 Corinthians 14, see Christian meetings as open to people with even slight interest, he does present a very definite sense in Romans of there being a specific bounded group who are Christians and hence "holy ones." Although he may be presenting the boundary as somewhat sharper than it was in reality, the pattern he presents seems likely to have been generally recognizable to the churches, especially in features such as labeling (οἱ ἅγιοι) and practice (baptism). Early Christian communities may not be such loosely bounded groups as some think.

The idea of group boundaries is often embarrassing to present-day churches. The ideal is often felt to be that the church is an unbounded group in which people of every view can be drawn progressively closer to God. Ceremonies of initiation, such as baptism or confirmation, often become public affirmations that are fairly arbitrarily located in a person's journey towards God. There is persistent stress on the need to avoid distinction in a congregation between people who are within any form of group boundary and people outside.

Theologically, underlying many of these views is the idea that all God's creatures, especially people, are holy: all that can be distinguished is, possibly, degrees of holiness, and these lie along a broad, incremental scale. Paul would agree that there is a certain degree of sanctity of all of creation: "the earth is the Lord's, and everything in it" (1 Cor 10:26, citing Ps 24:1). However, his application of holiness language to Christians represents a sharply defined boundary: all Christians are holy, non-Christians are not (with the possible exception of Israel, but that is a debate beyond this article). Churches that seek to build their theology on the Pauline tradition are committed to some idea of boundaries, both at the level of the Church worldwide, and consequently, at the level of the local congregation. How this works out in practice is clearly a complex and del-

15. Neyrey, *Render to God,* Appendix B.

icate matter. However, the Pauline tradition implies a theology and practice in which considerable significance is given to boundary and to boundary-crossing processes and rituals. Becoming one of "the holy people," in Paul's terms, is not a minor and unimportant matter.

Children of God

In Rome, "son of God" was a term in (or, indeed, on) common currency. When Octavian was seeking to establish his authority, he issued coins that prominently carried the words *Caesar divi f[ilius]*, "Caesar, son of the divine one."[16] The use that the Roman emperors made of their connection to their deified predecessors was a central expression of their own sacredness and claim to power. Octavian presented himself as greater than Antony because Octavian had inherited the name Caesar and was the son of the god, Julius Caesar.

This sonship was not a matter of birth. Augustus was born Gaius Octavius, only a great-nephew of Gaius Julius Caesar. However, Caesar's will adopted Octavius as his son. Octavius' name became Gaius Julius Caesar Octavianus. He could now claim to be the descendant of Julius Caesar. In fact, all but one of the Julio-Claudian emperors came to power via an adoption. As these and other prominent adoptions (e.g., that of the younger Pliny by the elder) show, in the first century, adoption was publicly recognized as making someone a child of the adoptive parent with a degree of completeness that is hard for us to grasp. If the parent was later deified, one became the child of a god.

The Israelites too were called "sons of God." Wisdom 18 uses both singular and plural. The Egyptians were forced to acknowledge θεοῦ υἱὸν λαὸν εἶναι, "the people to be God's son" (Wis 18:13). Earlier, they had imprisoned τοὺς υἱούς σου, "your [God's] sons" (18:4). As with οἱ ἅγιοι, however, the issue is more complex. In the Psalms, for example, the people of Israel as a nation are not called "sons of God," but the term is used of angelic beings (Ps 28:1 LXX = 29:1 MT; Ps 88:7 LXX = 89:6 MT), of the king of Israel (Ps 2:7), and of some figures such as judges (Ps 81:6 LXX = 82:6 MT).

Identity with the divine is the peak of holiness. Paul ties the Christians very emphatically into existence as God's sons or children (the two terms, υἱοί and τέκνα, seem to be used interchangeably in chapter 8). Seven times in chapter 8 he refers to this idea. Most of these are in 8:14-17.

---

16. E.g., H. Mattingly, *Coins of the Roman Empire in the British Museum (Augustus to Vitellius)* (London: British Museum, 1923), Augustus, no. 602 and no. 615.

ὅσοι γὰρ πνεύματι θεοῦ ἄγονται, οὗτοι υἱοὶ θεοῦ εἰσιν.
15οὐ γὰρ ἐλάβετε πνεῦμα δουλείας πάλιν εἰς φόβον
ἀλλὰ ἐλάβετε πνεῦμα υἱοθεσίας ἐν ᾧ κράζομεν· ἀββὰ ὁ πατήρ.
16αὐτὸ τὸ πνεῦμα συμμαρτυρεῖ τῷ πνεύματι ἡμῶν ὅτι ἐσμὲν τέκνα θεοῦ.
17εἰ δὲ τέκνα, καὶ κληρονόμοι·
κληρονόμοι μὲν θεοῦ, συγκληρονόμοι δὲ Χριστοῦ,
εἴπερ συμπάσχομεν ἵνα καὶ συνδοξασθῶμεν.

For those who are led by the Spirit of God, they are sons of God.
15For you did not receive a spirit of slavery again to fear,
but you received a Spirit of adoption, by which we cry, "Abba father!"
16The Spirit itself testifies with our spirit that we are children of God.
17If children, then also heirs;
heirs of God and fellow heirs with Christ,
since we suffer with him so that we shall be glorified with him.

The first thing we notice is that the son/child/adoption/father language is tied tightly to the activity of various "spirits": spirit of God; spirit of slavery; spirit of adoption; "the spirit itself;" our spirit. There are at least two spirits here: God's spirit and a human spirit. Looking at v. 16, and thinking about what Paul says earlier in the chapter about the "spirit of God" that is in Christians, and the "spirit of Christ" (apparently the same spirit) that Christians have (8:9), "the spirit itself" which "testifies with our spirit" (8:16) must be the spirit of God. "The spirit itself" in 8:16 seems to be "the spirit of adoption" in 8:15. Since these both seem to be terms for God's Spirit, I have capitalized them in my translation.

In 8:14-17, the Spirit does several things. It leads (8:14). That is, it is an active agent that does things or goes places and does so in such a way as to be able to be followed. Either its actions are perceptible, so that people can choose to follow the Spirit, or the Spirit acts as a power that can move people's lives (as, for example, Mark 1:12, where the Spirit sends out [ἐκβάλλει] Jesus into the wilderness). In Romans, Paul does offer moral choices (see 8:12-13). However, he seems more to associate the Spirit with power and action. The blessing at the end of the main section of the letter is for hope, which is produced ἐν δυνάμει πνεύματος ἁγίου, "by the power of the holy Spirit" (15:13). In that verse the holy Spirit has a power that produces hope, an echo of 5:5, where hope does not disappoint because God has poured his love into our hearts through the holy Spirit that he has given to us. We may be able to coordinate the presence of God's love in the Christian's heart with the Christian's membership in God's family. The holy Spirit's action is the means by which converts are put into a state of being beloved by God, children of God, having the status of being holy.

It is therefore no surprise that, in 8:14, Paul makes the boundary of the group who are holy, who are sons of God, the same as the boundary of the group led by the Spirit. He has already drawn the same boundary in 8:4. The boundary defining "us" is the boundary of the group who κατὰ πνεῦμα περιπατοῦσιν, "who walk according to the Spirit." This is an identical boundary to that of the group "led by the Spirit" in 8:14. The holy, the sons of God, are those who walk κατὰ πνεῦμα, a state that is enabled by the leading power, the δύναμις, of the holy Spirit.

In 8:15, the Spirit is the means by which we gain our voice to interact with God as child to father. That is, the Spirit is the power that enables the conduct of our relationship with God as his adopted children (reading ἐν ᾧ as "by which," cf. 8:26-27). Similarly, in 8:16, the Spirit is an agent that acts to reinforce our internal testimony to our belonging to God's family. The close relationship of 8:15 to the statement of sonship in 8:14, and the contrast with δουλεία, the state of slavery (rather than the process of enslavement), suggest that the receiving of a πνεῦμα υἱοθεσίας, "spirit of adoption," implies that Christians are in the state of being adopted sons. However, it is not immediately clear how this works grammatically — how the genitive, υἱοθεσίας, which is a property of the Spirit, relates to the state or quality that the receiver of the Spirit has. This has produced a fair amount of scholarly debate.[17] A look at the NT and LXX usage of πνεῦμα, in the sense of "spirit," with the genitive of abstract nouns is helpful here.

From a rough survey, in the NT there are probably seventeen instances of πνεῦμα, as "spirit," with a genitive of an abstract noun.[18] For the Septuagint, the figure is twenty-four. Apart from Rev. 19:10, with its curious reference to "the spirit of prophecy," and Isa 4:4, in which a "spirit of judgement" cleanses Jerusalem, all of the texts fit one of two patterns. In the more frequent of the patterns (fourteen times in NT, seventeen times in LXX), the spirit is something that comes into a person from outside. The genitive noun is a quality of the spirit that the spirit then produces in the person. In the less frequent pattern (twice in NT, six times in LXX), the spirit is already part of the person. The quality ascribed to the spirit is then also a quality of the person. Some examples will make the patterns clear. Exod 28:3 and 2 Tim 1:7 are good examples of the main pattern.[19]

17. J. M. Scott, *Adoption as Sons of God*, WUNT 2:48 (Tübingen: J. C. B. Mohr, 1992), pp. 244-66; Byrne, *Romans*, p. 252; G. D. Fee, *God's Empowering Presence: The Holy Spirit in the Letters of Paul* (Peabody, Mass.: Hendrickson, 1994; Carlisle: Paternoster, 1995), pp. 565-66.

18. My method was to search the NT (Nestlé-Aland 27) and LXX (Rahlfs) using Accordance 6.9 (Oaktree Software, 2005). The search criteria were for πνεῦμα, followed within two words by a feminine noun in the genitive. I then weeded out irrelevant texts.

19. For other examples see Exod 31:3; 35:31; Num 5:14, 30; Deut 34:9; Wis 7:7; Sir 39:6; Pss Sol 8:14; Zech 12:10; Isa 11:2; 19:14; 28:6; 29:10; Dan 13:44, 63; Luke 13:11; Rom 1:4 (?); 8:2, 15 (?); 11:8;

καὶ σὺ λάλησον πᾶσι τοῖς σοφοῖς τῇ διανοίᾳ οὓς ἐνέπλησα πνεύματος αἰσθήσεως καὶ ποιήσουσιν τὴν στολὴν τὴν ἁγίαν Ααρων.

And you, speak to all those who are wise in their thinking, whom I have filled with a spirit of perception, and they will make Aaron's holy robe (Exod 28:3).

οὐ γὰρ ἔδωκεν ἡμῖν ὁ θεὸς πνεῦμα δειλίας ἀλλὰ δυνάμεως καὶ ἀγάπης καὶ σωφρονισμοῦ.

For God has not given us a spirit of fearfulness but of power and love and self-control (2 Tim 1:7).

The second pattern is exemplified by Isa 61:3,

δοθῆναι τοῖς πενθοῦσιν Σιων . . . καταστολὴν δόξης ἀντὶ πνεύματος ἀκηδίας.

To give to the mourners of Zion . . . a garment of glory in place of a spirit of grief.

In this case the person's own spirit is described as a having the quality of grief. This means that the person himself or herself has the quality of grief, i.e., grieves. A similar example from the NT is where Paul urges the Galatians to set a sinning fellow Christian right ἐν πνεύματι πραΰτητος (Gal 6:1), "with a humble spirit."[20]

In almost every case, the use of πνεῦμα with the genitive of an abstract noun implies that the spirit has a quality and that the person who receives or possesses that spirit has a version of that quality. Either the spirit enters the person, bringing the quality to that person or, less frequently, the spirit is an aspect of the person which is described as the location of a quality that characterises the person.

In Rom 8:14-16, the "Spirit of adoption" is distinguished from the human spirit by the note about the cooperation of the two in 8:16. The phrase, "Spirit of adoption," therefore falls into the first of our categories of usage of πνεῦμα with the genitive of an abstract noun. This Spirit arrives from outside and conveys to the convert the quality of being someone who is adopted as a child of God.[21] It is clear from v. 14 that the Spirit of adoption must be the Spirit of

---

Eph 1:17; 1 John 4:6. For the "Spirit of truth" (John 14:17; 15:26; 16:13) and the "Spirit of grace" (Heb 10:29), the quality of the person is derived from that of the spirit, rather than identical.

20. For other examples, see Odes 7:39; Wis 1:5; Hos 4:12; 5:4; Bar 3:1; 2 Cor 4:13.

21. The examples of use of υἱοθεσία that are cited by Scott (*Adoption as Sons of God*, pp. 45-57) in his excellent survey suggest that although, strictly, the word denotes the process of adoption, in fact its use is generally to indicate the state of having been adopted.

God, whose leading makes us children of God. Thus the arrival of God's Spirit in a person is the arrival of a power that changes the person into a child of God. Since the peak of holiness is closeness to God, the action of the Spirit in making someone a child of God moves the person from the sphere of the ordinary to the sphere of the holy.

The Spirit is the Spirit of adoption that makes the Christian a child of God (8:14-16). The δύναμις, power, of the holy Spirit is the means by which God acts to bring the Christian's hope (15:13). The holy Spirit makes the gentiles holy (15:16). Such a coordination of ideas begins to pull in a wide range of threads in the argument of Romans, especially if one sees the δύναμις of the Spirit as somehow the δύναμις of the gospel (1:16) and if one links Paul's statement of his mission in 15:16 to other statements of it in 16:25-26 and 1:1-6.

The people of Rome knew of sons of gods: the emperors or figures such as the Egyptian Horus. What they did not know of was a divine son like Jesus, for whom God produced countless brothers and sisters. What is more, much more, the ordinary people of Rome — people not in mythical stories or in imperial palaces but on the streets and in the apartment blocks of the city — were invited to become these children of God. How did it feel, to live in the consciousness that one was an adopted son or daughter of God, a brother of the lord Jesus Christ? One of the most common plot elements of Graeco-Roman story-telling was that of the disguised deity, walking around among an ignorant populace. Christians who believed Paul's words would feel that they and their fellow Christians were like disguised deities, walking around the streets of Rome. In Romans 8, the main application of the discussion of the status of Christians as children of God is about having a sense of security and hence being strong under suffering. As part of God's family, Christians are secure in God's love. Paul also makes the point that as children of God, Christians have been given a central role in the liberation of the created order. It is unclear how this would have seemed to a poor craft worker or a slave. It may have given some sort of a sense of worth through having a place in the world's key events. The universality of divine sonship among Christians would also, one imagines, have had an impact on the issues of mutual respect that are dealt with in chapters 14 and 15.

Present-day churches would probably, if they thought of it, tend to be embarrassed by the idea of their members as disguised deities. Christian humility tells against extravagant claims of elevated status. Any church that decided to call itself "The Children of God" would be inviting suspicion as being a group of fanatics. However, for all churches, whether or not they want to follow Paul on the issue of defining boundaries (discussed above), the concept of being children of God must be an important one. Of course, there is scope for setting this alongside Paul's assertion, according to Acts, that all people are God's offspring

(Acts 17:28, citing Aratus, *Phaenomena* 5). However, Paul in Romans is very definite that participation in Christ, and so being led by the Spirit of God, constitutes the Christian as a child of God in some sense that Paul clearly does not think is shared by humankind as a whole. I do not want to return to the issue of boundaries at this point. The key issue here for churches is to reflect on the implications of all Christians being children of God: like disguised deities. As in Romans 8, this has implications for people's feelings of security, self-worth, and involvement in God's plans for the world. It also has implications for issues of mutual respect, as are raised in Romans 14 and 15. On a denominational scale and on a local scale there are clear implications for ecumenical relations (and for relations between churches within the same denomination!). Maybe more sharply still, there are implications for mutual respect within congregations. We are theologically insane to make the all-too-common judgements about the relative worth of various members of the congregation. How can one build a scale of relative worth when all are children of God and brothers or sisters of Christ?

Conclusion

Approaching Romans with a focus on holiness as a status that defines the people of God has led us to draw together three aspects of the letter: divine calling as marking off the Christians from the realm of the ordinary; adoption by God as linking Christians to the most holy being; designation of Christians by means of terminology that Jewish society used to describe the holy. Each of these three occupies an important place in the letter. Together they communicate a strong sense of the specialness, the sacredness, of the Christians at Rome and across Paul's world.

An effect of this study has been to draw attention to the role of the Spirit in moving the convert from the sphere of the ordinary to the sphere of the holy. This is seen most clearly in the Spirit's role in bringing adoption as sons and daughters of God. These pneumatological points, in turn, suggest directions for further reflection on the letter's soteriology. The power of the Spirit in making the convert holy seems likely to be linked to the power of Spirit as the means of God bringing life from death. This in turn leads us on towards the Christology of the letter and, particularly, the conjunction in 1:3-4 of the appointment of Jesus as son of God, power, the "Spirit of holiness" and the resurrection. All in all, a large number of interesting avenues are opened by consideration of holiness and ecclesiology. The idea of the Church as having the status of holiness is a neglected topic. If one is to understand what Paul writes about the people of God in Romans, then it is a topic that needs to be moved back closer to centre-stage.

Carnal Conduct and Sanctification in 1 Corinthians: *Simul sanctus et peccator?*

BRUCE W. WINTER

Given the catalogue of sinful behavior in the Christian community in Corinth that Paul addressed in 1 Corinthians, one is astonished by what he says of them on three occasions. He does not state that they *should be sanctified,* that they *will be sanctified* in heaven, but that *they are already sanctified* (1:2, 30; 6:10). This declaration seems to be a highly inappropriate, if not irresponsible, one to make in the light of their indulgence in fornication and adultery, which they justified on the basis of the popular aphorism that "all things are permitted for me" (6:12, 15; 10:8, 23). Paul's statement is all the more surprising because he clearly warns them immediately prior to the discussion of the former problem that those who commit fornication and other sins in a catalogue of vices, will not inherit the kingdom of God (6:9). How can Paul, in the light of this latter statement, not only believe but also tell the Corinthian Christians in their present spiritual condition on three occasions that they have been sanctified? Would we ourselves be comfortable informing Christians who are behaving as the Corinthians did that they "are sanctified" (1:2)?

It is also very unlikely that we would then immediately proceed, as Paul did, with a thanksgiving prayer for the grace of God given to them, affirming that he had "enriched them" in every way, "that the testimony of Christ was confirmed among them," and that God "will strengthen them to the end, so that they will be *blameless* on the Day of the Lord Jesus" (1:4-9).[1] As the letter unfolds it emerges that their behavior was unholy and culpable. Would we follow up the declaration of holiness in 1:2 with these affirmations of similar behavior in a Christian congregation today?

The Christian tradition to which the one who is being honored in this

---

1. P. T. O'Brien, "Thanksgiving for God's Grace Given: 1 Cor. 1:4-9," in *Introductory Thanksgivings in Paul,* NovTSup 49 (Leiden: Brill, 1977), pp. 107-37.

volume belongs gives more than notional assent to the doctrine of holiness and it does so at a time when the emphasis on the personal and corporate pursuit of holiness appears largely to have slipped from the agenda of wider Christianity. It has been replaced by what could be called "consumer" Christianity where Christians "shop" around for a church that suits them. This shift away from an emphasis on holiness simply reflects the focus of our contemporary society that is possessed by possessions and passions. The former is promulgated on the premise that need and greed are the engines that drive human beings because life is seen to consist in the abundance of possessions and pleasures. The latter has been endorsed by the dominant popular philosophical system of the past eighty years. It began with psychological hedonism that spawned the "Roaring Twenties" and was made even more culturally acceptable half a century ago by Hugh Heffner in his *Playboy* magazine which published his defense of hedonism in a series entitled "The playboy's philosophy." It was Walter Lippmann who astutely observed "that the pursuit of happiness is the most unhappy pursuit." Is it really the message of 1 Corinthians that the present pursuit of holiness is the most Christian pursuit, and is obligatory at the corporate and personal level? If so, how does one make sense of Paul's declaration to Christians that they are sanctified, even though their behavior is distinctly unsanctified, i.e., unholy? Carnality and holiness are surely antonyms in 1 Corinthians.

When used in this chapter, the term "carnality" covers the same range of meanings supplied by the *Oxford English Dictionary*, namely "sensual, unsanctified, worldly" and is not restricted to the first meaning. This is important because sanctification is so often seen in the Christian community as solely the antithesis to the first meaning when reading either 1 Corinthians or the larger Pauline corpus.

In order to unravel Paul's teaching on sanctification in this letter it is proposed (I) to highlight aspects of Corinthian culture that are reflected in the issues he discusses in order to understand that carnality covers more than sexual issues, and then to explore his teaching on Christian sanctification, (II) to discuss the concept of "Christ our sanctification," (III) to examine unsanctified conduct in the sanctified; and then (IV) to note the divine discipline exercised on those whose unsanctified living provokes the Lord's intervention. This chapter seeks to clarify Paul's teaching on the critical doctrine of sanctification in this penultimate era of salvation in which Christians now live.

I. The Extent of Christian Carnality

How carnal was Roman Corinth? While it is generally not known that "to Cretianize" in Greek was widely used as a first-century synonym "to tell lies,"[2] all seem to be aware that "to Corinthianize" had, for centuries, referred to having sexual intercourse with a prostitute.[3] The latter term originated from a Classical Greek play and belonged to the Greek era of Corinth, as did the story that on the Acrocorinth there was a temple of Aphrodite that housed one thousand prostitutes. This was a myth from the Greek period as there was no temple prostitution in the Corinth of Paul's day for two reasons — (i) The newly built first-century temple to Aphrodite was a small construction on the edge of the Acrocorinth overlooking this proud Roman colony; (ii) by this period Aphrodite, the patron of the new colony founded by Rome in A.D. 44 had been Romanized and was now known as Venus, the divine "mother" of the imperial family. No longer the naked sex icon of the Greek period, she was now a well-clad and highly respectable goddess.[4]

Taking cognizance of these facts is critical as there is a temptation to read 1 Corinthians as a letter written to a city that was saturated with prostitutes and whose male inhabitants were hopelessly addicted to promiscuity. It is then concluded that the conduct of those Christians was totally explicable and sexual purity was the main issue Paul addressed in his letter. Such a perception misreads the secular mores of Roman Corinth and obscures the important teaching on the breadth of Christian corporate and personal holiness that encompasses matters well beyond the sphere of their sexuality. This letter addresses critical issues concerning holiness in our contemporary church, just as it did for that nascent congregation in the A.D. 50s.

While statistical information does not tell the whole story, it is interesting to note that, based on the number of words that Paul used to address different issues, the three longest discussions in 1 Corinthians are devoted to divisiveness among Christians (1:10–4:21), the misuse of spiritual gifts (12–14), and eating in the idol temple as a matter of a "right" (8–11:1). Paul's responses occupy 19.6

---

2. Polybius, 16.18.15–22.2 and Plutarch, *Lysias* 20.2.

3. See the fourth-century B.C. plays of Philetaerus 13.559a and Poliochus, 7.31.3, "The Whoremonger (ὁ Κορινθιαστής)," and Plato, *The Republic*, 404C in which a "Corinthian girl" = a prostitute.

4. "Venus . . . is placed at the center of the city [Corinth] as the Mother of the Roman Nation, and as the mother of the Roman colony," C. K. Williams II, "A Re-evaluation of Temple E and the West End of the Forum of Corinth," in *The Greek Renaissance in the Roman Empire: Papers from the Tenth British Museum Classical Colloquium*, BICSSup 55, ed. S. Walker and A. Cameron (London: University of London, Institute of Classical Studies, 1989), p. 157.

percent, 18.5 percent, and 17 percent of the length of the letter respectively.[5] The first two problems show that sexual issues were not the only unsanctified matters Paul had to deal with at length and, even on the third matter, sexual misconduct was not the central problem.

Would our contemporary preachers have begun by first addressing the problem of "politics" in the church and not sexual issues? This is what Paul does in 1 Corinthians 1:10–4:21. It has to do with conduct that he describes as secular, i.e., "walking according to secular dictates," "behaving like [secular] men," and categorizing their conduct as "carnal" (σάρκινος/σαρκικός, 3:1-3). It came about with Christians importing mores governing the teacher/pupil relationship from secular education into their perception of ministry and discipleship in the church. That this should happen is entirely explicable because the students of the teachers at the secondary and tertiary levels of education were called by the same term used of the disciples of Christ (μαθηταί).[6]

Like the Trojan horse, along with that designation came secular conventions. They determined how an orator would relate to his pupils in this important era of the dawning of the Second Sophistic and how his students would slavishly follow him. They were expected to imitate his ways, to give exclusive loyalty to him and to be in competition with the disciples of other teachers as to whose instructor was superior — hence Paul's selection of the terms "strife" and "zealousness" drawn from the semantic domain of education (παιδεία) to describe what Paul saw as the cult of following Paul, Apollos, or Peter (1:11-13; 3:3-4). At the time of writing 1 Corinthians the Christians were playing the first two off against each other, as if they were in competition with one another for followers — just as secular teachers were (4:6).[7] Paul indicates that this giving of exclusive loyalty was idolatrous (1:13). He wanted no followers, because the ministers belonged to the church and not *vice versa* (3:21-23). There was nothing salacious involved in this major issue that Paul addressed first. It was very much a replication of their secular way of thinking and one that was destroying the Christian fellowship of brothers.[8]

---

5. For an analysis of 1 Corinthians see my "The 'Underlays' of conflict and compromise in 1 Corinthians," in *Paul and the Corinthians: Studies on a Community in Conflict, Essays in Honour of Margaret Thrall*, ed. T. J. Burke and J. K. Elliott (Leiden: Brill, 2003), pp. 140-49.

6. Dio Chrysostom, *Or.* 55:1, 3, 5.

7. Dio Chrysostom, *Or.* 8:9 records an incident in Corinth where the disciples of the sophists were fighting with those of rival sophists. For a discussion see my *Philo and Paul among the Sophists: Alexandrian and Corinthian Responses to a Julio-Claudian Movement*, 2nd ed. (Grand Rapids: Eerdmans, 2002), pp. 124-29.

8. From the evidence in 2 Corinthians 10–13 the problem seemed to be intractable. See my "Paul among the Christian Sophists," in *Philo and Paul*, pp. 203-39.

The serious issue of incest occupies the next section of the letter. What deeply troubled Paul was that some Christians boasted not about the sin but the status of the person sexually involved with his stepmother. It was he, and not she, who was to be excluded from the Christian community for we can presume that she was not a Christian. Exclusion from personal contact and table fellowship go well beyond the boundaries of incest and includes issues that are seen to be equally serious, i.e., covetousness, idolatry, verbal abuse, drunkenness, and swindling other people (5:10).[9]

Vexatious litigation over the smallest matters was a standard way of bringing into the public domain conflict situations between individuals, for interpersonal strife was very much part and parcel of first-century life.[10] Under Roman law such litigation was off limits between family members, hence the astonishment that in the family of God "brothers go to law against brothers and that before unbelievers" (6:6).[11] A judge determined the outcome of a case and jurors were elected to office by a wealth test. They were known to be corrupt in their decision-making process that was influenced by the rank and status of the respective contestants. They were "unjust" in their decisions and open to being influenced by bribes. Financial penalties were imposed on the person who lost the case (6:1-8).[12]

In 6:9-20 behavior is related to what ancient historians have designated "the unholy trinity" of eating and drinking and immorality.[13] That was expected of young men when they assumed the *toga virilis* on reaching manhood — food was for the belly and the belly for food and the body was made for sex.[14] Cicero argued that this had always been the case, when he wrote of those who rejected the well-known aphorism "it is permitted" *(licitum est).*

> If there is anyone who thinks that youth should be forbidden affairs even with courtesans, he is doubtless eminently austere, but his view is contrary

---

9. G. D. Fee, *The First Epistle to the Corinthians,* NICNT (Grand Rapids: Eerdmans, 1987), p. 220 rightly sees the whole of chapter 5 as a single unit as there is no break at 5:6.

10. D. F. Epstein, *Personal Enmity in Roman Politics 21-43 B.C.* (London: Routledge, 1989).

11. Cicero, *Fam.* 9.25.3.

12. See my "Civil Litigation in Corinth: The Forensic Background to 1 Cor. 6.1-8," *New Testament Studies* 37 (1991): 559-72.

13. "'The intimate and unholy trinity' of eating, drinking and sexual immorality" (A. Booth, "The Age for Reclining and its Attendant Perils," in *Dining in a Classical Context,* ed. W. J. Slater [Ann Arbor: University of Michigan Press, 1991], p. 105).

14. The young Corinthian men would have subscribed to the inscription on a sculpture of a phallic symbol now in the Archaeological Museum, Naples — "here dwells happiness" *(hic habitat felicitas).* See C. Mills and J. J. Norwich, *Love in the Ancient World* (London: Orion, 1997), p. 125.

not only to the license of this age, but also to the custom and concessions of our ancestors. For when was this not a common practice? When was it blamed? When was it forbidden? When, in fact, was it that what is permitted was not allowed *(quod licet, non liceret)?*[15]

Apart from Paul, Tacitus saw the temptations that opened up to young men on receiving the *toga virilis* as a persistent danger. "The elegant banquet . . . along with the use of the toga . . . are the enticements of Romanization to vice and servitude."[16] Nicholas of Damascus in his life of Augustus records at that age he was not "in attendance with the young men as they get drunk, not to remain at drinking parties past evening nor to have dinner . . . and he abstained from sex just at the time when young men were particularly sexually active."[17] We are certain that "it is permitted" was a popular aphoristic saying of young men that justified their excessive eating and drinking and after-dinner sex (6:2) — it was not a misunderstanding of Paul's gospel.[18] The sexual sin was not that of adultery but fornication because it created a one-flesh relationship through intercourse with a prostitute and was not a breach of marriage, i.e. adultery. The *Sitz im Leben* points to activities at feasts and not brothels.

Chapter 7 is Paul's longest discussion of marriage, singleness, divorce, and chaste conduct prior to marriage as well as the remarriage of widows, all of which are seen as a Christian "calling." He also addresses the issues of social pressures open to those concerned with "class," i.e., Jewish/Gentile identity, or bonded service and manumission and voluntary indentured service into a Roman household for a set period so that Provincials could secure Roman citizenship (7:17-24). It shows that some Christians were keen to be upwardly mobile in the established class system for reasons of personal and financial advantage and thus there was the need for standard teaching in all the churches, not just the church in Corinth (7:17).

Guests at major civic feasts sat down to eat and drink in the temple precincts and rose up "to play," i.e., engaged in what was politely called "after dinners" by courtesy of the traveling brothels.[19] However, Paul goes back to the core issue as to why some Christians were attending, i.e., to exercise their constitutional rights as Roman citizens. He confronts the arguments some put for-

---

15. Cicero, *Pro Caelio* 20.41.

16. Tacitus, *Agr.* 21.

17. F. Jacoby, ed., *Die Fragmente der griechischen historiker* (Berlin: Weidmannsche Bundhandling, 1926), II: 90.

18. *Contra* D. Wenham, *Paul: Follower of Jesus or Founder of Christianity* (Grand Rapids: Eerdmans, 1995), pp. 95-96.

19. Philo, *Vit.* 54.

ward as to why they should be present and then extrapolates at length on not exercising his rights as an apostle (chap. 9). He again rejects the popular aphorism that "all things are permitted" (10:23), and demands what was antithetical, i.e., they must give no offence to Jews or Greeks or to the church of God but seek the welfare of neighbors that they may be saved. He cites himself as an example. Therefore they must imitate him by not exercising their rights, just as he himself imitates Christ in this matter (10:32–11:1). Carnal conduct was not only manifested in their moral misconduct but in their worldly way of operating on the basis of their civic rights and not on their gospel responsibilities. As Roman society was founded on the basis of the constitutional "rights," Paul demands a major inversion of thinking.

In discussing the exercising of spiritual gifts at the expense of relationships in the Christian meetings, Paul makes a devastating judgment. In 13:1-3 he categorically states that however "gifted" the ministry of Christians may be, if it is not motivated by love then their words are empty and they themselves "are nothing." Even though they have prophetic powers and great faith, they gain nothing — however heroic their sacrifices (13:1-4). Their interpersonal conflicts surface at every point of interaction from the beginning of the letter (1:10; 6:1; 11:16, 18) to this point where Paul's concern is still about divisions among believers (12:25).

Paul's discussion of the resurrection of the body is often seen as a purely eschatological issue. However, as the argument unfolds, matters relating to eating, drinking and sexual immorality are again addressed as a central concern. Paul testifies to the fact that he himself needs self-restraint. He has "to die every day" and fights the beast, i.e., sexual passion.[20] The first set of injunctions in this lengthy discussion concerns matters he had raised earlier about the use of the body (5; 6:9-20; 7:36; 10:8). "Do not be deceived," he commands, because "bad company corrupts good morals" (15:33). This is a popular and apposite citation from Menander's *Thais* for the context was about going to prostitutes.[21] The next injunction is "wake out of drunkenness and stop sinning," a reference back to 6:13 and 10:7, "For some have no knowledge of God. I say this to your shame" (15:34). Paul alludes to the work done for the Lord in evangelism, on which he has touched earlier (9:19-22; 11:1), in contrast to their hedonistic activities. He again addresses the unholy trinity of first-century partying involving feasting and fornication or adultery (6:12-20; 10:7-8). His only other set of in-

---

20. Dio Chrysostom, *Or.* 5.16, 22, 24-7 and A. Malherbe, "The Beasts at Ephesus," *Journal of Biblical Literature* 87 (1968): 71-80.

21. For the text see A. Meineke, *Fragmenta comicorum Graecorum*, 2nd ed. (Berlin: De Gruyter, 1970), 1:73 and for both the text and discussion see my *After Paul left Corinth: The Influence of Secular Ethics and Social Change* (Grand Rapids: Eerdmans, 2001), pp. 98-100.

junctions in this chapter comes at the end of the whole discussion where he has been answering both the objections raised in 15:35 about how the dead are raised, the nature of the body, and the overall implications of the body for the Corinthians. They must "be steadfast, immoveable, always abounding in the work of the Lord" and not in their hedonistic lifestyle (15:58, cf. 15:32-3).[22] They are to follow Paul who at great cost brought the gospel to them (15:10-11) and they in turn must do the same so that others may have the knowledge of God (10:33–11:1). His concerns here are with the gospel responsibilities of Christians as *the* alternative to their first-century hedonistic lifestyle.

The immediate implication of chapters 1–4 concerning Apollos is spelt out in full in 16:12-18 where it first emerges that they wished him to return and, by implication, not Paul. Here the remedy for this zealousness over teachers and the sort of strife endemic in first-century relationships is dealt with in the call to be "alert, resolute in the faith, courageous and strong, and doing everything motivated by love" (16:13-14). What follows overturns the Roman social order with its emphasis on the protocol attached to rank and status. The head of the house of Stephanas took a servile position, and is commended by Paul as a paradigm (16:15-16), as are those who came from Corinth to Ephesus and refreshed Paul's spirit — an essential aspect of ministry (16:17-18).

The Christian community in Corinth seems not to have abandoned the pursuit of happiness that was derived from the philosophical schools of first-century Platonism and Epicureanism as well as the more ancient tradition of Greek Philosophical Hedonism. Its adherents were taught only to call off pursuits when they no longer brought them self-fulfillment or were the occasion of pain or difficulty.[23] This attitude applied not only to sexual matters but also to wider issues as has been demonstrated in this brief survey. The Corinthians were, after all, citizens of the secular city before they became citizens of heaven and their cultural preconditioning was responsible for their behavior.

In conclusion, it is a misreading of 1 Corinthians to see carnality purely in terms of the first definition offered by the *Oxford Dictionary of English*. This is critical for our subsequent discussion because the antithesis to carnality is central to Paul's solutions to a much wider field of activities. Not only unrighteous persons are listed: "fornicators, idolaters, adulterers, consenting sexually penetrated and penetrating homosexuals," but also "thieves, covetous people,

---

22. Paul uses ὥστε as a summary of the ethical demands that follow from his discussion here as well as at the end of those on the Lord's supper and spiritual gifts (11:33; 14:39).

23. "Nature . . . has also given man the senses, to be, as it were, his attendants and messengers . . . the special faculties and aptitudes of other parts of the body." Cicero, *Laws* 1.26-27. See also the *verbatim* account of Philo, *Det.* 32-4 citing the sophists of his day who integrated first-century Platonism and Epicureanism in a similar way to Cicero.

drunkards, those who are verbally abusive, and swindlers" (6:9-10). Six out of the ten sins are not sexual.

II. Christ Our Sanctification

If the problems in the Christian community were not monochrome, what solution does Paul provide in 1 Corinthians that would promote holiness? The issue of sanctification is certainly foremost in Paul's mind as his opening greeting in 1 Corinthians reveals. Corinthian Christians are defined as "sanctified in Christ Jesus" and as such are designated "saints" (1:2). The former statement is not reproduced elsewhere in the Pauline corpus. The question was asked at the beginning of this chapter — what did sanctification mean for the Corinthian Christians of whose sins and follies Paul knew as he commenced writing this letter? Had he simply declared that they were "justified," a term he was to use later in the letter (1:30; 6:11), we would not be at all surprised, but his use of "sanctified" is totally unexpected.

In 1:30-31 Paul again declares that "from Him [God] you yourselves are in Christ Jesus who is made wisdom to us from God, both justification and sanctification and redemption in order that just as it is written 'The one who boasts must boast in the Lord.'" The expectation would have been that justification and redemption would be linked but between these terms Paul inserts "sanctification" and uses τε καί which "provides a closer connection than simple καί."[24] Here Paul includes himself and the Corinthian Christians in these key theological terms that explain the work of God. Conzelmann calls sanctification "an alien wisdom" from God.[25] Therefore what the term "sanctification" means can be deduced in part from the role the other key terms of "wisdom," "justification," and "redemption" play. As a consequence those who boast can only boast in the Lord because this is his doing, as the apt citation from Jeremiah 1:31 reminded them. This summary citation fits well with the preceding discussion in 1:10-31.

In 6:11 "sanctification" occurs before "justification" as they are linked together to describe the Christians. Paul does not say that they "are washed, sanctified, and justified" but they "were washed, sanctified and justified in the name of the Lord Jesus and in the Spirit of our God." All are aorist passives that refer not to a sequence of events but to the past work of the Lord Jesus and the Spirit in them without drawing a distinction between the three terms used to describe

24. BDF, p. 230.
25. H. Conzelmann, *A Commentary on the First Epistle to the Corinthians*, Hermeneia (Philadelphia: Fortress, 1975), p. 50.

this divine work. If we look at the evidence cumulatively from 1:2-3, 30 and now 6:11 the Corinthian Christians are who they are now as a result of the former work of God the Father, the Lord Jesus, and the Spirit in them.

Peterson discusses these three passages appropriately under the heading of "New status in Christ." He wishes to argue not for a sequence by which God justifies, then sanctifies, and then redeems us. It is not the consistent order in the three passages. He concludes that "the sanctification in view here is not a process of moral change. The context is about belonging to God and being given a holy status. The focus is on God's saving activity, not our response."[26] That "calling" or "rank" in Christ is also expressed at the beginning of the letter where Paul designates them as "saints," i.e., Christians (1:2). They would have understood that "rank" was something that was bestowed in the secular world of Roman Corinth as an issue of social standing in this colony, a *terminus technicus* that Paul consciously used in 1:26 and again later in 7:17-24.

Part of the solution appears to have been in setting the overarching reality of their position in Christ not as the concluding perspective but that through which God sees those who are his children. It is clear that incorporation into Christ has alone brought these great benefits to the Corinthians, so that their status or position in Christ is the cause for genuine thanksgiving.

III. Correcting the Unsanctified Conduct of the Sanctified

It is not possible within the limits of this chapter to address all the ways in which Paul deals with the unsanctified patterns of behavior in 1 Corinthians, because he had no one pastoral method but approached each issue differently.[27] On some occasions he engages in prolonged arguments, in another instance he addresses an issue by interrogation, simply asking nine penetrating questions of those engaging in vexatious litigation against fellow Christians (6:1-8). Paul develops a sustained argument against "this right of yours" (8:9)[28] in which he

---

26. D. Peterson, *Possessed by God: A New Testament Theology of Sanctification and Holiness*, NSBT (Leicester: Apollos, 1995), pp. 42, 43-44.

27. For a detailed analysis of how Paul used different approaches to each of the pastoral issues see my forthcoming *After Paul Left Corinth: The Resolution of Conflict and Compromise in 1 Corinthians* as the sequel to *After Paul Left Corinth: The Influence of Secular Ethics and Social Change*.

28. It is not a "liberty" (which is ἐλευθερία in Greek) as 8:9 is sometimes wrongly rendered, but a "right" (ἐξουσία) to which he refers. The latter term occurs on numerous occasions where Paul uses it of his rights in 9:4, 5, 6, 12, 18. The cognate for "liberty," i.e., "free" is found in 9:1.

seeks to persuade them to abandon their destructive flirtation with idolatry and commands them to imitate him in discharging their gospel responsibilities as he himself has done in imitation of Christ (8:1–11:1). Rhetorical handbooks fail at this point because Paul does not adopt a standard approach; each case is handled differently.[29] I have suggested elsewhere there is a two-fold strategy to deal firstly with presenting issues one by one and at the end of the letter to address their underlying causes and the final solution to them in 1 Corinthians 15 and 16:12-18.[30]

As an example of how Paul counters unsanctified behavior we shall address the issues raised in 6:9-20. His arguments as to why young men should abandon feasting and fornication is an example of how he confronts issues of carnality. In 6:9 he cautions the Corinthians not to be deceived because "the unrighteous will not inherit the kingdom of God." We assume that Paul's call not to be deceived indicates that there were those who had or were in danger of being so. He then intervenes with reference to the work of the Lord Jesus and the Spirit that distances them from what they once were — sinners without a savior (6:9-11).

It is significant that there follows immediately a series of arguments as to why young men should not be involved with high-class prostitutes who plied their trade at dinners among the élite partying-going set of Corinthian playboys who had received the *toga virilis* as the right of passage not only to manhood but riotous living. He produces eight reasons why they must desist from this "unholy trinity" of eating, drinking, and fornication with female prostitutes.[31] He strongly counters their aphorism "everything is permitted" with the observations of two arguments, "but (ἀλλά) not everything is beneficial," "but (ἀλλά) I will not be enslaved by anything," referring to the destructive and addictive nature of fornication (6:12). They may argue that appetites are for nourishing the body and the body was made to receive food to justify their indulgence at dinners, but Paul counters strongly that God will do away with both and for the body was not designed for fornication "but" (ἀλλά) for the Lord (6:13).

---

29. For a general discussion of the issue of rhetoric see my "Revelation *v.* Rhetoric: Paul and the First-century Fad," in *Bible Translation Issues* (Wheaton: Crossway Books, 2005).

30. Paul deals with presenting problems in 1 Corinthians but addresses the underlying causes of compromises and conflicts in the concluding section of his letter. See my "The 'Underlays' of conflict and compromise in 1 Corinthians," pp. 139-55.

31. The term Paul uses in 6:12-20 is for fornicators (πόρνοι) — he distinguishes in 6:9 between "fornicators" (πόρνοι) and adulterers (μοιχοί) and the sexual partner in 6:15, 16 was a female prostitute (πόρνης). This is further supported by the fact that they thereby establish a "one flesh relationship" in 6:16. Had married men been involved, the charge here would have been adultery, which breaches the one flesh relationship.

The Christian playboys had forgotten that God will raise up their bodies, so the body and the deeds done in it are not inconsequential (6:14; cf. 2 Cor 5:10). Their new relationship with Christ to whom they are joined is exclusive. Being joined to Christ means that they are not permitted to have sexual intercourse with a prostitute because sexual intercourse establishes a one-flesh relationship (6:15-17). The command that follows demands that they flee immorality, because of the damage it inflicts on their bodies through casual sexual intercourse (6:18). They also have failed to take into account that the work of the Lord Jesus and the Spirit means that they are indwelt by the latter in the same way God's presence dwelt in the temple in the old covenant, and the Spirit they have in their body comes from God. They are therefore no longer owners but tenants in their bodies (6:19). The final argument Paul uses is that Christ's rescuing them means that they are no longer their own and on that basis they must glorify God by means of what they do with their bodies, i.e., live chaste lives (6:20).

Here is a series of powerful arguments that Paul uses to demolish the very popular aphorism that endorses the promiscuous behavior among the young Corinthian men. The deception they appeared to suffer from is strongly entrenched in their thinking but his arguments are formidable. Paul does not resort to ethical injunctions without the framework of sanctification. It is within the redemptive work of God that they are now positioned. It is now incumbent upon them to heed the cogent arguments as to why fornication is proscribed for subjects of the kingdom of God and they must now flee immorality because of the damaging effects upon them. Their task was to glorify God. There was a Christian alternative to the "unholy trinity."

In the light of this example it could never be said that any assertion by Paul of their position as "sanctified in Christ Jesus" permits them to persist in unsanctified sexual behavior. In fact, based on his affirmation of their sanctification in the preceding verses, he argues all the more strongly for them to live sanctified lives. The same is also true of other issues discussed in this letter that was written to deal with carnality. Paul in keeping with his approach has demolished every argument and every high thought that has been raised contrary to the knowledge of God and brought every thought captive in obedience to Christ (2 Cor 10:4-5).

IV. Divine Discipline for Unsanctified Living

There is no explicit statement in the letter indicating that genuine Corinthian Christians would lose their salvation because of their conduct. In fact their position in Christ indicates that they will not be condemned with the world

(11:32). Even in the case of incest Paul declares that the offender's spirit will be saved "on the day of the Lord" (5:5). Given that they are guaranteed justification, sanctification, and redemption, does this mean that God never intervenes because of the misconduct of Christians?

Paul asserts that the Lord "judges" many of the Corinthian Christians because of what they are presently doing. As we now explore the letter we see what those judgments are. In the case of the incestuous person, his flesh will be destroyed because he is handed over to Satan for that purpose (5:5). This implies the destruction of his body, i.e., his flesh and not just his exile from the community. Presumably his life is destroyed "in order that his spirit is saved in the day of the Lord" (5:5).

The young men who are sowing their wild oats as the result of the rite of passage to manhood inflict harm on themselves at the present moment with the unique sin that Paul says is damaging to the body — "he is sinning against his own body" (εἰς τὸ ἴδιον σῶμα ἁμαρτάνει), contrasting it with all other sins that are "outside the body" (6:18).

Paul warns the Corinthians that their exercising of dining rights in the temple will inevitably "provoke the Lord to jealousy" because they eat at the table of the *daimonioi* with its attendant idolatry and immorality (10:20-22). They must flee from that table because the history of Israel shows that where there is flirtation with idolatry and its accompanying pleasures there was the removal of many (10:8, 14, 20). Paul states that this experience in Israel's history was specifically recorded so that Christians would not crave evil things as they did (10:6). History does not have to repeat itself and those who are confident that they are unaffected by participation are warned. "So let everyone who thinks he stands, take heed that he does not fall" (10:12). What provokes the Lord to action in the old covenant does so in the new.[32] What happened to Israel provides the paradigm and does Paul have here in mind the same outcome as in the case of incest regarding the flesh and the spirit (5:5)?

Because of the abuses at the Lord's Supper some have already suffered at the Lord's hands. "Many are weak and sick" and quite a few are said to be "asleep," a euphemism for "death" (11:30). The verb "asleep" is used by Paul elsewhere only with reference to "believers" who are deceased (1 Cor 7:39; 15:6, 18, 20, 51; 1 Thess 4:13-15). It has happened "because of this," i.e., their conduct towards other believers. They were culpable since Paul had delivered to them the tradition of the Lord's Supper and they knew as a consequence how they should relate to one another in that celebration.

---

32. For an excellent study see B. S. Rosner, *Paul, Scripture and Ethics: A Study of 1 Corinthians 5–7,* AGJU 22 (Leiden: Brill, 1994), pp. 68-81 and 123-46.

So the overarching statement is that God "disciplines" (παιδευόμεθα) his children "in order that (ἵνα) we will not be condemned (κατακριθῶμεν) with the world" (11:32). We can assume from other evidence in 1 Corinthians that this is a principle that applies to conduct beyond abuses at the Lord's Supper. So it is right to speak of God now disciplining his children because of unsanctified conduct. This being the case one cannot argue that Paul's doctrine of sanctification lulls Christians into complacency and that he is indifferent to sinful conduct. They will not suffer final condemnation (κατακρίνω) but they will receive discipline from the Lord, a prospect that none would relish given the nature of it that is outlined in 1 Corinthians. God's discipline is always remedial, but it is discipline nevertheless.

If God's intervention is remedial, then Paul in concert with the Corinthian congregation also passes judgment "with you in spirit" on the incestuous man, indicating that he has already reached his verdict (5:4). The discipline imposed by the church was to deliver the offender over to Satan for "the destruction of the flesh" in order that the person will be saved ultimately (5:3-5). The church's discipline is to be done "in the name of the Lord Jesus . . . with the power of the Lord Jesus" (5:4), and like the divine discipline its aim is ultimately salvation of his spirit in the day of the Lord.

While Paul's teaching in 2 Corinthians is not within the purview of this essay, there Paul indicates that in the case of genuine repentance where the person is not "asleep," the church must also model the gospel. They do this by showing grace, encouraging the person, and reaffirming their love for him (2 Cor 2:7-8). Just as Paul passed judgment (5:3-5), so too he pronounced forgiveness in the presence of Christ, and the church must do the same. Satan must not be allowed to exploit that Corinthian situation, presumably by harassing the repentant into believing that he is not forgiven (2 Cor 2:10-11). So the reverse process to the one outlined in the previous paragraph must be replicated in the church.

The community was also commanded to withdraw from fellowship with those "brothers" who were out of fellowship with God because of their conduct (5:11), with Paul naming five other vices that were also listed in the following chapter (6:9-10). He explicates the sixth, i.e., "immorality" in 6:9 to include fornication, adultery, and homosexual intercourse. What therefore excludes non-Christians from the kingdom when committed by Christians obliges the community to now withdraw their fellowship, presumably for remedial purposes. Paul's arguments and commands in 1 Corinthians were given to remedy the carnal conduct of the sanctified. And Paul was to remind the same church in a subsequent letter addressed to "the saints" (2 Cor 1:1) that given the promises that God would walk among his people and he would be their God and they

197

would be his people, they on their part were commanded to "come out from among them and be separate" and "not touch the unclean thing." Having these promises and the two imperatives that flowed from them (2 Cor 6:16-17), he requires the Christians to "cleanse themselves from every defilement of the body and the spirit and to perfect holiness in the fear of the Lord" (2 Cor 7:1). These commands given to "the saints" and the call to perfect holiness out of reverence for God continued to provide no grounds for complacency.

V. Sanctification and the Contemporary Church

In theological terminology will *simul sanctus et peccator* succinctly but adequately represent the status of the Christian with respect to the nature of the Christian life in the penultimate era of salvation? From a pastoral perspective, nothing could be more supportive than to know that Christ is our sanctification positionally, especially when we are most conscious of the deficiencies of our lives in the past. Has the teaching office of the church also been alert, especially in our indulgent and "non-judgmental" age, to the fact that the pursuit of holiness is the most important Christian pursuit?

Some contemporary churches are vigilant with respect to consensual homosexual acts but not so in their treatment of members who fornicate or commit adultery. Some think that theft is relatively unimportant; while greed is just part of our affluent society and therefore covetousness is not really as serious as the sin of idolatry; drunkenness is wrong but verbal abuse is not as bad as sexual sins; and shady business deals, while fraudulent, are explicable since the Enron affair has revealed how widespread and almost inevitable it is where there is profit-obsessed capitalism. Yet the non-sexual offences in the catalogue in 6:9-10 are not regarded as sufficiently serious to be subject to discipline in the church.

However, sin still provokes divine action in the face of actual or material idolatry, resulting in weakness, sickness and even death in the case of those sinning grievously against the "mystical" body of Christ. It harms a person's body because of fornication and presumably adultery, and renders fruitless spectacular and even heroic ministries conducted at the expense of relationships that have to be nurtured by love.

At one time sexual misconduct would have automatically excluded Christians from the believing community, but not necessarily so in all branches of our contemporary church life. They are felt to be regrettable "lapses" but not life threatening. They are not seen as warranting church intervention and needing genuine repentance — after all the favorite text from a survey done among

Christians in the past decade was "judge not and you will not be judged" (Matt 7:1). In previous decades it was John 3:16.

The sobering reality for the teaching office of the contemporary church is that while the consequences of actions found in 1 Corinthians may not be the focus of teaching from the pulpit, they cannot be indulged in without God's disciplining hand being laid on the perpetrators at some point. This is regardless of whether it is taught or not taught or whether the church acts or does not act. Paul noted that God had already disciplined some Corinthian Christians because of their conduct — "that is why many of you are weak and sick and quite a few sleep" (11:30).

The pursuit of holiness by Christians might gain added incentive if all of Paul's teaching on sanctification in 1 Corinthians was resurrected. That would mean that Christians would look with confidence to the work of God in Jesus Christ for his people but at the same time would determine to abandon all those sins that stalked secular Corinth and the Christians who lived there because they come under the heading of "carnality."

So there are two errors into which Christian communities can fall on the doctrine of sanctification if all the teaching in 1 Corinthians is not incorporated into their understanding. The first error is that while justification "in Christ" is "positional," sanctification is not and therefore becomes a process that has to be secured by the individual Christian's own effort — this is hardly helpful to those with an oversensitive conscience or a negative perception of themselves which can be the result of a dysfunctional family background, abuse, or wrong instruction.

The other error is that sanctification is only "positional" and therefore the Christian is careless about personal holiness and indifferent to sinful conduct, because of the aphorism "once saved, always saved." It is significant that, on two occasions, Paul commands the Corinthian Christians not to be deceived. In the first instances he enumerates ten sins that exclude from the kingdom (6:9-10), some of which are present in their midst i.e., immorality (5:1; 6:13; 10:8; 15:33), idolatry (10:10), drunkenness (15:34), and cheating (6:8). Again he refers to the deleterious effects on good morals through the corrupting influence of inappropriate sexual liaisons (15:33). This is a reference to their activities previously referred to (6:15; 10:7-8). Was it that the Corinthians had happily embraced their positional sanctification and saw it as a license to do whatever they wanted, grossly underestimating the disciplining hand of God in the present moments of their lives? There is a similar deception in the contemporary Christian scene. 1 Corinthians provides a very timely and balanced perspective.

In conclusion, 1 Corinthians affirms that God is the author of justification, sanctification, and redemption and also the one who exercises remedial discipline with his erring children. Sanctification in 1 Corinthians is then the work of God in Christ, and the work of the Word of God, i.e., the Old Testament and the apostolic Word. If the Word of God is flagrantly set aside, then the work of God is seen in the divine disciplining of those who devalue the work of God in Christ as also part of sanctification. In all branches of the contemporary church the teaching office must draw attention to all three aspects of the work of God in sanctification if we are to recover for our generation the biblical teaching on holiness.

The People of God in a Pluralistic Society: Holiness in 2 Corinthians

J. AYODEJI ADEWUYA

What does it mean to *be* and *live* as people of God in a pluralistic society? By examining how the Corinthians wrestled with living in an environment whose moral values, religious convictions, and principles were opposed to theirs, this essay on 2 Corinthians attempts to shed light on how twenty-first-century believers might live in a morally polluted and pluralistic society.[1]

Paul's Rhetorical Strategy in 2 Corinthians

Although the particularities of the problems that Paul addressed in 2 Corinthians remain highly speculative, the social, cultural, and religious settings of the Corinthian Christians are increasingly clear. Paul's teaching on holiness in 2 Corinthians is intricately connected with its rhetorical and historical situations. Both, in turn, dictate his rhetorical strategy in 2 Corinthians and the teaching on holiness contained in it.

An essential component of a letter's rhetorical situation is its controlling exigency — "an imperfection marked by urgency; it is a defect, an obstacle, something wanting to be done, a thing which is other than it should be."[2] The exigency functions as the organizing principle: "It specifies the audience to be

---

1. With regard to 1 Corinthians, Michael J. Gorman notes that "in this letter we have more (relatively) clear windows into an early Christian community than in any other New Testament writing" (*Apostle of the Crucified Lord: A Theological Introduction to Paul and His Letters* [Grand Rapids: Eerdmans, 2004], p. 227). Gorman's comments are applicable to 2 Corinthians in as much as Paul is writing to the same congregation.

2. Lloyd F. Bitzer, "The Rhetorical Situation," in *Rhetoric: A Tradition in Transition*, ed. Walter R. Fisher (East Lansing: Michigan State University, 1974), p. 252.

addressed and the change to be effected."[3] Bitzer's analysis, when applied to 2 Corinthians, enables us to speak of multiple "controlling exigencies," to which the rhetorical situation of 2 Corinthians is inextricably linked. One urgent exigency in 2 Corinthians is that of the holiness of the congregation. When Paul wrote to the Corinthians, Corinth, although a Roman colony, maintained many ties with Greek religion, philosophy, and the arts. Consequently, their faith was influenced by a Hellenistic world-view. As observed and succinctly stated by Fee, "Although they were the Christian church in Corinth, an inordinate amount of Corinth was yet in them, emerging in a number of attitudes and behaviors that required surgery without killing the patient."[4] They were the *Christian* community in Corinth, but in a number of things their attitude was more determined by being Corinthians than by their Christian faith.[5] A closer examination of the historical situation will help us to see how the holiness of this congregation had become a pressing exigency in the rhetorical situation of 2 Corinthians.

As various studies on the history of Corinth have shown, religion was as diverse as Corinth's population.[6] As such, a serious problem in Corinth that faced both the Jews and the Corinthian Christians of the first century was that of religious pluralism and the imperial cult. Religious pluralism "was woven into the fabric of everyday life"[7] and presented difficult challenges to the Corinthian believers. Moreover, in Corinth, as in any cosmopolitan city then and now, vice and religion prospered side by side. The problem of food offered unto idols in 1 Corinthians 8–10 is a case in point. One serious challenge that the fledgling Christian communities faced was whether to compromise or capitulate.

While it is impossible to know precisely who constituted the audience of Paul's letter, the congregation is likely comprised of Jews and Gentiles. In 1 Corinthians, Paul addressed the audience directly as Gentiles (12:2), indicating that there were Gentiles in the Corinthian community. Pagan temples dominated the public space in Corinth so Paul's use of temple imagery would be understandable to them. However, bearing in mind Paul's citations of OT texts

---

3. Bitzer, "Rhetorical Situation," p. 252.

4. Gordon D. Fee, *The First Epistle to the Corinthians*, NICNT (Grand Rapids: Eerdmans, 1987), p. 4.

5. Fee, *First Epistle*, p. 4.

6. E.g., Jerome Murphy-O'Connor, *St. Paul's Corinth. Texts and Archaeology*, GNS 6 (Wilmington, Del.: Glazier, 1983); James Wiseman, "Corinth and Rome I: 228 B.C.–A.D. 267," *ANRW* I 7, pp. 438-548; Bruce W. Winter, "Responses to Religious Pluralism — 1 Cor. 8–10," *Tyndale Bulletin* 41 (1990): 207-26; Bruce W. Winter, "The Achean Federal Imperial Cult II: The Corinthian Church," *Tyndale Bulletin* 46 (1995): 169-78.

7. Winter, "Responses," p. 209.

and allusions to Jewish traditions (1 Cor 5:6-8; 10:1-5; 2 Cor 3:18; 6:14-17), some of the Corinthians may have been Jews, or at the least had some knowledge of Judaism. Paul's use of temple imagery is insufficient evidence to establish this but his use of temple linked to purity language is unintelligible without his Jewish roots. Purity was a dominant concern both in the Jewish Temple cult and for Paul the Pharisee and is an essential backdrop to his understanding of the church in 2 Cor 6:16.

Thus Paul's mission was not to pour his gospel into a religious vacuum but to contend with other religions for the truth of his gospel in a highly pluralistic setting. He wanted the Corinthians to be a good witness to the society in which they lived, but at the same time to protect them from compromising their faith by slipping into familiar pagan ways. This meant (1) being morally exemplary citizens, and (2) attacking any immorality that might compromise the witness to the city as well as the harmony of the community. Paul's goal was to persuade the Corinthians to embody the gospel of Jesus Christ that he had preached to them.[8] He, therefore, employs metaphors that both depict and define the character of the Corinthians as the people of God, pointedly describing the manner of living that is required.

Paul's Designation of the *Ekklēsia* in 2 Corinthians

It can be argued that the failure of the Corinthians to live holy lives is a result of an unclear understanding of both who they are, and who they are called to be. In short, the Corinthian Christians seemed to have suffered from an "identity-crisis." Since Paul's view of the *ekklēsia* is a controlling factor in his teachings on holiness in 2 Corinthians (and elsewhere in his writings), it is appropriate to identify and examine the way Paul designates the believing community in this epistle.[9]

Holy Ones

In 2 Cor 1:1 Paul identifies the recipients as the church of God in Corinth and the "holy ones" in Achaia (cf. Rom 1:7; 1 Cor 1:1). Two important observations emerge from his designation of the Corinthians as "holy ones." First, Paul uses

---

8. Gorman, *Apostle*, p. 227.

9. Although there are many metaphors used for the *ekklēsia* in 2 Corinthians (e.g., temple, virgin, bride), only two will be expanded upon due to limitation of space.

the word *hagioi* in relational and ethical senses.[10] Used with a relational nuance, to be holy means to belong to God as a result of a covenant relationship that is made possible through the Christ-event. The holiness of God's people is based on their relation to him. The Corinthian Christians, in the same manner as Old Testament Israel, have been brought into a special and new relationship with God "in Christ Jesus." They, like Israel, were holy because of God's gracious choice and therefore separated from the profane world around them. Their lives however, seemed to suggest otherwise. In the ethical sense, Paul uses *hagiazein* as something required of those who belong to God, thus showing that relationship to God, instead of excusing, actually demands a moral/ethical response. A holy life is one to be lived out in the market-place, testifying to the relationship that is present between the Holy God and those who claim to belong to him. God's people must live like God.

Second, Paul almost always uses the word *hagioi* in the plural when referring to human beings. He uses it only once in the singular in a reference to "every holy one" (Phil. 4:21). In other words, Paul's thinking on holiness is primarily communal. Although each person who belongs to Jesus Christ belongs to him personally, there is nothing individualistic about such relationship. As such, it is the church, collectively, that is called to holy living, the individual only being important as a constituent member of the community. In 2 Cor 1:1, the word *hagioi* is closely linked with *ekklēsia.* To be a "member of the church" then would be equivalent to "being a holy one," in which case it might be appropriate to translate both simply as the "people of God."

The People of God

Paul's explicit designation of the Corinthians as the "people of God" in 2 Cor 6:16 coheres with his previous designation of them as "holy ones" and the "church of God." In the OT "People of God" is the designation for Israel which knows itself to be chosen and called by God in its entire existence — which includes all of its social dimension. To be the people of God in the OT is to be possessed by God. In Exod 19:3-8 Israel is summoned to a special relationship with God, described by three phrases: a special possession among all peoples, a kingdom of priests, and a holy nation. Israel is to be God's own people, set apart from other nations for his own service just as priests were set apart from

10. For a more detailed treatment of Paul's use of *hagioi* and other holiness vocabulary in the Corinthian correspondence, see J. Ayodeji Adewuya, *Holiness and Community in 2 Cor. 6:14–7:1: Paul's View of Communal Holiness in the Corinthian Correspondence,* StBL 40 (New York: Peter Lang, 2001), pp. 129-62.

others and marked by a quality of life commensurate with the holiness of their covenant God.[11] As Deut 7:6-8 makes clear, "people of God" is to be understood as Israel. Israel was chosen and in choosing her from all nations and saving her from Egypt, God intended for Israel's conduct to correspond to his own liberating actions. Israel was to be a holy people with a social order which distinguished it from other nations. Furthermore, they were his son (Exod 4:22), or sons (Deut 14:1), his sheep or flock (Ps 95:7), and his holy people (Deut 14:2; 28:9, Isa 62:12). It is important to note that Paul transfers the concept of chosenness to the Corinthian congregation. As "people of God," the Corinthians, like the Israelites, have been brought into a covenant relationship with God. They are not merely to receive his goodness; more important, they are to live under his rule and so to be a testimony to the presence and character of God among all the nations. The question is: "How are the Corinthians, as the people of God, to explicate his holiness?"

Aspects of Holiness in 2 Corinthians

Holiness as Pure Motivation Resulting in Ethical and Religious Purity

The issue of motivation is a question that is as relevant today as it was for Paul. The first hint about holiness in 2 Corinthians is contained in Paul's boast about his integrity as he faces criticism from the Corinthians about the change in his travel plans. Because of his ministry to them Paul can make certain claims about the personal behaviour of himself and Timothy in 2 Cor 1:12, a passage important both for its content and also for the holiness terminology employed. The claims that Paul makes in the passage are not on the basis of others' testimony but, according to Paul, on the basis of the witness of their consciences. In this verse, Paul affirms the manner in which he and Timothy have lived — "in holiness[12] and sincerity before God." For classicists, "sincerity" *(eilikrineia)* was used to denote either unmixedness and purity or sincerity and uprightness.[13] In Wis 7:25 wisdom is described as "a pure emanation of the glory of the Almighty *(aporroia eilikrinēs).*"[14] Paul uses the term in 1 Cor 5:8: since Christ our paschal lamb has been sacrificed, let us celebrate the Passover, "not with the old leaven, the leaven of malice and evil, but with the unleavened bread of sincerity *(eilikrineias)* and truth." However, based on the entire context of 1 Cor 5:1-12, *eilikrineias* is better

11. B. S. Childs, *The Book of Exodus,* OTL (Philadelphia: Fortress, 1974), p. 367.
12. Reading ἁγιότητι rather than ἁπλότητι as in NA[27].
13. LSJ (1940) with supplement (1968), p. 486.
14. Unless otherwise noted, all translations come from the RSV.

translated as purity.[15] In that passage, Paul is more concerned with the purity of the Corinthians than with their sincerity. Therefore, when Paul uses *eilikrineia* in 2 Cor 2:17 to describe himself and Timothy, not as "peddlers of God's word; but as men of sincerity *(eilikrineia)* as commissioned by God, in the sight of God," "sincerity" may be in view, but the context can very readily accommodate the sense "ethical purity." As the aroma of Christ (2:15) there would be no place for a mixed fragrance. As those who speak from God in the presence of God in Christ (2:17b), the character of their entire lives would have to be unalloyed. Their lives could not be such as that of the peddler with his bag of salesman's tricks.[16] Paul testifies that the lives of Timothy and himself have been of high character before the Corinthians and before God in Christ. They have lived in ethical and religious purity; their lives have been lived in holiness.[17]

Their manner of living, "in holiness and purity," derives from God, which is especially emphasized by the following clause in 1:12b: "not by earthly wisdom but by the grace of God." In grounding the holiness of his life in the grace of God rather than in his own human achievement, Paul nullified any reproach for his boasting. Because the life of the risen Christ is now Paul's life (Gal 2:20; cf. 1 Cor 1:30) and because he seeks to allow the mind of Christ which has been given him from God to control his life so that he is an imitator of Christ (cf. 1 Cor 2:13-16; 10:31–11:1), he does not draw back from asserting that he and Timothy have lived in holiness. This is not a boast as to their achievement and consequently something for which they can claim credit. To the contrary, this is what the grace of God has worked in them.

The final clause of this verse is highly significant. Paul and Timothy have not lived in some isolated haven but have conducted themselves publicly "in the world" and especially "towards you." For Paul, therefore, withdrawal from society was not the key to holiness.[18] He relied upon the grace of God who worked in him, and gave him the victory he sought. Because of the enabling power of their God, Paul and Timothy behaved themselves toward all in ethical conformity to the will of their God and Savior.

---

15. Cf. F. F. Bruce, *1 & 2 Corinthians*, NCB (Grand Rapids: Eerdmans, 1971), p. 57: "[S]in must be a thing of the past, holiness the abiding quality of the present and future."

16. Cf. BDAG, p. 508, *kapēleuō*: "Because of the tricks of small tradesmen . . . the word comes to mean almost *adulterate*. . . ." Cf. Isa 1:22 LXX.

17. Cf. H. A. W. Meyer, *A Critical and Exegetical Handbook to the Epistles to the Corinthians* (Edinburgh: T&T Clark, 1879), who asserts that Paul speaks of moral holiness and purity and that ". . . of his *entire conduct* not *merely* of his teaching" (p. 146). So also Bruce, *1 & 2 Corinthians*, p. 180.

18. Although Paul would urge separation as we shall see below, he never advocates isolationism.

Holiness as Forgiveness and Restoration

In 2 Cor 2:5-11, Paul deals with an offender whose identity and nature of offence remain unresolved.[19] Two matters in the passage relate to the explication of holiness in 2 Corinthians. The first is Paul's willingness to forgive and how his forgiveness implies forgiveness by the entire congregation. Underlying Paul's readiness to forgive is his desire for reconciliation with the members of the Corinthian believing community. The second issue is Paul's anticipation of the unwillingness to forgive and how an unforgiving stance could lead to Satan taking an advantage, not just of the repentant offender but the entire congregation. What is the reason for this juxtaposition?

The sequence of Paul's thoughts in the passage is important. Paul expects the Corinthians to demonstrate forgiveness to keep that brother from going into despair, "that he will not be overwhelmed by excessive sorrow" (2:7a). They were by that means to communicate love (2 Cor 2:8) to him. If they were "obedient in everything" (2:9), their forgiveness would mirror the apostle's forgiveness, which would mirror Christ's forgiveness. Moreover, Paul says, forgiveness was to be, not only for the sake of the offender, but also for the benefit of the church. The phrase "for your sake" (2:10) probably implies that not only Paul but also the whole Corinthian church may have been adversely affected by the offender's punishment. Hence, implicit in Paul's call for forgiveness is that a failure by the Corinthian congregation to forgive the offender would constitute a threat to the very basis of their existence, which was the love and forgiveness of Christ. Without their own reflection of Christ's love and forgiveness towards each other, Satan would take advantage and exploit the situation. Thrall suggests that although Paul does not explain precisely how Satan would take advantage, "perhaps he has in view the promotion of dissension within the congregation, should the offender remain penalised."[20] However, in view of Paul's pastoral concern, he also intends to impress upon the Corinthians that if the church cannot be a living demonstration of forgiveness in a community, there is no compelling reason for the people in that community to want to be a part of the church. Thus, the distorted image of the church that results from a lack of forgiveness will be to Satan's advantage. Forgiveness is a product of Christian love and holiness, and strengthens the fellowship of believers as it reconciles the repentant to fellowship. Arrington's suggestion that "refusal to forgive the be-

19. Discussions on these issues can be found in major commentaries. For a special treatment see Colin G. Kruse, "The Offender and the Offence in 2 Corinthians 2:5 and 7:12," *Evangelical Quarterly* 86 (1988): 129-39.

20. Margaret Thrall, *A Critical and Exegetical Commentary on 2 Corinthians*, vol. I, ICC (Edinburgh: T&T Clark, 1994), p. 181.

liever who has sinned, and who is now repentant, or receiving him with cold-ness back into fellowship, works to Satan's advantage"[21] is on target.

Holiness as Reconciliation

Paul's appeal for reconciliation with the disaffected Corinthians, although em-bedded in the earlier part of the letter, continues in 5:11–7:16, the first subsec-tion of which is 5:11–6:2. The thought unit is held together by an inclusio (5:11, "we persuade men"; the two appeals of 5:20b and 6:1). It is built around two components: 5:11-12 and 5:13–6:2. Once again, Paul's defense of his ministry and character comes into focus. His intent in 5:13–6:2 is to provide the Corinthians the basis for answering those who boast in external appearances.

Paul is motivated by the love of Christ, a love which he defines in terms of his death for us. "Jesus Christ is here presented as the endangered benefactor who went to the outer limits of beneficence on behalf of humanity."[22] Such love compels Paul to see things differently. First, unlike his opponents, he can no longer judge by externals, that is, "according to the flesh" (5:16). Second, Paul goes further to define his ministry in terms of reconciliation based on the Christ-event. Reconciliation, Paul would argue, results from an inner transfor-mation. Although Paul does not make this point explicit here, in a later key pas-sage he ties reconciliation with God closely to the notion of "new creature/new creation" in 5:17-21. Indeed, reaching the climax of his argument in 5:21, Paul's point is that the Christ-event is God's way of making sinners into saints, i.e., making sinners into those "who embody and implement the covenant faithful-ness of the covenant God."[23] While on the one hand Paul here appeals to the Corinthians to be reconciled with him, on the other hand he later appeals to the non-Christian world to be reconciled with God because God, in the death of Christ, has already borne the cost of any debt owed him.

In 2 Cor 6:1-10, Paul continues with his apostolic defence as God's ser-vant. Verse 1 is crucial to the understanding of holiness. Paul exhorts the Corin-thians not to "receive the grace of God in vain." What exactly does that mean?

---

21. French L. Arrington, *The Ministry of Reconciliation: A Study of 2 Corinthians* (Cleve-land, Tenn.: Pathway, 1998), p. 42.

22. Frederick W. Danker, *2 Corinthians*, ACNT (Minneapolis: Augsburg, 1989), p. 79.

23. The language comes from N. T. Wright, *The Resurrection of the Son of God* (Minneapo-lis: Fortress, 2003), p. 306. Although unnecessarily limiting the language to Paul's experience of his apostolic vocation, he argues extensively for this understanding of *dikaiosunē theou* in 2 Cor 5:21 in "On Becoming the Righteousness of God: 2 Corinthians 5:21," in *Pauline Theology*, vol. II, *1 & 2 Corinthians*, ed. David M. Hay (Minneapolis: Augsburg/Fortress, 1992), pp. 200-208.

In the context of the preceding section, it is right to argue that Paul is suggesting that the Corinthians will have received the grace of God in vain if they refused to be reconciled with him — Christ's ambassador; for one cannot be in proper relation with God while at the same time rejecting the ambassador through whom God makes appeal for reconciliation. Paul uses Isa 49:8 to make his plea. In the same manner as the Servant, Paul calls the Corinthians to reconciliation with himself as a proof of their salvation. He wishes to have his damaged relationship with his beloved community restored. Here is the essence of holiness. A right relationship with God not only demands, but also results in, a right relationship with other believers. Furthermore, in this section, Paul continues to defend his call by returning to his paradoxical understanding of ministry (6:4-5; cf. 4:7-12). Since Paul clearly perceives his apostolic work as being an integral part of God's mission, he urges them not to receive the grace of God in vain.

Holiness as Relationship

Perhaps there is no passage that better encapsulates Paul's teaching on holiness in 2 Corinthians than 2 Cor 6:14–7:1. His choice of words in the passage is quite striking. Apart from Paul's description of the Corinthian congregation as the people and temple of God, he uses terms such as defilement, cleansing, holiness, and perfection. The focus throughout this text is the believing community — the church, not the individual believer. Paul sees humanity, in general, and in this instance, the Corinthian believers as beings-in-relation. Therefore, however one understands the passage, it must primarily be seen in terms of the church rather than the individual. Together, the Corinthians are the "people" and "temple" of God. With such designations, Paul wishes to acknowledge that the Christians at Corinth are God's chosen people in the same way that Israel had been (Exod 19:6), separated from all that is profane and consecrated to God, the Holy One of Israel (cf. Isa 6:3), present in the cult. The Corinthians belong to God in covenant relationship in the same way as did Israel. In designating the Corinthians as the people of God (2 Cor 6:16), Paul has attributed to the Corinthians a title which Israel considered to be an expression of its peculiar dignity. In the Old Testament, it was the covenant relationship that made Israel a holy community (cf. Exod 19:5-6). Its continued existence depended on the abiding presence of the Holy One in their midst, a presence that both makes holy and demands holiness in turn. This demand was formulated in the covenant law which stipulated how Israel was to live out the covenant relationship, making them God's holy people, separated from the nations. In the context of

Leviticus 19, the rule against an "unequal yoke" may simply be an effective way of telling the Israelites as a "people" to maintain their identity, that is, to be different. They must live up to their relationship. Thus, it is clear from Leviticus 19 that holiness entails being and keeping in proper relationship with God. However, as Leviticus 19 also shows, relating with God also necessitates relating properly with others both within and without the covenant community. There are clear echoes of this background in 2 Cor 6:14–7:1. By alluding to the Holiness Code, Isaiah, and Ezekiel, Paul wishes to recall the Corinthians to their unique covenant relationship with God. By his sanctifying presence which is denoted by his walking among them, God makes them holy and demands that they be holy (2 Cor 7:1). Paul leaves no doubt that when the community is "unequally yoked," it violates its covenant relationship with God and ceases to exist as the people of God, even though it continues to do so in outward form.

Holiness as Separation

In the antitheses of 2 Cor 6:14b-16a, Paul reinforces the incongruence of the association of Christians with "unbelievers." In typical Pauline fashion, he makes clear the unique identity of Christians by distinguishing them from all others (cf. Rom 6:19; 13:12; 1 Thess 4:2-8; 5:5; Eph 5:8).[24] Paul frequently employs dualistic terms in defining membership (1 Cor 1 :20-28; 2:12; 3:19; 5:10, 12-13; 6:1, 2; 7:12-15, 31, 33-34; 11:32; 2 Cor 4:4; 6:14; Gal 4:3; 6:14; 1 Thess 4:12; Eph 2:2; Col 2:8, 20; 4:5).[25] In this way, the new Christian life in faith is set against the background of a pagan past.

The purpose of the rhetorical questions in 2 Cor 6:14b-16 is to show the incongruity of such associations. For example, nothing can be more incongruous than light and darkness, whether in the literal or figurative meaning of the terms. Such incongruity is true of holiness and sin. Christ and Belial are discordant and opposite. How then can their followers agree? Elements so discordant can never be united into a harmonious whole. Paul is clearly thinking of associations that involve a partnership rather than a casual or occasional working re-

---

24. Such perspective was not lacking in early Christian paraenesis. For example, 1 Pet 2:4-11 contains the following: (a) Christians as God's house (v. 5); (b) holiness (vv. 5, 9); (c) contrast between believers and unbelievers (v. 10); (d) contrast between light and darkness (v. 9); (e) combination of flesh and soul (v. 11). Statements which draw a contrast between "once" and "now" (corresponding to what we term "us" and "them" in this place) form a pattern in parts of the NT.

25. N. A. Dahl, "Form-critical observations on early Christian preaching," in N. A. Dahl, *Jesus in the Memory of the Early Church* (Minneapolis: Fortress Press, 1976), pp. 33-34.

lationship (cf. 1 Cor 10:20-21 on the impossibility of uniting the service of Christ and the service of demons). In vv. 16-18 Paul asserts the incongruity of the association between believers and unbelievers by dwelling on the metaphor of the temple. Although the contrasts focus on the relationship between the Corinthians and the "unbelievers," implicit in these OT citations is Paul's way of describing the Corinthian Christians as God's holy people and his sons and daughters. Because the Corinthians are related together "in Christ," they cannot be so related to unbelievers in the same manner. To do so is to be contaminated and to compromise their holiness.

There is a certain ambiguity suggested in the Corinthians' relationship to the outside world.[26] While they must have the strong group boundaries of an eschatological sect, at the same time, they must maintain an openness to evangelize the people that surround them (see 1 Cor 5:9-13). Paul is not so much concerned that standards of the wider culture differ from those of the Christian movement as he is that the community adhere to its own principles, and live to its calling. The promise commenced in v. 17 is continued in v. 18. God declares that he not only will receive into his favour those who regard themselves as his temple and keep themselves aloof from all contaminating associations with the wicked, but that he will be a father to them. Hence, holiness in 2 Cor 6:14–7:1 must involve separation but certainly not isolation.

Paul's desire for the Corinthians to manifest holiness in terms of separation continues in chapters 10–13. Although these chapters deal primarily with Paul's answers to his critics, his objective nevertheless remains the same. This section reveals the danger that confronts the Corinthians. Things looked so bad that Paul says in 2 Cor 13:5, "Test yourselves and see if you are in the faith!" They have been influenced by liars who know how to speak smooth, logical, and clever speeches that appear so wise. It reminds one of Shakespeare's *Othello* where Iago, the villain of the play, gains the trust of Othello and others in order to destroy them. He is a master at disguising himself as an honest, beloved friend all the while working skilfully at evil and poisoning the minds of those who trust him until they do his wishes. In the end the hero, Othello, jealously kills his wife and himself because he believed Iago's lie that his wife was cheating on him. The opponents of Paul in 2 Cor 10–13 are undermining the truth and making those who once trusted in Paul turn away from him. But this was not Paul's main concern. The issue was not loyalty either to Paul or the false apostles but loyalty to Christ and the gospel. The spiritual progress of the Corinthians was at stake. The false teachers instil pride and a false sense of wisdom in those they influence, distort-

---

26. This is true of all Pauline communities. See W. A. Meeks, *The First Urban Christians* (New Haven: Yale University Press, 1983), pp. 97-103.

ing the way of Christ. They are dangerous deceivers who look impressive to the Corinthians and Paul desires that they separate themselves from these deceivers. Holiness, in this instance, has to do with sound teachings. Paul, with a God-given jealousy, was jealous for their purity in life and doctrine.

Continuing his "foolish" boasting, in 2 Cor 11:2, Paul describes the Corinthians collectively as a virgin, awaiting the consummation of their wedding ceremonies at Christ's Second Coming. In his appeal, he uses the imagery of betrothal that is in conformity with Jewish customs. In the OT, Israel is frequently depicted as betrothed to Yahweh (Isa 50:1; 54:1-6; 62:5; Hos 1–3). Paul now thinks of the Christian community, specifically, the Corinthian congregation as the pure bride of Christ, Christ as the bridegroom, and himself as one who is to present the bride to her husband.[27] According to the Jewish law, the violation of a betrothed virgin was no less serious than if the marriage had already been consummated.[28] Paul's usage of this OT "father and daughter" image (Deut 32:19; 2 Kgs 19:21; Isa 62:5; Jer 18:13; 31:4) underscores the intimate relationship that exists between him, and subsequently, Christ and the Corinthians. However, the point of the imagery is to show Paul's concern for the virginal purity of the Corinthians. As the bride is separated from all others to her husband alone, so the people of God are separated not only from every form of defilement but are completely devoted to him. Having accepted the gospel, the Corinthians have committed themselves totally to Christ, but they would be united fully with him only at his Second Coming. In the interval it was Paul's responsibility to ensure that they lived up to their engagement implicit in their baptism.[29] Hence, the purity language in 2 Cor 11:2-3 serves to heighten the Corinthians' sense of the proper boundaries of the community and underscores the separation aspect of holiness. In the same way that God was jealous for the undivided loyalty of Israel, so also is Paul with the Corinthians. As people who are incorporated into Christ, they must live as befits their status.

Holiness as Cleansing

Paul's presentation of the cleansing aspect of holiness comes to the fore in 2 Cor 7:1: "Since we have these promises, beloved, let us cleanse ourselves from every defilement of body and of spirit, making holiness perfect in the fear of God."

---

27. Victor P. Furnish, *2 Corinthians*, AB (Garden City, N.Y.: Doubleday, 1984), p. 499.

28. Philo, *Spec. Leg.* 1.107; 3.72.

29. Jerome Murphy-O'Connor, *The Theology of the Second Letter to the Corinthians* (Cambridge: Cambridge University Press, 1991), p. 108.

Here, Paul also continues to emphasize the separation aspect of holiness. The call to cleansing in 2 Cor 7:1, although applicable personally, is communal in nature. Paul is calling the Corinthians, who are both God's temple and people, to live as befits their calling. The basis for this exhortation lies in the fact that the believers are the recipients of the promises enumerated in 6:16b ("I will be their God and they shall be my people"), 17b ("then I will welcome you"), and 18 ("and I will be a father to you and you shall be my sons and daughters"). In response to the fulfilment of these promises, which were initially made to Israel "according to the flesh" (or to David, in the case of the last [2 Sam 7:14]), Israel was to have been obedient to the ethical and cultic demands of Yahweh.[30] Because the Corinthians, as members of the new church of God in Christ Jesus, have now become the recipients of these promises from God, they are likewise confronted with the responsibility to effect complete ethical and religious renewal in accordance with the directives of their God. In 1 Cor 6:11, Paul had reminded them that they had been washed *(apelusasthe),* sanctified, and justified. Here, Paul is addressing those who have experienced that initial renewal, so that in Christ they have his righteousness; they are in the light; they are believers; they are the temple of the living God (6:14-16a). They are the sanctified people of God in that they have been set apart to belong to God in Christ. They are consequently in a position to be confronted with an ethical imperative which they can be expected to fulfil.[31] Now their task is that they so cleanse themselves that they become holy in an ethical sense. This they may accomplish by the removal of every defilement of body and spirit.

Paul's demand for the cleansing of flesh and spirit is a reference both to the physical body and to the "seat of emotion and will."[32] In short, the total life of the believer is to be rendered free from anything which would make the believer objectionable in his or her person to his or her God. Thus, there is to be no phase of the Corinthians' lives which is to be ignored in their efforts to make themselves clean. He is exhorting the Corinthians to make the outward expression of their lives conformable to that which their "salvation-life" actually is. Without anymore turning back to a former way of life, they are to rid themselves of everything that would not be reflective of the nature of their Lord, Jesus Christ. By carrying out this cleansing process, they will increasingly come to be in the likeness of Christ. Therefore, cleansing, in this passage has to do with a

---

30. Cf. Lev 26:1, 11-12; Jer 32:31-41; 31:9, 23, 31-34; Ezek 11:9, 12, 17-21; 36:25-38; Isa 43:6-7.

31. Cf. Rom 8:6-13 and Phil 2:12-13 where Paul affirms that it is only the one who has received the Spirit of God and thereby has the power of God at work in him who can — only through that power — do that which is pleasing to God.

32. Cf. E. deWitt Burton, *A Critical and Exegetical Commentary on the Epistle to the Galatians,* ICC (Edinburgh: T&T Clark, 1921), p. 486.

proper use of the temple, the dwelling-place of the Holy Spirit through which God is to be glorified (cf. 1 Cor 6:15-20). Here, believers are made holy by the cleansing of every defilement, while living a life of reverence for God, i.e., submission to his Lordship. A decisive action of cleansing seems to be Paul's demand here and may be implicit in 1 Thessalonians. There he prays that the Thessalonians will stand before God at the Parousia with hearts "blameless in holiness" (1 Thess 3:13). Thus, as Greathouse suggests, holiness *(hagiosunē)* denotes a state of sanctity that would enable Paul's Thessalonian converts to anticipate Christ's return with confident joy.[33]

As Paul uses holiness *(hagiosunē)* here in 7:1 it expresses that essential character of God as separation from all evil, and his just dealings in his relationship with humanity, the likeness of which believers may possess in greater or lesser degrees in proportion to their conformity to the will of God. As a result of cleansing in body and spirit it will become increasingly possible to describe believers by the term *hagioi,* as people who live lives of *hagiosunē* — "holiness." Paul, of course, does not think of a holy church that is not comprised of holy people. He insists that the whole person, body and soul, is totally involved in worship. Spiritual needs are as important for the body as bodily needs are for the soul. But this context is communal, which means that in worship and sacrifice there is co-responsibility as each contributes to the whole in a spirit of mutual participation.

When Paul urges the Corinthians to bring holiness to completion, he is not suggesting that holiness and ethical impurity are compatible at any point for the community or persons in community. On the contrary, he is exhorting believers to pursue an ethical purity which is limited, but not tainted; an ethical purity which reflects a portion of the holiness of God and must come more and more to reflect God's holiness. Holiness may expand — indeed it must — as believers gain greater awareness of what constitutes defilement of flesh and spirit and subsequently cleanse themselves of that defilement. As used in 2 Cor 7:1, holiness is not "merely a static condition, a holiness obtained by observance of cultic practices . . . the context is not one of resting content with an unholy life . . . but one of acting out one's status in Christ."[34] It is therefore right to suggest that holiness *(hagiosunē)* in 2 Cor 7:1 refers to "a quality of life and character, arising from a relationship with the Holy One."[35]

33. William M. Greathouse, *Wholeness in Christ: Toward a Biblical Theology of Holiness* (Kansas City: Beacon Hill, 1998), p. 200.

34. S. E. Porter, "Holiness, Sanctification," in *Dictionary of Paul and His Letters,* ed. Gerald F. Hawthorne and Ralph P. Martin (Downers Grove: InterVarsity, 1993), p. 400.

35. David Peterson, *Possessed by God: A New Testament Theology of Sanctification and Holiness* (Leicester: Apollos, 1995), p. 78. Peterson is right only in so far as his observation on relationship with God is concerned.

In sum, the whole exhortation including the call to cleansing is to be seen as having ethical, relational, and corporate significance. Paul had acknowledged earlier (1 Cor 6:9-11a) that the Corinthians had been washed, a reference to their conversion-initiation experience. The whole exhortation in 2 Cor 6:14–7:1 stands in relation to the process aspect of holiness, as indicated by the present tense of the participle. Cleansing, in this passage, has to do with a proper use of the body as a temple, a dwelling-place of the Holy Spirit through which God is to be glorified (cf. 1 Cor 6:15-20).

Missional Holiness

It is important to note the relational image of God as a "father" in 2 Cor 6:18. Perhaps it may be suggested that implicit in the use of that image is the need for the Corinthians, in the same way as Israel, to mirror God and model his holiness. The Corinthians must live consistently as God's sons and daughters. Their behaviour must confirm his paternity and their covenantal relationship with him. Paul's call for holiness in 2 Corinthians forces us to recognize that the Christian church really has to be a contrast-society, with its own social forms and an alternative style of life.[36] However, just like Israel, the church's alternative life-style was to produce a missionary effect of revealing God to the idolatrous environment in which it lived. It was not to degenerate to asceticism. Simply put, God is to be made known by the Corinthians by their alternative lifestyle. Paul gives a hint of this in the previous chapter (2 Cor 5:18-20). In Christ, God forgives the Corinthians. But with that responsibility comes a purpose, namely to engage in "the ministry of reconciliation." Believers are to be living vessels pointing to God (2 Cor 5:18-19), his stand-in representatives for the rest of humankind. Their ministry of reconciliation is not limited to reconciling the lost to God, but also includes reconciling people to one another.

Implications for the Church Today

In 2 Corinthians, Paul's rebukes, instructions, and exhortations on holiness proceed from his understanding of the nature of the church as the people of God. Important implications flow from this study for the people of God today.

First, the church's self-understanding of its identity and purpose is cru-

---

36. G. Lohfink, *Jesus and Community: The Social Dimension of Christian Faith* (Philadelphia: Fortress, 1984), p. 136.

cial to its relationship with God and the wider society. The church must not primarily define itself over against a fallen world or the pluralistic society in which it is located, but in relation to God. In other words, the church must first answer the question of what it is called to be. As such, Pauline holiness must always be formulated in ecclesial terms. Although not excluded, for Paul, the primary sphere of holiness and moral concern is not the character of the individual, but the corporate obedience of the church.

Second, there are two grounds for the church being a holy people. On the one hand, there is the redemptive work of God through Christ (2 Cor 5:17-20). The church's holy status is found precisely in its being the people whom God chose to be his special possession (cf. Deut 7:6; 14:2) and to be his children (Deut 14:1). The church is holy because of its call to be God's own people. The holiness of the church does not stem from its members and their moral and religious behaviour. On the other hand, however, the relationship of believers with God has serious implications. Holiness is not only to be based on the church's relationship with God as a separate, distinct people but also on the actualization of that holiness in relationship with the wider society. The church's holiness demands that it really lives in accordance with the social order which God has given it, a social order which stands in sharp distinction with the pluralistic society in which it is located. Thus, the church's holiness is based on a dynamic, ongoing relationship with God — a relationship, which, in turn, is to govern believers' relationships with the wider society as well as those within their own community (cf. 1 Cor 5:9-13; 2 Cor 6:14–7:1; 10–13).

Third, and following from above, the church's holiness is to be a responsible (or required) one. It is difficult to argue that one may be related to God without a corresponding actual holiness that involves ethical decisions.[37] For Paul, holiness is not the status of the community only; it is not just the fact of being called to be God's people.[38] It is the character of God in which his children participate.[39] Holiness is something the church continues to pursue be-

---

37. Israel's example is important in this regard. Although God had declared that Israel had been selected to become his holy people, this declaration was hardly enough to make Israel holy. Israel, in order to achieve the holiness associated with God and his acts, would have to obey God's laws and commandments. Therefore, one may say that Israel's holiness has a required aspect. Israel was to be actively and intensely committed to God in loving obedience and trust. The call of Israel was to a people with a common goal and destiny and not just to individuals. Israel's holiness is to be understood as having a communal dimension manifested in social relationships. So also is Christian holiness.

38. Cf. C. K. Barrett, *A Commentary on the First Epistle to the Corinthians,* HNTC (New York: Harper and Row, 1968), p. 32.

39. Cf. 2 Cor 1:12; Heb 12:11.

cause God calls the church to the task of living into and out of the full power of the Holy Spirit. The church must display the reality of sanctification, a sanctification that is framed first and foremost in corporate terms.

Fourth, Christians in general, like the Corinthians, are to have the distinction of being the people of God — people who are in the world but are not of it. Believers are to live in the midst of unbelievers and interact with them, offering the message of reconciliation of the world to God through Christ. Nevertheless, the church must be watchful lest the world squeezes her into its own mould. There still remains a need for clear boundaries between believers and the secular culture in which they live. For Paul, there were some things with which the Corinthians could not compromise, and apparently, some people with whom they maintained no close ties. Such were matters of concern for them. They ought to be for us too. Without clear boundaries, the church loses her "prophetic" voice and moral ascendancy. As Gorman rightly suggests, holiness for Paul means a "countercultural cruciformity in expectation of the coming day of judgment and salvation."[40] Without doubt, "Paul's understanding of holiness reflects both his communal and eschatological understanding of the church."[41]

Fifth, the claim of the church to be holy demands that the church be an effective agent of reconciliation. Such reconciliation consists of two aspects. First, it must first cater to its own needs. The church must do more in restoring erring ones. But reconciliation goes beyond that. Therefore, second, for the church to live out her calling as the people of God, she must do so in reconciled relationship with God and one another, regardless of racial, ethnic, national, and gender identities. As Gelder rightly states, "our fragmented world needs to see that a community of diverse persons can live in reconciled relationship with one another because they live in reconciled relationship with God."[42]

Sixth, the church must take seriously what it means to be the "people of God." The division of the world along racial or ethnic lines, and institutionalized into national, political units, has taken, and continues to take its toll on the church. The "people of God" is to be formed around a different identity, one that transcends race, ethnicity, and nationalism. The church ought to be a detribalized community — a community that is comprised of diverse, racial, ethnic, national, and political identities.

Seventh, if the church is truly holy, it will take seriously the work of God in the world, rather than becoming inwardly focused and becoming preoccu-

40. Gorman, *Apostle*, p. 237.

41. J. Ayodeji Adewuya, *Transformed by Grace: Paul's View of Holiness in Romans 6–8* (Eugene, Ore.: Cascade Books, 2004), p. 85.

42. Craig Van Gelder, *The Essence of the Church: A Community Created by the Spirit,* repr. (Grand Rapids: Baker, 2004), p. 107.

pied with maintaining purity, as important as that is. Holiness is missional. God is about the mission of reconciliation in the world. Paul states that God has given to the church the "ministry of reconciliation, that is, in Christ God was reconciling the world to himself" (2 Cor 5:18-19). It is God's purpose to make all things new, reconciling everything to reflect his intention for the created order while looking forward to consummation. For those who are separated from God, this means being brought into right relationship with God and others.

Circumcision in Galatia and the Holiness of God's Ecclesiae

Troy W. Martin

A consideration of ecclesiology (Gal 1:2, 13, 22) in Galatians certainly seems appropriate, but a discussion of holiness may seem out of place since neither the word *holy* (ἅγιος) nor any of its cognates occur in Galatians. The absence of this word in Galatians is even more striking since it occurs in every other letter in the Pauline corpus. Even though Galatians does not use the word *holy*, Galatians presents a sustained discussion of holiness as a characteristic of the people or ecclesia of God.

The Galatian controversy is essentially a discussion about holiness. The word *holy* (ἅγιος, -ία, -ον) is an adjective referring to "the quality possessed by things and persons that could approach a divinity."[1] The word itself does not specify the quality or qualities necessary for a proper relationship with the divinity, and all religions that use this term engage in seemingly endless debates of how someone or something must be or of what someone or something must do to approach and remain in the presence of the deity. The word thus refers to the qualities necessary to being "in" rather than "out" with the deity but does not specify what these qualities are.

---

1. BDAG, p. 10.

I dedicate this essay to my former professor Alex Deasley. My studies with him impressed me with his slow, meticulous procedure of thoroughly moving through the sacred text. I learned from him that an exegete should not move too quickly but take time to examine carefully every feature of the text that presents itself. He has influenced my own approach to the sacred text, and for this I am grateful. I am also grateful for his sagacious advice that led me to the University of Chicago, where I received the exegetical skills that characterize my scholarship. In gratitude, I dedicate this essay on holiness and ecclesiology in Galatians to Alex and hope that he finds satisfaction in knowing that his influence extends far beyond the short time I studied with him.

The agitators[2] in Galatia want "to shut out" (Gal 4:17) the Galatians from the people of God because the Galatians are uncircumcised and hence do not possess in the agitators' opinion an essential quality necessary for a relationship with God. Paul responds that circumcision is not necessary for the Gentiles' being the people of God, but rather the necessities are faith in Jesus Christ (Gal 2:16) and possession of the Spirit as a counter to the flesh (Gal 3:2; 5:5, 22-25; 6:8). This controversy is essentially therefore a discussion about a necessary characteristic that marks the holiness of the people or ecclesia of God, and Galatians is arguably Paul's most sustained discussion of holiness.

This essay attempts to appreciate this discussion of holiness by examining the cultural repertoire of circumcision that informs the controversy. It then describes the positions of the agitators and the Galatians and explains Paul's proposed solution to the problem of circumcision as a characteristic of the holy people of God, concluding with some reflections on the theoretical and practical significance of the discussion of holiness in Galatians for the people or ecclesia of God in the contemporary world.

1. The Cultural Repertoire of Circumcision

In his extensive study of circumcision in the Priestly writings, Klaus Grünwaldt comments on the rich cultural repertoire of circumcision and observes different understandings of circumcision during the various periods of Israel's history.[3] In particular, he mentions three different connotations of circumcision that arise from the experiences of Abraham, the Babylonian Exile, and the arrival of the Greeks in Palestine. All three of these connotations inform the Galatian controversy.

1.1. Abraham's Circumcision

Interpreters are unprepared for the strange and unexpected introduction of circumcision into the biblical text. In Genesis 17, God cuts a covenant with Abra-

---

2. Labeling the advocates of circumcision as opponents may be inappropriate. See George Lyons, *Pauline Autobiography,* SBLDS 73 (Atlanta: Scholars Press, 1985), pp. 78-79. These individuals are traditionally called Judaizers, but James D. G. Dunn, *The Theology of Paul's Letter to the Galatians* (Cambridge: Cambridge University Press, 1993), p. 10, rejects this label. Mark D. Nanos, *The Irony of Galatians: Paul's Letter in First-Century Context* (Minneapolis: Fortress, 2002), p. 5 criticizes the labels of troublemakers and agitators, but (pp. 193-99) favors the neutral label of influencers. Much of this criticism is valid, but the present study adopts Paul's perspective and uses the term *agitators* because of clear textual references in Gal 5:10, 12.

ham and promises to give Abraham the land of Canaan in which Abraham wanders as a stranger. God then commands Abraham to circumcise himself and all the males of his social group as their obligation in this covenant.[4] Hence, this covenant becomes known as the covenant of circumcision. Some may wonder, "How odd of God to choose circumcision, the cutting off of the piece of skin called the prepuce or foreskin to expose the glans or corona at the extremity of the male reproductive organ." We may also wonder if Abraham negotiated with God, as he did on other occasions. Abraham, who is ninety-nine years old when God commands him to circumcise himself, could have responded, "God, is this circumcision thing negotiable? How about a pierced ear or even a nose ring?" Abraham does not negotiate, however, but promptly circumcises himself and all the males of his household (Gen 17:23-27). Readers are left to wonder, "Why circumcision?"[5]

Actually, God's choice of circumcision in this account is profoundly appropriate and brings Abraham to a decisive crossroad in his spiritual life. While the practice becomes characteristic of the cultures of the western Fertile Crescent,[6] it apparently does not spread eastward into Mesopotamia or become characteristic of the cultures of the eastern Fertile Crescent.[7]

According to Gen 11:31, Abraham originates in Ur of the Chaldeans at the eastern end of the Fertile Crescent and comes from a culture that does not practice circumcision.[8] Nevertheless, God promises him the land of Canaan, where circumcision is practiced. God's command to circumcise forces Abraham to demonstrate once and for all that he believes God. By circumcising himself, Abraham removes more than a piece of flesh; he severs himself from his former life and culture. After circumcision, he can never return home to Ur and "fit in" with that culture since the operation is not reversible.[9] Instead, his circumci-

---

3. Klaus Grünwaldt, *Exil und Identität: Beschneidung, Passa und Sabbat in der Priesterschrift, BBB* 85 (Frankfurt am Main: Anton Hain, 1992), p. 1.

4. Whether or not one accepts Grünwaldt's source critical conclusions (*Exil*, pp. 36-40, 54-55), Grünwaldt nevertheless supports the present essay in understanding Abraham's circumcision as an act of faith.

5. Andreas Blaschke, *Beschneidung: Zeugnisse der Bibel und verwandter Texte,* TANZ 28 (Tübingen: A. Francke Verlag, 1998), p. 89.

6. Blaschke, *Beschneidung,* p. 46.

7. Claus Westermann, *Genesis 12–36: A Commentary* (Minneapolis: Augsburg, 1985), pp. 264-65 and Robert G. Hall, "Circumcision," in *Anchor Bible Dictionary,* vol. 1, ed. D. N. Freedman et al. (New York: Doubleday, 1992), p. 1027. The lists of nations that practice circumcision in Jer 9:25 and Herodotus (*Hist.* 2.104) support this point.

8. Even if Abraham originated from another place such as Haran, as some argue, his uncircumcision demonstrates that he originates from a culture that does not circumcise.

9. Blaschke, *Beschneidung,* p. 88.

sion identifies him with the culture of Canaan.[10] Before circumcision, Abraham had always been a stranger in the land of Canaan. After circumcision, he belongs to this culture and is at home in Canaan, the land of God's promise.

Circumcision in Genesis 17 therefore is an act that demonstrates unwavering faith in God by which one decisively renounces one's former life and enters that new life promised by God. The account of Abraham's circumcision in Genesis 17 is an important part of the cultural repertoire that informs the understandings of circumcision in the Galatian controversy. This account, however, does not exhaust this cultural repertoire, and the circumstances of circumcision during the Babylonian Exile must also be considered.

1.2. Circumcision in the Babylonian Exile

Nebuchadnezzar, King of Babylon, exiles the people of Judah in 597 and 586 BCE and creates a new understanding of circumcision. Nebuchadnezzar brings Abraham's descendants back to the land of the Chaldeans, where Abraham originated and where circumcision is not practiced. Now, their circumcision no longer identifies these exiles with the dominant culture as in Canaan but distinguishes them from the Babylonians. Appalled by the rampant idolatry and disdain for Israel's God, the Jewish exiles distinguish themselves as the pure people of God from the impure Babylonians. The prophet Habakkuk (Hab 2:12-17) describes the Babylonians as faithless, wicked, merciless, and idolatrous as well as uncircumcised.[11] The distinction between Abraham's exiled descendents and the Babylonians transfers to circumcision, which assumes the connotation of purity, and to uncircumcision, which now connotes impurity.

Exilic prophets begin to distinguish the holy people of God from unholy others on the basis of circumcision.[12] Isaiah (52:1) encourages the exiles by exhorting: "Awake, awake, put on your strength, O Zion; put on your beautiful garments, O Jerusalem, the holy city; for there shall no more come into you the uncircumcised and the unclean" (RSV). Ezekiel (44:6-8) prohibits uncircumcised foreigners from serving or even entering the sanctuary in Jerusalem to avoid profaning this holy place. Ezekiel (28:10; 31:18; 32:19-32) foresees a particularly unpleasant end for the uncircumcised.

In contrast to Abraham's circumcision, circumcision in the Babylonian

---

10. On which, see Grünwaldt (*Exil,* p. 12) and Blaschke (*Beschneidung,* pp. 34-43).

11. Blaschke, *Beschneidung,* p. 48, translates Hab 2:16 MT as "[Babylonians,] show your foreskins."

12. See Grünwaldt, *Exil,* p. 11; Blaschke, *Beschneidung,* pp. 48-50.

Exile is no longer primarily an act demonstrating faith in God. Rather, the state of circumcision becomes primarily a mark of purity that distinguishes God's holy people from unholy others.[13] The state of circumcision as a mark of uncommon purity now joins Abraham's act of faith in the cultural repertoire of circumcision that informs the Galatian controversy. A complete description of this cultural repertoire, however, requires a consideration of the new understanding of circumcision occasioned by the arrival of the Greeks in Palestine.

1.3. Circumcision in the Hellenistic World

Like the Babylonians, the Greeks do not practice circumcision. However, the Greeks go a step further and actively oppose circumcision among the peoples they encounter. Herodotus (*Hist.* 2.104) reports that Phoenicians, who inhabit the land where circumcision probably originated, abandon the practice when they encounter the Greeks. A few centuries later, the Greek King Antiochus IV (Epiphanes) even outlaws circumcision among Abraham's descendants on penalty of death (1 Macc 1:48). Mothers and families that circumcise their infant sons are paraded around the city wall with the babies hung from their mother's necks, and then all are hurled from the wall to their death (1 Macc 1:60-61; 2 Macc 6:10). Many Jews abandon circumcision and seek to hide their circumcision by pulling the skin over the glans and attaching it permanently by epispasm, a surgical procedure, or temporarily by *fibulae,* clothespins (1 Macc 1:15).[14] Nevertheless, many in Israel stand firm and resolve in their hearts not to abandon or profane God's holy covenant by renouncing circumcision (1 Macc 1:62-63).

Several authors illustrate the Greek and later Roman negativity toward circumcision.[15] Strabo speaks glowingly about the religion Moses instituted but accuses Moses' successors of introducing circumcision as a result of their

---

13. As, e.g., in *Jub.* 15:25-34; 30:7-17 and 1QS 5:5. Blaschke (*Beschneidung,* pp. 64-105) correctly emphasizes that the exilic texts do not portray circumcision itself as a purification act but rather as a sign of belonging to Yahweh and Yahweh's holy and pure people.

14. For other texts that mention the use of epispasm or *fibulae,* see Hall, "Circumcision," p. 1029 and esp. Blaschke, *Beschneidung,* pp. 139-44. For the medical practice of epispasm, see Celsus, *Med.* 7.25.1; Soranus, *Gyn.* 2.34; and Dioscorides, *Mat. med.* 4.153. For the procedures presented in these texts, see Blaschke, *Beschneidung,* pp. 350-56. See also J. P. Rubin, "Celsus' Decircumcision Operation," *Urology* 16 (1980): 124 and David L. Gollaher, *Circumcision: A History of the World's Most Controversial Surgery* (New York: Basic Books, 2000), p. 16.

15. For an extensive list and discussion of these authors, see Blaschke, *Beschneidung,* pp. 323-60.

superstition.[16] Strabo describes circumcision as a mutilation of the male reproductive organ.[17] Josephus reports that Apion scorns the circumcision of the genitals.[18] Tacitus describes circumcision as a base and abominable custom of the Jews.[19] Finally, Juvenal cites circumcision of a son as one of the bad influences of a father enamored with Jewish customs.[20] It is worth asking why the Greeks and later the Romans as well are so opposed to circumcision.

The association of circumcision with male sexual arousal partially explains their negative attitude toward circumcision. The Greek word ψωλός and the Latin word *verpus* both refer to circumcision but literally mean with the glans exposed.[21] The word *glans* is the Latin word for acorn and refers to the shape of the extremity of the male reproductive organ. Although this exposure is only one aspect of male sexual arousal, synecdoche permits these words to refer to male arousal by describing only this one aspect. Hence, when the Greeks and Romans designate male sexual arousal by the visibility of the glans, circumcision by permanently exposing the glans makes a circumcised male appear perpetually sexually aroused.[22]

Even a modern urologist such as Dr. C. W. Vermuelen of Billings Hospital sometimes cannot distinguish circumcision from male sexual arousal when examining ancient nude figurines.[23] Martial plays upon this ambiguity in his denunciation of a poetic rival, whom he addresses four times in eight lines as *verpe poeta,* circumcised or sexually aroused poet. Martial emphasizes the appropriateness of this address because the poet was born in Jerusalem and sodomizes Martial's servant boy.[24] This association of circumcision with permanent male sexual arousal partially explains why Greeks and Romans viewed circumcision as socially unacceptable and an affront to decency.[25]

In the Hellenistic World, the pressure of social conformity and the accusation of moral indecency challenge the practice of circumcision. Those who circumcise face ridicule of shameful proportions and appear to the Greeks and

16. Strabo, *Geog.* 16.2.37; M. Stern, *Greek and Latin Authors on Jews and Judaism,* vol. 1 (Jerusalem: The Israel Academy of Sciences and Humanities, 1974), pp. 295, 300.

17. Strabo, *Geog.* 16.4.9; Stern, *Authors,* vol. 1, p. 312.

18. Josephus, *Ag. Ap.* 2.14 (137); Stern, *Authors,* vol. 1, p. 415.

19. Tacitus, *Hist.* 5.2; Stern, *Authors,* vol. 2, pp. 19, 26.

20. Juvenal, *Sat.* 14.96-106; Stern, *Authors,* vol. 2, pp. 102-3.

21. J. N. Adams, *The Latin Sexual Vocabulary* (Baltimore: Johns Hopkins University Press, 1982), pp. 12-14, 36.

22. Gollaher, *Circumcision,* pp. 13-14.

23. Reported by Jack M. Sasson, "Circumcision in the Ancient Near East," *Journal of Biblical Literature* 85 (1966): 476.

24. Martial, *Epig* 11.94.

25. Blaschke, *Beschneidung,* pp. 346-49, esp. 360.

Romans as sexually perverse and as slaves to their boundless sexual passions. In such a challenging context, those who practice circumcision demonstrate their total devotion to God and God's commandments. After the Greeks arrive in Palestine, circumcision becomes a practice of distinction between those uncompromisingly committed to God and those who abandon the traditions of Israel.[26] It distinguishes those who resolutely maintain their former traditions from those who abandon their former devotion to God to "fit in" with the dominant Greco-Roman culture. This new perspective of circumcision as a practice of distinction represents an essential component of the cultural repertoire of circumcision and an important aspect of the Galatian controversy.

1.4. Summary

This cultural repertoire reflects several different connotations for the circumcision word group that informs the discussion of holiness in Galatians. With Abraham, circumcision is first an act that demonstrates faith in God by which one renounces one's former life and enters that new life promised by God. In the Babylonian Exile, the state of circumcision then becomes a mark of the purity of God's people. With the arrival of the Greeks, circumcision becomes a practice of distinction that differentiates the apostates from the faithful who maintain an uncompromising commitment to God. The verb περιτέμνειν (to circumcise) and the noun περιτομή (circumcision) therefore refer either to an act, or a state, or a practice.[27] An as act, circumcision relates to the physical operation itself. Following this surgery, a person then lives in a state of circumcision.[28] Even though circumcised persons have no choice but to live in a circumcised state, they still must decide if they will practice the distinctions associated with the covenant of circumcision (Gen 17:14). These connotations expressed in the cultural repertoire of circumcision are relevant for understanding the perceptions and positions of the participants in the Galatian controversy about the holiness of God's people.

---

26. See Grünwaldt's (*Exil,* pp. 13-14) discussion of this meaning of circumcision.

27. Jost Eckert, *Die urchristliche Verkündigung im Streit zwischen Paulus und seinen Gegnern nach dem Galaterbrief,* BU 6 (Regensburg: Friedrich Pustet, 1971), pp. 49-53; Charles E. B. Cranfield, *The Epistle to the Romans,* vol. 1, ICC (Edinburgh: T&T Clark, 1975), p. 171 n. 4; and Joel Marcus, "The Circumcision and the Uncircumcision in Rome," *New Testament Studies* 35 (1989): 74-75.

28. Joseph B. Tyson, "'Works of the Law' in Galatians," *Journal of Biblical Literature* 92 (1973): 428.

2. The Participants in the Controversy

2.1. The Agitators

While the agitators accept the full cultural repertoire and the various connotations of circumcision, Paul portrays their position in the debate as emphasizing the practice of circumcision to distinguish the holy people of God from those outside. The participle περιτεμνόμενοι in Gal 6:13a describes the position of the agitators in Galatia.[29] Because they are already circumcised, the participle cannot mean *become circumcised* or *let oneself be circumcised*.[30] Thus, this participle cannot refer to the act of circumcision. Neither can it designate the state of circumcision since Paul would then be including himself among the opponents of the Galatians.[31] Consequently, only the meaning of circumcision as the practice of distinguishing between circumcised and uncircumcised makes sense in Gal 6:13a. Even the present tense of this participle implies the ongoing, continuous nature of this action.[32] Therefore, the best translation of the participle in 6:13a is *those who practice the distinctions of circumcision*.[33] The agitators' position in the controversy emphasizes the practice of circumcision to distinguish themselves as the people of God from the uncircumcised Galatians (Gal 4:17).

This understanding of the practice of circumcision explains the use of

---

29. Heinrich Schlier, *Der Brief an die Galater*, KEK 7 (Göttingen: Vandenhoeck & Ruprecht, 1962), p. 281; Eckert, *Verkündigung*, p. 34 n. 4; and F. F. Bruce, *The Epistle to the Galatians*, NIGTC (Grand Rapids: Eerdmans, 1982), pp. 269-70. Neither the view of Ernest de Witt Burton, who contends that this participle refers to the Galatians and not to the agitators (*A Critical and Exegetical Commentary on the Epistle to the Galatians*, ICC [Edinburgh: T&T Clark, 1921], pp. 352-54) nor the view of E. Hirsch, who concludes that the participle designates the Gentile converts of the Judaizers ("Zwei Fragen zu Gal 6," *Zeitschrift für die neutestamentliche Wissenschaft und die Kunde der älteren Kirche* [1930]: 192-97), is persuasive.

30. Dunn (*Theology*, pp. 8-12) argues along with the majority of scholars that the troublemakers are Jewish Christians. However, Johannes Munck (*Paul and the Salvation of Mankind* [Richmond: John Knox, 1959], pp. 87-89) contends that the agitators are Gentiles since the present middle participle always means "those who receive circumcision." George Howard (*Paul: Crisis in Galatia*, SNTSMS 35 [Cambridge: Cambridge University Press, 1990], p. 17) adequately critiques Munck's proposal. Furthermore, Munck's argument is refuted by Gal 5:3 where this participle does not mean "those who receive circumcision."

31. So Robert Jewett, "The Agitators and the Galatian Congregation," *New Testament Studies* 17 (1971): 202.

32. While some manuscripts place this participle in the perfect tense, the textual evidence favors the present tense.

33. Even though the agitators are primarily in view, this meaning of the participle would not exclude any Jew who practices the distinctions of circumcision. See Albrecht Oepke, *Der Brief des Paulus an die Galater*, THKNT 9 (Berlin: Evangelische Verlagsanstalt, 1957), p. 160.

περιτέμνω in 5:2-3. In 5:2 Paul says, "If you practice circumcision, Christ will be of no benefit to you." In 5:3 he says, "Every man who practices circumcision is obligated to observe the whole law." Many commentators understand the middle voice of these verbal forms in 5:2-3 as causative or permissive middles and understand περιτέμνω as a reference to the surgical operation or act of circumcision. They then translate the finite verb περιτέμνησθε as *you become circumcised* or *you permit yourself to become circumcised*.[34] Correspondingly, they translate the participle περιτεμνομένῳ as *one who becomes circumcised* or *one who lets oneself be circumcised*. These commentators then apply these circumcision references in 5:2-3 to the Galatians and not to the agitators in spite of the participle's use in 6:13 as a clear reference to the troublemakers.[35]

These commentators' discussion fails to explain why the Galatians would be excluded from Christ's benefit if they become circumcised while Paul, as a circumcised person, enjoys these same benefits.[36] After all, the Galatians' submission to circumcision really should not matter since in Christ neither circumcision nor uncircumcision makes any difference (5:6; 6:15; cf. 3:28).[37] Thus, the references in Gal 5:2-3 cannot relate to the act or state of circumcision as almost all commentators assume because Paul receives Christ's benefits and does not consider himself obligated to observe the whole law even though he is circumcised. Rather, the references in Gal 5:2-3 relate to the agitators' practice of circumcision in distinguishing the holy people of God.[38]

The correspondence in the second chapter of Galatians between the agitators in Syrian Antioch and the agitators in Galatia illustrates the agitators' emphasis on the practice of circumcision. The reference to circumcision in Gal

34. Pierre Bonnard, *L'Épitre de Saint Paul Aux Galates*, CNT 9 (Paris: Delachaux & Niestlé, 1972), p. 103; Burton, *Galatians*, pp. 272-74; Bruce, *Galatians*, 1982, pp. 228-29; Dieter Lührmann, *Galatians*, CC (Minneapolis: Fortress, 1992), pp. 94-96; and Joseph B. Lightfoot, *The Epistle of St. Paul to the Galatians*, ZC (Grand Rapids: Zondervan, 1957), pp. 203-4.

35. The practice of circumcision is a distinguishing characteristic of the agitators (6:13; 2:12) and indicates that Paul addresses the agitators in 5:2-3, not the Galatians. If Paul addresses the agitators in 5:2-3, as these references to circumcision indicate, then the agitators are probably also addressed in the entire section of 4:21–5:6 as I demonstrate in my article "Apostasy to Paganism: The Rhetorical Stasis of the Galatian Controversy," *Journal of Biblical Literature* 114 (1995): 450-56; repr. in *The Galatians Debate: Contemporary Issues in Rhetorical and Historical Interpretation*, ed. Mark D. Nanos (Peabody, Mass.: Hendrickson, 2002).

36. Heikki Räisänen, *Paul and the Law* (Philadelphia: Fortress, 1983), p. 190.

37. See my article "Covenant of Circumcision (Gen 17:9-14) and the Situational Antitheses in Gal 3:28," *Journal of Biblical Literature* 122 (2003): 111-25.

38. H. Dieter Betz, *Galatians*, Hermeneia (Philadelphia: Fortress, 1979), p. 258; Oepke, *An die Galater*, p. 118; Franz Mußner, *Der Galaterbrief*, HTKNT 9 (Frieburg: Herder, 1988), p. 346; Hermann N. Ridderbos, *The Epistle of Paul to the Churches of Galatia*, NICNT (Grand Rapids: Eerdmans, 1956), p. 187.

2:12 must relate to practicing the distinctions of circumcision since any other meaning does not differentiate between the agitators at Antioch on the one hand and Paul, Peter, and Barnabas on the other.[39] This reference indicates that the practice of circumcision includes more than simply performing the physical act itself. Practicing circumcision also means maintaining distinctions between the circumcised and the uncircumcised (Gen 17:14), especially by refusing to engage in table fellowship. Paul states that before some of James' people arrived, Peter and the other Jews were not observing the distinction of circumcision and did not exclude the Gentiles. Out of fear for those who practice circumcision (τοὺς ἐκ περιτομῆς, 2:12), however, Peter and the other Jews separate themselves from the uncircumcised.[40] The correspondence between the situation in Syrian Antioch and in Galatia illustrates the Galatian agitators' emphasis on the practice of circumcision in the controversy in Galatia.

The agitators' position in the Galatian holiness controversy focuses primarily on circumcision as a practice that distinguishes God's people from those outside. The agitators' position is that the uncircumcised Galatians should and must submit to the act of circumcision to properly relate to God. According to the agitators, the Galatians should be excluded or "shut out" (Gal 4:17) from the holy people of God if they refuse to submit to circumcision. The Galatians' reaction to the position taken by the agitators thus becomes important for understanding the controversy about holiness in Galatia.

2.2. *The Galatians*

While Paul clearly portrays the agitators' position in the debate, his portrayal of the Galatians' reaction is more obscure. J. Louis Martyn represents the traditional conception of the Galatians' reaction. Martyn conceives of the Galatians as eager to become circumcised after deserting Paul for the circumcision gospel. Martyn's conception of the Galatians' reaction, however, fails to explain

---

39. See Dunn, *Theology*, pp. 73-74; "The New Perspective on Paul," in *Jesus, Paul, and the Law* (Louisville: Westminster, 1990), pp. 198, 200; and "The Incident at Antioch," *Journal for the Study of the New Testament* 18 (1983): 3-41; repr. in *Jesus, Paul, and the Law* and in Nanos, ed., *The Galatians Debate.*

40. Walter Schmithals's suggestion that *circumcision* in Gal 2:12 refers only to Jews and not to Jewish Christians should be rejected (*Paul and James*, SBT 46 [Naperville, Ill.: Alec R. Allenson, 1965], pp. 66-68). For the association between the positions of the agitators at Antioch and Galatia, see Schlier, *An die Galater*, p. 84 and M. Bachmann, *Sünder oder Übertreter*, WUNT 59 (Tübingen: J. C. B. Mohr [Paul Siebeck], 1992), p. 110. See also the similar perspective of the party in Acts 11:2-3.

why none of the Galatians has submitted to circumcision at the time of Paul's writing the letter.[41] The operation requires only a few minutes to complete. His conception also fails to explain why Paul accuses the Galatians of returning to their former pagan time-keeping scheme (Gal 4:10). The immediate context of Gal 4:10 argues for the pagan character of this list. In 4:8, Paul mentions the former pagan life of the Galatian Christians. In 4:9, he asks them how they can desire their former life again. Paul then proposes their observance of the time-keeping scheme in 4:10 as a demonstrative proof of their reversion to their old pagan life.[42]

The most serious problem with Martyn's conception of the Galatians' reaction, however, is his failure to explain how an entire group of Greco-Romans could eagerly desire circumcision.[43] Considering the physiological perception that circumcision renders a male permanently sexually aroused, how can exegetes assume that the Galatians would eagerly submit to circumcision? Do these exegetes really think that the Galatians would be enthusiastic about entering a public bath or participating in the gymnasium in a sexually excited state? Should they not more reasonably conclude that the social ridicule would have simply been so overwhelming that the Galatians were not about to submit to circumcision no matter how much pressure the agitators exert? Martyn's con-

---

41. Paul's failure to address a means of reintegrating the Galatians who have already submitted to circumcision strongly argues that none of the Galatians has become circumcised.

42. On which, see my article "Pagan and Judeo-Christian Time-keeping Schemes in Gal 4:10 and Col 2:16," *New Testament Studies* 42 (1996): 105-19 and my monograph *By Philosophy and Empty Deceit: Colossians as Response to a Cynic Critique*, JSNTSup 118 (Sheffield: Sheffield Academic Press, 1996), pp. 124-34. Nanos (*Irony*, pp. 267-68) agrees with my identification of this time-keeping scheme as pagan rather than Jewish. In contrast, J. Louis Martyn (*Galatians: A New Translation with Introduction and Commentary*, AB [New York: Doubleday, 1997], pp. 414-18) argues that Paul objects to the Teachers' solar calendar based on Gen 1:14. Martyn assumes that Paul and his communities operated without a calendar, an assumption undermined by the evidence from Paul's letters and Acts (*By Philosophy and Empty Deceit*, pp. 125-29). Paul and his communities operated with a Jewish time-keeping scheme, and Paul would need to explain the incompatibility of the Jewish solar calendar with his own if indeed Gal 4:10 were to describe such a solar calendar. The lack of such an explanation in Galatians is evidence that Gal 4:10 describes a pagan rather than a Jewish time-keeping system. Martyn's interpretation presumes that the Galatians could astutely discern the subtle distinctions among various Jewish time-keeping schemes while being completely ignorant of the issues associated with circumcision.

43. Neil J. Mceleney ("Conversion, Circumcision and the Law," *New Testament Studies* 20 [1974]: 321-23) provides no examples of the conversion of an entire group of Gentiles except at the point of a sword. No historical analogy exists for an entire community of Gentiles submitting willingly to circumcision. Cf. the similar conclusion of Paul W. Barnett ("Jewish mission in the era of the New Testament and the apostle Paul," in *The Gospel to the Nations: Perspectives on Paul's Mission*, ed. Peter Bolt and Mark Thompson [Downers Grove: InterVarsity, 2000], p. 276).

ception of the Galatians' reaction appropriately emphasizes the importance of circumcision in the debate but leaves several crucial problems unresolved.

Understanding Paul's portrayal of the Galatians' reaction in the debate as totally unwilling to submit to the act of circumcision resolves these problems.[44] Paul portrays the Galatians as deserting him for the circumcision gospel and as accepting this gospel as the valid Christian gospel (Gal 1:6-9). Because of their aversion to circumcision, however, Paul portrays them as refusing to submit to circumcision, apostatizing from Christianity, and returning to their former paganism (4:8-11). This understanding of the Galatians' reaction explains why none of the Galatians has submitted to circumcision and why they could recognize without elaboration that their pagan time-keeping scheme mentioned in Gal 4:10 is incompatible with Paul's Jewish time-keeping scheme and a demonstration of their return to paganism. This understanding of the Galatians' reaction avoids the problems associated with Martyn's traditional conception and provides a more historically responsive description of the Galatians' participation in the controversy by taking seriously both the Jewish and Greco-Roman cultural repertoire of circumcision.

2.3. Paul

Paul enters this controversy about holiness subsequent to the exchanges between the agitators and the Galatians, when their positions are already established. The agitators accept circumcision as an act of faith in God, a mark of purity for the people of this God, and a practice of distinction that differentiates this God's people from others. The agitators have successfully convinced the Galatians to accept this view of circumcision as essential to the valid Christian gospel of this God. In contrast to the agitators' cultural repertoire, however, the Galatians have been socialized to view circumcision as morally unacceptable and an affront to decency. Consequently, they decide to associate themselves with this God no longer but to return to their former gods instead. Thus, the agitators identify a quality necessary to being the holy people of God with which the Galatians cannot comply without denying their own sense of morality. The disparate positions between the agitators and the Galatians in this controversy seem insurmountable.

Paul engages this holiness controversy and argues that circumcision is not

---

44. Martin, "Apostasy to Paganism," pp. 437-61. See also my article "The Voice of Emotion: Paul's Pathetic Persuasion (Gal 4:12-20)," in *Paul and Pathos*, SBLSymS 16, ed. Thomas H. Olbricht and Jerry L. Sumney (Atlanta: Society of Biblical Literature, 2001), pp. 183-84.

an essential quality of holiness for the people of God. For Paul, the very composition of the people of God that includes both Jews and Gentiles denies circumcision as a requirement for holiness. If Gentiles are forced to submit to circumcision and become Jewish proselytes, then the gospel is only for Jews and not for both Jews and Gentiles. According to Paul, the truth of the gospel (Gal 2:5, 14; cf. 5:7) is that both Jews and Gentiles are justified by faith in Jesus Christ and not by circumcision (2:15-16).[45] In the Antioch incident, Paul views the separation of the circumcised from the uncircumcised as hypocrisy (2:13-14) since both are justified by faith in Christ and not from observance of the law (2:16). For Paul, the practice of circumcision that requires separation from the uncircumcised in the Christian community is contrary to the true, inclusive gospel of Jesus Christ (2:14).[46] Therefore, circumcision cannot be an essential quality of holiness for God's people composed of both Jew and Gentile.

Paul further argues that circumcision is not an essential quality of holiness because, as an act, it does not demonstrate the Galatians' faith but rather causes their faith to waver. By leaving their former gods (Gal 4:8-9), the Galatians demonstrate their faith in God. Only after they become convinced that their new faith requires the immoral, indecent act of circumcision do they decide to abandon their new faith and return to their paganism.[47] Rather than demonstrating their faith as with Abraham, the act of circumcision destroys their faith.

Paul communicates to the Galatians that they can exercise their faith apart from circumcision just as Abraham did before his circumcision. Paul quotes Gen 15:6, which states that Abraham believed God and that his faith established him in a right relationship with God. Abraham is uncircumcised at this time and does not receive the covenant of circumcision until later as narrated in Genesis 17. Paul explains that just as with Abraham, God justifies uncircumcised peoples who respond in faith to God (Gal 3:8). Thus, Paul argues that circumcision is not an essential quality of holiness because as an act it is not essential to the demonstration of faith even with Abraham.

Finally, Paul argues that circumcision is not an essential quality of holiness because the fruit of the Spirit and not circumcision marks the purity of the people of God. Paul reminds the Galatians that it was on account of the weakness of their flesh that he preached the gospel to them (Gal 4:13).[48] He further

---

45. Moisés D. Silva, "The truth of the gospel: Paul's mission according to Galatians," in *The Gospel to the Nations*, ed. Bolt and Thompson, pp. 56-57.

46. Dunn, "Incident," pp. 35-37.

47. Martin, "Apostasy to Paganism," pp. 440-45.

48. For a defense of this reading of Gal 4:13, see my article "Whose Flesh? What Temptation? (Gal 4.13-14)," *Journal for the Study of the New Testament* 74 (1999): 65-91.

reminds them that those who engage the works of the flesh are not the people of God (5:19-21). Rather, the people of God are those who receive the Spirit in their hearts (4:6) and produce the fruit of the Spirit (5:22-25). Even Hagar's son who was circumcised was cast out because he was born according to the flesh rather than according to the Spirit (4:21-31). Hence, Paul argues that the fruit of the Spirit rather than circumcision marks the purity of the people of God.

Through experiential and scriptural arguments, Paul attempts to persuade the participants in the Galatian holiness controversy that the act and the state of circumcision are irrelevant to being the people of God (3:28-29; 5:6).[49] According to Paul's arguments, because the practice of circumcision requires separation from the uncircumcised in the Christian community, it is even contrary to the true, inclusive gospel of Jesus Christ (2:14; 5:2-6).[50] To resolve the controversy, Paul proposes faith in Jesus Christ (Gal 2:16) and possession of the Spirit (Gal 3:2; 5:5, 22-25; 6:8) rather than circumcision as the essential qualities of God's holy ecclesiae.

Assessing the success of Paul's proposed solution to the Galatian controversy is difficult. The contribution of the Galatian churches to the Jerusalem offering (1 Cor 16:1) indicates the acceptance of Paul's solution by the Galatians, who evidently maintained their faith in Jesus Christ and their spiritual purity even though uncircumcised.[51] The success of Paul's solution among the agitators is less demonstrable. What is more demonstrable is that Paul's solution profoundly impacted the church from his day until the present in the unwavering faith and uncommon purity of many uncircumcised individuals who compose the holy people of God.

3. Implications for the Contemporary Church

3.1. Theoretical Implications

The Galatian holiness controversy is ancient history and yet similar debates play out over and over again in the contemporary church whenever a decision must be made about the qualities necessary to being the holy people of God. Disputed issues arise and subside as new issues occupy their place. Older holiness debates about outward adornment or harmful substances have yielded to

49. Martin, "Covenant of Circumcision," pp. 111-25.
50. Dunn, "Incident," pp. 35-37.
51. Eung Chun Park (*Either Jew or Gentile: Paul's Unfolding Theology of Inclusivity* [Louisville: Westminster John Knox, 2003], p. 53) evaluates the evidence less positively.

more recent discussions about abortion and homosexuality. Even though the Galatian controversy cannot resolve all of these subsequent debates, it is a rich resource for understanding how these debates shape a community into a people who embody the holiness of God.

First, the Galatian controversy demonstrates that the people of God constantly need to engage the issue of what quality or qualities characterize a holy ecclesia. Reticence to engage such debates detracts from the holiness of God's people and results in confusion about the character and nature of the church. Only by engaging such debates can the church realize its true identity. The Galatian controversy results in a new understanding of the church composed of both Jew and Gentile and enables a realization of the promise of God to Abraham (Gal 3:8-9, 15-18). Such debates may be messy, but they are absolutely necessary for the realization of a holy ecclesia.

Second, the agitators in Galatia demonstrate that simply maintaining older positions and practices may not conform to the holiness of God's people. By not fully appreciating the significance of the coming of Christ for the people of God (Gal 3:19-29), the agitators cling to a "holy" practice that damages the ecclesiae by hindering the recruitment and retention of new converts. Determining which practices and behaviors should be excluded from a holy life and which should not is a continual challenge and requires continuous debates since changing situations require new considerations of the requirements of holiness.

Third, the Galatians demonstrate the necessity in these debates of considering the perceptions and sensitivities of the many diverse peoples who comprise the people of God. In an increasingly pluralistic world, holiness debates must recognize that not everyone possesses the same worldview or social location and that some holiness practices and positions may even be perceived to be immoral. Pluralism provides not only a challenge to holiness but also a wonderful opportunity to embody holiness in many different contexts and situations and to realize the full flowering of God's holiness in the human race.

Finally, Paul's arguments in the controversy demonstrate that the resolution of such debates should not change the tradition but appropriate the tradition in a more authentic way. Many in Paul's day and since consider him to have radically altered his received traditions. However, Paul's theological and scriptural arguments prove that his solution to the Galatian holiness controversy did not change God's original intention but rather realized more completely God's full intention to bless all the peoples of the world through Abraham. By careful consideration of Christian theology and scriptural exegesis, holiness debates can and should result in a more authentic embodiment of the holiness tradition in the ecclesiae of God.

As in Galatia, holiness debates are usually characterized by strong emotion, intensity, and, on occasion, acrimony. Desiring to maintain the façade of unity among God's people, many may seek to avoid these debates. The holiness controversy in Galatia, however, sets a precedent that such debates facilitate rather than deprecate the realization of holiness among God's people, and it is unlikely such debates will ever be totally avoided until Christ is fully formed in the holy ecclesiae of God (Gal 4:19).

3.2. Practical Implications

The controversy about holiness in Galatia is indeed ancient history, and neither the situation nor the participants are ever again exactly replicated in the experiences of the holy people of God. Nevertheless, this controversy can inform at least two current debates about embodying holiness in the contemporary church. Paul's strategy and position in the Galatian controversy offer some pastoral insights for engaging these contemporary debates.

The first contemporary holiness debate informed by the Galatian controversy concerns divorce. Those who hold divorce to be incompatible with holiness appeal to Jesus' words in Mark 10:9 that prohibit the separation of a couple God has joined together and to Malachi's words in Mal 2:16 about God's hating divorce. Based on the exception in Matt 5:32 and 19:9, some allow divorce on the grounds of sexual unfaithfulness or adultery but for no other reason. Thus, a man may severely abuse his wife emotionally and even physically, but unless he is sexually unfaithful, she may not divorce him. Several who hold this view cite 1 Pet 3:1-2 and 1 Cor 7:16 to instruct the wife that her suffering will lead her husband to repentance and to renounce his abuse. Those who prohibit divorce enable an abusive husband to inflict unimaginable pain on his wife and provide her with no way to escape.

Many outside the church and some inside the church assess this prohibition of divorce as immoral. Nancy Nason-Clark asks a very penetrating question, "The evangelical family is sacred, but is it safe?"[52] She answers negatively by pointing out that the evangelical desire to keep the family together and avoid divorce at all costs encourages spousal abuse and enables it to continue. She calls on evangelical church leaders "to recognize the prevalence and seriousness

52. Nancy Nason-Clark, "The Evangelical Family Is Sacred, but Is It Safe?" in *Healing the Hurting: Giving Hope and Help to Abused Women,* ed. Catherine Clark Kroeger and James R. Beck (Grand Rapids: Baker, 1998), p. 109. See also Catherine Clark Kroeger and Nancy Nason-Clark, *No Place for Abuse: Biblical and Practical Resources to Counteract Domestic Violence* (Downers Grove: InterVarsity, 2001).

of abuse among families of faith."[53] David Instone-Brewer observes, "Too many generations of husbands and wives have been forced to remain with their abusing or neglectful partners and have not been allowed to divorce even after suffering repeated unfaithfulness."[54] He calls on the church to repent of its immoral position on divorce.

Those who hold rejection of divorce as an essential mark of God's holy people risk condemnation by a culture that increasingly views prohibiting divorce to abused spouses to be immoral. As with circumcision in Galatia, prohibiting divorce in circumstances of abuse may hinder the recruitment and retention of new converts as well as damage the reputation and image of the church in a culture that views such a prohibition as immoral. God's holy people must determine if prohibiting divorce is necessary to remain faithful to the tradition or if the tradition offers an alternative as Paul proposed in Galatia.

The biblical tradition does offer an alternative in Exod 21:10, but this alternative has been obscured by focusing on Jesus' comment on Deut 24:1-4 in Mark 10:2-12 and Matt 19:3-12. Some Pharisees want to draw Jesus into the debate about the interpretation of Deut 24:1-4. One group interprets this passage as allowing divorce only for a matter of sexual misconduct while another understands this passage as allowing divorce for any cause. Jesus clearly sides with the former group and rejects divorce for any cause but allows divorce for the cause of sexual misconduct. Unfortunately, these Pharisees did not ask Jesus about his opinion of Exod 21:10, which must have also informed Jesus' position on divorce.

Since the grounds for divorce in Exod 21:10 were commonly accepted in the first century and Jesus never specifically rejected the teaching of this passage, Jesus probably also accepted these grounds, which Instone-Brewer summarizes as follows:

> The law of Exodus 21:10-11 was used to apply for divorces in New Testament times by both men and women. The law was applied in two categories — material neglect and emotional neglect. The material matters of food and clothing were grouped together, and emotional neglect appears to have been widened to include cruelty by both the wife and the husband. If a man or woman succeeded in showing that a partner had neglected his or her material or emotional needs, a divorce could be granted.[55]

---

53. Nason-Clark, "The Evangelical Family," p. 118.

54. David Instone-Brewer, *Divorce and Remarriage in the Bible: The Social and Literary Context* (Grand Rapids: Eerdmans, 2002), p. 314.

55. Instone-Brewer, *Divorce and Remarriage,* p. 110.

Jesus' position on divorce, therefore, probably allowed divorce not only for sexual unfaithfulness but also for material and emotional neglect including cruelty.

These alternative grounds for divorce in Exod 21:10-11 allow God's holy people to be faithful to the tradition while permitting divorce in circumstances of abuse and thus to avoid being condemned as immoral. Divorce in circumstances of material or emotional abuse need not be incompatible with living the holy life. Like circumcision in the Galatian controversy, prohibiting divorce in abusive marriages is not an essential mark of God's holy people, who need not continue advocating a position considered immoral by much of contemporary culture.

Another contemporary holiness debate informed by the Galatian controversy concerns the role of women in the ministry of the church. Those who exclude women from preaching and sometimes even teaching in the church appeal to passages in the Pauline corpus such as 1 Cor 14:33-36 and 1 Tim 2:11-15. Those who view these exclusions as an essential mark of God's holy people risk condemnation by a culture that views such exclusion as gender biased. As in Galatia, such a practice by God's people hinders both the recruitment and retention of new converts and damages the reputation and image of the church in a culture that views such exclusion as immoral. God's holy people must determine if exclusion of women in certain types of ministry is necessary to remain faithful to the tradition or if the theological and biblical tradition offers an alternative, as Paul proposed in Galatia.

Indeed, Paul himself offers alternatives in at least two passages. In 1 Cor 11:2-16, Paul recognizes that women may pray or prophesy in the worship service if they are modestly attired.[56] Many solutions have been proposed to resolve the tension of this passage with other passages in the Pauline corpus that recommend the silence of women. Nevertheless, this passage offers God's holy people an alternative to the exclusion of women from ministry positions that involve preaching or teaching. In Gal 3:28, Paul states that women have full membership in the body of Christ.[57] While Paul does not specify what full membership encompasses, involvement of women in the full range of ministries in the church would seem to be at least envisioned. Like circumcision in the Galatian controversy, exclusion of women from ministry is not an essential mark of God's holy people, who need not continue holding a position considered immoral by much of contemporary culture.

56. See my article "Paul's Argument from Nature for the Veil in 1 Corinthians 11:13-15: A Testicle Instead of a Head Covering," *Journal of Biblical Literature* 123 (2004): 71-80.

57. Martin, "Covenant of Circumcision," pp. 111-25.

4. Conclusion

The Galatian holiness controversy understood against the cultural repertoire of circumcision in the first century can inform at least two debates about how best to embody holiness in the contemporary church. Similar to the agitators' view of circumcision, some Christians consider rejection of divorce and exclusion of women from ministry as essential characteristics of the holy people of God. Similar to the Galatians' view of circumcision, many outside and even some inside the church now consider these characteristics as immoral. Paul's strategy and position in the Galatian controversy do indeed offer some pastoral insights for engaging these contemporary debates and seeing new alternatives that permit God's holy people to remain faithful to the tradition and at the same time to avoid the charge of immorality.

Church and Holiness in Ephesians

George Lyons

Ephesians has long figured prominently in discussions of biblical ecclesiology. And with good reason: It has a greater density of references to church than any major New Testament book,[1] and is second only to 1 Thessalonians within the Pauline corpus in the density of holiness terminology. But there is considerable debate about what Ephesians has to say on both subjects. An essay of brief scope can call attention to the major issues; it certainly cannot solve them all.

Debated Issues

The Church as Local or Universal in Ephesians?

Scholars debate whether the word ἐκκλησία, translated "church" throughout the NT, had any religious connotations before Christians appropriated it as a self-designation. Its use in the Septuagint referring to the assembly of Israel is of doubtful importance, since Jews well before the first century normally used "synagogue" (συναγωγῆς) for their gatherings, even in Aramaic. There is little reason to believe Christians adopted the term ἐκκλησία as a claim to being the "true Israel." It simply identified the church as an "assembly" or "gathering" of people.

Paul's letters preserve the earliest surviving literary evidence for the Christian use of the term ἐκκλησία, although he was almost certainly not the first to apply the term to gathered Christian communities. Scholars debate whether Paul actually wrote Ephesians, in part, because of its allegedly novel, non-Pauline ecclesiology. Most assume that the generally accepted Pauline let-

---

1. Based on Logos Bible Software calculations using the NA²⁷/UBS⁴ critical text.

ters always use "church" to refer to local Christian gatherings, whereas Ephesians always refers to the universal church.[2] The consensus fails to explain how either Paul or some later disciple could apply a term previously referring to individual gatherings to the disparate collection of Christian communities scattered throughout the Mediterranean world. This failure presents a serious objection to the view that "church" refers to a universal entity in Ephesians.[3]

This essay takes the minority view that Ephesians does not use ἐκκλησία in the later sense as a universal or invisible church encompassing all true believers of all time and in every place — living or dead, scattered or gathered.[4] Clearly Ephesians uses the term to refer to more than a local gathering of believers. But this is not an entirely unprecedented development. Ephesians merely expands the notion of an earthly assembly to include "a *heavenly assembly.*" Living Christians concurrently *already* participate (Eph 1:3, 22, 23; 2:5-6; 3:10) in this heavenly church in some sense in anticipation of the eschatological consummation. "Christians belong both to a heavenly church which is permanently in session and to a local church which, though it meets regularly, is intermittent in character."[5] Each local church is a tangible expression of the heavenly church,[6] a notion already anticipated in the generally accepted Pauline letters.[7] This, in turn, prepared the way for the later development of the concept of a universal church.

The Eschatology of Ephesians

Scholars generally do not take seriously enough Ephesians' repeated references to the church's existence in "heavenly places" (ἐπουράνιος — 1:3, 20; 2:6; 3:10;

---

2. E.g., Victor Paul Furnish, "Ephesians, Epistle to the," in *The Anchor Bible Dictionary,* vol. 2, ed. D. N. Freedman et al. (New York: Doubleday, 1992), pp. 535-42.

3. This essay does not defend either position in the debate on authorship.

4. So also Robert Banks, *Paul's Idea of Community* (Greenwood, S.C.: Attic Press, 1980), pp. 44-47.

5. Banks, *Paul's Idea,* p. 46.

6. So Banks, *Paul's Idea,* pp. 46, 47; P. T. O'Brien, "Church," in *Dictionary of Paul and His Letters,* ed. Gerald F. Hawthorne, Ralph P. Martin, and Daniel G. Reid (Downers Grove: InterVarsity, 1993), pp. 125-26. See, however, Kevin Giles's (*What on Earth is the Church? An Exploration in New Testament Theology* [Downers Grove: InterVarsity, 1995], pp. 127-47) challenge to this minority view.

7. Andrew T. Lincoln (*Ephesians,* WBC [Dallas: Word, 2002], p. 67), who otherwise accepts the consensus, allows that Gal 1:13; 1 Cor 10:32; 12:28; 15:9; and Phil 3:6 may have a more universal application. Similarly, Rudolf Schnackenburg (*The Church in the New Testament,* trans. W. J. O'Hara [New York: Herder & Herder, 1965], p. 84) follows the majority, but suggests Gal 4:26-27 and Phil 3:20 as Pauline analogies to the church existing in the heavenly realm.

6:12; and οὐρανός — 3:15; 4:10; 6:9). To do so requires us to imagine how Christians participating in the heavenly gathering around Christ may also go about their daily lives. Perhaps an explanation may be found in part within Jewish apocalyptic eschatology, which was conceived both spatially and temporally.[8] That is, "Heaven" was visualized as above in contrast to the world below. But it was also visualized as reserved for the future age to come in contrast to the present evil age.

Ernst Käsemann's essay "On the Subject of Primitive Christian Apocalyptic"[9] rightly argued that the fundamental issue in apocalyptic was, "To whom does the sovereignty of the world belong?"[10] This explained for him Paul's concern for bodily existence and ethics. The human body is "that piece of the world which we ourselves are and for which we bear responsibility."[11] Thus, the bodily obedience of Christians was for Paul the essential expression of worship to God the Creator in the world of everyday. Christ's heavenly lordship finds visible expression only when it takes personal shape in us in this present world and makes the gospel credible. The bodily obedience of Christians is an expression of the power of the Resurrection. Resurrection is not just about the reanimation of the dead, but about the reign of Christ. Because Christ already reigns as Lord, "his own are already engaged today in delivering over to Christ by their bodily obedience the piece of the world which they themselves are."[12] In so doing Christians bear witness to his lordship over the entire world and anticipate the future reality of the Resurrection and the uncontested reign of Christ.[13]

Believers participate in Christ's destiny as the representative of the new world that is coming. Thus, "membership in the Church *is* membership in this divine new world."[14] Paul does not conceive of humans as solitary individuals. As specific pieces of the world, they are always determined from the outside, by the lordship to which they surrender themselves. Human life is "a stake in the confrontation between God and the principalities of this world," and thus, "mirrors the cosmic contention for the lordship of the world."[15]

---

8. Both schemes coexist within the same Jewish apocalypses (e.g., 1 and 2 Enoch and 2 Esdras/4 Ezra). Lucien Cerfaux (*The Church in the Theology of St. Paul,* trans. Geoffrey Webb and Adrian Walker [Freiburg: Herder and Herder, 1959], p. 357) considers the heavenly church a counterpart to the Jewish apocalyptic notion of a heavenly Jerusalem.

9. In *New Testament Questions of Today,* trans. W. J. Montague (Philadelphia: Fortress, 1969), pp. 108-37.

10. Käsemann, "On the Subject," p. 135.

11. Käsemann, "On the Subject," p. 135.

12. Käsemann, "On the Subject," p. 135.

13. Käsemann, "On the Subject," p. 135.

14. Käsemann, "On the Subject," p. 128.

15. Käsemann, "On the Subject," p. 136.

So far, so good. But Käsemann's attempt to distinguish the eschatological understanding of Paul from that of the "Hellenistic enthusiasts" that preceded and followed him,[16] including the authors of Ephesians and Colossians, is unpersuasive. He claimed that enthusiasm's overly-realized eschatology made the body and bodily obedience inconsequential. It was preoccupied with individual freedom, overvalued ecstasy, and miracles, had little regard for ethics, and was unconcerned about the eschatological future.[17] Because even radical enthusiasts could not ignore the world not yet subjected to Christ, they felt particularly obligated to missionary activity. The problem is that none of this portrayal of enthusiasm fits Ephesians as well as Käsemann's description of Paul's apocalyptic view of the church.

Believers already possess their future inheritance by incorporation into the church. The unique emphasis of Ephesians is its spatially conceived eschatology, in which the church here and now experiences what the temporal eschatological scheme reserves for the coming age. Not only have believers already been saved (2:5, 8; 6:17), they have been raised (1:19, 20; 2:5, 6) with Christ. It is true that Ephesians never mentions the parousia hope, but there is ample evidence that its eschatology is not entirely realized and the future completely collapsed into the present. The church is the new community toward whom God intends in the ages to come to show the immeasurable riches of his grace in kindness in Christ Jesus (2:7). Like the uncontested letters of Paul, Ephesians distinguishes this evil age and the age to come (1:21; 5:16; 6:12), places a strong emphasis upon future hope (1:18; 2:12) and "the kingdom of Christ and of God" (5:5), sees growth in Christian maturity as essential to God's intentions for the church (4:11-16), expects Christians to obey the Holy Spirit in preparation for the future "day of redemption" (4:30), and looks forward to future judgment (6:8, 9).

Ephesians cherishes no illusion that sharing in Christ's victory removes the church from the sphere of conflict. Those who have been seated with Christ in heavenly places are at the same time those who continue to walk in the world (2:10; 4:1, 17; 5:2, 8, 15). They must stand in the midst of a continuing battle against the rulers of this dark world *and* against the spiritual forces of evil in heavenly places (6:12). G. B. Caird correctly insists that the "Hebraic hyperbole" here must not be misunderstood to suggest that Christians no longer struggle with the threats of pagan neighbors or with temptation, or that "spiritual" battles alone matter. Ephesians merely warns that, when the church is under attack from human enemies, the real enemies are "the spiritual forces in the background. *The heavenly places* are the territory in which invisible powers compete

16. Käsemann, "On the Subject," pp. 124-37.
17. Käsemann, "On the Subject," p. 127.

for" human allegiance and control. Christ's heavenly victory over the powers is "a representative victory," which must "be repeated in the lives of his followers."[18] Only an ongoing tension between the already and not yet makes sense of the intercessory prayer that concludes the first half of Ephesians (3:14-21) and the parenesis that follows in the second half (chaps. 4–6). Ephesians is easily as concerned about the ethical dimensions of holiness as are the generally accepted Pauline epistles.

Implicit References to Church in Ephesians

To incorporate uncritically everything Ephesians asserts about believers into its ecclesiology would be to make its specific affirmations about the church and holiness inconsequential. The word "church" is first mentioned only in Eph 1:22; it does not appear again until midway through chapter 3; and it appears nowhere in chapters 4 or 6. Nonetheless, we cannot simply ignore the insights into the church and holiness that come by way of what is said about "us" and "you" believers indirectly.

Ephesians' opening salutation closely resembles that of a typical Pauline letter, except for the designation of its addressees,[19] who are "the holy ones who are also faithful in Christ Jesus" (cf. Rom 1:7; Phil 1:1; Col 1:2). If the letter was an encyclical, as some have concluded, it merely identifies its audience as God's people who are believers in Christ Jesus. The expression "holy ones" — traditionally "saints" — characteristically refers to those we would today call believers, Christians, or God's people.[20] Ephesians has sixteen occurrences of terms from the Greek word-family (ἁγι-/ἁγν-) translated holy, holiness, sanctify, sanctification in English. The church is defined in terms of holiness.[21] Like the uncontested letters of Paul, Ephesians applies holiness terminology to the everyday activities of believers.

18. G. B. Caird, *Paul's Letters from Prison*, NClaB (Oxford: Oxford University Press, 1976), p. 92.

19. On the absence of "in Ephesus" in the textual tradition, see Bruce M. Metzger, *A Textual Commentary on the Greek New Testament: A Companion Volume to the United Bible Societies' Greek New Testament (third edition)*, corrected ed. (London/New York: United Bible Societies, 1975), p. 601.

20. Paul S. Minear (*Images of the Church in the New Testament* [Philadelphia: Westminster, 1960], p. 136) adds: "Wherever the church is spoken of as the saints, the power of the Holy Spirit is assumed to be at work within it" (p. 137).

21. Robert Hodgson, Jr., "Holiness (NT)," in *The Anchor Bible Dictionary*, vol. 3, ed., D. N. Freedman et al. (New York: Doubleday, 1992), pp. 249-54.

The author implicitly associates himself and his readers by using the first-person plural pronoun. In Eph 1:3-10 "we"/"us"/"our" refers to "all Christians, irrespective of national origin."[22] This changes in 1:11–2:10, where "we" refers more narrowly to Jewish Christians in contrast to "you" Gentile Christians. But 2:11-22 refers to Christ's creation of "one new humanity" (15), neither Jewish nor Gentile, but uniting Jews and Gentiles into a church that second-century Christians would call a *tertium genus* — "third race."[23]

Although the OT sometimes uses "saints" to designate "Israel as the people of God," we should not conclude that members of the church called themselves "saints" merely to claim the blessings once reserved for Israel.[24] Gentile believers, brought near to God through the death of Christ (2:13), become "citizens with the saints and also members of the household of God" (2:19). But since this holy church is a "new humanity" (2:15), the terms "saints" and "household of God" cannot refer simply to the existing, historical people of God plus Gentiles. What is this *new* community of which both Jewish and Gentile believers become fellow citizens if it is not merely an expanded or redefined Israel? The LXX and New Testament use of "holy ones" to refer to the company of angels,[25] God's heavenly entourage, and the departed spirits of believers provides the only plausible answer — the assembly in heavenly places.

Ephesians takes for granted that the church consists not only of God's people on earth, but of believers in Heaven — the church militant and the church triumphant, to use anachronistic language. God is "the Father, from whom every family in heaven and on earth takes its name" (3:14-15; NRSV). Ephesians presumes the existence of both earthly and heavenly assemblies. In Heaven, church is constantly in session, whereas the earthly church exists only as scattered believers who come together sporadically. The image of believers as a household concerns not merely their relationship to one another, but also to God. God's household is not confined to this world; it exists also in Heaven, and includes angels and glorified believers.[26]

---

22. Arthur G. Patzia, *Colossians, Philemon, Ephesians*, GNC (San Francisco: Harper & Row, 1984), p. 134.

23. Giles, *What on Earth*, p. 138. Ernest Best (*A Critical and Exegetical Commentary on Ephesians*, ICC [Edinburgh: T&T Clark, 1998], p. 269) agrees that the author of Ephesians "would not . . . have rejected the traditional term for the church: the third race." Markus Barth, however, argues that the church has been incorporated into historical Israel, which includes all Jews, believing and unbelieving (*The People of God*, JSNTSup 5 [Sheffield: JSOT Press, 1983]).

24. So Giles, *What on Earth*, p. 133.

25. E.g., Job 15:15; Ps 88:6, 8; Isa 57:15; Amos 4:2; Dan 8:13. In the NT this seems to be the meaning of "saints" in 1 Thess 3:13; 2 Thess 1:7, 10; and Col 1:12 (Lincoln, *Ephesians*, p. 60). Best (*Ephesians*, p. 278) argues that "saints" in Eph 1:18 and 2:6 (and possibly 2:19) refers to angels.

26. Best, *Ephesians*, pp. 278, 379.

The abrupt change of metaphors for the church from family to building and temple in Eph 2:19-22 is "facilitated by the triple meaning of the word οἶκος ('household', 'house', 'temple')."[27] Kinship imagery changes to architectural as the newly defined household becomes "a holy temple in the Lord." This sanctuary is clearly metaphorical, as the expression "spiritually" in 2:22 indicates. Its "foundation" is the preaching of "the apostles and prophets" (2:20). And "Christ Jesus himself" is the ἀκρογωνιαῖος of this temple. Whether Christ is imaged as the "cornerstone" or the "capstone" of the building,[28] the explicit point of the metaphor emphasizes Christ's crucial role in making the church "a dwelling place for God." God is not inaccessible in Heaven somewhere; people encounter God, no longer in a literal building, but in the community gatherings of Christians.[29]

As members of the heavenly church, believers' everyday lives are sanctified by the presence of God. But the church is holy, not merely by virtue of its unique relationship with God — positional holiness. It is the community God chose in Christ before creation to be holy and blameless before him in love (1:4). The church is not holy by definition alone; it is called to grow in personal holiness (2:21; 4:17-24). Ephesians defines a holy community as one that is distinguished by mutual love (3:17; 4:2, 15, 16), obedient to God's gracious call, and pleasing to him (4:1-32) — "imitators of God" and the model of self-giving love seen in Christ (5:1-2). The church consists of those who have put off their old lives of sin to be clothed in a new humanity, created in the likeness of God "in true righteousness and holiness" (here from ὁσιότης; 4:24). The church is destined by God to live for the praise of his glory (1:12). God's Spirit lives in the church (2:22), empowering it to love (3:16-19) and to live worthy of its call to holiness (4:1). The Spirit provides the ethical power the church needs to experience wholesome and loving mutual relations and to refrain from evil of every kind (4:1–5:2, 15-21). The Spirit is the source of its strength in the face of its cos-

27. Caird, *Paul's Letters*, pp. 60-61.

28. Best (*Ephesians*, pp. 284 [nn. 85 and 86], 285) lists defenders of both positions. Jerome's *Commentary on Ephesians* presumes a deliberate ambiguity, because Christ both founds and finishes the church. This is consistent with the double-meaning of the head metaphor in which Christ is both the source of the body's growth (Eph 1:22; 4:15; 5:23) and the objective of its growth (Eph 4:13-16). Christ is its beginning and end (David J. Williams, *Paul's Metaphors: Their Context and Character* [Peabody, Mass.: Hendrickson, 1999], p. 116).

29. Assuming the reading in 2:21 of that of the earliest manuscripts and NA[27] (i.e., "every building" — every local church — being "built up into a holy sanctuary in the Lord") rather than the textual variant followed by most translations, which refers to "the whole building" (i.e., the universal church). The sense of the former reading is that as each local church provides God with a spiritual dwelling place in that location (Eph 2:22), all these churches grow together into one holy sanctuary.

mic battle with spiritual forces (6:10-18) and the foretaste of its final redemption (1:14, 17; 4:30).[30] Because the holiness of the church is God's doing and brings credit to him, "the ethical definition of the church"[31] is not about human achievement.

Personal holiness is the achievement of the Triune God in the corporate life of the Christian community.[32] God the Father of our Lord Jesus Christ has blessed the church with every spiritual blessing in the heavenly places in Christ (1:3). These blessings are not "spiritual" because they are invisible and inward only, but because they are the work of the Holy Spirit in the church (1:13, 14; 5:19). They are "heavenly" because they originate with God, not because they are reserved for the future age. The blessings once expected only in the age to come have already become a present heavenly reality for believers through the fulfilled promise of the Spirit.[33] In Ephesians 2:11-22 the unity of the church is similarly articulated in Trinitarian terms.[34] Through Christ both Jews and Gentiles "have access in one Spirit to the Father" (2:18). As a result of what Christ has done, Gentiles are "no longer strangers and aliens" (2:19). "In Christ," the church is "joined together and grows into a holy temple in the Lord" (2:21), "built together in the Spirit into a dwelling place for God" (2:22).

The church is a graced community, enabled by God to live lives characterized by good works he planned for them to do (2:10). The church has been gifted by the ascended Christ so that "the holy people" that make up its membership might do "the work of ministry," thereby "building up the body of Christ . . . in love" (4:7-16). As in the generally accepted Pauline letters, grace is not a divine indulgence that makes sin inconsequential, but God's transforming work in the lives of believers that allows them to understand and actually do God's will.

Giles claims that Ephesians 4:1-16 "says more specifically on the church than any other part of this epistle," although the word "church" nowhere appears here. The focus is on the unity of the church described using the images of "body" (4:4, 12, 16), "building" (4:12, 16), "fullness of Christ" (4:13), and "new humanity" (4:13). The affirmations about the church are organized in a Trinitarian fashion — from the Spirit, through Christ, to God the Father. The church is one, but must constantly work to preserve this unity, utilizing the as-

---

30. Giles, *What on Earth*, p. 145.

31. Giles, *What on Earth*, p. 144.

32. Since all three persons of the Trinity appear throughout the passage, dividing 1:3-14 along Trinitarian lines is neither necessary nor persuasive.

33. So Lincoln, *Ephesians*, pp. 19-20; contra, among others, Caird (*Paul's Letters*, p. 33).

34. For the Trinitarian pattern of thought, see Lincoln, *Ephesians*, pp. 40-42. Cf. also Patzia (*Colossians, Philemon, Ephesians*, p. 128).

cended Christ's gifts. The unity of the church is an expression of the holiness to which it has been called (4:1; 1:4).

The unity of the church comprised of Jews and Gentiles is the work of Jesus Christ accomplished by his death on the cross — "he is our peace" (2:14). Gentiles were brought near to God "by the blood of Christ" (2:13). "In his flesh he has made both groups into one" (2:14). He reconciled both groups to God "through the cross" and put to death the hostility between the two "through it" (2:16).[35] In 2:14-16 the benefits of Christ's death are described by way of two metaphorical results: the destruction of the wall that divided the two groups[36] and the creation of "one new humanity" reconciled to God "in one body through the cross." Christ brought an end to the hostility separating Jews and Gentiles by abolishing laws that kept them separate and giving them shared access to God.[37]

Ephesians does not depict this unified community as gathering together to worship God, but presumes that worship takes place primarily in everyday life. It applies traditional worship terminology to the saving work of Christ (Eph 5:2) and to the new lifestyle of believers that is characterized by love (cf. Eph 4:1-16; Rom 12:1-10). The holy church worships God by living to the praise of his glory (Eph 1:6, 12, 14) *in the world.* In typical Pauline fashion (e.g., Rom 14:19; 15:2; 1 Cor 14:3-5, 12, 17, 26; 1 Thess 5:11), Ephesians depicts the church gathering together for mutual upbuilding (οἰκοδομή) — edification (cf. 2:21; 4:29). The church gathers to be equipped to bring praise to God by its life in this world in anticipation of its future communion with God and the saints in the heavenly world. It gathers to be prepared for the battle it faces.

Appealing to OT imagery,[38] Eph 6:10-19 exhorts the community as a whole (using the "you" plural throughout) to defend itself against the attacks of its spiritual enemies by putting on "the whole armor of God" (6:11, 13). If Roman military practice served as a model, the size and normal use of the shield in battle presumes a defensive formation that offered protection for soldiers

---

35. It is unclear here whether Jesus' mission and ministry is an essential prerequisite to the crucifixion. Does Christ's proclamation of peace (2:17) refer to Jesus' preaching or to the church's proclamation of his death and resurrection?

36. Many see here an allusion to Temple wall which divided the Court of the Gentiles from the inner courts open to Jews only (e.g., J. L. Houlden, *Paul's Letters from Prison: Philippians, Colossians, Philemon, and Ephesians,* WPC [Philadelphia: Westminster, 1977], p. 90).

37. Space does not permit consideration of the claim that Christ's death "abolished the law" (2:15). Ephesians insists upon the end of those "commandments and ordinances" — purity laws — that maintained the separation of Jews and Gentiles.

38. Isa 11:5; 59:16-19; Wis 5:17-23; cf. 1 Thess 5:8; 2 Cor 6:7; Rom 13:12.

acting in concert, not individually.[39] A command to "be strong in the Lord" (6:10) summarizes well the thrust of Eph 6:10-19. The church struggles against overwhelming odds. Evil would be overpowering without the more than sufficient strength available from the Lord (6:10-12). The ancient weapons of warfare serve as metaphors describing the spiritual resources God provided believers to face the struggles of life in "this dark world" (6:12; see 6:13-17). All of this imagery seems directed to one end — to urge the church to call upon the incalculable resource of divine might available through unceasing prayer (6:18-20; see 3:20-21).

"The sword of the Spirit" (6:17) is the only offensive weapon among the panoply, and the only weapon that is explained: It is "the word of God" (see Isa 11:4; 49:2; Hos 6:5; Rev 1:16; 19:15). The Holy Spirit as the church's sword (see Heb 4:12, 13) comes to its aid in the struggle against evil, inspiring it to speak the words God wants it to speak (see Mark 13:11; Luke 12:11, 12; Isa 49:2; 51:16). Spirit-inspired persuasive speech rather than threats of violence (see 6:9) is the only offensive weapon the church is allowed.

Explicit References to Church in Ephesians

The Church as the Body of Christ

Ephesians' first explicit reference to "church" provides an equation, identifying the "church" as "his body." The passage raises a number of exegetical puzzles, not the least of which is whether this equation should be taken metaphorically or literally. But before we address this question, there are some even more basic issues.

A fairly literal translation of Eph 1:22-23 points out the initial problem — antecedent ambiguity. "And 'he subjected all things under his feet' and made him head over all things to the church, which is his body, the fullness of him who fills all things in everything." Deciding what is the antecedent of each of the third-person pronouns "he," "his," and "him" — is no easy task, since the pronoun serves as both the subject and object of the sentence and also appears as a genitive modifier.

There is no explicit subject in the Greek sentence equivalent to the pro-

---

39. The point is not to urge Christians to aggression and violence, but to adopt the discipline, mutual support, preparedness, dedication, and self-sacrifice that marked the reputation of soldiers as portrayed in philosophical discourse. This point was drawn to my attention by my student Brian Mackey in his unpublished senior theology paper (December, 2005).

noun "he"; it is only implicit in the verbs ὑπέταξεν — "he subjected" — and ἔδωκεν — "he made"[40] or "he appointed."[41] The apparent antecedent — the last explicit preceding subject — is "God" in 1:17. Thus, God must be the active agent, and Christ, the recipient of God's activity. God made "him," αὐτὸν — Christ — "head" over all things to the church. And the "feet" and the "body" must be Christ's — αὐτοῦ/"his." The four actions of God in Eph 1:20-22 are probably "not temporally successive but simultaneous."[42] God raised Christ from the dead, seated Christ at God's right hand, subjected all things under Christ's feet, and made Christ head over all things to the church.[43]

The corporal and spatial imagery of the passage is indebted to the metaphorical language of Pss 8:6 and 110:1. As in the Ancient Near East in general, Christ's seat at God's right hand (1:20) places him in a position of ultimate authority.[44] Just as the victor placed his foot on the necks of defeated foes, God has put everything under Christ's feet,[45] making him the master of the universe who rules over everything. In short, he is Lord.

But what are we to make of the phrase, "God has made Christ head over all things"? Does "head" function within this corporal imagery as merely another metaphor to distinguish the master from his subjects?[46] Is the point of all these body-part metaphors simply to assert that God designated Christ as the cosmic Lord of all that exists? Is the issue Christ's lordship over the universe on behalf of the church or his rule over the body, the church,[47] as in 4:12-16?

The Septuagint meaning of "head" (κεφαλή) as "ruler" or "leader"[48] makes perfect sense in Col 2:10, where Christ is called "the head of every ruler and authority." He is the Lord of lords. But when the Hebrew connotations of "head" underlie the Greek term, it may instead be synonymous with ἀρχή and

---

40. BDAG, ὑποτάσσω 1 (p. 847), δίδωμι 5 (here used as an equivalent of τιθέναι, p. 193).

41. Best, *Ephesians*, p. 181.

42. Best, *Ephesians*, p. 182.

43. Although the church is clearly Christ's body (v. 23a), the precise meaning of v. 23b remains unclear and cannot be taken up here in detail.

44. Robert G. Bratcher and Eugene Albert Nida, *A Translator's Handbook on Paul's Letter to the Ephesians* (London/New York: United Bible Societies, 1982), p. 35.

45. Konrad Weiss, "πούς," in *Theological Dictionary of the New Testament*, vol. 6, ed. Gerhard Friedrich; ed. and trans. Geoffrey W. Bromiley (Grand Rapids: Eerdmans, 1976), p. 626. See also Best, *Ephesians*, p. 180.

46. Most ancient people did not think of the head as the part of the body that controlled other bodily parts, although such ancient medical writers as Hippocrates and Galen illustrate that some physicians did indeed espouse this then novel view (So Markus Barth, *Ephesians 1–3*, AB 34 [Garden City, N.Y.: Doubleday, 1974], pp. 186-92).

47. So also Lincoln, *Ephesians*, pp. 67-68 and Best, *Ephesians*, p. 182.

48. E.g., Deut 28:13; Judg 10:18; 11:11; 2 Sam 22:44; Isa 7:8, 9.

have the force of "source" or "origin." The body is not only subject to the head, but "derives its growth and development from its head."[49] There are no ancient parallels to the notion that bodily growth originated from the head of the body as Col 2:19 and Eph 4:15-16 insist.[50]

The "newer" medical view of the head was not the traditional Greek view and certainly not that of the OT. The head of a family in a patriarchal society was in charge of the family by virtue of being the biological source of the rest of the family — the family owed its existence to him.[51] The head of a river was not the decision maker, but the source of the river's water. Hence, outside the NT the metaphorical uses of "head" include both lordship and source or origin. In Col 1:15-20 Christ's headship over the cosmos is parallel to ἀρχή and πρωτότοκος.[52] Christ's headship of both cosmos and church derives from his status as mediator of the original creation (Eph 2:10, 15; 4:24; cf. Col 1:16) and the new creation (Eph 2:15; 4:24), giving him the right to rule both the cosmos and the church.

Focusing on the image of the church as Christ's body (2:23a),[53] some scholars insist that this is not imagery at all, but that the church is the literal continuation of the incarnation.[54] But there is no justification in Ephesians for making "*church* and *body* interchangeable."[55] If Christ is Lord of "all things," this must include the church. And a church that is subject to him must be distinguishable from him. In any case, if the imagery is metaphor and not allegory, its essential point is clear enough: The earthly church shares Christ's heavenly status now (1:22-23; 2:15-16) and already reveals God's future purposes in the heavenly places (3:10-11).

Ephesians' fourth explicit reference to church repeats earlier claims that Christ is "the head of the church"; and the church, "the body" of Christ (5:23; cf. 1:22). But it adds another role to Christ's résumé: Here Christ is "the Savior" of the church — the only place in the NT where he is so identified. That Christ is the Savior of the body clearly distinguishes him from the church.[56]

49. Lincoln, *Ephesians*, p. 70.

50. Lincoln, *Ephesians*, pp. 68-72.

51. Cf. Best, *Ephesians*, p. 193.

52. Best, *Ephesians*, p. 195.

53. On the possible origin(s) of the imagery of body as applied to the church, see Lincoln, *Ephesians*, pp. 70-72.

54. E.g., J. A. T. Robinson, *The Body* (London: SCM, 1957), pp. 51, 58; Pierre Benoit, *Jesus and the Gospel*, trans. Benet Weatherhead (Bristol: Herder and Herder, 1973), pp. 53-58; Schnackenburg, *The Church*, p. 175; Cerfaux, *The Church*, pp. 262, n. 1; 263, 282, 323, 330, 347, 349, 357.

55. Minear, *Images of the Church*, p. 185.

56. Best, *Ephesians*, p. 537. Ephesians 5:23 seems to be a midrash on Gen 2:18-24: Woman was created from the source (i.e., "head") of the man to be his companion (Caird, *Paul's Letters*,

The Church as the Community of Salvation

In the second explicit reference to church in Eph 3:8-10, Paul's grace-enabled preaching is said to concern "the fathomless riches of Christ" — the all-inclusive message of universal salvation, of Christ's willingness to save all people, even Gentiles. The purpose of Paul's mission was to preach the good news of "the plan of the mystery hidden for ages in the God who created all things." This plan[57] was "that the diverse wisdom of God might now be made known to the rulers and authorities in the heavenly places *through the church*."[58] Elsewhere in the Pauline corpus, "rulers and authorities" normally refer to angelic and demonic spirits. Are we to imagine heavenly spectators witnessing the earthly church or the church's heavenly presence? Regardless, the crucial point is that through the church the long unknown intentions of God have become public knowledge. The secret is out: God wants to save everyone. The Creator of the universe intends also to be its Re-creator.

Paul's preaching of the gospel brought "the church" into existence, a church that included Gentiles in its ranks. The church is to play a mediating role in accomplishing God's purposes by making God's wisdom known to the rulers and authorities in the heavenly places. But how? Is it by the preaching of the gospel, by the mere existence of a unified community, or by the unified church's worship in the world — i.e., its life of ethical holiness? In any case, the church demonstrates "that one day cosmic divisions will also be overcome."[59]

Perhaps because Ephesians celebrates what God has already accomplished in the unified church, it does not emphasize evangelism directed toward unbelievers. Its exhortation not to associate with the disobedient (5:6-7) should not be taken as a warrant against missionary activity.[60] Rather, as in 1 Cor 5:9-13 and 2 Thess 3:6-10, its concern is more probably with shunning professing believers who do not take the Christian ethic seriously. Christians are not to "participate in the unfruitful works of darkness, but rather to speak out

---

p. 88). The church "is subject to Christ" not because he is its "head," according to 5:24, but because he is its Savior (Best, *Ephesians*, p. 535).

57. The terms "mystery," "will," "purpose," and "plan" all make "the point that God's purpose has been hitherto concealed, but now declared in Christ" (Houlden, *Paul's Letters from Prison*, p. 268).

58. Caird, *Paul's Letters*, p. 66 (emphasis added). Caird also insists, "It is hardly an exaggeration to say that any interpretation of Ephesians stands or falls with this verse." He is adamant that ". . . *the heavenly places* are not some region remote from the life of earth, but the spiritual environment in which unseen forces compete for man's allegiance."

59. Giles, *What on Earth*, p. 138.

60. Against Furnish, "Ephesians," p. 540.

against them" (5:11). Ephesians calls for Christians to speak the truth to their neighbors (4:25) and to speak in ways that build up and give grace to all who hear them (4:29). Equipped with the whole armor of God, Christians will be "ready to proclaim the gospel" (6:15; NRSV) with persuasion (6:17) and boldness (6:19, 20).

The third reference to church in Ephesians appears in the doxological conclusion of Paul's prayer-report in 3:14-21. God's worthiness to be praised is demonstrated by the very existence of the church. Doxology is not so much what the church says directed toward God as what others recognize as true about God because the church exists as an expression of praise to God. God is to be forever recognized for who he is as truly and faithfully in the church as in Christ. God provides the church more than adequate power to accomplish his purposes. God is present, his rule recognized, and his glory manifested in the church.

The Church as the Bride of Christ

All five of the remaining explicit references to the church appear in close proximity to one another within Ephesians' analogy of the relationship of husband and wife to that between Christ and the church in 5:21-33. This passage emphasizes the intimate nature of the marriage-like relationship between Christ and the church.

The fifth explicit reference asserts as a fact that "the church is subject to Christ" (5:24), presuming that the church lives in voluntary obedience to Christ whereas the sixth explicit reference to "church" appeals to the example of Christ, commanding husbands to love their wives "as Christ loved the church and gave himself up for her." "This is the only place in the NT where the church and not individuals is named as the object of Christ's activity,"[61] and it raises a number of difficulties that cannot be addressed in detail here.[62] In any case, any interpretation that limits salvation to the sovereign and arbitrary decisions of God is challenged by Ephesians' insistence that holiness is the purpose of Christ's love for the church. "Christ loved the church and gave himself up for her in order to sanctify her by cleansing with the washing of

61. Best, *Ephesians*, p. 541.

62. E.g., does this presume a preexistent church chosen beforehand by God to be receptive to his offer of salvation and therefore the only ones toward whom the love and death of Christ are directed? While the issue is indeed complex, if God's choice alone is sufficient apart from any human response, it is impossible to make sense of the salvation by grace through faith insisted upon in Eph 2:8-9.

water by the word" (5:25-26).[63] His love was intended to have the consequence of making the church holy and fit to belong to himself. Prior to responding to Christ's love, "the church" was not the church or not the kind of church Christ intended it to be.

The seventh explicit reference to "church" (5:27) again connects the church and some ethical and personal sense of holiness. Christ intends the church to be glorious and "without a spot or wrinkle" — "holy and without blemish." Ephesians 5:26-27 describe Christ's death as having three purposes/results (each introduced by ἵνα).

The first has a double effect: Christ's death "sanctified" and "cleansed" the church. Since both these verbs are aorists, it is impossible to distinguish them sequentially. The terms are probably intended to be mutually interpretive — i.e., sanctification effects moral cleansing. It is a matter of interpretation when this sanctifying cleansing was accomplished. Was it when Christ died — as a potential benefit, or was it when the believer was baptized — as an actualized benefit? If this is an allusion to the bath of baptism, the imagery is complicated by the fact that "baptism is an individual matter."[64] Whatever the precise meaning, the point is that Christ's death provides for the sanctification of believers (cf. Heb 13:12).

The second purpose/result is the presentation of the church to Christ as a bride (5:27). Unlike 2 Cor 11:2, in which the church's marriage is imaged as a future prospect, here, the marriage is an accomplished fact. No longer just his fiancée, the church-bride has already become the wife of Christ. While there are difficult questions raised by this analogy,[65] it is clear from 5:32 that the church-bride, prepared by moral cleansing, is presented to her Lord-husband within "this world of space and time. . . . The church is already the bride of Christ."[66] "The bride is Christian believers viewed corporately as an entity."[67] Thus, the personal, ethical holiness of the church is not to be expected only in the age to come, but in this present world.

The third purpose/result of Christ's sanctifying death repeats the descrip-

---

63. It is unclear which "word" is intended — the baptismal formula — "I baptize you in the name of Jesus Christ/Father, Son, and Holy Spirit," or the preaching that accompanies baptism.

64. Best, *Ephesians*, p. 543.

65. E.g., Was the "marriage" consummated at the death of Christ, the moment of baptism, or some other such decisive moment in the Christian walk? Since the latter two "moments" are individual rather than corporate experiences, associating them with this "marriage" makes little sense of the analogy. Perhaps the analogy simply breaks down (Best, *Ephesians*, p. 546).

66. Giles, *What on Earth*, p. 143.

67. Giles, *What on Earth*, p. 144.

tion of believers given in Eph 1:4. Christ died so that the church might be "holy and without blemish" (5:27). This connects what is said about the church with what the book's opening benediction says about "us." "God chose us in Christ before the creation of the world in order that we might be holy and blameless before him in love" (1:4).

In this context in which the church as the bride of Christ is the dominant metaphor, the eighth explicit reference to "church" (5:29-30) returns to the imagery of the church as the body of Christ. This has the effect of equating the book's two prominent images of the church. Beyond this, it clarifies the character of Christ's love for the church asserted in the sixth reference concerning Christ's love for the church. Human care for one's own body becomes the basis for the claim, "No one ever hates his own body, but he nourishes and cherishes it, just as Christ does the church, because we are members of his body." That we are *members of* Christ's body clarifies the first explicit reference to church, which identifies it simply *as* Christ's body. Here the author and his readers as members of Christ's body are a part of the church. But the church and Christ are as clearly distinguishable as the members are from one another.

The ninth and final explicit mention of "church" in Ephesians (5:32) applies the mysterious one-flesh union of husband and wife to Christ and the church. It asserts that although the two are distinguishable, they are in some profound sense actually one. If the mystery of the church's relationship with Christ could be adequately described without resorting to imagery, a prosaic explanation would be satisfactory. Perhaps the same might be said of the church's simultaneous earthly residence and heavenly reality. Mysteries may be asserted but never fully explained.

Conclusion

Christ's paradoxical victory over the forces that resist God through his death on the cross has created the possibility for universally sinful humanity to participate in a new human community through the power of the Holy Spirit. Ephesians presents the church as a diverse, earthly community of renewed people, who gather together in unity and fellowship with the Triune God and in concert with the hosts of heavenly angels and glorified believers. Transformed by faith in Christ's gracious offer of salvation, the church submits to his lordship and lives worthy of his call to holiness. Christ has given the church gifted leaders who offer mutual edification that enables believers to grow out of his resources in increased unity, moral maturity, love, and Christlikeness. Despite its diverse membership, the spiritually unified church may be compared to a healthy body, well-constructed building, holy Temple, well-ordered family, loving marriage, or disciplined military unit. The scattered community, equipped for "the work of ministry," lives in the world so as to bring praise to God. Regular participation in the life of Heaven empowers the community of believers to anticipate the life of the age to come with lives of personal holiness and love, even in the face of opposition from sinister forces.

Ephesians presents a vision of the church in a world transformed by the good news that Christ already reigns as Lord. In Heaven he reigns unchallenged, despite continuing resistance on earth. The church makes visible Christ's presence in the world and anticipates the final consummation of his rule.

The earthly church's participation in the heavenly assembly has profound ethical implications for its daily life. Far from libertine imaginations of heavenly self-indulgence that Käsemann supposed arose from the over-realized eschatology of "Hellenistic enthusiasm," Ephesians envisions an entirely different understanding of Heaven. It is not a world in which every human sensual craving is gratified; instead the mutual love of the saints seeks the well-being of others. Heaven is not the church's literal address, but heavenly values and priorities have already created a human community that mirrors the life of Heaven. Ephesians' celebration of the church's heavenly existence reminds it of its earthly responsibilities.

If the obvious excesses of the Corinthian church sprang from the seeds of over-realized eschatology, as many scholars presume, Käsemann's caution would be warranted. But can the origin of the ethical and theological problems in Corinth be so easily diagnosed? No NT book emphasizes the realized dimensions of eschatology as unmistakably as John's Gospel. But it certainly lends no support to ethical indifference. John encourages believers, who live in this world, not to be of this world. Christians are to live, in intimate heavenly unity with the Triune God and with other believers, a life distinguished by holy love (John 17).

The excesses of the under-realized and overly literalistic eschatology of Dispensational Premillennialism are a more real and present danger to contemporary Christianity than the alleged realized eschatology of Ephesians. Too many Christians evade the implications of holy living here and now by investing all their attention on speculative theories about the unfolding of future events in this latter-day apocalyptic misunderstanding.

Some modern scholars equate pietistic Christian spirituality with an abuse they dismiss as "enthusiasm." But there is no reason to presume that those who take seriously an authentic personal relationship with God and are convinced that God's Spirit empowers them to live the life of Heaven in this present world have misunderstood the NT's view of the Christian life. Certainly excessive subjectivity, emotionalism, and mystical fantasies have led to aberrant forms of Christianity. But so have excessive rationalism and humanism.

No thinking Christian of the twenty-first century seriously imagines that Heaven is somewhere up in outer space. But the NT nowhere makes such an overly literalistic modern reading of the imagery of Scripture an article of faith. Unless we begin with the assumptions of atheistic rationalism, it is not absurd to take seriously the existence of God. And it is not impossible for modern believers to share the conviction of Ephesians that earthbound believers may nonetheless participate in the reality in which God resides, however we may define it.

Ephesians offers no geography of heavenly places, but it does characterize the heavenly life of the church. This life is not marked by selfish sensual indulgence, but by an other-centered love like that modeled by the self-giving life of Christ. The very fact that Ephesians uses the human body and the intimacy of marriage to image the church of Christ is evidence against the notion that it might endorse a gnostic dismissal of material existence as inherently sinful. On the contrary, the Holy Spirit of God so sanctifies human existence that the earthly church lives in this present world to the praise of his glory.

Ephesians explicitly rejects as antithetical to the life of Heaven a wide range of self-indulgent behaviors (4:17–5:14) that not only characterized ancient paganism, but as certainly characterize the normal lifestyle of most in the affluent modern West. The same heavenly ethic that excludes the sexually immoral from the kingdom of Christ and God also excludes the greedy (5:3-5). Were ancient pagans who bowed at idolatrous shrines any more deceived by empty promises than are those who greedily pursue individual fulfillment at the temples of modern consumerism — the shopping mall? Ephesians calls the Christian community to wake up and expose all such unfruitful works of darkness, not to participate in them (5:6-14).

Ephesians' concern that Christians reflect the holiness of Heaven in the world of everyday may account for its two most prominent images of the church — the body of Christ and the bride of Christ. Because the church is the body of Christ, it shares in his representative victory over the forces of evil and his exaltation to Heaven. But if his victory is to be repeated in the lives of his followers on earth, the church must live in voluntary submission to Christ's lordship. Just as Christ represents the church in Heaven, the church represents Christ on earth. God's holy people must actually live lives of holiness, replicating the life of Heaven on earth.

Because the church is already the bride of Christ, it has been cleansed and equipped to fulfill its holy calling. But the unified church is also a building in progress, so there is still room for growth in personal holiness. The demands of love are not exhausted in one heroic act, but call for daily expressions of humility, gentleness, patience, and tolerance (4:1-6).

Marriage, the most domestic of human relations, illustrates the mysterious relationship between Christ and his church, because its holiness is the fruit of his love. Ephesians describes the life of holiness in terms of loving community relations. The unity of the church composed of both Jews and Gentiles is the most visible expression of this. Christ's love serves as the model for the church in its mutual relations and in its life in the world. Ephesians reminds us that holiness must find expression in the daily lives of believers. It is primarily in the world that the church worships God, not in its gatherings, which celebrate its corporate life and equip it for its mission to embody Christ in the world. It is in this equipped and serving holy community, not in a literal building, that the world encounters the Triune God. If it is love that distinguishes the church from other communities, this must be encountered in a local church living out the life of Heaven on earth, not in the abstract notion of some universal entity.

Working Out Salvation:
Holiness and Community in Philippians

J. ROSS WAGNER

Writing to the church in Philippi, Paul addresses his dear friends as "the holy ones (ἅγιοι) in Christ Jesus" (1:1; cf. 4:21). Whatever their background,[1] their identity is now determined by the gracious work of salvation that God has accomplished for them in Christ. Paul avers that as God has begun a good work among them, God will certainly also bring that work to completion (1:6). And yet, while the apostle never wavers in his insistence that God is the initiating and primary agent in their salvation, Paul also calls this community of "holy ones" to expend every effort in pursuing holiness in their common life. They are to "live as citizens in a manner worthy of the gospel of Christ" and to "work out [their] own salvation with fear and trembling" (2:12).

As Morna Hooker perceptively observes, "Whatever we may wish to say about Christ's death as a unique saving act is not diminished by the recognition that what [Christ] does *for* us has to be worked out *in us*."[2] My purpose in this essay is to explore how Paul seeks to form the Philippian community so that their identity as God's holy people comes to expression in a communal life of holiness, as together they increasingly embody the pattern of Christ's self-giving love. Taking my cue from Professor Hooker, I will pose the focal question for this investigation in the following way: "How, in Paul's view, is what God does *for* us worked out *in us?*"

My interest here centers not on the *initial* and decisive transformation of humans by God: that is, God's singular[3] rectifying work of freeing them from

---

1. On the social composition of the Philippian church, see Peter Oakes, *Philippians: From People to Letter,* SNTSMS 110 (Cambridge: Cambridge University Press, 2001).

2. Morna D. Hooker, "A Partner in the Gospel: Paul's Understanding of His Ministry," in *Theology and Ethics in Paul and His Interpreters: Essays in Honor of Victor Paul Furnish,* ed. E. H. Lovering, Jr. and J. L. Sumney (Nashville: Abingdon, 1996), pp. 83-100 (emphasis original).

3. J. Louis Martyn rightly insists that "God's rectification is not God's response at all

slavery to sin and death "in Adam," and giving them new life by uniting them to Christ through the Spirit. To be sure, this is a central concern of Paul's soteriology, but it is something that I will presume here. In this essay, I am primarily interested in exploring how salvation plays out in the ongoing lives of those whom God has decisively transformed, those whose existence is now determined by their union with the crucified and risen Christ, those whose lives are now to be lived in the power of God's Spirit.

Paul's answer to the question, "How is what God does *for* us worked out *in* us?" centers on a transformed community. That is, at the heart of Paul's gospel of a rectified cosmos are restored relationships, not only one's relationship with God, but also one's relationships with fellow human beings. Salvation manifests itself in a community that takes on the character of Christ both in its interactions among its members and in its relationship to the world at large. Paul addresses his exhortation and teaching in Philippians not to isolated individuals, but to individuals in community.[4] As the Philippians work out their own salvation, they do so as a community. They are to "live as citizens," that is, to conduct their public, communal life, in a manner "worthy of the gospel" (1:27). It is in standing firm together, striving together for the faith of the gospel (1:27), devoting themselves to one another's interests (2:3-4), living peaceably with one another (2:14-16), that the gospel becomes visible. The community of God's "holy ones" is the vanguard of the outworking of God's rectification of the cosmos.

Work out your own salvation . . . for
God is the one who is working in you.

I will structure my investigation around a key text in Philippians that brings sharply into focus the question: "How is what God does *for* us worked out *in* us?"

Philippians 2:12-13:

12Ὥστε, ἀγαπητοί μου, καθὼς πάντοτε ὑπκούσατε, μὴ ὡς ἐν τῇ παρουσίᾳ μου μόνον ἀλλὰ νῦν πολλῷ μᾶλλον ἐν τῇ ἀπουσίᾳ μου, μετὰ φόβου καὶ τρόμου τὴν ἑαυτῶν σωτηρίαν κατεργάζεσθε· 13θεὸς γάρ ἐστιν ὁ ἐνεργῶν ἐν ὑμῖν καὶ τὸ θέλειν καὶ τὸν ἐνεργεῖν ὑπὲρ τῆς εὐδοκίας.

[whether to human faith or to human observance of the Law]. It is the *first* move; it is God's initiative, carried out by him in Christ's faithful death" ("God's Way of Making Things Right," in *Theological Issues in the Letters of Paul* [Nashville: Abingdon, 1997], pp. 141-56, here p. 151).

4. There is, in fact, only one address in the entire letter to a singular "you" (4:3).

12And so, my beloved, just as you have always obeyed, so now — not only as those who do so just in my presence, but now much more in my absence — continue to work out your own salvation with fear and trembling, 13for God is the one who is working among you both [your] willing and [your] working, for his good pleasure (author's translation).

This exhortation immediately follows Paul's poetic recitation of the story of Christ (2:6-11) — the narrative that shapes their communal identity and that must determine their communal mindset (2:5). He now brings this story directly to bear on the Philippians' ongoing experience of God's saving work (2:12-18).

Paul begins by connecting their communal life to the story of Christ. His reference to their consistent "obedience" (2:12a) echoes the focus on Christ's own "obedience" at the center of the "Christ hymn" (2:8); their obedient pattern of life offers clear evidence that the distinctive pattern of Christ's life is already being manifested in their community. Convinced that this has not been simply an accommodation to his presence with them, but that it is indeed a genuine, persistent characteristic of their communal life, Paul urges them in 2:12b, "Continue to work out your own salvation." The question of how they are to do this, practically speaking, will occupy us shortly. But if we are to understand the logic of Paul's soteriology rightly, it is necessary first to attend to the assertion about God's acts that undergirds Paul's urgent insistence that they act.

God Is the One Who Is Working in You

In a striking play on words, Paul avers that the Philippians' continuing efforts to "work out" (κατεργάζεσθαι, 2:12) their salvation are grounded in, enabled by, and infused with God's own "work" (ἐνεργεῖν, 2:13) among them: "work out your own salvation . . . for God is the one who is working among you." Indeed, it is this ongoing work of God (ὁ ἐνεργῶν) that actually generates the Philippians' own "willing" (τὸ θέλειν) and "working" (τὸ ἐνεργεῖν).[5] In Paul's view, God stands right at the center of human volition and action; divine and human agency are inextricably woven together in the lives of those whom God is saving.[6] All that the Philippians do to work out their salvation is at

5. The first occurrence of ἐνεργεῖν (ὁ ἐνεργῶν) is transitive; its direct objects are the two articular infinitives.

6. Compare 1 Thess 2:13: παραλαβόντες λόγον ἀκοῆς παρ' ἡμῶν τοῦ θεοῦ ἐδέξασθε οὐ λόγον ἀνθρώπων ἀλλὰ καθὼς ἐστιν ἀληθῶς λόγον θεοῦ, <u>ὃς καὶ ἐνεργεῖται ἐν ὑμῖν τοῖς πιστεύουσιν</u>.

one and the same time an outworking of God's prior and continuing work in their midst.

The weighty final phrase of this sentence, "for good pleasure" (ὑπὲρ τῆς εὐδοκίας), draws attention to the sovereign initiative of God in all of this. God's εὐδοκία — a standard term in the lexicon of divine election — is the ultimate frame of reference for divine activity (the participle) as well as for human volition and action (the infinitives).[7] God's work among them is a sign of his gracious purpose for them; at the same time, because of God's empowering presence, they work together with God for the accomplishment of God's gracious will in and through their community.

That God's action precedes, undergirds, and permeates the Philippians' own actions is a pervasive theme in this letter so replete with moral exhortation, as a survey of key passages will make clear. In the letter opening (1:1), Paul, whose own existence is defined by slavery to Christ, calls the Philippians "holy ones," addressing them as a community created by God's act of claiming them as his very own people "in Christ Jesus."[8] The prayer for grace and peace "from God our father and the Lord Jesus Christ" (1:2), as well as Paul's thanksgiving for the Philippians' partnership in the work of the gospel (1:3-5), underlines the fact that the fellowship and love Paul and the Philippians share is grounded in the identity and redemptive activity of the one God and one Lord whom they serve.[9] The Philippians have been Paul's partners in the work of the gospel "from the first day until now" (1:5), but this partnership is itself rooted in the initiative of God, "who began a good work among you" (1:6a). Indeed, no matter what Paul will later say about the urgency and indispensability of the Philippians' participation in the outworking of their own salvation, all of Paul's strategies of moral formation in this letter are grounded in the conviction that, ultimately, it is God who works to "bring [that good work] to completion until the day of Christ Jesus" (1:6b). Paul prays unceasingly for the Philippians, for God is the one who must cause their love to increase in all knowledge and discernment so that they can test and approve what really matters and live blamelessly until Christ's coming (1:9-10). And it is through the agency of Jesus Christ that they will be filled

---

7. εὐδοκία, Matt 11:26; Luke 10:21; Eph 1:5, 9; cf. εὐδοκέω, Matt 12:18; 17:5; Mark 1:11 par.; Luke 12:32; 1 Cor 1:21; Gal 1:15; Col 1:19; LXX Ps 43:4; 67:17; 151:5; 2 Macc 14:35; 3 Macc 2:16.

8. Cf. Exod 19:6; 1 Cor 1:30.

9. Similarly, when the apostle adds to his expression of deep longing for them the qualifier "with the compassion of Christ Jesus" (1:8), or when he refers to the Philippians' boast on his account "in Christ Jesus" (1:26), or when he asks them to welcome Epaphroditus "in the Lord" with all joy (2:29), he does so out of a bedrock conviction that the only true basis for their relationship is the life they share by virtue of the fact that God has united them all to Christ.

with "the fruit of righteousness" that brings glory and praise to God, from whom all this comes (1:11; cf. 2:11; 4:20).

As Paul relates the details of his own affairs (1:12-26), God's providential activity is everywhere presumed. Paul's imprisonment "in Christ" (1:13) has actually "resulted" in the advance of the gospel (1:12).[10] He has "been appointed" (κεῖμαι) for the defense of the gospel (1:16). He trusts that "this will turn out for [his] deliverance" (1:19).[11] Here Paul links the Philippians' prayers for him to "the supply of the Spirit of Jesus Christ," revealing once again the conjunction of divine and human actors in the outworking of God's purposes.[12] Similarly, Paul's confidence that he will in no way "be ashamed" rests on his earnest hope that God will be faithful to continue to work so that, now as always, Christ will "be exalted" through Paul's own bold speech and in Paul's very body, whether Paul lives or dies (1:20).

When the apostle turns to address the Philippians' affairs directly, God is to be found right at the center of their circumstances as well. In his absence, Paul urges them to "live as citizens" (πολιτεύεσθε, 1:27; cf. 3:20) — that is, to conduct their public, communal life in Philippi — in a manner "worthy of the gospel of Christ." This they will do only if they stand firm in the one Spirit of God[13] and together, with one soul, struggle fearlessly for the faith of the gospel, even in the face of strong opposition (1:27-28). Much of the rest of the letter is devoted to shaping the Philippians' behavior by unpacking this exhortation and driving it home with both positive and negative examples (2:1–4:3). And yet, Paul calls the community to fidelity and perseverance precisely because this "evidence of . . . [their] salvation" itself comes "from God" (1:28). Their vindication rests secure in the hands of God, who has graciously granted to them not only to trust in Christ but also to suffer for Christ's sake (1:29). God is before, behind, in, with, and under all that the Philippians are called to be and to do.

It is through the encouragement that is theirs in Christ, the comfort that comes from [God's ?] love,[14] and their sharing in the Spirit, that the Philippians are able to adopt Christ's pattern of humble self-giving service in their interactions with one another (2:1-4). Such a frame of mind expresses the reality of their belonging together "in Christ" (2:5). Their mutual forbearance, unity, and

---

10. μᾶλλον εἰς προκοπὴν τοῦ εὐαγγελίου ἐλήλυθεν.

11. τοῦτό μοι ἀποβήσεται εἰς σωτηρίαν. Cf. Job 13:16 LXX, where in the wider narrative context Job stubbornly places his hope for vindication in God alone.

12. On "supply" (ἐπιχορηγία) here, see Gordon D. Fee, *Paul's Letter to the Philippians,* NICNT (Grand Rapids: Eerdmans, 1995), pp. 134-35.

13. The parallel in 4:1, as well as Paul's usage of πνεῦμα elsewhere, suggests that the Holy Spirit is meant here. So also Fee, *Philippians,* pp. 164-66.

14. Cf. 2 Cor 13:13.

steadfast faithfulness to the gospel stems from their new identity, "children of God," and it reveals that identity to the "crooked and perverse generation" among whom they live (2:14-16). Even the Philippians' sacrificial service to Paul (2:17, 25, 30; 4:18), enacted in the mission of Epaphroditus, is to be understood as "the work of Christ" (2:30), a "fruit of the righteousness that comes through Jesus Christ" (1:11; cf. 4:17).

In chapter 3, Paul characterizes himself and the Philippians as those who worship "by the Spirit of God"[15] and "boast in Christ Jesus" rather than rely on any human status or accomplishment (3:3). The agent at the center of Paul's own story of transformation is none other than God. Because of God's apocalyptic invasion of Paul's own life, he has "suffered the loss" of all things (3:8) that he might "be found" in Christ (by God's gracious act),[16] having a righteousness that has nothing to do with his own achievement, but everything to do with God's: "the righteousness that comes through the faith of Christ: the righteousness that is from God on the basis of faith" (3:9). To have this righteousness, Paul explains, is to know Christ, to experience the power of his resurrection, to share in his sufferings, being conformed (by God! cf. 3:21) to Christ's death, that one may also come to share in Christ's resurrection from the dead (3:10-11).

Paul himself participates vigorously in God's ongoing work of transformation, single-mindedly pursuing "God's upward call in Christ Jesus" (3:12-14). But he strains forward with all his effort to grasp the goal (εἰ καὶ καταλάβω) precisely because he himself has already been grasped (κατελήμφθην) by Christ (3:12). Paul is confident that the Philippians will share his outlook (φρονεῖν) and recognize that God's transforming work in their lives calls them to bold action (3:15a); but even if they do not yet have this mature frame of mind, he rests assured that God himself will reveal (ἀποκαλύπτειν) even this to them (3:15b).

That God will complete his transforming work in Paul's life, and in the lives of the Philippians, Paul has no doubt, for his confidence rests on the fact that God has already claimed them as his people and bestowed on them a heavenly "citizenship" (3:20; cf. 1:27). Now they await a savior from heaven, "the Lord Jesus Christ, who will transform [their] humble bodies in conformity (cf. 3:10) to his glorious body." Christ will do this "by the effective power (ἐνεργεία,

---

15. Compared with Galatians, Romans, and 1–2 Corinthians, there is a curious lack of emphasis on the Spirit in Paul's moral exhortation in Philippians. Yet although he does not speak of "walking in the Spirit" or "living according to the Spirit" in Philippians (note, however, κοινωνία πνεύματος, 2:1), Paul is no less insistent in this letter that God's empowering presence is fundamental to their ongoing life in Christ.

16. For "be found" in the context of eschatological judgment, see 2 Cor 5:3; 1 Pet 1:7; 2 Pet 3:10, 14.

cf. 2:13) that enables him to subject all things to himself" (3:21). Their hope firmly fixed on Christ's sovereignty over every principality and power, earthly or heavenly,[17] Paul's beloved brothers and sisters in Philippi can, and must, "stand firm in the Lord" (4:1; cf. 1:27).

Paul's closing instructions remind the Philippians yet again that their on-going communal life is empowered by the presence and activity of God. Paul exhorts them to "rejoice in the Lord" (4:5) and to live lives of moderation and gentleness because "the Lord is near" (4:5). They are not to worry but constantly to lift up their needs to God with thankful hearts; if they do so, "God's peace will guard [their] hearts and minds in Christ Jesus" (4:6-7). They are to set their minds on worthy things and imitate Paul's manner of life; as they do, "the God of peace will be with [them]" (4:8-9). Even as he thanks his friends for their gift, Paul cannot pass up an opportunity to offer himself as an example of one who is "self-sufficient" (αὐτάρκης) through dependence on God's power and provision alone: "I can do all things through the one who strengthens me" (ἐνδυναμοῦν, 4:13).[18] And while Paul gratefully acknowledges the Philippians' financial support as an expression of their partnership with him in the work of the gospel, he reframes their gift as a sacrifice offered to God, an oblation that is itself the fruit of righteousness that comes through Jesus Christ and results in the glory of God (4:17; cf. 1:11).[19] Appropriately, the final words of the letter are devoted to God's working and God's glory: "My God will fully supply all of your need according to his riches in glory in Christ Jesus" (4:19); "to our God and father be glory for ever and ever" (4:20); "the grace of the Lord Jesus Christ be with your spirit" (4:23).

We are now in a position to appreciate the full force of Paul's admonition to "work out your own salvation *with fear and trembling*" (2:12). This is the language of theophany.[20] God is present and active among them. God's working precedes and follows, interpenetrates and undergirds, the Philippians' active participation in the ongoing realization and outworking of the salvation God has wrought for them. Cognizant that God dwells in their very midst, the Philippians cannot but respond with reverent fear and holy awe.[21]

---

17. The echoes here of Psalm 8/110 (cf. 1 Cor 15:23-28; Eph 1:20-23) may point to Christ's victory over cosmic enemies. (I owe this insight to my colleague Beverly Gaventa.)

18. For God's δύναμις, see also 3:10, 21.

19. Note Paul's use elsewhere of cultic language to describe the Philippians' service to Paul (2:17, 25, 30; 4:18).

20. Cf. Exod 15:16; Ps 2:11; Isa 19:16; 66:2, 5; Dan 4:37a; 10:11; PrMan 4; JosAs 14:10. See further Peter T. O'Brien, *Commentary on Philippians*, NIGTC (Grand Rapids: Eerdmans, 1991), pp. 282-84.

21. Compare the line of thought in 1 Pet 1:13-17.

Work Out Your Own Salvation

And yet, if we are to understand Paul's view of how what God does for us is worked out in us, it is crucial to recognize that nothing Paul says about God's prevenient and persistent acting renders the Philippians' own acting superfluous or insignificant. God is working among the Philippians, not apart from, but in and through their own volition and action. And so, Paul calls on the community to participate in God's saving work among them by deliberately seeking together to conform their attitude and behavior to Christ's own pattern of life: "just as you have always obeyed, so now . . . continue to work out your own salvation" (2:12).

Addressing the Philippians as competent moral agents, Paul frames the task of working out their salvation as a matter of "obedience." The term Paul uses here for "work," κατεργάζεσθαι, has the sense, "achieve, accomplish, bring about, produce."[22] As employed by moral philosophers, it carries the notion of exercising, practicing, developing, perfecting a skill or faculty.[23] The Philippians' obedient response is thus to exert persistent, purposeful, painstaking effort toward the full realization in their communal life of the salvation that God has begun and is bringing to completion among them.

What then, practically speaking, does Paul expect the Philippians to do? It is my contention that Paul's practices of moral formation, embodied in his apostolic ministry (including this letter), are deeply rooted in his soteriology.[24] Before examining these practices more closely, then, two preliminary remarks are in order.

First, Paul's conviction that God is at work among the Philippians

22. See Rom 7:15-18; 15:18. Cf. BDAG, p. 531; LSJ, p. 924.

23. So Plato, *Ti.* 88c. Compare Epictetus' use of the related compound, ἐξεργάζεσθαι, in the sense "exercise, develop, perfect": *Discourses* 1.4.18 (//ἐκπονεῖν); 1.7.31 (//ἀργυπνεῖν, πονεῖν); 2.20.21; 3.13.8; 3.15.13 (//φιλοπονεῖν); 3.22.44 (//ἐπιμελεῖσθαι, ζητεῖν); 4.4.26 (//γυμνάζειν); 4.10.13; *Ench.* 29.7 (//φιλοτεχνεῖν).

24. In this respect, Epictetus provides a fascinating counterpoint to Paul. As A. A. Long persuasively argues, Epictetus' approach to moral formation receives its distinctive shape from his theology, that is, his understanding of the nature of the cosmos and the place of humans in it (*Epictetus: A Stoic and Socratic Guide to Life* [Oxford: Oxford University Press, 2002]). To bring these two figures into dialog would prove immensely illuminating, but this is a task that cannot be pursued here. For an interesting probe along these lines, see Troels Engberg-Pedersen, "Self-sufficiency and Power: Divine and Human Agency in Epictetus and Paul" (version of 12 July 2004; available online at http://www.abdn.ac.uk/divinity/Gathercole/paper-EP.htm). In my view there is much interesting work still to be done in order to account for both the striking similarities and the no less crucial differences between these two brilliant moral theologians.

grounds his approach to moral formation. Paul is not attempting to impose a foreign pattern on this community from the outside. Rather, he cooperates with God in the work of conforming them to Christ, to whom they have already been united.[25] By the grace of God, who has begun and who is continuing to complete this good work among them, Christ's life, suffering, death, and resurrection now determine the pattern of the Philippians' own lives. In urging the Philippians to work out their own salvation, Paul is calling them to embody in their experience who they already are, by God's grace, in Christ.

Second, while Paul does not devote sustained attention to an analysis of the problem (as he does, for example, in Galatians 5 or Romans 6–8), it is clearly a presumption of his moral exhortation that, although God has united the Philippians to Christ and is working to conform them to the pattern of Christ, there is still another way of living open to the Philippians, foreign though it may be to their new life in Christ. This is the old way of "the flesh," the way of ambition, pride, self-interest, and factionalism. It is displayed by "some" of the brothers who see in Paul's imprisonment an opportunity for their own advancement (1:15, 17) and by those who (in contrast to Timothy) seek their own interests rather than those of Jesus Christ (2:21). It is the frame of mind centered on earthly things (οἱ τὰ ἐπίγεια φρονοῦντες, 3:19; cf. Rom 8:5), devoted to the gratification of selfish appetites, that is evident in more extreme form among those whom Paul characterizes as "enemies of the cross of Christ" (3:18). In exhorting the Philippians to work out their salvation, Paul urges: "Do nothing from selfish ambition and conceit (2:3; cf. 1:15, 17); do not look to your own interests (2:4; cf. 2:21); do everything without grumbling and disputing (2:14)." The disciplined rejection of these old patterns of thought and life stands as the necessary corollary to embodying the new pattern that is now their own by virtue of their union with Christ.

Paul's strategy of moral formation in Philippians centers on the call to adopt a frame of mind, an outlook on the world, that leads to habits of living that conform to the pattern of Christ's obedience to God in self-giving for others. The theme of a renewed mind is sounded from the very beginning of the letter, where Paul prays that their love will increase yet more and more in knowledge and discernment so that they can test and approve what really matters (1:9). He urges them repeatedly to "think/be intent on" (φρονεῖν) the same thing (2:2; 4:2; cf. Rom 12:16; 15:5; 2 Cor 13:11)/the one thing (2:2; cf. 3:13), which is not simply a general exhortation to concord, but a call to unity based on having *this* attitude among themselves (2:5; 3:15): the attitude displayed by Jesus Christ (2:6-11) that is their own by virtue of their union with Christ (2:5b; 4:2,

25. This point is emphasized by Hooker, "Partner," pp. 98-99.

ἐν κυρίῳ) and that is modeled before them by Paul and by those who emulate Paul's pattern of life (3:4-17).[26]

Throughout the letter, Paul seeks to foster this attitude of mind that leads to right action — that is, to lives lived in conformity to Christ's. Like other good moral philosophers of his day, he approaches the task of moral formation from a number of different angles, employing an array of interlocking strategies.

Central to Paul's whole approach to moral formation is his retelling of the story of Jesus.[27] Whatever speculations one may entertain about the pre-Pauline origin of the so-called "Christ hymn," Paul offers it to the Philippians as the foundational paradigm for "living as citizens in a manner worthy of the gospel" (1:27).[28] In humility (ταπεινοφροσύνη), they must regard (ἡγεῖσθαι) others as better than themselves, so that they carefully attend to (σκοπεῖν) the interests of others rather than to their own interests (2:3-4). This is so because Christ himself did not regard (ἡγεῖσθαι) equality with God as something to be exploited for his own advantage, but instead humbled (ταπεινοῦν) himself and became obedient, even to death on the cross, for the sake of others (2:6-8).[29] Just as Jesus relied on God alone for vindication (2:10-11), so the Philippians are called to struggle courageously side by side for the faith of the gospel, patiently enduring opposition and suffering for Christ's sake, eagerly awaiting the appearing of their heavenly deliverer (1:27-29; 3:20-21).[30]

The story of Christ is played out again and again in the lives of others whom the Philippians are called to imitate. Throughout the letter, Paul offers a series of human examples whose conduct the Philippians must either emulate or eschew. Each is laid to the touchstone of Jesus' pattern of life. Timothy, who

26. In his perceptive study, "Transformation of the Mind and Moral Discernment in Paul" (in *Early Christianity and Classical Culture: Comparative Studies in Honor of Abraham J. Malherbe*, ed. J. T. Fitzgerald et al. [Leiden: Brill, 2003], pp. 215-36), Luke Timothy Johnson characterizes Paul's viewpoint in the following terms: "The human νοῦς is in process of renewal by the mind of Christ, so that the expression of φρόνησις within the community that is the body of the Messiah is to act according to the pattern of life demonstrated above all in the obedient faith and self-disposing love of Jesus" (p. 231).

27. Cf. Wayne A. Meeks, *The Origins of Christian Morality: The First Two Centuries* (New Haven: Yale University Press, 1993), p. 196.

28. See Stephen E. Fowl, *The Story of Christ in the Ethics of Paul*, JSNTSup 36 (Sheffield: Sheffield Academic Press, 1990), pp. 77-101.

29. Although Paul does not speak here explicitly of Christ's death "for others," it is implicit in the rhetoric of the passage as a whole, which exhorts the Philippians to give themselves for one another. Moreover, basic to Paul's conception of the cross is the notion that Jesus "loved me and gave himself for me" (Gal 2:20; cf. "for us," 1 Thess 5:10; Gal 3:13; 2 Cor 5:21; Rom 5:8; "for our sins," Gal 1:4; 1 Cor 15:3). It is inconceivable that such an idea would be absent here.

30. Living in expectation of the *parousia* of the Lord is a recurrent theme in this letter (1:6, 10; 2:16; 4:5).

together with Paul is named a "slave" of Christ in the letter opening, recalls Jesus' own self-emptying in taking on the form of a slave (2:7). Paul commends his coworker as one who "serves as a slave" in the work of the gospel (δουλεύω, 2:22). Moreover, Timothy displays the Christ-like characteristics that Paul exhorts the Philippians to embody: unlike those who seek their own interests, Timothy is genuinely concerned with the Philippians' interests, precisely because he seeks "the interests of Jesus Christ" (2:20-21).

Paul further encourages the Philippians to see the pattern of Christ's self-donation working itself out in Epaphroditus, who risked his life, drawing near "to the point of death" (μέχρι θανάτου) for Paul's sake (2:30; cf. 2:8). He tells them to welcome Epaphroditus back with joy and hold him in honor, along with all "such people" (2:29). Paul's comment suggests that there are still other worthy examples of this cruciform pattern of life to be found; indeed, there are some among the Philippians themselves. The Philippians are actively to seek out such people, carefully observe their manner of life, and imitate their conduct (3:17; cf. 4:9).

Paul views himself as having a unique, formative role in shaping the Philippians' manner of life in Christ.[31] He explicitly calls the Philippians to join him in imitating Christ[32] and to pay careful attention to those who live according to the same christomorphic pattern (τύπος) that they have in Paul (3:17). Not simply Paul's teaching, but his whole manner of life displays the pattern of Christ, and so they are to model themselves after the things they have learned and received and heard and seen in Paul (4:9).

Even in his absence, Paul continues to play this paradigmatic role for them through his letter. Just as he prays that they will grow in love and knowledge and perception so that they can discern "what really matters" (1:9-10), so also Paul models for them such devotion to the interests of Christ as he reports on his own circumstances. Though he languishes in prison, what matters is that the gospel is advancing; though some proclaim Christ from envy and rivalry, what matters is that Christ is proclaimed; though he faces a possible death sentence, what matters is that Christ will be exalted through him by life or by death (1:12-20). Just as Paul urges the Philippians to seek others' interests rather than their own, he himself considers the Philippians' need for him to remain with them for their progress in the faith to matter more than his own

31. See Beverly Roberts Gaventa, "Apostle and Church in 2 Corinthians," in *Pauline Theology Volume II: 1 & 2 Corinthians*, ed. D. M. Hay (Minneapolis: Fortress, 1993), pp. 182-99, esp. pp. 193-99; John H. Schütz, *Paul and the Anatomy of Apostolic Authority*, SNTSMS 26 (Cambridge: Cambridge University Press, 1975).

32. For a defense of this translation of συμμιμηταί μου γίνεσθε, see Hooker, "Partner," pp. 93-94.

desire "to depart and be with Christ," which from his point of view is "far better" (1:21-26).

Most striking is the way in which Paul narrates his own life story in chapter 3 so that it corresponds to the pattern of Jesus' story told in the Christ hymn.[33] As Jesus did not regard (ἡγεῖσθαι) equality with God as something to be employed for his own advantage, but emptied himself by becoming a slave (2:6-7), so Paul, Christ's "slave" (1:1), regards (ἡγεῖσθαι) everything he once valued, but now has lost for Christ's sake, to be less than worthless in view of the surpassing value of knowing Christ (3:7-8). God manifests the power of Christ's resurrection in Paul's life in paradoxical fashion, by conforming him to Christ's death, as Paul comes to share in the sufferings of Christ (3:9-10).[34] Yet Paul presses on in the hope of fully sharing in Christ's resurrection, because it is for this very thing that Christ has laid hold of him (3:11-14). In relating his own story in this manner, Paul does not present himself as a lone, heroic figure who imitates Christ out of his own immense reservoir of individual virtue and strength.[35] Rather, Paul's life replicates the pattern of Christ's only because Paul has been united to Christ. His righteousness is not his own, but Christ's, and it is Christ who now lives in him, working that righteousness out to its glorious consummation.[36] Because the Philippians stand in the same relationship to Christ as does Paul, and because God has granted to them also the grace of suffering for Christ (1:29), Paul can present himself to them as one whose mindset and way of life is a pattern for all who, with him, are pressing on toward maturity in Christ (3:15-16).

Even where Paul cites a negative example to serve as a warning, he evaluates the conduct the Philippians are to shun in light of the story of Christ. The unnamed "many" in 3:18-19 are "enemies of the cross of Christ" precisely because in adopting a frame of mind (φρονεῖν) that is fixed on earthly things — the satisfaction of their own appetites — they reject the way of obedient, self-giving service to God and to others that is the way of the cross. In contrast, Paul asserts, our "citizenship," that is, our "body politic," our "commonwealth"

---

33. On Paul's "christomorphic historiography," see John M. G. Barclay, "Paul's Story: Theology as Testimony," in *Narrative Dynamics in Paul: A Critical Assessment,* ed. B. W. Longenecker (Louisville: Westminster John Knox, 2002), pp. 133-56.

34. Cf. 2 Cor 4:7-18 and the illuminating study by Steven J. Kraftchick, "Death in Us, Life in You: The Apostolic Medium," in *Pauline Theology Volume II: 1 & 2 Corinthians,* ed. D. M. Hay (Minneapolis: Fortress, 1993), pp. 156-81.

35. On the incompatibility of the way of Christian discipleship with the classical tradition of individual virtue represented by Aristotle, see Samuel Wells, "The Disarming Virtue of Stanley Hauerwas," *Scottish Journal of Theology* 52 (1999): 82-88.

36. Cf. Karl Barth's comments on Phil 3:9b in *The Epistle to the Philippians,* trans. J. W. Leitch (Richmond: John Knox, 1962), pp. 99-103.

(πολίτευμα), is in the heavens, and from it we eagerly await our savior. However, this expectant waiting does not lead to quietistic escapism, but rather to "standing firm" (4:1; cf. 1:27; 3:16) and "living as citizens" in a manner worthy of the gospel (1:27), which is to say: living lives in union with Christ, sharing his humiliation and sufferings, being conformed to his death, all in the firm hope of sharing his resurrection, when he will transform "the body of our humiliation" and conform it to "his body of glory" (3:20-21).

The call to adopt a frame of mind and a pattern of living in conformity to Christ is clearly central to what Paul means by "working out your own salvation." Imitation of Christ's life and of other lives that display this pattern of faithful, self-giving obedience, is the ongoing task of the community.[37] A number of other features of Paul's moral exhortation in Philippians are noteworthy as interconnected strategies that support and sustain the formation of this frame of mind and pattern of living. I will mention six. There is space to touch on them only briefly:

(1) Paul stresses the importance of *forming right habits of mind.* In examining the call to imitation, we have already encountered this theme in the language of "adopting a mindset" (φρονεῖν), "regarding" (ἡγεῖσθαι), "carefully considering" (σκοπεῖν). In 4:8, the apostle widens the scope of his exhortation to encompass *whatever* is true, honorable, just, pure, lovely, commendable, excellent, worthy of praise. These are the things on which they must fix their minds (λογίζσθαι). Such worthy objects of contemplation are by no means abstractions: they are epitomized in what the Philippians have learned and received and heard and seen in Paul's own life (4:9). Indeed, in the following section of the letter, Paul himself exemplifies this discipline of mind to which he calls them. He has learned (μανθάνειν) contentment; he knows (οἰδέναι) how to handle both abasement and abundance; he has become an initiate (μυεῖν) in the art of living well in every circumstance, through fellowship with the one who gives him strength (4:11-13). This discipline they too are called to master through unceasing, prayerful dependence on the God who will supply all of their needs (4:6-7; 19).

(2) Along with right thinking, Paul's moral discourse stresses *diligent practice of the cruciform life.* His exhortation to "keep thinking about these

---

37. In addition, Paul alludes to a number of scriptural examples, both positive and negative: Job (1:19; cf. Job 13:16 LXX); Daniel (2:15; cf. Dan 12:3 LXX); the wilderness generation (grumbling, 2:14 [cf. Exod 15:22–16:12, etc.]; blameless children, 2:15 [contrast Deut 32:5]). It is unclear whether any of the Philippians would have recognized these allusions, but at minimum, they show the impact of scriptural paradigms on Paul's thinking about the shape of life in Christ. In other letters, the appeal to scriptural figures as patterns for those in Christ is more explicit (e.g., 1 Corinthians 10; Gal 4:21-31; Romans 4).

things" (ταῦτα λογίζεσθε, 4:8) is matched in the following verse with another: "The things you have learned and received and heard and seen in me — keep doing these things" (ταῦτα πράσσετε, 4:9). The Philippians' life in Christ is a journey that requires a disciplined, persevering practice of the faith. Paul devotes himself to their progress (προκοπή) and joy in faith (1:25; cf. 1:12). He depicts their life as a community in Philippi as an athletic event in which they strive side by side for the faith of the gospel (1:27), struggling in the same contest in which Paul himself is engaged (1:29-30; 4:3).[38] They, together with Paul, are running flat out in a race whose completion demands a single-minded focus on grasping the goal at the finish line (3:11).

(3) As Paul's language of "striving side by side" (συναθλεῖν) suggests, this is not a solitary journey or an individual athletic event.[39] Paul's practice of moral formation in Philippians relies heavily on *fostering significant relationships* within the community. Paul employs familial language throughout the letter: the Philippians are "children of God" (2:15), Paul's "brothers and sisters" (1:12; 2:25; 3:1, 13, 17; 4:1, 8, 21; cf. 1:14). God is their common "father" (1:2; 2:11; 4:20).[40] And although Paul does not use the term "friend" or "friendship," he employs many of the themes and conventions of ancient friendship.[41] The Philippians' relationships with Paul and with one another are embodied in practices such as partnering in a common task, offering help and encouragement, expressing practical concern for one another's welfare, refraining from grumbling and disputing, exchanging letters and personal visits, sharing resources, and praying for one another. These relationships play a vital role in their ongoing transformation.

(4) A further notable feature of Paul's moral exhortation in Philippians is the repeated *exhortation to rejoice*. Joy characterizes Paul's attitude toward the Philippians themselves, whom he names "beloved and longed-for brothers and sisters, my joy and my crown" (4:1). He rejoices in their partnership in the gospel

---

38. Note the parallel between their being granted by God to suffer for Christ's sake (1:29) and Paul's sharing in Christ's sufferings and so being conformed to his death (3:10).

39. Cf. "fellow soldier" (2:25).

40. Note also Paul's reference to his relationship with Timothy as that of "father" and "child" (2:22).

41. See L. Michael White, "Morality Between Two Worlds: A Paradigm of Friendship in Philippians," in *Greeks, Romans, and Christians: Essays in Honor of Abraham J. Malherbe*, ed. D. L. Balch et al. (Minneapolis: Fortress, 1990), pp. 201-15; John T. Fitzgerald, ed., *Friendship, Flattery, and Frankness of Speech: Studies on Friendship in the New Testament World*, NovTSup 82 (Leiden: Brill, 1996); idem, ed., *Greco-Roman Perspectives on Friendship* (Atlanta: Scholars, 1997). Stephen E. Fowl, *A Commentary on Philippians*, The Two Horizons New Testament Commentary (Grand Rapids: Eerdmans, 2005) offers a theological commentary on Philippians that devotes careful attention to the theme of friendship.

(1:4; 4:10); he seeks their progress and joy in faith (1:25); he appeals to them to make his joy full by their conformity to Christ (2:2). Such joy must also characterize the Philippians' attitude toward one another (2:28-29). Paul rejoices at the progress of the gospel through God's sovereign control over the circumstances of his own imprisonment (1:18), and he commands the Philippians to rejoice together with him as the genuineness of their own faith is made manifest in the day-to-day circumstances of their lives (2:17-18; 3:1; 4:4). Paul's repeated command to "rejoice in the Lord" flows from the heart of his soteriology. Because God has put right the Philippians' relationships with God and with one another — because God is actively at work in all of their working and striving — because the beginning and the end of their salvation is in God's hands, they *must* rejoice. Progress in joy is something for which they must labor and strive, for it is progress in the life of faith to which they have been called in Christ (cf. 1:25).

(5) In their striving for joy, Paul exhorts them to *the discipline of constant prayer* (4:6). They are to banish anxiety by thankfully bringing their requests before God in every circumstance (4:6). As they do so, God will grant them the peace that will preserve them in the frame of mind that is properly theirs in Christ Jesus (4:7), and God will prove faithful to meet their needs (4:19). Their private and communal prayers, assisted by the Spirit of Jesus Christ, play an essential, effective role in working out God's purposes for Paul's salvation (1:19). Similarly, Paul intercedes earnestly, yet with thankfulness and joy, for them, knowing that God will be faithful to use his prayers in bringing to completion the good work that God is doing in their midst (1:3-11).

(6) Finally, both an outgrowth of the Philippians' transformation by God and a means to their further transformation is their continued *participation in the work of the gospel.* As a result of the work God has begun among them, the Philippians have been partners with Paul in the work of the gospel right from the very beginning (1:5). From the time Paul left Philippi, they have participated in Paul's mission through their financial support (4:15-16) and through their prayers (1:19). Among the Philippians are some whom Paul names explicitly as "coworkers" (2:25; 4:3). But all of them share with the imprisoned Paul the grace of defending and confirming the gospel in the very heart of imperial power (1:7; 4:22) by helping to bear the burden of Paul's affliction (4:14) through their giving and through their intercession (1:19). What is more, God has granted to them all the privilege of suffering together on Christ's behalf in Philippi. Though they have different roles to play than that of Paul the apostle, they too struggle in the same contest of faith in which Paul is engaged (1:29-30). Paul does not need to exhort the Philippians to engage in mission. As they work out their own salvation together in unity and peace with one another — as they are conformed by God to the self-giving, suffering, and rising of Jesus — they

271

themselves *are* a proclamation of the rectifying power of God.[42] They shine like stars in the universe, holding fast the word of life (2:12-16).[43]

Working Out Salvation in Contemporary North America

I began this study by quoting one Methodist biblical scholar, theologian, and preacher. It is perhaps fitting that I conclude by appealing to another. How is what God does *for* us worked out *in* us? John Wesley answers Morna Hooker's question with an apt homiletical epitome of Pauline soteriology: "God works, therefore we *can* work; God works, therefore we *must* work."[44] To this, I would add a third affirmation that is absolutely crucial to Paul's thought: God works, therefore we *do* work.

God is at work: God's work of salvation manifests itself in a community of "holy ones" who have been decisively transformed through union with Christ, a community that God continues to transform so that their lives increasingly conform to the pattern of Christ's life, death, and resurrection as they participate together with Paul in the work of the gospel.

Therefore, we can and must and do work also: Paul calls the Philippians to holiness. They are to participate in God's saving work among them by striving together to conform their frame of mind and thus their pattern of life to Christ's own. In seeking to form a christomorphic community, Paul employs a wide array of strategies of moral exhortation, but all are rooted in his deepest convictions about what God has done and continues to do for the salvation of the entire cosmos.

Although Philippians was written to a particular community of believers living in a far distant time and place, contemporary North American Christian communities rightly read Paul's letter as addressed to us also, for we too are members of the one universal Church to which Paul and the Philippians belong.[45] Like Paul and his brothers and sisters in Philippi, we are to understand

---

42. Cf. 2 Cor 3:1-3.

43. Note also 4:5, τὸ ἐπιεικὲς ὑμῶν γνωσθήτω πᾶσιν ἀνθρώποις. For further reflections on the question of the Philippians' involvement in Paul's mission, see James P. Ware, *The Mission of the Church in Paul's Letter to the Philippians in the Context of Ancient Judaism,* NovTSup 120 (Leiden: Brill, 2005); Michael D. Barram, *Mission and Moral Reflection in Paul,* StBL 75 (New York: Peter Lang, 2005).

44. "On Working Out Our Own Salvation" (1785), in *John Wesley's Sermons: An Anthology,* ed. A. C. Outler and R. P. Heitzenrater (Nashville: Abingdon, 1991), pp. 486-92.

45. See Robert Jenson, "The Religious Power of Scripture," *Scottish Journal of Theology* 52 (1999): 89-105, here pp. 98-99.

our identity as God's holy people as a gift, the result of God's singular work of rectification in freeing us from sin and death and uniting us to Christ by the Spirit, a work that God continues to bring to completion in our midst through conforming our lives, corporate and individual, to the pattern of Christ. And because God is at work among us, we too are called in our own context to holiness: to "live as citizens" — that is, to conduct our public, communal life — in a manner "worthy of the gospel of Christ" (1:27).

Paul's letter challenges contemporary communities of faith to ask, "What would it mean for us, as God's holy people, to 'work out' together, in our particular setting and circumstances, the salvation that God is working among us?" Although the answers to this question will be many and varied, just as the contexts of individual churches vary, Philippians suggests a number of characteristics that should be evident in all communities seeking to grow in conformity to Christ.

First, such churches recognize that God's prior and on-going saving work is the ground of the community's identity as God's holy people, the basis for all of our own striving increasingly to embody holiness in our life together. The call to "work out our own salvation" is not an invitation to focus on ourselves or to trust in our own powers and abilities; it is a summons to a radically God-centered manner of life that exalts the supremacy of God in all things and that relies wholly on the sufficiency of God's grace to us in Christ in every circumstance. Far from christianizing our culture's messages of self-help, self-reliance, and self-sufficiency, such communities will proclaim and embody a gospel that focuses on God's work of redeeming the cosmos for God's own glory, a gospel that leads people continually to place their hope in God alone.

Moreover, these churches understand that hope in God and reliance on God's grace does not promote quietism or permit disengagement from the world. Rather, such churches deliberately and energetically work out their salvation together by engaging in practices that cooperate in God's work of conforming them to the pattern of Christ's life. As we saw in our brief survey above, such practices are best learned through imitation and sustained through significant, ongoing, face-to-face and heart-to-heart relationships. Fostering such intimate community among church members is no small challenge in our individualistic culture, but it is vital to the formation and nourishment in Christian disciples of the "frame of mind" that is ours by virtue of our union with Christ.

This frame of mind comes to expression in a christomorphic pattern of life that is deeply engaged in God's mission in the world. Again and again in this letter, Paul emphasizes that union with Christ leads to a joyful embodiment of Christ's own self-giving love for others, both inside and outside the community. As the Philippians demonstrate solidarity with one another in a context of deprivation and suffering,[46] as their extreme poverty overflows in generous part-nership with Paul in mission,[47] as their allegiance to a crucified Lord challenges every pretension to power and glory based on violence and oppression, they themselves *are* a proclamation of the gospel. Churches that understand their identity and calling as God's holy people recognize that mission is not one of a number of things the church does; mission belongs to the church's very nature as God's holy people in the world.[48]

Inevitably, churches that embody the pattern of Christ's faithful, self-disposing love will come to share in Christ's sufferings. This too is a gracious gift from God (1:29-30). It is embraced in the sure knowledge that there is a deep fellowship with Christ himself in the midst of suffering and in the firm confidence that we who in this way are being conformed to Christ's death will also share in Christ's resurrection (3:10-11; 3:20–4:1). Animated by this hope, God's holy people press on to lay hold of that for which Christ Jesus has laid hold of us, confident that God, who began this good work among us, will in-deed carry it on to completion until the day of Christ Jesus.

---

46. For a convincing argument that the Philippians' suffering was largely, though not ex-clusively, economic, see Oakes, *Philippians*, pp. 77-102.

47. Note also the deep commitment to sharing economic resources expressed in their ea-ger participation in Paul's collection for the poor among the saints in Jerusalem (2 Cor 8:1-5).

48. For the recovery of this insight in a post-Christendom North American context, see the publications of the Gospel and Our Culture Network (http://www.gocn.org), including Darrell L. Guder et al., *Missional Church: A Vision for the Sending of the Church in North America* (Grand Rapids: Eerdmans, 1998); Lois Y. Barrett et al., *Treasure in Clay Jars: Patterns in Missional Faithfulness* (Grand Rapids: Eerdmans, 2004).

The Sanctification of the Imagination in 1 Thessalonians

Andy Johnson

At a theology conference where the nature of ecclesial holiness was being discussed, a pastor from Guyana told the following story. One of their (outdoor) worship services was interrupted when a man ran toward them. A second man with a pitchfork was chasing him screaming threats that he was going to murder the first man. The whole assembly moved between the two men, placing their very bodies in harm's way, refusing to allow the second man to carry out his threats. They also began to talk to both men, exploring the nature of the dispute and seeking to effect reconciliation. Enabled by the Spirit, their very concrete, embodied action displayed the cruciform character of the Holy God in their social context. In addition, by means of that action (which literally required a network of communal relations to be carried out), the Holy Spirit was at work shaping, transforming, indeed, *sanctifying the imaginations* of individuals within that *ekklēsia*.

My intentional framing of this story with this sort of theological language arises from my reading of 1 Thessalonians. This essay argues that Paul's discourse in 1 Thessalonians indicates that God effects sanctification/holiness for the *ekklēsia* as a whole and for persons within it through grace-enabled, embodied practices that require a network of communal relations.[1] Paul depicts

---

1. While I am not using the word "practice" in any technically precise way, my appeal to "embodied practices" has similarities with the broad movement that Nicholas M. Healey calls the "new ecclesiology," e.g., Lindbeck, Hauerwas, Hütter, Tanner ("Practices and the New Ecclesiology: Misplaced Concreteness?" *International Journal of Systematic Theology* 5 [2003]: 287-308). Cf. also Sam Powell and Michael Lodahl, *Embodied Holiness: Toward a Corporate Theology of Spiritual Growth* (Downers Grove, Ill.: InterVarsity, 1999).

I consider it an honor to dedicate this essay to Alex Deasley, teacher, mentor, and friend. Without his patient instruction, encouragement, and confidence in me, I could not have become a teacher of the NT.

his audience as *one* eschatological instantiation of Israel reconfigured around a crucified Lord.[2] As such they are called to be an embodiment of the holiness/ character of God, a holiness reconfigured as "cruciformity." Crucially, Paul depicts such holiness/sanctification as happening in the life of this *ekklēsia*. In short it occurs when God *transforms* the character, dispositions, and allegiances of *persons* within the *ekklēsia* through grace-enabled, embodied, practices. Such transformation might best be referred to as *the sanctification of the imagination,* a divine activity that requires an *ecclesial* framework. Hence, while God does indeed seek to sanctify individual persons, the church is not simply an external aid to what is essentially an internal, asocial, sanctification.[3] Rather, God's primary aim is to create alternative, sanctified, social bodies in which God's cruciform character is visibly embodied, i.e., "colonies of cruciformity."[4]

An Eschatological Instantiation of Israel in Thessalonica

Israel was brought into existence as a people when, in faithfulness to the covenant with the patriarchs (Exod 2:24), God led them out of Egypt and gave them Torah at Sinai to provide the pattern for their life together. This covenant-keeping faithfulness and liberating activity manifest in the Exodus was for God's people "a transparent window into God's own character."[5] And it was God's very character that defined holiness, a holiness or character that was also to be the mark that distinguished God's elect covenant people from the nations around them (e.g., Lev 11:44-45; 19:2; 22:31-33). Their life together was to be characterized by actions that mimicked God's faithful actions toward them in the Exodus (e.g., Lev 19:33-37). Acknowledging the failure of the nation as a whole to mirror the holiness of God, some second temple Jews drew on a common prophetic tradition that in the messianic age God would restore his people's holiness by pouring out God's Spirit on/into them (Ezek

2. By "eschatological instantiation of Israel," I mean one specific embodiment/example of what Israel was to become among the nations in the messianic age according to a common prophetic tradition (see below). I do not mean that this particular church or the Church as a whole has displaced Israel as God's elect. The language of "reconfiguration" comes from Terence L. Donaldson, *Paul and the Gentiles: Remapping the Apostle's Convictional World* (Minneapolis: Fortress, 1997), p. 236.

3. Here I have modified the language of Miroslav Volf, *After Our Likeness: The Church as the Image of the Trinity* (Grand Rapids: Eerdmans, 1998), p. 172.

4. Michael J. Gorman, *Cruciformity: Paul's Narrative Spirituality of the Cross* (Grand Rapids: Eerdmans, 2001), p. 349.

5. Joel B. Green, *Salvation* (St. Louis: Chalice, 2003), pp. 72-73.

36–37; Joel 2:28-29). In Ezekiel 36–37 (LXX) Yahweh promises to take his people "out of the nations" (36:24), give them "a new heart" (36:26) and to "give my Spirit in/into you all" (36:26-27, 37:6).[6] The end result of all of this is expressed in 36:23b where Yahweh says: "And the nations will know that I, myself, am the Lord *when I manifest my holiness by means of you (pl.)* before their eyes." Hence, the result of all this was to be the public display of Yahweh's character/holiness before the eyes of the nations by means of their life together. In the messianic age Israel was to become an eschatological instantiation of the holiness of God.

For Paul that messianic age had arrived, but in a most unexpected way, i.e., via a crucified messiah. When Paul and the earliest church claimed that God was in *the crucified messiah* (2 Cor 5:19), that the one who had experienced crucifixion and death at the hands of the Roman Empire was *Lord*, it was scandalous and foolish (1 Cor 1:23).[7] This one was "the *Holy* one of God," the one in whom the Holy Spirit came to dwell.[8] For Paul, this Jesus is the exalted *Lord* who, then and now, remains marked by a cruciform character; he is "messiah having been *and remaining* crucified" (1 Cor 1:23).[9] And this crucified messiah has become for us, among other things, holiness (ἁγιασμὸς) from God (1 Cor 1:30). He reveals the very character of the God of Israel, and thereby the nature of God's holiness. Therefore *the Jew from Nazareth who hangs on the cross does so as a public display of God's holiness, revealing the character of Yahweh to be cruciform.*[10] In Stephen Barton's terms, holiness has been dislocated and relocated in the *crucified Lord*.[11] Hence, the character of the sanctity/holiness which derives from this God may best be described as "cruciformity."[12]

In 1 Thessalonians Paul is clearly concerned with the holiness of his audience. Although this audience is predominantly, if not wholly, made up of

---

6. Unless otherwise noted, all translations are my own.

7. On the early ("binitarian") treatment of Jesus as divine in the context of Jewish monotheism, see Larry W. Hurtado, *Lord Jesus Christ: Devotion to Jesus in Earliest Christianity* (Grand Rapids: Eerdmans, 2003).

8. On which, see Kent Brower, "The Holy One and His Disciples: Holiness and Ecclesiology in Mark," in this volume, pp. 57-75.

9. The effect of the perfect tense participle, ἐσταυρωμένον. Cf. Mark 16:6.

10. So Gorman, *Cruciformity*, pp. 17-18.

11. Stephen C. Barton, "Dislocating and Relocating Holiness: A New Testament Study," in *Holiness Past and Present*, ed. Stephen C. Barton (London: T&T Clark, 2003), pp. 193-213, (p. 205).

12. Cf. Paul Minear, "The Holy and the Sacred," *Theology Today*, 47 (1990-91): 5-12, (8) as well as Gorman's reflections (*Cruciformity*, p. 18, n. 29). For the further development of similar reflections along trinitarian lines, see Michael Gorman's essay in this volume, "'You Shall Be Cruciform for I Am Cruciform': Paul's Trinitarian Reconstruction of Holiness," pp. 148-66.

Gentiles, he depicts them as a part of God's *elect* people in covenant relationship with Yahweh (1:4). Indeed, he depicts them in such a way that one can almost read their story out of the portions of Ezekiel 36–37 (LXX) referred to above.[13] They have turned "away from idols to be enslaved to the *living* and true God" (1:9) and their call by this God was not to impurity (4:7). Hence, in Ezekiel's terms, they have been cleansed/saved from their impurities and idols.[14] Depicted as no longer among the "nations/gentiles who do not know God" (4:5), they have (in some sense) been "taken out of the nations" who do not know this God,[15] who "gives his Holy Spirit into you all" (4:8).[16] Indeed, one might even say that in the transformation of their imaginations (on which see below) God has given them a "new heart."[17] Such allusions suggest that Paul understands his Thessalonian audience as having been "grafted into" the elect people of God (to use his later language from Romans 11) and to function as one local eschatological instantiation of that people, albeit one now reconfigured around a crucified Lord.[18] As such, enabled by the giving of the eschatological Holy Spirit, and the conversion and sanctification of their imaginations/hearts, the result was to be the same as that expressed by Ezekiel, i.e., the public display of *this Lord's* character/holiness before the eyes of the nations by means of their life together. They were to be an embodiment of the very holiness of

13. For what follows, cf. Jeffrey A. D. Weima, "'How You Must Walk to Please God': Holiness and Discipleship in 1 Thessalonians," in *Patterns of Discipleship in the New Testament*, ed. Richard N. Longenecker (Grand Rapids: Eerdmans, 1996), pp. 98-119, (pp. 110-12).

14. Compare Ezek 36:25b (καθαρισθήσεσθε ἀπὸ πασῶν τῶν <u>ἀκαθαρσιῶν</u> ὑμῶν καὶ <u>ἀπὸ πάντων τῶν εἰδώλων</u> ὑμῶν) and 36:29a (καὶ σώσω ὑμᾶς ἐκ πασῶν τῶν <u>ἀκαθαρσιῶν</u> ὑμῶν) with 1 Thess 1:9 (καὶ πῶς ἐπεστρέψατε πρὸς τὸν θεὸν <u>ἀπὸ τῶν εἰδώλων</u>) and 4:7 (οὐ γὰρ ἐκάλεσεν ἡμᾶς ὁ θεὸς <u>ἐπὶ ἀκαθαρσίᾳ</u>).

15. Compare 1 Thess 4:5 (τὰ ἔθνη τὰ μὴ εἰδότα τὸν θεόν) with Ezek 36:24a (λήμψομαι ὑμᾶς ἐκ τῶν ἐθνῶν).

16. Compare 1 Thess 4:8 (διδόντα τὸ πνεῦμα αὐτοῦ τὸ ἅγιον εἰς ὑμᾶς) with Ezek 37:6 (δώσω πνεῦμά μου εἰς ὑμᾶς). Cf. also Ezek 36:26a, 27a.

17. In Ezekiel "new heart" obviously does not refer to a "conversion" as with this predominantly Gentile audience, but instead to a new disposition enabling the people of Israel to keep the commands of Yahweh. Whether Paul is appropriating the language of Ezekiel 36–37 consciously or unconsciously in this epistle, he is refracting Israel's scriptural traditions through the lens of "an ecclesiocentric hermeneutic" (Richard Hays, *Echoes of Scripture in the Letters of Paul* [New Haven: Yale University Press, 1989]).

18. I am aware that such language can be read as "supersessionist" and am also aware of the complexity of this issue which cannot be addressed here in detail. I can only say that I reject a strong supersessionist reading of Paul. Hence, with the language above, I do not mean to imply that this audience or all of Paul's predominantly Gentile audiences as a whole, is what now constitutes Israel without remainder. That is, I do not mean that these churches or the Church as a whole has now displaced Israel as God's elect people.

God, a public display of the cruciform God in Thessalonica. We turn now to a more detailed description of the way this unfolds in the letter.

Response to the Gospel: Enslavement to God

In 1:6 Paul portrays his audience as one, who after receiving his message (λόγον) in much "much tribulation/pressure," "became imitators of us and of the Lord." The result of this imitation was that *their corporate life together, their ecclesial body as a whole,* became an example[19] to all those who are faithful/ believe in Macedonia and Achaia (v. 7). In v. 8, Paul then says that from this audience the same message (λόγος) about the Lord went out and that their πίστις to God has gone forth in every place. Paul has no need to speak about their πίστις because it is being announced by others outside their city in their report of the kind of entrance Paul and his companions had with his audience (v. 9). This entrance is further described[20] with the long phrase, "how you turned to God away from idols to be enslaved to the living and true God and to await his Son from heaven" (vv. 9-10). It is the totality of this phrase which defines their πίστις in this context. Hence, their πίστις is defined in terms of three verbs: "turned," "to be enslaved," "to await."

Since religion permeated every aspect of city life in this culture, a "turning to God away from idols" that can be announced by others outside their city is not only a reference to an inner change of disposition. Rather, it also refers to actions that would have been publicly visible resulting in "much tribulation/ pressure" (1:6).[21] For example, no longer making sacrifices to the emperor or the goddess Roma would signal their disloyalty to the empire.[22] Refusing to cel-

---

19. Reading τύπον with NA[27] rather than τύπους on which, see Bruce M. Metzger, *A Textual Commentary on the Greek New Testament: A Companion Volume to the United Bible Societies' Greek New Testament (third edition)*, corrected ed. (London/New York: United Bible Societies, 1975), p. 629.

20. Taking the καὶ as explicative.

21. Such θλῖψις was likely characterized by social ostracism, verbal harassment, possible political sanctions, and perhaps even sporadic physical violence (Todd Still, *Conflict at Thessalonica: A Pauline Church and Its Neighbors*, JSNTSup 183 [Sheffield: Sheffield Academic Press, 1999], p. 217; cf. John Barclay, "Conflict in Thessalonica," *Catholic Biblical Quarterly* 55 [1993]: 512-30, [513-16]).

22. On the influence of the imperial cult in Thessalonica and the challenge Paul's language would have presented to it, see J. R. Harrison, "Paul and the Imperial Gospel at Thessaloniki," *Journal for the Study of the New Testament* 25 (2002): 71-96; K. P. Donfried and Howard Marshall, *The Theology of the Shorter Pauline Letters* (Cambridge: Cambridge University Press, 1993), pp. 15-18; Still, *Conflict*, pp. 260-66. On the political setting and implications of

ebrate the various feasts and festivals in honor of city gods, thereby invoking their wrath on the city, would indicate disloyalty to their city.[23] Any artisans in the *ekklēsia* who refused to honor the patron god/goddess of their trade guild would have risked economic hardship. In addition, if the patriarch of their extended household was not a member of the *ekklēsia*, refusing to honor one's household gods would cause domestic tensions in the household.[24]

Paul, then, is likely depicting his audience as moving away from their normal civic duties, "to be enslaved to (δουλεύειν) the living and true God." With the present infinitive δουλεύειν, Paul portrays others as depicting the state of the Thessalonian *ekklēsia* as one of *ongoing enslavement to God*, i.e., as exhibiting unconditional obedience and loyalty toward God. It is not that their πίστις "'*results*' in turning from idols, etc., but that faith [πίστις] *is* the turning from idols to serve the living God of Israel."[25] Hence, what those outside are announcing is their faithfulness/loyalty/obedience to the God of Israel. While the semantic range of πίστις includes belief and trust, in 1 Thessalonians Paul most often uses πίστις and its cognate, πιστεύω, in this sense of faithfulness/loyalty.[26] Michael Gorman's words appropriately describe the way Paul uses πίστις in this letter: "Faith is humanity's appropriate posture before God. It is devotion, total commitment, faithfulness. . . ."[27]

This understanding of the πίστις of this audience also coheres closely with Paul's characterization of the *ekklēsia* in 1:6 as being an "imitator of us and of the Lord." Enslaved to (δουλεύειν) God, they maintained a fidelity to God in the face of serious tribulation/pressure. Such fidelity is analogically related to that displayed by Christ who also took the form of a slave (δοῦλος) and exhibited a similar loyalty to God by obediently going to his death on a cross (Phil 2:6-8).[28] Their

---

Paul's rhetoric more generally, see Richard A. Horsley, ed., *Paul and Empire: Religion and Power in Roman Imperial Society* (Harrisburg, Pa.: Trinity Press International, 1997); Richard Horsley, ed., *Paul and Politics: Ekklēsia, Israel, Imperium, Interpretation* (Harrisburg, Pa.: Trinity Press International, 2000).

23. Barclay, "Conflict," p. 515; Still, *Conflict*, pp. 255-60.

24. Abraham Malherbe, *Paul and the Thessalonians: The Philosophical Tradition of Pastoral Care* (Philadelphia: Fortress, 1987), p. 50; Still, *Conflict*, pp. 251-55.

25. Douglas Harink, *Paul Among the Postliberals* (Grand Rapids: Brazos, 2003), p. 36, n. 26 (my emphasis).

26. Πίστις has this sense in 1:3, 8, 3:2, 5, 6, 7, 10 and possibly in 5:8. Πιστεύω takes this meaning in 1:7, 2:4, 10, 13. In 4:14 πιστεύω followed conspicuously by ὅτι, refers specifically to "believing" something, namely, the resurrection of Jesus.

27. *Cruciformity*, p. 101.

28. I understand the contested phrase, πίστις (᾿Ιησοῦ) Χριστοῦ, as a subjective genitive yielding the translation, "faith/faithfulness of Christ." See the illustrative exchange between James Dunn (who defends the objective genitive) and Richard Hays (who defends the subjec-

ekklēsia as a whole exhibits a similar pattern of faithfulness as that of Jesus in his rectifying display of loyalty/obedience/faithfulness to the God of Israel.[29] As a "non-identical repetition"[30] of the πίστις of Jesus, their πίστις may be characterized as an "an initial and ongoing cruciformity, grounded in the faithfulness of Jesus the Messiah."[31] As Douglas Harink maintains:

> The point to emphasize here is that for Paul the Thessalonian believer's participation in God's gracious work through Christ and the Spirit is not focused upon or localized in a single form of human response, that is receptive faith (or "faith in Christ," a phrase which appears nowhere in the letter); rather it is depicted as spread over the whole range of human life, active and passive, attitudinal and bodily, inner and outer, personal, social, and political.[32]

Paul so unequivocally affirms this audience's fidelity to God until 3:10 that it is a bit surprising to hear him express his desire there to "see your face and make complete (καταρτίσαι) the things lacking in your πίστις." The verb, καταρτίσαι, occurs often in educational contexts to refer to the teacher completing the student's instruction so that he or she could live fully as an adult (cf. Luke 6:40).[33] Such language, coupled with the completely positive portrayal of the audience's πίστις throughout the epistle until this verse, points away from any *intentional* disloyalty to God. Instead, given their relatively recent conversion and its accompanying new value system, it points toward *a lack in their ability to discern* how their πίστις should be embodied in each circumstance that might confront them. After Paul left, and even after Timothy had brought back nothing but a positive report about their πίστις (3:6-8), Paul could anticipate that numerous issues might arise in their social context about which he had not given them specific instructions,[34] issues they might not even recog-

---

tive) in the two essays now conveniently reproduced in the appendix of Richard Hays, *The Faith of Jesus Christ: The Narrative Substructure of Galatians 3:1–4:11*, 2nd ed. (Grand Rapids: Eerdmans, 2002), pp. 249-97. For a concise summary of the advantages of taking the phrase as a subjective genitive, see Gorman, *Cruciformity*, pp. 110-19.

29. This "rectification" language reveals the influence of J. L. Martyn and Richard Hays on my thinking.

30. This phrase is originally John Milbank's introduced to me via Stephen Fowl and Michael Gorman.

31. Gorman, *Cruciformity*, p. 95 (cf. also p. 387).

32. Harink, *Paul*, p. 35.

33. Gene L. Green, *The Letters to the Thessalonians*, PillarNTC (Grand Rapids: Eerdmans, 2002), p. 174.

34. See Bruce Winter, *After Paul Left Corinth: The Influence of Secular Ethics and Social Change* (Grand Rapids: Eerdmans, 2001).

nize as possible threats to their loyalty to God. Such "lacking things," then, are *not* activities in which they are *currently* engaged manifesting their disloyalty to God. Rather, they have to do with incomplete aspects of their ability to discern what sorts of practices might lead to, or actually constitute, a display of disloyalty toward God. Paul, therefore, says that he prays constantly that God will allow him to see them again, presumably for a more extended time of instruction, and "make complete (καταρτίσαι) the things lacking in your πίστις." In the meantime, he uses the rest of the epistle to initiate that completion.

With this issue ringing in the ears of his audience, Paul moves directly into a wish-prayer in which he prays that their hearts will be established "blameless in holiness" before God at the *parousia* of the Lord Jesus (3:11-13). The context, then, points toward a relationship between the completion of the things lacking in their πίστις and the establishment of their hearts "blameless *in holiness*" at the *parousia*. Hence, what remains incomplete in their πίστις is the "sanctification of their imagination."

The Sanctification of the Imagination: Practicing Holiness in the *Ekklēsia*

It is difficult to overemphasize the radical change that had recently taken place in the lives of this audience. As Wayne Meeks observes, "[b]eing or becoming religious in the Greco-Roman world did not entail either moral transformation or sectarian resocialization."[35] So for Gentiles in the Roman Empire to worship a crucified and risen Jewish peasant as the one Lord would have been surprising enough, but to undergo a radical resocialization in which they became a part of a community whose moral life was to be characterized by a cruciform pattern would have required no less than a "conversion of the imagination."[36] One's "imagination" (or "life world") often operates invisibly at an unacknowledged level giving shape to one's intentions and dispositions, as well as to the practices that flow out of them.[37] Hence, these Thessalonians' whole epistemological[38]

35. *The Origins of Christian Morality: The First Two Centuries* (New Haven: Yale University Press, 1993), p. 28.

36. This phrase is from Richard Hays, "The Conversion of the Imagination: Scripture and Eschatology in 1 Corinthians," *New Testament Studies* 45 (1999): 391-412; cf. Green, *Salvation*, p. 117.

37. Green, *Salvation*, p. 72.

38. On the Spirit's role in epistemological transformation, see my "Turning the World Upside Down in 1 Corinthians 15: Apocalyptic Epistemology, the Resurrected Body, and the New Creation," *Evangelical Quarterly* 75 (2003): 291-309 (292-96).

and volitional apparatus (i.e., their imaginations) through which they made cognitive/volitional judgments and construals about their world had to be re-shaped by the Holy Spirit.[39] In NT terms, this *roughly* corresponds to saying that their hearts (καρδίαι) had to be changed.[40] By the power of the Spirit working in and among them, one "life world" had to be unlearned and another learned.[41] Otherwise they could not begin discerning what faithfulness/loyalty to the one God of Israel actually entailed, much less decide to enact such faithfulness. In short their whole embodied life (inner and outer) had to be initially and continuously transformed.

Paul expects his wish-prayer in 3:12-13 to be voiced publicly when the letter is read in the assembly (5:27). Hence, with it he explicitly makes holiness/sanctification a matter of public concern for the *ekklēsia*. The prayer connects the language of holiness (ἐν ἁγιωσύνῃ) with both καρδία (or "imagination") and with communal practices and proceeds as follows: "May the Lord enable you to increase and to abound in love (ἀγάπη) for one another and for all just as we (were enabled by the Lord to increase and abound in love) for you all *in order that*[42] he might strengthen your hearts (τὰς καρδίας) in holiness (ἐν ἁγιωσύνῃ) to be blameless (ἀμέμπτους) before our God and Father at the *parousia* of our Lord Jesus together with all his holy ones." That Paul understands the sort of love (ἀγάπη) referred to here as self-giving *practices* is sug-

---

39. I agree with Healey's caution against a focus on "practices" that doesn't also address the inner work of the Holy Spirit in forming right dispositions and intentions of those performing such practices ("Practices," p. 305).

40. The correspondence between "heart" and what I am calling "imagination" is rough partially because Paul's usage of anthropological terms in reference to "inner" aspects of persons is often imprecise. As in the LXX, καρδία in the NT generally refers to "the *inner person,* the seat of understanding, knowledge and will, and takes on as well the meaning *conscience*" (A. Sand, *EDNT* 2, p. 250, his emphasis). Paul uses καρδία with both volitional (e.g., 1 Thess 2:4; 1 Cor 4:5) and cognitive (e.g., Rom. 10:8-9) nuances, demonstrating that he can use the term to refer to the inner aspect of one's intentions, dispositions, and cognitive judgments. However, he does not use "inner" anthropological terms (e.g., καρδία, ψυχή, πνεῦμα, νοῦς) in precise ways, nor does he bracket off the inner activities associated with these from their embodiment in public practices. That Paul understands persons as embodied wholes can be seen in the obvious parallels between the wish-prayers in 3:12-13 and 5:23-24. The establishment of their *hearts* (καρδίαι) blameless (ἀμέμπτους) in holiness (ἐν ἁγιωσύνῃ) at the *parousia* (3:13) is hardly different from their entire sanctification (ἁγιάσαι) in which their whole *spirit, soul,* and *body* will be kept blameless (ἀμέμπτως) at this same *parousia* (5:23).

41. Cf. Gorman's contention that the Pauline communities met especially to hear prophecy, i.e., "to *unlearn* the ancient culture of honor and status and to *learn* what it means to exist as an exclusive alternative community . . ." (*Cruciformity,* p. 356).

42. The NIV and NRSV miss the connection between the two optative verbs and the εἰς τὸ στηρίξαι.

gested earlier in 2:6-12 where he narrates his own actions for the sake of the Thessalonians. These actions have a "cruciform" structure, a narrative pattern that parallels that of the Christ hymn in Philippians 2.[43] That is, *although* Paul could have made weighty demands based on his status as an apostle (1 Thess 2:7), *rather* he treated his audience like a nurse caring for her children, sharing his own self with his beloved (ἀγαπητοὶ) addressees as he worked day and night to keep from being a burden to them while he proclaimed to them the life-giving gospel of God (2:8-9). This pattern of life exhibited by Paul is a "non-identical" repetition of that exhibited by Christ. It simultaneously exhibits both his πίστις (toward God) and his love toward others and Paul goes on in 2:10 to describe this behavior as not only "*holy* (ὁσίως) and righteous (δικαίως),"[44] but also "blameless (ἀμέμπτως)," a word whose adjectival form occurs in 3:13. Hence, Paul's depiction of his own actions in 2:6-12 as "blameless (ἀμέμπτως)" has a bearing on how one should understand 3:13.[45]

Paul's prayer is that the Lord will enable the Thessalonians to increase in analogous self-giving actions, both toward each other *and toward those outside* the *ekklēsia*.[46] The purpose for the Lord's action in the community is to establish their hearts "blameless in holiness . . . at the *parousia*." Here, then, Paul is imploring the *crucified* and risen Lord to enable the *ekklēsia* to increase in *cruciform* practices in order that, at the *parousia,* the hearts/imaginations of those in it will be *blameless in holiness.* These are practices that Paul depicts them as *already engaged in* (1:3; 3:6; 4:9-10), practices which, as I have suggested, would assume an initial and continuing transformation of their hearts/imaginations in order to be sustained. Here we should note *the reciprocal movement* of Paul's prayer. The movement is *from* being engaged in grace-enabled self-giving practices *to* the establishing of their hearts/imaginations as blameless in holiness at the *parousia*. In the prayer, then, Paul depicts God as sanctifying those who

---

43. I.e., the pattern manifest in the loving action of Christ's faithfulness on the cross in order to achieve God's purposes: "refusing to exploit status for selfish gain, freely renouncing such status, and preferring others over self by emptying himself in 'incarnation' . . . and by humbling himself in death" (Gorman, *Cruciformity,* p. 169, see pp. 192-95 for the cruciform pattern of Paul's actions in 1 Thess 2:6-12).

44. The terms ὁσίως and δικαίως may simply refer to Paul's keeping divine and human law respectively (so Charles A. Wanamaker, *The Epistles to the Thessalonians: A Commentary on the Greek Text,* NIGTC [Grand Rapids: Eerdmans, 1990], p. 105). However, given Paul's concern for his audience's holiness, they may indicate that Paul's behavior was conformed to the character/image of God (cf. Eph 4:24; Wis 9:3).

45. As well as 5:23, the only other place in the letter where Paul uses ἀμέμπτως.

46. To clarify, these are actions done: by the *ekklēsia* as a whole; by persons within the *ekklēsia* for the sake of others within it; by individuals within the *ekklēsia* for the sake of others outside it.

constitute the *ekklēsia* in the context of grace-enabled practices in a way that continues the transformation of their hearts/imaginations. Hence, the Lord's enabling them to increase in love would continue God's transformation of them into a holy community blameless at the *parousia* because its very communal life is shot through and through with self-giving actions.[47] As such it would be permeated with God's own character/holiness as definitively revealed in the faithfulness of Jesus. It would be a "colony of cruciformity," an eschatological instantiation of the holiness of God.

There is a similar pattern of thinking in 4:1-8 although these verses have in view the avoidance of certain practices.[48] In vv. 1-2, the audience, knowing what commands Paul has previously given them, is *currently* "walking in a way that is pleasing to God" (vv. 1-2).[49] In these verses, Paul encourages them to continue doing so more and more as they live their lives in accordance with these commands. With the word "for" (γὰρ) Paul connects their living in accordance with these commands to the language of sanctification and the prohibitions that follow in vv. 3-8. "*For* this," he says, "is the will of God, your sanctification (ἁγιασμὸς)." If, as seems likely, ἁγιασμὸς is best understood here as the process whereby they are becoming sanctified,[50] continued adherence to the prohibitions that follow are depicted as *necessary conditions* for God to bring it about.[51] While the exact nature of these prohibitions is much debated,[52] I agree with

47. "Although no direct link between the exhortations to love and the cross appears in 1 Thessalonians, the love to which Paul calls the Thessalonians — the love that he showed them — is clearly cruciform love: selfless, others-centered, edifying, and nonretaliatory" (Gorman, *Cruciformity,* p. 218).

48. Verses 1-2 flow directly out of Paul's concern for the sanctification of the audience's imagination expressed in 3:12-13. While more closely related to vv. 3-8, these verses broadly introduce the rest of the paraenetic material through 5:22.

49. Using present-tense verbs (περιπατεῖν, ἀρέσκειν, περιπατεῖτε) and a complimentary paraenetic style appropriate for exhorting friends, Paul portrays the audience as continuing to live in a way that is "pleasing to God" (cf. Abraham J. Malherbe, *The Letters to the Thessalonians,* AB 32b [New York: Doubleday, 2000], p. 220). The "threatening tone" of vv. 6-8 notwithstanding, Paul does not imply that some in the audience are *currently engaging* in the practices he warns them against in 4:3-8 (contra Green, *Letters,* pp. 184, 186-87, 200; Wanamaker, *Epistles,* pp. 158-59).

50. So I. Howard Marshall, *1 & 2 Thessalonians,* NCB (Grand Rapids: Eerdmans, 1983), p. 106; Malherbe, *Letters,* p. 225; Wanamaker, *Epistles,* p. 150.

51. *Necessary,* but *not sufficient,* conditions since Paul clearly understands ἁγιασμὸς as involving more than abstention from certain sexual practices.

52. Part of the debate revolves around how to translate σκεῦος κτᾶσθαι in 4:4a. Is Paul counseling (the males in) his audience to "acquire/hold (κτᾶσθαι) a wife (σκεῦος)" or to "gain mastery over (κτᾶσθαι) his own body/sexual organ (σκεῦος)?" While I am more inclined to the latter view (so NRSV, NIV), my argument here would not be substantially affected if one accepts most versions of the former view.

those who understand them all in sexual terms⁵³ rather than taking 4:6a as a reference to business/trade practices.⁵⁴ In addition, while I take them as directed primarily toward intra-communal practices, Paul would also have sufficient reason to reiterate any of his previous warnings against the dangers of πορνεία (any form of sexual relations outside marriage) outside the community context.⁵⁵

Paul equates God's will with their sanctification and then moves on to (partially) define their sanctification with a series of three infinitive clauses that unfold with increasing specificity in vv. 3-6.⁵⁶ The first is a general admonition in v. 3 to completely abstain from πορνεία (any form of sexual relations outside marriage). The next infinitive clause in vv. 4-5 stands in apposition to this general admonition explaining what is involved in completely abstaining from πορνεία. In this second infinitive clause, Paul commands each of them to learn how to gain mastery over their own body in holiness (ἐν ἁγιασμῷ) and honor, not in passionate lust "like the Gentiles who do not know God." Then, in the third infinitive clause in v. 6a, Paul admonishes them not to "wrong or exploit one's ἀδελφὸν in this particular matter." Such language suggests that vv. 3b-6 are *primarily* concerned with prohibiting πορνεία *within* the *ekklēsia*, i.e., with intra-communal practices.⁵⁷ This third infinitive clause stands in apposition to v. 4 specifying in negative terms what would be involved in a failure to obey Paul's admonition in vv. 4-5. Hence, whatever the exact nature of the sexual practices in vv. 3-5, a failure to abide by Paul's admonitions in those verses would result in doing what v. 6a prohibits, viz., wronging or exploiting another member of God's household. Therefore, in vv. 3-5 Paul is likely prohibiting intra-communal practices which reflect the opposite of cruciformity, the opposite of the character of the Holy God reflected in the faithfulness of the Lord Jesus.⁵⁸

53. E.g., Malherbe, *Letters*, pp. 226-33; Marshall, *1 & 2 Thessalonians*, pp. 106-12; Wanamaker, *Epistles*, pp. 150-56; Weima, "How You Must Walk," pp. 106-10.

54. E.g., Willi Marxsen, *Der Erste Brief an die Thessalonicher*, ZBK 11.1 (Zürich: Theologischer Verlag, 1979), p. 61; Traugott Holtz, *Der Erste Brief an die Thessalonicher*, EKKNT 13 (Zürich: Benziger, 1986), pp. 161-62.

55. In that case, however, one need not appeal to sexual practices associated with the cults of Cabirus or Dionysus to account for Paul's exhortations (e.g., Karl P. Donfried, "The Cults of Thessalonica and the Thessalonian Correspondence," *New Testament Studies* 31 [1985]: 336-56). The typically (although not universally) tolerant attitude toward sexual activity outside of marriage in non-Jewish society at large would be enough to explain his concern.

56. These summary comments on vv. 3-6a are indebted to Marshall, *1 & 2 Thessalonians*, pp. 106-112.

57. Adultery is most probably in view (Green, *Letters*, pp. 195-97).

58. Cf. Gorman's comments to this effect in this volume: "Holiness is taking on a cruciform shape, without thereby losing other, more traditional meanings such as sexual virtue" ("'You Shall Be Cruciform,'" p. 155).

Such practices do not reflect the character of God, but rather the pattern of life outside the *ekklēsia,* life among "the Gentiles who do not know God" (4:5).

In vv. 6b-8 Paul gives three reasons why the audience must avoid the prohibited practices.[59] Utilizing a familiar biblical pattern when the (lack of) holiness of God's people is in view,[60] Paul first reminds his audience of what he had told them before, namely, that "the Lord is an avenger in all these things" (4:6b). That is to say, the *crucified* Lord, to whom this audience owes its very existence as a people, will avenge activity within the corporate life of this people that violates his own character. Second, in v. 7, Paul reminds the audience that God did not call us to impurity (ἐπὶ ἀκαθαρσίᾳ),[61] but rather "into the sphere where God's sanctification takes place" (ἐν ἁγιασμῷ).[62] Finally, rejecting these prohibitions amounts to a rejection of the God who, in Ezekiel-like language, "gives his Holy Spirit into you all" (4:8).[63] Hence, to engage in prohibited intra-communal sexual practices would be tantamount to rejecting the gift of the eschatological Spirit whose purpose was to sanctify them, i.e., to enable their life together to publicly display *this Lord's* character/holiness before the eyes of the nations.

In 4:9-12 Paul continues with more compliments and exhortations. In vv. 9-10 he portrays them as an audience whose "brotherly love" (φιλαδελφίας) is not in question, an audience taught by God to love (εἰς τὸ ἀγαπᾶν) one another. In fact their "doing this" (i.e., these loving practices) is on public display extending to brothers and sisters throughout the whole of Macedonia. Paul then exhorts them to continue these practices more and more before addressing an intra-communal issue in vv. 11-12 in which some in the community have apparently become idle. Whatever the precise reason for their idleness,[64] the

---

59. Marshall, *1 & 2 Thessalonians,* pp. 112-14; Weima, "How You Must Walk," p. 110.

60. Cf. the pattern manifest in God's dealings with exilic Israel: "Just as God had warred against Egypt so as to deliver Israel, so, when Israel patterned its life after oppressive Egypt, God had clashed with Israel" (Green, *Salvation,* p. 73).

61. While Paul can use ἀκαθαρσία with non-sexual nuances (e.g., 1 Thess 2:3), he most often uses it in contexts where sexual immorality is in view (e.g., Rom 1:24; 2 Cor 12:21; Gal 5:19-20; cf. Eph 4:19, 5:3; Col 3:5).

62. Wanamaker's language, *Epistles,* p. 157. As the above translation indicates, I do not take ἐπὶ and ἐν as synonymous (contra Green, *Letters,* p. 199). One reason for this is because I do not understand "impurity" as the actual opposite of "holiness" (on which, see Richard Bauckham, "The Holiness of Jesus and His Disciples in the Gospel of John," in this volume, pp. 95-98).

63. Compare the language in 4:8 (διδόντα τὸ πνεῦμα αὐτοῦ τὸ ἅγιον εἰς ὑμᾶς) with Ezek 37:6 (δώσω πνεῦμά μου εἰς ὑμᾶς). As indicated above, 4:5-8 shares numerous affinities with the language of portions of Ezekiel 36–37.

64. See the discussion in Malherbe, *Letters,* pp. 252-60.

upshot of these verses is that Paul counsels some to engage in the same manual labor (ἐργάζεσθαι) that he depicted himself as engaged in when he brought the gospel to them (2:9, ἐργαζόμενοι) *in order to avoid burdening any of them*. In these verses, then, Paul interprets the φιλαδελφία and ἀγάπη in which they should remain engaged as an activity (i.e., manual labor) exhibiting love which enables persons within the *ekklēsia* to avoid becoming an economic burden to each other. He assumes that such behavior would make a favorable impression on those outside the community (v. 12a).

Paul does not return to explicit holiness language until his wish-prayer in 5:23. While space prohibits a thorough investigation of 4:13–5:22, some brief comments with regard to the practices Paul encourages among the Thessalonians are in order. To begin with, it is worth noting that on the basis of what he says in both sections dealing with the *parousia*/day of the Lord (4:13-18, 5:1-11), Paul commands the audience to "encourage one another" (4:18, 5:11) and to "build each other up" (5:11). Such practices, as well as the practices to which Paul refers in 5:12-14, are concrete manifestations of love for those within the community and for the *ekklēsia* as a whole.[65] In 5:15 Paul directs the audience to see to it that "no one repays evil for evil but always seek the good for each other *and for all.*" In light of the extreme social pressure they are enduring, if the *ekklēsia* as a whole engaged in this practice, not only intra-communally but *"for all,"* it would clearly distinguish them as a group from those outside who were "doing evil" to them. It would represent a "non-identical repetition" of the pattern of costly, self-giving love that defines the character of the God to whom they are faithful. In this case, an alternative, sanctified, social body in which God's character is visibly embodied would be on display.

Paul's exhortations in 5:16-22 relate to two primary practices, i.e., prayer in vv. 16-18 and the hearing and evaluating of prophetic utterances in vv. 19-22.[66] In the first of these, Paul exhorts his audience to pray continuously (v. 17), prayer that should be characterized by joyous acceptance (v. 16) and thanksgiving in the midst of every circumstance (v. 18). Practicing this kind of prayer in the midst of extreme social pressure is only possible on the basis of, and would exemplify, an utter dependence on God and the hope of God's coming public vindication of the faithful (as Paul describes in 4:13–5:11). It would both flow from, and continue to engender, a transformation of this audience's imagination. Although commenting on prayer in Acts, Joel Green's words are apropos here: "Prayer of this sort *allows for the infusion of a worldview* centered on the gracious God, on dependence on God, on the imitation of God, and on

---

65. Cf. Gorman, *Cruciformity,* p. 217.
66. Malherbe, *Letters,* pp. 329-36.

the disclosure of God's purpose for humanity, all understood against an eschatological horizon in which the coming of God in sovereignty and redemption
figures prominently."[67] One might say, then, that the practice of prayer in this
context is an activity through which the Spirit continues to effect the sanctification of the audience's imagination.

In vv. 19-22 Paul turns his attention to the practice of hearing and evaluating prophetic utterances. He exhorts the audience not to "quench the Spirit,"
which would occur in this context if they regularly "despised the prophetic utterances" they heard when they assembled together.[68] The hearing of Spirit-
inspired prophetic utterances was an important source for improving their
ability to discern how their πίστις should be embodied in each circumstance
that might confront them. When the assembly met to hear prophecy, it met "to
unlearn the ancient culture of honor and status and to *learn* what it means to
exist as an exclusive alternative community, worshipping the one God,
grounded in the cross of Christ, and infused by the cruciform Spirit."[69] Hence,
through the communal practice of hearing and testing prophetic utterances,
the Spirit was at work transforming/sanctifying the audience's imagination.
Such a practice better equipped them to "hold fast to the good and to abstain
completely from the very appearance of evil" (vv. 21-22).

Paul's wish-prayer in 5:23-24 must be understood in light of his former
wish-prayer in 3:11-13 as well as in light of his concrete exhortations in 4:1–5:22.
As we have seen, adherence to these concrete exhortations would result in practices that both presuppose and continue the transformation of his audience's
imagination. Hence, when Paul says in 5:23, "May the God of peace himself,
sanctify (ἀγιάσαι) you all entirely," the aorist infinitive, ἀγιάσαι,[70] should be
taken as referring to the *whole reciprocal process* to which Paul has been referring. Keeping in mind the similar language of 3:13, the following clause (5:23b)
is best taken as explicating the preceding one[71] and translated as "that is, may
your whole spirit, soul, and body be kept blameless at the coming of our Lord
Jesus Christ." Accordingly, Paul's use of "spirit, soul, and body" is not a precise
anthropological classification but a way of emphasizing that God is out to sanctify one's whole embodied self.[72] Hence, 5:23 refers to the culmination of the reciprocal process in which God is sanctifying those who constitute the *ekklēsia* in
the context of grace-enabled, embodied practices in a way that both presup-

---

67. Green, *Salvation,* p. 117 (my emphasis).
68. Malherbe, *Letters,* p. 331.
69. Gorman, *Cruciformity,* p. 356.
70. On the common use of the aorist infinitive in wish-prayers, see BDF 337.4.
71. So Malherbe, *Letters,* p. 338.
72. See Malherbe, *Letters,* pp. 338-39.

poses and continues the transformation of their imaginations. Because this God is faithful (v. 24), the result will be a people of God, kept blameless *both now and at the eschaton* because their communal life is constituted by self-giving actions.[73] In this way, the community as a whole and the transformed persons within it would reflect the character of the Holy God as revealed most fully in the faithfulness of Jesus Christ.

Practicing Holiness in the Church Today

God's call on local churches in the twenty-first century remains the same as that of God's call on the church in Thessalonica. God calls local churches to an instantiation of holiness, i.e., to a life together that publicly displays their *Lord's* character/holiness before the eyes of the nations. It is a call to persons within the *ekklēsia* as well as to the *ekklēsia* as a whole to exhibit a "non-identical repetition" of the pattern of costly, self-giving love that defines the character of the God to whom they are faithful. The fulfillment of this call only happens through the work of the eschatological Spirit who, in a reciprocal movement, both empowers, and is active in, embodied practices by which God brings about the sanctification of the imagination and thereby creates "colonies of cruciformity."

There are no short cuts to this goal. It is complicated by the fact our imaginations have been formed not only by Christian influences but also by a variety of personal experiences and by simultaneously being a part of various non-Christian cultures and sub-cultures. In the West in particular, not only these cultures and sub-cultures, but large segments of the Church itself, have an entrenched commitment to an individualism that understands the self as an autonomous construction by the individual. For the most part, as church leaders we have failed to take intentional steps that would frame our communal life in ways that nurture day-to-day renewal in our insight into, and embodiment of, the holiness/character of God.[74] How might observing the way that Paul engages in this theological task in 1 Thessalonians help us in this regard?

---

73. Cf. the concluding words of Andrew Chester: "Paul's vision in the end is of a community that exemplifies God's Spirit in action, and Christ's self-giving love as pervading its whole way of life, in difficult everyday circumstances" ("The Pauline Communities," in *A Vision for the Church: Studies in Early Christian Ecclesiology in Honor of J. P. M. Sweet*, ed. Markus Bockmuehl and Michael B. Thompson [Edinburgh: T&T Clark, 1997], p. 120). Cf. also the comments of Dwight Swanson, "Holiness in the Dead Sea Scrolls: The Priorities of Faith," in this volume, p. 35.

74. Here, I have modified language from Green, *Salvation*, p. 133.

Perhaps most important, we should take a cue from Paul and make the holiness/sanctification of the *ekklēsia* a matter of public concern by actually using such language publicly to frame various activities in our communal life. This might take a variety of forms, the first of which could be to imitate Paul by publicly praying for the sanctification of our church's imagination when we are gathered for worship in a way that connects it to self-giving practices. Such prayer would itself be a "grace-enabled" practice through which we would implore the Triune God to conform us to this God's own character. In this type of prayer, we would acknowledge the initial and ongoing reciprocal movement whereby the transformative power of the Spirit both enables us to engage in such practices and continues transforming our imaginations through them. One word of caution is in order here, i.e., our prayers should also include a petition that the Spirit would stand against us if our practices are not faithfully embodying the character of God.

As this note of caution acknowledges, what truly counts as a cruciform practice requires discernment and might vary from one ecclesial context to the next. The individual and corporate ability to engage in such discernment is supplied by the Spirit and nurtured in a variety of traditional church practices (e.g., catechism, Bible reading, proclamation, sacraments). Assuming those practices to be a regular part of the life of the local church, one resource we often overlook is that of shared storytelling.[75] We ought purposely to allow space in our public gatherings for telling stories of persons and whole communities who have discerned clearly what constitutes cruciform actions in their particular social context and faithfully embodied them in "non-identical repetitions" of the story of their crucified Lord. The story in the introduction about the church in Guyana is one example of such stories. Others might include well-known examples of individual Christians (e.g., Dietrich Bonhoeffer, Mother Teresa) and whole church bodies (e.g., the German Confessing Church). They ought also to include stories about the transformed lives and self-giving actions of individual Christians in the local church, stories like that of my own grandmother who, in the midst of the depression in the 1930s, took the new shoes off her young son (who had an old pair at home) and gave them to another child in the church (who had none). Here, however, another word of caution is in order. We should also tell stories that illustrate the failure of various local churches to embody the character of God in their social context. In conjunction with the more traditional catechetical practices of the church, such shared storytelling

---

75. On this practice, as well as numerous other helpful reflections along these lines, see Tod E. Bolsinger, *It Takes a Church to Raise a Christian: How the Community of God Transforms Lives* (Grand Rapids: Brazos, 2004), pp. 130-32.

would help our people better discern what counts as cruciform practices. Moreover, it is also itself a practice through which the Spirit continues the process of transforming/sanctifying our imaginations. We should explicitly acknowledge this by again framing such times with prayer, praying that through them the Spirit will sanctify our imagination.

Another obvious step we might take is simply to plan and engage in communal activities that intentionally display a pattern of costly, self-giving love in the social context within which the church is located and then publicly frame these activities with the language of sanctification and holiness. For example, asking for true sacrificial giving from its members, a local church in the North American suburban context could engage in a major capital campaign to finance improvements in one community in the two-thirds world (e.g., clean water sources, schools, self-sustaining businesses). This corporate action would be an attempt to intentionally display the character of God in this social context.[76] It also would need to be publicly framed with, and explicitly connected to, the language of the Spirit's enabling and sanctifying activity in which we would acknowledge that the Spirit is at work sanctifying the imaginations of individuals within the community through this project.

Through such practices our life together would begin to embody God's holiness and, only because we trust God's faithfulness (1 Thess 5:24), we could confess that the Spirit is at work sanctifying our imaginations, shaping the totality of who we are (our "spirit, soul, and body") into "a living exegesis"[77] of the narrative of the crucified Christ. Indeed, if contemporary research on the brain is on the right path, it would not be far-fetched to say that through these practices, the Spirit acts *on and in* our very bodies.[78] As the Spirit enables us to engage in these activities as a part of this ecclesial web of relationships, the synapses in our brains are being formed in ways that reconstruct our very selves shaping our intentions, dispositions, allegiances, and attitudes. Hence, individuals are sanctified only as a part of a community which is on its way to becoming an eschatological instantiation of the character/holiness of the cruciform God.

76. Capital campaigns to build or improve local church facilities for legitimate ministry purposes are common (and necessary) in the suburban context and often result in significant sacrifice for many. However, for non-Christians in this social context, such campaigns often look like simply another church building program rather than a display of the cruciform character of God.

77. Gorman's language (*Cruciformity*, p. 92).

78. Cf. Joseph LeDoux, *Synaptic Self: How Our Brains Become Who We Are* (New York: Viking, 2002).

The Perfection of Christ and the Perfecting of Believers in Hebrews

GORDON J. THOMAS

Unlike many of Paul's epistles, Hebrews does not seem to be addressed to the pastoral particularities of a specific congregation. Problem individuals are not mentioned by name. Rather, it tackles a tendency which is threatening a category of people — Jewish believers who are being tempted to revert to their ancestral faith. At first glance, therefore, Hebrews offers little for those seeking help with a biblical ecclesiology. However, holiness in Hebrews is firmly grounded in Christ, and Hebrews, more than any other NT book, grapples directly with the relationship between a holy people and Christ's life, death, and ascension. Christology and soteriology are enriched by this complex document. If the church today is to live up to its "holy, catholic and apostolic" billing, it may be less in need of books, seminars, and conferences on "how to do church" than of a much surer grasp of who Jesus is, what he has done, and what he is currently doing for us. A consideration of the integral connection between the perfection of Christ and the perfecting of believers may turn out to be pertinent to the holiness of the church after all.

The writer to the Hebrews is anxious to press on to deeper teaching based on Psalm 110 about Christ's unique role as high priest after the order of Melchizedek, but there is a problem. It would appear that many of his readers

---

This chapter is an expanded and revised version of three shorter articles originally published in *The Flame* 70.2 (Apr.-Jun., 2004) and 70.3 (July-Sept., 2004) as part of the "Re-Minting Christian Holiness" series.

It is a privilege to contribute something to a volume dedicated to Alex Deasley, one of the best Christian role-models of my formative years. The gradual growing sense of being called by God to teach scripture in general and holiness in particular, which has shaped my life, probably owes most to my parents. However, Alex's example and influence cannot be far behind them, and, like many others, I thank God for exposing me to his ministry of God's Word.

are rapidly losing momentum in their Christian journey. They have failed to build on the excellent foundation that apostolic preaching and teaching laid for their faith (Heb 2:1-4). They are a case of arrested spiritual development. So far are they from spiritual maturity that the writer has serious concerns about their future well-being. With a combination of encouragement and warning, he tries to prod them into forward motion again. As he meditates on Psalm 95, he has a horrible premonition that these believers might end up replicating the fate of the Israelites who were delivered from slavery in Egypt but never made it as far as the Promised Land.

In this light, the pastoral strategy adopted by this NT writer is twofold. First, he moves to cut off any potential retreat into Judaism for his readers. From slipping back through negligence right through to bold-faced apostasy and everything in between, every kind of retrogression is proscribed. Typologically a clear parallel is drawn between such movement and the actions of the ancient rebels in the Sinai desert who hankered after the flesh-pots of Egypt. Second, he fixes his readers' minds on Jesus — who he was, what he achieved, and what he is currently doing.

1. The Perfection of Christ

Hebrews concentrates on the person and work of Christ. Most of the major themes are introduced in 1:1-4, which functions like an overture to the whole work. Through Christ, God's ultimate revelation to the human race has been given: "in these last days he (God) has spoken to us by a Son, whom he appointed heir of all things, through whom he also created the worlds. He is the reflection of God's glory and the exact imprint of God's very being, and he sustains all things by his powerful word" (1:2-3a).[1] There can be little doubt that that writer wishes to draw attention right from the start to the infinite superiority of the son, not only of this final revelation. The language is close in meaning to that of John 1:1-4. This spokesperson is superior to all of God's earlier spokespersons — he is the creator and sustainer of all things — and unmistakable in his godness. Such an emphasis is crucial for the soteriology that the writer sets out in subsequent chapters. God's action in Christ is not through mediators — the contrast is with angels (1:5–2:5), however exalted. This is the Son. The second half of v. 3 then tells us that "When he had made purification for sins, he sat down at the right hand of the Majesty on high . . ." — which introduces the important subject of Jesus' atoning death for sin.

---

1. Unless otherwise noted, all citations are from the NRSV.

Jesus' Death: Unbeatable and Unrepeatable

In a fairly compressed way, Hebrews portrays Jesus as dealing with every conceivable aspect of the sin problem. His atoning death on the cross dealt first with the power of sin as personified in the devil: "Since, therefore, the children share flesh and blood, he himself likewise shared the same things, so that through death he might destroy the one who has the power of death, that is, the devil, and free those who all their lives were held in slavery by the fear of death" (2:14-15). Here salvation is understood as dealing with death, the ultimate expression of human alienation from the sources of life. Jesus needs to enter fully into the human condition and its subjection to death, experience death himself, and thereby remove its terror. Although the resurrection is not mentioned here, the implication is that this is precisely how the fear of death and the power of the devil in using death as a weapon of terror are defeated. Death is still experienced by flesh and blood, but it no longer has the final word (see 1 Thess 4:13-18; 1 Cor 15:20-58).

Second, his death was incomparably more effective in dealing with the penalty of sin than the old animal sacrifices which it superseded, "For it is impossible for the blood of bulls and goats to take away sins" (10:4). For the writer to the Hebrews, all such OT rituals were merely anticipations of the one true, unique and unrepeatable sacrifice for all sin for all time. They needed to be repeated *ad infinitum* but "he has appeared once for all at the end of the age to remove sin by the sacrifice of himself" (9:26).

Third, because sin not only offends a holy God but contaminates the sinner, the death of Jesus also provided a means of purification from sin. Unlike other parts of the New Testament which emphasise the importance of human consecration (e.g., Rom 12:1) or of the ministry of the Holy Spirit in producing sanctification (e.g., 2 Thess 2:13), the main thrust of Hebrews is to attribute the sanctification of believers to the all-sufficient sacrifice of Christ. For this writer, sanctification is christocentric and the sanctification of believers is positional in that they are sanctified by being in Christ. This bases the sanctification of the believers in the atoning work of Christ rather than the presence or absence of any experience or on the basis of greater human effort. Chapter 10 boldly declares that "it is by God's will that we have been sanctified through the offering of the body of Jesus Christ once for all" (10:10). And four verses later we are told that "by a single offering he has perfected for all time those who are sanctified" (10:14).

A strikingly unusual analogy for Jesus' sacrificial death that is used more than once in Hebrews is with the red heifer of Numbers 19. This was a specialised form of the sin/purification offerings of bulls, goats, and other animals prescribed in Leviticus 4. It was used especially for dealing with ceremonial uncleanness. The heifer would be slaughtered and burnt outside the Israelite camp and its ashes would be kept there for future use. Anyone who was defiled by touching a dead body would need to be sprinkled on the third and seventh days with a mixture of heifer-ash and running water. It was not necessary to kill a red heifer every time there was a death in the community. The death and ashes of one animal were sufficient to cleanse countless defiled people. The symbolism seems to lie unobtrusively behind the choice of words in the final chapter: "Therefore Jesus also suffered outside the city gate in order to sanctify the people by his own blood" (13:12). In Heb 9:13-14, however, it stares the reader in the face: "For if the blood of goats and bulls, with the sprinkling of the ashes of a heifer, sanctifies those who have been defiled so that their flesh is purified, how much more will the blood of Christ . . . purify our conscience from dead works to serve the living God."

Jesus' Life: A Painful Perfecting Process

The effectiveness of Jesus' death as an atoning sacrifice depended entirely on who it was who was dying. Theologians down through the centuries have demonstrated a fondness for focusing on the beginning and end of Jesus' life — hence all that has been written on the Person and Work of Christ or the Incarnation and Atonement. However, the theology of Hebrews sets great store by what happened in between the birth and the death. It suggests that Jesus had to be made ready for his role as the sacrificial victim on the cross.

In Heb 2:10 we read that "it was fitting that God . . . should make the pioneer of their salvation perfect through sufferings." This may raise questions as to whether Jesus could ever have been anything less than perfect. It probably helps if we read "perfect" in its Hebrew sense of "being fit for its purpose," rather than as "beyond improvement." If dying for sin was the ultimate purpose of Jesus' life, then suffering en route was an unavoidable aspect of his preparation. Thus the anguish of Gethsemane is invoked as symptomatic of a painful life: "In the days of his flesh, Jesus offered up prayers and supplications, with loud cries and tears, to the one who was able to save him from death, and he was heard because of his reverent submission. Although he was a Son, he learned obedience through what he suffered; and having been made perfect, he became the source of eternal salvation for all who obey him" (5:7-9).

Does this imply, as some commentators suggest, that Jesus had some disobedience that needed to be knocked out of him?[2] Definitely not! But morally

---

2. See, for example, Ronald Williamson, "Hebrews 4^{15} and the Sinlessness of Jesus," *Expository Times* 86 (1974-5): 6, who asks, "do not the statements made about Jesus' having 'been

and spiritually the implication is that baby Jesus was not the finished article. If he was fully human, then like all of us he had to grow and learn in order to reach maturity (cf. Luke 2:52).

His perfecting or maturing also relates to his vocation as the unblemished sacrifice for sin. If he had ever yielded to temptation, then he would automatically have been disqualified as an unfit sin-offering, like a diseased bull or injured goat (cf. Mal 1:13). In addition, his experience of human weakness, tiredness, and suffering qualifies him perfectly to be a sympathetic high priest today (4:15a). Somehow Jesus had to be both fully human and fully sinless. How could that have been possible?

Jesus' Person: Fully Human and Fully Sinless

While in no doubt whatsoever about Jesus' deity before his incarnation, Hebrews insists absolutely that the incarnate Jesus was fully human. It is part of the argument about his suitability to be our high priest. It states that "he had to become like his brothers and sisters in every respect *(kata panta),* so that he might become a merciful and faithful high priest in the service of God, to make a sacrifice of atonement for the sins of the people" (2:17).

The writer then goes on to affirm that "we do not have a high priest who is unable to sympathize with our weaknesses, but we have one who in every respect *(kata panta)* has been tested as we are, yet without sin" (4:15). This is an essential plank in the argument that Christ was superior to the regular high priests, because they had to offer sacrifices for their own sins first but he, being "holy, blameless, undefiled," did not need to do so (7:26-27). Fully human? Fully tempted? Definitely. The Greek expression *"kata panta"* is literally "according to all things" and means "in every respect." Yet despite the comprehensiveness of his temptation, Jesus was "without sin."

When Jesus was born, was he like Adam before or after the Fall? Many Christians instinctively say "before."[3] Because Adam was disobedient, and Jesus lived as a perfectly obedient human, it must be that he was born like Adam before the Fall. But we are not like Adam before the Fall; we are fallen human beings. Hebrews clearly states that Jesus had to become and therefore did become

---

made' perfect and having to learn obedience imply that there was a time in his experience when the perfect, sinless obedience to which he finally won through on the Cross was not yet his?"

3. Cf. David Peterson: "It is possible that our writer viewed the manhood of Jesus as comparable to that of Adam before the Fall, Christ achieving the dominion that Adam lost through sin" (*Hebrews and Perfection: An Examination of the Concept of Perfection in the Epistle to the Hebrews,* SNTSMS 47 [Cambridge: Cambridge University Press, 1982], p. 190).

"like his brothers and sisters in every respect" and that can only mean like us in our fallenness. But how then could he be sinless? In terms of basic logic the problem could be stated like this:

> All humans are sinful by nature.
> Jesus was fully human.
> ∴ Jesus was not fully sinless.

Alternatively:

> All humans are sinful by nature.
> Jesus was fully sinless.
> ∴ Jesus was not fully human.

Popular theological thinking leaves little room to have a Jesus who is both fully human and fully sinless. Yet that is precisely what the writer to the Hebrews declares. If his *"kata panta"* is no artistic flourish and he is telling the plain truth about Jesus' humanity and sinlessness, then in our writer's mind it seems likely that fallenness is not to be equated with sinfulness and sin therefore is not an intrinsic part of what it is to be a human.

It seems truer to the book of Hebrews to affirm that all humans are fallen, that Jesus shared our fallenness and our temptations completely, but that in him fallenness did not lead automatically to sinfulness. Immediately we want to ask "why not?" but Hebrews does not tell us. What it does tell us is that our Saviour is made like us in every respect . . . yet without sin.

That being the case, how do all the achievements of our perfect Christ translate into holy living by Christians? For now, suffice it to say that Jeremiah's prophetic hope of God's law being written on human hearts has been fulfilled by Jesus, "the mediator of a better covenant" (8:6, 8-12). In triumphing over Satan and sin, our forerunner (6:20) lived a holy life all the way to the finishing-line and in so doing made holy living possible also for us who follow in his footsteps.

2. The Perfecting of Believers

Entering the Rest of Faith — An Analogy for Holiness? (3–4)

The question of holiness in Hebrews has been particularly influential in the thinking and preaching of those in the Wesleyan-holiness tradition. For them, Hebrews 3 and 4 provide a paradigm for the life of the individual who comes to faith and moves on to experience the rest of faith promised by God on the analogy of the people of God set out in these chapters.

This pattern can be seen in Charles Wesley's hymn on Hebrews 3–4 which begins like this:

> Lord, I believe a rest remains
> To all thy people known,
> A rest where pure enjoyment reigns,
> And Thou art loved alone.
>
> A rest, where all our soul's desire
> Is fixed on things above;
> Where fear, and sin, and grief expire,
> Cast out by perfect love.
>
> *O that I now the rest might know,*
> *Believe, and enter in!*
> *Now, Saviour, now the power bestow,*
> *And let me cease from sin.*[4]

Hebrews 3 and 4, in quoting Psalm 95, warn Christians against repeating the folly of the Israelites. They hardened their hearts in the wilderness and were prevented from entering God's rest. In its original context that "rest" was entry into the Promised Land, but the writer of Hebrews expands the notion so that it will also apply to his readers, who are in danger of reverting from Christianity to Judaism. The two key statements of chapter 4 are in vv. 3 and 9: "For we who have believed enter that rest" (v. 3); "So then, a sabbath rest still remains for the people of God" (v. 9). Verse 11 then goes on to encourage people to *make every effort to enter that rest.*

In the Wesleyan-Holiness tradition, many have followed Charles Wesley's example and equated "the rest of faith" with what is sometimes called a "second blessing" experience of entire sanctification. In his commentary on Hebrews, a prominent theologian from this tradition, H. Orton Wiley, wrote: "This 'rest of faith' is a personal, spiritual rest of the soul in God. It is promised as an inheritance to all who are the sons of God by the 'new birth' — a second definite crisis in the lives of true believers."[5]

The majority of recent New Testament scholars fail to see anything of a

---

4. Charles Wesley, "Lord, I Believe a Rest Remains," in *Wesley Hymns*, compiled by Ken Bible (Kansas City: Lillenas Publishing, 1982), p. 36.

5. H. Orton Wiley, *The Epistle to the Hebrews*, rev. ed. (Kansas City: Beacon Hill, 1984), p. 126.

"second crisis" in these difficult verses. Indeed, recent Wesleyan scholarship reads the text differently.[6] Wayne McCown writes,

> The use of Hebrews 3–4 as a holiness text is generally based on an allegorical interpretation of the passage. . . . Its basis is a presumed analogy between Israel's experience as a nation and each Christian's spiritual pilgrimage. Israel was first delivered from bondage, and only after a period of wandering in the wilderness entered into the Promised Land victorious over her enemies. Normal Christian experience follows a similar pattern. In the first work of grace, God grants deliverance from the bondage of sin. Customarily, there follows a period of struggle, characterized by ups and downs, and wandering in relation to God's perfect will. But the Christian is exhorted to move beyond that stage, to victory over inbred sin. Thus, beyond the state of inner turmoil, he/she is promised spiritual rest, as a second work of grace.[7]

According to Judith Wray, "Entering into the rest becomes a participation, a to-be-maintained participation in the completed cosmic work of God."[8] Not everyone agrees with this, however. "Commentators are divided about whether the emphatic εἰσερχόμεθα should be understood as a real present . . . or as futuristic. . . . Nowhere else does the author suggest a full and unconditional realization of the Christian hope in the present. . . . It is therefore preferable to understand εἰσερχόμεθα as an emphatic equivalent of the future tense."[9] It is hard to imagine arguing for a "full and unconditional realization of the Christian hope in the present" in Hebrews, since so much seems to depend on whether the readers persevere or fall back. However, a certain amount of realised eschatology is surely demanded by the author's insistence that, thanks to Christ, the Jeremianic new covenant is now in operation. Through Christ, who has made it across the finishing-line, we now have access to God the Father in the Holy of Holies.

In context, therefore, the rest appears to be a metaphorical way of referring to salvation. It has *a present aspect* as something we enter now and *a future aspect* as something that remains to be entered. This "already" and "not yet" tension perhaps reminds us of Matthew's similar use of "the kingdom of

---

6. See, for example, Wayne McCown, "Holiness in Hebrews," *Wesleyan Theological Journal* 16 (1981): 58-78.

7. McCown, "Holiness in Hebrews," p. 63.

8. Judith Hoch Wray, *Rest As a Theological Metaphor in the Epistle to the Hebrews and the Gospel of Truth: Early Christian Homiletics of Rest*, SBLDS 166 (Atlanta: Scholars Press, 1998), p. 91.

9. P. Ellingworth, *The Epistle to the Hebrews: A Commentary on the Greek Text,* NIGTC (Grand Rapids/Carlisle: Eerdmans/Paternoster, 1993), p. 246.

heaven" and John's use of "eternal life." Hebrews has a great deal to say about sanctification and holiness but not necessarily in these two chapters.

Going On to Perfection — A Synonym for Sanctification? (6:1)

Another passage often used by a previous generation of holiness preachers is Heb 6:1, which reads: "Therefore let us go on toward perfection (τελειότητα), leaving behind the basic teaching about Christ." The key word can mean either "perfection" or "maturity." So which meaning does the context support? Looking back at chapter 5 we find the author in verse 10 wanting to launch into a deep and learned exposition of Jesus as the fulfilment of Ps 110:4, the high priest after the order of Melchizedek. However, his style is cramped by the spiritual ignorance and immaturity of his readers, who still need spiritual milk, rather than solid food (vv. 11-14). Ellingworth agrees that "the context clearly requires that τελειότητα mean, not 'perfection' in contrast with sin, but 'maturity' in contrast to the state of the νήπιοι (5:13)."[10] The application of the metaphor of human development that our writer uses in this passage is difficult to equate to static events as if one could be born at one instant, then made adult at another. In this passage, it is hard to resist the implication then that 6:1 is a call for the immature to go to maturity, rather than for converts to seek a second blessing.

The Cleansing of the Conscience/Consciousness (9:13-14)

In pastoral work one occasionally comes across a Christian tortured by guilt. For some sin committed years ago continues to haunt the memory and the conscience. At a practical level it can help the person to make a full confession to a minister/counselor in front of a trusted friend (see Jas 5:16) and to be told authoritatively that, having satisfied the biblical conditions for forgiveness, they are truly forgiven (see John 20:23). The cleansing of that guilty conscience is achieved, however, neither by the penitence of the guilty party nor the compassion of those seeking to help but through the Holy Spirit applying the benefits of Christ's sacrificial death on the cross to the defiled conscience: "For if the blood of goats and bulls, with the sprinkling of the ashes of a heifer, sanctifies

---

10. Ellingworth, *Hebrews*, p. 312. This seems much more convincing in context than Hugh Montefiore's opinion that "The maturity towards which advance must be made is the perfection of Christian doctrine . . ." (*The Epistle to the Hebrews*, BNTC [London: A. & C. Black, 1964], p. 104).

those who have been defiled so that their flesh is purified, how much more will the blood of Christ . . . purify our conscience from dead works to serve the living God" (9:13-14).

A different problem for many people these days is not a tormented conscience but a traumatised consciousness. Despite seeking forgiveness for their own sins, these people often feel emotionally scarred for life by the sins committed against them by other people. Violence, sexual abuse, rape, torture, physical degradation are happening all around us no matter where we live, but most of it goes undetected and unpunished. What is the good news of Jesus Christ for the victims?

C. A. Pierce believes that in the NT conscience is "the painful reaction of man's nature, as morally responsible, against infringements of its created limits."[11] Peterson agrees that the writer of Hebrews "is fundamentally concerned with conscience as a register of man's guilt before God — with the *accusing conscience*."[12] Paul Ellingworth has a less rigid understanding of conscience than others: "Συνείδησις . . . is one of a group of terms available to describe the inward aspect of human nature."[13] An even broader definition is offered by Lane. He labels it "the human organ of the religious life embracing the whole person in relationship to God."[14]

If the Greek word for "conscience" in 9:14 is translated "consciousness" in 10:2, does our writer also imply that the blood of Christ could purify someone's consciousness from dead works? No commentators seem willing to proffer "consciousness" as a possible translation in 9:14, despite the fact that it is the unanimous preference for the same word in 10:2. But might this also be a benefit of the blood of Christ? Purifying the conscience is the standard translation but purifying the consciousness might well be a neglected aspect of holiness in Hebrews.[15]

Having Been Sanctified/Being Sanctified by a Single Unrepeatable Offering (10:10, 14)

The first part of this chapter concentrated on the perfection of Christ. As we move on to consider the perfecting of believers, the inescapable conclusion is

11. C. A. Pierce, *Conscience in the New Testament,* SBT 15 (London: SCM, 1955), p. 108.
12. Peterson, *Perfection,* p. 135.
13. Ellingworth, *Hebrews,* p. 442.
14. W. L. Lane, *Hebrews 9–13,* WBC (Dallas: Word Books, 1991), p. 240.
15. The pastoral implications of this alternative reading might be significant. For an account of one such pastoral application, see G. J. Thomas, "Purifying the Consciousness," *Healing and Wholeness* 16 (1994): 20-21.

that Hebrews grounds the sanctification of human beings utterly and completely in what was achieved by Jesus' death on the cross and subsequent offering of his own blood to the Father in the heavenly sanctuary after his ascension (8:2; 9:11-12, 24).

In chapter 10 we read of how Jesus came to do his Father's will, in fulfilment of Ps 40:8. Verse 10 goes on to say that ". . . it is by God's will that *we have been sanctified (hēgiasmenoi esmen)* through the offering of the body of Jesus Christ once for all." Verse 14 then declares that ". . . by a single offering *he has perfected (teteleiōken) for all time those who are* (or, *are being) sanctified (tous hagiazomenous)."*

In a very influential book published towards the end of the nineteenth century the evangelical Bishop of Liverpool, J. C. Ryle, made such statements as: "Sanctification is always a progressive work" and "Sanctification is an imperfect work, comparatively, and will never be perfected until we reach heaven."[16] While there is clearly some truth in these remarks, they fail to do full justice to what the writer to the Hebrews is affirming. According to him in some very real sense what Jesus did two thousand years ago through a single offering has changed every believer. Although many are prepared to accept the significance of Jesus' work in sanctification in a positional sense, not all are prepared to speak of transformation of the sanctified. But our writer is not describing what Jesus has done *for* us all that time ago but what he has done *to* us. The grammar in the text is instructive. The verbs are in the perfect tense: We *have been* sanctified (v. 10); he *has* perfected us for all time (v. 14).[17] This indicates an action completed in the past, the effects of which continue until the present. "Those who are sanctified" *(tous hagiazomenous)* are the direct object of Christ's action of perfecting. It is inadequate therefore to assert that Jesus made provision for our sanctification back then. The writer to the Hebrews is saying that *we have been changed* for the better (made holy, perfected)[18] as a direct consequence of Jesus' self-offering on our behalf.

Taken in isolation that might convey the impression that any Christian is the finished article with no possibility of spiritual growth. The remainder of Hebrews, especially chapter 12, and the grammar of 10:14 tell against this view.

---

16. J. C. Ryle, *Holiness* (London: James Clarke, 1952), pp. 39, 31.

17. Montefiore's comment that "in this Epistle there is no realised eschatology . . ." is hard to square with these affirmations (*Hebrews*, p. 83).

18. See Robert P. Gordon, *Hebrews,* Readings (Sheffield: Sheffield Academic Press, 2000), p. 113: "The perfection in question is that of being made fit for the presence and the worship of God." Peterson, *Perfection,* p. 167, defines it as "The definitive consecration to God that the work of Christ makes possible . . ." in fulfillment of the Jeremiah 31 prophecy.

The people described as having been perfected are also those who are *"being sanctified."*[19]

This is a present participle, which indicates continuous, ongoing, or repeated action.[20] It may thus be understood in different ways. On the one hand, "the word 'sanctified' may be regarded as durative; that is, the time element enters into it. It would then be translated 'being sanctified,' in the sense of being in the process of sanctification."[21] It can also be read as "iterative, or a timeless act repeated, and would then mean those who from time to time are sanctified."[22] The durative reading may support the view that sanctification should be viewed as a process carried on through life, and not as a single definite act of faith in the blood of Christ. The iterative reading has been used by Wiley and others to suggest the writer is referring "to those who are being sanctified from time to time."[23] Some in the Wesleyan-Holiness tradition explain this as those who one after another experience sanctification as a second blessing,[24] but that is not the plain sense of the text. The iterative interpretation, applied by Wiley to a second definite work of grace, is also favoured by Peterson, although not to a second work of grace. He regards it as part of a comprehensive conversion-package, whereby sinners are not only forgiven but "possessed by God."[25] If vv. 10 and 14 are considered together, the text suggests that Christians have been sanctified and are being sanctified.[26]

Holiness seems to be truest to scripture and the most intelligible to ordi-

19. According to Robert Jewett, *Letter to Pilgrims: A Commentary on the Epistle to the Hebrews* (New York: Pilgrim, 1981), p. 168, "The two terms have virtually identical definitions in the usage of Hebrews, but in this sentence they are used to express the dynamic tension between the absolute givenness of renewed relationship and the requirement to hold fast to that relationship. . . ."

20. But see Lane, *Hebrews*, p. 268, who views this as "a timeless description of the community of faith."

21. Wiley, *Hebrews*, p. 290.

22. Wiley, *Hebrews*, p. 290.

23. Wiley, *Hebrews*, p. 290.

24. See Wiley, *Hebrews*, p. 290: "it seems to me that the true meaning of 'being sanctified' is also iterative and can only refer to those who are being sanctified from time to time. Otherwise it appears inconsistent for the writer to say that he has perfected or completed those who are as yet only in the process of being sanctified."

25. See David Peterson, *Possessed by God: A New Testament Theology of Sanctification and Holiness*, NSBT 17 (Leicester: Apollos, 1995), p. 35.

26. This is by no means the consensus of commentators on Hebrews, however. Peterson is representative of those who place the emphasis heavily on the former. Thus, "10:14 clearly locates this perfecting in the past with respect to its accomplishment and in the present with respect to its enjoyment" (*Perfection*, p. 167). But Hebrews portrays a definitive change of standing achieved by Christ in the past leading to an ongoing change of state for Christians in the present.

nary Christians when described in relational terms. Since God alone is holy in himself (Rev 15:4), all human holiness depends on a *right relationship* with this holy God. Hebrews recounts how the sacrifice of Christ opened a way into the Holy of Holies in heaven for each one of us who follows in his footsteps. If one finds evidence of unlimited atonement in the Bible (i.e., that Christ died for the sins of the whole world and that the gospel invitation is for every creature), that might imply that all human beings have been sanctified already. Clearly that conflicts both with daily experience of life, not to mention many other Bible passages. So, is there some implicit narrowing of the field? Verse 10 would seem to say so. Who are those who have been sanctified? Answer: "we," i.e., the writer and his Christian readers, all of whom received the message of salvation from apostles, which was confirmed by signs, wonders, miracles, and gifts of the Holy Spirit (2:3-4). Another way of defining this group is as those who laid a foundation of repentance and faith, who had been enlightened and had shared in the Holy Spirit (6:1-5). The sanctification of those who have been sanctified is therefore not just something *achieved* by Jesus but something *received* by his followers.

Let Us Lay Aside Every Weight (12:1)

Chapter 12 is framed rather imposingly. It begins by confronting the reader with a sense of being surrounded by a great crowd of faithful witnesses[27] and ends with a picture of the heavenly Jerusalem and all its inhabitants. The reader is reminded in v. 28 that a holy God ought to be approached in worship with reverence and awe. He is not to be trifled with, "for indeed our God is a consuming fire" (v. 29). In between there is a call to "run with perseverance the race that is set before us" (v. 1), a pertinent exhortation for Jewish Christians who are tempted to abandon their Christian faith and revert to their ancestral religion. The way in which we are to run the Christian race encompasses many vital aspects of holiness teaching.

The term "weight" *(ongkos)* is left deliberately vague.[28] In its original context it could refer either to clothing or to a spare tire around the midriff. The

---

27. See F. F. Bruce, *The Epistle to the Hebrews,* rev. ed. (Grand Rapids: Eerdmans, 1990), p. 333, who does not regard these witnesses as spectators of our efforts but as those who "by their loyalty and endurance . . . have borne witness to the faithfulness of God."

28. See Lane, *Hebrews,* p. 409, who writes: "The qualifying adjective πάντα, 'all,' indicates that the writer did not have any particular consideration explicitly in mind. . . . The combined expression covers any encumbrance that would handicap a runner, and by analogy anything that would interfere with responsible commitment to Jesus Christ."

non-essential thing that hinders one person's progress may be very different from another's.[29] If one wants biblical chapter and verse to define and ban spiritual weights, he or she will look in vain. They are morally neutral objects or activities, which may be a source of harmless pleasure at certain times, but which impede our progress at other times. Only the Holy Spirit can identify them for us. When he does so, the person who is serious about pursuing holiness will offload them quicksharp.

Let Us Lay Aside the Sin That Clings So Closely (12:1)

If they are to complete the Christian race, the second thing to be laid aside is the sin that clings so closely or that so easily distracts. In athletics the equivalent is the illegal substance, the performance-enhancing drug. The problem might begin innocently enough with something of medicinal value, like a preparation that helps muscle-tears heal more quickly. But the person who supplies this can soon be offering something else which crosses the line of illegality. Before they know it, the athlete is trapped in the shady world of anabolic steroids and masking agents.

The Shorter Catechism paints a gloomy picture of Christians being doomed to sin daily in word, thought, and deed. Indeed, in much Western Christian thought indwelling sin remains in the Christian until one's dying day. The sin mentioned here though is not something that remains in the Christian after conversion. The earlier account of the superiority of Christ's atoning sacrifice rules that out. The blood of goats and bulls was powerless to take away sins (10:4) but Jesus "has appeared once for all at the end of the age *to remove sin* by the sacrifice of himself" (9:26). As a consequence Christians may now approach the presence of God himself "with a true heart in full assurance of faith, *with our hearts sprinkled clean* from an evil conscience and our bodies washed with pure water" (10:22).

So where are we to locate the sin which the Christian runner must lay aside? The following verses in chapter 12 make that quite clear. Verse 3 describes Jesus enduring hostility against himself from *sinners* and v. 4 parallels that with a reference to the readers' "struggle against *sin.*" Sin is still a hostile and aggressive external threat on all sides, since we do not yet see all things subject to man/ the Son of Man/Christ (2:8). If the Christian then or now has been compro-

---

29. So Bruce, *Hebrews*, p. 336, "It may well be that what is a hindrance to one entrant in this spiritual contest is not a hindrance to another; each must learn for himself what in his case is a weight or impediment."

mised by yielding to temptation, the standard required by 12:1 is zero tolerance for sin. Lay it aside! Get rid of it!

Endure Trials for the Sake of Discipline (12:3-11)

The readers of Hebrews are finding the Christian race tough going. They have the spiritual equivalent of blistered feet and a stitch in their side. So the temptation to drop out of the race is enormous at times. Maybe they were expecting a bed of roses and all kinds of blessings in the kingdom of God's Son. The writer shows no sympathy, however. He tells them that hardship is par for the course and is actually good for them. No pain, no gain! In v. 7 he challenges them to *endure trials for the sake of discipline.*

Why does God allow (or, perhaps, subject us all to) all sorts of unpleasant and painful circumstances in our lives? The thorny problem of whether God *brings* these circumstances or *allows* them to come cannot be solved here. At the very least, the writer believes that God uses these things for our own good. That may not necessarily be the outcome, unfortunately. Scripture and experience alike testify to the fact that suffering can lead to rejection of the way of the cross. But because Jesus, the pioneer, has walked this way and through suffering learned obedience, this can also be the positive outcome for his followers. For our writer, the answer lies in verse 10: "he disciplines us for our good, in order that we may share his holiness."[30] Holiness is not just about having a right relationship with a holy God. It is also a matter of developing a Christ-like character. Unfortunately for those seeking an easy ride, there is nothing so character-forming as suffering. The hardships of life can be used by God for his good purposes in our lives.

---

30. Over the years I have taught this passage many times and I have asked my students how many of them can identify some painful trials in their lives as God's discipline. So far the only person who has even given me a clear answer to my question is George, a Christian businessman who became obsessed with his business. He borrowed and expanded, borrowed and expanded some more. Slowly he became so busy that God was getting squeezed out of his life. Then came a disastrous downturn in the economy. Businesses started to fail left and right, and George's business among them. If you talk to George today, he is still a businessman but these days a more godly one. The collapse of his business was a painful process of discipline, for which George is profoundly grateful, because it helped him to share God's holiness. See Tom Wright, *Hebrews for Everyone* (London: SPCK, 2003), p. 153, for a not wholly dissimilar story of a friend "who had firmly and finally decided not to join the ordained ministry but to become a chartered accountant. Almost at once he was struck down by a strange disease which forced him to stay in bed for a week, by the end of which not only his mind, but also his heart, and the direction of his life to this day, had been changed."

Pursue Peace with Everyone and the Holiness
without Which No One Will See the Lord (12:14)

According to Heb 12:14 with its dire warning, holiness is a pre-requisite for seeing God. This view is taken by F. F. Bruce, who wrote: "The sanctification without which no man shall see the Lord is, as the words themselves make plain, no
optional extra in the Christian life but something which belongs to its essence."[31] The verb "pursue" *(diōkete)* corrects any misconception that Christ
did everything for our sanctification and we need do nothing. On this reading
of the text, those who are part of God's holy people must respond in holy living.
Not all scholars agree, however.

William Lane, for example, asserts that "In Hebrews ἁγιασμός does not
possess an ethical significance" and that pursuing holiness means "earnestly to
hold firmly the gift of Christ through which believers have been made holy."[32]
This is unconvincing. Bruce is much closer to the mark when he writes, "Here,
as in v. 10, practical holiness of life is meant, the converse of those things against
which a warning is uttered in the verses which follow."[33] The word means to
make strenuous efforts and the fact that grammatically it is a present imperative means that we must keep doing so continuously.

That, however, is just half of the verse. It is just as important to maintain
peace with everyone.[34] According to Lane, "In this context 'peace' is an objective reality that results from the redemptive accomplishment of Christ in his
sacrificial death on the cross. It is the gift of eschatological salvation as well as a
sign that points to the presence of the new age and to the future perfection. . . ."[35] On Lane's reading of the two halves of the imperative, pursuing
peace entails pursuing the gift of eschatological salvation and pursuing holiness
means holding on to the gift of having been made holy. The cultic lens through
which he views this command robs it of any meaningful, practical, and ethical
application in the present. But peace must be more than an abstract soteriological concept. Rather, the exhortation is to pursue right relations with other

31. Bruce, *Hebrews*, p. 364. In similar vein, note Packer's declaration that "holiness is every Christian's calling. It is not an option, but a requirement. God wants his children to live up
to his standards and to do him credit in the eyes of the watching world. . . ." J. I. Packer, *A Passion
For Holiness* (Nottingham: Crossway Books, 1992), pp. 90-91.

32. Lane, *Hebrews*, p. 450.

33. Bruce, *Hebrews*, p. 348.

34. Lane, *Hebrews*, pp. 437-38, disagrees with those who interpret this as seeking peace
with everyone. In his opinion the author's preference for the preposition *meta* rather than *sun*
justifies the translation, "Pursue peace along with everyone."

35. Lane, *Hebrews*, p. 449.

people, as it is to do so with God. That makes sense because Jesus does not give loving God wholeheartedly and loving one's neighbor as oneself as alternative expressions of the greatest commandment.

In some older publications, sermons and essays may be found on "striving for . . . holiness without which no one will see the Lord." The three dots are the surest possible evidence that holiness is being misconstrued as private piety, rather than corporate godliness. To delete "peace with everyone" from the verse is to emasculate it. Peace and holiness are held in tandem. If the essence of holiness is a right relationship with a holy God, then the vital tangible expression of holiness is right relationships with other people. The pursuit of God's holiness, then, can never be individualistic. God's peace, his *shalom*, is only evident in our lives in the nexus of relationship. In the context of this section of Hebrews, it points to the need of the community to maintain wholeness within it. He exhorts his readers to "lift your drooping hands and strengthen your weak knees, and make straight paths for your feet" (12:12).

The converse of this is highlighted in the following verses: "See to it that no one fails to obtain the grace of God; that no root of bitterness springs up and causes trouble, and through it many become defiled" (12:15). Through this allusion to a warning in Deut 29:18, our writer again urges his readers to continue on the journey rather than turning aside in apostasy. But those individuals who are tempted to turn aside are to be gathered up and brought along with their fellow pilgrims on this journey, "so that what is lame may not be put out of joint, but rather be healed" (12:13).

To what extent should this pursuit of peace and holiness be seen in a wider context? Robert Jewett interprets peace in both an individualistic and a global sense, defining it as "The harmonious sense of health and well-being that comes to the person who accepts adversity as divine discipline" and as "an end to social inequalities and injustice and the recovery of brotherliness and goodwill."[36] These fine-sounding ideals are indeed part of the wider implications of Christian holiness and find their anchor in the teaching of Jesus. They are, therefore, essential to any full-orbed discussion of Christian holiness. It must be acknowledged, however, that they are not self-evidently the original emphases of this author whose interest is much more directed to the health of the community on its journey to the city of God. Montefiore seems more attuned to the immediate context — "Peace here is enjoined not with all comers but between members of the church, for v. 15 (which in the Greek is dependent on this verse) is only concerned with matters inside the ecclesiastical community."[37]

36. Jewett, *Letter to Pilgrims*, p. 220.
37. Montefiore, *Hebrews*, p. 223.

One of the supreme tests of sanctification is how Christians get along with their fellow-Christians. Even the most Spirit-filled Christians can have diametrically-opposed opinions and they find it very hard to back down, if they believe that a matter of principle is at stake. It was ever thus. Hence the bust-up between Paul and Barnabas in Acts 16 over whether to give John Mark a second chance. That particular story had a relatively happy ending in that Paul came to value Mark in the end. However, for every reconciliation, how many wounds in the Body of Christ remain as open sores?

The implications of this for the care of the weak and the failing within the community of faith are enormous. Those who are in danger are to be helped and strengthened. Those who have stumbled are to be lifted up. Through his attention to the cloud of witnesses and the community throughout, our writer insists that this is a journey of holiness together rather than an individual pursuit of the beatific vision.

Benediction (13:20-21)

There can be no better way to round off a pilgrimage through holiness in Hebrews than with this wonderful anonymous church leader's word of blessing on his readers in 13:20-21: "Now may the God of peace, who brought back from the dead our Lord Jesus, the great shepherd of the sheep, by the blood of the eternal covenant, make you complete in everything good so that you may do his will, working among us that which is pleasing in his sight, through Jesus Christ, to whom be the glory forever and ever. Amen."

Living as Exiles:
The Church in the Diaspora in 1 Peter

JOEL B. GREEN

Irrespective of their importance to the biblical witness and to significant streams of Christian tradition, today the language and practices of holiness suffer a debilitating anemia. This is especially true when it comes to any sense of community-based holiness — to the holiness of a people in contrast to personal piety, and to the holiness of God's people in the public realm.

We can trace the cause of this malaise along several lines. For example, as Yale law professor Stephen Carter observed a decade ago, in the United States both political and legal systems compel believers to subordinate their personal religious views to a public faith largely devoid of religion.[1] For the Christian community, this means that, while I might be encouraged to exercise my beliefs in the privacy of my inner life or home, powerful forces press me to hang my religious commitments at the door prior to leaving my house each morning. More broadly, we have learned to compartmentalize sacred from secular, and thus to imagine that some aspects of life, such as the gathering of God's people for worship or the solitude of prayer, are permeated with holiness in a way not available in or appropriate to our workaday lives. We could point as well to our cultural inheritance from the Enlightenment, leading us to drive a wedge between the scientific study of our faith and the exercise of that faith in such time-honored practices of discipleship as the reading of Scripture, Lord's Supper, and hospitality. The widespread emphasis on the individual, so important in modernity, works against any notion of community holiness, too. Where shall we find a standard for holiness in a world system bereft of its moorings in any standard of holiness outside the individual's own inclinations? "I am what I am and I ain't what I ain't," claims Popeye the Sailor Man, speaking for many of us. More profoundly, philosopher Charles Taylor finds that personal identity has

1. Stephen L. Carter, *The Culture of Disbelief* (New York: Anchor, 1994).

come to be based on presumed affirmations of the human subject as self-sufficient and self-engaged.[2] Basic to our notions and experience of authentic personhood are self-autonomy and self-legislation. If we have found it increasingly difficult to welcome or even contemplate an authority external to ourselves (our own conscience, our own experience, our own desires), if "growing up" is tied to achieving independence and autonomy, then we may not be surprised to discover that we hear so little of the holiness of God's people. The church may not be "of the world," but on these matters its contemporary views and practices have very much been shaped on the potter's wheel of the modern world.

These forces and others beside make it difficult for us to hear, and even more so to be shaped by, the witness to holiness found in 1 Peter. This is true even though, as commentators readily agree, holiness is a principal concern of the letter.[3] The words on the page are clear enough — "as he who called you is holy, be holy yourselves in all your conduct; for it is written, 'You shall be holy, for I am holy'" (1 Pet 1:15-16)[4] — but who can hear them? Who can embody them? In fact, we have been reared and formed in ways that predispose us against hearing clearly and living out Peter's call to holiness. The trivializing of religious faith in American culture, intellectual habits that confuse learning with the amassing of facts, the schism between secular and sacred — such lessons as these, deeply embedded in our shared conversations and common life, distance us from engaging 1 Peter in meaningful ways. Umberto Eco speaks of good reading as the practice of those who are able to deal with texts in the act of interpreting in the same way as the author dealt with them in the act of writing.[5] Such a reader — a Model Reader, to use Eco's term — is the precondition for actualizing the potential of a text to engage and transform us. This requires that readers read themselves into the text, so to speak, tuning their ears to the bandwidth of the text. Writing of "understanding" in her novel, *The Telling*, Ursula K. LeGuin makes a similar point: "*To learn a belief without belief is to sing a song without the tune. A yielding, an obedience, a willingness to accept these notes as the right notes, this pattern as the right pattern, is the essential*

2. Charles Taylor, *Sources of the Self: The Making of the Modern Identity* (Cambridge, Mass.: Harvard University Press, 1989).

3. For example, Peter H. Davids, *The First Epistle of Peter*, NICNT (Grand Rapids: Eerdmans, 1990), pp. 17-19; I. Howard Marshall, *1 Peter*, IVPNTC (Downers Grove: InterVarsity, 1991), pp. 26-27; Pheme Perkins, *First and Second Peter, James, and Jude*, Interpretation (Louisville: John Knox, 1995), pp. 19-21.

4. Biblical citations are from the NRSV, unless otherwise noted.

5. For example, Umberto Eco, *The Role of the Reader: Explorations in the Semiotics of Texts*, Advances in Semiotics (Bloomington: Indiana University Press, 1979), pp. 7-11.

gesture of performance, translation, and understanding. The gesture need not be permanent, a lasting posture of the mind or heart; yet it is not false. It is more than the suspension of disbelief needed to watch a play, yet less than a conversion. It is a position, a posture in the dance."[6]

Engaging 1 Peter as its Model Reader, understanding (that is, standing under) its message, requires just such a posturing on our part, whereby we adopt its perspective on our world. Hence, I want first to explore the situation of Peter's audience, not as an antiquarian exercise, but especially in order to press the question whether we are willing to be that audience and so to be addressed by its message. If we are, then we can take more seriously the second section of this chapter, where I will examine Peter's alternative perspective on the reality of his readers. I want to show that Peter presents us with a paradox. He sets side-by-side two competing versions of the same reality, with our experience of the world portrayed as both the worst of times (ostracism, life on the margins, rejection) and the best of times (new birth, living hope, our lives as a journey of joy and faithfulness). Competing interpretations of the same situation rest on different perspectives from which to observe and make sense, and Peter wants his readers, us, to read our contemporary lives from within the perspective of the scriptural story of God and the life of Jesus. If we do, then we see that this lived reality, however perplexing and painful it may be, is deeply rooted in God's saving purpose. In the final section of this chapter, then, I want to ask, What is the nature of holiness in this world? I will show that it is precisely in the day-to-day experience of this paradoxical situation that God's people are to carve out their vocation of holiness of heart and life.[7]

Peter's Model Readers: Diaspora and Its Challenges

Peter deploys a range of images to characterize his audience, to map their identity, so to speak, and the location of Peter's readers as *strangers in a strange land* is among the most prominent. Linguistically, this motif is marked by such terms as "exile" (1:1; 2:11), "dispersion" (or "diaspora") (1:1), and "alien" (2:11). Troy Martin highlights the importance of this concept by identifying it as the

---

6. Ursula K. LeGuin, *The Telling* (New York: Harcourt, 2000), pp. 97-98; emphasis original.

7. In preparing this chapter, I have drawn from my earlier work, especially "Identity and Engagement in a Diverse World: Pluralism and Holiness in 1 Peter," *Asbury Theological Journal* 55 (2000): 85-92; and "Faithful Witness in the Diaspora: The Holy Spirit and the Exiled People of God according to 1 Peter," in *The Holy Spirit and Christian Origins*, ed. Graham Stanton, Stephen Barton, and Bruce Longenecker (Grand Rapids: Eerdmans; London: T&T Clark, 2005).

letter's "controlling metaphor."[8] Martin's assessment, though overstated, help-fully presses us to map Peter's readers in terms of both their social location and their theological habitation within the grand narrative of God's project. These come into focus in the experience of exile.

In what sense are Peter's Model Readers "exiles" and "strangers"? Precur-sors in the Old Testament include the expulsion of Adam and Eve from Eden (Gen 3:24), Abraham's life among the Hittites as "a stranger and alien" (Gen 23:4), and the wandering Israelites en route to the land of promise, for example, as well as the more recent Babylonian exile and, at the time of Peter's writing, the realities of Jewish life under Roman rule.[9] On the one hand, Peter's audi-ence does not share with their forerunners in Israel the experience of exile in the sense of their having been forcibly removed from their homes. Nor is there any hint in 1 Peter that the status of Peter's readers as exiles rested on their lack of faithfulness to the covenant. The opposite is closer to the mark. Their elec-tion by God serves as the theological basis of their life as aliens. Nevertheless, they identify with, or are called upon to identify with, Israel-in-exile. And, bor-rowing the language and promise of exodus and new exodus,[10] Peter sets before them the hope of salvation that marks exile's end.

Thus, those believers to whom Peter addresses this letter have not been drawn into a new geographical space; rather, his Model Readers, both past and present, have been born anew (1:23) within the space they had previously in-habited. They belong, but they do not belong. As Miroslav Volf helpfully ob-serves, "Christians do not come into their own social world from the outside seeking either to accommodate to their new home (like second generation im-migrants would), shape it in the image of the one they have left behind (like colonizers would), or establish a little haven in the strange new world reminis-cent of the old (as resident aliens would)."[11] Peter's exiles are not "Jews" living among "Gentiles" in the expected sense of these terms, then, as though the au-thor were concerned with their ethnic or national status. Moreover, attempts to

8. Troy W. Martin, *Metaphor and Composition in 1 Peter,* SBLDS 131 (Atlanta: Scholars, 1990). See also Reinhard Feldmeier, *Die Christen als Fremde: Die Metapher der Fremde in der antiken Welt, im Urchristentum und im 1. Petrusbrief,* WUNT 64 (Tübingen: J. C. B. Mohr [Paul Siebeck], 1992); Miroslav Volf, "Soft Difference: Theological Reflections on the Relation be-tween Church and Culture in 1 Peter," *Ex Auditu* 10 (1994): 15-30.

9. For evidence of the understanding that Israel's exile was still in progress in the first century CE, see Craig A. Evans, "Jesus and the Continuing Exile of Israel," in *Jesus and the Resto-ration of Israel: A Critical Assessment of N. T. Wright's "Jesus and the Victory of God,"* ed. Carey C. Newman (Downers Grove, Ill.: InterVarsity, 1999), pp. 77-100.

10. Cf. Rikki E. Watts, "Exodus," in *New Dictionary of Biblical Theology,* ed. T. D. Alexan-der and Brian S. Rosner (Downers Grove, Ill.: InterVarsity, 2000), pp. 478-87.

11. Volf, "Soft Difference," pp. 18-19.

find in Peter's descriptive terms a reference to his readers' economic status[12] founders similarly on a problem of category. One's social status was a product of numerous, intersecting considerations, relative income or access to the means of production being only one of them. In fact, there is no basis within the letter itself for suggesting that Peter's audience occupied any rung on the ladder of economic measurement other than the broad middle of those living in Asia Minor. The basis for their life as strangers in a strange land lies elsewhere.

John Barclay has analyzed the way in which diaspora Judaism responded to its environment with reference to *assimilation* (i.e., a measurement of social integration, including social interaction and practices), *acculturation* (i.e., the degree of linguistic, educational, and ideological achievement), and *accommodation* (i.e., the practical utility of acculturation, whether to embrace or resist one's surrounding culture).[13] We may gather from this sort of analysis that identity and boundary maintenance are pivotal: Who are *we* in relation to *them?* What is the basis of *our* constitution as a community? What are *our* characteristic practices? By what strategies are these maintained? The metaphorical world within which Peter's Model Readers dwell is qualified, on the one hand, by the temporal nature of the experience of diaspora in which the people of God are depicted as a journeying people (for example, 1:3-12); and, on the other, by the social and religious threat confronting a people challenged with the ever-present possibility and threat of assimilation and defection.[14] In fact, a profound irony rests in the fact that the markers and practices that give this people a cohesive identity (the disciplined life of a distinctive people) actually serve to locate those thus identified on the margins of honorable society.

In his biblical theology of exile, Daniel L. Smith-Christopher observes that "a stronger sense of 'community identity' arises under circumstances of minority, stateless existence."[15] We are not surprised, then, that Peter encourages his audience to the sort of faithfulness that had traditionally attached itself to discourse in the Jewish diaspora. As exilic identity is a matter of disciplined life oriented toward survival as a distinct people, so, in the present, they are to embody the call to Israel in Exodus and Exile to be holy. As a priestly people, a

---

12. As in, say, John H. Elliott, *A Home for the Homeless: A Sociological Exegesis of 1 Peter, Its Situation and Strategy* (Philadelphia: Fortress, 1981).

13. John M. G. Barclay, *Jews in the Mediterranean Diaspora: From Alexander to Trajan (323 BCE to 117 CE)*, Hellenistic Culture and Society (Berkeley: University of California Press, 1996), pp. 92-102.

14. Cf., for example, Martin, *Metaphor and Composition*, pp. 150-61.

15. Daniel L. Smith-Christopher, *A Biblical Theology of Exile*, OBT (Minneapolis: Fortress, 2002), p. 141.

holy nation, they would embrace the missional vocation to be "holy" — that is, "different," or "distinctive" — in the midst of the Gentiles (for example, 2:9-12).

Thus, on the positive side of the ledger, dispositions and behaviors encouraged throughout the letter are grounded in the identity of Peter's Model Readers as God's people, while, on the negative side, those very dispositions and behaviors had become the impetus for the hostility with which they have become intimate. Thus, Peter writes, "If you are reviled for the name of Christ, you are blessed, because the spirit of glory, which is the Spirit of God, is resting on you. But let none of you suffer as a murderer, a thief, a criminal, or even as a mischief maker. Yet if any of you suffers as a Christian, do not consider it a disgrace, but glorify God because you bear this name" (4:14-16; cf. 2:23; 3:9, 16). In the household of the Roman empire, status was achieved via conformity to habits of life that had become so conventional that they were largely unspoken, "what everyone knows." Then, as now, fitting in was important, and noncompliance and other forms of social distinctiveness were valued negatively. Within the empire, Peter envisions an audience that lives as though they belonged to another household, one headed by God the Father (1:1-2; 1:13–2:10). Their transformed loyalties and practices located them on the margins of acceptable society. They had become the victims of social ostracism, their allegiance to Christ having won for them slander, animosity, reproachment, scorn, vilification, and contempt.

The result of life in these terms is a crisis of faith and, with it, the threat of assimilation and defection.

Life in the "Realm of Holiness": Remapping Peter's Readers

It is important for Peter that his Model Readers identity themselves with Israel, but this is not merely so that they might identify with Israel in their crisis. Rather, for Peter the narrative of Israel is itself determined by the story of Jesus and by the journey of salvation and hope it engenders. That is, the Israel into whose history Peter writes his audience is *Israel as interpreted* by the suffering, death, resurrection, ascension, and pending revelation of Jesus Christ. Similarly, although Peter sketches a number of characteristic dispositions and behaviors for his readers, it is of real significance that his concern is not so much to segregate Christian communities from the larger world as it is to tie them firmly to their center. To put it differently, Peter works less to construct boundaries for the people of God as to define their center, and he does this by locating his audience on the map — not so much as persons of the diaspora, but rather as persons "in Christ." In other words, alien status or diasporic life does not constitute the "controlling metaphor" for Peter's message in 1 Peter. That designation belongs to another point of orientation by which Peter has mapped the location of his readers. Peter's Model Readers certainly comprised "a stateless minority in the context of a massive empire,"[16] but, for Peter, the lives of these followers of Christ are determined decisively not by their location in the empire but by their habitation of a space he designates in 3:16; 5:10, 14 as "in Christ."

Given that Peter devotes so much attention to describing his audience as aliens, strangers, outsiders, the ostracized, we might justifiably ask, Where might they be "at home"? Ultimately, of course, one might reply that Peter locates the "inheritance" of his readers "in heaven" (1:4), but this is not the whole story. Certainly, he disallows any suggestion that they might find a home or gain their bearings "among the nations" (2:11-12), as it is such people whose lives are characterized by "licentiousness, passions, drunkenness, revels, carousing, and lawless idolatry" (4:3), as well as "excesses of depravity" and blasphemy (4:4). Indeed, reference to "in" (in Greek, *en*, referring to boundedness within a container, whether spatial, temporal, or a state or condition) implies an "out," and "among the Gentiles" may designate "the outside." Perhaps better, the phrase "among the Gentiles" serves as a summary description of that place within which those who follow Christ cannot but be strangers. Just as the letter begins by declaring its Model Readers as strangers of the diaspora, so it ends with a climatic declaration of their true home; their life is "in Christ" (5:10, 14) — a life defined, then, throughout the letter in christological terms with particular reference to the redemptive and exemplary journey of Jesus through suffering and death to his exaltation.

Already, then, we see that Peter casts his eyes upon the challenging circumstances of his audience in order to give himself to making sense of them. The paradox of his position is present already in the opening of his letter, where he places side-by-side two competing descriptions of his audience: chosen and exile (1:1). It is unfortunate that most translations, including the NRSV, obscure the oxymoron Peter uses, by separating the two terms in a way that does not represent well the Greek text. In the intimate alignment of these two terms we find the apparent contradiction that Peter addresses throughout the letter: chosen by God, rejected by humans. This is the story of Israel. This is the story of Jesus. And, we now discover, this is the ongoing story of God's people. Our difficulty in hearing Peter's letter lies especially in the fact that God's people, including ourselves, do not embrace rejection easily. We want to belong. We want to be chosen. We want status. We do not want to be strangers, aliens, people for whom "home" is not and can never really be "home."

16. So Smith-Christopher characterizes the Hebrews in exile (*Biblical Theology of Exile,* p. 144).

Our proclivities and sensibilities resist the combination of these apparent opposites: chosen and marginal, elect and alien. In order to move forward with faith and in faithfulness, we need new ways of making sense of things, new values and commitments, and this is what Peter seeks to provide. He works to re-form the way we see things, the imaginations by which we make sense of life, in two, interrelated ways.

(1) Peter Narrates the Story of Israel as Though It Were Our Story

Scientist-theologian Anne Foeret refers to humans as "*Homo Narrans Narrandus* — the storytelling person whose story has to be told," who tells stories to make sense of the world and to form personal identity and community. Given the central role of narrative in the way we are formed as a people, a crucial question is, What story is Peter telling? What narrative do we find in 1 Peter? Obviously, 1 Peter is a letter, so our concern is not with the form of 1 Peter per se, but rather with the narrative it presumes and projects and into which Peter works to induct his Model Readers. The question is, For Peter, what story ought we to inhabit? What story ought to shape our lives and do so decisively? For Peter, the main elements of this story would include the following:

- The Life of Israel, Foreshadowing Jesus' Death, Resurrection, and Glory, as well as the Model Readers' Present Plight
- Jesus' Death and Resurrection (New Exodus)
- Present, Exilic Journey
- The End/Glory/Revelation of Christ

Several important observations can be made.

First, although Peter does not write a "history of Israel," he is nonetheless engaged in the historian's task of sorting out the pivot-points in Israel's story and articulating their meaning. Like historians of all kinds, then, Peter studies the past with an eye to serving the present, and especially to showing the continuity between followers of Jesus and Israel of old.[17] There, in that story, will Christians find their true identity and learn the way of faithfulness. Indeed, for Peter, "the language and hence the reality of Israel pass without remainder into the language and hence the reality of the new people of God."[18] Peter collapses

---

17. See David Lowenthal, *The Past Is a Foreign Country* (Cambridge: Cambridge University Press, 1985).

18. Paul J. Achtemeier, *1 Peter*, Hermeneia (Minneapolis: Fortress, 1996), p. 69.

the historical distinctives between ancient Israel and contemporary Christians in favor of theological unity.

The Old Testament thus gives Peter's Model Readers their true identity by narrating their past. The Old Testament also serves a foreshadowing role. Foreshadowing is an interpretive device available to us only after the fact; that is, we do not experience foreshadowing in life, but can see in retrospect how events happen as a consequence of things to come. For Peter's audience, this means that their present calamity is neither a surprise to God nor a contradiction of their relationship to him as his chosen people. Even scorn and animosity from humans can be folded into the grand narrative of God's work. Rejection by others loses its power when one realizes one's status as stranger in a strange land. The accusation, "You do not belong," holds little surprise for persons who know already that their true homeland is elsewhere. And the loss of honor among men and women loses its sting when this loss is parried by the reception of honor from God.

In 1 Peter, the unity of ancient Israel and contemporary people of God comes into focus especially in 2:9-10: "But you are a chosen race, a royal priesthood, a holy nation, God's own people, in order that you may proclaim the mighty acts of him who called you out of darkness into his marvelous light. Once you were not a people, but now you are God's people; once you had not received mercy, but now you have received mercy."[19] This affirmation, a virtual collage of numerous Old Testament texts (for example, Exod 19:5-6; Isa 43:20-21; Hos 1:6, 9; 2:1, 23), is made of Peter's audience just as it had been made of Israel of old. This community and that community are one. A similar role is played by the description of the Christian community as God's temple: "Come to him, a living stone, though rejected by mortals yet chosen and precious in God's sight, and like living stones, let yourselves be built into a spiritual house, to be a holy priesthood, to offer spiritual sacrifices acceptable to God through Jesus Christ" (2:4-5; see 4:17). Peter's Model Readers ("you") draw their identity from the Old Testament categories of priesthood (called of God), sacrifice (offered to God), and temple (built by God); they have become the dwelling place of God's presence among humanity.

A second observation concerning Peter's "narrative" is that the present time is characterized as life in the diaspora. This is the marginal life of aliens and exiles, among whom the threat of assimilation and apostasy is constant and concerns with identity, boundaries, and faithful witness are paramount. But it

---

19. For a thorough discussion of this material, see Jo Bailey Wells, *God's Holy People: A Theme in Biblical Theology*, JSOTSup 305 (Sheffield: Sheffield Academic Press, 2000), pp. 208-40.

is also an existence qualified by its temporal nature. It will come to an end at the revelation of Jesus Christ. This in-between time, then, is depicted as a journey of growth, of suffering, and of hope. Christians are "on the way," not at home. Consequently, they must exercise discernment as they sit loosely in relation to the institutions and ways of life that are respected and regarded as "at home" in this world. And they must work out the terms of faithfulness according to the values and commitments determined by the age to come.

Third, the axis of Peter's "narrative" is Jesus Christ. His readers are to find their home "in Christ." The warrant for his directives concerning faithful living is Jesus' own suffering, death, resurrection, and triumph. And Jesus is the interpretive matrix for understanding the pattern of God's story, the lens through which to read our story within the story of God.

Elements of the story of Jesus that Peter highlights include Jesus' pre-existence (1:11; cf. 1:20), his life of faithfulness (1:2), his suffering and death (1:2, 11, 19; 2:4, 7, 21-25; 3:18-19; 4:1; 5:1), his ascension (3:22), and his pending, final revelation (1:7, 11, 13; 5:1). Among these, of special importance is Jesus' suffering and death, and especially its relationship to the eternal purpose of God — which Peter documents repeatedly.[20] Jesus' suffering is at one and the same time *exemplary*, providing a model for his followers of innocent suffering (2:19-20; 3:16-17; 4:1-2, 13-16); *redemptive*, providing a model for his followers of effective suffering (2:12, 15; 3:1-2); and *anticipatory*, providing a model for his followers of how God will vindicate the righteous who suffer (2:20; 4:13-14; 5:1, 10). This means that, although it is true that Peter draws heavily on the holiness tradition available in the Old Testament, it is equally true that this tradition is now fundamentally branded by the crucifixion of Jesus. The consequence is that holy life in the world is marked not by withdrawal or separation, but by an engagement of such profundity that it is capable of leading to ostracism, rejection, banishment, even wrongful death.[21]

(2) Peter Underscores the Work of the Holy Spirit, to Make Us Holy

In his opening salutation, Peter characterizes his audience as "elect strangers" — that is, as persons whose status before God and in the world is:

20. See 1:11, 19 (Isa 52:13–53:12); 2:4-10 (Ps 118:22; Isa 8:14); 2:21-25 (Isa 52:13–53:12); 4:1-2, 17.

21. This point is made more generally in Stephen C. Barton, "Dislocating and Relocating Holiness: A New Testament Study," in *Holiness Past and Present*, ed. Stephen C. Barton (London: T&T Clark, 2003), pp. 193-213.

according to the foreknowledge of God the Father,
in the sanctification of the Spirit,
because of the obedience and sprinkling of blood of Jesus Christ.

(1:1-2; my translation)

Here, as in 4:12-14, the Spirit is identified as the agent of God's power. In this case, the Spirit is oriented toward the work of "making holy" — a motif of significance elsewhere in the letter (1:15, 16, 19, 22; 2:5, 9; 3:15). This includes the exegesis of scriptural material in 2:4-10, where holiness is lumped together with human rejection and divine election. Evidently, the antidote to the threats of exilic life is the empowering work of the Spirit, who enables God's people not only to survive as a distinct people, but to embody the call to Israel in exodus and exile to be holy. This way of thinking surfaces in 4:11-14, where Christian speech in the midst of testing draws on "the strength that God supplies," "because the spirit of glory, which is the Spirit of God, is resting on you" (cf. Isa 11:2).

In many translations of 1:2, the role of the Spirit is instrumental, as in the NRSV: "sanctified by the Spirit." Remembering Peter's concern to locate his readers on the map, so to speak, we might press for an alternative reading — namely, "in the sanctification of the Spirit." In terms of meaning, this phrase would be a close cousin of that other "place," "in Christ." To put it differently, "because of the obedience and sprinkling of blood of Jesus Christ," Peter's Model Readers have been relocated in a new space: "in the realm of holiness engendered by the Holy Spirit."[22] This way of putting things prepares for Peter's reference to believers as a "spiritual house" in 2:5, where the modifier "spiritual" bars us from hearing in Peter's words a reference to an architectural structure while at the same time ensuring that we grasp that the construction of this temple is the work of the Spirit. Clearly, the Spirit effects election and holiness in God's people, forming them into the "place" where the holy God is present.[23]

Peter's task, then, is to pull back the curtain on the contemporary lives of God's people so that they might see what only the eyes of faith allow. His Model

---

22. Thus, taking πνεύματος as a genitive of production; for this construction, cf. Daniel B. Wallace, *Greek Grammar beyond the Basics: An Exegetical Syntax of the New Testament* (Grand Rapids: Zondervan, 1996), pp. 104-6.

23. See Wells, *God's Holy People,* 216-17. This idea, that the wilderness of exile is the place for the Spirit to make people holy, was not original to Peter. For example, Peter's theology resonates well with that of another wilderness community: Qumran, whose *Rule of the Community* has it that the Spirit is integral to cleansing and holiness (for example, 1QS 3.7-8; 9.3-4); see John R. Levison, "Holy Spirit," in *Dictionary of New Testament Background,* ed. Craig A. Evans and Stanley E. Porter (Downers Grove, Ill.: InterVarsity, 2000), pp. 507-14 (pp. 513-14); Matthias Wenk, *Community-Forming Power: The Socio-Ethical Role of the Spirit in Luke-Acts,* JPTSup 19 (Sheffield: Sheffield Academic Press, 2000), pp. 102-5.

Readers are suffering, ostracized, people on the margins. No one needed to explain this reality to them, however; their calamitous state of affairs was well known to them already! Rather, they needed to make sense of it all. Peter's work, then, was not to deny the reality of suffering, but rather to put the painful experience of marginal existence into perspective, to fill it with new meaning. This he does by overlooking what might seem to be the natural, social, and historical chasm separating Israel of old and a contemporary, largely Gentile church, in favor of a theological unity by which God's people, old and new, then and now, Gentile and Jew, could be seen as one continuous people. His strategy is to induct his readers into the story of Israel as though it were their story, so that they might recognize themselves in Israel's Scriptures as the "you" to whom God speaks and the "we" who respond. They, we, are the fruit of the Spirit's generative work, for it is the Spirit who forms a holy people into a residence for God's presence.

The Nature of Holiness in the World

For 1 Peter, the purpose for the Spirit's work in forming a holy people among whom God may dwell is that they might "offer spiritual sacrifices acceptable to God through Jesus Christ" (2:5). What is the nature of those offerings? Peter works out the nature of holy living in three ways.

(1) Holiness as Human Vocation

First, Peter takes the positive route of characterizing his Christian audience in relation to God's call to holiness, to be like God. Thus, the directive against conformity to the desires of this world (1:14) is balanced by the exhortation to "live in referent fear during the time of your exile" (1:17), and the warrant for both rests in God's words, "You shall be holy, for I am holy" (1:16). In this way, he locates the Christian vocation squarely in the context of God's call upon Israel since, in order for Israel to fulfill its mission of being Yahweh's priesthood in the midst of the nations, they were to be "holy" — that is, "different," or "distinctive." This was not at root a call for retreat from the world, but a vocation to identify with God's own character. In order to make a difference in the world of nations, Israel was to be different — in the words of C. J. H. Wright, "recognizably, visibly, and substantively different, as the people belonging uniquely to Yahweh and therefore representing his character and ways. . . ."[24]

24. Christopher J. H. Wright, "Old Testament Ethics: A Missiological Perspective," *Catalyst* 26 (2, 2000): 5-8 (6).

(2) Holiness as Conversion and Engagement

Peter adopts a negative stance *vis-à-vis* the former lives of his audience, but he does not engage in invective rhetoric against "the world at large," as though we might define Christian identity and behavior in opposition to non-Christians. He does not counsel separation from the world, as though the demands of holiness might necessarily or even possibly be parlayed into patterns of isolation. Nor does Peter imagine that his readers can simply wipe the slate clean, so to speak, as though they could erect a new moral and political world from the ground up, a world that would be more conducive to or even reflect Christian faithfulness. We are, Peter urges, called to work out the nature of holiness as aliens in this world, where we are here and now. We anticipate with hope that "imperishable, uncorrupted, and unfading inheritance kept in heaven" (1:4), but this time and this place are not it. Hence, Peter insists on a conversion of our deepest allegiances, our character, and our practices — even if this involves suffering injustice precisely because we repudiate violence by refusing to "repay evil for evil or insulting for insulting" (3:9).

In the past, Peter's audience gave room for those desires that led to "doing what the Gentiles like to do" (1:14; 4:3), but now they live out holiness toward one another in constant love, hospitality, humility, and mutual service (4:8-9; 5:1-7), and toward the world in faithful witness. Indeed, Peter is confident that honorable conduct in the world, even when that conduct is belittled by others, will lead others to faith (for example, 2:12; 3:5, 15b-18a). Hence, although it is true that Peter's identification of his readers as the chosen people of God brings with it a warning against the dangers of falling into forms of behavior that would jeopardize the future promised them by God, it is also true that Peter is able to conceive of alternative, more faithful ways of being in the world. This is because of Jesus Christ, who both demonstrates and makes possible a holiness of engagement.

(3) Holiness as the Imitation of Christ

Finally, Peter points to the work of Jesus, which for him is effective both in the generation of this new people and for modeling the way of life expected of his followers. Ultimately, Christian identity and practice are not defined negatively *vis-à-vis* those who reject the ways of Yahweh, but positively in relation to the way of Jesus Christ. Peter discusses the life of Jesus not as a speculative exercise, but precisely in order to draw out its relationship to the new lives of those who are enabled and called to follow Christ. Paul Achtemeier summarizes well: "The theological logic of 1 Peter is grounded in the events of the passion of Jesus Christ: his suffering (2:21) and death (1:19), and his subsequent resurrection (1:21) and glorification (3:21). The logic thus grounded structures both the new reality and consequently the new behavior of those who follow Christ."[25] For this reason, Peter devotes significant attention to the redemptive and exemplary journey of Jesus through suffering and death to his exaltation: ". . . Christ suffered on your behalf, leaving you a pattern so that you might follow in his footsteps" (2:21).

We are not against the world; the holiness of God's people is thus not found in reciprocal animosity with their opponents. We do not withdraw from the world. We do not work out our identity and sense of mission simply by negating the beliefs and behaviors of others. If we are different from the world, it is not because we set out to be so, but rather because our lives rest ultimately in a God who is different and we follow in the footsteps of Jesus Christ.

Conclusion

Some interpreters of 1 Peter find Peter's message one of accommodation or conformity to societal expectations:[26] When in Rome, do as the Romans, so as not to create unrest or to draw upon oneself or one's community dreaded negative attention. I find it hard to imagine how a letter in which the death of Jesus Christ figures so prominently — the death of Jesus by crucifixion at the hands of the Romans — could adopt such a perspective on life in the world. In fact, the holiness of engagement to which Peter gives witness would seem to disallow such an interpretation.

Take, for example, the admonition to "honor the emperor" (2:17). Obviously, this advice represents no less than what was expected of all who lived under Rome's imperial rule. On the surface, Peter seems to be abdicating the rule of Christ for the rule of Rome: When in Rome, do as the Romans. We should take care to note, though, that almost with the same stroke of the pen, Peter also wrote, "Honor everyone" (2:17). It is hard to imagine a more devastating critique of the Roman way, of "the way things are done," for with the pairing of these two directives Peter has flattened the status pyramid of the Roman world. He has just made one's response to the emperor nothing more than one's re-

---

25. Achtemeier, *1 Peter,* p. 66.

26. For example, David L. Balch, *Let Wives Be Submissive: The Domestic Code in 1 Peter,* SBLDS 26 (Chico, Calif.: Scholars, 1981).

sponse to the slave next door — or, perhaps better, he has made one's response to the slave next door no less than one's response to the emperor!

Peter's perspective is neither escapism nor accommodation. It is, rather, a hammering out of the good news within the lived realities of ordinary life. This is a holiness of engagement.

Holiness and Ecclesiology
in Jude and 2 Peter

Ruth Anne Reese

Many scholars easily link Jude and 2 Peter since they share a large swath of similar text between them,[1] but a close examination of each text reveals that each epistle also has distinct approaches and addresses different topics and situations. They are written to different people who find themselves in different circumstances and the proposed actions that each church should undertake have significant variations between them. At the same time, both epistles share an urgency about holy living in an unholy world, and this urgency is directed towards the church. Because the letters address different situations, I will address them separately while also giving attention to their contribution in our contemporary context. The contemporary church is challenged by both internal and external difficulties; together, these two books speak to those situations. In the twenty-first-century context, the church experiences division at local and worldwide levels. In addition, the church faces challenges from religions and philosophies of life outside the Christian faith. In North America many of the ways that believers live out the life of the church together are failing. What will replace that life (secularism, humanism, individualism, or a renewed and revitalized understanding of the life of the church as the people of God)? In this context, these two epistles have much to say to the church in the twenty-first century.

---

1. Jude 5-19 and 2 Peter 2 share significant similarities that are almost certainly the result of borrowing from one document to the other. Which borrowed from the other is not significant for this essay. For a complete discussion of the issue see Richard Bauckham, *2 Peter, Jude,* WBC (Waco: Word Books, 1983), pp. 141-43.

Jude: A Letter to the Divided Church

Initial Overview of Jude's Ecclesial Situation

The epistle of Jude is written to a church that finds itself internally divided. Some in the church have turned away from the self-giving practices that build up the community and their faith, and have turned away from pursuit of the love of God. Instead, they have taken up ways of life that are self-affirming and that have at their root a denial of Jesus Christ. These people are described as those who shepherd themselves and pursue a way of life that is designed to bring them increases in status and wealth. Among other examples, they are compared with Balaam and Korah. These people are still, to some extent, within the boundaries of the church. The epistle opens using the language of secrecy to describe them. They have slipped in secretly among the beloved (v. 4) and remain with them enjoying the benefits of the church and partaking of the love feasts that should be the embodiment of the community (v. 12). Understanding that the opponents are hidden within the boundaries of the community will foster a particular reading of the epistle that differs from those who draw strict boundaries between the beloved and the opponents. The letter never encourages the people who are addressed as the beloved to excommunicate or exclude those who are engaging in unholy and divisive acts, yet the letter clearly indicates that these are people in their midst. Instead, the beloved (and, I would argue, all those who wish to define themselves as the beloved) are encouraged to engage in acts that build up their faith, that resonate with their position as beloved and kept, and that reach out to rescue those who are in need of salvation and mercy (namely, those who have been living ungodly lives and causing divisions within the church). Such a response can only arise out of their position as those who are beloved by God and kept by Jesus Christ.

Setting Ecclesial Life within a Larger Narrative

The author begins by identifying himself as the slave of Jesus Christ and by addressing his audience as those who identify themselves as the called community: those who are loved by God the Father and who are kept by Jesus Christ. But after this opening, Jude does very little to explore the significance of Jesus' life, death, or resurrection. Instead, when Jude turns to address the problem that confronts the church, he turns first of all to the history that he expects them to share. He sets the problems that the community faces inside the larger narrative, which he expects them to acknowledge as their own. He draws on their understanding of Scripture and tradition to communicate with the community the dangerous position of those who deny Jesus and who are a law unto themselves. This is a narrative that he expects them to know already (v. 5), and he sees Jesus as having a part in this narrative both in the Exodus and in the description of the one who will come with his myriad of angels to address all the ungodly people and their ungodly deeds (vv. 14-15).[2] The narrative that begins with the events of the Exodus carries through to the point at which the author encourages the audience to remember the words of the apostles so that they do not find themselves taken by surprise. While there is limited reflection on Jesus or the events of Jesus' life in this short letter, the author assumes that the readers will recognize the significance of Jesus as master, as Lord, and as one who has been present in history and who will come to rectify the problems of ungodliness that they now face. At the heart of the community's identity is its relationship to the one who has called them and who now keeps them for that time when they will be presented before God pure and joyful and holy (v. 24).

There is a strong contrast between the final holy presentation of the beloved people of God and those who are described as ungodly throughout the epistle. The writer has drawn deeply on the resources of scripture and tradition to describe the ungodly as people who have engaged in the deepest and most awful types of sin. Most notably, they have participated in the type of sin that led to the destruction of Cain, in the paradigm of rebellion against the faithfulness of God,[3] and in the prideful actions of self-promotion and destruction of the community (e.g., grumbling, discontent, and boasting, v. 19). It is also clear from the author's presentation that such deliberate and ongoing sin will not go unpunished. Repeatedly, the author refers to segments of Israel's history where the ungodly have reaped the consequences of their actions. The unbelieving generation was destroyed (v. 5); the angels who rebelled were kept in prison (v. 6); Sodom and Gomorrah suffered destruction by fire (v. 7); Korah was swallowed up (v. 11); and the ungodly experienced the judgment of God (vv. 14-15). While the author does not encourage the beloved to excommunicate the ungodly, he makes it abundantly clear that the actions of previous ungodly generations have not gone unnoticed by God, nor has God failed to respond to those actions. The ungodly people who are participating in the actions that are denying God and destroying the community would do well to take note of the

---

2. Jude's use of κύριος should be seen as a reference to Jesus, and in this sense Jesus is understood to be present in some pre-existent fashion at such events as the Exodus and the destruction of Sodom and Gomorrah.

3. J. D. Charles, *Literary Strategy in the Epistle of Jude* (London: Associated University Presses, 1993), p. 112.

implied judgment that God has reserved for all those who rebel against him. At the same time, this is not a book that pronounces a judgment upon sinners from which there is no return.

Differentiating between the "Holy" and "Unholy" in Jude

The issue of holiness is intimately connected with the church community in this epistle. The opening segment separates out two groups: the first is a called out community who are loved by God and kept by Jesus; the second is a group who have slipped into this same community and denied the very God who bought them (he is the master, an obvious reference to the slave-master relationship in the Greco-Roman world) and who keep themselves instead of allowing Jesus to keep them. This separation between two groups only seems to be further upheld by the rhetorically fiery description of these ungodly people in vv. 5-19. Yet, there are several nuances that cause the reader to pause in this stringent separation of the two groups who can be labeled as the "holy" and the "unholy."

The first is the secret nature of the opponents' presence (vv. 4, 12). The implication of their secret presence among the beloved is that they too are present when this letter is read to the whole church — the community consists of both the beloved and the ungodly.

The second nuance is the instructions at the end of the book. While the instructions are addressed to the beloved (v. 20), the ungodly people who had slipped in secretly would also hear the instructions read out to the beloved. At the same time, the instructions themselves may help us to see a less rigid separation than is easily envisioned in the first portion of the epistle. The beloved people are given four instructions. Three of these instructions are participles, but one of these is an imperative. The beloved are to build themselves up in their faith and to pray in the Holy Spirit (v. 20). This is followed by the imperative; they are to keep themselves in the love of God. At the beginning of the epistle they were described as those who are loved by God, but now they are instructed to remain in this love. Throughout the epistle Jesus or the Lord (κύριος) has been described as the one who keeps both the beloved and the ungodly (vv. 1, 6, 13) but now it is the beloved who must keep themselves in the love of God. This tension between the opening segment of the epistle and the closing instructions may serve to arouse tension in the readers or hearers themselves.

Every reader wants to be identified as one of the beloved, as one of those who is kept by God, but at the end of the epistle, the reader is required to take responsibility for her position. This suggests that the ungodly are offered a route back into the called out community of the beloved via the same instructions that are given to the beloved themselves. The ungodly may participate in building others up in the faith instead of causing division, grumbling, and argument while engaging in self-promotion, licentiousness, and status seeking. They too may seek to build others up by praying in the Holy Spirit. They too may remember their history and seek not to live into the litany of groups and people who have gone astray. These are the types of activities that those who are beloved engage in to keep themselves in the love of God. And if the ungodly seek to live in this way, then they too may join with the beloved in the act of waiting. For the last instruction that the beloved are given is the instruction to wait for the mercy of the Lord Jesus Christ. This is the mercy that will lead them into eternal life. The called out community is instructed to live in such a way that they will be able to wait together for the final redemption that Christ will bring them.

The third nuance that should give pause to the reader who wishes to see a stringent and permanent separation of the two groups in Jude is vv. 22-23. While it is possible that the ungodly may come to a sudden realization of their position upon hearing the letter read out, this is not the most likely scenario. After all, human hearts are often stubborn and entrenched. Here the beloved are instructed to show mercy towards some who are doubting, to save some by snatching them out of the fire, and to have mercy on some even while they despise the garment that is stained by the flesh. In other words, they have an ongoing responsibility to rescue their brothers and sisters from destruction. This responsibility is not abrogated when the brothers or sisters fall into doubt, danger, or sin; instead, these are the very ones towards whom the beloved are instructed to show mercy and salvation. Ungodliness does not make the ungodly untouchable. The beloved reach out to rescue those in need. Following this command for the beloved to demonstrate mercy and salvation, Jude identifies God as Savior, and makes it clear that access to that salvation is through Jesus Christ (v. 25). In some ways, the rescue of the ungodly that the beloved are to effect is analogous to Jesus' own presentation of the beloved as pure and spotless in the presence of God.

Shaping Contemporary Ecclesial Life in Holy Ways: Resources from Jude

The context of this letter is a divided church. There are two sides, both of whom are sure to look at themselves as being in the right. Those who identify themselves as the beloved understand the ungodly to be Jesus-denying, lawless self-promoters. The ungodly are portrayed as taking advantage of the beloved and causing general chaos in the community. Addressing this issue of division, sin, and heresy (for it is an obvious heresy to deny Jesus) in the church, Jude provides a general set of resources that should be considered when division has occurred within the community — whether two thousand years ago or in the twenty-first century.

First, the church must be able to see and name the wrongdoing that is being perpetrated by a particular group, especially within specific contexts. For example, the ungodly were using the love feasts as a place for self-care and self-promotion instead of building up the other members of the body of Christ. Specific naming of sin helps make the problem concrete and addressable.

Second, the church needs to recognize that God is able to judge, discipline, and punish those who are ungodly in his own time. Whether that judgment is more immediate, after a period of time, or on the final day of judgment, believers must continue to affirm that God's judgment will come and will be visited on those who are ungodly. However, it is not the responsibility of the beloved to mete out that judgment or any consequent punishment.

Third, those who want to live out a godly, holy life as the beloved people of God must find ways to build each other up in their faith. Faith can be strengthened by naming those things that are antithetical to it (denying Jesus Christ, lawlessness, lack of faith in God's provision, division, murmuring, self-promotion, and greed, to name some of the issues addressed by Jude). At the same time, faith needs to be fed and strengthened by positive activity as well. This includes praying in the Holy Spirit (v. 20). Some commentators have suggested that the participle, προσευχόμενοι, is causal. Thus, it is by praying in the Holy Spirit that the faith of the beloved is built up.[4] Elsewhere in the New Testament, it is the Holy Spirit who teaches believers and reminds them of the truth Jesus *taught* (John 14:26); it is through the Holy Spirit that God's *love* has been poured into our hearts (Rom 5:5); and it is the Holy Spirit who helps us *to pray* when we do not know what words to use (Rom 8:26). Hence, part of the way that the church builds itself up and encourages its members is by inviting the Holy Spirit to be at work in its midst in such a way that the whole congregation knows the work of the Holy Spirit in teaching, love, and prayer. In addition, the church engages in the kinds of actions that will keep them in the love of God (v. 21). Since these actions are not specifically spelled out, we might assume that they are the opposite of the actions that the ungodly people in Jude have pursued. So, for example, the beloved might keep themselves in the love of God by affirming with their lives their faith in Jesus Christ, by living according

---

4. Douglas J. Moo, *2 Peter, Jude,* NIVAC (Grand Rapids: Zondervan, 1996), p. 284.

to his law (i.e., the new commandment "to love one another," John 13:34), and by speaking in ways that give hope, bring peace, encourage truthfulness, and serve the other members of the community.

These types of actions undertaken by faith and through the grace of Jesus Christ will enable the church to be the called out community of God's people. As the called out community that is building rather than tearing down faith in Jesus, they are to await the mercy of Jesus that leads to eternal life.[5] The beloved are to wait together for Jesus to visit them with his heart of compassion, i.e., his mercy that leads them to eternal life. They do not earn their life, not even by engaging in acts of godliness; instead they wait and receive their life from Jesus as a gift given out of his mercy.

Fourth, it is the task of this community of the beloved to gather up the ungodly into their midst and work for their transformation. They are to do this by offering the ungodly mercy and salvation. Having been instructed to wait and be open to receiving the mercy of Jesus themselves (v. 21), they are to demonstrate mercy to the ungodly who do not deserve it (vv. 22-23). The instruction to show mercy frames this last set of commands. The beloved are to show mercy to those who doubt, to those who are in two minds, who are ambivalent, undecided, and unsure what to think, and they are to show mercy to others who are deeply stained. However, that mercy is to be tinged with fear, not offered lightly. When the sins of the ungodly have been named, then the godly can offer mercy with fear because they know the kinds of places to which they can be drawn by the sins of the ungodly. They too recognize their own susceptibility to the stained life; such recognition allows them to offer mercy without thereby being drawn into the sinful life of the ungodly. Hence, the salvation that they are to offer the ungodly is framed by mercy. Salvation in this context is clearly rescue from destruction since the beloved are instructed to snatch some from the fire associated with the judgment of God (v. 23; cf. v. 7). Thus, the beloved are to do all they can to rescue the ungodly and enable them to join them in patiently awaiting the final mercy of Jesus Christ that will bring them to eternal life. They are to do this in the context of the community (all the instructions are in the plural) with love, encouragement, and healthy fear. They are to trust the one who is able to present them in the presence of God without blemish and with joy.

These steps can be taken in the twenty-first-century church just as they were taken in the first-century church. Some are unwilling to name sin and heresy because it is easier to live with it and avoid the pain of confrontation, but this does not lead to a strong Christian body. Frequently, people in the western

---

5. Mercy is the quality of showing kindness or compassion to someone at their point of need.

church do not even know when they have apostatized nor how they lead others astray. They see their own perspective and are inclined to think that they are right and others are wrong. There are many elements within the western church: both different denominations and different commitments within and across those denominations. Words like "fundamentalist," "evangelical," and "liberal" have been used to mark off stringent boundaries of one group from another. Too often such words are used to demarcate the "holy" from the "unholy," to say "those of us on this side of the line are okay, but the ones on the other side are not." The challenge may be to ask ourselves how we who identify ourselves as being on a particular side of a line also deny our master Jesus Christ. Are we so committed to "simple faith" in God's absolutes that we are unwilling to see any complexity in the life of faith? Do we work so hard at the practical elements of faith (the three point sermon and seven clues for effective living) that we fail to understand the ambiguity of faith? Conversely, are we so aware of the mystery and unintelligible parts of faith that we have become convinced that there are no absolutes and find ourselves denying the truth of parts of both Scripture and tradition? Each of these can be its own form of sin, which needs to be named and dealt with. Each can be a denial of the master who has bought us with his life and called us to be holy. Any mercy that we offer without naming and dealing with the sins that are present presents a danger to the body: the danger of assimilating sin as a normal part of the life of the community.

On the other hand, in an effort to "preserve holiness" in the community, some believers name sin solely for the purpose of judgment and punishment rather than to enable mercy and salvation. In this case, sin is named but lives are not rescued nor changed by the naming of sin.[6] Once sin is named, however, it is vitally important for the church to engage in living practices that affirm our faith in both word and deed and embody the holiness to which we are called. We must encourage each other to grow in faith, to pray in the Holy Spirit, to keep ourselves in the love of God, and to wait for the mercy of Jesus. Furthermore, we must do all we can as the local community of Christ's body to rescue the ungodly by engaging in acts that demonstrate the kindness of Christ at their point of need (whether they are torn between divided opinions or deeply stained by the sins in which they engage). Finally, as the twenty-first-century church, we need to be aware that the ungodly may be as much within our midst as without, and it is always important to ask ourselves if our own actions and ways of life embody the instructions to the beloved or move us in directions that deny our master, Jesus Christ.

6. See L. Gregory Jones, *Embodying Forgiveness* (Grand Rapids: Eerdmans, 1995), pp. 145-50 for a discussion of the judgment of grace.

The epistle of Jude is one short book in a diverse canon. It is certainly not the only book dealing with issues related to holiness and ecclesiology. In any particular circumstance in the church, it is important to consider the range of comments and positions that the Scripture offers on a particular issue. The circumstances that faced the church addressed by the epistle of 2 Peter are quite different, for example, from the circumstances faced in the epistle of Jude.

2 Peter: A Letter to the Church Enticed by the World

There are both similarities and differences between the books of Jude and 2 Peter. Both recipients are described as people who are called (Jude 1; 2 Pet 1:3); both face people who have slipped into their midst and denied Jesus (Jude 4; 2 Pet 2:1); both encounter teachers who proclaim a self-serving fulfillment of their own desires over care for others and love of Jesus (Jude 4; 2 Pet 2:2, 13); both are reminded that the apostles had told them that there would be mockers in the last days who would follow their own desires (Jude 18; 2 Pet 3:3); and both are warned to be wary of those who might cause them to stumble (Jude 23; 2 Pet 3:17). But the situations are also different. The recipients of the book of Jude are told to build up their faith and practice mercy and salvation towards those who might be rescued (vv. 20-23). On the other hand, the recipients of 2 Peter are given far greater instruction about the assets available to them through knowledge of Jesus Christ (1:3-11) and are encouraged to live pure, righteous lives (3:11). They are not instructed to show mercy or salvation to those who might tempt them to leave the faith but are instead instructed to be on guard against such people (3:17). It appears that some new converts in 2 Peter are being enticed away from faith in Jesus (2:18-21) and Peter provides them, along with all Christians, with resources to respond to the specific threats that they experience. These resources are rooted in their status as equal believers in Jesus, their knowledge of Jesus Christ, and the narrative of Scripture from creation to eschaton with a focus on Jesus Christ.

The Audience and the Present Crisis
Engendered by Their Opponents

At the outset of the letter, Peter[7] draws attention to the status of those whom he addresses. They are identified as ones "who have received faith that is of equal

---

7. Many contemporary commentators have argued that 2 Peter is a pseudepigraphical book (e.g., Bauckham et al.) written by someone who is using the name of Simon Peter. A few

honor with our own" (1:1). This is particularly interesting if a fair number of the recipients are recent Christians as it emphasizes that the faith that they all belong to is one in which status is shared equally between both apostles and new believers. At the same time, the apostle recognizes his unique role as one who was an eyewitness to the ministry of Jesus Christ, and so he pens this letter as a reminder and resource to the community. The status of faith is shared equally, but there are different roles within the community.

The community is one whose members are described as "established in the truth" (1:12). This affirmation is important because as we read on in the epistle, we discover that the believers are confronted by people who distort the truth and who intend to deceive them and lead them astray. The opponents taunt them by saying that there will be no second coming and that the world will go on in the same unchanged state that they have always known (3:4). Since it is obvious to the opponents that nothing is going to change, they tempt the believers to leave the life of faith and holiness behind in exchange for a life of pleasure. Those who want to stand firm and retain their honorable position within the faith will be best served by relying on their life-changing knowledge of Jesus Christ (1:3, 8; 3:18) and by trusting in the promises and power that he gives them (1:4; 3:9, 13). The community is already established in the truth, and they have been assured at the outset that everything they need for life and godliness has already been provided through their knowledge of the one who called them (1:3-4).

The audience's knowledge of Jesus Christ is essential in this short epistle. The author reminds them of it in the opening sentence when he expresses the desire that "grace and peace be multiplied" to them in their "knowledge of God and of Jesus our Lord" (v. 2). 2 Peter uses two Greek words for knowledge (ἐπίγνωσις and γνῶσις). The first, ἐπίγνωσις, has been shown by Picirelli to have the sense of "full knowledge" or perhaps even "saving knowledge" in 2 Peter.[8] Each time that it is used in 2 Peter it has as its object either God or Jesus Christ. On the other hand, the second word, γνῶσις, has the sense of knowing in a broad or general sense rather than in the intensified sense that ἐπίγνωσις seems to carry in 2 Peter. The audience of 2 Peter is to grow in their full knowledge of God and of Jesus Christ. This growth comes about as the community focuses on Jesus Christ and observes his glory and his moral goodness. Where other books might turn to the cross or to the resurrection as the events to be known,

---

(e.g., Michael Green, *2 Peter, Jude,* 2nd ed. [Downers Grove, Ill.: InterVarsity, 1987]) have argued that it is written by Simon Peter himself. I am in agreement with this latter position and have therefore referred to the author as Peter throughout this essay.

8. Robert E. Picirelli, "The Meaning of 'Epignosis,'" *Evangelical Quarterly* 47 (1975): 85-93.

Peter focuses upon the person of Jesus, upon his honor and virtue and upon the divine fellowship that is offered to believers. This participation in the divine comes about because of the promises and gifts that Jesus gives to believers that enable them to have both life and godliness. Jesus demonstrates the divine life as one that is full of both glory and moral excellence. He then makes available the means for his followers to share in the divine nature, both its glory and its virtue.[9] Faithful people in this epistle are those who have knowledge of both God and Jesus Christ and who have been impacted by their encounter with salvation and righteousness. It is the power of Jesus that has made available to believers everything that they need to pursue life and godliness (1:3), and this is most fully demonstrated in the glory and moral virtue of Jesus, the one who calls them (1:3).

In contrast to the life lived in light of the full knowledge of God and Jesus Christ, the reader need only turn to the second chapter for an opposite picture. Here are a group of people who have chosen to live relying on their own power and making their own promises. The motives that drive them are described as greed and pleasure (2:2-3, 10, 13-14, 18); their aims are for the destruction of others (2:1). They are people who are unjust and whose end is destruction, yet the promises they make to others are offers of freedom that they can never fulfill (2:18-22). This is life apart from the knowledge of God.

The Basis of Peter's Response to Their Present Crisis

An Appeal to Share in the "Glory" of the Son

The believers are invited to share in that divine nature, which has just been described as one of glory and virtue. One of the ways that the glory of God has been understood since the Old Testament is as the presence of God with his people.[10] In the New Testament, God's presence is manifested in the person of Jesus. This is clearly seen in books like the Gospel of John (particularly 1:1-18)

---

9. The phrase γένησθε θείας κοινωνοὶ has been an important part of the Orthodox theology. Protestants have often been wary of this doctrine because they feared that it meant "becoming like God." Jürgen Moltmann (*The Coming of God: Christian Eschatology* [Minneapolis: Fortress, 1996]) rightly helps us to understand that participation with the divine means that "The divine characteristics of non-transience and immortality therefore become benefits of salvation for human beings" (p. 272). It is clear from 2 Peter and other NT texts that through Jesus humans share some characteristics with God and these are to be received with thanksgiving and treasured as part of God's work with humanity.

10. A. M. Ramsey, *The Glory of God and the Transfiguration of Christ* (London: Longmans, Green and Co., 1949).

and Hebrews 1:1-4, but it is also part of other New Testament books as well. In 2 Peter the glory of Jesus is coupled with his ability to live a life of moral virtue. Now, Jesus provides the resources for his followers to do the same.

In the one scene from Jesus' life that is recounted in 2 Peter, glory is one of the major themes. Peter writes, "he received honor and glory from God the Father" (1:17), when the "Majestic Glory" announced Jesus as his beloved Son. The Father is present in the world in the person of his Son and bestows on him the honor and glory that reveals both the power and presence of God in the world. It is worth noting that in the Greco-Roman world power was concentrated in the father, who was the head of his household and exercised power over his sons until the time of his death.[11] The father could bestow or withhold power and position from his son. Here, we see Jesus' father announcing his pleasure in his son and indicating the relationship between them that is characterized by the glory they share. The writer's reflection on the glory and power of Christ is his testimony before those who assert that the events of Jesus' life are simply myth or fable. His eyewitness account focuses attention on the reliability of Jesus and his prophetic word.

The writer's reflection on this scene from Jesus' life is not simply about what Jesus did or who he is but is instead focused on the resources he provides in the present for daily living. In addition, the author reminds the readers of the promises that Jesus gives them. These promises include the return of Jesus to establish a kingdom of righteousness (3:9-13) and the gift of the Holy Spirit.[12] Knowledge of Jesus is not just for the present but is for the future realization of the kingdom of God as well. The provision of God is for now and for eternity. The knowledge and promises of Jesus enable believers to live out the instructions to add to their faith such characteristics as moral virtue, knowledge, self-control, endurance, godliness, and brotherly love.

An Appeal to God's Reliability in the History of His People

At the same time that Peter focuses upon the glory and power of Jesus as living resources for the community, he also draws upon elements of the history of Is-

---

11. Paul Veyne, *The Roman Empire* (Cambridge, Mass.: Harvard University Press, 1987), p. 29.

12. Ἐπάγγελμα (*epangelma*, "promise") only occurs in 2 Pet 1:4 and 3:13 and does not occur at all in the LXX. Ἐπαγγελία (*epangelia*, "promise") occurs in about fifty New Testament verses and eight times in the LXX. Even as a verb the word is only used about fifteen times in the New Testament (once in 2 Pet 2:19) and ten times in the LXX. Despite the infrequency of its usage, it recurs in contexts that share two particular themes: the promise of the Holy Spirit (cf. Luke 24:49 and Acts 1:4) and the promise/s made to Abraham and his descendants.

rael to shape their response to the present crisis. He begins the epistle by reminding them of the glory and majesty that Jesus embodied and then turns to the power of God in history. The Lord God rescues the godly and judges the unrighteous. The angels that sinned were judged (2:4). The generation of Noah was condemned, but the righteous man Noah along with his family was rescued (2:5). The cities of Sodom and Gomorrah were destroyed, but the righteous man Lot was delivered (2:6-8). God sees the just and the unjust, the godly and the ungodly, and he rescues the just and judges the unjust (2:9-10). The opponents in 2 Peter 2 are compared with the angels, the ancient world, and the cities that were destroyed; they are portrayed as empty, vain, sensuality-seeking, greedy deceivers. There is no doubt by the end of the chapter that the group that confronts the church in this epistle is a sly, charming one that embraces new believers with silky words that promise freedom from rules, regulations, and boundaries. There is also little doubt that God sees such ungodliness for what it is and is prepared to judge those who engage in it.

An Appeal to God's Reliability in Creation and New Creation

After outlining the sins of the ungodly, Peter turns in chapter 3 to the specific argument that they have been using to persuade believers to join their way of thinking. The opponents mock belief in the second coming of Christ (3:3-4). They taunt the believers with the observation that it hasn't happened yet. To drive their point home, they add that there isn't any reason to expect it to happen in the near future since nothing has changed since the fathers fell asleep. In other words, since the time of the ancients the world has gone on just as it always has and there is no reason to expect anything different. Peter has already demonstrated the power of God to discern good and evil and judge accordingly either for destruction or for salvation. He has shown how God has acted in history to vindicate the just and to punish the unjust. Now, Peter turns even farther back, to the beginning of history, in order to remind his readers that the God that they follow is the one who has created the world as they know it (3:5-6). He formed it by his word and by water. Just as he has power over people to rescue or destroy, so too God has power over his creation. And once before he chose to destroy that which he had made by means of a flood. The opponents should not forget this, for just as he rescues and judges, so too he creates and destroys. What he has done once, he can do again (3:7).

Here, Peter points his readers toward the future, reminding them that the Lord will return and that his return will be accompanied by an undoing of the world as they know it and the institution of a new world in which justice dwells (3:8-13). Neither the believers nor their opponents should forget that their history demonstrates a God of power, that they can draw on his power through Jesus Christ for their present endurance in a hostile world, and that his power will be fully demonstrated when the world is remade. Christians belong to God's narrative of justice, and they are called to live accordingly. That narrative begins with the creation of the world, continues through the story of God's judgment of Noah's generation, and through the destruction of Sodom and Gomorrah. It is a narrative that is made known in the prophetic words of the ancient prophets and continues with the revelation of Jesus as the Son who is the glory of God. This narrative will have its end when justice has been fully rewarded, injustice done away with, and this state of affairs is the permanent condition of the new creation. This is the narrative that those who have the knowledge of God and Jesus Christ live into. It is the narrative of promise; the narrative of salvation. It is the narrative that God desires for all people.

A Call to Holiness

Since Jesus has saved these believers and since their knowledge of him has brought them into a position where they share a faith of equal honor with the apostles, they are called to new lives that are characterized by the virtues of the first chapter (i.e., self-control, godliness, etc.), by purity and blamelessness (3:14). They live these lives in response to the One who has already acted in history and who therefore they can trust to act again in the future. Holiness is the proper response of a people who are aware of God's power to save and judge.

From the beginning of this letter the hearers have been called to life and godliness. The call to a holy and righteous life touches on all aspects of their life together. It is about the whole of their life (ζωή) and not only about their religious life (εὐσέβεια). The call to holiness is concerned with their ethical behavior, with their communal practices, and finally with the ultimate fulfillment of God's purposes. None of these can be compartmentalized from the others. The virtues of the first chapter have several results when they are put into practice. First of all, like the majority of this epistle the virtues are addressed to the whole community (ὑμῖν) rather than solely to individual believers, and the practice of these virtues has present effects. Those who put these things into practice will be productive and fruitful (1:8). The community that practices these virtues will find itself in a place where it can be used by God and where it will produce fruit for the kingdom. Indeed, those who practice these virtues and who live in such a way as to be certain of his calling (the noun form of the calling they already received in 1:3) will not stumble.

The virtues act as a safeguard against the temptations that arise in the second and third chapters — the temptation to pursue pleasure over faithfulness, greed over sacrifice, and injustice over justice. Furthermore, a virtuous way of life will have ongoing results into the future as it will secure for them entrance into the eternal kingdom of the one who saves them, Jesus Christ (1:11). It is always clear that entrance into the kingdom is ultimately dependent upon Jesus and his gracious gifts while at the same time holy living is the right and expected response to the calling of Jesus upon the lives of the community.

The audience of this letter finds themselves, like those in the epistle of Jude, facing an enemy that has slipped into their assembly secretly. The threat against them is even more specific in this epistle. Those they face are false teachers who deny Jesus and advocate unbridled license, while being greedy and deceitful. Furthermore, they tempt new believers with promises of freedom that the opponents cannot honor because they themselves are enslaved. In this environment, Peter reminds his audience of the basics of life and godliness: growth in the knowledge of Jesus Christ, steadfast reliance on the promises of God, realization of the believers' participation in the divine nature and fellowship, and the admonition to diligently add to their faith the virtues of a godly life.

Shaping Contemporary Ecclesial Life in Holy Ways: Resources from 2 Peter

While the book of 2 Peter may be almost two thousand years old, it has much within its small confines that should engage the twenty-first-century church, particularly the western church. The western church is plagued with the temptations of pleasure, self-gratification, greed, and self-deception. Pleasure, enjoyment, and indulgence are the norm, and simplicity, contentment, and consistent effort to grow in faith seem to be reserved for either the super-spiritual or the poor. We may even go so far as to recognize the ways in which our material goods distract us from the life of godliness, but there is little incentive for change. The powers of our world shout at us in myriad forms (TV, advertisements, billboards, the structure of our shopping experiences, the expectations of our family and friends, etc.), and they are usually enticing us to spend more, enjoy ourselves more, be more sexy, and engage more fully in the world around us. Most of us know the slogans of the world: "If it feels good, do it"; "You deserve a break today"; "be all you can be."

These are just samples of the world's messages. Few of us take enough time to analyze the messages we hear, to ask whom they are serving and why, or to ask questions about the larger story to which they belong (for example, the narratives of continual progress or of individual success). We think that such messages go in one ear and out the other, but they are much more powerful than we acknowledge, especially since they are ubiquitous. (Even the ancients knew the power of pithy proverbs to make a point as Peter himself demonstrates with his reference to the saying "a dog returns to its vomit" [2:22].) Advertisers and organizations are quite aware of the power of a catchy jingle. In an environment where those around are enticing believers with catchy promises, intriguing arguments, and interesting speculations, 2 Peter takes the believer back to the person of Jesus Christ. Ultimately, the strength for life and godliness lies in relationship with Jesus. 2 Peter reminds believers that their very life and any godliness that it may contain comes as a gift from Jesus, the one who gives both the promises and the power needed for daily life. It also reminds us that the words that are spoken to us are often spoken to serve the purposes of another agenda and are not for our benefit. The words of the world are often self-serving, greedy, and deceitful. Owning a new car will not make someone more sexy (it's more likely to make them more indebted — but that truth does not sell cars) or fulfilled. Such false messages are more easily rejected in light of the relationship that comes about from the full knowledge of Jesus Christ and from the experience of living within his power and promises. Such knowledge is only fully known in the context of the community of Christ's body. The false messages of the world are more easily understood for what they are when believers are embedded in the narrative of Scripture. Knowing the narrative of Scripture as our own story enables us to point out the inconsistencies and the false promises offered by those who have either rejected or never known Jesus Christ.

These enticing messages tend to be directed at individuals in the highly individualized western world. But there are also messages that affect the church itself more directly. For example, the church has been enticed into thinking that faith is a private matter, the business of the individual in the home and private life.[13] Alongside this comes a message of tolerance: "all roads lead to heaven"; "you believe your way, I'll believe my way." These are the messages that encourage believers to be passive about their faith, to keep it to themselves and to make sure that it happens at the appropriately segregated time and place (church, home group, Bible study rather than work, gym, and book club). The message of 2 Peter is addressed to the church as a whole. It encourages the whole community to grow up into the life of virtuous faith, and it directs the church to look to Jesus both as their example for that life and as the power that makes that life possible. The church that lives together in the power and prom-

---

13. On which, see Trevor Hart, *Faith Thinking: The Dynamics of Christian Theology* (Downers Grove, Ill.: InterVarsity, 1995); Rodney Clapp, *Border Crossings: Christian Trespasses on Popular Culture and Public Affairs* (Grand Rapids: Brazos, 2000).

ises of Jesus will find itself an effective and fruitful community that will be poised to enter the eternal kingdom of God.

Like believers from the first century, contemporary Christian believers also share in the narrative of the work of God. We too can draw on the power of God that was demonstrated with the first act of creation; we too can be reminded that God has rescued the godly and judged the ungodly and that this is both the history that we come from and the history that we live into. We too are reminded that a day is coming when the new order will be an order of justice filling the whole earth. As the body of Christ, we live into this picture of future justice by our implementation of the virtues in chapter 1. If justice is about being in right relationship with God and with each other, and if this includes all forms of relationship (i.e., economic, emotional, familial, etc.), then the virtues as they are lived out in community can be understood as some of the elements of justice. We practice moral goodness, self-control, endurance, and brotherly love, and these virtues when added to faith lead to the fruits of peace and justice among the people of God.

Jude and 2 Peter: A Message for the Church

These two short epistles are often overlooked as resources for the church, but their voices are especially pertinent in this time when so much of the western church is tempted by the pleasures of the world. These books are even more relevant since many western Christians have been able to justify or rationalize their unanalyzed participation in the socio-cultural structures of pleasure and self-gratification. In these books, the temptation to self-indulgence is linked with the sin of denying Christ (Jude 4; 2 Pet 2:1-4). These temptations come from people who are both within and outside of the church, and these two books provide significant instructions about how to deal with such temptation. The act of building up the body of believers in faith, prayer in the Holy Spirit, and works of mercy and salvation is a clear response to those who would mislead the followers of Jesus. At the same time, believers must be able to clearly see the misinformation, lies, and deceit that are offered as truth by those who would persuade them to leave behind the life of faith for the life of pleasure and self-indulgence. Such false messages are best countered by a full knowledge of the person Jesus Christ and of his power and promises. These must be put into practice in the virtuous life of faith that is lived in such a way as to hasten the coming of the day when God's righteous justice will dwell in the new heaven and the new earth.

"On Earth as It Is in Heaven": Holiness and the People of God in Revelation

Dean Flemming

The theme of the holiness of God's people in the book of Revelation has been largely underreported. One reason for this — particularly among evangelicals — is the perception that Revelation's "focus is too much on the future" to supply much teaching on sanctification in the present.[1] When the Apocalypse is seen mainly as a description of what will happen in the end-time future, then reflecting God's holy character in our current life circumstances easily becomes a peripheral concern. The problem is compounded by popular dispensational interpretations of Revelation, in which the "church" to which John is writing is caught up to heaven at the beginning of chapter 4 ("Come up here," 4:1), thereby escaping the task of holy living on earth.

In contrast, this essay will suggest that Revelation is deeply concerned with the call to Christian holiness in this world. Furthermore, it proposes that what it means to live a holy life is seen in the first place, not in individual terms, but as the corporate and public embodiment of the holiness of God, a holiness that is profoundly ethical in its character. What then does it mean for John's audience to be the holy people of God in the midst of their day-to-day cultural and social world? And how might Revelation's vision of a holy church help to form communities of faith that incarnate God's holiness in *our* world?

---

1. Donald Guthrie, *New Testament Theology* (Downers Grove, Ill.: InterVarsity, 1981), p. 674.

It is a privilege to offer these few thoughts in gratitude to Alex R. G. Deasley, my longtime example and friend. Since my days as a seminary student under his tutelage, I have been inspired by his passion for interpreting and proclaiming the message of scriptural holiness as a living possibility for the people of God.

Revelation's Rhetorical Perspective

For John's readers the call to holiness is heard and lived out in a particular social context, that of Roman Asia, most likely near the end of the first century.
John is not just a visionary and a prophet; he is also a pastor, whose message
addresses the needs of churches (*ekklēsiai;* 1:4; 2–3; 22:16) he knows well. Contrary to much traditional interpretation of Revelation, the main problem facing these Christian communities was not official persecution from Rome —
although sporadic local oppression was certainly possible (2:10; 3:10). For the
majority of these churches, the greatest threat was the temptation to compromise with the dominant Roman culture.[2] Christians in Western Asia Minor
were under daily social and economic pressure to participate in Roman public life, which was tightly bound to the imperial cult and worship of various
traditional gods.[3] What the seer sees — and many of his readers do not — is
that by making peace with the ways of the empire, these *ekklēsiai* are guilty of
collusion with an entire system of religious, political, and economic power —
another kingdom/empire, which demands an allegiance that is due to God
alone.

Consequently, in addition to other cosmic conflicts, a *rhetorical* battle
is being waged in Revelation. It is a battle for the minds and hearts, the
imaginations and loyalties of communities of Christians.[4] Through his "revelation of Jesus Christ," John offers these churches an alternative vision of
the world from the deceptive imperial worldview that saturated the cities of
Asia. Revelation unveils reality *as it really is,* from the standpoint of God's
future and God's throne. Richard Bauckham captures this apocalyptic perspective well:

> John (and thereby his readers with him) is taken up into heaven in order to
> see the world from the heavenly perspective. He is given a glimpse behind
> the scenes of history so that he can see what is really going on in the events
> of his time and place. He is also transported in vision into the final future

2. David A. deSilva, *The Hope of Glory: Honor Discourse and New Testament Interpretation* (Collegeville, Minn.: Michael Glazier/Liturgical Press, 1999), pp. 179-82; G. K. Beale, *The
Book of Revelation,* NIGTC (Grand Rapids: Eerdmans, 1999), pp. 28-33.

3. See Wes Howard-Brook and Anthony Gwyther, *Unveiling Empire: Reading Revelation
Then and Now* (Maryknoll, N.Y.: Orbis, 2001), pp. 102-11, 115-18; David A. deSilva, "The Social
Setting of the Revelation to John: Conflicts Within, Fears Without," *Westminster Theological
Journal* 54 (1992): 286-96; A. Y. Collins, *Crisis and Catharsis: The Power of the Apocalypse* (Phila-
delphia: Westminster, 1984), pp. 84-104.

4. Loren L. Johns, "The Lamb in the Rhetorical Program of the Apocalypse of John," *SBL
Seminar Papers* 37, Part 2 (Atlanta: Scholars Press, 1998), p. 784.

of the world, so that he can see the present from the perspective of what its final outcome must be, in God's ultimate purpose for human history.[5]

Thus John's prophetic vision of the glorified saints in heaven and of God's universal end-time kingdom not only reveals the church's hope of things to come. It also gives ecclesial communities a counter-imagination that defines who they are in the present. The question confronting John's readers is this: which vision of reality will shape their personal and corporate life, along with their perception of the world — the vision of Christ's victorious kingdom or the values of the dominant culture? Will they be Christian assemblies who comfortably cohabit with the idolatrous world around them, or will they live in light of God's final purpose for his people? These critical issues form the backdrop for Revelation's portrayal of a holy people of God.

A Holy God

Holiness begins with God. In Revelation, holiness is not in the first place an ethical ideal, but the identity and character of God.[6] The church is holy only as it is in relationship with a holy God. God's holiness is spotlighted above all in John's vision of the heavenly throne room in chapters 4 and 5, the theological heart of the book. Echoing another throne room scene from Isaiah 6, the heavenly worshipers extol God the Almighty with the threefold "holy, holy, holy" (4:8; cf. Isa 6:3). God is exceedingly holy, distinct from his creation. The heavenly pyrotechnics that emanate from God's throne only help to underscore the point (4:5; cf. 8:5; 11:19; 16:18-21).

From John's perspective, what is true in heaven must come to earth. Bauckham keenly observes that Revelation's prophetic vision might be viewed as a fulfillment of the first three petitions of Jesus' prayer: God's name be hallowed, his kingdom come, his will be done *on earth as it is in heaven* (Matt 6:9-10).[7] But the "facts on the ground" were different: "John and his readers lived in a world in which God's name was not hallowed, his will was not done, and evil ruled through the oppression and exploitation of the Roman system of power."[8] Because of his absolute holiness and righteousness, God cannot toler-

---

5. Richard Bauckham, *The Theology of the Book of Revelation* (Cambridge: Cambridge University Press, 1993), p. 7.

6. Thomas Söding, "Heilig, heilig, heilig: zur politschen Theologie der Johannes-Apokalypse," *Zeitschrift für Theologie und Kirche* 96 (1999): 54.

7. Bauckham, *Theology,* p. 40.

8. Bauckham, *Theology,* p. 40.

ate evil and the ungodly forces that dominate the world. Thus, in the remainder of the book after the throne room vision, God's holiness expresses itself in judgment on an idolatrous and sinful world. The God who sits on the throne is the Holy One whose judgments are true and just (16:5-7; cf. 6:10; 15:3-4; 19:11).

John not only envisions a holy Creator God, but also an exalted Christ who shares the same character of holiness. Christ speaks to the church in Philadelphia as "the Holy One, the True One" (3:7). He appears in blazing splendor as Daniel's "one like the Son of Man" (1:12-16; 14:14; cf. 2:18), and as the Divine Warrior who judges evil and wages war in righteousness (19:11-16). Yet, although awesome and holy, he is not distant from his people. Revelation pictures Christ standing in the midst of the seven lampstands, which represent the seven churches (1:13, 20; cf. 2:1). Jesus, the one who is present among them, calls the churches to repent and to embody their Lord's own holy character (chaps. 2 and 3).

In Revelation, the only appropriate response to a holy God and to Christ the slaughtered Lamb is *worship*. Throughout the Apocalypse, the saints and heavenly beings who acknowledge God's sovereignty are engaged in acts of worship, which acclaim God's holiness and righteous judgments (e.g., 4–5; 7:11-17; 11:16-18; 15:3-4; 19:1-8). For the churches in Roman Asia, worship is a political, as well as a religious act. David Aune has shown that Revelation's heavenly throne room scene bears so many resemblances to the ceremonial practice of the Roman imperial court and cult that John's readers could not help but make the connection.[9] Later, worship of the one holy God in heaven is set in blatant contrast to the idolatrous worship of the beast on earth (13:4, 8, 12, 15; 14:7, 9, 11; 16:2; 19:20), embodied for John's readers in the emperor cult. The message is clear: if God is on the throne, then Caesar isn't. God's people must choose whom they will serve. Revelation's picture of the saints' unbroken service/worship (*latreuein;* 7:15; 22:3) of God and the Lamb signifies that all of life must be lived under divine lordship and for the praise and glory of God. Worship involves both adoration and obedience.

9. David E. Aune, "The Influence of Roman Imperial Court Ceremonial on the Apocalypse of John," *Biblical Research* 28 (1983): 5-26. Common practices include, e.g., the presentation of gold crowns, prostration, and the singing of hymns. See also Howard-Brook and Gwyther, *Unveiling Empire,* pp. 202-7.

A Holy People

A Communal Holiness

A holy God requires a holy people and the seer understands this well. In Revelation the holiness of Christians is portrayed largely in corporate terms. This is consistent with John's belief that the church stands in continuity with Israel, as the end-time people of God. John repeatedly co-opts Old Testament language and images, then reapplies them to the church as God's new eschatological community. Twice, for example, he identifies the church as a "kingdom" and "priests" (1:6; 5:10; cf. 20:6). This language draws the book's readers back to the foundational covenant passage of Exod 19:5-6, in which God sets Israel apart from all other peoples as his treasured possession and a "holy nation." As a kingdom, the church both acknowledges and shares in Christ's rule (2:26-27; 3:21; 5:10; 20:4, 6). As priests, the whole people of God — not just a class of religious specialists — are consecrated to a vocation of worship and of offering prayers (5:8; 8:4) and sacrificial service to God (cf. Isa 61:6). Moreover, as Israel was marked out to be a holy and priestly nation mediating God's light to the Gentiles, the new community of priests conveys God's presence to the nations through its distinctive and faithful witness (5:9-10; cf. 7:9; 14:6-7; 15:4; 21:24-26).[10] The basis of their creation as a royal and priestly people is not a divine deliverance from Egypt, but a new exodus, a redemption from sin purchased by the blood of Christ, the Passover Lamb (5:10; cf. 1:5-6).[11] Jesus' loving sacrifice has freed them *from* sin (1:5) *for* the task of embodying God's rule and becoming priests to the world.[12]

Other biblical ideas and images reinforce this picture of a community set apart by God and for God. The word "people" *(laos)* represents the church on just two occasions, but both are weighty in their significance. In 18:4, a heavenly message comes to "my people," commanding them to separate from the sins of Babylon, just as God's people Israel were called to distance themselves from the depravity of the pagan nations around them (e.g., Isa 52:11; Jer 50:8; 51:45; Ezek 20:41). Later, when John describes the end-time community of the New Jerusalem in 21:3, he shifts to the plural "peoples" *(laoi)*. Here Revelation stunningly redefines the identity of God's holy people from Israel, a single elect nation (e.g., Lev 26:11-12; Ezek 37:27), to a multicultural chorus of worshipers drawn

---

10. Beale, *Revelation*, p. 193.

11. See J. M. Ford, "The Priestly People of God in the Apocalypse," *Listening* 28 (1993): 248-51; Bauckham, *Theology*, pp. 70-71.

12. Ben Witherington III, *Revelation*, NCBC (Cambridge: Cambridge University Press, 2003), p. 76.

from all the peoples of the world (cf. 5:9; 7:9; 14:6). But this is not simply a heavenly state of affairs. Since Christ has *already* won the decisive victory in his sacrificial death and resurrection, he has constituted the eschatological people of God who are gathered from all nations (5:5, 9-10; cf. 1:5-6). Elsewhere the Lamb's followers are the "called and chosen," his special possession (17:14). They are stamped with a seal and the name of God is inscribed on their foreheads (7:3; 14:1; 22:4; cf. 3:12; Ezek 9:4-6). This symbolizes not only God's protection, but also a radical belonging to him. Those who are "sealed" are also God's "slaves" (*douloi;* 7:3; cf. 22:3); they give complete allegiance to their divine Master, unlike the "earth-dwellers," whose foreheads bear the brand of the beast (13:16-17).

John's communal understanding of holiness is expressed particularly in the term "saints" (*hagioi,* literally, "holy ones"). This word, more than any other, designates the true church in Revelation (5:8; 8:3, 4; 11:18; 13:7, 10; 14:12; 16:6; 17:6; 18:20, 24; 19:8). Above all, it speaks of the church's relationship to a holy God. When *hagios* refers to people, it regularly occurs in the plural and indicates not merely a collection of individual saints, but a holy community.[13] Like Israel of old, the saints are "a people holy to the Lord" (Deut 7:6; 14:2, 21; cf. Ps 34:9); they are chosen and set apart to belong to God in a special way. For John, as for the New Testament as a whole, the "saints" are not a subset of especially holy individuals or martyrs within the wider company of Christians; they are the *only* true Christians.[14] They are *hagioi* because they participate in the holiness of God. At the same time, the saints are set apart in order to *be* a holy people, as God is holy — a perspective to which we will return shortly.

Other images that John applies to the church — the seven lampstands (1:20; 2:5; cf. 11:4), the sealed 144,000 of Israel (7:4-8; 14:1-5), the woman who gives birth to the Messiah (12:1-6), the bride of the Lamb (19:7-8; 21:2, 9; 22:17), the temple (3:12, 11:1-2; cf. 21:3), the holy city, New Jerusalem (3:12; 21:1-2, 10), a brotherhood or family (6:11; 12:10; 19:10) — reinforce the corporate nature of the people of God in Revelation. This does not mean, however, that Revelation lacks any concern for the individual's relationship to God or for personal holiness. The exalted Christ can speak of "a few persons" (lit. "names") within the church of Sardis "who have not soiled their clothes" (3:4). The church as kingdom will reign with Christ (1:6; 5:10; 20:6), but individual believers within the communities must "conquer" and continue to do his works in order to share in

13. The two exceptions to the use of the plural, *hagioi,* are 20:6 and 22:11. In the "makarism" of 20:6, however, those who are "holy" *(hagios)* are still conceived primarily in corporate terms, as the plural references to the same people as "priests," who will corporately reign with Christ suggest.

14. Söding, "Heilig, heilig, heilig," p. 63.

his kingdom rule (2:26-27; 3:21). Even the seemingly deterministic language in the book's conclusion, "Let the evildoer still do evil . . . and the holy *(ho hagios)* still be holy" (22:11), should be taken as a rhetorical warning and challenge. Every reader must decide whether she or he will enter the holy city or remain outside with the wicked (cf. 22:14-15).

An Ethical Holiness

We have seen that a major rhetorical goal of Revelation is to call its readers to resist compromise with the earthly powers and to motivate them to faithfulness and obedience in light of God's ultimate purpose for his creation. Given this aim, it is hardly surprising that we discover a heavy accent on ethical holiness. The saints, who are holy by virtue of their relationship to God, must reflect that holiness in their character and their conduct. Holiness is both gift and task for the people of God.

This moral element comes into highest visibility in Christ's prophetic messages to the churches in chapters 2 and 3. Christ, speaking through the Spirit (e.g., 2:6), knows the "works" of the churches individually (2:2, 19; 3:1, 8, 15). He can commend the Thyatirans' good works of love, faith, service, and endurance (2:19; cf. 2:2-3), but in other cases, churches' deeds are judged to be morally defective. Thus Sardis — more corpse than living church — has works that are not "perfect" in God's eyes (3:1-2), and Laodicea's deeds are so putrid, they make Christ sick (3:15-16). The specific sins that John spotlights in Pergamum and Thyatira are idolatry and immorality. Both of these are linked to the churches' toleration of false teachers who are apparently promoting a lifestyle of cozy compromise with the idolatrous culture around them (2:14-15, 20-23). For the Ephesians, moral failure has to do with abandoning their former love for God and toward one another (2:4-5). The Spirit's remedy for ethically deficient churches is communicated in a variety of appeals — wake up (3:2, 3), hold firm (2:25), obey what you have heard (3:3; cf. 2:26), remember and return to your first works (2:5; cf. 3:3), and, above all, repent (2:5, 16, 21, 22; 3:3, 19). Repentance means not only the turning of hearts toward God, but also turning away from doing evil and embracing a new lifestyle of obedience (2:5, 21; 9:20-21; 16:11). The call to repent is extended in the first place to the whole congregation, not just to individuals. What is more, repentance is a matter of life and death. A church that refuses to repent and persists in its unholy practices is in danger of having its lampstand removed from its place (2:5); in other words, of facing the same judgment reserved for the pagan world that is in league with Satan and the beast (9:20-21; 16:10-11). On the other hand, a church that turns to the Lord is promised the Spirit's renewing power. Nearly comatose Sardis is thus assured that Christ "holds the seven spirits of God" (3:1; cf. 1:4; 4:5, 5:6), which probably refers to the fullness of the divine Spirit at work in the community. Jesus offers the perfection and power of the Spirit to revive the church in Sardis from the dead.[15]

The theme of ethical holiness continues throughout the rest of the book (4–22), but instead of focusing on the moral character of local Christian assemblies, it plays out on a cosmic stage. Faithfulness and purity are necessary to endure the eschatological battle being waged between God and the Lamb on the one hand and the Devil and his earthly allies on the other. The saints, who represent the true people of God, are defined as those who "keep the commandments of God and hold fast to the faith of Jesus" (14:12; cf. 12:17). They endure the onslaughts of the beast (13:10; cf. 13:7; 14:12), and they are draped in righteous deeds (19:8). In light of Jesus' soon return, the "righteous" *(ho dikaios)* must act rightly, and the "holy" *(ho hagios)* are to persist in holy living (*hagiasthētō;* 22:11).[16] From Revelation's perspective, the notion of "saints" who are relationally holy but *not* ethically holy isn't a possibility worth contemplating.

The seer fleshes out this portrait of an ethically pure church with a number of compelling images. In 14:1-5 he envisions the saints as a 144,000-strong army of redeemed followers of the Lamb. They are pictured as holy warriors "who have not defiled themselves with women" (14:4). Just as Israel's warriors were called to ritual purity through abstaining from sexual relations during battle (Deut 23:9-10; 1 Sam 21:5), so the church must be morally pure in order to be victorious over the Lamb's enemies.[17] The additional reference to their being "virgins" *(parthenoi;* 14:4) may also point to the church's role as the Lamb's unsullied bride (19:7-8). Furthermore, like the Lamb they follow, they are without deceit (14:4-5; cf. Isa 53:9; Zeph 3:13). Their integrity cuts a bold contrast to the lies and illusions of a whole cast of deceptive characters in Revelation, including Jezebel (2:20) their Jewish persecutors (3:9), Satan (12:9; 20:3, 8, 10), the false prophet (13:14; 19:20), and the whore Babylon (18:23). In short, they are "blameless" *(amōmoi;* 14:5) — a term borrowed from the language of Old Testament sacrificial offerings, which now characterizes the moral purity of the saints.

15. Grant R. Osborne, *Revelation,* BECNT (Grand Rapids: Baker Academic, 2002), pp. 36, 173.

16. Osborne rightly observes that the aorist imperative verbs in Rev 22:11 "are global, emphasizing lives that are characterized by these activities" (*Revelation,* p. 787). The ethical significance of the "holy" is further underscored by its contrast with the "filthy" *(rhyparos),* a term that refers to moral impurity.

17. Bauckham, *Theology,* pp. 77-78. Contra A. Y. Collins, who takes 14:4 as a literal idealizing of sexual asceticism (*Crisis and Catharsis,* pp. 127-31).

The necessity of the church's purity and avoidance of defilement comes to particular expression in John's clothing metaphor which we might say weaves its way through Revelation like a white thread. Christ commends the faithful few in Sardis whose clothes are not soiled and who will walk with him "dressed in white." For these well-clad Christians, conquering will mean being garbed in white robes, a symbol of both purity and victory (3:4-5; cf. 3:18; 6:11). John later envisions a numberless multitude of saints who "have washed their robes and made them white in the blood of the Lamb" (7:14; cf. 7:9, 13); "that is, purified themselves from the sins of the idolatrous culture and attached themselves to the Lamb in holiness."[18] Clean robes are also the required "dress code" for entry into the holy city (22:14). The church in her end-time purity is revealed as a chaste bride, adorned in clean, bright linen that is woven from the righteous deeds of the saints (19:7-8; 21:2, 9; cf. Isa 61:10; Ezek 16:7-14; 2 Cor 11:2; Eph 5:25-27).[19] When that image is juxtaposed against the promiscuous whore Babylon, decked out in her purple and scarlet (17:1-5; cf. 18:16), the contrast could not be more striking. Throughout the Apocalypse, outer garments symbolize the inward moral character of the church.

A Public Holiness

Among the New Testament writings, Revelation is without rival in its emphasis on the public and political dimensions of holiness. As I noted earlier, Revelation's theology of holiness is closely tied to the context John addresses. For the seer, the church lives out its holy calling in a world dominated by a Roman Empire that had absolutized its power and hijacked the claim to supreme sovereignty that belongs to God and Christ alone.[20] This self-deifying order was demonstrated above all in the Caesar cult, which was particularly virile in the cities of Asia. In John's time, the emperor cult was not simply a "religious" matter; it was heavily intertwined with Roman politics and economics. Wes Howard-Brook and Anthony Gwyther summarize this relationship:

18. David A. deSilva, *Honor, Patronage, Kinship and Purity: Unlocking New Testament Culture* (Downers Grove, Ill.: InterVarsity, 2000), p. 303.

19. Craig R. Koester, *Revelation and the End of All Things* (Grand Rapids: Eerdmans, 2001), p. 195. Given the connection between clean, white robes and moral purity in Revelation, "the righteous deeds of the saints" refer to acts of obedience and endurance in 19:8 (cf. 22:11), rather than specifically to martyrdom. Contra Robert M. Royalty Jr., *The Streets of Heaven: The Ideology of Wealth in the Apocalypse of John* (Macon, Ga.: Mercer University Press, 1998), p. 214.

20. For the critique of the Roman system of power in Revelation, see Bauckham, *Theology*, pp. 35-39.

[T]he Roman imperial cult served as the propaganda mechanism for the empire itself. Everywhere one looked, the message was found inscribed in stone and metal, proclaimed in public ritual, and announced as "good news": the Roman Empire was the most powerful and blessed reality imaginable; refusing to worship it was to engage in heresy and treason at the same time. Thus, the political and economic functions of empire were propagated as "holy" by the practices of religion.[21]

We should not be surprised, then, that the formidable beast, which is linked to Rome's political and military might, attracts the worship of the "whole earth." It inspires words of adoration that parody the praise of God: "Who is like the beast, and who can fight against it?" (13:3-4; cf. Exod 15:11; Ps 71:19; 89:8). Closely related is the Roman system of commerce, which is especially symbolized by the harlot Babylon (chaps. 17–18). In Revelation, "Babylon the great" (18:2) represents the fallen, human city. It was embodied in the past by cities like Babel, Sodom, Tyre, and Babylon, but it is presently incarnated by Rome, whose evil outstrips them all.[22] In return for bringing peace and prosperity to the Mediterranean world, Rome expected and often received loyalty from her grateful subjects, particularly in Asia. John, however, prophetically unmasks Rome as a city that enriches itself on the back of violence against the innocent, oppression of the powerless, and economic exploitation of the empire. At the expense of others, she indulges her lust for luxury and wanton consumption (18:3, 7).[23]

How are God's people to respond to the constant pressure to compromise with evil in the form of Roman power and idolatry? John, in continuity with the Old Testament concern for holiness as a distinctive pattern of life in relation to the surrounding peoples, wants the saints to live as an alternative community. Consequently, Revelation draws sharp boundaries between the church and the world, between empire and community of faith. It is in this light that we can understand the warnings to the churches in Pergamum and Thyatira against eating food sacrificed to idols (2:14-15, 20-21). Christians in Asia Minor could encounter idol meat at a variety of settings — public celebrations, social dinners at the temple, local guild feasts — which involved honoring the em-

21. Howard-Brook and Gwyther, *Unveiling Empire*, p. 238.

22. See Bauckham, *Theology*, p. 130.

23. On Revelation's economic critique, see, e.g., Richard Bauckham, *The Climax of Prophecy: Studies on the Book of Revelation* (Edinburgh: T&T Clark, 1993), pp. 338-83 as well as his "The Fallen City: Revelation 18," in *The Bible in Politics: How to Read the Bible Politically* (Louisville: Westminster John Knox, 1989), pp. 85-102; Christopher R. Smith, "Reclaiming the Social Justice Message of Revelation: Materialism, Imperialism and Divine Judgement in Revelation 18," *Transformation* 7 (1990): 28-33.

peror and various pagan gods.[24] Unlike the teachers in their midst (the Nicolaitans, 2:15; Jezebel, 2:20-23) who apparently encouraged accommodation as a way of surviving in the Roman world, Revelation calls for separation from such "normal" cultural practices. Through John's prophetic eyes, they represent a sell-out to state-sponsored idolatry.[25] Revelation reinforces the need for God's people to be a countercultural community by lumping together the specific sins of Jezebel and the Nicolaitans — idolatry and fornication — with God's enemies doomed for destruction, including the beast (13:4, 8) and Babylon the harlot (14:8; 17:1-5; 18:3, 9; 19:2; cf. 21:8; 22:15).[26] Likewise, the Laodiceans, who boast in their riches (3:17), see in John's vision of fallen Babylon a reflection of their own arrogance and self-indulgent consumption (Revelation 18).[27]

For the churches of Asia Minor, the call to holiness is an appeal to "come out" of Babylon, forsaking her sins and so avoiding her judgment (18:4; cf. Jer 51:6, 45). Their exodus is not from a physical city, but from the allurements of the empire, with its unholy systems of greed, idolatry, and injustice. But what does this mean for John's readers? Is this simply the "extremist call" of a radical sectarian?[28] Does John expect Christian communities to withdraw from the public world and passively wait for God to destroy Babylon in the end? On the contrary, Revelation's answer for the church is not to retreat into a cocoon of pious irrelevance, but to *resist* Rome's dominant ideology through its prophetic witness *(martys)*. This witness in the first place means giving verbal testimony to the truth and holiness of God, as well as obeying God's commands (12:17).

24. See Philip A. Harland, "Honouring the Emperor or Assailing the Beast: Participation in Civic Life among Associations (Jewish, Christian and Other) in Asia Minor and the Apocalypse of John," *Journal for the Study of the New Testament* 77 (2000): 118-19.

25. Unlike Paul's more nuanced argument in 1 Corinthians 8–10, Revelation does not consider any possible scenarios in which eating sacrificial food might *not* involve idolatrous worship (cf. 1 Cor 10:23-30). Revelation's contextual theological argument apparently requires a more uniform and radical stance.

26. See Harry O. Meier, *Apocalypse Recalled: The Book of Revelation after Christendom* (Minneapolis: Fortress, 2002), pp. 81-85. It is difficult to be certain as to whether "fornication" *(porneia)* in 2:14 and 20 should be taken literally or as a figure for religious infidelity and idolatry, as is often the case in the Old Testament. Since fornication is typically used figuratively elsewhere in Revelation (e.g., 17:2, 4; 18:3, 9), the latter meaning is more likely.

27. J. N. Kraybill has argued that John's audience may have included Christians who "had (or were tempted to have) dealings with Rome through maritime trade or other commercial ties." Consequently, in chapter 18 John urges Christians to dissociate from Rome's economic structures, which were saturated with the influence of the imperial cult (*Imperial Cult and Commerce in John's Apocalypse,* JSNTSup 127 [Sheffield: Sheffield Academic Press, 1996], here p. 16); cf. Bauckham, *Climax of Prophecy,* pp. 376-77.

28. Greg Carey, "Teaching and Preaching the Book of Revelation in the Church," *Review and Expositor* 98 (2001): 90.

However, Jesus' faithful witness led him to the cross, and those who follow him must also be willing to suffer. They are to hold fast to the "testimony of Jesus" (12:17; 19:10; cf. 1:2, 9), which means not only their testimony *to* Jesus, but also their bearing Jesus' own witness to the truth through their words and through their lives.[29]

It is in the public arena that this costly witness must sound forth. John is convinced that when the church prophetically testifies to God's truth and righteousness against the injustices of Rome, against the beast's false claim to the whole world, the result may be the shedding of the blood of the saints (6:9). But through their very suffering and death, God's people participate in Christ's triumph over Satan and evil: "they have conquered him (Satan) by the blood of the Lamb and by the word of their testimony, for they did not cling to life even in the face of death" (12:11). Bauckham comments perceptively on Revelation's counter-perspective on the church's witness:

> Is the world a place in which military and political might carries all before it or is it one in which suffering witness to the truth prevails in the end? . . . While rejecting the apocalyptic militancy that called for literal holy war against Rome, John's message is not, "Do not resist!" It is, "Resist! — but by witness and martyrdom, not by violence." On the streets of the cities of Asia, John's readers are not to compromise but to resist the idolatry of the pagan state and pagan society. In so doing they will be playing an indispensable part in the working-out of the Lamb's victory.[30]

It is easy to imagine how the churches to which John is writing — largely politically powerless and marginalized communities — might be tempted either to cave in to the pressure to conform to the outlook of the great empire on the one hand, or to opt out of the struggle by focusing on their own personal holiness on the other.[31] But Revelation assures its readers that the character of the church's life in the world is determined not by the values of political and economic power, but by the sacrificial witness of the Lamb. This is not an introspective brand of holiness. Resisting captivity to fallen Babylon means that the saints must challenge the ungodly cultural and political ideologies that dominate their world. But they will do so at a cost. God's holy warriors "follow the Lamb *wherever* he goes" (14:4). The way of holiness is the way of the cross; it is

29. See A. A. Trites, *The New Testament Concept of Witness,* SNTSMS 31 (Cambridge: Cambridge University Press, 1977), pp. 156-64.

30. Bauckham, *Theology,* pp. 91-92.

31. See Christopher Rowland, *Radical Christianity: A Reading of Recovery* (Maryknoll, N.Y.: Orbis, 1988), p. 81.

the way of conquering through suffering, victory through defeat, overcoming through cruciform love. For John's readers, active separation from Babylon may result in economic hardship, social exclusion, persecution, martyrdom. But those who persevere and overcome are assured that they will join in the Lamb's triumph over evil. What is more, the saints' loving and faithful witness even to the point of death will have the magnetic effect of drawing people from the world's nations to worship the one true God (11:3-13; 15:1-4). Public holiness is a powerful instrument of mission.

A Holy City

It is only in the stunning image of the New Jerusalem that Revelation's vision of a holy church reaches its fulfillment (21:1–22:5). In contrast to the present *ekklēsiai* in chapters 2 and 3, which need to repent of their evil deeds, the coming holy city represents the church in its eschatological fullness and perfection.[32] It is *all* holy space. The city is patterned after Ezekiel's vision of the Jerusalem to come (Ezekiel 40–48), but there is a profound difference. Ezekiel's holy city is built around a holy temple where God dwells; this is its dominant feature. But John unveils a city in which there is "*no* temple . . . for its temple is the Lord God the Almighty and the Lamb" (21:22). Ezekiel's temple morphs, so to speak, into the Almighty's throne. In fact, the entire New Jerusalem, with its perfect cubic shape, becomes a sanctuary like the holy of holies, permeated with the splendor and unimpeded presence of God. In this city, boundaries between the sacred and the secular dissolve. The whole city is sanctified through the presence of God and the Lamb; every inhabitant is a "high priest" with unrestricted access to the inner sanctuary; all, like Moses, will see the glorious and holy God face to face (21:4).[33]

Moral purity is the hallmark of the New Jerusalem. The new holy city fulfills all of the ancient longings for the ideal human community, which was characterized not only by physical beauty, but especially by the ethical lives of the citizens.[34] Even more, it is the final reversal of the story of human sin that separated human beings from the holy presence of God.[35] The city is also the Lamb's bride (21:2, 9), who is adorned with the saints' "righteous deeds" (19:8),

32. See e.g., Pilchan Lee, *The New Jerusalem in the Book of Revelation,* WUNT 129 (Tübingen: Mohr Siebeck, 2001), pp. 304-5; Beale, *Revelation,* pp. 1039, 1041, 1045.

33. Elizabeth Schüssler Fiorenza, *Revelation: Vision of a Just World,* Proclamation Commentaries (Minneapolis: Fortress, 1991), pp. 112-13.

34. For ancient references, see Meier, *Apocalypse Recalled,* pp. 193-94.

35. Koester, *Revelation,* p. 200.

as well as dazzling jewels, which symbolize "the glory of God in all its radiance and purity" (21:19-21).[36] Only those who wash their robes are invited to enter its gates (22:14), but everything unclean is barred from the holy presence of God (21:27). Three catalogs of sins — or more precisely, "sinners" (21:8, 27; 22:15) — draw boundaries between those who are "inside" and those who are "outside" (22:15) the city's walls. The warning for John's readers is plain: those who persist in practicing Babylon's sins have no home in the holy Jerusalem; they must also share Babylon's punishment.

But John's vision of the New Jerusalem is about more than just the exclusion of the unrighteous from the holiness of heaven. It is a picture of human wholeness, which is an important dimension of its holiness.[37] In contrast to ancient Babylon (Babel), whose builders tried to achieve paradise on their own terms (Gen 11:1-9), the wholeness of heaven comes down to humanity, as a gracious gift of God (21:2, 10; cf. 3:12). With echoes of Eden resounding, John describes the new creation as a realm of healing and life (22:1-2). It features the river of life and the tree of life, whose leaves offer healing for the nations and a removal of humanity's curse (22:2-3). The city's gates are ever open, and its radiance attracts the world's nations to glorify God and to walk in his light (21:23-26; cf. 15:4). The New Jerusalem reveals a restored and transformed human community; it symbolizes the saints in full loving fellowship with one another, with God at the very epicenter of their shared life. Above all, God's servants (douloi) enjoy an unimpeded relationship with God. Those who bear God's name on their foreheads "also come to bear the impress of his nature on their lives" (22:3-4; cf. 1 John 3:2; 2 Cor 3:18).[38] Intimate communion with a holy God requires a people who are conformed to God's own likeness.

If the New Jerusalem is John's prophetic vision of the final perfected people of God,[39] must his readers wait until God judges wicked Babylon in the end to enter its gates? Yes and no. Although the holy city belongs to the future, it stands for a vision of reality that must shape the church's present life in the

---

36. Osborne, *Revelation*, p. 749.

37. M. Robert Mulholland, Jr., *Revelation: Holy Living in an Unholy World* (Grand Rapids: Francis Asbury Press, 1990), pp. 52-53, 321.

38. G. B. Caird, *The Revelation of St. John the Divine*, HNTC (New York: Harper and Row, 1966), pp. 280-81.

39. There is some debate as to whether the New Jerusalem is an image of the saints themselves or the place where they reside. Despite Royalty's arguments that Revelation conceives of the New Jerusalem mainly in a spatial sense (*Streets of Heaven*, pp. 215-18), John's identification of the New Jerusalem with the bride (21:9-10; cf. 21:2) suggests that he is thinking more about community than place. I like Ben Witherington's suggestion that "community creates place, rather than the reverse" (*Revelation*, p. 263).

world.[40] By "entering" God's future city, John's readers gain the perspective from which to recognize and resist the illusions of the dominant culture. Embracing their future will mean receiving the grace to live as citizens of the coming holy Jerusalem in the midst of an unholy world (cf. Phil 3:21).[41]

John spotlights the alternatives facing the *ekklēsiai* of Asia by telling a "Tale of Two Cities" — the holy city and the harlot city. The moral contrasts are especially pungent. Babylon is the "great whore," clothed in seductive luxury (17:1, 4), but Jerusalem is the chaste bride, arrayed in righteousness and justice (19:8; 21:2, 9). The harlot's splendor comes from exploiting her subjects (17:4; 18:9-19), while the bride's radiance is from the glory of God in her midst (21:11-21). Babylon corrupts and deceives the nations of the world (18:3, 23; 19:2), but the nations walk by the New Jerusalem's light (21:24). Wicked Babylon is filled with abominations, impurities, and illusion (17:4-5; 18:2, 23), but the new holy city banishes everything false and unclean (21:27; cf. 21:8, 22:11). Babylon the prostitute intoxicates the nations with her wine of immorality and idolatry (14:8; 17:2; 18:3), but in the heavenly Jerusalem the nations are beckoned to drink from the water of life and to be healed by the tree of life that grows beside the river (21:6; 22:1-2).[42]

John's readers face a stark choice: which city will determine their allegiance in the present and fashion their destiny for the future? To be the holy people of God within the cities of Roman Asia means embodying the character and values of the city to come, which is already their true home. But there is a tension here. Gregory Beale shows that Revelation's picture of the New Jerusalem is also brimming with contrasts to the faltering and imperfect local *ekklēsiai* John addresses in chapters 2 and 3.[43] It is therefore no coincidence that God's people are only called "saints" *after* chapter 3, when Revelation sets the true community of God in sharpest distinction from the sinful world.[44] By un-

---

40. Bauckham, *Theology,* pp. 129-30. In spite of many valuable insights on the significance of the New Jerusalem for John's audience in the Roman Empire, I cannot agree with Howard-Brook and Gwyther's reduction of the New Jerusalem to a symbol of God's activity in *present* human history (Howard-Brook and Gwyther, *Unveiling Empire,* pp. 158-59, 184; cf. William Stringfellow, *An Ethic for Christians and Other Aliens in a Strange Land* [Waco: Word Books, 1973], pp. 48-58). John's vision of the New Jerusalem (e.g., "death will be no more," 21:4) will not be fully realized until the coming of "a new heaven and a new earth."

41. See Mulholland, *Revelation,* pp. 53, 347-48 and passim.

42. For fuller lists of parallels and contrasts between the two cities, see Howard-Brook and Gwyther, *Unveiling Empire,* pp. 159-60; Bauckham, *Theology,* pp. 131-32.

43. Beale, *Revelation,* p. 1119.

44. Conversely, the term *ekklēsia* ("church"), which occurs twenty times in Revelation, is confined to chapters 1–3 and a single reference in the epilogue (22:16); it only refers to historical Christian communities.

veiling the contrasts between the bride and the whore, between the conquering saints and the compromising *ekklēsiai*, Revelation urges its readers to stop accommodating with the worldly powers. Instead, they are to incarnate the purity and wholeness of their glorious future in anticipation of it. Within the Roman world, local assemblies of believers are called to be outposts of another kingdom, another empire than that of Caesar and Satan — the empire of God and the Lamb. Their corporate life is to model real peace and justice, and the true human community that embraces the world's diverse peoples (e.g., Rev 21:3), of which Caesar's empire could only make counterfeit boasts.[45] Their obedient witness offers a foretaste of the future, when the holy city comes down from heaven and the transforming presence of God fills the whole earth.

Implications for the Church Today

We have seen that Revelation challenges local *ekklēsiai* in Asia Minor to resist the pressure to compromise with Roman idolatry and live as the holy people of God in light of the coming redemption and judgment. But how might this contextualized message continue to shape communities of believers into churches that embody God's holiness in the twenty-first century? Sharply put, what is the Spirit still "saying to the churches" (2:7)?

First, then and now, the church's call to holiness must flow out of its vision of the holy God seated on the throne. God's altogether holy and just character, not any human standard of ethical behavior, provides both the measure and motivation for a holy people. Such a vision liberates us from settling for a squinty, codified version of holiness. At the same time, it means that God requires of his people nothing less than separation from sin and compatibility with his own nature.

Second, Revelation teaches us that it is in the community's *worship* of the Holy One that we affirm that God and the Lamb must be enthroned in every aspect of life. Worship in Revelation is consistently pictured in direct antithesis to worship of the idols of this world. When Christians worshiped the one true God in the cities of Roman Asia, they were at the same time professing that the emperor had no clothes and the self-deifying myths of the empire were false. Far from being an escape from the day-to-day public world, the church's worship is an open declaration that it refuses to bow down to the idolatries of the

45. See N. T. Wright, "Paul's Gospel and Caesar's Empire," in *Paul and Politics: Ekklesia, Israel, Imperium, Interpretation*, ed. R. A. Horsley (Harrisburg, Pa.: Trinity Press International, 2000), pp. 182-83; Howard-Brook and Gwyther, *Unveiling Empire*, pp. 223-35.

age.[46] In modern Western societies, such idols take many forms — wealth, success, hedonistic pleasure, celebrities, political and economic power, to name just a few. Worship of the thrice-holy God excludes all other affections, all competing loyalties. Thus, worship is much more than what happens at a weekly gathering of the Christian community. True worship transforms all of life into a living sacrifice, holy and acceptable to God (Rom 12:1).

Third, Revelation's theology of holiness has a strong communal emphasis. Drawing richly on Old Testament covenant language and Israel's corporate story, the seer pictures the church as a community of saints, set apart from the ethos of the dominant culture in order to radically belong to God. This vision culminates in John's image of the New Jerusalem, in which a purified people from every nation is gifted with an abundant shared life in the intimate presence of God. Revelation's notion of ecclesial holiness stands as a needed corrective to traditions in which sanctification is primarily limited to the inward experience of the individual believer. Revelation shows us that personal holiness only has true meaning in relation to the character and life of the Lamb's community. When believers focus solely on cultivating a personal relationship to Christ, but are at the same time not rightly related to other members of Christ's body, they settle for something far less than biblical holiness. John Wesley's claim that "the gospel of Christ knows of . . . no holiness but social holiness"[47] still rings true.

Fourth, Revelation is unequivocal about the nature of the church's holiness. A people that is graciously in relationship to God must be like the Holy One they worship; those redeemed by the slaughtered Lamb are to follow Jesus' pattern of sacrificial love. God's people must be "saints" in reality as well as in name. As a result, not only individuals, but communities of faith as a whole, must still heed Christ's warnings to wake up and repent of their sins, lest they ultimately face God's righteous judgment. In First World societies, local congregations are more apt to identify with the churches of Revelation that are in danger of compromise with pagan society than those that are facing persecution because of their faithful witness. Too much of Western Christianity has become all but indistinguishable from the dominant culture in its values and its lifestyle. We seldom swim against the stream. How many modern-day Laodicean churches, for instance, are enamored with their own numerical success, buildings, budgets, and influence? When the presence of God among his people does not translate into a visibly different pattern of thinking, valuing,

---

46. Bauckham, *Theology,* p. 161.

47. John Wesley, *The Works of John Wesley,* vol. 14, 3rd ed. (Kansas City: Beacon Hill, repr., 1979), p. 321.

and living, how can the church bear the authentic witness of Jesus to the world? Revelation forcefully reminds us that the church is called to be Christ's holy bride, adorned in righteous deeds and purified by its vision of the Holy One on the throne.

Fifth, Revelation's appeal to come out of Babylon (18:4) is still a call to publicly oriented holiness. Rather than being simply a retreat into personal piety, holiness helps to define the church's relationship to its cultural, political, and social world. Separating from Babylon means more than just avoiding certain activities; it is also about the church exposing and resisting the powers and ideologies that challenge God's rule in the world. In the first place, we must prayerfully discern where Babylon is to be found — it may be closer than we think. Rome was not the only actor to play Babylon's part.[48] Babylon and her sins are recast in new roles again and again in human history, including on our own world stage. Wherever governments or global conglomerates fill their own coffers at the expense of powerless people; wherever political or commercial empires behave in ways that demand idolatrous allegiance;[49] wherever nations use military, economic, or political coercion as a tool of self-serving policies; wherever societies or individuals embrace an ethos of greedy consumption — there is Babylon reborn. J. Nelson Kraybill is surely right that for churches situated in relatively powerful, comfortable, and secure societies, "it may be difficult to hear or accept John's radical critique of imperial power, a critique that seems logical to many people in the two-thirds world."[50] But the church's prophetic witness of word and life must always side with God's righteousness against the idolatries and injustices of the age. Of course, the political and social dynamics of our post-colonial world are not identical to those of the Roman Empire. Communities of faith will need to work out *how* to bear an authentic witness to God's holiness and compassion within their particular contexts. We should not be amazed, however, if that countercultural testimony to the truth becomes costly and unpopular. It has always been so with followers of the slain Lamb.

Sixth, Revelation weds holiness to hope. It continues to give the church an alternative way of seeing the world, which in turn shapes its character and daily practice. It is a vision of the New Jerusalem to come — a city perfect in its proportions, liberated from sin, filled with God's wholeness. John pictures heaven coming down to a redeemed and transformed creation, and a healing of the world and its peoples. As Ben Witherington remarks, the New Jerusalem "is . . .

---

48. Craig Keener, *Revelation*, NIVAC (Grand Rapids: Zondervan, 2000), p. 434.
49. See Kraybill, *Imperial Cult and Commerce*, p. 22.
50. Kraybill, *Imperial Cult and Commerce*, p. 10.

about the invasion of earth by heaven, thereby finally entirely sanctifying the earthly realm" (21:2-3).[51] This is a radical optimism in the grace of God, which reshapes the possibilities of grace for God's people and his creation even now. John would have little time for eschatologies that look to the church's rapture into the next world as an escape from the earth and its problems or as an excuse for abdicating responsibility toward God's creation. He would not be impressed with otherworldly spiritualities that ignore the cries of human misery and injustice while believers blissfully march on to heavenly Zion.[52]

To be sure, Revelation reminds us that there is a wholeness that will be imparted to God's people only when they "see his face" in the future (Rev 22:4; cf. 1 John 3:2), when finally "the kingdom of the world has become the kingdom of our Lord and of his Christ" (11:15). Holiness must live in hope of its completion. But John's vision of the copious beauty of future life in God's presence beckons congregations of Christians to reflect the beauty of holiness as they daily enflesh God's love, justice, and *koinōnia* in their world. The transforming vision of New Jerusalem calls the church to be an agent for the "healing of the nations" (22:2), even as it eagerly expects a time when peoples from every language, tribe, and nation will worship the holy God and the Lamb around the throne. The church is the presence of God's eschatological future in the world. As Kraybill rightly affirms, "The heavenly New Jerusalem breaks into present reality whenever people take seriously the Lord's Prayer, 'Your will be done, on earth as it is in heaven' (Mt. 6.10)."[53] A holy church embodies the life to come in its everyday world.

Finally, Revelation offers contemporary churches not only a theology of ecclesial holiness, but also a way of communicating that theology. Eugene Peterson reminds us that Revelation is largely *theological poetry,* teeming with imagination and sensation.[54] Its impact is greatest when it is performed, heard, experienced (1:3), rather than simply read as a written work. The most powerful rendering of Revelation I have encountered was that of an aged preacher who acted out the Apocalypse by memory from beginning to end. John draws upon a whole arsenal of striking ecclesial metaphors — bride, kingdom, priests, city, lampstands, holy warriors, virgins, woman, wearers of white robes — in order to transform his readers' theological imagination regarding the church that embodies its holy calling. Particularly in the world's East and South, the church has learned that signs, ritual, drama, and colors sometimes express the realities

51. Witherington, *Revelation,* p. 276.
52. See Witherington, *Revelation,* p. 277.
53. Kraybill, *Imperial Cult and Commerce,* p. 221.
54. Eugene Peterson, *Subversive Spirituality* (Grand Rapids: Eerdmans, 1994), pp. 93-100.

of the gospel more compellingly than the language of principles and proposi-
tions. At the same time, Revelation might provide a first-century model for
how to communicate a theology of holiness to a twenty-first-century
postmodern generation of visual and interactive learners — people who are
shaped largely through symbols, stories, and sensory experiences. The question
remains. Do we have ears to hear and eyes to see what and how the Spirit would
speak to the churches in Asia, Europe, and North America today?

Index of Authors

Achtemeier, Paul, 323
Adewuya, J. Ayodeji, 204n.10
Allison, Dale C., Jr., 37
Aratus, 183
Aristotle, 139, 268n.35
Arrington, French L., 207
Aune, David, 346

Barclay, John, 315
Barrett, C. K., 125
Barth, Markus, 243n.23
Barton, Stephen, xix, 49, 71, 73, 277
Bauckham, Richard, 97n.9, 326n.1, 344-45, 351n.20, 354
Beale, Gregory, 357
Best, Ernest, 243n.23
Betz, Hans Dieter, 46n.10
Bitzer, Lloyd F., 202
Blaschke, Andreas, 223n.13
Borg, Marcus J., 66, 70
Botey Vallès, Jaume, 165-66
Boyarin, Daniel, 130, 145
Broadhead, Edwin K., 57-58
Brooke, George J., 8n.15
Brower, K., xviii-xix, 49
Bruce, F. F., 20, 122, 305n.27, 306n.29, 308
Bryan, Steven, 63
Burton, Ernest de Witt, 226n.29

Cadbury, H., 129
Caird, G. B., 241, 250n.58

Calvin, John, 125
Carroll, John, 89
Carter, Stephen, 311
Celsus, 223n.14
Cerfaux, Lucien, 240n.8
Chester, Andrew, 290n.73
Cicero, 188, 189n.15, 191n.23
Coloe, Mary, 107
Conzelmann, H., 192
Crossan, John Dominic, 161

Davies, W. D., 37
Deasley, Alex R. G., 20-21, 117n.10
Dio Chrysostom, 187nn.6-7, 190n.20
Dioscorides, 223n.14
Dunn, James D. G., 70, 71n.70, 81n.25, 150n.16, 162n.52, 171, 226n.30, 280n.28

Eco, Umberto, 312
Ellingworth, Paul, 301-2
Epictetus, 72n.72, 139, 264nn.23-24
Evans, O. E., 128

Fee, Gordon, 154, 202
Flemming, Dean, xxiii
Fletcher-Louis, Crispin H. T., 15n.34, 27
Foeret, Anne, 318
France, R. T., 63

Galen, 248n.46
García-Martínez, Florentino, 28

363

Index of Scripture References and Ancient Texts